TARRASCH'S
BEST GAMES OF CHESS

DR. TARRASCH

Siegbert Tarrasch

TARRASCH'S
BEST GAMES OF CHESS

Selected and annotated by

FRED REINFELD

1947

CHATTO & WINDUS

LONDON

To the memory of
GEORGE E. SMITH
Chess Editor of *The Field*
1925–1946

FOREWORD

SINCE Tarrasch had an active chess career extending over half a century, it seems strange indeed that this is the first definitive collection of his best games published in either English or German. (Both his *Dreihundert Schachpartien* and *Die Moderne Schachpartie* cover only limited parts of his career.) Tarrasch played so many fine games that the selection of the outstanding specimens was necessarily a very laborious task! In many cases I was able to follow Tarrasch's own analyses and comments in my annotations; but in all instances I have examined them carefully and made revisions and corrections where they seemed necessary. Thus, while many of the good points in these notes are due to Tarrasch, the responsibility for mistakes falls on the writer.

This foreword would be hopelessly incomplete without an acknowledgment of my gratitude to the late Mr. G. E. Smith, Amos Burn's worthy successor as Editor of the distinguished chess column in *The Field*. It is literally true that without Mr. Smith's assistance this book could not have been written. He first proposed the idea of this work, arranged for its publication, gave valuable advice regarding the selection of games, carefully revised the typescript and read the proofs. I am also indebted to Mr. Harold Raymond, of Messrs. Chatto and Windus, for his invariably friendly and helpful attitude.

FRED REINFELD

NEW YORK, *August*, 1946

CONTENTS

PART II. MATCH GAMES

CONTENTS

CONTENTS

BIOGRAPHICAL INTRODUCTION

SIEGBERT TARRASCH was born in Breslau on March 5, 1862. He came into the world with a club foot, which, as he remarks in his *Dreihundert Schachpartien*, did not hinder him from making rapid progress. He was a good scholar, excelling in all subjects but mathematics. At the age of fifteen, he learned how to play chess. Actually he had become familiar with the game during an earlier period, but in later years he preferred to date his introduction to chess from the time that he had made the "astonishing discovery" that books were written about the fascinating pastime.

Young Tarrasch had always been an enthusiastic reader, and he began to devour in an unsystematic but highly efficient way all the chess literature on which he could lay his hands. The atmosphere of his native town was propitious for his studies: the immortal Anderssen had been born in Breslau, and had devoted his life to teaching at one of its *gymnasia*. Tarrasch was to see Anderssen only once, and we may imagine with what awed reverence he must have beheld the legendary hero. Tarrasch displayed a marked aptitude for chess from the very start, and became so absorbed in the game that he had little time left for such trifles as homework. However, he made up for the lost time by more diligent study. As a mature man, he was to pay tribute (tongue-in-cheek, perhaps) to his instructors, for "always stressing clarity of thought and expression". He completed his *gymnasium* studies brilliantly in 1880.

Young Tarrasch had selected medicine as his profession and the University of Berlin as the institution where he would complete his studies. Judging from the sequel, his choice must have been based on a number of considerations. He found the lectures dull, the amusements of a great city inviting and the lure of chess irresistible. Most of his time was spent at the cafés where he met the great and near-great of the day: Winawer, B. Lasker, Riemann, Schallopp and others whose names and deeds are all but forgotten today. Two semesters were sadly neglected by Tarrasch while he prepared for the Hauptturnier of the German Chess Association, held in Berlin, 1881. But here stark disappointment awaited him, for he failed to win the coveted first prize.

Crushed by failure, Tarrasch returned to the university. Here he had the good fortune to meet a professor, Dubois-Reymond, whose brilliant lectures fired his interest and induced him to resume his studies. For a year and a half Tarrasch worked busily to make up for his previous idleness. So industrious did he become that he decided to leave the great city and its distractions. He transferred to Halle, which had a fine medical department and was small enough to make concentration not too difficult. He continued to work hard at his studies, leaving himself a reasonable amount of time for chess. At the Hauptturnier at Nuremberg in 1883, his patience was rewarded, and he won the first prize and the title of master in really scintillating style.

By the time that Tarrasch sent in his entry for the international tournament held at Hamburg in 1885, he had passed all his examinations and was a full-fledged physician. Then and later, he was to know how taxing it is to combine tournament chess with the practice of another profession. The masters looked askance at this "also-master" ; he was 23, a doctor without tournament experience —what kind of master was that ? !

The official masters had their answer soon enough. Tarrasch played phenomenal chess, scoring win upon win to end in a quintuple tie with Blackburne, Englisch, Mason and Weiss, half a point behind Gunsberg, the tournament victor ! So strict a judge as Steinitz acclaimed the young man's play, and Zukertort's comments were equally enthusiastic.

In his next tournament, at Frankfort, 1887, Tarrasch's play·was uneven and fumbling. But he managed to tie for fifth prize—an excellent showing in a strong tournament. The following year he won a small tournament at Nuremberg ; but here again his play was rather unsteady. At Leipzig, the same year, his showing was catastrophically bad : he came last ! Such a failure was bound to make a deep impression on a man as boundlessly ambitious as Tarrasch, and he began play in the strong Breslau tournament of 1889 with a keen determination to do better. It was here that he began the series of great tournament victories which gave him his pre-eminence in the chess world : Berlin, 1889 ; Manchester, 1890 ; Dresden, 1892 ; Leipzig, 1894. Even his tie-match with Tchigorin in 1893 added to his fame ; for at that time the Russian was at the top of his form. The games of this match are among the most interesting of Tarrasch's whole career ; they were a duel not only of two players, but two philosophies of chess. The games outline vividly the strong and weak points of both masters.

It was during this sensationally successful period that Tarrasch was invited to play Steinitz for the world championship at Havana. Tarrasch's professional duties made it impossible to accept, but it is fascinating to speculate on the outcome. The probabilities were all in his favor, for it is very doubtful whether the Steinitz of 1890 could have held his own against the Tarrasch of 1890. In any event, the Steinitz of 1894 turned out to be no match for the Lasker of 1894. And with the coming of the great Emanuel Lasker, Tarrasch was destined to play second fiddle for the rest of his life.

It was a galling situation for Tarrasch : he had come so far, and yet it was not far enough. At the famous tournaments of Hastings, 1895, and Nuremberg, 1896, Tarrasch was a distinguished also-ran while Pillsbury took top honors in the first, and Lasker scored decisively in the second. True, he had one more great triumph—in the famous marathon tournament at Vienna, 1898. This monster tourney, held to celebrate the fiftieth year of Franz Joseph's reign, provided for no less than 20 players in a double-round event. The exacting ordeal, which lasted two months, was the occasion of some of Tarrasch's finest chess. Even the British Chess Magazine, which could never forgive Tarrasch for dimming the already faded glories of Blackburne, Bird and Mason, grudgingly paid tribute to Tarrasch's play.

In the new century, only two more significant successes remained for Tarrasch ; in 1905, he defeated Marshall overwhelmingly in their match, and two years later, he won the Ostend Championship Tournament in impressive style. But, although his active playing career continued until 1928, it was not his formal successes to which Tarrasch owed his enormous prestige in the chess world. That fame rested on his books, which in turn depended on two fundamental and inter-acting elements : his *games* and his *teachings*.

Tarrasch's teachings are by far the most important feature of his distinguished chess career. He was the first man to appreciate, to assimilate and to pass on to others the revolutionary positional theories of Steinitz. It is difficult for us, living six decades later, to appreciate the magnitude of Tarrasch's achievement. Steinitz had aroused ill-will and opposition ; Tarrasch was more persuasive in getting the new theories accepted. Two generations of chessplayers have been brought up on the teachings of Tarrasch. What was once the private knowledge of a few outstanding men is now public property, available to any tyro who spends a little time on one of the many first-class chess manuals which are available nowadays.

It is true that part of Tarrasch's persuasiveness was based on the efforts of his predecessors. In the post-Morphy era there was at least partial understanding of the need for development; in the post-Steinitz era, there was at least partial understanding of the need for soundness in the formation of an attack. Tarrasch did not have the dreary task of starting at the very beginning.

Tarrasch's teachings can be reduced to a number of simple rules (the simplicity is of course in the phraseology, not in the contents !) :

1. *Mobility is all-important.* Superior mobility is an asset ; lack of mobility a serious defect. Tarrasch parted company with Steinitz in evaluating the importance of mobility ; for the younger man preferred mobility plus a weakness, to constricted positions without weaknesses.

2. *Mobility confers the initiative.* Mobility gives you the greater options, the greater freedom of choice. You lay down the law, your opponent submits. If you have more mobility and more space, you must increase your advantage ; you must constrict your opponent's terrain until he runs out of viable moves.

3. *Mobility creates its own plans.* When you have more mobility and more space, the game plays itself ; for the possession of the initiative carries the duty of maintaining and intensifying that initiative.

4. *Planning technique must be mastered.* If you are to utilise the initiative by planning, you must become a master of planning methods. Otherwise your initiative will be frittered away as your superiority fades. Winning prospects will be replaced by equality or loss.

These are the elements of Tarrasch's doctrines, and they appear over and over again in his games, always taking on new guises. The formula is the same, the problem is always new. As we scrutinise these simple elements, we must again be careful not to minimise Tarrasch's achievements. Today these propositions are self-evident; in the '80s they were incomprehensible to some, distasteful to others.

The chief concern of this book, however, is not with Tarrasch's career nor even with his teachings. Tarrasch and his rivals are dead, the leaves of the tournament books faded, cracked and withered (perhaps bombed out of existence). But the *beauty* of the games still remains.

So many of these games are classics, but to me they are more : they are old friends. Among such a luxurious richness of material, it is difficult to pick and choose, to say which games are outstanding ;

they all have their memorable and endearing qualities. And this despite the fact that so many of them depend on *technical display* for their strongest effects. But this should not surprise us, for the great artists infuse a creative element into even what is banal.

Which of these games is the "best" ? Is it perhaps No. 18 with Thorold, in which a "dry" Rook and Pawn ending is played with such chiselled perfection ? Or No. 27, the flawless game in which a backward Pawn leads to defeat virtually by force ? Or No. 29, the little-known gem which demonstrates with such telling effect the weakness of the hostile centre ? Or No. 77, which illustrates so excitingly the crisp attacking prowess of Tarrasch's old age ? Or the games of the match with Tchigorin, in which we are enchanted with the interplay of massive preparations, resourceful defences, far-seeing counter-attacks and surprising conclusions ? Who can say which is "best"—who wants to ? They are all games which will stand playing and replaying and always evoke delight.

What, in the last analysis, gives these games their eternal attraction ? I think the source is Tarrasch's own enormous zest and passion for the game of chess. All his love for chess went into these masterpieces. Tarrasch, like all other human beings, had serious faults of character. But he had at least one great redeeming quality : he had an unbounded urge to communicate to others all the pleasure which he received from chess. He devoted a whole lifetime to that task.

"Chess is a form of intellectual productiveness," he wrote in his last book *The Game of Chess*, "therein lies its peculiar charm. Intellectual productiveness is one of the greatest joys—if not the greatest one—of human existence. It is not everyone who can write a play, or build a bridge, or even make a good joke. But in chess everyone can, everyone must, be intellectually productive and so can share in this select delight. I have always a slight feeling of pity for the man who has no knowledge of chess, just as I would pity the man who has remained ignorant of love. Chess, like love, like music, has the power to make men happy."

The last sentence is the key to Tarrasch's games.

TARRASCH'S TOURNAMENT AND MATCH RECORD

Tournaments

	Rank	Won	Lost	Drawn	Total
Nuremberg, 1883 (Minor)	1	8	3	1	12
Hamburg, 1885	2–6	11	5	1	17
Frankfort, 1887	5–6	11	7	2	20
Nuremberg, 1888	1	5	3	2	10
Leipzig, 1888	8	2	5	0	7
Breslau, 1889	1	9	0	8	17
Manchester, 1890	1	12	0	7	19
Dresden, 1892	1	9	1	7	17
Leipzig, 1894	1	13	3	1	17
Hastings, 1895	4	12	5	4	21
Nuremberg, 1896	3–4	9	3	6	18
Budapest, 1896	8	4	4	4	12
Vienna, 1898	1	23	3	14	40
Monte Carlo, 1902	5–7	11	5	8	24
Monte Carlo, 1903	1	17	3	6	26
Ostend, 1905	2–3	14	4	8	26
Nuremberg, 1906	10	3	4	9	16
Ostend, 1907	1	8	3	9	20
Hamburg, 1910	10	5	5	6	16
San Sebastian, 1911	5–6	3	3	8	14
San Sebastian, 1912	4	9	5	5	19
Breslau, 1912	4–5	9	4	4	17
St. Petersburg, 1914	4	5	6	7	18
Mannheim, 1914	8–9	4	4	3	11
Berlin, 1918	4	0	3	3	6
Berlin, 1920	5–7	4	4	1	9
Gothenburg, 1920	4–7	5	3	5	13
Pistyan, 1922	11	5	6	7	18
Mannheim, 1922	1	3	0	1	4
Hastings, 1922	5	1	3	6	10
Teplitz-Schönau, 1922	13	1	4	8	13
Vienna, 1922	4–6	6	2	6	14
Carlsbad, 1923	11	5	6	6	17
Mährisch-Ostrau, 1923	7–8	4	4	5	13
Trieste, 1923	4	5	2	4	11
Meran, 1924	10	2	3	8	13
Baden-Baden, 1925	16–17	3	8	9	20
Breslau, 1925	10	1	5	5	11
Semmering, 1926	6–7	8	5	4	17
London, 1927	—	4	2	9	15
Bad Kissingen, 1928	11	0	4	8	12
		273	152	225	650

TARRASCH'S TOURNAMENT AND MATCH RECORD

Matches

	Won	Lost	Drawn	Total
Tchigorin, 1893	9	9	4	22
Walbrodt, 1894	7	0	1	8
Marshall, 1905	8	1	8	17
Dr. Lasker, 1908	3	8	5	16
Schlechter, 1911	3	3	10	16
Mieses, 1916	7	2	4	13
Dr. Lasker, 1916	0	5	1	6
	37	28	33	98

TARRASCH'S
BEST GAMES OF CHESS

PART 1

TOURNAMENT GAMES

1. NUREMBERG, 1883

(Minor Tournament)

FRENCH DEFENCE

It was on the basis of his excellent showing in this tourney that Tarrasch was invited to the International Tournament at Hamburg two years later. This and the following game are an indication of the fine chess Tarrasch produced in his first international test.

	White	*Black*
	Dr. S. Tarrasch	S. Löwenthal
1.	P—K 4	P—K 3
2.	P—Q 4	P—Q 4
3.	Kt—Q B 3	Kt—K B 3
4.	B—Kt 5	B—K 2
5.	P—K 5	K Kt—Q 2
6.	B×B	Q×B
7.	B—Q 3	

Old-fashioned. For Tarrasch's adoption of the modern move 7. Q—Q 2, see Game 70.

7. ......   P—Q R 3

Tarrasch recommends 7. ...O—O, pointing out that an attempt by White to reinforce the centre would be faulty: 8. Q Kt—K 2, P—Q B 4; 9. P—Q B 3, P—B 3; 10. P—K B 4, Q B P×P; 11. B P×P, P×P; 12. B P×P, Q—Kt 5 ch; 13. Q—Q 2 ?, R—B 8 ch.

8. Q Kt—K 2   Q—Kt 5 ch

The acceptance of the Pawn offer involves considerable loss of time, but it seems feasible in the hands of a good defensive player.

| 9. | P—B 3 | Q×Kt P |
| 10. | P—K B 4 | Kt—Kt 3 |

This move and its sequel involve a loss of valuable time. ...Q—R 6—K 2, with chances of securing a normal development, was in order.

| 11. | P—Q R 4 ! | Kt—B 5 |
| 12. | B×Kt | P×B |

The point of White's 11th move is now clear : Black's Queen can no longer retreat to K 2 *via* R 6. What is still more important : Black will be unable to defend the advanced Q B P by means of ... P—Q Kt 4.

| 13. | Kt—B 3 | Q—Kt 3 |
| 14. | O—O | Q—B 3 |

Black's position is very difficult. After 14. ...O—O ; 15. Kt—Kt 3 he would be subjected to a powerful attack and would be dangerously behind in development.

15. Kt—Kt 3   P—K Kt 3

He is anxious to keep the Knight out of K R 5, even at the cost of seriously weakening the black squares.

| 16. | Q—Kt 1 ! | P—Kt 3 |
| 17. | Q—Kt 4 ! | |

The presence of the Queen on this square is intolerable : ...O—

O is prevented, ...P—Q Kt 4 is impossible, and Kt—Q 2 is threatened.

17.	P—Q R 4
18. Q—R 3	B—Kt 2
19. R—B 2	

Freeing his K Kt for action.

| 19. ...... | Kt—R 3 |

Superficial, as the Knight has no scope here. ...Kt—Q 2 was surely better.

| 20. Kt—Kt 5 ! | Q—Q 2 |
| 21. Kt(Kt 3)—K 4 ! | B×Kt |

Relinquishing this Bishop is the price Black must pay for castling. If 21. ...O—O—O ? ; 22. Kt—B 6 winning the exchange.

22. Kt×B	O—O—O
23. Q—R 2 !	Q—Q 4
24. Kt—Q 2	Kt—Kt 1

While White plays to regain the sacrificed Pawn, Black flounders around. Lacking good squares for his pieces, he has no plan at his disposal.

| 25. R—Kt 1 | K—Q 2 |
| 26. Kt×P | K—K 1 |

And now the King is back where he started ! But White was threatening R×P etc.

27. Q—K 2	K—B 1
28. Kt—K 3	Q—K 5
29. R—K 1	P—R 4

This move is unavoidable, as White's forces must be denied access to K Kt 4. But Black's King's side is sadly weakened at the same time.

| 30. Q—R 2 | K—Kt 1 |
| 31. Q—Q 2 | Q—B 3 |

32. P—B 5 !

Smashing up Black's King's side, no matter how he replies. Against 32. ...K P×P Tarrasch intended 33. Kt×P !, P×Kt ; 34. R×P ! with a winning attack.

32.	R—R 2
33. P×Kt P	P×P
34. R—B 6	Q—K 1
35. Q—R 2	R—K 2
36. P—Q 5 !	

There is no good reply to this decisive stroke. Thus if 36. ...Kt—Q 2 ; 37. R×P, Kt×P ; 38. R×R, Q×R ; 39. P—Q 6 ch, Q—B 2 ; 40. P×P, R—Q B 1 ; 41. Kt—Q 5 and wins (Tarrasch).

36.	K—Kt 2
37. P×P	Kt—B 3
38. Kt—Q 5	Kt×P

A last attempt, which is refuted by Tarrasch's admirable play. He has held the whiphand throughout.

| 39. Kt×R | Q×Kt |

If 39. ...K×R ; 40. Kt—
Q 5 ch winning the exchange or a
piece.

```
40. R(B 6)—B 1    Q—Kt 4
41. Q—K 2         R—Q 4
42. Q—K 4         Kt—Q 6
```

The plausible 42. ...R—B 4
would have allowed the following
fine finish planned by Tarrasch :
43. Q—Q 4 (threatening P—R 4),
P—R 5 ; 44. R×Kt !, R×R (if
44. ...Q×R ; 45. R—K 1, Q×Q
ch ; 46. P×Q and the K P
queens !) ; 45. R—K 1, K—B 3 ;
46. Q×R ch, Q×Q ; 47. R×Q,
K×R ; 48. P—K 7 etc.

```
43. P—K 7        Kt×R
44. P—K 8 (Q)    Resigns
```

2. NUREMBERG, 1883

(Minor Tournament)

FRENCH DEFENCE

In the course of his very long career
as a master, Tarrasch produced so
many fine games that it would be
difficult to single out any special
group as being his very best. But
if any set of games deserves that
honour, it might well go to the
games that he played with the
French Defence. Few masters
have penetrated so deeply into
the spirit of this opening as did
Tarrasch.

White	Black
Dr. S. Tarrasch	T. von Scheve

```
1. P—K 4      P—K 3
2. P—Q 4      P—Q 4
3. Kt—Q B 3   B—Kt 5
```

It is customary to think of this
move as the last word in modernity,
but it appeared often in the tournament chess of the '70's and '80's.

```
4. P×P        P×P
5. Kt—B 3     Kt—K B 3
6. B—Q 3      O—O
7. O—O        B—Kt 5
8. B—K Kt 5
```

White has adopted a colourless
continuation, and Black could now
obtain an excellent position with
...P—B 3 followed by ...Q Kt—
Q 2. Instead, he decides on a
faulty exchange which leads to
inextricable difficulties.

```
8. ......      B×Q Kt
9. P×B         Q Kt—Q 2
10. Q—Q 2      P—B 3
```

This leads to a demonstrably
inferior position ; hence he should
have played ...B×Kt at all costs.
True, White would have had two
wide-ranging Bishops and the open
K Kt file ; but his Pawns would
have been weak, and Black would
have had the consolation of being
rid of the sickly Q B.

```
11. Kt—K 5     Q—B 2
12. P—K B 4    P—K R 3
```

White was threatening to win the
B with P—K R 3 etc.

```
13. B—R 4      P—B 4
```

Hoping for counterplay ; the
game has reached the critical stage.

```
14. P—K R 3    B—R 4
15. P—Kt 4     P—B 5
16. B—B 5      B—Kt 3
17. B×Q Kt !
```

This was played after a profound
study of the position. Most play-

ers would have continued unthinkingly with the gain of a Pawn, but Tarrasch sees much more profoundly into the position. After 17. B×B, P×B ; 18. Kt×Kt P, Kt—K 5 Black has an excellent game, and after 17. Kt×B, P×Kt ; 18. B×Kt P White will have to play P—B 5 sooner or later, permitting ...Kt—K 5. This correct but far from obvious reasoning leads Tarrasch to adopt a seemingly weaker continuation.

17.	Kt×B
18. Kt×Kt	Q×Kt
19. P—B 5	B—R 2
20. P—B 6 !	

This move is the key to White's plan. 20. ...P—K Kt 4 ? is refuted by 21. B×P, P×B ; 22. Q×P ch, B—Kt 3 ; 23. Q—R 6. Or if 20. ...P×P ? ; 21. Q×P wins. Note that the fact that the Bishops are of opposite colour plays no part.

| 20. ...... | B—Kt 3 |
| 21. R—B 2 ! | |

Tarrasch points out that the immediate 21. P×P, K×P ; 22. B—B 6 ch, K—R 2 would be ineffectual. White must bring greater pressure to bear on the weak point.

| 21. ...... | Q R—K 1 |
| 22. Q R—K B 1 | R—K 5 |

[*See diagram in next column.*]

23. B—Kt 3 !

This powerful retreat accomplishes White's purpose.

23.	K—R 2
24. P×P	K×P
25. B—B 4	K—R 2

POSITION AFTER 22. ...R—K 5

Black has no choice, for if 25. ...R—K R 1 ; 26. B—K 5 ch wins the exchange.

26. B×P	R—K Kt 1
27. B—Kt 5	Q—K 3
28. B—B 6	R—K 6

White threatened instant destruction with Q—Kt 5—R 4 ch. The manner in which he now winds up the game is very fine.

29. R—Kt 2 !   R×R P

Or 29. ...R—K 1 ; 30. B—K 5, R×R P ; 31. R—B 3, R—R 3 ; 32. R—R 2, Q×P ch. ; 33. R—Kt 3 and wins (Tarrasch).

30. R—B 3 !	R—R 3
31. Q×R ch !	K×Q
32. R—R 2 ch	B—R 4
33. R×B ch	K—Kt 3
34. R—Kt 5 ch	K moves
35. R—R 3 mate	

Tarrasch has neatly rounded off a well-played game.

3. HAMBURG, 1885

FRENCH DEFENCE

ONE can imagine with what excitement Tarrasch must have begun this, his first tournament game. He acquitted himself so worthily that in later years he considered it one of his best efforts. Incidentally, Réti selected this game for *Masters of the Chessboard* as representative of Tarrasch's style.

White	Black
Dr. S. Tarrasch	Dr. Noa

1. P—K 4   P—K 3
2. P—Q 4   P—Q 4
3. Kt—Q B 3   Kt—K B 3
4. P—K 5   K Kt—Q 2
5. Q Kt—K 2

As will be demonstrated later, this attempt to support the centre is faulty. Steinitz's continuation 5. P—B 4, P—Q B 4 ; 6. P×P is better.

5. ......   P—Q B 4
6. P—Q B 3   Kt—Q B 3

The correct line, pointed out by Pirc more than half a century later, is 6. ...P—B 3 ! 7. P—K B 4, P×Q P ; 8. P×Q P, P×P ; 9. B P×P, B—Kt 5 ch !, so that 10. Kt—B 3 or B—Q 2 can be answered by ...Q—R 5 ch !

7. P—K B 4   P×P

But here the exchange is faulty. Tarrasch recommends ...Q—Kt 3.

8. P×P   B—Kt 5 ch
9. B—Q 2

Against 9. Kt—B 3 Black has the following variation, which was fashionable at the time : 9. ... O—O ; 10. Kt—B 3, P—B 3 ; 11. B—Q 3, P×P ; 12. B P×P, R× Kt ! ; 13. P×R, Q—R 5 ch ; 14. K—B 1, Kt×Q P ; 15. P—B 4,

Q—R 6 ch ; 16. K—B 2, B—B 4 ; 17. B—K 3, Kt×P ! ; 18. P×Kt, B—Q 2 followed by ...R—B 1 ch.

9. ......   Q—Kt 3
10. Kt—K B 3   O—O
11. B×B

Now that Black's King is removed from the centre, White is willing to offer the exchange of Queens.

11. ......   Q×B ch
12. Q—Q 2   Kt—Kt 3
13. Kt—B 3   R—Q 1
14. Kt—Q Kt 5   B—Q 2

Tarrasch bases his hopes for the ending on the fact that this Bishop is ineffectual, being hemmed in by the Black Pawns on K 3 and Q 4.

15. Kt—Q 6   Q R—Kt 1
16. R—B 1   Q×Q ch
17. K×Q   Kt—B 1

More exact would be ...P—Q R 3 followed by ...Kt—B 1.

18. Kt—Q Kt 5   P—Q R 3
19. Kt—B 3   Kt(B 1)—K 2
20. B—Q 3   Q R—B 1
21. P—Q Kt 3

In order to play Kt—Q R 4 without having to fear ...Kt×P in reply. The next phase of the struggle centres about the attempt of each player to post a Knight on Q B 5. White has the better prospects here, as his Q B 5 is not commanded by the hostile Bishop.

21. ......   Kt—Kt 5
22. P—Q R 3   Kt(Kt 5)—B 3

Better than ...Kt×B, which would leave White with two

strongly functioning Knights against a Knight and an ineffectual Bishop.

23. P—Q Kt 4

Black's apparent waste of time with the Q Kt has compelled Tarrasch to renounce his plan temporarily, for if 23. Kt—Q R 4, Kt—R 4; 24. Kt—B 5, R×Kt !

23. ...... P—R 3

Creating a target for a later King's side Pawn advance by White ; but if Black is to play his King to the centre, he must sooner or later do something to guard the K R P.

24. P—K R 4 Kt—Kt 1

Black wants to double Rooks on the Q B file, but the immediate ... R—B 2 could be answered by Kt—R 4. Incidentally, ...P—K R 4 here or later would not be good : White would play a Rook to the K Kt file and continue with P—Kt 4.

25. K—K 3 !

Preparing for the ensuing trip of the K Kt to Q B 5.

25.	R—B 2
26. R—B 2	R(Q 1)—Q B 1
27. K R—Q B 1	K—B 1
28. P—Kt 4	B—K 1

Black's game is being systematically constricted, and his Bishop continues to be useless.

29. Kt—Q 2	Kt—Q 2
30. Kt—Kt 3	Kt—Q Kt 3
31. Kt—B 5	Kt—B 5 ch

This is not good, but nothing can affect the outlines of White's plan : advancing on the King's side and opening up a file in that sector.

32. B×Kt	P×B
33. Kt(B 5)—K 4 !	P—Q Kt 4
34. Kt—Q 6	R—Kt 1

Now that the K Kt has reached an even better square, White is ready for the final assault.

35. P—B 5 !

Beginning the final assault. After the earlier constriction of his game, Black is in no position to offer sturdy resistance.

35.	B—Q 2
36. R—B 2	Kt—Q 4 ch
37. Kt×Kt	P×Kt

Black has avoided the opening of a file—for a few moves.

38. P—Kt 5	P—K R 4
39. R(B 1)—B 1	K—Kt 1
40. P—Kt 6 !	

Forcing an entry no matter how Black replies.

| 40. ...... | P—B 3 |
| 41. R—K 2 | |

The patient shifting of White's Rooks is curious. Who would have foreseen that the K file would be the highway to victory ? [1]

41.	B—B 3
42. R(B 1)—K 1	R—Q 1
43. K—B 4	P×P ch
44. R×P !	K—B 1
45. Kt—B 7	R—K 1
46. Kt—Kt 5	R(B 2)—K 2 ?

Putting an end to his resistance, but Black could not have continued much longer, as Tarrasch shows : 46. ...R×R ; 47. P×R ! R— K 2 ; 48. P—B 6 ! P×P ; 49. P×P, R×R ; 50. Kt—R 7 ch, K— K 1 ; 51. P—B 7 ch, K—Q 2 ; 52. P—B 8 (Q), R—B 8 ch ; 53. K— Kt 5, R×Q ; 54. Kt×R ch, K— K 2 ; 55. P—Kt 7, K—B 2 ; 56. K—R 6, K—Kt 1 ; 57. Kt—Kt 6 and wins.

| 47. Kt—R 7 ch. | Resigns |

4. HAMBURG, 1885

SCOTCH GAME

TARRASCH shows admirable self-control in defending himself against a violent attack and then shifting to a powerful offensive.

| White | Black |
| DR. S. TARRASCH | M. WEISS |

1. P—K 4	P—K 4
2. Kt—K B 3	Kt—Q B 3
3. P—Q 4	P×P
4. Kt×P	

Even at the time this game was played, it was common knowledge that the Scotch is an opening which offers the second player very little trouble. Tarrasch was fond of it in his early days, however—doubtless because of its simplicity.

4.	Kt—B 3
5. Kt×Kt	Kt P×Kt
6. B—Q 3	P—Q 4
7. Kt—Q 2	

Obviously too slow ; nor is 7. Q—K 2 much better. 7. P— K 5, Kt—Kt 5 actually gives Black the initiative, while 7. Kt—B 3, B— Kt 5 ; 8. P × P, Q—K 2 ch ! is also quite satisfactory for him. All of which testifies to the innocuous character of this line of play.

| 7. ...... | B—Q B 4 |
| 8. P—K R 3 | |

Unnecessary timidity, played because Tarrasch was still under the spell of the old masters.

8.	O—O
9. O—O	R—K 1
10. Q—B 3	R—Kt 1

Black has developed his game admirably, whilst White's pieces are awkwardly situated. In order to develop the Q B, he must move his Knight, which in turn necessitates renouncing his original intention of not exchanging Pawns in the centre.

| 11. P×P | P×P |
| 12. Kt—Kt 3 | B—Q 3 |

He wants to be able to answer B—K Kt 5 with ...B—K 4.

13. B—K 3	P—Q R 3
14. B—Q 4	Kt—K 5
15. P—B 4 !	Q—R 5

Black has built up a fine attacking position, but this sortie is premature. ...P—Q B 3 would have been preferable. It must be admitted that Black's plan is an attractive one, the threat being 16. ... Kt—Kt 4 ; 17. Q—Q 1, Kt×P ch and wins.

16. B—K 3   Kt—B 3

The critical position has been reached, as Black threatens ... B—K Kt 5, or else ...P×P and wins. But Tarrasch has a satisfactory reply !

17. K R—B 1 !   B—K 4

There was still time for ...P—B 3.

18. P×P   R—Kt 5

If 18. ...B×Kt P ; 19. R—B 4.

19. R—B 2 '   B—Kt 5 ?

...B—Kt 2 is correct. The move actually made has been expected by Tarrasch, who is fully prepared for it.

20. P×B   Q—R 7 ch
21. K—B 1   R×Kt
22. P×R   Q—R 8 ch
23. K—K 2   Q×R

So far, so good ; but now White takes over.

24. P—Kt 5 !   Kt—Q 2
25. B×P ch   K×B

25. ...K—B 1 ; 26. B—B 5, Kt—Kt 3 (not 26. ...R—K 2 ?; 27. Q—R 3 etc.) ; 27. B—K 6, R—K 2 ; 28. P—Kt 6 ! would not be much better.

26. Q—B 5 ch   K—Kt 1
27. Q×Kt   R—Kt 1
28. P—Kt 6 !   Q—R 8

There was no good move : if 28. ...P×P ; 29. Q—K 6 ch ; if 28. ...R—K B 1 ; 29. P×P ch, R×P ; 30. Q—K 8 ch ; if 28. ... K—R 1 ; 29. Q—R 3 ch etc. (Tarrasch). White now wins as he pleases.

29. Q×P ch   K—R 1
30. Q—B 5   B—Q 3
31. R—B 1   Q—R 7
32. R—B 4   R—K B 1
33. Q—Kt 5   Resigns

5. HAMBURG, 1885

ENGLISH OPENING

THE opening of this game is played in such original style by Tarrasch that it might well pass for a Nimzovich game ! Of Tarrasch's first 13 moves, 11 are with Pawns. The important point is, however, that the objective (cramping the enemy's position) is speedily achieved.

White   *Black*
S. TAUBENHAUS   DR. S. TARRASCH

1. P—Q B 4   P—K 3
2. Kt—Q B 3   P—Q 4
3. P—K 3

P—Q 4 is the strongest move.

| 3. ...... | P—Q B 4 |
| 4. Kt—B 3 ? | |

Here P—Q 4 was absolutely essential. Apparently Taubenhaus did not anticipate the following reply.

4.	P—Q 5 !
5. Kt—K 2	Kt—Q B 3
6. Kt—Kt 3	P—K R 4
7. P—Q R 3	

P—K R 4 was better. White's Q Kt is getting terribly harassed.

7.	P—R 5
8. Kt—K 2	P—K 4
9. P—Q 3	P—R 4

The advance of both R Ps in the opening is rarely seen! The text enables Black to answer a possible P×P with ...B P×P, as the reply P—Q Kt 4 is prevented.

| 10. P—R 3 | B—Q 2 |
| 11. P—K 4 | P—B 3 |

Preventing the freeing exchange which would result from B—Kt 5 etc.

| 12. Kt—R 2 | P—K Kt 4 |
| 13. B—Q 2 | P—R 5 |

Black's powerful and orignal opening play has consisted almost exclusively of Pawn moves, with the result that White can never hope to get his pieces into proper play. The frantic efforts which Taubenhaus now makes to escape his grim fate, and the manner in which Tarrasch exploits these efforts, give the remaining part of the game a fascinating quality.

14. Kt—B 1	B—Q3
15. B—K 2	Q Kt—K 2
16. B—R 5 ch	K—B 1

The inability to castle is no hardship, as will be seen.

17. B—K Kt 4	Kt—Kt 3
18. Q—B 3	K—Kt 2
19. P—K Kt 3	

If White continues in peaceful vein, ...P—Kt 4 will give him a strategically lost game. Hence he tries to conjure up some attacking possibilities on the King's side.

19.	R—Kt 1
20. B×B	Q×B
21. Q—Kt 4	Q—K 2
22. P×P ?	

After this the fate of White's K R P is sealed.

| 22. ...... | R×P |
| 23. Q—Kt 2 | |

Intending Kt—B 3 followed by P—R 4. But Black's reply spoils this plan.

| 23. ...... | K—B 2 ! |
| 24. Kt—K 2 | Q—Q 2 |

Increasing the pressure on the K R P and making room for the development of the Knight, which will in turn make possible the doubling of the Rooks on the K R file.

25. Kt—K B 3   R—R 3

...R—R 2 would give White some chances (26. B × P).

26. Kt—Kt 3   Kt(Kt 1)—K 2
27. R—K Kt 1

Since ...Q R—K R 1 will decide the fate of the K R P in any event, Taubenhaus tries to get some compensating attack.

27. ....   Kt—B 5

27. ...Q × P ; 28. Q × Q, R × Q ; 29. B × P, R × Kt ; 30. R × R, P × B ; 31. Kt × Kt P ch is too unclear.

28. B × Kt   K P × B

Black is now ready to capture the K R P, hence the following desperate diversion.

29. P—K 5   P × Kt
30. P × B   Q—K 3 ch !
31. K—Q 2

K—B 1 is answered advantageously in the same way.

31. ......   P × P
32. Q × B P   Kt—B 4 !
33. Q R—K 1   Q—K 6 ch !
34. Q × Q   P × Q ch

This new K P is destined to play an important rôle in the ensuing end game.

35. K—B 3   R × P
36. Q R—K B 1   K—Kt 3

As tranquil play will leave Black with an easy win, Taubenhaus now embarks on a desperate combination.

37. R × P ch ! ?   P × R
38. Kt—K 5 ch   K—Kt 2
39. R × Kt   R—K B 1

Tarrasch's play hereabouts is rather weak ; doubtless the effect of excitement and fatigue. 39. ... R—R 8 (threatening mate) followed by ...P—K 7 is immediately decisive.

40. R × P ch

If 40. P—Q 7, R—R 8 ! 41. K—B 2, R × R ; 42. P—Q 8 (Q), R—B 7 ch and mate next move. Or 41. P—Kt 4, R × R ; 42. P—Q 8 (Q), R × Kt and wins.

40. ......   K—B 3
41. Kt—Q 7 ch   K × R
42. Kt × R   R—R 1

Quicker was 42. ...R—R 8 ! ; 43. K—B 2, P—K 7 ; 44. P—Q 7, R—B 8 ch ;   45. K × R, P—K 8 (Q) ch ;   46. K—B 2, Q—B 7 ch followed by ...Q × Kt (Tarrasch).

43. Kt—K 6 ch   K—Kt 5
44. P—Q 7   K—B 6
45. Kt—Kt 5 ch   K—Kt 7
46. Kt—K 4   R—K Kt 1

Superfluous.

47. K—B 2   K—B 8
48. Kt—Kt 3 ch   K—K 8
49. P—Q 4   P × P
50. Kt—B 5   R—Q 1
51. Kt × Q P   R × P
52. Kt—Kt 5   P—K 7
53. Kt—B 3   K—B 8
      Resigns

6. HAMBURG, 1885

RUY LOPEZ

In the course of his début, Tarrasch disposed of famous veterans with the greatest ease. A case in point :

	White	*Black*
	H. E. Bird	Dr. S. Tarrasch

1.	P—K 4	P—K 4
2.	Kt—K B 3	Kt—Q B 3
3.	B—Kt 5	P—Q R 3
4.	B—R 4	Kt—B 3
5.	Q—K 2	

A move which was destined to become really fashionable almost half a century later.

5.	......	B—B 4

Offering a rather dubious gambit : 6. B×Kt, Q P×B ; 7. Kt×P, Q—Q 5 ; 8. Kt—Q 3, B—R 2. But Bird was more eager to make sacrifices than to accept them !

6.	P—B 3	P—Q Kt 4
7.	B—B 2	

Too slow ; B—Kt 3 should be played. With his next four moves, Black seizes the initiative at a remarkably early stage.

7.	......	O—O
8.	P—Q 3	P—Q 4 !
9.	B—Kt 5	P—Q 5
10.	P—K R 3	

White's position is already inferior, but this move does not help matters. Q Kt—Q 2 followed by O—O is better.

10.	......	Q—Q 3
11.	Q Kt—Q 2	Kt—Q 2 !
12.	P—K Kt 4	P—B 3 !

White's Q B will now be out of play for the remainder of the game.

13.	B—K R 4	P×P !
14.	P×P	B—R 6

Threatening ...B—Kt 7. Black is angling for control of his Q 5, and the manner in which this is achieved is quite interesting.

15.	Kt—B 1	Q—B 4

Not 15. ....B—Kt 7 ? ? ; 16. B—Kt 3 ch.

16.	B—Kt 3 ch	K—R 1
17.	Q—Q 2	P—Kt 5 !

This gains control of Q 5, the temporary exile of the K B being of minor importance.

18.	P—B 4	Kt—Q 5
19.	Kt×Kt	Q×Kt
20.	Q R—Kt 1	

White's wretched position is untenable. Neither of his Bishops has any scope, his King is not secure and his Q P is fatally weak.

20.	......	Kt—B 4

If now 21. B—B 2, P—Q 4 ! (threatening P—Kt 6 ! followed by B—Kt 5).

21. K—K 2

21.	......	Kt×K P

"This sacrifice has been called 'brilliant' and 'remarkable' and the like by various annotators. It is nothing of the sort, being quite obvious. But the fine preparatory moves, the whole logical development of the attack and the striking originality of which this game is redolent—these are noteworthy features" (Tarrasch).

22. P×Kt	Q×K P ch
23. Kt—K 3	B—Kt 2
24. Q R—Kt 1	Q R—Q 1
25. Q—B 2	Q—B 6 ch
26. K—K 1	B—K 5

Every move tells : White is being driven back all along the line.

27. Q—K 2	Q—B 5
28. B—Kt 3	Q—R 3
29. R—R 2	

Tarrasch suggests B—B 2 as offering more hope of holding out.

| 29. ...... | B—Q 6 |
| 30. Q—B 3 | B—Kt 7 ! |

This Bishop now comes in with decisive effect.

31. Kt—Q 5

If Kt—Q 1, Q—B 8 is conclusive.

| 31. ...... | R×Kt |
| 32. B—B 4 | |

Since White cannot play 32. P×R ? because of 32. ...B—B 6 ch and mate next move, he ought to resign.

32.	B—B 6 ch
33. K—Q 1	B—K 5 ch
34. K—B 1	B—Q 7 ch !

35. K—Kt 2	B×B
36. Q×Q B	R—Q 7 ch
37. K—Kt 1	B×R
38. P—Kt 5	Q—Kt 3
39. Q×Q	P×Q
40. R—Kt 4	

White resigned without awaiting his opponent's reply. A crushing defeat.

7. HAMBURG, 1885

FRENCH DEFENCE

THIS game is fittingly described as a flawed masterpiece. Tarrasch plays some magnificent moves here, but his loss of one crucial tempo spoils a well-nigh perfect game.

| *White* | *Black* |
| F. RIEMANN | DR. S. TARRASCH |

1. P—K 4	P—K 3
2. P—Q 4	P—Q 4
3. Kt—Q B 3	Kt—K B 3
4. B—Kt 5	B—K 2
5. B×Kt	B×B
6. Kt—B 3	

Too slow. White's fifth move is an old continuation which has again come into favour in recent years ; but the modern preference is for 6. P—K 5, B—K 2 ; 7. Q—Kt 4 followed by O—O—O with attacking possibilities.

6.	O—O
7. P—K 5	B—K 2
8. B—Q 3	P—K B 3

This ambitious move presages a bitter fight for control of the centre. ...P—Q B 4 is simpler.

9. Kt—K 2

Weak. O—O followed by R—K 1, with the idea of exerting pressure along the K file, was better. However, Black might continue with 9. ...P—K B 4.

9.	P—Q B 4
10. P—B 3	P×K P
11. P×K P	

This is also questionable. Kt×P was in order.

11. ...	Kt—B 3
12. Kt—Kt 3	B—Q 2
13. Q—Kt 1	Q—B 2 !

This calm reply reveals that White's last move was simply a positional mistake. Tarrasch willingly submits to a seemingly dangerous attack because he knows that the advantage of securing a centre Pawn against a wing Pawn will have more lasting effects. Thus he follows the teachings of the great Steinitz.

14. B×P ch	K—R 1
15. P—K R 4	

15. Q—Kt 6 looks formidable but is answered easily enough : 15. ...Kt×P (...B—K 1 is even safer) ; 16. Q—R 5, Kt×Kt ch ; 17. P×Kt, Q—B 5 etc.

15.	Kt×P
16. Kt—Kt 5	P—B 5

In order to answer B—Kt 8 with ...Kt—Q 6 ch.

17. Q—Q 1	R—B 3
18. P—B 4	

Kt—R 5 would be effectively answered by ...R—R 3 ; 19. B—B 2, B—K 1. White's desperate attempts to work up an attack only postpone the onset of Black's coming counter-action.

18.	Kt—B 3
19. B—B 2	

Against 19. Q—R 5 Black has several good defences, of which the following, offered by Steinitz, is the simplest : 19. ...R—R 3 ; 20. Kt—B 7 ch, K×B ; 21. Kt×R, P×Kt ; 22. Q—B 7 ch, K—R 1 etc.

19.	B—K 1
20. Kt—K 2	B—Q 3 ?

A serious loss of time. Correct was 20. ...B—R 4 ! forcing 21. P—K Kt 3. As Tarrasch points out, Black would then have the agreeable choice between either ... R—Q 1 followed by ...P—K 4, or ...Q—Kt 3 followed by ...B—B 4, as in the text.

21. P—K Kt 3	Q—Kt 3 !

The primary purpose of this move is to answer 22. Q—Q 2 with ...B—B 4, preventing White from castling on the Queen's side.

22. P—Kt 3	B—R 4 ! ?

Involving a sacrifice which has become unavoidable. If 22. ... P×P ; 23. P×P threatening P—R 5 followed by Q—Q 3 ; or if 22. ...R—Q 1 ; 23. P—R 5.

Steinitz has this interesting comment : "Dr. Tarrasch has never entered a great tournament before. To judge from the present game and from his excellent general score in the Hamburg Tournament, he is evidently a rising star who will most probably develop into one of first magnitude. The power of combination evinced by Black in the present instance is of the highest type, though it seems that his position judgement is not ripe yet. The depth of the fine move in the text will be appreciated later on, but we are not quite certain that the plan of attack is analytically as sound as it turned out successful in practice."

23. P×P   P×P

24. R—Q Kt 1

Not 24. Q×B ?, R—Q 1 ; 25. Q—R 3, Q—K 6 ; 26. R—R 2 (if 26. B—Q 1, R×B ch ! and mate in four), B × Kt and wins. 24. Kt—K 4 would be answered by 24. ...R—Q 1.

24. ......   Q—B 2
25. Kt—K 4   R—Q 1
26. Kt×R   P×Kt

Threatening to win the Queen with ...B—R 6.

27. Q—B 1   B—B 4
28. P—B 5 ?

Losing quickly. After 28. R—Kt 5 the issue would still be in doubt.

28. ......   Q—Kt 2 !

Threatening 29. ...B×Kt ; 30. K×B, Q—Kt 5 ch and wins.

29. Q—B 4   Kt—K 4 !
30. R—K B 1

There is no defence : if 30. K—B 1, Kt—Q 6 ; 31. Q×P, B×Kt ch ; 32. K×B, Q×P ; 33. B×Kt, Q—B 7 ch ; 34. K—Q 1, B—K 6 forcing mate. Or 30. Kt—Q 4, B×Kt ; 31. P×B, R×P ; 32. Q—K 3, Kt—B 6 ch ; 33. K—B 1, Q×P ; 34. Q—R 6 ch, K—Kt 1 ; 35. Q×B, Kt—R 7 ch ; 36. R×Kt, R—B 5 ch ; 37. K—K 2, Q×R ch ; 38. K—K 1, Q—Kt 6 ch ; 39. K—Q 2, P—B 6 ch ; 40. K—Q 1, R—B 8 ch ; 41. K—K 2, R—B 7 ch ; 42. K any, Q—Kt 8 mate (Tarrasch).

30. ......   Kt—Q 6 ch
31. B×Kt   P×B
32. P—Kt 4

Amusing would be 32. Kt—Q 4, P—K 4 ; 33. Kt—K 6, Q×P ch (or simply 33. ...P×Q ; 34. Kt×Q, P—Q 7 mate) ; 34. Q×Q, P—Q 7 mate.

32. ......   P×Kt
33. P×B

White should resign.

33. ......   P×R (Q) ch
34. K×Q   R—Q 6

Not 34. ...Q—Kt 8 ch ; 35. K—K 2, Q×R ; 36. Q—R 6 ch K—Kt 1 ; 37. Q—Kt 6 ch, K—B 1 ; 38. Q×P ch, K—K 1 ; 39 Q—Kt 6 ch ! and Black must accep a draw in order to save his Queen

35. Q—Kt 8 ch   Q—Kt 1
36. R×P   R—Q 1
37. Q—R 2   Q—Kt 5

White resigns. "The greater part of this game qualifies it as a masterpiece of very rare stamp" (Steinitz).

8. FRANKFORT, 1887

FRENCH DEFENCE

THIS is one of Tarrasch's most famous early games. It is an absorbing if imperfect example of his youthful attacking style.

White	Black
DR. S. TARRASCH	I. GUNSBERG

1.	P—K 4	P—K 3
2.	P—Q 4	P—Q 4
3.	Kt—Q B 3	P×P

For other examples of this variation, see Games 116 and 117.

4.	Kt×P	Kt—K B 3
5.	B—Q 3	Q Kt—Q 2
6.	B—K 3	

This rather unusual move could be answered by ...P—K 4 without any apparent danger.

6.	......	Kt×Kt
7.	B×Kt	Kt—B 3
8.	B—Q 3	B—Q 2
9.	Kt—B 3	B—Q 3

Black's last two moves have been rather thoughtless; he does not seem to realize that these "developing" moves will turn out to be of little value.

10.	O—O	Kt—Kt 5 ?

Waste of time.

11.	B—K Kt 5 !	P—K B 3

Creates a lasting positional weakness. ...B—K 2 was better, although Black's position would still have been inferior.

12.	B—Q 2	Q—K 2
13.	P—K R 3	Kt—R 3

Now we have the same kind of situation as in Game 125, where Tarrasch also refuses to capture the Knight.

14.	P—B 4	P—B 3
15.	P—Q Kt 4 !	O—O—O

"Castling into it." However, after 15. ...B×P; 16. B×B, Q×B; 17. R—Kt 1, Q—Q 3; 18. R×P, O—O; 19. Q—B 2, P—K B 4 (recommended by the Tournament Book as relatively best) Black is helpless: 20. P—B 5, Q—Q 4 (if 20. ...Q—K 2; 21. Kt—K 5, K R—Q 1; 22. Kt× P); 21. B—B 4, Q—K 5; 22. Q—B 1 (threatening to win the Queen with R—K 1), B—B 1; 23. R—Q B 7, P—B 5; 24. R—K 1, Q—Kt 3; 25. R × B !, Q R × R; 26. R × P and wins (Tarrasch).

16.	R—K 1 ? !	

"Nowadays I would not offer the Pawn, but would continue with the simpler P—B 5, P—Q R 4 and P—Kt 5. The conclusion would not be so pretty, but the winning process would be more certain" (Tarrasch).

16.	......	B×P
17.	R—Kt 1	B×B
18.	Q×B	K—Kt 1

The threat was 19. Q—Kt 2, B—K 1 (if 19. ...P—Q Kt 3; 20. P—B 5 with a terrific attack); 20. R×P etc.

19. P—B 5	B—B 1
20. R—Kt 3	Q—Q B 2
21. K R—Kt 1	K—R 1

According to Steinitz, this is a defensive move too many. He recommends ...Kt—Kt 1—K 2—Q 4.

| 22. R—Kt 6 ! | P—K 4 |

Black gasps for counterplay. Of course if 22. ...P×R ? ; 23. P×P wins.

| 23. R(Kt 1)—Kt 4 | K R—K 1 |

And not 23. ...P×R ; 24. P×P followed by 25. R—R 4 ch, K—Kt 1 ; 26. R—R 8 ch !, K×R; 27. Q—R 5 ch and mate next move. White's attack is beginning to look quite menacing.

24. P×P	P×P
25. R—Q R 4	P—K 5
26. Q—R 5	Q—Kt 1
27. B×P	B—B 4 ?

This loses ; the proper course was 27. ...R—Q 8 ch ; 28. Kt—K 1, Kt—B 4 with about even chances.

28. R—R 6 ! !

Black's last move is "outgeneralled by Dr. Tarrasch with admirable depth and ingenuity. The beauty of this splendid move (28. R—R 6 ! !) can only be fully appreciated about eight moves on each side later on" (Steinitz).

| 28. ...... | R—Q 8 ch |

All of Black's remaining moves are practically forced !

| 29. Kt—K 1 | R×Kt ch |
| 30. Q×R | B×B |

No better is 30. ...R×B ; 31. R×R, P×R ; 32. R—K 8 etc. (Steinitz).

31. R×B	R×R
32. Q×R	P×R
33. Q×P ch	Q—Kt 2
34. Q—K 8 ch	Q—Kt 1
35. Q—K 4 ch	Q—Kt 2
36. P—B 6	

The point.

36.	Q—Q B 2
37. Q—K 8 ch	Q—Kt 1
38. Q—Q 7 !	Q—Kt 8 ch
39. K—R 2	Kt—B 4
40. P—B 7	Resigns

A delightful finish.

9. NUREMBERG, 1888
SICILIAN DEFENCE

ONE of the most difficult arts for the great chess master to acquire is the ability to repulse the desperate onslaught of an adversary who knows that he is positionally beaten. When the opponent is Mieses, the master who courts victory must be doubly on his guard.

White	*Black*
Dr. S. Tarrasch	J. Mieses
1. P—K 4	P—Q B 4
2. Kt—K B 3	Kt—Q B 3
3. Kt—B 3	

P—Q 4 is more exact, as the text might well be answered by ... P—K 4 !

3.	Kt—B 3
4. P—Q 4	P×P
5. Kt×P	P—K 4 ?

An experiment which turns out miserably ; Black will have no compensation for his coming Pawn weaknesses. Either 5. ...P—Q 3 or ...P—K 3 was in order.

6. K Kt—Kt 5   P—Q R 3

Or 6. ...P—Q 3 ; 7. B—Kt 5, P—Q R 3 ; 8. B×Kt, P×B ; 9. Kt—R 3, P—Q Kt 4 ; 10. Kt—Q 5 and the outlook for Black is very poor.

| 7. Kt—Q 6 ch | B×Kt |
| 8. Q×B | Q—R 4 |

...Q—K 2 ; 9. Q×Q ch would leave Black with a hopelessly inferior ending ; the text leads to much the same result.

9. B—Q 2   Q—Kt 5

One can hardly blame Mieses for wanting to avoid the distasteful middle game which faces him ; but his endgame prospects are, if anything, even drearier !

| 10. Q×Q | Kt×Q |
| 11. O—O—O | |

Tarrasch has one of those happy positions which play themselves : he has two Bishops, his development is more rapid and effective,

and he will have a field day exploiting the weakness of Black's Q 3 and Q 4. Black's Pawn position is ruined by the backwardness of his Q P and the weakness of his black squares, particular Q 3 and Q Kt 3.

11. ......   P—Q Kt 4

In order to prevent the powerful manœuvre Kt—R 4—Kt 6. Unfortunately the text creates a new weakness, but what is to be done ? If 11. ...P—Q 4 ? ; 12. P—Q R 3 wins a Pawn ; if 11. ...P—Q 3 ; 12. B—K Kt 5 is embarrassing ; and if 11. ...Kt—Kt 5 ; 12. B—K 1 and Black is very quickly driven back.

12. B—Kt 5   Kt—Kt 5

The threat was 13. B×Kt, P×B ; 14. P—Q R 3, Kt—B 3 ; 13. Kt—Q 5 winning a Pawn. True to his style, Miese defends in aggressive fashion.

13. B—R 4	P—B 3
14. B—K 2	Kt—R 3
15. P—R 4 !	

Exacting the penalty for Black's 11th move.

| 15. ...... | P×P |
| 16. Kt×P | B—Kt 2 ! ? |

A more conservative player would resort to ...K—K 2 and ...P—Q 3. But Mieses prefers a more lively course.

17. Kt—B 5

If instead 17. P—K B 3, R—Q B 1 ; 18. R—Q 2, Kt—B 3 ; 19. Kt—B 5, R—Q Kt 1 (Tarrasch).

17. ......   R—Q B 1 !

c

So that if 18. Kt×B, R×P ch etc.

18. B—R 5 ch !	P—Kt 3
19. Kt×B	R×P ch
20. K—Kt 1	P×B
21. B×P	O—O !

If 21. ...R—K B 1 ? ?; 22. Kt—Q 6 mate ! If 21. ...R—Kt 1 ; 22. B×P is a satisfactory reply. The text compels White to play with great care.

| 22. B×P | K R×P |

White was threatening B—Q 6. Black's " attack " is really sham, as White's Bishop is admirably posted for attack or defence.

| 23. R×P | Kt—B 2 |

Not 23. ...R×P ; 24. Kt—Q 6, R(B 7)—B 7 ; 25. R—Q B 1 (threatening 26. R—Q 8 ch, R—B 1 ; 27. R×R ch, K×R ; 28. B—B 6 followed by mate), R—B 1 ; 26. Kt—B 8 !, R—K 1 ; 27. Kt—K 7 ch, K—B 2 ; 28. Kt—Kt 6 ch and wins. Or 24. ...Kt—B 3 ; 25. R—Q B 7, K—B 1 ; 26. B—B 6 and wins (Tarrasch).

24. B—B 3	Kt—B 3
25. K R—Q 1	Q Kt—K 4
26. R—K 7 !	K—B 1

If 26. ...Kt—K 3 ; 27. R—K 8 ch followed by the victorious advance of the K P.

| 27. R—B 7 ! |

Not 27. R×Kt, R×B !

| 27. ...... | R×B |

Black has no choice but to get rid of this Bishop.

| 28. P×R | R×P |
| 29. Kt—Q 8 ! | Kt—Kt 4 |

Not 29. ...R×P ; 30. R—K B 1. Black's position is hopeless.

| 30. P—R 4 | Kt(K 4)—B 6 |

Resignation. If 30. ...Kt(Kt 4)—B 2 ; 31. R—K B 1, R—Kt 2 ; 32. Kt—K 6 ch, or, if 30. ...Kt (Kt 4)—B 6 ; 31. Kt—K 6 ch and 32. R—Q 8 mate (Tarrasch).

31. P×Kt	Kt—Q 7 ch
32. K—B 2	Kt×P ch
33. K—Kt 3	Resigns

Tarrasch has shown himself a good strategist in the first part of the game, and a good tactician in the second.

10. NUREMBERG, 1888

FRENCH DEFENCE

HERE is another of Tarrasch's famous games. Despite certain flaws, this game was considered the last word on the variation it exemplifies, until Nimzovich refuted Tarrasch's line of play twenty-four years later. Some ten years later Nimzovich refuted his own views!

White	Black
L. PAULSEN	DR. S. TARRASCH

1. P—K 4   P—K 3
2. P—Q 4   P—Q 4
3. P—K 5 ? !

One of the most controversial moves in the whole realm of the openings! Paulsen and Steinitz were pioneers in adopting it but failed to impress the chess world. Later Nimzovich championed the move, endowing it with a wealth of typically original motifs and scoring some notable victories.

3. ......   P—Q B 4
4. P—Q B 3   Kt—Q B 3
5. Kt—B 3   Q—Kt 3
6. B—Q 3

B—K 2 is better, as the text only wastes a move.

6. ......   P × P !

Undertaking to demonstrate that White's Q P is weak. 6. ...B—Q 2 ? is less exact : 7. P × P !, B × P ; 8. O—O, P—B 3 ; 9. P—Q Kt 4, B—K 2 ; 10. B—K B 4 with advantage (Nimzovich-Salwe, Carlsbad, 1911).

7. P × P   B—Q 2
8. B—K 2

B—B 2 looks attractive, but then 9. ...Kt—Kt 5 forces the exchange of the Bishop (10. B—Kt 3, B—Kt 4).

8. ......   K Kt—K 2
9. P—Q Kt 3   Kt—B 4
10. B—Kt 2   B—Kt 5 ch
11. K—B 1

Necessary in order to save the Q P. Needless to say, however, the renunciation of castling has certain disagreeable aspects.

11. ......   B—K 2

In order to answer 12. P—K Kt 4 with ...Kt—R 5. The whole conception is over-elaborate, however, and would properly be replaced by Nimzovich's recommendation 11. ...O—O ; 12. P—Kt 4, Kt—R 3 ; 13. R—Kt 1, P—B 3 ! (the attack on White's centre continues) ; 14. P × P, R × P ! ; 15. P—Kt 5, R × Kt ; 16. B × R, Kt—B 4 ; 17. R—Kt 4, B—K 1 ! and Black has the better game despite his material inferiority.

12. P—Kt 3   P—Q R 4

This move looks stronger than it really is. Paulsen's courageous reply gives his pieces a powerful point of support at Q Kt 5 which amply compensates for the resulting weakness of his Q Kt P.

13. P—Q R 4 !   R—Q B 1
14. B—Kt 5   Kt—Kt 5

Black naturally strives to loosen White's hold on his Q Kt 5.

15. B × B ch ?

Weak. Paulsen was apparently afraid to play 15. Kt—B 3 because of the continuation 15. ...B × B ; 16. Kt × B, Kt—B 7. But as Nimzovich points out, there could then follow 17. R—B 1, Kt—K 6 ch ; 18. P × Kt, Kt × P ch ; 19. K—K 2, Kt × Q ; 20. R × R ch, K—Q 2 ; 21. R × R, Kt × B ; 22. R—Q B 1 and wins.

| 15. ...... | K × B |
| 16. Kt—B 3 | Kt—B 3 ! |

16. ...Q—R 3 ch; 17. K—Kt 2, Kt—Q 6 looks inviting, but after 18. Q—Q Kt 1 ! (forced; if 18. Q—B 2 or Q—Q 2, B—Kt 5—while if 18. Q—K 2 ? R × Kt !; 19. B × R, Kt—B 5 ch etc.), B—Kt 5 ; 20. Kt—Q Kt 5 ! White is safe (Tarrasch).

| 17. Kt—Q Kt 5 | Kt—R 2 |
| 18. Kt × Kt ? | |

18. Q—Q 3 ! (Nimzovich) is much better.

| 18. ...... | Q × Kt |
| 19. Q—Q 3 | |

Possibly overlooking Black's rejoinder, but White's game is bad in any event. Black threatens ...Q—R 3 ch, followed by doubling his Rooks on the Q B file with a strategically won game.

| 19. ...... | Q—R 3 ! |

The winning move. After the forced exchange of Queens (20. K—K 2 ? ?, R—B 7 ch) Black has a number of decisive advantages: the open Q Kt file, command of the seventh rank and the fact that White's Bishop is at a disadvantage. Add to these factors the permanent weakness of the Q P, and it is clear that White is in a bad way.

| 20. Q × Q | P × Q |

The fact that Black has a doubled and isolated Q R P is of no importance.

21. K—Kt 2	R—B 7
22. B—B 1	R—Q Kt 1
23. R—Q Kt 1	R—B 6
24. B—Q 2	R(B 6) × P
25. R × R	R × R
26. B × P	R—Kt 7

26. ...R—R 6 seems stronger, but it would allow the annoying reply R—Q B 1 !

27. B—Q 2

If 27. R—Q B 1, Kt—K 6 ch followed by ...Kt—B 5. The command of Q B 5 is a key to the ending which follows.

| 27. ...... | B—Kt 5 |

Not 27. ...Kt × Q P ? ?; 28. B—B 3.

| 28. B—B 4 | P—R 3 |

This gives White some counter-chances. Tarrasch later recommended ...R—R 7.

29. P—Kt 4	Kt—K 2
30. R—R 1	Kt—B 3
31. B—B 1	R—B 7
32. B—R 3	R—B 5

White can no longer avoid the loss of a Pawn ; nevertheless ... B × B would have been simpler.

33. B—Kt 2	B—B 6
34. B×B	R×B
35. R—Q Kt 1	

His only chance is to play aggressively.

| 35. ...... | K—B 2 |
| 36. P—Kt 5 ! | R—B 5 |

Not 36. ...P—K R 4 ; 37. P—Kt 6 !, P×P ; 38. Kt—Kt 5, Kt×Q P ; 39. R—Q 1, R—B 5 ? ; 40. R×Kt (Tarrasch).

| 37. P×P | P×P |
| 38. P—R 5 ! | R—R 5 |

Better than 38. ...Kt×R P (if 38. ...Kt×Q P ; 39. R—Kt 6) ; 39. R—Q R 1, K—Kt 3 ; 40. R—Kt 1 ch, K—R 2 and Black will have technical difficulties.

39. K—Kt 3	R×R P
40. K—Kt 4	R—R 6
41. R—Q 1	

In order to guard the Q P so that he can move the Knight and play K—R 5.

41.	R—Kt 6
42. P—R 4	Kt—K 2 !
43. Kt—K 1	Kt—B 4
44. Kt—Q 3	

The traps continue. If now 44. ...Kt×Q P ; 45. Kt—B 5 regaining the Pawn.

44.	P—R 4
45. Kt—B 5	R—Q B 6
46. R—Q Kt 1	

In view of the threatened ...R—B 5 he has nothing better.

46.	Kt × Q P
47. Kt—R 6 ch	K—Q 1
48. R—Kt 8 ch	R—B 1

If 48. ...K—K 2 ; 49. R—Kt 7 ch, K—B 1 ; 50. Kt—B 7, with unpleasant threats to Black's King.

49. R—Kt 7	K—K 1
50. Kt—B 7 ch	K—B 1
51. Kt—Kt 5	Kt × Kt
52. R×Kt	R—R 1
53. P—B 4	

R—Kt 3 would be slightly better.

53.	P—R 5
54. R—Kt 1	P—R 6
55. P—B 5	

White is playing for stalemate possibilities ; there is nothing else left !

55.	P—R 7
56. R—Q R 1	R—R 5 ch
57. K—R 5	

On other King moves, Black simply plays his King to the Queen's side with an easy win.

57.	K—Kt 2
58. P×P	P×P
59. R—Kt 1 ch	K—R 1 !

Tempo move.

60. R—Q R 1	K—R 2
61. R—K Kt 1	P—R 8 (Q)
62. R—Kt 7 ch	K—R 1

White resigns. The endgame has been interesting. A bitter battle !

11. LEIPZIG, 1888.

FRENCH DEFENCE

THE modern player has difficulty in understanding why the colourless

Exchange Variation was so popular a line of play against this defence. White's chances of obtaining the initiative are so microscopic that the simplifying move 3. P×P is virtually an admission that White is embarrassed for an effective continuation as early as the third move !

White	Black
J. Minckwitz	Dr. S. Tarrasch

1.	P—K 4	P—K 3
2.	P—Q 4	P—Q 4
3.	P×P	P×P
4.	Kt—K B 3	Kt—K B 3
5.	B—Q 3	B—Q 3
6.	O—O	O—O
7.	Kt—B 3	P—B 3

Turning away from symmetry—a necessary step if drawish positions are to be avoided.

8.	Kt—K 2	Q—B 2
9.	Kt—Kt 3	B—K Kt 5
10.	P—K R 3	B—K 3

Against 10. ...K B×Kt White can advantageously reply 11. BP× B, with good attacking chances.

11.	Kt—B 5	B×Kt
12.	B×B	Q Kt—Q 2

Despite the apparently level character of the position, White's game has already become slightly inferior. He has lost time with his Q Kt's peregrinations, and his Q B has rather slender prospects.

13. B—Kt 5

Black's obvious reply shows the pointlessness of this move. B—K 3 was better.

13.	......	Kt—K 5
14.	B×Q Kt	

Not an attractive move, but after 14. B—K 3, Q Kt—B 3 the coming ...P—K Kt 3 will be embarrassing.

14.	......	Q×B
15.	B—K 3	P—K B 4
16.	Q—Q 3	Q R—K 1

Black clearly has the better game.

17. Q R—K 1   P—K R 3 !

Intending to play ...P—K Kt 4 —5 and thus exploit the weakness created by White's 10th move. The advance of the K Kt P will not weaken Black's castled position, as White's game is barren of attacking possibilities.

18.	Kt—R 2	Q—Q B 2
19.	Kt—B 3	Q—B 2
20.	R—B 1	

A further attempt to eject Black's annoying Knight would be futile : 20. Kt—R 2, P—K Kt 4 ; 21. P—K B 3, Q—B 2 ! and Black wins a Pawn.

20. ......   P—Q Kt 4

The notion of preventing White's demonstration on the Queen's side is attractive but does not prove feasible. Hence he might well have played ...P—K Kt 4 at once.

21.	P—Q Kt 3	P—Kt 4
22.	P—B 4	Kt P×P

23. P×P

23. ......   P—Kt 5 !

This carefully prepared thrust is decisive.

24. R P×P   B P×P
25. Kt—K 5

There is little choice : if 25. Kt—Q 2, Q—R 4 ; 26. P—Kt 3, B×P ; 27. P×B, Kt×P and White must resign.

25. ......   Q—R 4 !

Much stronger than ...B×Kt. Black is now poised for the deadly move ...P—Kt 6.

26. P×P

Or 26. P—Kt 3, Q—R 6 with the fatal threat of ...R—B 4—R 4.

26. ......   B×Kt
27. P×B   P—Kt 6 !
28. P×Kt P   Kt ×P
29. R—B 3

The only move ; but White's resistance is ebbing rapidly.

29. ......   R×R
30. P×R   R—K B 1

Threatening mate in two.

31. P—B 4   Kt—K 7 ch
32. K—B 2   Kt×P !

The quickest way.

33. R—Kt 1 ch   K—R 1
34. B×Kt   R×B ch
35. K—K 1   Q×P ch

White resigns, as he must lose his Queen. A good example of what happens when the first player allows the initiative to slip out of his hands.

12. BRESLAU, 1889

PETROFF DEFENCE

THIS game is instructive because of the way in which Black's apparently minor difficulties in the opening are built up into definite inferiority.

	White DR. S. TARRASCH	*Black* J. MASON
1.	P—K 4	P—K 4
2.	Kt—K B 3	Kt—K B 3
3.	Kt×P	P—Q 3
4.	Kt—K B 3	Kt×P
5.	P—Q 3	

Although it is rarely adopted, this move has its points.

5.	......	Kt—K B 3
6.	P—Q 4	P—Q 4
7.	B—Q 3	B—K 2

The chief virtue of White's 5th move lies in the fact that if Black wishes to continue along standard Petroff lines with 7. ...Kt—K 5, he will find himself a whole tempo behind the usual variations.

| 8. O—O | B—K Kt 5 |
| 9. P—B 3 | Q Kt—Q 2 |

The more natural 9. ...Kt—B 3 would allow the embarrassing reply 10. B—Q Kt 5.

| 10. R—K 1 | O—O |
| 11. B—K B 4 | |

A fine square for this Bishop. Note that without having committed any overt mistake, Black finds himself in a highly uncomfortable position, without a constructive plan at his disposal.

11.	R—K 1
12. Q Kt—Q 2	Kt—B 1
13. Q—Kt 3	P—Q Kt 3 ?

A wholly satisfactory reply to the annoying sortie of the Queen was not available, but this disastrous weakening of the Pawn formation at once leads to insurmountable trouble.

| 14. Kt—K 5 | Kt—K 3 |

Cutting off the Q B from the Queen's side, but even after the somewhat preferable ...Kt—Kt 3, Black would not be happy.

| 15. B—Kt 3 | P—Q R 3 |

White was threatening (among other things) 16. B—Kt 5, R—K B 1 ; 17. B—B 6, R—Kt 1 ; 18. Kt×B, Kt×Kt ; 19. B×Q P etc. But a Pawn must fall in any event.

| 16. Kt×B | Kt×Kt |
| 17. B—B 5 | B—Kt 4 |

An unsuccessful attempt to complicate matters.

18. Kt—B 3 !

Simpler and more effective than the win of a piece by 18. P—K B 4, B×P ; 19. B×B, Kt×B ; 20. B×Kt (not 20. R×R ch, Q×R ; 21. B×Kt, Q—K 6 ch), Q—Kt 4 ; 21. B—B 3, Kt—R 6 ch ; 22. K—B 1, Q×Kt ; 23. P×Kt, Q×R P (Tarrasch)—for Black could still put up a good fight.

18.	Kt—R 3
19. B×Kt	P×B
20. B×P	Q×B
21. Kt×B	Q—Q 3
22. Q—B 2 !	

Still further intensifying the weakness on Black's black squares.

| 22. ...... | P—Kt 3 |
| 23. Q—Q 3 | Kt—B 2 |

White threatened 24. Q—R 3, K—Kt 2 ; 25. Q×Kt ch !

| 24. Kt×Kt | K×Kt |

Black's game is obviously hopeless : he is a Pawn down and his pieces are tied to the defence of his pitiably vulnerable Pawns.

| 25. R—K 5 | R—R 2 |
| 26. Q R—K 1 | K—Kt 2 |

The threat was 27. Q—B 3 ch followed by R×Q P.

27. Q—K 2

Compelling his helpless opponent to part with a second Pawn.

27.	Q R—K 2
28. Q×P	Q—B 3
29. Q—K 2	P—Q Kt 4
30. P—K R 4 !	Q—B 5

As White has just announced his intention of smoking out the hostile King, Black desperately plays for the exchange of Queens. But of course this is equivalent to resignation.

31. P—R 5	Q×Q
32. R(K 1)×Q	K—B 3
33. R(K 2)—K 3	R—Q R 1
34. P—R 3	R—Q Kt 1
35. K—B 1	

Tarrasch calmly prepares to bring his King to Q Kt 4 !

35.	R—Q R 1
36. K—K 2	R—K Kt 1
37. K—Q 3	R(Kt 1)—K 1
38. K—B 2	R—Q B 1
39. K—Kt 3	R—B 3
40. R—B 3 ch	K—Kt 2
41. R—Kt 5	R—B 1

Or 41. ...K—R 3 ; 42. R(B 3)—Kt 3, P×P ? ; 43. P—K B 4 followed by R—R 3 with mate in the offing (Tarrasch). White's objective is to force the exchange of a pair of Rooks, so that his King can advance to Kt 4 with decisive effect.

42. P×P	P—R 3

42. ...P×P ; 43. R(B 3)—Kt 3 is equally hopeless.

43. R—Kt 4	R—B 5

In order to hold back White's King.

44. R—B 7 ch	R×R
45. P×R ch	K×P
46. R—Kt 3	R—R 5
47. R—R 3	K—Kt 3
48. R—B 3	K—Kt 2
49. K—B 2	

The King begins a new Odyssey, this time headed for the key square K 5.

49.	R—R 1
50. K—Q 3	K—Kt 3
51. K—K 3	K—Kt 2
52. K—B 4	K—B 3

Or 52. ...R—B 1 ch ; 53. K—K 5, R×R ; 54. P×R, P—R 4 ; 55. K—B 4 and wins (P—Kt 3 followed by P—R 4).

53. R—R 3	R—K R 1
54. P—Kt 4	R—R 2

If 54. ...K—B 2 ; 55. K—K 5 and White wins as he pleases.

55. R×P ch	Resigns

13. BRESLAU, 1889

FRENCH DEFENCE

DESPITE its flaws, this difficult game abounds in so much absorbing play that failure to include it would be a grave loss to a collection of Tarrasch's best games. Like the game that follows, it illustrates the dramatic conflict between two opposing schools of thought.

White	Black
J. MIESES	DR. S. TARRASCH

1. P—K 4	P—K 3
2. P—Q 4	P—Q 4
3. P×P	P×P
4. B—K 3	Kt—K B 3
5. B—Q 3	B—Q 3
6. Kt—K 2	O—O
7. Q Kt—B 3	

The system of development adopted here by Mieses is one of which he was very fond. It has little to recommend it, and such success as he achieved with it was due to his ability, rather than to any merit in the variation.

7.	P—B 3
8. Q—Q 2	B—K 3
9. B—K B 4	B—Q Kt 5
10. O—O	

One would have expected an aggressive player like Mieses to castle on the other wing, with exciting play in the offing.

10.	Kt—R 4
11. Q R—K 1	Kt—Q 2
12. B—K Kt 5	Q—R 4
13. Kt—Kt 3	Kt×Kt
14. R P×Kt	K R—K 1
15. K—R 2	

True to his somewhat primitive attacking style, Mieses prepares to utilise the open K R file.

15.	P—B 3
16. B—R 4 ?	

For the sake of provoking an unsound reaction, Mieses condemns this Bishop to what may turn out to be permanent inactivity. B—K 3 was in order.

16.	Kt—B 1

Tarrasch realises that 16. ...P—K Kt 4 ? would be premature : 17. B×P, P×B ; 18. Q×P ch, K—R 1 ; 19. B×P !, K×B ; 20. R—K R 1 ! He therefore waits for a more propitious moment in which to exploit the Q B's unfortunate position.

17. R—K R 1	B—Q 3
18. K—Kt 1	Q—B 2

Forcing the following rejoinder, as ...P—K Kt 4 is now a real threat.

19. P—B 4	B—K Kt 5 !

Nailing down the Q B by preventing a future P—K Kt 4.

20. Kt—K 2	

B—K 2 seems no better, as Black can simply reply ...P—K R 4 or ...Q—Q 2.

20.	R—K 2
21. P—B 4	

Mieses desperately strives to open up the game ; his great fear is that passive play will lead to a position in which he will find himself virtually a piece down.

21.	P×P
22. B×B P ch	K—R 1
23. Kt—B 3	Q R—K 1
24. R×R	

K—B 2 is a little better.

24.	Q×R
25. K—B 2	B—Kt 5 !

Elimination of the Knight is essential for the execution of the following manœuvres by Black.

26. P—R 3	B×Kt
27. Q×B	P—Q Kt 4
28. B—Kt 3	

Unavoidable—if 28. B—B 1, P—Kt 4 ; 29. P×P, P×P ; 30. P—Q 5 ch, K—Kt 1 and wins.

28.	Q—K 7 ch

If 28. ...P—Kt 4 ; 29. P×P, P×P ; 30. P—Q 5 ch, Q—K 4 ; 31. B×P etc.

29. K—Kt 1	Q—K 8 ch
30. K—R 2	

Forced ; if 30. Q×Q, R×Q ch ; 31. K—R 2, R×R ch ; 32. K×R, P—K R 3 ; 33. P—B 5, B×P ; 34. B—Q 1, P—Kt 4 ; 35. P—K Kt 4, B—K 5 ; 36. B—K B 2, Kt—K 3 and Black wins easily.

30.	Q×Q
31. P×Q	P—K R 3
32. P—B 5	

The only move to save the Bishop. Black could now simply play ...B×P, but he has a stronger line.

32.	R—K 6 !
33. B—Q 1 !	B×B

...P—K R 4, keeping the Bishop imprisoned, was more in the spirit of the play up to this point.

34. R×B	R×B P
35. P—Q 5	P×P ?

But here Tarrasch falters. The text allows White to get such strong play with his pieces that he soon acquires a clearly drawn position. The right way, says Tarrasch, was 35. ...P—B 4 ! ; 36. P—Q 6, Kt—

Q 2. If, then, 37. R—K 1, R—Q 6, holding everything.

36. R×P	K—Kt 1

If 36. ...P—R 3 ; 37. P—R 4 !, P×P ; 38. R—R 5 or else 37. R—Q 8, K—Kt 1 ; 38. P—Kt 4, K—B 2 ! (not 38. ...R×P ? ; 39. B—Kt 3 and there is no defence to the double threat of B—Q 6 or R×Kt ch !) ; 39. B—K 1, R—B 2 ; 40. B—Kt 4 or 40. R—R 8 and White should draw.

37. R×P	R×R P
38. P—Kt 4	

One can understand White's eagerness to liberate the Bishop, yet 38. R—Kt 8 ! was the proper drawing move. If, then, 38. ...R—R 5 ; 39. P—Kt 4 !, R×P ; 40. B—K 1, K—B 2 ; 41. R—Kt 7 ch, K—K 1 ; 42. R—Kt 8 ch, K—B 2 ; 43. R—Kt 7 ch and Black can make no headway ; or 38. ...R—Q 6 ; 39. P—Kt 4, K—B 2 ; 40. B—B 2, R—Q 2 ; 41. B—B 5, Kt—R 2 ; 42. R—Q R 8 ! (not 42. R—K R 8, as Black simply leaves the Knight *en prise* and answers 43. R×Kt ? with ...K—Kt 1) and White draws (Tarrasch).

38.	Kt—Q 2
39. B—Kt 3	Kt—Kt 3
40. B—B 2	R—R 3

There is nothing better, for example, 40. ...Kt—B 5 ; 41. B—Q 4, P—Q R 4 ; 42. R—Kt 8 ch, K—R 2 ; 43. R—Kt 7, Kt—K 4 ; 44. B×Kt, P×B ; 45. P—B 6 etc. (Tarrasch).

41. R—B 5	Kt—Q 2
42. R—B 8 ch	K—R 2
43. R—B 7	Kt—K 4
44. K—R 3 ?	

Missing his last drawing chance :
44. R×P, Kt×P ch ; 45. K—
Kt 3 (Tarrasch) and it does not
seem that Black has any winning
chance.

44.	R—R 6 ch

45. K—R 4

After this the win is fairly easy.
Tarrasch gives the following problem-like win after 45. P—Kt 3 ;
45. ...R—R 7 ; 46. B×P, Kt—
B 6 ; 47. P—Kt 5, Kt×P ch ; 48.
K—R 4, R—R 5 ch ; 49. K—R 5
(if 49. P—Kt 4, R—R 6 forces
mate), Kt—K 5 ; 50. P—Kt 4 (if
50. K—Kt 4, Kt—Q 3 ch followed
by ...Kt—Kt 4), R—R 6 ; 51.
P—Kt 5 (if 51. K—R 4, Kt—Kt 4
followed by ...R—R 6 mate),
R P×P ; 52. K—Kt 4 (if 52. B—
Q 4, R—R 5 ; 53. R—Q 7, Kt—
Kt 6 ch ; 54. K—Kt 4, Kt—K 7 ;
or 52. B—Kt 8 ?, R—R 6 ch ; 53.
K—Kt 4, Kt—B 7 mate), R—
Kt 6 ch ; 53. K—R 5, Kt—Q 3 ;
54. B—Q 4 (if 54. R—B 5, Kt×
P !), Kt—Kt 4 ! ; 55. R—Q 7, Kt
×B ; 56. R×Kt, R—R 7 ch ; 57.
K—Kt 4, R—R 5 ch and wins.
An exquisite line of play !

45.	R—R 5

46. R×P	R×P ch
47. K—R 3	R—K B 5
48. B—B 5	R×P

Black has an easy win now.

49. B—B 8	R—Kt 4
50. R—Q B 7	Kt—Q 6

This soon leads to the fall of the
last Pawn.

51. P—Kt 3	Kt—B 7 ch
52. K—R 2	Kt—K 5
53. B—K 7	R—Kt 3

Capture of the Pawn would be
answered by B×P.

54. K—R 3	R×P ch
55. K—R 4	P—B 4
56. R—Q 7	R—Kt 8
57. K—R 3	Kt—Kt 4 ch
58. K—R 2	Kt—B 6 ch
59. K—R 3	P—B 5

Threatening mate on the move.
White's faint hopes of stalemate
hardly justify his continuing play.

60. B—R 4	Kt×B

At last the unfortunate Bishop
departs !

61. K×Kt	R—Kt 3
62. K—R 5	P—B 6
63. R—Q 2	R—K B 3
64. R—K B 2	R—B 5

Threatens mate.

65. R—K Kt 2	R—B 4 ch !

White resigns. A monumental
struggle !

14. BRESLAU, 1889

FRENCH DEFENCE

THIS game is absorbing not only because of the alert way in which Tarrasch seizes the initiative and the delightful mating possibilities at the conclusion of the attack ; there is a clash here between the old and the new, between the rather superficial attacking style of the nineteenth-century romantics and the more thoughtful and logical methods of development characteristic of their successors.

| *White* | *Black* |
| E. SCHALLOPP | DR. S. TARRASCH |

1. P—K 4	P—K 3
2. P—Q 4	P—Q 4
3. Kt—Q B 3	Kt—K B 3
4. P—K 5	

Steinitz's continuation, very popular at the time this game was played. Black gets a good game without much effort.

4.	K Kt—Q 2
5. P—B 4	P—Q B 4
6. P×P	Kt×B P

...B×P is more customary, but the text has its points ; White's attacking plans with Q—Kt 4 and B—Q 3 are neutralised.

| 7. Kt—B 3 | Kt—B 3 |
| 8. B—K 2 | Q—Kt 3 |

Temporarily restraining White from castling.

| 9. R—Q Kt 1 | Kt—Q 2 |

To prevent B—K 3. If now 10. Kt—Q Kt 5, with the idea of playing Q Kt—Q 4 (as recommended by the *Handbuch*), Black simply replies ...B—B 4 with a very fine game.

| 10. B—Q 2 | P—B 3 |

The right move, as the following exchange frees Black's game considerably.

| 11. P×P | Kt×P |
| 12. Kt—Q R 4 | |

Driving away the hostile Queen from its annoying post, but at the cost of leaving the Knight out of play at Q R 4.

12.	Q—B 2
13. O—O	B—Q 3
14. Kt—Kt 5	

Pointless. P—K Kt 3 should have been played here or at the next move.

| 14. ...... | O—O |
| 15. P—B 4 | P—K R 3 |

To this White's best reply is 16. Kt—R 3, leaving Black with the better game because of the more harmoniously centralised position of his pieces.

| 16. P—Q B 5 ? | |

A positional blunder which allows Black to obtain two united passed Pawns.

16.	P×Kt
17. P×B	Q×P
18. P×P	Kt—K 5
19. R×R ch	

Making a bad position still worse. B—K 3 at once held out a bit more hope.

19. ......   Q×R
20. B—K 3   Q—K B 4 !

This Queen move is very strong, as will be seen.

21. P—R 4

Against Schallopp's later recommendation 21. Q—B 2, Kt—Kt 5 ; 22. Q—B 7, Kt—Kt 6 ; 23. R—K 1, Tarrasch suggests 23. ... Kt×B ch ; 24. R×Kt, Q—Kt 8 ch ; 25. B—B 1, Kt—Q 6 ; 26. R—Q B 2, B—Q 2 ! with much the better game.

21. ......   B—Q 2
22. Kt—B 5

Apparently a useful simplifying move ; but he has overlooked Tarrasch's clever reply !

22. ......   P—Q 5 !
23. Kt×B

23. B×P ? would cost a piece ; while if 23. Kt×Kt, Q×Kt ; 24. B—B 2, Kt—K 4 ! ; 25. B×P, B—B 3 (Tarrasch) with a winning attack.

23. ......   P×B
24. B—B 3

Or 24. Q—K B 1, Kt—Kt 6 ! ; 25. Q×Q (if 25. Q—K 1, Kt×B ch still wins a piece), Kt×B ch ; 26. K—B 1, Kt—Kt 6 ch etc.

24. ......   Kt—Q 7
25. R—B 1   Kt—Q 5 !

The invasion of the second Knight leads to a sparkling finish in which the Knights appear to advantage.

26. K—R 2

26. B×P would lead to pretty mating positions : 26. ...Q—B 7 ch ; 27. K—R 2, Kt—K 7 ; 28. Q—K 1, Kt—B 8 ch ; 29. K—R 3, Kt—B 5 ch ; 30. K—Kt 4, Kt—R 7 mate ! Or 27. K—R 1, Kt—K 7 ; 28. Q—K 1, Kt—Kt 6 ch ; 29. K—R 2, Kt(Q 7)—B 8 ch ; 30. K—R 3, Q—B 4 mate ! (Tarrasch).

26. ......   Q—B 5 ch
27. K—R 3   Kt(Q 7)×B
28. P×Kt   P—K 7

White resigns, forestalling Tarrasch's intention of concluding with 29. Q—K 1, Q×B P ch ; 30. K—R 2 (if 30. Q—Kt 3, Q—B 8 ch), Q—Kt 5 ; 31. R—B 3, Kt—B 6 ch ; 32. R×Kt, Q×R ; 33. K—Kt 1, R—Q 1 etc.
Schallopp's illogical development has been forcefully refuted.

15. BRESLAU, 1889

THREE KNIGHTS' GAME

Tarrasch's simultaneous play on both wings stamps this game as thoroughly modern in spirit. Such strategy was so novel at the time

TOURNAMENT GAMES
31

that even thirty years later it was
still a source of praise and wonder-
ment !

| White | Black |
| Dr. S. Tarrasch | I. Gunsberg |

1. P—K 4   P—K 4
2. Kt—K B 3   Kt—Q B 3
3. Kt—B 3   P—K Kt 3
4. B—B 4

Old-fashioned and tame. Stronger
is 4. P—Q 4, P×P; 5. Kt—
Q 5!, B—Kt 2; 6. B—K Kt 5,
P—B 3; 7. B—K B 4 and White
has a fine game.

4. ......   B—Kt 2
5. P—Q R 3

To preserve the K B against a
possible ...Kt—R 4.

5. ......   P—Q 3
6. P—Q 3   B—K 3

This does not turn out too well,
as the resulting doubled Pawns are
unwieldy and potentially weak.
But it may be that Black's 8th move
is the real mistake.

7. B×B   P×B
8. B—Kt 5   K Kt—K 2 ?

After this, Black's Knights are
destined to play a feeble part
throughout the game. ...Kt—
B 3 should have been played, with
the intention of following up with
...P—K R 3: White would either
have to exchange, or else retreat his
Bishop, permitting Black to obtain
a measure of freedom.

9. Kt—K 2   O—O
10. Q—Q 2

Tarrasch reveals in his notes that
he purposely postponed castling in
order to keep Gunsberg in the dark
as to his intentions.

10. ......   Q—K 1
11. B—R 6

He dismisses the attack by P—
K R 4 etc. as Black's pieces would
be well posted for defensive purposes.

11. ......   Kt—Q 1
12. B×B   K×B
13. Kt—Kt 3   P—B 4

It is difficult to see what Gunsberg hoped to gain by this move.
It creates a target for a subsequent
P—Kt 4. Steinitz's recommendation ...P—Q 4 follows by ...
Kt—B 2 would have been somewhat preferable.

14. Q—K 3   R—B 1
15. Kt—Q 2   Kt—Kt 1

The Knight is finally headed for
its best square, but after much loss
of time. In view of the fact, however, that White's K Kt now gets a
highly effective post at Q B 4, it
would have been worth while to
play 15. ...P—Q Kt 4.

16. Kt—B 4   Kt—B 2
17. P—Q R 4 !   Kt—B 3
18. O—O   P—K Kt 4

Angling for a King-side attack
which in the nature of things must
remain no more than a vain hope.
...P—Q 4 was better, although
after 19. Kt—Q 2, 20. Kt—B 3
and 21. K R—K 1, Black would
hardly be able to avoid ...P—Q 5,
leading to much the same kind of
position as arises after the text.

19. Q—K 2

In order to prevent ...P—K R 4.

19. ......   R—Q 1
20. K R—K 1   Kt—R 1

Now that ...P—Q 4 has been discouraged, Black strives for ... Kt—Kt 3—B 5.

21. Q—Q 2 !

Gaining time by the attack on the K Kt P and at the same time preparing for P—Kt 4.

21. ......   Q—Kt 3

...P—K R 3 would have been better, for a number of reasons : it would leave open the possibility of ...Kt—Kt 3, it would leave the Queen free to guard the Queen's side, and it would avoid the uneconomical protection of the K Kt P by the Queen.

22. P—Kt 4 !   P—Kt 3

White's Queen's side attack is very strong. 22. ...P×P would not do because of 23. Q×Q Kt P, winning a Pawn. The text, while unavoidable, permits the following powerful infiltration by White's Q R.

23. P—Kt 5 !

Fixing the target.

23. ......   Kt—B 2
24. P—R 5   Kt—Q 2
25. P×P   P×P
26. R—R 7

Very strong. Black cannot play 26. ...P—Q 4 because of 27.

P×P, P×P ; 28. Kt×P, either Kt×Kt ; 29. R×Kt etc.

26. ......   P—R 4

Hoping for ...P—R 5—6 followed by ...P—Kt 5 and Kt—Kt 4. However, the attack is mostly sham and White has little trouble disposing of it.

27. R—Kt 7   P—Kt 5
28. Kt—B 1   K—R 1
29. Q—K 3   P—R 5
30. K—R 1

In order to prevent ...P—R 6. Tarrasch does not give his opponent the slightest chance.

30. ......   P—Q 4

Realising that his " attack " is futile, Gunsberg plays to give up a Pawn temporarily. He has little choice, as his Q Kt P is condemned in any event.

31. Kt×Kt P   P—Q 5
32. Q—K 2   Kt×Kt
33. R×Kt(Kt 6)   R—Q Kt 1
34. R×R   R×R
35. R—Kt 1   Kt—Q 3
36. P—Kt 6   Kt—B 1

The Q Kt P is now lost, and it is quite an interesting problem to see how White can maintain the advantage. Thus if 37. P—Kt 7, Kt—Q 3 ; 38. R—Kt 6, R×P ! ; 39. R×Kt, R—Kt 8 ; 40. K—Kt 1, P—R 6 ; 41. P—Kt 3, Q—R 3 and White's position is very difficult ; or 37. Q—Q 2, R×P ; 38. R×R, Kt×R ; 39. Q—R 5, Q—B 3 ! ; 40. Q×Kt, Q×P ; 41. Q—Kt ! ? (White should take a draw by perpetual check), P—R 6 ! and wins (Tarrasch).

37. P—K B 3 !

This unexpected move is decisive ! If now 37. ...P—Kt 6 ; 38. P×P, P×P ; 39. Q—Q 2 and wins (39. ...R×P ; 40. R×R, Kt×R ; 41. Q—R 5 and wins).

37. ......   P×P
38. Q×P   K—Kt 2

Or 38. ...Kt×P ; 39. Kt—Q 2, Kt—Q 2 ; 40. R×R ch, Kt×R ; 41. Q—B 8 ch, Q—Kt 1 ; 42. Q—R 6 ch, Q—R 2 ; 43. Q—B 6 ch, Q—Kt 2 ; 44. Q×P ch and wins (Tarrasch).

39. Kt—Q 2   R×P

If 39. ...Kt×P ; 40. Kt—B 4, Kt—Q 2 ; 41. R×R ch, Kt×R ; 42. Kt×P winning easily.

40. R—K B 1 !   Kt—Q 3
41. Kt—B 4 !   Resigns

For if 41. ...Kt×Kt ; 42. Q—B 8 ch, K—R 2 ; 43. R—B 7 ch etc.

16. MANCHESTER, 1890
RUY LOPEZ

ONE can hardly call this a game ; it s really a fragment. However, since several generations of chess players have chuckled over it, its inclusion in this collection is eminently appropriate.

White	*Black*
DR. S. TARRASCH	I. GUNSBERG

1. P—K 4	P—K 4
2. Kt—K B 3	Kt—Q B 3
3. B—Kt 5	P—Q R 3
4. B—R 4	Kt—B 3
5. O—O	Kt×P
6. P—Q 4	P—Q Kt 4
7. B—Kt 3	P—Q 4
8. P×P	B—K 3
9. P—B 3	B—K 2
10. R—K 1	

This is the move which in later years became the point of departure for the famous Breslau Variation (see Games 87 and 176).

10. ......   O—O
11. Kt—Q 4

White's last move sets his opponent quite a problem. 11. ... Kt×K P loses a piece after 12. P—B 3, while 11. ...Kt×Kt ; 12. P×Kt leaves Black with a very poor Pawn position.

11. ......   Q—Q 2 ??

This is the position of the famous

Tarrasch Trap. Black loses a piece by force.

12. Kt×B   P×Kt

Or 12. ...Q×Kt ; 13. R×Kt with the same result.

13. R×Kt   Resigns

Tarrasch had already won in the same way from Zukertort in the Frankfort 1887 Tournament ! Incidentally, the reader who is curious about the solution of Black's difficulties in the diagrammed position should study the games quoted above. Surprisingly enough, Black must have recourse to the complicated mazes of the Breslau Variation (11. ...Kt×K P ; 12. P—B 3, B—Q 3 etc.).

17. MANCHESTER, 1890

PETROFF .DEFENCE

THIS game is interesting not only because it illustrates Tarrasch's happy knack of gradually and systematically increasing an opening advantage, but also because it must have been much more difficult to play than appearances indicate. The ability to steer clear of apparently advantageous continuations in order to find the single move which really maintains the pressure, is one of the hall-marks of a great master.

White	*Black*
DR. S. TARRASCH	J. MASON
1. P—K 4	P—K 4
2. Kt—K B 3	Kt—K B 3
3. Kt×P	P—Q 3
4. Kt—K B 3	Kt×P
5. P—Q 4	P—Q 4

6. B—Q 3	B—K 2
7. O—O	O—O
8. R—K 1	Kt—K B 3

White's last move, despite its seemingly simple and obvious character, is not an easy one to meet. See Game 105 for the alternative 8. ...B—K B 4.

9. B—K B 4

Good enough to maintain the advantage, but 9. Kt—K 5 is more aggressive and has the additional advantage ˉ of preventing ...B—K Kt 5.

| 9. ...... | B—K Kt 5 |
| 10. Q Kt—Q 2 | Kt—R 4 ? |

This move is out of place and at best loss of time. ...B—R 4, intending ...B—Kt 3, does not seem a bad idea here. ...Kt—B 3, completing his development, was also playable.

11. B—K 3   Kt—Q B 3

Black is evidently reluctant to admit his mistake, else he would have played 11. ...Kt—K B 3, hoping that his loss of time would be compensated for by the less effective posting of White's Q B. 11. ...P—K B 4 would be answered by 12. P—K R 3.

12. P—K R 3

Simple and strong. If now 12. ...B—K 3 ; 13. Kt—K 5, Kt—B 3 ; 14. P—Q B 3 followed by P—K B 4 with a promising game.

| 12. ...... | B×Kt |
| 13. Q×B | P—K Kt 3 |

Had the Knight retreated, White would have brought his Knight to K B 5 by way of B 1 and Kt 3. The text avoids this, but weakens the black squares.

14. P—B 3

A necessary precaution against ...Kt—Kt 5.

14.	Q—Q 2
15. Kt—B 1	Kt—Q 1
16. B—K R 6	Kt—Kt 2
17. Kt—K 3	P—Q B 3
18. Kt—Kt 4	Kt(Q 1)—K 3

White has built up considerable pressure against the hostile black squares, but it is not easy to find the most effective way to continue the attack. Thus if 19. Q—B 6, Q—Q 3 (not 19. ...Q—Q 1; 20. B × Kt, B × Q; 21. B × B, threatening Kt—R 6 mate) and White's Queen must retreat. Or 19. Kt—B 6 ch, B × Kt; 20. Q × B, K R—K 1 (not 20. ...Q—Q 1; 21. B × Kt, Kt × B; 22. R—K 7. with a strong initiative). Or finally 19. Q—K 3 (threatening 20. B × Kt, K × B; 21. Q—K 5 ch and wins), K R—K 1 (so as to answer B × Kt with ...Kt × B). In all these instances, Tarrasch points out, Black has a difficult but not necessarily a lost game.

19. R—K 2 !

He intends to double on the K file before undertaking any decisive action.

19. ...... Q—Q 1

...P—K B 4 would allow Kt—K 5 with powerful effect.

20. Q R—K 1   B—Kt 4

Threatening to win the exchange with ...P—K B 4.

21. B × B   Kt × B

Or 21. ...Q × B; 22. Kt—B 6 ch, K—R 1; 23. Kt—Q 7, K R—K 1; 24. Kt—K 5, R—K 2; 25. Kt × P ch, R × Kt; 26. Q × R, R—K B 1; 27. P—K R 4 !, Q × P; 28. P—K Kt 3 ! with a won game (Tarrasch).

22. Q—B 6 !

Forcing an easily won ending. Less good was 22. Q—B 4 (if 22. Kt—B 6 ch, K—R 1; 23. Q—B 4, Kt(Kt 4)—K 3; 24. Q—R 4 ?, Kt—R 4, winning a piece), Kt—R 4 ! (better than 22. ...Kt(Kt 2)—K 3; 23. Q—K 5, P—B 3; 24. Q—Kt 3, Kt—Kt 2; 25. P—K R 4, Kt—B 2; 26. R—K 7 with a strong attack, or 22. ...Kt(Kt 4)—K 3 ?; 23. Kt—R 6 ch and 24. Kt × P ch) and Black stands well; 23. Q—K 5, P—B 3; 24. Q—K 7, Kt—B 5 ! and the advantage has changed hands (Tarrasch).

22.	Q × Q
23. Kt × Q ch	K—R 1
24. R—K 7	Kt(Kt 4)—K 3

The Pawn could not have been saved, for if 24. ...K R—Q Kt 1 ; 25. P—K R 4, Kt(Kt 4)—K 3 ; 26. Kt—Q 7, R—K 1 ; 27. R×P—or 24. ...P—Kt 3 ; 25. B—R 6 etc.

25. R×Kt P   Q R—Kt 1

Black's game is quite hopeless. Thus if 25. ...K R—Q Kt 1 ; 26. R×B P, R×P ? ; 27. R(K 1)×Kt, Kt×R ; 28. R×P mate.

26. R×R P   R×P
27. Kt—Q 7   R—B 1
28. Kt—K 5   R(Kt 7)—Kt 1

He cannot avoid the loss of a second Pawn, for if 28. ...P—B 3 ; 29. Kt×P, R×Kt ; 30. R—R 8 ch winning both Knights !

29. Kt×B P ch   K—Kt 1
30. Kt—R 6 ch

An experiment to see whether Black will play 30. ...K—B 1 ? allowing 31. R—B 7 ch, K—K 1 ; 32. R×Kt winning both Knights !

30 ......   K—R 1
31. Kt—B 7 ch   K—Kt 1
32. Kt—K 5   R—R 1

White was threatening 33. Kt—Q 7, R—R 1 ; 34. R—Kt 7 with the idea of Kt—B 6 ch and wins.

33. R×R   R×R
34. Kt×B P   R×P
35. Kt—K 7 ch   K—B 1
36. Kt×P   R—R 6

Threatening ...Kt×P, but the end is near.

37. B—B 4   P—R 3
38. Kt—Kt 6 !   Resigns

If the attacked Knight moves, there follows 39. Kt—Q 7 mate. If 38. ...K—B 2 ; 39. P—Q 5, Kt—Q 1 ; 40. P—Q 6 ch, K—B 3 ; 41. Kt—Q 7 ch and wins. White's agile Knight has made no less than 15 moves !

18. MANCHESTER, 1890

FRENCH DEFENCE

THERE are times when " mere " technique becomes so refined that it is transmuted into great artistry. The little-known ending which concludes this game is a case in point. No better example of Rook and Pawn play could possibly be recommended to the student ; and those who have on occasion allowed a win to slip through their hands will marvel at the exactitude and patience with which Tarrasch gradually approaches his goal.

| *White* | *Black* |
| DR. S. TARRASCH | E. THOROLD |

1. P—K 4   P—K 3
2. P—Q 4   P—Q 4
3. Kt—Q 2

This move, which was revived so successfully in the later '20's by Spielmann, was a great favourite with Tarrasch at this stage of his career.

3. ......   P—Q B 4
4. K P×P   Q×P

A reply recommended by some authorities in order to avoid the isolated Q P which generally results from ...K P×P. 4. ... BP×P would not be good because

of 5. B—Kt 5 ch, B—Q 2 ; 6.
P×P !, B×B ; 7. Q—R 5.

5. K Kt—B 3

This temporary Pawn sacrifice is
almost compulsory, since 5. P×P
would give Black too good a game.

5. ......   P×P
6. B—B 4   Q—K R 4

The moderns rightly prefer the
more modest retreat ...Q—Q 1.
The Queen is rather exposed after
the text, and Black soon finds himself in difficulties.

7. O—O   Kt—Q B 3

If 7. ...P—K 4 ; 8. Kt×K P.

8. Kt—Kt 3   P—K 4
9. Kt×K P !   Q×Q
10. R×Q   Kt×Kt
11. R—K 1   P—B 3
12. P—B 4   B—Q Kt 5

While White devotes some time
to regaining the piece, Black utilises
this interval to promote his development.

13. B—Q 2   B×B
14. Kt×B   B—B 4
15. P×Kt   O—O—O
16. B—Q 3   B×B
17. P×B   P×P

Black has defended well thus far,
but the advanced Q P will be weak,
requiring careful handling on
Black's part.

18. Q R—B 1 ch !

A clever interpolation. Black's
King is driven away from the
centre, for if 18. ...K—Q 2 ; 19.

R×P, Kt—B 3 ; 20. R—B 4 winning the Q P. Or 19. ...Kt—
K 2 ; 20. Kt—B 3, Kt—B 3 ; 21.
R—K 4, K R—K 1 ; 22. R—Kt 4 !
winning a Pawn.

18. ......   K—Kt 1
19. R×P   Kt—B 3
20. Q R—K 1   K R—K 1 ?

A very poor move which leads to
a lost ending. After 20. ...R—
Q 2 ; 21. R—K 7, K R—Q 1 the
win would be much more difficult,
if at all possible.

21. R×R   Kt×R

If 21. ...R×R ; 22. R×R ch,
Kt×R ; 23. Kt—Kt 3 and the
Q P falls.

22. R—K 7   P—Q R 3

Black is powerless : the loss of a
Pawn is unavoidable.

23. Kt—Kt 3   P—Q Kt 3
24. Kt×P   R×Kt
25. R×Kt ch   K—B 2

Although White has won a Pawn,
the ending is far from easy. The
following play readily divides into
the following phases :
1. White protects the Q P with

his Rook and then brings his King to K 3, relieving the Rook.

2. The Rook moves along the third rank in order to attack the hostile Pawns and weaken them by forcing their advance.

3. The Q P, which looks so weak, soon appears in its proper rôle of formidable passed Pawn. It is advanced so as to protect the Rook at K 5. Once the Rook is free to move along the fifth rank, it can simultaneously attack Black's Pawns and guard White's.

4. By this time, Black's pieces will be completely tied up, and White will be in a position to advance the passed Pawn, convoyed by King and Rook.

5. Above all, Tarrasch strives throughout to lessen his opponent's mobility. Black's terrain is systematically constricted until he is virtually left without a move.

26. R—K 3 !

26. R—K 7 ch looks strong, but after 26. ...K—Q 3 ; 27. R×P, R×P ; 28. R×P, R—Q 8 ch ; 29. K—B 2, R—Q 7 ch followed by ...R×Q Kt P the ending is unclear : White should win, but Black has drawing chances and the play must be calculated with great exactitude.

26.   K—Q 2
27. K—B 2   P—Kt 3
28. R—R 3 !   P—K R 4

Thus the K Kt P has been weakened. ....

29. K—K 3   R—Q 3
30. P—Q 4   R—K 3 ch
31. K—Q 3   R—K 8

A futile attempt at counterplay.

32. R—Kt 3   R—K 3
33. R—K 3   R—Q 3
34. R—K 5   R—K B 3
35. P—Q R 4 !

The ending has proceeded according to schedule. Now Tarrasch is ready to advance the Queen's side Pawns to take the sting out of any invasion of his second rank.

35. ......   R—B 7
36. R—K 2   R—B 3
37. P—Q Kt 4   R—B 8
38. R—K 5   R—B 7

38. ...R—Q R 8 would be answered by P—R 5 ; or if 38. ... R—Q Kt 8 ; 39. P—Kt 5.

39. R—K Kt 5

Repulsing the counter-attack and forcing Black's Rook to retreat. Note that this has been made possible by the advance of the Queen's side Pawns.

39. ......   R—B 3
40. P—R 3

A useful tempo move. 40. P—Q 5 could be answered by ...R—B 5, or if 40. K—K 4, R—K 3 ch ; 41. R—K 5, R—Q B 3. After the text, Black must disturb the position of either his Rook or King.

40. ......   K—Q 3
41. K—K 4   R—K 3 ch
42. R—K 5   R—B 3
43. P—Q 5   K—Q 2

He had no choice, since Rook moves would be answered by R—K 6 ch.

44. R—Kt 5!

The Rook is to go to K B 3, driving the hostile Rook off the only available open file.

44.	K—Q 3
45. R—Kt 3	K—K 2
46. R—K B 3	R—Q 3
47. K—K 5	R—Q 1

R—B 7 ch was threatened.

48. P—Q 6 ch   K—Q 2

Of course, if 48. ...R×P ; 49. R—B 7 ch with an easily won King and Pawn ending.

49. R—B 7 ch	K—B 1
50. R—B 7 ch	K—Kt 1
51. R—B 2	R—K 1 ch
52. K—B 6	P—Q Kt 4

Quite hopeless. Resignation is in order.

53. P—Q 7	R—R 1
54. K—K 7	R—R 2 ch
55. K—Q 6	R—R 1
56. R—K 2	Resigns

The technical perfection of Tarrasch's endgame play is seen here to good advantage.

19. MANCHESTER, 1890

RUY LOPEZ

TARRASCH's treatment of the ending is a model for the exploitation of the advantage of the exchange. Blackburne is gradually constricted and thrown back all along the line until further resistance is no longer feasible.

| *White* | *Black* |
| DR. S. TARRASCH | J. H. BLACKBURNE |

1. P—K 4	P—K 4
2. Kt—K B 3	Kt—Q B 3
3. B—Kt 5	P—Q 3
4. P—Q 4	P×P
5. Kt×P	B—Q 2
6. Kt—Q B 3	Kt—B 3
7. O—O	B—K 2
8. P—Q Kt 3	O—O
9. B—Kt 2	

This development of the Bishop, attributed to Mackenzie but popularised by Tarrasch, is doubtless more effective than B—Kt 5. At Kt 2 the Bishop cannot be exchanged so easily, and it is trained menacingly on Black's King's side.

9. ......   Kt—K 1

Black cannot hope to free his position with such retiring moves. Relatively better is ...R—K 1 and ...B—K B 1, as played by Schlechter in an analogous position in Game 24.

10. Kt—Q 5 !

As Black retreats, White advances. The presence of this outpost is quite burdensome for Black.

| 10. ...... | Kt×Kt |
| 11. B×B | Q×B |

11. ...Kt×B P ; 12. B×Kt, Kt×R ; 13. B—Kt 5, P—Q B 3 ; 14. Kt×B ch, Q×Kt ; 15. B—Q 3 would, of course be in White's favour.

12. Q×Kt   B—Q 1

Black wants to drive away the irritating Knight with ...P—

Q B 3, but since he will weaken the Q P thereby, he naturally desires to retain his Bishop.

13. Q R—Q 1   Q—K 3

White's last move has made it possible to answer 13. ...P—Q B 3; 14. Kt—K 3, B—B 3 with 15. P—K 5.

14. Q—Q 3   P—Q B 3

Weakening the Q P; but if 14. ...P—K B 4; 15. K R—K 1, P× P; 16. R×P or 15. ...P—B 5; 16. P—K 5 with distinct advantage for White in either event.

15. Kt—K 3   P—B 3

A new weakening move, which Blackburne must have played with the greatest reluctance; however, with Kt—B 5 and Q—Kt 3 in the offing, White's Bishop has become too dangerous. Furthermore, if 15. ...B—B 3; 16. B×B, Q×B; 17. Kt—B 4, R—Q 1; 18. P—K 5 with a winning game.

16. Kt—B 5   B—B 2
17. K R—K 1   R—Q 1
18. P—Q B 4   R—B 2
19. Q—R 3 !   K—R 1 ?

Missing the point of White's last move. ...Q—B 1 should have been played to avoid the loss of the exchange.

20. Kt—R 6 !   Q×Q

Or 20. ...R—K 2; 21. Q×Q, R×Q; 22. Kt—B 7 ch still winning the exchange. The text at least has the merit of splitting White's Pawns.

21. Kt×R ch   K—Kt 1
22. P×Q   K×Kt
23. P—B 4   K—K 3
24. K—Kt 2   P—K Kt 3
25. K—B 3   Kt—Kt 2
26. R—K 2

Tarrasch is consolidating his game before undertaking decisive action. His material advantage can make itself felt only after some new lines are opened.

26. ......   K—B 2
27. R(K 2)—Q 2   R—K 1
28. B—R 3 !

An important move. The following forced reply intensifies the weakness of the Q P and reduces the scope of the Bishop.

28. ......   P—Q B 4
29. B—Kt 2   Kt—K 3
30. P—K R 4

Tarrasch's next step is to prepare a breakthrough on the K Kt file. Black is able to prevent this, but only at the cost of weakening his position.

30. ......   P—Q R 3
31. R—Kt 2   P—Q Kt 4

The advance of these Pawns is poor policy, as the ultimate result is a fine open file for White's Rooks.

32. B—B 3   P—Kt 5
33. B—Kt 2   P—Q R 4
34. Q R—K Kt 1

Threatening 35. P—B 5, Kt—B 1; 36. P—R 5, P—Kt 4; 37. P—R 6 ! followed by P—K R 4. This breakthrough would have been interesting because of the utilisation of the doubled K R P. In order to prevent this advance, Blackburne resorts to a desperate expedient.

| 34. | ...... | P—Q 4 ? ! |
| 35. | B P×P | Kt×P |

Black has gained some freedom, but he has given White a strong passed Pawn and left his Q B P exposed to attack.

36.	R—Q 2	B—Q 3
37.	R(Q 2)—Q 1	P—R 5
38.	B—B 1	

The Bishop will now be more useful on its original diagonal.

| 38. | ...... | Kt—R 4 |
| 39. | R(Kt 1)—K 1 | |

R—Kt 2 would have been simpler, but the text is good enough : if now 39. ...B×P ; 40. B—K 3, B—Q 3 (or 40. ...B—Kt 6 ; 41. R—K Kt 1, B×P ; 42. R—Kt 4 and White wins easily) ; 41. R—Q B 1 etc.

39.	......	R—Q R 1
40.	R—K 2	P×P
41.	P×P	R—R 8
42.	R(Q 1)—K 1	Kt—Kt 2

After this Tarrasch forces winning simplifications, but if 42. ... B—K 4 ; 43. B—K 3, R—R 6 ;

44. R—Q Kt 1, B—Q 3 ; 45. R—Q B 2 and wins.

43.	B—B 4 !	R×R
44.	R×R	K—K 2
45.	R—Q R 1	

At last Tarrasch has the desired position. His Rook penetrates into Black's game, and the cooperation of White's King and Q P adds the final touch.

45.	......	B×B
46.	K×B	Kt—K 1
47.	R—R 7 ch	K—Q 3
48.	R—R 6 ch	K—Q 2
49.	P—K 5	P×P ch
50.	K×P	Kt—B 2
51.	R—Q B 6	Kt—Kt 4
52.	R×B P	Kt—B 6
53.	R—R 5	Kt—K 7
54.	R—R 7 ch	K—B 1
55.	P—Q 6	Resigns

20. DRESDEN, 1892

RUY LOPEZ

THE precision and clarity with which Tarrasch winds up this ending from move 16 on, make this game worthy of careful study. His opponent, on the other hand, plays carelessly and misses several opportunities.

| *White* | *Black* |
| M. PORGES | DR. S. TARRASCH |

1.	P—K 4	P—K 4
2.	Kt—K B 3	Kt—Q B 3
3.	B—Kt 5	Kt—B 3
4.	O—O	Kt×P
5.	P—Q 4	Kt—Q 3

This variation was a great favourite with Tarrasch and Pillsbury. It leads to simplifying exchanges which relieve Black of the difficulties he usually encounters in the Berlin Defence ; and his two Bishops and Queen's side majority give him chances in the endgame.

6. B×Kt   Q P×B
7. P×P   Kt—B 4
8. Q×Q ch

For 8. Q—K 2, Kt—Q 5, see Game 48.

8. ......   K×Q

The King is well placed here for the ending, and with the Queens removed, is in no danger. Thus if 9. B—Kt 5 ch, K—K 1 ; 10. Kt—B 3, P—K R 3 ; 11. B—B 4, B—K 3 ; 12. Q R—Q 1, R—Q 1 ; 13. Kt—K 4, P—B 4 etc. (Harmonist-Tarrasch, Breslau, 1889).

9. Kt—B 3   P—K R 3

In order to prevent Kt—Kt 5 in reply to his next move.

10. P—Q Kt 3   B—K 3
11. B—Kt 2   B—K 2
12. Q R—Q 1 ch   K—B 1
13. K R—K 1

Mechanical play ; Tarrasch recommends Kt—K 2 with a view to Kt—B 4 or Q Kt—Q 4, striving for the exchange of Black's Q B.

13. ......   P—K Kt 4 !

Preventing an eventual Kt—B 4 and also neutralising a possible advance of the K B P at a later stage.

14. Kt—K 4

Kt—K 2 would now be answered by . . .P—B 4—the customary policy of taking away squares from a hostile Knight when one has the two Bishops.

14. ......   P—Kt 3 ?

A hasty move, instead of which . . .R—Q 1 should have been played.

15. Kt—Q 4 ?

Missing the excellent reply 15. Kt—Q 6 ch ! which is best answered by . . .B×Kt with equality. Because of the position of Black's K R on the long diagonal, 15. . . . Kt×Kt ? would cost him a piece, while 15. . . .P×Kt ; 16. P×P would leave White with the better game.

15. ......   Kt×Kt
16. R×Kt   K—Kt 2

Now the game is once more proceeding satisfactorily and Tarrasch is soon able to establish and augment an advantage.

17. Kt—B 6   P—Q R 4
18. P—Q R 4   P—B 4
19. R—Q 3   P—B 5

The undoubling of this Pawn leaves Black with an effective Queen-side majority which soon leaves him with a clearly winning position.

20. P×P   B×P
21. R—Q 4

If 21. R—Q 7, B—Kt 5 ; 22. P—B 3, B—Q B 4 followed by . . . B—K 3 (Tarrasch) with a fine game.

| 21. ...... | B—K 3 |
| 22. Kt—K 4 | K R—Q 1 |

Further simplification is now the guiding theme.

23. K R—Q 1

| 23. ...... | B—K B 4 ! |

The decisive move. Black threatens to win a piece with ... B×Kt, and the threatened Knight cannot move.

| 24. P—K B 3 | B×Kt |
| 25. R×R | |

P×B ? would be a blunder because of ...B—B 4.

25.	R×R
26. R×R	B×R
27. P×B	K—B 3

Black calmly proceeds with his plan.

| 28. B—R 3 | P—Kt 4 ! |

Creating a passed Q R P against which White is helpless.

29. P×P ch	K×P
30. K—B 2	K—B 5
31. B—Kt 2	B—K 2

All clear, simple and logical.

32. K—B 3	P—R 5
33. P—R 4.	P—R 6
34. B—R 1	B—Kt 5
35. P×P	P×P

White resigns ; there is nothing to be done against ...B—B 6.

21. DRESDEN, 1892

RUY LOPEZ

THIS game has been known for decades as " the Dresden trap ". Although it rarely occurs in actual play, it plays a basic rôle in the treatment of the Steinitz Defence.

| *White* | *Black* |
| DR. S. TARRASCH | G. MARCO |

1. P—K 4	P—K 4
2. Kt—K B 3	Kt—Q B 3
3. B—Kt 5	P—Q 3
4. P—Q 4	B—Q 2
5. Kt—B 3	B—K 2
6. O—O	

6. B×Kt, B×B ; 7. Q—Q 3 is an advantageous alternative.

| 6. ...... | Kt—B 3 |
| 7. R—K 1 | O—O ? |

Black hopes to maintain the centre, but the game demonstrates conclusively that this policy is not feasible.

| 8. B×Kt ! | B×B |

...P×B loses a Pawn.

| 9. P×P | P×P |
| 10. Q×Q | Q R×Q |

For 10. ...K R×Q see the concluding note.

11. Kt×P   B×P

Not 11. ...Kt×P ? ; 12. Kt×
B winning a piece.

12. Kt×B   Kt×Kt

Obviously the Knight cannot be
taken. But apparently Marco's
calculations have taken him no
further than this stage !

13. Kt—Q 3 !   P—K B 4

Forced.

14. P—K B 3   B—B 4 ch

15. Kt×B !

Simple and effective. Tarrasch
points out that 15. K—B 1 would
not be good enough because of 15.
...B—Kt 3 ; 16. P×Kt (if 16.
Kt—B 4, Kt—Q 7 ch), P×P ch ;
17. Kt—B 4, P—K Kt 4 ; 18. R×
P, P×Kt ; 19. K—K 2 (if 19.
B×P, R—Q 7 or 19. R×P, R—
Q 8 ch ; 20. K—K 2, R×R ; 21.
K×R, R—B 7), K R—K 1 ; 20.
R×R ch, R×R ch etc.

15. ......   Kt×Kt
16. B—Kt 5   R—Q 4

If now 17. P—Q B 4, R—Q 2 ;
18. B—K 7, Kt—Q 6.

17. B—K 7   Resigns

Black must lose the exchange (if
17. ...R—K 1 or ...R—B 2 ; 18.
P—Q B 4).

Curiously enough, Tarrasch had
published the whole variation as
analysis about a year and a half
earlier in the *Deutsche Schach-
zeitung*. Since that time, Black's
inability to avoid giving up the
centre has been one of the fundamental motifs of the play against
this defence.

Note that if Black had played 10.
...K R×Q there would have fol-
lowed 11. Kt×P, B×P ; 12. Kt×
B, Kt×Kt ; 13. Kt—Q 3, P—
K B 4 ; 14. P—K B 3, B—B 4 ch ;
15. K—B 1 !, R—K B 1 ; 16. K—
K 2 winning a piece.

22. DRESDEN, 1892

QUEEN'S PAWN GAME

THIS was one of Tarrasch's favourite games. In later years, as Tarrasch's doctrines became more and
more diffused, such games were
produced as a matter of course
by younger masters. After such
masterpieces became almost common place, the capacity to admire
Tarrasch's pioneering efforts likewise lessened.

White	*Black*
T. VON SCHEVE	DR. S. TARRASCH

1. P—Q 4.	P—Q 4
2. Kt—K B 3	P—Q B 4
3. P—B 3	

Rather slow. P—B 4 is the best way to play for the initiative.

3.	P—K 3
4. B—B 4	Q—Kt 3
5. Q—B 2	

Q—Kt 3 is more likely to lead to equality, which is all that White can now hope for. The position of the Queen on the Q B file is soon made highly uncomfortable by the opposition of Black's Q R on the same file. This explains the following capture.

5.	P×P !
6. P×P	Kt—B 3
7. P—K 3	B—Q 2
8. Kt—B 3	R—B 1
9. B—K 2	

B—Q 3 looks more natural, but then the reply ...Kt—Kt 5 would deprive White of the K B's services.

9.	Kt—B 3
10. O—O	B—K 2
11. P—Q R 3 ?	

White advances the wrong R P. He should have played P—K R 3 in order to preserve his Q B from exchange. The text (apparently played as a preparation for B—Q 3) creates a seemingly slight weakness on the Queen's side of which Tarrasch takes masterly advantage. 11. Kt—K 5 would be effectively met by ...Kt×Kt followed by ...Kt—K 5 !

11.	Kt—K R 4
12. B—Kt 3	Kt×B
13. R P×Kt	O—O
14. B—Q 3	

White's attempts at King's side attack are refuted easily enough, whereas Black's coming action on the Queen's side has definite grounds for a successful conclusion.

14.	P—Kt 3
15. K—R 2	

Initiating a fantastic scheme of attack which has no hope of success and cuts off the K R from the scene of hostilities. K R—B 1 was the logical move.

15.	Kt—R 4 !

Provoking the following reply, which only loses time for White.

16. Kt—K 5 ?	B—K 1
17. R—R 1	P—B 3

Played with gain of time because of White's 16th move.

18. Kt—B 3

18. Kt×Kt P ?, P×Kt ; 19. B×P, K—Kt 2 leaves White with inadequate compensation for the piece.

18.	Kt—B 5

Taking advantage of 11. P—Q R 3 ?. The reply P—Kt 3 would lose a Pawn.

19. Q R—Q Kt 1	Q—R 4

Practically forcing the following exchange because of the threat of ...Kt×R P or ...Kt×Kt P.

20. B×Kt	R×B

Now Black has two Bishops against two Knights, and this will soon tell heavily in his favour.

| 21. | Q—Q 2 | B—B 2 |
| 22. | R—R 1 | K R—B 1 |

Tarrasch's objective is now to force the removal of White's Knight from Q B 3, assuring complete control of the Q B file by Black.

23. P—K Kt 4

Still continuing with his fallacious plan. K R—Q B 1 was still the proper course.

23. ......   P—Kt 3

An incomprehensible-looking move, but Tarrasch explains that he had intended 23. ...P—Q Kt 4 ?, noting as he touched the Pawn that its advance two squares would be answered by 24. Kt× Q P !

24. P—K Kt 3

Possibly with some idea of playing 25. P—Kt 5, P×P ; 26. Kt—K 5 which, if played at once, would have been met by ...B—Q 3 pinning the Knight.

| 24. | ...... | P—K Kt 4 |
| 25. | Kt—K Kt 1 | P—Kt 4 |

Now that White's Queen is unguarded, this advance is playable.

26.	K Kt—K 2	Q—Kt 3
27.	K—Kt 2	P—Q R 4
28.	R—Q R 2	

Momentarily delaying ...P—Kt 5, for if 28. ...P—Kt 5 ; 29. P×P, P×P ; 30. Kt—R 4, Q—B 3 ; 31. P—Kt 3, R—B 7 ; 32. R×R, Q×R ; 33. Q×Q, R×Q ; 34. R—K 1 and it is clear that Black has not made the most of his advantage.

| 28. | ...... | Q—B 3 |
| 29. | Q—Q 1 | B—Kt 3 |

Again ...P—Kt 5 would be premature : 30. P×P, P×P ; 31. Kt—R 4, R—B 7 ; 32. Kt—B 5 etc.

30.	Q—R 1	P—Kt 5
31.	P×P	P×P
32.	R—R 6	Q—K 1

The results of Black's play in the Q B file and White's faulty defence are now apparent : if 33. Kt—Q 1, B—Q 6 ; 34. R—K 1 (or 34. K—B 1, R—B 8), B×Kt ; 35. R×B, R—B 8 and wins. If 33. Kt—R 4, R—B 7 ; 34. Kt—Kt 6 (if 34. Kt —Kt 1, B—K 5 ch ; if 34. Q—Q 1, Q—Kt 4 is decisive), R—Q 1 ; 35. R—K 1, Q—Kt 4 and wins.

What follows is sheer despair. .

33.	R×K P	P×Kt
34.	Kt×P	Q—Q 2
35.	R—Kt 6	B—Q 1
36.	R—Q R 6	Q×P
37.	P—B 3	Q—B 4
38.	P—K 4	P×P
39.	P×P	Q—Kt 5
40.	Q—K 1	R×P
41.	R—R 7	B×P ch
42.	K—Kt 1	B—Q Kt 3

White resigns—none too soon.

23. DRESDEN, 1892

BISHOP'S GAMBIT

THE ability to defend oneself against a protracted attack is found, as a rule, in only the greatest masters. Cool judgment, steadiness under fire, a wary eye for potential threats, stubborn resistance to withering attacking moves and patient hope for the moment when the counter-attack can set in—these are the qualities which a great defensive player must possess.

White	Black
S. WINAWER	DR. S. TARRASCH

1.	P—K 4	P—K 4
2.	P—K B 4	

Evidently Winawer has made up his mind that his best chance against his redoubtable opponent lies in playing for the attack.

2.	......	P×P
3.	B—B 4	P—Q 4
4.	B×P	Q—R 5 ch

The old-fashioned line, which has gradually been dropped in favour of ...Kt—K B 3. The latter move gives Black a quick development and avoids the creation of any organic weakness.

5.	K—B 1	P—K Kt 4
6.	Kt—K B 3	Q—R 4
7.	P—K R 4	B—Kt 2

Not 7. ...P—K R 3 ? 8. B× P ch !, Q×B ; 9. Kt—K 5 followed by Q—R 5 ch and wins.

8.	P—Q 4	Kt—K 2
9.	Kt—B 3	P—K R 3
10.	K—Kt 1	

At last threatening P×P. At first sight 10. ...P—Kt 5 looks like a good reply, but this would lead to the loss of the K B P without any compensation.

10.	......	Q—Kt 3
11.	Q—Q 3	P—Q B 3

A move that has given rise to considerable argument in this and similar positions. Tarrasch discarded the alternative 11. ... Q Kt—B 3 on the grounds that after 12. Kt—Kt 5 he would either have to embark on an unclear course with 12. ...O—O, or else expose himself to harassing attacks with 12. ...K—Q 1. He points out that after this latter move, White would have good attacking chances with 13. P—R 5, Q—B 3 ; 14. P—K 5, Q—B 4 ; 15. B—K 4.

12. P—R 5 ? !

This looks attractive because it drives Black's Queen to a very poor square. On the other hand, Black's advanced Pawns are stabilised, and White's K R P soon becomes weak.

12. ......   Q—R 2 !

12. ...Q—Q 3 ; 13. P—K 5, Q—B 2 ; 14. B—K 4 would be inferior. Tarrasch indicates the amusing possibility 14. ...O—O ; 15. Kt×P, P×Kt ; 16. P—R 6, B—R 1 ? ; 17. B—R 7 mate !

13.	B—Kt 3	O—O
14.	Kt—K 2	B—Kt 5
15.	B—Q 2	Kt—Q 2

The crisis. Black now threatens ...Kt—B 3, winning the K R P.

Winawer finds the only way to spoil this plan.

16. B×P!

Forestalling ...Kt—B 3. White gets only two Pawns for the piece, but he has a lasting initiative, a strong Pawn centre, and superior mobility. Black's task from now on will be an onerous one.

16. ......   P×B
17. Kt×P   B×Kt

Partly for purposes of simplification, and also because it is now difficult to make good use of the Bishop. Thus if 17. ...Kt—B 3; 18. Kt—K 5 with good attacking prospects; or 17. ...Q R—Q 1; 18. Kt—R 2, Kt—Q B 4; 19. Q—Kt 3, regaining the piece, for if 19. ...Kt×B; 20. Kt×B, threatening to win the Queen (Tarrasch).

18. P×B   Q R—Q 1
19. Q—K 3

The exchange of his valuable Bishop could not be avoided, for if 19. Q—B 4, Kt—Q Kt 3 wins the Q P.

19. ......   Kt—Q B 4!
20. P—B 3   Kt×B
21. P×Kt   P—R 3

Now the worst is over for Black, but his position is still exasperatingly passive in character.

22. R—K R 2   K R—K 1
23. Kt—K 2   Kt—Q 4

The Knight begins a long tour for the purpose of guarding against White's projected advance of the centre Pawns.

24. Q—B 2   Kt—B 2
25. Kt—Kt 3   Kt—K 3

Gaining time for his next move because of the threat of ...Kt×P.

26. Kt—B 5   Kt—Kt 4

Now the struggle centres about Black's desire to prevent the advance of the K B P; White's Pawns must be held back.

27. K—R 1   K—R 1

If 27. ...R×K P; 28. P×R, Kt×P; 29. Q—R 4! and not 29. Q—B 3?, Q×Kt! (Tarrasch).

28. R—Kt 2   B—B 3!
29. Kt—K 3

Threatening P—K 5 followed by P—K B 4.

29. ......   Kt—K 3!

Crossing White's plan. If now 30. P—K 5, B—Kt 4 followed by ...B—B 5; or if 30. P—Q 5, P×P; 31. Kt×P, R×Kt; 32. P×R, Kt—B 5; 33. R—Kt 4, Q—B 4 (Tarrasch) and the initiative has passed to Black.

30. R—Kt 4

Again threatening P—K 5 followed by P—K B 4. Black's reply disposes of the threat and compels White to avoid an exchange.

30. ......   B—Kt 4
31. Kt—B 5   R—K Kt 1

Tarrasch had intended to play 31. ...B—B 5 at this point, but he now realised that 32. R×B, Kt×R; 33. Q—R 4, Kt—K 3 (not 33.

...Kt—Q 4 ; 34. P—Q B 4) ; 34. Q—B 6 ch, K—Kt 1 ; 35. R—Kt 1 ch, K—B 1 ; 36. Kt×P would give him a very difficult game.

32. Q—R 2 ?

Thus far Winawer has made the most of his chances, but here he misses the best line, which in Tarrasch's opinion was 32. P—K B 4, B—B 3 ; 33. Q R—K Kt 1, R× R ; 34. R×R, R—K Kt 1 ; 35. R×R ch, Q×R ; 36. Q—B 3, and the outcome of the game would still be in doubt.

32. ......   B—B 3
33. Q R—K Kt 1

If instead 33. R×R ch, R×R ; 34. P—K B 4, R—Kt 5 with a winning counter-attack. Compare this with the previous note.

33. ......   R—Kt 4 !

Confronting White with a terrible choice : shall he capture the Rook, weakening his R P and forever renouncing P—K B 4, or shall he permit Black to double the Rooks on the all-important K Kt file ? !

34. P—K B 4

He tries to solve the problem in another way, but now Tarrasch can at last seize the initiative.

34.	R×Kt !
35. P×R	Q×P
36. R(Kt 1)—Kt 2	Kt—Kt 2
37. R(Kt 4)—Kt 3	

In order to answer ...Kt×P with R—R 3. The protection of the weak Pawns is a troublesome task.

37.	Q—Kt 8 ch
38. R—Kt 1	Q—K 5 ch
39. R(Kt 1)—Kt 2	Q—Kt 8 ch
40. R—Kt 1	Q—K 5 ch
41. R(Kt 3)—Kt 2	

Having gained time to complete the second hour, both players are able to study the position more carefully. At first sight 41. Q—Kt 2 looks more promising than the text, for example, 41. .... Q×B P ? ; 42. R—K B 1, leaving Black with a far more difficult game than in the text. However, Black simply answers 41. Q—Kt 2 with 41. ...Q×Q ch ; 42. R(Kt 1)×Q, R—Q 4 ; 43. R—R 3, R—K B 4 ; 44. R—K B 2, Kt—K 3 with an easy win.

41. ......   R—Q 4

Immediately decisive.

42. P—B 5	R×B P
43. Q—Kt 8 ch	K—R 2
44. R—Q 1	R×P ch
45. K—Kt 1	Q—K 6 ch
46. R—B 2	B—R 5

White resigns. A finely contested game.

24. LEIPZIG, 1894

RUY LOPEZ

As is well known, Tarrasch did a great deal of valuable work in elaborating White's play against the Steinitz Defence. This is one of the classic games which illustrate his procedure against cramped positions.

	White DR. S. TARRASCH	*Black* C. SCHLECHTER
1.	P—K 4	P—K 4
2.	Kt—K B 3	Kt—Q B 3
3.	B—Kt 5	P—Q 3
4.	P—Q 4	B—Q 2
5.	Kt—B 3	Kt—B 3
6.	O—O	B—K 2
7.	R—K 1	Kt × Q P

As Tarrasch had already demonstrated in a famous game (no. 21), Black can no longer maintain the centre with 7. ...O—O. The underlying idea of the text is to obtain some freedom by exchanging two pieces.

| 8. | Kt × Kt | P × Kt |
| 9. | B × B ch | Q × B |

In later years it came to be realised that the objective of playing ...P—Q 4 was too ambitious, and that Black would do better with 9. ...Kt × B. The latter mode of recapture gives him very fair chances : the Bishop goes to K B 3, the K R to K 1, and the Knight to K 4 or Q B 4.

| 10. | Q × P | O—O |

A position which has undergone considerable investigation. White has the advantage, based on the fact that his position is freer and his pieces have greater possibilities of powerful utilisation. Thus, White's Queen is more aggressively posted than its Black counterpart. White's Rooks may possibly be swung over to the King's side for direct attacking purposes, his Knight is headed for K B 5 or Q 5—more aggressive posts than the corresponding squares K 4 or Q B 4 which are reserved for Black's Knight ; finally, White's Bishop has a magnificent diagonal reserved for it.

Finally, White's K P is a bastion for White's pieces and at the same time controls important enemy territory (Q 5 and K B 5). Black's Q P, on the other hand, does little more than confine his Bishop. The final diagnosis is therefore : considerable positional advantage for White.

| 11. | P—Q Kt 3 ! | |

Following the course adopted in Game no. 19.

| 11. | ...... | K R—K 1 |
| 12. | B—Kt 2 | B—B 1 |

Kt—Q 5 threatened to be annoying.

| 13. | Q R—Q 1 | Q—B 3 |

P—K 5 was threatened.

| 14. | R—Q 3 | R—K 3 |

Imitating White's manœuvre with the Rooks, partly to keep the K P under observation and partly to add strength to the potential freeing moves ...P—Q 4 or ... P—K B 4. Schlechter handles the defence very ably.

15. Q R—K 3   Q R—K 1
16. P—K R 3 !

With the double object of pre-venting ...Kt—Kt 5 and later sup-porting a King's side attack.

16. ......   Q—Kt 3

Tarrasch points out that the attempt to oppose Bishops on the diagonal would turn out badly : 16. ...P—K Kt 3 ; 17. Kt—Q 5, B—Kt 2 ; 18. P—Q B 4, Kt—R 4 ; 19. Q—Q 2, B×B ; 20. Q×B threatening P—K Kt 4.

17. Q—Q 3   P—B 3

Beginning a new phase in the struggle to free himself : he means to play ...P—Q 4, which explains White's next two moves.

18. Kt—R 4 !   Q—B 2
19. P—Q B 4 !   Kt—Q 2

Tarrasch considers that ...P—K Kt 3 followed by ...B—Kt 2 would have been preferable, now that White's Queen is removed from the long diagonal.

20. K—R 1 !

A mysterious move ! Since ... P—K B 4 will soon be a threat, White prepares for P—K Kt 4 and also for R—K Kt 1.

20. ......   P—B 3

In order to break the diagonal of White's Bishop ; but the move has the drawback of creating a target for White's coming attack.

21. Q—B 2 ? !

Tarrasch wants to bring his Knight to K B 5, but the imme-diate Kt—B 3 could be well an-swered by ...Kt—B 4 ; therefore Tarrasch first plays away the Queen, in the hope that Schlechter will lose patience and play his Knight to the less useful square K 4.

Nevertheless, the text is inferior to Q—Kt 1 ! for reasons that will soon became apparent.

21. ......   Kt—K 4
22. Kt—B 3   Kt—B 2 !

So as to answer Kt—K 2 with ...P—K B 4, achieving freedom at last.
23. P—K Kt 4 ? !

There was still time for Q—Kt 1.

23. ......   Q—R 4 ?

Missing his great opportunity. Réti points out that 23. ...P—Q 4 ! could have been played here : 24. K P×P (had Tarrasch played 21. Q—Kt 1 ! he would have 24. B P×P, P×P ; 25. Kt×P at his disposal, making 23. ...P—Q 4 altogether impossible. Thus it is the unprotected position of the Queen at B 2 which makes 23. ... P—Q 4 ! possible), R×R ; 24.

R×R, R×R; 25. P×R, Q—Kt 6 etc.

24. R—Q 1

In order to be able to play Kt—K 2; another move which would have been unnecessary with White's Queen at Kt 1.

24. ......   Q—Kt 3
25. P—K R 4 !

25. Kt—K 2 would still have been premature, for then 25. ... Kt—Kt 4 would have forced the Knight back to B 3. Tarrasch's favourite stratagem of limiting Pawn moves plays an important rôle in this game.

25. ......   Kt—K 4
26. R—Kt 3   Kt—B 2
27. P—B 3

Now that the K P is solidly protected, White can proceed with his Knight's tour.

27. ......   Kt—R 1

Black wants to make room for the Queen to defend the King's side—a futile hope. ...P—Kt 3 would keep the hostile Knight out, but the eventual P—Kt 5 would still have deadly effect.

28. Kt—K 2   Q—B 2
29. R(Q 1)—K Kt 1 !

Kt—Q 4 ? would be careless because of the reply ...P—Q 4.

29. ......   Q—B 2
30. Kt—Q 4   R(K 3)—K 2
31. P—Kt 5

Opening the K Kt file, which

breaks Black's resistance very quickly.

31. ......   P×P
32. R×P   P—K Kt 3
33. Kt—B 5   R—K 4

Despair. If 33. ...R—K 3; 34. Q—B 3, R—K 4; 35. P—B 4 or 33. ...R—Q 2; 34. Q—B 3, B—Kt 2; 35. Kt×B, winning the exchange in either case.

34. P—B 4 !   R×Kt
Or 34. ...R×P; 35. Q—B 3 etc.

35. P×R   B—Kt 2
36. P×P   Resigns

If 36. ...P×P; 37. P—K B 5 wins easily (but not 36. R×P ?, Kt×R; 37. R×Kt, R—K 8 ch; 38. K—Kt 2, R—K 7 ch). A very interesting encounter in this, the first game between these two celebrated masters.

25. LEIPZIG, 1894
RUY LOPEZ

IT is evident from quite a few Tarrasch games of this period that Steinitz's insistence on the value of the two Bishops did not sit well with his contemporaries. Nowadays the realisation of the strength of this piece has filtered down to the lowest ranks.

White	Black
J. BERGER	DR. S. TARRASCH

1. P—K 4	P—K 4
2. Kt—K B 3	Kt—Q B 3
3. B—Kt 5	P—Q R 3
4. B—R 4	Kt—B 3
5. P—Q 3	B—B 4

Tarrasch loathed the cramping move ...P—Q 3 and avoided it wherever possible. The text, however, has the drawback that 6. B—K 3 ! can force the exchange of Bishops, for if 6. ...B—Kt 3 ? ; 7. B×B, P×B ; 8. B×Kt, Q P× B ; 9. Kt×P, and there is no way to recover the Pawn. After 6. ... B×B, however, White would have some advantage because of the open K B file.

6. O—O	P—Q Kt 4
7. B—Kt 3	P—Q 3
8. B—Kt 5	

This colourless move has little to recommend it. P—B 3 or Kt—B 3 was better.

| 8. ...... | P—R 3 |
| 9. B×Kt ? | |

A superficial move which facilitates Black's development and leaves him with two effective Bishops. B—K 3 would have been preferable.

9.	Q×B
10. Kt—B 3	Kt—K 2
11. Kt—Q 5	Kt×Kt
12. B×Kt	R—Q Kt 1
13. Kt—Q 2	

Else ...B—K Kt 5 threatens to be annoying. White's game is already uncomfortable.

| 13. ...... | P—K R 4 ! |

Highly unconventional. Tarrasch is not interested in the banal notion of castling ; instead he plays to get his K R into attacking formation by means of ...R—R 3— K Kt 3.

| 14. Q—K 1 | |

This could wait until ...B— K Kt 5 has actually been played. P—B 3 or K—R 1 would have been more useful.

| 14. ...... | R—R 3 |

Tarrasch observes here that this unusual development of the Rook is often found in his games.

| 15. K—R 1 | R—K Kt 3 |

The position has already become quite dangerous for White, for example, 16. Kt—Kt 3 ?, R×P ! ; 17. K×R, B—R 6 ch ! and mate follows.

16. P—Q B 3	Q—Kt 4
17. R—K Kt 1	R—B 3
18. P—Q 4 ? !	

The patient R—K B 1 would have been somewhat better, but White is anxious to shake off the pressure, even at the cost of a Pawn or two.

| 18. ...... | B—Kt 3 ! |

Tarrasch prefers to avoid clearing up the position in the centre, thus adding to White's perplexity. If, instead, 18. ...P×P ; 19. Kt— B 3 creates complications.

| 19. Q—K 2 | |

Again R—K B 1 was in order. After the text, Black has the win well in hand.

| 19. ...... | Q—B 5 ! |

This embarrassing move cannot be met adequately, for if 20. Q R— K B 1, P×P ; 21. P×P, B×P and Black has won a Pawn without danger. Or 20. P×P, P×P and the K B P falls.

20. K R—K B 1   P×P
21. P—K Kt 3

Hoping for attack, White nervously opens lines which will, however, benefit only the enemy.

21. ......   Q—R 3
22. P—K 5   P×K P
23. Q×K P ch

23. ......   K—B 1 !

Much stronger than the routine ...B—K 3. Black now threatens ...R—B 4, followed by ...R×B. 24. Kt—K 4 ? would be answered by ...R—B 4 winning the Queen, while if 24. Q R—K 1, B—K 3 or 24. Q—K 2, B—R 6, in either case with considerable advantage.

24. Kt—B 3   R—B 4

White's remaining moves are forced. Tarrasch winds up neatly.

25. Q—K 4   R×B !
26. Q×R   B—Kt 2
27. Q—B 5   Q—Kt 3 !

Taking advantage of White's terrible weakness on the long diagonal.

28. Q—B 4   Q—Q B 3
29. K—Kt 2   P—Kt 4 !

Winning the Knight.

30. Q—B 5   P—Kt 5
31. P×P   Q×Kt ch
32. Q×Q   B×Q ch
33. K—Kt 1   B×P

White resigns. A triumph for the Bishops.

26. LEIPZIG, 1894

KING'S GAMBIT DECLINED
(IN EFFECT).

ALTHOUGH Tarrasch was admittedly influenced by Steinitz in many ways, he differed strongly from the older master on a number of doctrines. One of these was Tarrasch's life-long insistence that freedom of action more than outweighs weaknesses in Pawn structure. The following game indicates that Tarrasch often succeeded in making out a good case for his views.

White	*Black*
R. TEICHMANN	DR. S. TARRASCH

1. P—K 4   P—K 4
2. Kt—Q B 3   Kt—K B 3
3. B—B 4   B—B 4

Apparently not fancying the dull line 3. ...Kt×P ; 4. Q—R 5, Kt —Q 3 ; 5. Q×K P ch, Q—K 2 etc., Tarrasch prefers to seek complications.

4. P—B 4   P—Q 3
5. Kt—B 3   Kt—B 3
6. P—Q 3   B—K Kt 5
7. P—K R 3   B—K 3

A judicious retreat, for, as is well known, after 7. ...B×Kt; 8. Q×B, Kt—Q 5; 9. Q—Kt 3! White has good attacking chances. However, an alternative at least equally as good as the text was discovered many years later: 7. ...B×Kt; 8. Q×B, P×P! If now 9. Q×P?, Kt—K R 4 followed by ...Q—R 5 ch and wins, or 9. B×P, Kt—K 4, forcing a favourable exchange.

8. B—Kt 5.

Declining the challenge: 8. B×B, P×B; 9. P×P would leave Black with an isolated K P, but with good play on the open K B and Q files. However, 8. B—Kt 3 or 8. B×B, P×B; 9. Kt—Q R 4 (making castling possible) would give White a more comfortable game than results from the text.

8. ......   P—Q R 3
9. B×Kt ch   P×B
10. P×P

Judging from the following play, Teichmann might have accomplished more with 10. P—B 5, B—B 1; 11. P—K Kt 4. The text leaves Black with a dubious Pawn structure, to be sure, but his two Bishops and open lines give him fine prospects.

10. ......   P×P
11. Kt—K 2

Not 11. Kt×P??, Q—Q 5 and wins. If 11. Q—K 2 (threatening Kt×P and also preparing for B—K 3) Black has the embarrassing reply ...Kt—R 4.

11. ......   Q—Q 3
12. P—Q 4 ?!

In his desperate groping for freedom, White resorts to an ingenious but two-edged move which gives the game a wholly new turn. The basic idea is that if 12. ...P×P? or ...B×P? White will win a piece; likewise, if 12. ...Kt×P?; 13. Q—Q 3! (stronger than 13. P×B, Q×Q ch; 14. K×Q, Kt—B 7 ch; 15. K—K 1, Kt×R; 16. K—B 1) Black must lose a piece.

12. ......   B—Kt 3 !

Simple and good: if 13. Kt×P, Kt×P or if 13. P×P, Q×Q ch; 14. K×Q, Kt×P.

13. Q—Q 3   Kt—Q 2
14. P—B 3

Necessary to support the centre, but the position of his Queen now becomes precarious.

14. ......   O—O
15. B—K 3

Castling would be premature because of 15. ...P—Q B 4!; 16. B—K 3 (not 16. P—Q 5??, P—B 5 ch), B P×P; 17. P×P, P×P and White dare not recapture because of ...P—Q B 4 winning a piece.

15. ......   P—K B 4 !

White's " mighty " centre is being smashed up by means of blows from the wings.

16. K P×P   B×B P
17. Q—Q 2   P—K 5 !

This Pawn looks rather shaky, but it has a cramping effect on White's game and puts his K Kt out of play for a long time to come.

18. Kt—R 2	B—K 3
19. B—B 4	Q—Q 4
20. O—O	P—B 4 !
21. B—K 3	P×P
22. P×P	P—B 4 !

This move has several good
points : Black completes the demolition of the hostile centre and
makes possible the powerful posting
of his Knight at Q 6.

23. Kt—Q B 3

If 23. P×P ?, B×B P with a
powerful game, for example, 24.
K—R 1, R×R ch ! ; 25. R×R,
Q—Q 6 ! ; 26. Q×Q, P×Q ; 27.
Kt—Q 4 (if 27. B×B ?, P×Kt
wins a piece), B×Q R P etc.

23.	Q—Kt 2
24. P—Q 5	B—B 4
25. P—Q Kt 3 ?	

Thus far Teichmann has withstood the onslaught well ; but here
Kt—R 4 was more promising by
far.

| 25. ...... | Kt—K 4 |
| 26. P—K Kt 4 ? | |

Another error of judgment ;
White must have thought that the
win of the K P was not far off.

| 26. ...... | B—Kt 3 |
| 27. Q—K Kt 2 | Kt—Q 6 |

The Knight is magnificently
posted. Black does not fear 28.
Kt×P ? because of ...Q—K 2 !
winning a piece.

28. R×R ch	R×R
29. R—K B 1	R—K 1
30. R—Q 1 ?	

The final blunder which allows
Black to force the game. Some
such move as Q—Kt 3 or K—R 1
was in order.

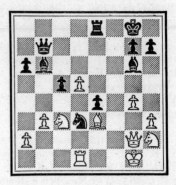

30. ......   P—B 5 !

This wins a Pawn. If now 31.
B×B, Q×B ch ; 32. K—R 1, P×
P ; 33. R—Q Kt 1, P×P !

31. Q—Q 2	P×P
32. P×P	B×B ch
33. Q×B	Q×Kt P

Black must now win additional
material. White's next move is
virtually forced, but it relinquishes
the blockade of the K P.

34. Q—Q 4   P—K 6 !

At last. the passed Pawn comes
into its own. The following loss of
the exchange is unavoidable.

35. R×Kt	B×R
36. Q×B	P—K 7
37. Kt—B 3	P—K 8(Q) ch
38. Kt×Q	R×Kt ch
39. K—B 2	R—K 4

The seemingly crushing 39.
...R—B 8 is met by 40. Q—K 3 |

40. P—Q 6   Q—Kt 3 ch
41. K—Kt 2   Q—B 3 ch
42. K—Kt 3

This loses outright. However, after 42. K—B 1, R—K 1 Black would soon be ready to advance his Q R P with an easy win in sight.

42. ......   R—K 3

White resigns, for if 43. P—Q 7, Q—Q 3 ch wins the Q P. A highly interesting game.

27. LEIPZIG, 1894

QUEEN'S GAMBIT DECLINED

TARRASCH considers this game one of his best ; the iron consistency which characterises his play here from beginning to end makes the game really noteworthy.

White	Black
DR. S. TARRASCH	T. VON SCHEVE

1. P—Q 4   P—Q 4
2. P—Q B 4   P—K 3
3. Kt—Q B 3   Kt—K B 3
4. Kt—B 3   B—K 2
5. B—B 4

Regarding this outmoded move, see also Game 46. The reply 5. ...P—B 4 gives Black a satisfactory position.

5. ......   P—B 3

At the time this game was played, the Queen's Gambit was only on the point of being " discovered ". Hence the text, which results in a cramped game.

6. P—K 3   Q Kt—Q 2
7. P—K R 3

In order to preserve the precious Bishop ; but Black's reply gives the game a wholly different orientation.

7. ......   Kt—K 5 ?

" The decisive mistake. After the following exchange, Black is left with a weak K P which requires protection. If it is to be maintained permanently, ...P—K B 4 must be played, but then P—B 3 renews the attack. Black must capture, whereupon the K Kt file is opened for White. The result is a combined and irresistible attack with both Rooks, Queen and Q B against K Kt 7. In all chess literature I do not know of another game in which, after the eighth (!) move, it is possible to conceive a plan in such detail, almost leading to mate, and which in the remaining 20 moves consistently leads up to a catastrophe " (Tarrasch).

8. Kt × Kt   P×Kt
9. Kt—Q 2   B—Kt 5

The disappearance of this Bishop makes a bad position worse, since the weak black squares are deprived of adequate protection ; hence the immediate ...P—K B 4, distasteful as it is, should be played.

10. P—R 3   B×Kt ch
11. Q×B

Now White has the two Bishops —an additional advantage.

11. ......   O—O
12. Q—B 2 !   P—K B 4

If 12. ...Kt—B 3 ; 13. B—K 5

(not 13. B—Kt 5 ? ?, Q—R 4 ch) wins the K P.

13. B—Q 6 !

Emphasising the weakness of the black squares and preventing the freeing manœuvre ...Q—K 2 followed by ...P—K 4.

13. ......   R—K 1

...R—B 2 was somewhat better.

14. O—O—O   Kt—B 3

14. ...Q—B 3 appears preferable, but after 15. P—B 5, P—K 4 ; 16. B—B 4 ch, K—R 1 ; 17. P—Q 5 ! Black's position is wretched.

15. B—K 5   B—Q 2
16. P—B 3 !

The time has come to open the K Kt file.

16. ......   P×P
17. P×P   P—Q Kt 4

A pathetic attempt at counterplay which is naturally unavailing.

18. R—Kt 1   R—K B 1
19. R—Q 2 !   R—B 2
20. Q R—Kt 2   P—Q R 4
21. Q—B 2 !

Planning the following decisive intrusion of the Queen.

21. ......   Kt—K 1

...R—R 2 at once would be more economical, but the vulnerable point K Kt 2 cannot be protected indefinitely.

22. R—Kt 5 !   Q—K 2

Or 22. ...P—R 3 ; 23. R—Kt 6, K—R 2 ; 24. Q—Kt 3, Q—K 2 ; 25. R×R P ch ! (Tarrasch).

23. Q—R 4

Threatening Q—R 6 followed by R—R 5.

23. ......   Kt—B 3
24. Q—R 6   R—R 2

There was no good defence : if 24. ...P—Kt 3 ; 25. R×P ch, P×R ; 26. R×P ch, R—Kt 2 ; 27. B×Kt wins ; if 24. ...B—K 1 ; 25. B×Kt, Q×B ; 26. Q×Q, R×Q ; 27. R×P ch, K—B 1 ; 28. R×P with an easy win.

25. B—Q 6 !

Crushing. It has been truly said that in a good position, the good moves come of themselves.

25. ......   Q×B
26. R×P ch   K—B 1

Avoiding 26. ...K—R 1 ; 27. Q×P ch !, Kt×Q ; 28. R—Kt 8 mate.

27. R×P ch !   K—K 2
28. R×R ch   K×R
29. R—Kt 7 ch   K—K 1
30. Q×Kt   Resigns

For if 30. ...Q—B 1 ; 31. Q—Kt 6 ch (made possible by 27. R×P ch !) wins the Queen. Note that White's K B never moved ! But the agility of his other Bishop on the enfeebled black squares more than makes up for the K B's inactivity.

28. LEIPZIG, 1894

GIUOCO PIANO

It is characteristic of great players that they can adopt a harmless opening and obtain a winning position in quick time. The secret lies, of course, in the fact that no position, no matter how harmless in appearance, can support a series of weak moves. The innocent-looking positions are particularly insidious in that respect, since their apparent lack of distinctive character is conducive to carelessness.

White	*Black*
Dr. S. Tarrasch	H. Süchting

1.	P—K 4	P—K 4
2.	Kt—K B 3	Kt—Q B 3
3.	B—B 4	B—B 4
4.	Kt—B 3	Kt—B 3
5.	P—Q 3	P—Q 3
6.	B—K Kt 5	

In recent years this has come to be known as the Canal Variation, so called because of a number of impressive successes scored by the Peruvian master against inferior opposition. The continuation recommended is 6. ...P—K R 3 ; 7. B×Kt, Q×B ; 8. Kt—Q 5, Q—Q 1 ; 9. P—B 3, Kt—K 2 with level prospects.

| 6. | ...... | Kt—Q R 4 |

| 7. | B—Kt 3 | Kt×B |
| 8. | R P×Kt | P—B 3 |

This leads to difficulties later, but was perfectly playable if followed up properly.

| 9. | P—Q 4 | |

Laudably enterprising, and not without risk in view of the fact that opening up the position gives the opponent's Bishops more scope.

| 9. | ...... | P×P |
| 10. | Kt×P | Q—Kt 3 |

Black does not fear the possible continuation 11. Kt—R 4, Q—B 2 ; 12. Kt×B, P×Kt ; 13. B×Kt, P×B ; 14. Kt—B 3, K R—Kt 1. His open lines would compensate for his poor Pawn position.

| 11. | B×Kt | P×B |
| 12. | Q Kt—K 2 | Q—Q 1 ? |

A pathetically colourless move. 12. ...R—K Kt 1 was in order, and if then 13. K—B 1 (Tarrasch's suggestion), B—K 3 followed by ...O—O—O with an interesting struggle in prospect.

| 13. | O—O | B—K 3 |
| 14. | Kt—B 4 ! | |

Gratefully taking advantage of Black's feeble play to seize the initiative.

| 14. | ...... | K—Q 2 ? |

Black is going to pieces. 14. ... Q—K 2 followed by ...O—O—O was quite playable.

| 15. | P—Q B 3 | Q—K Kt 1 |

Tarrasch makes the interesting observation that even ...P—Q R 4 would not prevent P—Q Kt 4, for example : 15. ...P—Q R 4 ; 16. P—Q Kt 4 !, P×P ; 17. R×R, Q×R ; 18. P×P, B×P ? ; 19. K Kt×B, P×Kt ; 20. Q—Kt 3 etc.

16. P—Q Kt 4   B×Kt ?

Losing a Pawn outright and with a desperately poor game in the bargain. It must be admitted, however, that after 16. ...B—Kt 3 ; 17. Kt—R 5, Q—Kt 3 ; 18. Q—B 3, K—K 2 ; 19. P—R 3 (threatening, among other things, K R—K 1 followed by Kt—B 5 ch) Black would likewise be in a bad way.

17. Q×B	Q—Kt 4
18. Kt×B	P×Kt
19. P—K B 4	Q—Kt 2
20. K R—Q 1	

Tarrasch is in no hurry to snatch a Pawn which cannot run away ; before capturing the Pawn, he first pauses to strengthen his position.

20.	Q—K 2
21. R×P	R×R
22. Q×R	K—B 2

Black may be relying on the presence of the heavy pieces to prolong his resistance. This is a faulty speculation, as White has a strong attack.

23. Q—R 5 ch	K—Kt 1
24. R—R 1	R—Q 1
25. Q—R 7 ch	K—B 2

Or 25. ...K—B 1 ; 26. Q—Kt 6, K—Kt 1 ; 27. R—R 7 followed by Q—R 5 (Tarrasch).

26. P—B 4 !

This move proves decisive in a very short time.

26.	R—Q Kt 1
27. P—Kt 5	P—Q B 4

If 27. ...P×P ; 28. P×P, followed by 29. R—R 6 wins.

28. R—R 6 !   Resigns

There is no good defence to the threat of R—B 6 ch. If 28. ... Q—Q 1 ; 29. Q—Kt 6 ch wins. If 28. ...K—B 1 ; 29. R—B 6 ch.

29. LEIPZIG, 1894

CENTRE COUNTER GAME

THIS is one of those beautiful games which are a happy blend of logic and psychology. The manner in which Tarrasch demonstrates the weakness of White's apparently strong centre is infinitely instructive.

White	Black
E. SCHIFFERS	DR. S. TARRASCH

1. P—K 4	P—Q 4

Evidently an experiment. It is almost the only instance on record of Tarrasch's adopting this move.

2. P×P	Q×P
3. Kt—Q B 3	Q—Q R 4
4. P—Q 4	Kt—K B 3
5. B—Q 3	B—Kt 5
6. P—B 3	B—R 4
7. K Kt—K 2	P—B 3

Creating a retreat for the Queen, which is likely to be exposed in this opening.

8. O—O	P—K 3
9. Kt—K 4	Q Kt—Q 2
10. B—K B 4	Kt×Kt

A sly move, which tempts White to retake with the Pawn and thus create an impressive-looking centre. The less ambitious but safer 11. B×Kt would have led to about an even game.

11. P×Kt	B—Kt 3 !

Not 11. ...P—K 4 ?? ; 12. P× P, Kt×P ; 13. B×Kt, Q×B ; 14. R—B 5 etc.

12. P—B 3

P—K 5 would have prevented the following important stroke ; but then ...P—Q B 4 would be an effective reply.

12.	P—K 4 !

Now White's centre begins to look shaky ; after 13. P×P, Kt×P the K P would be isolated and Black would have a fine post at K 4 for his pieces.

13. P—Q Kt 4 ?

Initiating a wholly incorrect plan. The motivation for this move is plausible but superficial : he wishes to drive back the Queen to B 2 (the only square from which to protect the K P), after which, so he thinks, Black will be embarrassed by the presence of his Queen and White's Q B on the same diagonal. But this difficulty is easily relieved by ...B—Q 3 ; after which White discovers that not only is his centre weak, but his Queen's side Pawns also need protection and his Knight is practically stalemated.

13.	Q—B 2
14. B—Kt 3	B—Q 3
15. Q—B 2	O—O

White's position doubtless makes a favourable impression at first sight, but actually it is already inferior because of the defensive and rather ineffectual placing of all his pieces.

16. P—Q R 4	K R—K 1

Beginning the assault on the centre.

17. Q R—K 1	P—Q R 4 !

A difficult move to meet adequately. 18. Kt P×P leaves a weak Q R P ; or if 18. P—Kt 5, P—Q B 4 ! (threatening to win the K B with ...P—B 5—a striking commentary on the congested position of White's pieces).

18. Q—Kt 3	R P×P
19. B P×P	Kt—B 3

Continuing the pressure. "Chess is a terrible game," Tarrasch remarks, " If you have no centre, your opponent has a freer position. If you do have a centre, then you really have something to worry about ! "

20. P×P   K B×K P

After this inevitable exchange of Pawns, the weakness of the K P becomes clearer than ever. On the other hand, White has some compensation in attacking chances which are not to be underestimated. All the more admirable, therefore, is the masterly way in which Tarrasch combines attack on the weak Pawn, occupation of K 4, attack on the diagonal Q R 2—K Kt 8 *and* a refutation of White's attack !

21. Kt—B 4   Q R—Q 1

Black's pieces are too well placed. White must do something, and he hits on the idea of attacking K B 7, which at once forces a crisis.

22. Kt×B   P×Kt
23. B—Q B 4   B×B
24. P×B   R—K 4 !

Threatening to win at least a Pawn by 25. ...Q—Kt 3 ch ; 26. Q—K 3 (26. K—R 1 ? ?, R—R 4 mate—or if 26. R—K 3 or 26. R—B 2, Kt—Kt 5 etc.), Q×P.

Tarrasch indicates 25. R—B 4 as White's best reply here.

25. P—R 5   P—Q Kt 4 !

This simple but extraordinarily effective answer refutes White's last move. There is no satisfactory reply, for if 26. B—Q 3, Q—R 2 ch wins, while if 26. B—K 2 the K P falls. White decides to die like a hero.

26. P×P e.p.   Q×P ch
27. Q—K 3   Q×P
28. B—R 2   Kt—Kt 5 !

Absolutely decisive, since White's Queen can no longer prevent the fatal check on the diagonal.

29. R×P   K—R 2 !

Wins more quickly than 29. ... Kt×Q ; 30. R—Kt 7 ch, K—R 2 ; 31. R×Q, Kt—B 7 etc.

30. Q—K 2   Q—Q 5 ch

White resigns, for if 31. K—B 1, Kt—R 7 mate ; or 31. R—B 2, R—K B 1 ; 32. R—K B 1, R×R ; 33. R×R, R×P ; 34. Q—Q 2, Q×Q ; 35. R×Q, R—K 8 mate (Tarrasch).

One of Tarrasch's little known masterpieces.

30. LEIPZIG, 1894

RUY LOPEZ

THIS unpretentious game is a convincing indication of how far ahead of his contemporaries Tarrasch was. His winning plan is simple and clear, and arises out of an apparently harmless position.

White	*Black*
Dr. S. Tarrasch	G. Marco
1. P—K 4	P—K 4
2. Kt—K B 3	Kt—Q B 3
3. B—Kt 5	P—Q R 3
4. B—R 4	Kt—B 3
5. Kt—B 3	B—Kt 5
6. Kt—Q 5	B—K 2
7. P—Q 3	P—Q 3
8. P—B 3	

8. Kt—Kt 4, B—Q 2 ; 9. Kt×
Kt, B×Kt ; 10. B×B ch, as
played by Tarrasch against Berger
at Breslau 1889, gives White somewhat better chances because of his
potential pressure against Black's
vulnerable Queen's side Pawns.

8.	O—O
9. Kt×Kt ch	B×Kt
10. O—O	Kt—K 2
11. B—K 3	Kt—Kt 3
12. P—Q 4	B—Kt 5

Up to this point the game has
been about even, but the text is a
step in the wrong direction. Black
should continue with ...Q—K 2 or
...B—K 3, with approximately
equal chances.

13. P—K R 3   B×Kt

Graceful acknowledgment of his
error was in order. ...B—K 3 or
...B—Q 2 should have been
played.

14. Q×B   B—Kt 4

Seeking a second exchange for
simplifying purposes and also to
exchange one of White's pair of
Bishops.

15. P—K Kt 3   B×B
16. P×B

Tarrasch realises that the possibilities of exploiting the K B file
outweigh the highly theoretical
weakness of the Pawn at K 3.
However, it should be mentioned
that Q×B followed by P—K B 4 is
an attractive alternative.

16.	K—R 1
17. R—B 2	P—Q B 3
18. B—Kt 3	P—B 3

Giving White's Bishop a key
square ; but the move is unavoidable as a means of minimising
White's pressure on the K B file.

19. B—K 6   R—K 1 ?

This allows an exchange which
makes Black's loss inevitable, and
must therefore be condemned. ...
Q—K 2 was somewhat better.

20. B—B 7 !	R—K 2
21. B×Kt !	P×B

What has White gained with his
last two moves ? The following
advance of the K R P gives us a
clue.

22. P—K R 4 !

This fixes Black's K Kt P on

K Kt 3. White is to occupy the K R file and play P—R 5. Black will then have the sorry choice of playing ...P×P and submitting to a winning attack on the K R file, or else of playing ...P—K Kt 4 and allowing the smash-up of the King's side with P—R 6! There is no satisfactory defence to this threat.

22. ......   Q—K 1

Black's counter-demonstration against the K P is destined to have no success ; just as he wins this Pawn, he has to resign !

23. R—K 1   K—Kt 1
24. R—Q 2 !

A feint. White pretends to be interested in the Q P, but his real objective is to close the Q file.

24. ......   Q—B 2

24. ...P×P ; 25. K P×P, P— Q 4 ; 26. R(Q 2)—K 2, P×P ; 27. R×P, R×R ; 28. R×R, Q—Q 2 might have been better, although its passive character is not attractive.

25. P—Q 5 !   P—Q B 4

Inevitable, as he cannot permit White to double on the Q file and play P×P with pressure on the weak Q P. But now that all counterplay on the Queen's side is stifled, White can work undisturbed on the other wing. Black's rapid downfall comes as a great surprise because of the drawish possibilities of the material still left on the board.

26. R—K B 1   Q—K 1
27. R—R 2   R—Q 1
28. Q—Kt 4

If at once 28. P—R 5, P×P ; 29. R×P, Q—Kt 3 with good chances. Hence the text.

28. ......   P—Q Kt 4
29. K—Kt 2 !

And not 29. P—R 5, P—Kt 4 ; 30. Q—B 5 (if 30. P—R 6, Q— Kt 3 !), Q—Q 2 ; 31. Q—Kt 6, Q—Kt 5 ! (Tarrasch).

29. ......   P—Kt 5
30. P—B 4   Q—R 5

Despair. Passive play would not have held out very long in any event.

31. P—R 5 !

Tarrasch is interested in opening up lines rather than in the win of the Pawn. If now 31. ...P×P ; 32. Q×P, and wins.

31. ......   P—Kt 4
32. P—R 6

Conclusive.

32. ......   Q—B 7 ch
33. R—B 2   Q×B P
34. P×P   K×P

If 34. ...R×P ; 35. Q—K 6 ch wins.

35. Q—B 5   K—Kt 1
36. Q×B P   Q×P ch
37. K—Kt 1   Resigns

With this victory, Tarrasch made certain of the first prize. The attack with the heavy pieces has been interesting.

31. HASTINGS, 1895

(Second Brilliancy Prize)

RUY LOPEZ

As the reader notes the ineptitude with which Tarrasch conducts much of this game, he may well wonder how it came to receive a prize. The answer lies in the magnificent closing combination, with which Tarrasch convincingly redeems himself.

White	*Black*
DR. S. TARRASCH	C. A. WALBRODT

1.	P—K 4	P—K 4
2.	Kt—K B 3	Kt—Q B 3
3.	B—Kt 5	P—Q R 3
4.	B—R 4	Kt—B 3
5.	Kt—B 3	P—Q 3
6.	P—Q 4	B—Q 2

Transposing into the Steinitz Defence Deferred. 6. ...P—Q Kt 4 ; 7. P×P leads to a rather lifeless game in which White's position is preferable.

7.	B×Kt	B×B
8.	Q—K 2	

Not best ; Q—Q 3 exercises much more lasting pressure on Black's game.

8.	......	P×P
9.	Kt×P	B—Q 2
10.	O—O	B—K 2
11.	P—Q Kt 3	O—O
12.	B—Kt 2	P—Q Kt 4

A sly move, the threat being 13. ...P—B 4 followed by ...P—Kt 5 and ...B—Kt 4 winning the exchange.

13.	P—Q R 4	P—Kt 5

With this move Black seizes the initiative. His present objective is to hurl back the Knights, at the same time obtaining more scope for his Bishops.

14. Kt—Q 1

14. Kt—Q 5 has been recommended, but after 14. ...P—B 4 ; 15. Kt—K B 3 (if 15. Kt×B ch ?, Q×Kt and Black wins a Pawn), Kt×Kt ; 16. P×Kt, B—K B 3 ; 17. B×B, Q×B Black has a very promising game.

14.	......	P—B 4
15.	Kt—K B 3	B—B 3 !

Black has an excellent position. If now 16. P—K 5, Kt—Q 4 with a fine game.

16.	Kt—Q 2	P—Q 4 !
17.	P—K 5	

It may be, as the critics claim, that 17. P×P was better. But in that event Black would have an ideal two-Bishop game. The object of the text is to strive for a close position in which Black's Bishops will not have too much scope. This turns out to be an impossible goal.

17.	......	Kt—K 1
18.	Kt—K 3	Q—Q 2
19.	Q R—Q 1	P—Q 5 !

While this move has the drawback of giving White's Knights a good square at Q B 4, that defect is far outweighed by the beautiful diagonal made available to Black's Q B—not to mention the virtual stalemate of White's Bishop. Yet it is this buried Bishop which is destined to win the game !

F

20. Kt(K 3)—B 4   Q—K 3
21. P—B 4   P—B 4
22. Kt—R 5   B—Q 4
23. Q—Q 3   K—R 1 !

Walbrodt has full freedom of
action in his barricaded position,
and takes advantage of the opportunity to build up a lasting attack.
The opening of the K Kt file is
indicated.

24. Q—Kt 3   R—R 2 !
25. Kt(R 5)—B 4   R—Kt 1
26. Q R—K 1

If 26. P—R 4, Q—R 3 winning
the K R P.

26. ......   P—Kt 4 !
27. R—K 2   B—Q 1
28. Q—Q 3   Q R—K Kt 2
29. P—Kt 3   P×P ?

Not the best; Tarrasch subsequently pointed out that ...P—
Kt 5 followed by ...P—K R 4—5
would have led to a quick win.

30. R×P   R—Kt 4
31. R(K 2)—B 2

Black's hasty 29th move has
allowed White counterplay in the
form of pressure on the K B P.

31. ......   Kt—Kt 2
32. Kt—Q 6   Q×P ?

Not 32. ...R—B 1 because of
33. Kt(Q 6)—K 4 ! But 32. ...
B—B 2 ! was better.

33. Kt×P   Kt—R 4 ?

This loses—in an amazing manner, to be sure. His best line was
33. ...Kt—K 3; 34. R—K 4, B
×R; 35. Q×B, Q×Q; 38. Kt×

Q with about even chances, despite
White's loss of the exchange. The
text is followed by a magnificent
finish.

34. R×P !!   Kt×P

As will be seen, Walbrodt relies
too much on this move. If, however, 34. ...P×R; 35. B×P wins
the Queen; if 34. ...Kt—B 3;
35. R×B Q×B; 36. R×B wins
a piece; if 34. ...B—K B 3; 35.
R×B, Q×B; 36. Kt—K 4 with
decisive advantage.

35. Kt×Kt !   R×Kt ch
36. P×R   R×P ch
37. K—B 1 !   R×Q
38. R—Kt 4 !!!   Resigns

A superb finish. It must literally have been the thrill of a lifetime to have witnessed this conclusion as it actually unfolded over
the board.

32. HASTINGS, 1895

FRENCH DEFENCE

THIS game, played in simple but
vigorous style by Tarrasch, is a
good example of his ability to make
the most out of a somewhat freer

position. The final combination has pleasing points.

White   *Black*
DR. S. TARRASCH   J. H. BLACKBURNE

1. P—K 4   P—K 3
2. P—Q 4   P—Q 4
3. Kt—Q B 3   P×P

Tarrasch had a lifelong aversion to this move, claiming that it gives White a wellnigh decisive advantage in terrain ! It is interesting to see how he sets about substantiating his claim.

4. Kt×P   Kt—Q 2
5. Kt—K B 3   K Kt—B 3
6. B—Q 3   P—B 4
7. O—O   P×P
8. Kt×Kt ch   Kt×Kt
9. Kt×P   B—B 4 ?

The first of a series of superficial "developing" moves. This Bishop belongs at K 2.

10. Kt—B 3   Q—B 2

Pointless at this stage.

11. Q—K 2   B—Q 2 ?

Aimless. This Bishop can be developed more effectively (bearing on the centre) later on by ...P— Q Kt 3 and ...B—Kt 2.

12. Kt—K 5   B—Q 3 ?
13. P—K B 4   O—O
14. B—Q 2   Q R—Q 1

At all events, Black does not add Pawn-grabbing to his sins (14. ... Q—Kt 3 ch ; 15. B—K 3, Q× P ? ; 16. Kt—B 4, Q—Kt 5 ; 17. Q R—Kt 1 winning a piece).

15. K—R 1   B—B 1

See the note to move 11.

16. R—B 3

White has steadily increased his command of the board and now begins to think of a direct assault.

16. ......   P—K Kt 3

Doubtless in order to break the diagonal of White's K B. But he creates a weakness which will be troublesome, in view of the cramped and ineffective position of his pieces.

17. P—B 4 !

Increasing his control of the centre. He can now play B—B 3 without being bothered by ...Kt— Q 4. Black's position is a difficult one to handle properly. He lacks terrain and hence prospects for his pieces. Such situations require enormous patience.

17. ......   B×Kt ? ?

A strange positional blunder from a master of Blackburne's ability. He opens up the K B file for White (more terrain !) and weakens his black squares irretrievably. ...K R—K 1 followed by ...B— B 1—Kt 2 was decidedly better.

18. P×B   Kt—Q 2
19. B—B 3   Kt—B 4
20. B—B 2   B—Q 2
21. P—Q Kt 3   K—Kt 2
22. Q—K 3   R—K R 1
23. Q R—K B 1   B—K 1
24. B—K 1 !

Having disposed his forces effectively, Tarrasch is now ready for a decisive attack. The text threatens B—R 4—B 6 ch. *Note the weakness of the black squares.*

24. ......   Q—K 2
25. R—B 6

Again threatening B—R 4.

25. ......   P—K R 3
26. B—R 4   P—K Kt 4

The advance of this Pawn is bound to have fatal effects, but on 26. ...Q—B 2 Tarrasch would have utilised his superior mobility in the following manner : 27. R(B 6)—B 3, P—K Kt 4 (otherwise the exchange is lost) ; 28. B× P, P×B ; 29. Q×P ch, K—B 1 ; 30. R—Kt 3 and Black is helpless against the threatened Q—Kt 7 ch (if 30. ...P—B 4 ; 31. B×P).

27. R×R P !

A really elegant conclusion.

27. ......   P×B

If instead 27. ......R×R ; 28. B×P, Q—B 2 ; 29. B—B 6 ch ! forcing mate.
Or 27. ...K×R ; 28. B×P ch ! and wins.

28. R×R   Resigns

For if 28. ...K×R ; 29. Q— R 6 ch, K—Kt 1 ; 30. B—R 7 ch and mate in 3.
The move 3. ...P×P has suffered a fearful catastrophe !

33. NUREMBERG, 1896

QUEEN'S PAWN GAME

TARRASCH considered this his best game in the tournament. It is most unorthodox in character, and bristles with unexpected moves and sly threats.

White	*Black*
G. MARCO	DR. S. TARRASCH

1. P—Q 4   P—Q 4
2. B—B 4   P—Q B 4
3. P—K 3

Far better than 3. P×P ?, Kt— Q B 3 ; 4. Kt—K B 3, P—B 3 ! ; 5. P—K 3, P—K 4 (Mason—Steinitz, London, 1883), when Black's command of the centre leaves White with a very poor game.

3. ......   P—K 3
4. Kt—K B 3   Q—Kt 3
5. P—Q Kt 3

Truly an ugly move, to quote Tarrasch ; it weakens the Queen's side permanently, and is out of place since White's Q B will not be fianchettoed. Q—B 1 was preferable.

5. ......   Kt—K B 3
6. B—Q 3   Kt—B 3
7. O—O   B—Q 2
8. P—B 3   R—B 1

Tarrasch is developing his position along the same lines as in Game 22.

| 9. | Q—K 2 | B—K 2 |
| 10. | P—K R 3 | |

Creating a retreat, if need be, for the Q B.

| 10. | ...... | O—O |
| 11. | Q—Kt 2 | |

Certainly a peculiar-looking move ; but Marco feared that after 11. Q Kt—Q 2, Q—R 4 his Queen would be cut off from the protection of the weak Queen's side.

| 11. | ...... | P—B 5 |
| 12. | B—K 2 | |

B—B 2 would keep the Bishop on the more aggressive diagonal, but White's Queen would be sadly hemmed in.

12.	......	Kt—K 5
13.	Kt—K 1	P×P
14.	P×P	Kt—R 4
15.	P—B 3 !	

The position is becoming quite interesting. If now 15. ...Q× Kt P ? ; 16. Q—R 2 wins a piece ; if 15. ...Kt×Kt P ; 16. P×Kt, Kt×R ; 17. Q×Kt, P×P ; 18. Kt—Q 2, P—B 4 ; 19. Kt—B 2 followed by R—Kt 1 and White stands well.

| 15. | ...... | Kt—Q 3 |

Tarrasch prefers to maintain the pressure on the Queen's side.

16. B—Q 1 ?

Surely the protection of the

Q Kt P by the natural developing move Kt—Q 2 was better. White's pieces are now awkwardly jumbled together, while his threat to win a piece with Q—R 3 can be parried easily enough.

| 16. | ...... | P—Kt 4 ! |

This surprising move forces the following exchange ; for if 17. B—Kt 3, Kt(Q 3)—B 5 ; 18. Q— R 2, Kt×K P ; 19. Q×Kt, Kt×B etc.

| 17. | B×Kt | B×B |
| 18. | Q—R 2 | B—B 2 |

Black's Bishops have enormous power : the immediate threat is ...Q—Q 3, creating new weaknesses in White's game.

19.	Q—R 3	B—Kt 4
20.	R—B 2	Kt—B 3
21.	Q—B 1 ?	

Marco touched his Queen inadvertently and had to move it, with the resulting loss of the exchange. An attempt to prevent Black's next move with 21. P—K B 4 would not do because of 21. ...P×P ; 22. P×P, Kt×P ! ; 23. P×Kt, Q× Q P ; 24. Kt—Q 2, B—Kt 3 and wins. 21. Kt—B 2 was his best chance.

21.	B—Kt 6
22. B—B 2	B×R ch
23. K×B	P—B 3 !

Preparing the following strong advance in the centre. White's game is still so disorganised that he cannot hold out much longer.

24. Kt—Q 2	P—K 4
25. Kt—B 1	P×P
26. B P×P	Kt×P !

Leads to a quick finish.

27. P×Kt	Q×P ch
28. Kt—K 3	K R—K 1
29. P—Kt 3	P—B 4

There is no good defence against the threatened ...P—B 5. On the other hand, 29. ...R×Kt ? ; 30. Q×R, Q×R would not do because of 31. Q—K 6 ch.

| 30. R—R 5 | P—Q R 3 |
| 31. Kt—Kt 2 | |

Or 31. P—B 4, P×P ; 32. P× P, Q×P ch ; 33. Kt—B 3, R×Kt etc.

| 31. ...... | P—B 5 |
| 32. P×P | P×P |

White resigns ; a smartly played game by Tarrasch.

34. NUREMBERG, 1896

QUEEN'S GAMBIT DECLINED

PERHAPS emboldened by Pillsbury's example at Hastings the previous year, Tarrasch played 1. P—Q 4 in all his games with the white pieces in this famous tourney.

White DR. S. TARRASCH	*Black* E. SCHIFFERS
1. P—Q 4	P—Q 4
2. P—Q B 4	Kt—Q B 3

Schiffers adopts the unusual defence favoured by his great compatriot Tchigorin.

| 3. Kt—K B 3 | B—Kt 5 |
| 4. P×P | |

In later years 4. Q—R 4 became popular at this point.

4.	B×Kt
5. Kt P×B	Q×P
6. P—K 3	P—K 4
7. Kt—B 3	B—Kt 5
8. B—Q 2	B×Kt
9. P×B	P×P

Otherwise White plays P—Q B 4 followed by P—Q 5. Black has a twofold problem now : he must restrain the Bishops, and he must not allow any advance of White's imposing centre Pawns. White's difficulty, on the other hand, is that if he advances too precipitately, he may find that his King is dangerously exposed.

10. B P×P	Kt—B 3
11. B—K 2	O—O
12. R—Q Kt 1 ?	

A superficial move which leaves White in a very embarrassing situation. Correct was O—O followed by B—B 3 !, P—K 4 and P—Q 5 with a very superior game.

12.	Q×R P
13. R×P	Q R—Kt 1
14. R—Kt 5	R×R
15. B×R	R—Kt 1 !

Black has secured a dangerous initiative and Tarrasch must play with great care to hold the position together. He cannot go in for 16. B×Kt ? because of 16. ...R—Kt 8 ; 17. B—B 1, Q—B 5.

16. B—Q 3	R—Kt 7

If now 17. B—B 3 ?, R×P ! ; 18. B—Kt 1, R×R P ! wins.

17. Q—B 1 !	P—Kt 3 !

White threatened 18. Q×Kt, R×B ; 19. Q—R 8 ch and mate follows.

18. B—B 4	

The Bishops are working effectively now. White is ready to castle.

18.	Q—Kt 8
19. O—O	

19. K—K 2, Q×Q ; 20. R×Q, Kt—Q R 4 ; 21. K—Q 3, Kt×B ; 22. R×Kt, R—Kt 2 ; 23. R—Kt 4 would also lead to a favourable ending.

19.	Q×Q
20. B×Q	R—Kt 5
21. B—K 2	Kt—Q 4
22. P—B 4	R—Kt 8
23. B—B 3	Kt(B 3)—Kt 5

White is slowly getting the better game, as his Bishops and the weakness of the hostile Queen's side Pawns augur well for him. But Schiffers offers sturdy resistance—up to a point.

24. B—Q 2	R—Kt 7
25. R—Q 1	P—K B 4
26. B—K 1	P—B 3
27. Q B×Kt	

Beginning simplifying exchanges which lead up to a fascinating endgame.

27.	Kt×B
28. R—Q B 1	R×P
29. K×R	Kt—Q 6 ch
30. K—K 2	Kt×R ch
31. K—Q 2	Kt—R 7

The question now arises : is Black's passed Q R P enough compensation for the superiority of the Bishop ?

32. P—Q 5 !	

This clever move gains several tempi in comparison to the trite B×P.

32.	P—B 4
33. K—Q 3	K—B 2
34. K—B 4	K—K 2
35. K×P	K—Q 1
36. P—Q 6	Kt—B 6
37. B—B 6	Kt—K 5 ch ?

A mistake which leaves White with a clearly won King and Pawn ending. ...Kt—Q 8 was indicated, although White would still retain the advantage.

38. B×Kt	P×B
39. K—B 6	

Black is helpless. If 39. ...P—Q R 4 ; 40. K—Kt 5, K—Q 2 ; 41. K×P, K×P ; 42. K—Kt 5, K—Q 4 ; 43. K—Kt 4 and wins : 43. ...P—R 3 ; 44. P—R 4, P—R 4 ; 45. K—Kt 5, K—Q 3 ; 46. K—B 4, K—K 3 ; 47. K—Q 4,

K—B 4 ; 48. K—Q 5, K—Kt 5 ;
49. K×P, K×P ; 50. K—B 3,
K—R 6 ; 51. P—K 4, K—R 7 ;
52. P—K 5, P—R 5 ; 53. P—K 6,
P—R 6 ; 54. P—K 7, K—Kt 8 ;
55. P—K 8(Q), P—R 7 ; 56. Q—
K 1 mate.

| 39. ...... | P—K R 3 |
| 40. P—R 4 ! | P—K R 4 |

White threatened to win with
P—R 5 ! etc.

41. K—Q 5	K—Q 2
42. K×P	K×P
43. K—Q 4	K—K 3
44. P—K 4	

Not 44. K—B 4 ?, K—B 4 etc.

44.	K—Q 3
45. K—B 4	K—B 3
46. K—Kt 4	K—Kt 3
47. K—R 4 !	

Simpler than the obvious P—
K 5, for White reserves the possibility of playing P—B 5 in some
variations. For example, if Black
now plays 47. ...K—R 3 ; 48.
P—B 5 wins. If 47. ...P—R 4 ;
48. P—K 5 leaves Black in *Zugzwang*, and similarly if 47. ...P—
R 3 ; 48. K—Kt 4, K—Kt 2 ; 49.
K—R 5, K—R 2 ; 50. P—B 5 etc.

| 47. ...... | K—B 4 |

A last despairing try.

48. K—R 5	K—Q 5
49. P—K 5	K—Q 4
50. K—R 6	K—K 3
51. K×P	K—B 4
52. K—Kt 7	K×P
53. P—K 6	K—Kt 5
54. P—K 7	K×P
55. P—K 8(Q)	P—Kt 4
56. Q—K 1 ch	K—Kt 5
57. Q—Kt 1 ch	K—B 5
58. Q—R 2 ch	K—Kt 5
59. K—B 6	Resigns

A delightful fighting game.

35. NUREMBERG, 1896

QUEEN'S GAMBIT DECLINED

DESPITE the early exchange of
Queens, this game takes a highly
interesting course. Tarrasch's
handling of the endgame from the
20th move on is imaginative and
forceful.

| *White* | *Black* |
| DR. S. TARRASCH | R. TEICHMANN |

1. P—Q 4	P—Q 4
2. P—Q B 4	P—K 3
3. Kt—Q B 3	Kt—K B 3
4. B—Kt 5	B—K 2
5. Kt—B 3	O—O
6. P—K 3	Q Kt—Q 2
7. R—B 1	P—B 3

At the time this game was played,
and for many years thereafter, ...
P—Q Kt 3 was generally played at
this point.

| 8. B—Q 3 | P×P |

In later years, after the variation had become the object of intensive study, the saving of a tempo by some such move as ...R—K 1 was far more fashionable than the text.

9. B×P	Kt—Q 4
10. B×B	Q×B
11. O—O	K Kt—Kt 3
12. B—Kt 3	P—K 4
13. Kt—K 4	P×P

Despite Black's success in achieving the freeing move ...P—K 4, his position is still cramped. In order to release his Q Kt from the burden of guarding the K P, he therefore decides to venture an exchange which will free his position at the cost of a weakened Pawn structure.

14. Q×P	Kt—B 3
15. Kt×Kt ch	Q×Kt
16. Q×Q	P×Q
17. K R—Q 1	B—Kt 5

If 17. ...B—K 3 ; 18. Kt—Q 4 is a good reply. If then 18. ...B×B ; 19. Kt×B, K R—Q 1 ; 20. Kt—B 5 and Black's position is difficult.

18. R—Q 6	K—Kt 2
19. Q R—Q 1	K R—K 1
20. P—K R 3	B×Kt

This leads to a clearly inferior game for Black, as the opening of the K Kt file and the strength of White's Bishop assure him a lasting initiative. However, 20. ...B—K 3 would be answered by 21. Kt—Q 4 with possibilities analogous to those in the previous note.

21. P×B	P—Q B 4
22. K—R 2	P—B 5
23. B—B 2	R—K 3

White threatened 24. R—Kt 1 ch and 25. R×P.

24. R(Q 6)—Q 4

Tarrasch points out that after 24. R—Kt 1 ch, K—R 1 ; 25. R—Q 4, R—K Kt 1 ; 26. R—R 4, R×R ; 27. R×P ch, K—Kt 1 ; 28. K× R, R—Q 3 (threat : ...R—Q 7) Black would have dangerous counterchances.

24.	R—K 4
25. P—B 4	R—Q Kt 4
26. R—Kt 1 ch	K—R 1
27. P—Kt 3 !	

Not 27. B×R P ?, P—B 4 etc. Not (instead of 27. ...P—B 4) 27. ...K×B because of 28. P—B 5 and wins.

27.	P—B 6

Dangerous, since it will soon be apparent that the advanced Pawn is in a very shaky state. ...P×P had to be tried.

28. B—K 4 !

This surprising move wins a Pawn, for if 28. ...R—Q Kt 1 ; 29. B×Kt P !, R×B ? ?, 30. R—Q 8 mate.

28. ......   P—B 4
29. B×Kt P   R—Q Kt 1
30. B—B 3   P—Q R 4
31. R—Q B 1

Beginning a new phase of the
struggle, which will centre about
the advanced Q B P.

31. ......   R—Q B 1
32. R—Q 3   R(Kt 4)—B 4
33. R—Q 6   R—Kt 4

If instead 33. ...R—Q Kt 1 ;
34. R—Q B 6. Or if 33. ...Kt—
R 1 ; 34. B—Q 5 followed by B—
B 4 and Black's proud Pawn falls by
the wayside.

34. B—K 2   R—Kt 5
35. R—Q 3   P—B 7
36. R—Q 2   P—R 5
37. R(Q 2)×P   R×R
38. R×R   P×P
39. P×P   R×Kt P
40. B—R 5 !   K—Kt 2

Or 40. ...P—B 3 ; 41. R—B 5
etc. (If at once 40. R—B 5, then
...R—Kt 7 is a good reply.)

41. R—B 7   Kt—Q 4
42. R×P ch   K—R 3
43. R×P   Resigns

Black's weaknesses have been
exploited inexorably.

36. NUREMBERG, 1896

GIUOCO PIANO

A MAGNIFICENT struggle between
these two famous rivals. The
rather colourless opening gives no
hint of the dramatic doings which
are to enliven the middle game.

	White	*Black*
	M. TCHIGORIN	DR. S. TARRASCH

1. P—K 4   P—K 4
2. Kt—K B 3   Kt—Q B 3
3. B—B 4   B—B 4
4. P—B 3   Kt—B 3
5. P—Q 3   P—Q 3
6. B—K Kt 5   B—K 3
7. Q Kt—Q 2

Tchigorin's adoption of the
Giuoco Pianissimo is in accordance
with the fashionable dictates of the
period. It is, however, not an
opening to give one's opponent the
slightest difficulty whatever.

7. ......   Q—K 2
8. Q—K 2   P—K R 3
9. B—K 3   B—Kt 3
10. K B×B   Q×B
11. Kt—B 4   Kt—K 2
12. O—O   O—O
13. P—Q R 4   Kt—Q 2 !
14. P—R 5   B×B
15. Kt×B

Judging from the sequel, White
would have been better advised to
play P×B, neutralising Black's
coming utilisation of the K B file.
But Tchigorin, true to his style,
prefers to invite nebulous complications.

15. ......   P—K B 4

Hoping to seize the initiative.
This game was played towards the
end of the tournament, with Tchigorin a point and a half behind
Tarrasch, and with both players in
the running for a high prize. This
accounts for the aggressive mood of
the following play.

16. P×P   Kt×P
17. Kt×Kt   Q×Kt

Not 17. ...R×Kt ? ; 18. Kt—Q 4.

18. P—Q 4 !

Beginning a very dangerous phase with the threat of Q—B 4 ch.

18. ......   P—K 5 !
19. Kt—Q 2   Q R—K 1 !

Intending to answer 20. P—B 3 with ...P—K 6, or if 20. Q—B 4 ch, R—B 2 ; 21. Q×P ? ?, Q—B 5 (threatening ...Q×Kt as well as ...Kt—B 4, winning the Queen) ; 22. Kt—B 4, Kt—K 4 winning a piece.

20. P—R 6 !

Creating an outpost which may lead to a critical position for Black on the Queen's side.

20. ......   P—Q Kt 3
21. Q R—K 1   P—Q 4
22. P—Q B 4 !

Realising that Black's Rooks are more effectively posted and that the K P has a cramping effect on his game, Tchigorin plays for counter-chances on the Queen's wing. The pressure mounts steadily.

22. ......   P—B 3
23. R—B 1

White is apparently making headway. He intends 24. P×P, P×P ; 25. R—B 7 or 24. ...Q×P ; 25. Q—B 4 with a good ending.

23. ......   K—R 1 !

Avoiding the exchange of Queens.

24. P×P   Q×P
25. Q—B 4   Q—K Kt 4 !

Quite a surprise. If now 26. Q×P, Q×Kt ; 27. Q×Kt, R—Q 1 ; 28. Q×P, R×B P ; 29. R×R, Q×Q R ch ; 30. R—B 1, Q×P and the Q P will fall. Black has good winning chances, despite the powerful Q R P.

26. Q—B 3   Kt—B 3
27. Kt—B 4   Kt—R 4
28. R—B 2   R—B 6
29. Kt—K 3   R—Q B 1
30. K—R 1   R(B 6)—B 1

Black now threatens ...Q—Kt 4 or else ...Kt—B 5—Q 6. The critical part of the game now begins.

31. P—Q 5 !

31. ......   P×P !

Tchigorin has just begun a long combination ; but Tarrasch sees further ahead.

32. Q×R   R×Q
33. R×R ch   K—R 2
34. R—B 7 !

His best chance. If instead 34. R—Q 1, Kt—B 5 ; 35. R—B 7, Kt—Q 6 ; 36. K—Kt 1, P—Q 5 ; 37. Kt—B 1, Q—B 5 (Tarrasch) and wins.

34. ......   P—Q 5

If now 35. Kt—B 2, Q—Kt 4
and wins. Tchigorin therefore decides that abandoning his Knight to
its fate is his best course.

35. R×P   Q—Kt 4 !

A surprising reply. Tchigorin
expected 35. ...P×Kt ; 36. P×
P, Q—Kt 4 ; 37. K—Kt 1 with a
winning position (if 37. ...Kt—
B 3 ; 38. R×Kt etc.), as the Q R P
cannot be stopped.

36. K—Kt 1   Kt—B 5 !

Tarrasch is maddeningly delib-
erate about capturing the Knight,
which still cannot move because of
the reply ...Kt—K 7 ch—Kt 6 ch.

37. R—K B 7   P×Kt
38. P×P

If 38. R×Kt, P—K 7 ; 39. R—
R 1, Q—R 4 ! wins. Or if 38.
P—R 7, P—K 7 ! still wins.

38. ......   Kt—K 7 ch
39. K—R 1

Or 39. K—B 2, Q×Kt P ! ; 40.
P—R 7, Kt—B 5 ch ; 41. K—
Kt 3, Q×P ch ; 42. K×Kt, Q×
R ch ; 43. K×P, Q—R 3 and
wins (Tarrasch).

39. ......   Q×R P
40. R(B 7)—B 2

Threatening R—K 1. But the
Knight has a means of escape, leaving White's game in a hopeless
state.

40. ......   Q—B 5 !
41. R—K 1   Kt—B 8
42. R—Q 2   Kt—Q 6
43. R(K 1)—Q 1   Q—Kt 6

Threatening ...Kt—B 7 ch.

44. R—K B 1   P—Q Kt 4
45. P—R 3   P—Kt 5
46. P—Kt 3   Q—K 3
47. K—Kt 2   Q—K 4
48. R—Q Kt 1   Q—Q B 4
49. R—K B 1

Or 49. R—K 2, Kt—B 8 ; 50.
R—K 1, Q—B 7 ch and wins.

49. ......   Q×P

White resigns. A difficult and
absorbing game.

37. NUREMBERG, 1896

INDIAN DEFENCE

THE Indian Defences might have
come into favour much sooner than
they actually did, had it not been
for the fact that they were so badly
misplayed on the rare occasions
when they were adopted in the
" good old days."

| White | Black |
DR. S. TARRASCH	R. CHAROUSEK
1. P—Q 4	P—Q 3
2. P—K 4	Kt—K B 3
3. Kt—Q B 3	P—K Kt 3
4. P—B 4	B—Kt 2
5. Kt—B 3	O—O
6. B—K 2	

Thus far the game has proceeded
on recognisably Indian lines, although in modern play P—Q B 4 is
almost invariably interpolated before bringing out the Q Kt. Black
should now play ...Q Kt—Q 2
with a view to ...P—K 4 or ...
P—B 4.

6. ......   P—Q 4 ?

But this is a violation of the spirit of the opening, resulting in a cruelly cramped game for Black.

7. P—K 5   Kt—K 1

If 7. ...Kt—K 5 ?; 8. Kt×Kt, P×Kt; 9. Kt—K Kt 5, winning a Pawn.

8. B—K 3   P—K 3
9. P—K R 4 !   Kt—Q B 3

Black should at least try ...Kt—Q 2 followed by ...P—Kt 3 and ...P—Q B 4. 9. ...P—K R 4 would be useless because of 10. P—K Kt 4.

10. P—R 5   Kt—K 2
11. P—K Kt 4   P—K B 4

Black is powerless against the coming assault, as his pieces are not properly posted for defence.

12. R P×P   Kt×P

Or 12. ...R P×P; 13. Kt—K Kt 5 and White wins as he pleases.

13. B—Q 3   P—K R 3

If 13. ...P×P; 14. Kt—K Kt 5 winning in quick time.

14. P—Kt 5   K—R 2
15. Q—K 2   R—R 1
16. Q—Kt 2 !   P—B 4
17. P×P   Resigns

Black must lose a piece : if 17. ...B×R P; 18. Q—Kt 5 ! or if 17. ...B—B 1 ; 18. Kt—Kt 5 ch, K—Kt 1 ; 19. Kt×K P etc. A catastrophe for Charousek !

38. VIENNA, 1898

RUY LOPEZ

In chess it is so often true that " a little knowledge is a dangerous thing." Thus, for example, there is a popular misconception that Bishops of opposite colour automatically ensure a draw. This is by no means the case in all or even most instances.

White	*Black*
Dr. S. Tarrasch	D. G. Baird

1. P—K 4   P—K 4
2. Kt—K B 3   Kt—Q B 3
3. B—Kt 5   P—Q R 3
4. B—R 4   Kt—B 3
5. O—O   B—K 2
6. Kt—B 3   P—Q 3

Modern theory considers that Black has better chances with ...P—Q Kt 4 followed by ...P—Q 3.

7. B×Kt ch   P×B
8. P—Q 4   P×P

For Tchigorin's move ...Kt—Q 2 see Game 103.

9. Kt×P   B—Q 2
10. P—B 4

This and the next move constitute a rather daring conception. More usual are 10. B—Kt 5, 10. Q—Q 3 and 10. P—Q Kt 3.

10.	O—O
11. P—K 5	P×P
12. P×P	B—K Kt 5

Despite the isolated K P, Black's game is uncomfortable. After 12. ...Kt—K 1 the Knight would be out of play for a long time, while 12. ...Kt—Q 4 ; 13. Kt—K 4 would give White good attacking prospects.

| 13. Q—Q 3 | B—Q B 4 |
| 14. B—K 3 | B×Kt |

Virtually compulsory. If 14. ...Kt—Q 4 ; 15. Kt×P !, B× B ch ; 16. K—R 1, Q—Q 2 ; 17. Kt×Kt, B—Q B 4 ; 18. Q—K 4 White would be a Pawn to the good.

| 15. B×B | Kt—Q 4 |
| 16. Q—Kt 3 | |

The exchange of Knights is unavoidable, in view of the threat of ...Kt—Kt 5 followed by ...Kt× B P.

| 16. ...... | Kt×Kt |
| 17. B×Kt | |

Not 17. Q×B ? ?, Q×B ch !

| 17. ...... | B—K 3 |
| 18. K—R 1 | |

White has good attacking chances, as his opponent's King's side is rather vulnerable. Tarrasch's chief object is to force ...

P—Kt 3. The manner in which this is accomplished is highly interesting.

18.	Q—Q 4
19. Q—R 4	Q R—Q 1
20. R—B 3	Q—B 5

R—Q 3 was threatened. The following manœuvres of Black's Queen hold back the attack for a while.

| 21. Q—B 2 | Q—K Kt 5 |
| 22. P—K R 3 | Q—Kt 3 |

Not 22. ...Q—R 4 ; 23. Q—R 7 winning a Pawn.

| 23. R—Kt 3 | Q—R 4 |

23. ...Q—B 4 ? would be refuted by 24. Q×Q, B×Q ; 25. P—K 6 with the double threat of R×P ch and P—K 7.

| 24. Q—B 6 ! | |

At last succeeding in forcing the desired weakness.

24.	R—Q 8 ch
25. K—R 2	P—Kt 3
26. R×R	Q×R
27. R—Q 3 !	

Beginning a beautiful combination to take advantage of Black's glaring weakness on K Kt 2.

| 27. ...... | Q×P |
| 28. B—Q 2 ! ! | |

Of course, if now 28. ...Q×R ; 29. B—R 6 forces mate.

35. K×P	Q—B 7 ch
36. K—Kt 4	P—B 4 ch
37. K—Kt 5	Q—Kt 6 ch
38. K—B 6	Q—R 5 ch
39. B—Kt 5	Resigns

Tarrasch has conjured up an interesting game from rather unpromising material.

28.	B×K R P !
29. R—Q 8 !	B×P
30. K×B ?	

Time pressure mars a fine finish. 30. P—K 6 !, as was later pointed out, would have won at once : 30. ...R×R (White threatened Q× B P ch as well as P—K 7) ; 31. P×P ch, K—B 1 ; 32. B—R 6 mate.

30.	P—K R 4
31. K—Kt 3	R×R
32. Q×R ch	K—R 2
33. P—K 6	

This still wins. Capture of the Pawn would lead to mate or loss of the Queen.

33.	Q—B 4

Or 33. ...Q×P ; 34. P—K 7, Q—K 4 ch ; 35. K—B 3, Q—B 4 ch ; 36. B—B 4, Q—R 6 ch ; 37. K—B 2, Q—R 5 ch ; 38. B—Kt 3, Q—B 3 ch ; 39. K—Kt 2, Q— Kt 7 ch ; 40. B—B 2 and wins (Marco).

34. P—K 7 !	P—R 5 ch

Queen checks would be met by the flight of White's King to the Queen's side.

39. VIENNA, 1898

RUY LOPEZ

THE games which Steinitz played in his last phase against his most famous disciples are rather pathetic. He violated his own rules, and was frequently defeated with his own weapons. A sad fate !

White	*Black*
Dr. S. Tarrasch	W. Steinitz

1. P—K 4	P—K 4
2. Kt—K B 3	Kt—Q B 3
3. B—Kt 5	P—Q 3
4. P—Q 4	B—Q 2
5. Kt—B 3	Kt—B 3
6. O—O	B—K 2
7. R—K 1	P×P
8. Kt×P	O—O
9. Kt×Kt	

B×Kt, as in Game 38, is more customary. The text has its points, however, as the further course of the game reveals. The K B is to be preserved for attacking purposes.

9.	P×Kt
10. B—Q 3	R—K 1

This move, as well as the manœuvre of which it is an integral part, is of doubtful value. 10. ...Kt— Kt 5 (intending ...Kt—K 4 supplemented by ...B—B 3) would be better. 11. P—B 4 would be a plausible but inferior reply, as 11. ...B—B 3 ! would involve the dangerous threat of 12. ...B—Q 5 ch.

11. P—K R 3 !

Depriving Black of the opportunity just mentioned.

11. ......   B—K B 1
12. B—K Kt 5 !

This move sets up a troublesome pin which reduces Steinitz's contemplated rearrangement of his pieces (...P—Kt 3 and ...B—Kt 2) to pointlessness.

12. ......   P—K R 3
13. B—R 4   R—Kt 1
14. R—Kt 1   P—Kt 4 ?

False pride. It would have been better to admit his error by playing ...B—K 2 and continuing with ...Kt—R 2 or ...Kt—Q 4. The text obviously constitutes a serious weakening of Black's King's position.

15. B—Kt 3   P—Kt 5

This is apparently the move Steinitz depended upon, reckoning only on 16. P×P, Kt×Kt P.

16. B—R 4 !

An unexpected reply. If now 16. ...P×P ; 17. P×P, B×P ? ; 18. Q—B 3 and Black loses a piece.

16. ......   P—K R 4
17. P×P   P×P
18. P—B 4 !

Now Black finds himself in a dis-

agreeable predicament, for if 18. ...P×P e.p. ; 19. Q×P and Black must choose between dangerously exposing his King with 19. ...B—K 2, or else losing the exchange after 19. ...B—Kt 2 ; 20. P—K 5 ! P×P ; 21. Kt—K 4, R—K 3 ; 22. B—B 4.

18. ......   B—K 2
19. B—B 2 !

A kind of move peculiar to Tarrasch. The immediate P—K 5 would allow Black to exchange pieces with ...Kt—Q 4. The text, by gaining time as a result of the attack on the Q R P, avoids any exchange.

19. ......   P—R 4
20. P—K 5   P×P
21. P×P

21. ......   Kt—R 4

Losing quickly, but the recommended alternative ...Kt—R 2 is not much better. There would follow 22. P—K 6 !, B×P ; 23. R×B, P×R ; 24. Q×P ch, Kt—Kt 4 (if 24. ...K—R 1 ; 25. Q—R 5 wins) ; 25. B—R 4, R—K B 1 (Kt—K 4 is threatened) ; 26. Kt—K 4, R—B 4 ; 27. Kt×Kt with an easy win in sight.

22. P—K 6 !	B×P
23. R×B	P×R
24. Q×P ch	Kt—Kt 2

Now Black must do penance for his sins of omission and commission. The attack ends victoriously in quick time.

25. Q—Kt 6	R—Kt 5

His last hope.

26. R—K B 1 !	R—K B 5
27. Q—R 7 ch	K—B 1

Or 27. ...K—B 2; 28. B—Kt 6 ch, K—B 3; 29. B—R 4 ch and wins.

28. B—Kt 6	Resigns

40. VIENNA, 1898

FOUR KNIGHTS' GAME

ALTHOUGH it was notoriously difficult to win a game from Schlechter, Tarrasch makes it look like a very simple task indeed ! The simplicity of the procedure conceals a certain subtle artistry.

White	*Black*
DR. S. TARRASCH	C. SCHLECHTER
1. P—K 4	P—K 4
2. Kt—K B 3	Kt—K B 3
3. Kt—B 3	

Since Tarrasch considered the Petroff definitely inferior, his avoidances of it were rare indeed.

3.	Kt—B 3
4. B—Kt 5	B—Kt 5
5. O—O	O—O
6. P—Q 3	B×Kt
7. P×B	P—Q 3
8. R—K 1	

Varying from the almost obligatory and rather hackneyed 8. B—Kt 5.

8.	B—Q 2

A lifeless continuation. More in the modern spirit would have been 8. ...Kt—K 2; 9. P—Q 4, P—B 3; 10. B—Q B 4, Q—B 2.

9. P—Q 4	Kt×Q P
10. Kt×Kt	P×Kt
11. B×B	Q×B
12. P×P	K R—K 1

It is already apparent that Black has gone wrong. White's centre Pawns are strong, and the Knight has less scope here than the Bishop. In addition, Black has kindly undoubled White's Q B Ps.

13. P—K B 3	P—Q 4
14. P—K 5	Q—K 3
15. R—Kt 1	P—Q Kt 3
16. R—B 1	Kt—Q 2
17. P—K B 4	P—K B 4

Although White has a strong centre and his K P is passed, Schlechter has at least succeeded in bringing about a Pawn position which seems to leave White's Bishop little scope behind the chain of Pawns. Tarrasch, however, solves this problem very neatly.

18. Q—B 3 !	P—Q R 3

18. ...P—B 4 is the natural move, but then comes 19. P—B 4 !, Q P×P; 20. P—Q 5, Q—K 2; 21. Q—B 3 recovering the Pawn advantageously.

19. B—R 3	P—Q Kt 4

If 19. ...P—B 4; 20. P—B 4 !,

Q P×P ; 21. P—Q 5, Q—K 2 ;
22. P—K 6 followed by R×P with
a fine game.

20. K—R 1

Now that his projects on the
Queen-side have come to a stand-
still, Tarrasch prepares for the characteristic break-through on the
other wing.

20. ......   K—R 1
21. R—Kt 1   R—K Kt 1
22. Q R—K B 1   P—Q R 4

Schlechter is naturally anxious to
drive the Bishop off its fine diagonal.

23. P—Kt 4   P—Kt 3

If 23. ...P—Kt 5 ; 24. P×P,
Q×B P ; 25. B—B 1, P—B 3 ; 26.
R—B 2 with an advantageous posi-
tion.

24. P—B 3   Q R—Kt 1

Still preoccupied with the same
plan.

25. R—Kt 2   P—Kt 5
26. B P×P   R P×P

At last Black has achieved his objective ; but the result is a weak
Q Kt P.

27. P×P !

This well-timed exchange gives
White exclusive occupation of the
K Kt file, as Black's Q R cannot
leave the Q Kt file.

27. ......   P×P

...Q×B P would prevent the
manœuvre White has in mind, but

in that event White would soon
succeed in advancing the K B P
with irresistible force.

28. R×R ch   Q×R
29. R—K Kt 1   Q—B 2
30. B—B 1   R—Kt 3
31. B—Q 2   R—Q R 3

Against other lines, White would
win in much the same way with B—
K 1, Q—Kt 2 and B—R 4.

32. B×P

Now the Bishop is once more
free, so that White's pieces can
cooperate to bring about a forced
win.

32. ......   R×P

33. Q—K Kt 3 !

With the nasty threat of P—K 6 !

33. ......   Kt—B 1

Or 33. ...R—R 3 ; 34. B—
Q 6 ! and wins.

34. B—K 7 !   Kt—Kt 3
35. B—B 6 ch   K—Kt 1
36. P—R 4   K—B 1
37. Q—Kt 3   R—R 1
38. Q—Kt 4 ch ! Resigns

For if 38. ...K—K 1 ; 39. Q—
Kt 7 wins. An admirable game by
Tarrasch.

41. VIENNA, 1898

QUEEN'S GAMBIT DECLINED

So fine a judge as Marco says of
this game : " A beautiful game by
Tarrasch, deeply conceived and
flawlessly executed."   Although
Tarrasch was considered a pillar
of orthodoxy, his play is highly unconventional throughout.

White	Black
A. Burn	Dr. S. Tarrasch

1.	P—Q 4	P—Q 4
2.	P—Q B 4	P—K 3
3.	Kt—Q B 3	P—Q B 3
4.	P—K 3	B—Q 3
5.	Kt—B 3	P—K B 4

The well-known Stonewall Variation, the theoretical drawbacks of
which are not exploited by Burn in
this encounter.

6. B—K 2

Too passive ; better is 6. Kt—
K 5 followed by P—B 4, and
White's initiative in the centre (his
Q B P is on the fourth rank, while
Black's Q B P is on the third) gives
him promising perspectives.

6.	......	Kt—Q 2
7.	O—O	Q—B 3
8.	Kt—K 1	

Intending P—B 3 followed by
P—K 4. This advance, if carried
out successfully, will leave Black
with a strategically lost game. The

unconventional manner in which
Tarrasch meets this plan is highly
interesting.

| 8. | ...... | Q—R 3 |
| 9. | P—K Kt 3 | |

Had Burn foreseen the consequences of this move, he would
have played P—B 4, thereby renouncing his plan of advancing the
K P.

9. ......   P—K Kt 4 !

Surprising, but, as will be seen,
quite logical. 10. B—R 5 ch, K—
B 1 would merely be loss of time
for White.

| 10. | P—B 3 | Kt—K 2 |
| 11. | P—K 4 | P—B 5 |

This is the basis of Black's counter-play.   He   obtains   attacking
chances and deprives White's pieces
of some good squares.

12. P—K 5 ?

A very great error of judgment.
This advance can seriously limit
Black's command of the board only
if played in conjunction with P—
B 5, but this latter move does not
prove feasible throughout the entire
game.   Hence it would have been
preferable to maintain the status
quo in the centre and continue with
K—Kt 2.

| 12. | ...... | B—B 2 |
| 13. | P—K Kt 4 | |

Not 13. P—B 5, says Mieses, because of the continuation 13. ...
P—Kt 3 ; 14. P—Q Kt 4, KtP×

P ; 15. Q Kt P×P, P×P ; 16.
P×P, Q—R 6 ; 17. K—B 2, Kt×
B P ! ; 18. P×Kt, B×P and wins.
The text prevents the above varia-
tion, but allows Black to work up a
powerful attack by opening up the
K R file.   Hence K—Kt 2 was still
in order.

13. ......   Q—Kt 2 !

Preparing for ...P—K R 4 and
also keeping an eye on the centre.
Thus if 14. P—B 5, P—Kt 3 ; 15.
P—Kt 4, P×P ; 16. Kt P×P, Kt
×K P ! ; 17. P×Kt, B×P etc.

14. R—B 2   P—K R 4
15. R—Kt 2   Kt—K Kt 3

The Knight plays an important
rôle from now on.

16. Kt P×P   R×P
17. B—Q 3   Kt—R 5
18. R—Q B 2

After 18. R—Kt 4 Tarrasch
would have continued advantageously with 18. ...Q—R 3 ; 19.
Q—B 2, P×P ! ; 20. K B×P, B—
Kt 3.

18. ......   P×P !

A move that few players would
hit on, since it apparently frees
White's game.   But the establishment of a vulnerable target in the
form of the weakened Q P is more
important.

19. B×Q B P   Kt—K B 4 !

Losing no time. The threat is
...Kt×Q P.

20. K—R 1   B—Kt 3 !

21. B×K P

Against 21. R—Q 2 Tarrasch
had planned the following pretty
finish : 21. ...Kt×K P ! ; 22. P×
Kt, Kt—Kt 6 ch ; 23. K—Kt 2,
R×P ch ! ; 24. K×R, Q—R 3 ch ;
25. K—Kt 2, Q—R 8 mate.

21. ......   Kt×Q P
22. B—Kt 4   R—R 1
23. R—Q 2   Kt×K P !

The play with the Knights is elegant. If now 24. R×Kt, B×R
(not 24. ...Kt×B ; 25. R—K 4
ch, Kt—K 4 ; 26. Q—K 2) ; 25.
Q×B, B×B ; 26. P×B, R×P ch ;
27. K—Kt 1, Q—R 1 ; 28. Q—
K 4, O—O—O and wins.

24. B×B   R×B
25. R×Kt   B×R
26. Q×B   R×P ch
27. K—Kt 1   Q—R 1 !

Threatening 28. ...R—R 8 ch ;
29. K—B 2, Q—R 5 ch. White's
position is hopeless.

28. B×P   P×B
29. Kt—K 4

29. Q×B P, R—R 8 ch ; 30.

K—B 2, R—B 2 would also win quickly for Black.

| 29. | ...... | R—R 8 ch |
| 30. | K—B 2 | Kt—Kt 5 ch |

White resigns. A " hyper-modern " game !

42. VIENNA, 1898
PETROFF DEFENCE

THIS is one of the classic constriction games which Réti used in *Masters of the Chessboard* to illustrate Tarrasch's style. Eager students of later generations were to be deeply impressed with the methodical manner in which Tarrasch steadily increased the pressure and reduced his opponent's mobility.

| *White* | *Black* |
| DR. S. TARRASCH | G. MARCO |

1.	P—K 4	P—K 4
2.	Kt—K B 3	Kt—K B 3
3.	Kt×P	P—Q 3
4.	Kt—K B 3	Kt×P
5.	P—Q 4	B—K 2

...P—Q 4 is more customary, but Marco is apparently obsessed with the idea of not putting the fine square K 4 at the disposal of White's K Kt. The result is a cramped game for Black and diminished scope for his K B.

| 6. | B—Q 3 | Kt—K B 3 |
| 7. | O—O | O—O ? |

Had Marco realised the implications of Tarrasch's next move, he would have played the more exact ...B—Kt 5 here.

8. P—K R 3 !

Now the Q B has no good square for development. The text must have come as a great surprise to Marco, for while advances of the R Ps were common up to about 1880 to prevent pins, Steinitz had laboured mightily against such moves and had impressed the younger generation with his arguments. *The advance of the K R P is bad when that Pawn can become a target for attack and thus weaken the castled position ;* but since Black has no attacking prospects here, the text has purely constructive features.

8. ......   B—K 3

A developing move of sorts. It has its drawbacks, as will soon be apparent.

9. P—B 4 !

Another good move. The natural development ...Kt—B 3 or ...Q Kt—Q 2 would now lose a piece by P—Q 5. ...P—Q 4 can be answered by P—B 5, leaving Black with a cramped game.

9. ......   P—B 3
10. Kt—Kt 5 !

Tarrasch is consistent in carrying out his plan. He wants to play P—B 4 and P—K B 5, further reducing Black's terrain ; at the same time, he hopes to provoke ...P—K R 3.

10. ......   Kt—R 3

After 10 ...P—K R 3; 11. Kt×B, P×Kt Black would have a wretched Pawn position.

| 11. | Kt—Q B 3 | Kt—B 2 |
| 12. | P—B 4 | P—K R 3 |

Marco can no longer resist the temptation to rid himself of the annoying Knight ; but the advance of the Pawn seriously weakens his position, since White's pieces will soon be posted for a powerful attack. Note the distinction between 9. P—K R 3 and 12. ... P—K R 3.

13. Kt—B 3 !

This is the kind of move that can be made only by a tyro or a great master. Tarrasch deliberately refrains from obtaining two Bishops and retreats the Knight with a loss of several tempi. But what is really important is the weakening of Black's position (...P—K R 3) and the cramping effect of the coming P—K B 5.

13. ......   Q—B 1
14. Q—B 2   R—Kt 1

Planning what turns out to be an ineffectual Queen's side advance. If 14. ...P—Q 4 ; 15. P—Q B 5, P—Q Kt 3 ; 16. P—Q Kt 4, P—Q R 4 ; 17. Kt—Q R 4 with advantage to White (Mieses).

15. P—K B 5   B—Q 2
16. B—B 4

This is reminiscent of Steinitz : the Q B is developed very late, but to a beautifully effective post.

16. ......   P—Q Kt 4
17. P—Q Kt 3   P—B 4 ? !
18. P—Q 5 !

Tarrasch can win a Pawn here with 18. Q P×P here, but he rightly reasons that keeping up the pressure is stronger policy.

18. ......   P—Kt 5
19. Kt—K 2   P—Q R 4
20. P—Kt 4 !

Beginning the process of taking advantage of ...P—K R 3.

20. ......   Kt—R 2

Only this retreat can hold up the Pawn-storming attack for a while.

21. P—K R 4   Q—Q 1
22. B—Kt 3   P—R 5

Note that Black's advance on the Queen's side (in contradistinction to Tarrasch's advance on the other wing) has no value.

23. K—R 1   R—R 1
24. Q R—K 1 !

Tarrasch naturally is not going to permit the exchange of his Rook, which is destined to be more useful than Black's Q R.

24. ......   Kt—K 1
25. Kt—B 4 !

The pressure mounts ominously. Note how smoothly White's pieces assume strong posts and cooperate harmoniously.

25. ......   B—K B 3

26. Kt—K 6 ! !

Lightning out of a clear sky !

26. ......   P×P

As Mieses shows, Black cannot take the Knight and escape un-scathed :
I. 26. ...P×Kt ; 27. B P×P, B—B 1 ; 28. B×Kt ch, K—R 1 ; 29. P—Kt 5 !, B—K 2 ; 30. Q—Kt 6 and wins.
II. 26. ...B×Kt ; 27. B P×B, P—Kt 3 ; 28. P×P ch, R×P ; 29. B×Kt P, R—K 2 ; 30. R×R, Q×R ; 31. R—K 1, B—K 4 ; 32. Kt×B and wins.

27. P×P   Q—Kt 3
28. Kt×R   K×Kt

Or 28. ...Kt×Kt ; 29. P—Kt 5 etc.

29. P—Kt 5 !

This advance forces a quick win.

29. ......   P×P
30. P×P   Kt×P

If 30. ...B×Kt P ; 31. P—B 6 !, P—Kt 3 ; 32. B×Kt P, P×B ; 33. Q×P winning.

31. Q—K R 2 !   K—Kt 1
32. Kt×Kt   B×Kt
33. P—B 6 !   P—Kt 3
34. B×Kt P   Resigns

If 34. ...Kt×P ; 35. R×Kt. An impressive victory.

43. VIENNA, 1898

HUNGARIAN DEFENCE

THIS encounter took place two rounds after the preceding game.

Curiously enough, it was played in much the same style by Tarrasch ! Years later he wrote of it : "A game in which combinations are absent. Yet, after a modest beginning, White cramps his opponent's game more and more until it is com-pletely crippled—and all this with-out any noticeable blunder on Black's side. That is the highest triumph of chess strategy."

White   *Black*
DR. S. TARRASCH J. W. SHOWALTER

1. P—K 4   P—K 4
2. Kt—K B 3   Kt—Q B 3
3. B—B 4   B—K 2

An unusual defence, adopted to evade the well-worn paths of the Giuoco Piano. Its drawback is that it leaves Black with rather a cramped game—a very dangerous condition against so great a master of constriction strategy as Tar-rasch.

4. P—Q 4   P—Q 3

...P×P would surrender the centre and give White a percept-ibly freer position.

5. P—Q 5

Rarely is a definitive policy laid down so early in a game. Tarrasch at once announces his policy of diminishing Black's terrain.

5. ......   Kt—Kt 1
6. B—Q 3 !

The freeing reply ...P—K B 4 must be hindered.

6. ......   Kt—K B 3
7. P—B 4   O—O
8. P—K R 3 !

As in the previous game, Tarrasch prevents ...B—Kt 5. In addition, he is now prepared to meet ...Kt—K 1 with P—K Kt 4, preventing ...P—K B 4.

Even at the cost of renouncing the two Bishops, Showalter should have played 7. ...B—Kt 5.

8. ......   P—B 3

Contemplating counterplay on the Queen's side, a project which is later foiled by Tarrasch.

9. Kt—B 3   Kt—R 3
10. B—K 3   Kt—B 2

...Kt—B 4 ? would lose a Pawn after B×Kt ; the Knight must therefore content himself with an inferior square.

11. O—O   K Kt—K 1

Hoping to play ...P—K B 4, which is at once prevented by Tarrasch. ...B—Q 2 followed by ...Q—K 1, intending ...P—Q Kt 4, was the alternative plan.

12. Q—B 2   P×P
13. B P×P   P—K Kt 3

Still striving for ...P—B 4.

14. B—K R 6   Kt—Kt 2
15. P—K Kt 4 !

Black's one chance to free himself (...P—B 4) is now permanently prevented. Now Tarrasch proceeds to the second, and much more difficult, phase of utilising his greater command of the board.

15. ......   Kt(B 2)—K 1
16. K—R 2   K—R 1
17. R—K Kt 1

White's task is to open a file on the King's side. This requires considerable preparation.

17. ......   B—Q 2
18. R—Kt 2   R—B 1
19. Q R—K Kt 1   P—Kt 3 ?

A feeble move which leads to a fatal weakening of the white squares in Black's game. A cramped position cannot stand the additional drawback of organic weaknesses.

20. Q—Q 2 !

White wants to play Kt—K 1 followed by P—B 4. But he first prevents ...B—K Kt 4 as a reply to Kt—K 1. Tarrasch is thus following out the maxim : *when your opponent has a cramped game, avoid exchanges.*

20. ......   Kt—B 3
21. Kt—K 1   Kt—Kt 1
22. B—K 3   P—K Kt 4

Preventing P—B 4, but the move has several serious flaws : (*a*) it weakens the white squares ; (*b*) it limits the scope of Black's K B ; (*c*) it creates a target for the opening of a file. These factors point to White's coming procedure : (*a*) exchange of Black's Q B, to intensify the weakness of the white squares ; (*b*) opening of the K R file.

23. Kt—B 3   P—B 3
24. P—K R 4 !   P—K R 3
25. R—K R 1   K—R 2

Black prepares to flee : the King's side is getting too hot for him. However, it must be borne in mind that it will not be an easy task to break down Black's well barricaded position.

26. K—Kt 1   K—Kt 3
27. Kt—R 2

The Knight is headed for K B 5 —a manœuvre to be executed in conjunction with the elimination of Black's Q B.

27. ......   R—Q B 2
28. Kt—B 1   Q—B 1
29. Q—K 2 !

Protecting the K Kt P and at the same time beginning to apply himself to the problem of the white squares. P—B 3 is more obvious, but would take away the square K B 3 from White's pieces.

29. ......   K—B 2
30. B—R 6   Q—Kt 1
31. Kt—Kt 5 !   B × Kt

Black has no choice. But now Tarrasch has achieved his objective of controlling the weak white squares.

32. B × B   K R—B 1
33. P × P   R P × P

Now White is able to exploit the K R file in its entirety, but after ... B P × P he would triple his major pieces on the K R file and finally break through decisively with R × P.

34. B—B 6   B—B 1
35. Q—B 3 !

[*See diagram in next column.*]

35. ......   R × B

Played in the desperate realisation that he has no good reply to the threat of B × K Kt P. Thus if 35. ...K—Kt 3 ; 36. R(Kt 2)—R 2 and wins :

POSITION AFTER 35. Q—B 3 !

I. 36. ...Kt—K 2 ? ; 37. R— R 6 ch, K—B 2 ; 38. Q × P ch, K—Kt 1 ; 39. R—R 8 mate.

II. 36. ...R—Q 1 ; 37. R— R 8, B—K 2 forced ; 38. R(R 1)— R 7, Q—B 1 (Q—B 5 ch ! ! was threatened) ; 39. R × Kt ch, K × R ; 40. Q—R 3 and Black is helpless.

These variations show the power of the open file.

36. P × R   Kt—K 3
37. R—R 7 ch   B—Kt 2

If 37. ...K—K 1 ? ; 38. Q— B 5 wins.

38. Kt—Kt 3   R × P
39. Kt—B 5

The Knight has arrived !

39. ......   Q—Q B 1
40. R(Kt 2)—R 2   Kt—K 2

40. ...K—Kt 3 would have lost in either of the following ways :
I. 41. B × K K Kt P !, P × B (if 41. ...Kt × B ? ; 42. R × B mate ; if 41. ...K × B ; 42. Kt × B) ; 42. Kt—R 4 ch ! !, K × R ; 43. Q— B 5 ch followed by Kt—Kt 6 mate.
II. 41. Q—R 3 (threatening Q—

R 5 mate), K—B 2 ; 42. Q—
R 5 ch, K—B 1 ; 43. Q—Kt 6,
R—B 2 (if 43. ...Q—Q 2 ; 44.
R×B, Kt×R ; 45. R—R 7) ; 44.
Kt×B, Kt×Kt ; 45. R—R 8.

The first variation is of course the
more conclusive, but both lines of
play are instructive because they
shed so much light on the nature of
White's advantage.

41. Kt×B   Kt×Kt
42. B×K Kt P   Q—K 3

Black resigns without waiting for
43. B—R 6 to win a piece—not to
mention the possibility 43. B×P,
Q×B ; 44. R×Kt ch, K×R ; 45.
R—R 7 ch. Tarrasch's exploitation of the enemy's crowded position has been masterly.

44. VIENNA, 1898

RUY LOPEZ

THERE were few victories that Tarrasch prized more highly than this
beautiful game with his great rival
Pillsbury. It was played in the
33rd round (!) of this magnificent
struggle, and Tarrasch needed a
win in order to remain in the running.

White	*Black*
DR. S. TARRASCH	H. N. PILLSBURY

1. P—K 4   P—K 4
2. Kt—K B 3   Kt—Q B 3
3. B—Kt 5   Kt—B 3
4. O—O   Kt×P
5. R—K 1

Beginning an experimental line
which was just beginning to go out
of fashion at this time. The
chances are that Tarrasch, desper-

ately needing a win, was anxious to
avoid the continuation 5. P—Q 4,
Kt—Q 3 ; 6. B×Kt, Q P×B ; 7.
P×P, Kt—B 4 ; 8. Q×Q ch, K×
Q. Both Tarrasch and Pillsbury
were partial to Black's chances in
this ending.

5. ......   Kt—Q 3
6. Kt×P   B—K 2
7. B—Q 3

A typically "bizarre" move
credited to Steinitz. Black's position is uncomfortable for a while,
but he should establish equality
fairly quickly.

7. ......   Kt×Kt
8. R×Kt   O—O
9. Kt—B 3   P—Q B 3

Pillsbury intends to rearrange his
pieces by playing ...Kt—K 1, ...
P—Q 4 and ...B—Q 3.

10. Q—R 5   P—K Kt 3

Tarrasch considers this weakening of the black squares too dangerous and recommends ...P—K R 3.
However, the text is playable if followed up carefully.

11. Q—B 3   Kt—K 1
12. P—Q Kt 3   P—Q 4
13. B—Kt 2   B—K 3
14. Q R—K 1   Kt—Kt 2 ?

An error of judgment which is
remarkable in a master of Pillsbury's stature. Schlechter recommends 14. ...Q—Q 2 ; 15. P—
K R 3 (otherwise ...B—B 3 followed by ...B—Kt 5 wins the exchange), B—B 3 ; 16. R(K 5)—
K 2, B—Kt 2 ; 17. B—R 3, Kt—
Q 3 and Black has achieved the

proper placing of his minor pieces in a highly satisfactory manner.

15. R(K 5)—K 2   B—B 3
16. B—R 3   R—K 1
17. Kt—Q 1 !

The Knight begins a tour to K Kt 4 to take advantage of the weaknesses of the black squares in the hostile position.

17. ......   B—Q 5

Black is in quite a quandary. He cannot move his Queen while the K B is at B 3, hence the text; but the removal of the K B leads to a further weakening of the King's side. The error at move 14 begins to take on ever gloomier implications.

18. P—B 3   B—Kt 3
19. Kt—K 3   Q—Q 2
20. P—R 3   P—Q B 4

Creating a target for White's attack and leading to an increase of the scope of his Bishops, as Tarrasch's later play demonstrates.

21. B—B 1

The Bishop will be used to good effect later on its original diagonal.

21. ......   B—B 2
22. Kt—Kt 4   B×Kt

Since White's Bishops soon prove too powerful, it would have been better to avoid this exchange, either by means of 22. ...Kt—R 4 or else (as suggested in the Tournament Book) by 22. ...Q—Q 3.; 24. Kt—R 6 ch, K—R 1 ; 25. P— Kt 3, R—K B 1. But Pillsbury seems to play this game in a

strangely defeatist mood, quite different from his usually dynamic style.

23. P×B   R—K 3 ?

There was really nothing better than a double exchange of Rooks. Doubtless Pillsbury feared the power of the Bishops in an ending (a comment, by the way, on his previous move), but they prove fearsome enough as the game actually proceeds.

24. P—B 4 !

With this and his next move, Tarrasch seizes the initiative and the Bishops come into play very strongly.

24. ......   P—Q 5

Judging from the continuation, ...P×P might have been preferable.

25. B—K 4 !   R—Kt 1
26. P—Q 3

Of course not 26. B×Q Kt P ?, R×B ; 27. Q×R, B—R 7 ch.

26. ......   P—Kt 3
27. P—Kt 3

In order not to be interrupted later on by the mating threat ... Q—Q 3.

27. ......   P—K R 4

Pillsbury is naturally not content to sit by idly and watch White's attack develop. Nevertheless, the text weakens the King's side still more, and hence the patient ...

Q R—K 1 would have been preferable.

28. P×P   Kt×P
29. B—Q 5

This must be played before ...
Kt—B 3.

29. ......   R×R

There is nothing better than surrendering the file, for if 29. ...R—
K B 3 ; 30. Q—Kt 2, B—Q 3 ; 31.
B—Kt 5, R—B 4 ; 32. P—B 4 followed by B—K 4.

30. R×R   K—Kt 2

If 30. ...R—K 1 ? ; 31. B—
B 6. White's pieces are working
together harmoniously, whilst
Black's are scattered and ineffectual. The result cannot
therefore be in doubt.

31. B—Kt 5 !

31. ......   P—B 3

If 31. ...R—K B 1 ; 32. R—
K 7 wins (32. B—K 7 is also good
enough).
    Against 31. ...B—Q 3 or 31.
...B—Q 1 Tarrasch planned the

following fine win : 32. R—K 7 !,
B×R ; 33. Q×P ch, K—R 1 ; 34.
Q×P, B×B ; 35. Q×Kt ch, Q—
R 2 ; 36. Q×B, R—K 1 ; 37.
B—K 4 ! and wins :
    I. 37. ...Q—K 2 ; 38. Q—
R 6 ch, K—Kt 1 ; 39. B—Q 5 ch.
    II. 37. ...R×B ; 38. Q—
Q 8 ch !, K—Kt 2 ; 39. Q—Q 7
ch, K—Kt 1 ; 40. Q×Q ch etc.

32. R—K 6 ! !

Another fine stroke which main-
tains the pressure on Black's weak-
ness. If now 32. ...P×B ; 33.
Q—K 4, Kt—B 3 ; 34. R—K 7 ch,
K—B 1 ; 35. R×Q, Kt×Q ; 36.
R×B with a won ending.

32. ......   B—K 4
33. B—Q 2

This quiet retreat wins a piece, as
Black's Knight cannot be saved.
Thus if 33. ...K—R 1 ; 34. P—
K Kt 4, Kt—Kt 2 ; 35. Q—
R 3 ch ; or 33. ...Q—Q B 2 ; 34.
R—B 6 ! followed by P—K Kt 4.
Pillsbury therefore makes a last
despairing bid for attack.

33. ......   R—K R 1
34. P—K Kt 4   Q—Q B 2
35. P×Kt   R×P
36. R—K 8   Q—Q 2
37. R—Kt 8 ch   K—R 2
38. Q—Kt 2   Q—B 4
39. B—K 4   R—R 7
40. R×P !

Very pretty.

40. ......   R×Q ch
41. R×R   Resigns

An unconventional finish to a
fine game by Tarrasch.

45. VIENNA, 1898

FRENCH DEFENCE

A GENERATION ago, it was still customary to speak of Tarrasch's superb games in this great tournament with something approaching awe. In his notes to this game, Mieses, for example, concludes with the comment : "Almost every game played by Tarrasch in this tournament is a veritable pearl of chess artistry."

White	Black
DR. S. TARRASCH	E. SCHIFFERS

1. P—Q 4	P—K 3
2. P—K 4	P—Q 4
3. Kt—Q B 3	Kt—K B 3
4. B—Kt 5	B—K 2
5. P—K 5	K Kt—Q 2
6. B×B	Q×B
7. Kt—Kt 5	

A somewhat old-fashioned move which allows Black to obtain a good game with proper play. For the alternative 7. Q—Q 2, see Game 70.

7.	Kt—Kt 3
8. P—Q B 3	P—Q R 3
9. Kt—Q R 3	P—Q B 4
10. Kt—B 2	Kt—B 3
11. P—K B 4	P×P

Black shows his hand too soon. He should leave open the choice between capturing in the centre, pushing by or maintaining the tension. The proper course would be to mobilise the Queen's side with 11. ...Kt—R 5 ; 12. R—Kt 1, P—Q Kt 4 with promising possibilities.

12. P×P	B—Q 2
13. P—Q Kt 3 !	

Beginning the characteristic process of constriction. Q—Q 2 or B—Q 3 would not be so good because of the reply ...Kt—B 5 ; whereas after the text, Black's Knights are destined to be useless throughout the game.

13.	R—Q B 1
14. Q—Q 2	O—O
15. Kt—B 3	P—B 4

Played in order to block the attacking diagonal of the hostile Bishop, White's P—K Kt 4 may now be expected as the logical continuation of his attacking plans.

16. B—Q 3	R—Q B 2

Schiffers realises that the Q B file is his best chance of counterplay.

17. O—O	K—R 1
18. K—R 1	B—K 1

Black is excessively cautious. ...K R—B 1 would have been more to the point.

19. P—K R 3	

In order to be able to answer ...B—R 4 with Kt—R 2 followed by P—K Kt 4.

19.	Kt—R 2 ?

Vainly hoping for ...B—Kt 4 or ...Kt—Kt 4. Since Tarrasch's reply is obvious, the text is simply waste of time.

20. P—Q R 4	Kt—B 3
21. P—K Kt 4	

In contrast to his opponent's vacillation, Tarrasch continues his business-like preparations for storming the King-side.

21. ......   P—Kt 3
22. P—R 5 !

Only a supremely confident player could resort to such a move. The text cramps Black's game, but at the cost of making his Q Kt 4 accessible to his pieces.

22. ......   Kt—B 1
23. R—K Kt 1   Kt(B 3)—R 2

Black is at last ready for some counterplay on the Queen's side ; the intensity of the struggle increases at every move.

24. R—Kt 3   P×P ?

Black changes horses in midstream. He doubtless feared that after 24. B—Kt 4 ; 25. P×P, Kt P×P (after 25. ...KP×P ; 26. Kt—K 3 followed by P—R 4—5 White's attack would be stronger) ; 26. Q R—K Kt 1 White's command of the K Kt file would give him formidable attacking chances. Yet Black would have a good defensive formation—certainly far more promising than what he actually obtains.

25. P×P   B—Kt 4
26. P—B 5 !

Tarrasch sees that the crisis is at hand and, unlike his timid opponent, boldly strives for the initiative. If 26. ...K P×P ; 27. P×P, P×P ; 28. Q R—K Kt 1, P—B 5 ; 29. R—Kt 4, B×B ; 30. Q×B with splendid attacking chances : White dominates the K Kt file and Black's Knights cannot accomplish a great deal.

26. ......   B×B

This much-maligned move has at least the merit of forcing Tarrasch to continue in an inspired vein which few players could emulate.

27. P—B 6 !

Very fine. If now 27. ...R× P ; 28. P×R, Q—Q 3 (seemingly very strong) ; 29. Kt—K 5 !, B× Kt (or 29. ...R×Kt ; 30. Q×B winning easily, while if 29. ... B—K 5 ch ; 30. K—Kt 1, R×Kt ; 31. Q—R 6, R—B 2 ; 32. P—B 7 etc.) ; 30. Q—R 6, B—K 5 ch ; 31. K—R 2, K—Kt 1 ; 32. R—K B 1 and wins ! Or 30. ...K—Kt 1 ; 31. R—K B 1, Q—B 1 (if 31. ... B—K 5 ch ; 32. K—R 2 and we have transposed into the previous variation) ; 32. P—B 7 ch, R×P ; 33. Kt×R and wins.

Here and in the remaining play, the helplessness of Black's Knights is a curious and important factor.

27. ......   Q—K 1
28. Q×B   Kt—Kt 4

The crisis. Black threatens ... R—B 6 very strongly. How is White to meet this threat ?

29. Kt—Kt 5 ! !

Very fine. Tarrasch meets the

threat by ignoring it ! If now 29.
...P—R 3 ; 30. R—K R 3 wins.
Black therefore has nothing better
than to win the Queen.

29. ...... R—B 6
30. Q×R

This sacrifice, which is both
forced and forcing, had of course
been calculated by Tarrasch some
time previously. Its effectiveness
rests on the power of the advanced
K B P, which paralyses Black's
defensive possibilities.

30. ...... Kt×Q
31. R×Kt P—R 3

Black cannot defend himself
against the simultaneous threats of
R—K R 3 and R—B 7. Thus if
31. ...P—R 4 ; 32. R—B 7, P×
P ; 33. K—Kt 2 and wins. Or
32. ...Q—Kt 4 ; 33. P×P, P×P
(if 33. ...Q—K 7 ; 34. R—
R 7 ch, K—Kt 1 ; 35. P×P wins) ;
34. R—R 7 ch, K—Kt 1 ; 35. R—
K Kt 1 and White wins pretty
much as he pleases. If 35. ...Q—
Q 6 ; 36. Kt—K 1, Q×Q P ; 37.
Kt(K 1)—B 3, Q—Q 6 ; 38. R—
Kt 7 ch, K—R 1 ; 39. Kt—R 4.
If 37. ...Q—K B 5 ; 38. P—
B 7 ch wins.

32. R—K R 3 Q—B 3

If 32. ...P—R 4 ; 33. R—
K Kt 1 and wins, the chief threat
being 34. P×P, P×P ; 35. Kt×
P, R—B 2 or ...R—Kt 1 ; 36.
Kt—Kt 7 and wins.

33. R×P ch K—Kt 1
34. R×P ch K—R 1
35. Kt—K 1 Kt—K 2

Despair. White threatens R—
R 2—R 2 mate.

36. R—R 6 ch K—Kt 1
37. Kt—Kt 2 !

The most elegant of the winning
methods at White's disposal, although the prosaic 37. P×Kt, R—
B 8 ch ; 38. K—Kt 2 would be
good enough.

37. ...... Q—B 6
38. R—K 1 Kt—B 3
39. R—Kt 6 ch K—R 1
40. R—K 3 Q×R
41. Kt×Q Resigns

A game in which Tarrasch reveals the serene self-confidence and
the iron nerves of the great master.

46. VIENNA, 1898

QUEEN'S GAMBIT DECLINED

TARRASCH produced many masterpieces devoted to the theme of
exploiting greater command of the
board. The following is one which
particularly impressed Réti. Incidentally, this game was played in
the last round of the great tournament, and Tarrasch had to win in
order to tie with Pillsbury for first
place.

	White	*Black*
	DR. S. TARRASCH	C. A. WALBRODT
1.	P—Q 4	P—Q 4
2.	P—Q B 4	P—K 3
3.	Kt—Q B 3	Kt—K B 3
4.	Kt—B 3	B—K 2
5.	B—B 4	

An old-fashioned move which

was destined to undergo virtual extinction a few years later. Black's best reply is ...P—B 4, obtaining a free game very quickly. Instead, Walbrodt resorts to tortuous moves and cramping manœuvres.

5.	P—B 3
6. P—K 3	Q Kt—Q 2
7. P—K R 3 !	

A characteristic Tarrasch move. He wants to preserve the Bishop from exchange by ...Kt—R 4.

7.	Kt—B 1
8. P—B 5	

Encouraged by Black's timid play, Tarrasch announces his policy of encirclement.

8.	Kt—Kt 3
9. B—R 2	Q—R 4

As will be seen, Black is greatly handicapped by his Q B's lack of mobility. Hence the following continuation suggests itself : 9. ...P—Kt 3 ; 10. P—Q Kt 4, P×P ; 11. Kt P×P, Q—R 4 ; 12. Q—Q 2, B—R 3. In this way Black would rid himself of his outstanding difficulty.

10. P—R 3	Kt—K 5
11. B—Q 3 !	

Disregarding the pin, for excellent reasons.

11.	Kt×Kt
12. Q—Q 2	Kt—K R 5

Black is at last taking steps to free his game by simplifying exchanges. But this Knight has made no less than four moves for the sole purpose of disappearing !

13. Kt×Kt	B×Kt
14. P—Q Kt 4	Q—Q 1
15. Q×Kt	O—O
16. O—O	Q—Q 2

Planning the ensuing exchange of his K B. But the cardinal defect of his position (the Q B's lack of mobility) continues to plague him.

17. Q—B 2 !

This move is more than a transparent threat. Black must now advance one of his King-side Pawns, thereby creating a target for a later Pawn advance. In this way Tarrasch ensures the subsequent opening of a file.

17.	P—B 4
18. K—R 1	

Preparing for P—Kt 4 etc. See the previous note.

18.	B—Q 1
19. B—K 5 !	B—B 2
20. P—B 4	B×B
21. B P×B	

Note that Tarrasch has permitted the exchange in a manner which has increased his command of the board.

21.	Q—K 2
22. P—Kt 4	

The attack begins. Black apparently has ample defensive measures at his disposal, but sooner or later he will be unable to meet all threats. The way in which Black is reduced to helplessness deserves close study.

22.	P—K Kt 3
23. R—B 4 !	

Réti has an instructive comment here which emphasises the importance of this move. The banal 23. P×P would be answered by ... Kt P×P, enabling Black to oppose Rooks on the K Kt file with a likely draw in the offing. Tarrasch therefore postpones the exchange of Pawns until he has posted his Rooks to good advantage. Black, on the other hand, cannot utilise this interim to improve the position of his Rooks because he lacks space in which to do so.

23.	B—Q 2
24. R—K Kt 1	K—R 1
25. Q—K Kt 2	P—Q R 4

An attempt at counterplay which turns out to be ineffectual.

26. B—Kt 1	R P×P
27. R P×P	R—R 5
28. P×P !	

Well timed. Black cannot reply 28. ...Kt P×P, for then 29. R—B 3 would very quickly be decisive : 29. ...B—K 1 (if 29. ...R×P ; 30. R—Kt 3 followed by R—Kt 7); 30. R—Kt 3, B—Kt 3 ; 31. R—Kt 5 and Black is helpless against P—R 4—5.

| 28. ...... | K P×P |

Now White's K P has become passed and his occupation of the K Kt file cannot be opposed.

| 29. Q—Q 2 | R—K Kt 1 |
| 30. Q—K 1 ! | . |

Preparing for the advance of the R P.

| 30. ...... | B—K 3 |
| 31. P—R 4 | Q R—R 1 |

32. R(B 4)—B 1	R—Kt 2
33. R—Kt 2	Q R—K Kt 1
34. R—K R 2	Q—Q 2
35. B—Q 3	R—R 1
36. Q—Kt 3	

After a brief spell of consolidation, Tarrasch systematically goes about the business of placing his pieces in the most effective manner.

36.	Q—K 2
37. R—K Kt 1	Q R—K Kt 1
38. R(R 2)—K Kt 2	R—K B 1 ?

Black has not managed to rise above the level of hackneyed moves. Here, for example, ...P—R 3 would have prolonged his resistance.

| 39. Q—B 4 ! | Q R—K Kt 1 |
| 40. Q—R 6 | B—Q 2 |

Black apparently has reason to be contented with the solidity of his defensive dispositions, for P—R 5 would lead to nothing more than general exchanges on the K Kt file. Tarrasch therefore evolves a truly inspired plan :

41. K—R 2 ! !

The King is to be brought to K B 4 *before* the general exchange

H

on the K Kt file. As Black cannot imitate this manœuvre, the resulting ending will be quite hopeless for him. Truly a masterly conception !

41.	B—K 3
42. R—Kt 5 !	B—Q 2
43. K—Kt 3 !	B—K 1
44. K—B 4 !	B—Q 2
45. P—R 5	

All according to schedule. If now 45. ...P×P ; there is a pretty sacrificial finish : 46. Q×P ch ! and mate next move.

45.	B—K 1
46. P×P	B×P
47. B—K 2 !	

The final step.

| 47. ...... | Q—Q 1 |
| 48. B—R 5 | B×B |

The proverbial swindle before resignation. If now 49. R×R ?, Q—R 5 ch ; 50. K×P, R—B 1 ch wins the Queen.

49. Q×B !	R×R
50. R×R	R×R
51. Q×R	Q—K B 1

If 51. ...Q×Q ch ; 52. K×Q, K—Kt 2 ; 53. K×P, K—B 2 ; 54. K—Kt 5, K—Kt 2 ; 55. P—K 6, K—B 1 ; 56. K—R 6, K—K 2 ; 57. K×P, K×P ; 58. K—Kt 6, K—K 2 ; 59. K—B 5, K—B 2 ; 60. K—K 5, K—K 2 ; 61. P—Kt 5, K—Q 2 (if 61. ...P×P ; 62. K×P and wins) ; 62. P×P ch, P×P ; 63. K—B 6, K—B 2 ; 64. K—K 7, K—B 1 ; 65. K—Q 6, K—Kt 2 ; 66. K—Q 7 and wins

(Tarrasch)—a little lesson in "the opposition."

| 52. P—K 6 | Resigns |

An unusually instructive game.

47. MONTE CARLO, 1903

FOUR KNIGHTS' GAME

In this game, Marshall's ill-judged attack is speedily repulsed and Black is left with a lost game for his pains.

| *White* | *Black* |
| Dr. S. Tarrasch | F. J. Marshall |

1. P—K 4	P—K 4
2. Kt—K B 3	Kt—Q B 3
3. Kt—B 3	Kt—B 3
4. B—Kt 5	Kt—Q 5

While Marshall played this defence years before Rubinstein adopted it, the latter master perfected the variation, scored brilliant successes with it and thus gave it its vogue.

5. B—R 4

A later but characteristic example of the variation is the following : 5. B—B 4, B—B 4 ; 6. Kt×P, Q—K 2 ; 7. Kt—Q 3, P—Q 4 ; 8. Kt×P, Q×P ch ; 9. Kt—K 3, B—Q 3 ; 10. O—O, P—Q Kt 4 ! ; 11. B—Kt 3, B—Kt 2 ; 12. Kt—K 1, Q—R 5 ; 13. P—Kt 3, Q—R 6 ; 14. P—Q B 3, P—K R 4 ! ; 15. P×Kt, P—R 5 ; 16. Q—K 2, Q×R P ch ! and mate in two (Belsitzmann—Rubinstein, Warsaw, 1917).

| 5. ...... | B—B 4 |
| 6. P—Q 3 | |

To play for the win of a Pawn
with 6. Kt×P, O—O ; 7. P—Q 3,
P—Q 3 ; 8. Kt—B 3, B—K Kt 5
or 7. Kt—Q 3, B—Kt 3 is very unattractive.

6.	Kt×Kt ch
7. Q×Kt	P—B 3
8. O—O	P—Q 3
9. B—K 3	B×B

If 9. ...B—Kt 3 ; 10. Kt—Q 5
with a good game.

10. P×B	B—Kt 5 ?

After 10. ...O—O the position
would be fairly level. But Marshall prefers to embark on a more
ambitious but really foolhardy
course.

11. Q—Kt 3	P—K R 4

Not 11. ...O—O ? because of
12. R×Kt. But now Black cannot very well castle on the King's
side without suffering from a
serious weakness : the advanced
K R P.

12. Kt—Q 5 !	

The beginning of a well-thought-
out plan which yields White a clear
advantage.

12.	Kt×Kt
13. P×Kt	Q—R 4
14. B—Kt 3	P×P
15. P—K 4 !	

Regaining the Pawn advantageously, since Black dare not capture.

15.	B—K 3

Thus Black admits that his expedition at move 10 was futile.

16. P×P	Q—B 4 ch
17. K—R 1	B—Kt 5

If 17. ...B×P ; 18. Q×Kt P
wins either the K B P or the K R P.

18. P—B 3	O—O
19. Q R—K 1	Q R—K 1
20. P—K R 3	B—Q 2
21. Q—Kt 5	

Decisive—the K R P is lost (if
21. ...P—K Kt 3 ; 22. B—Q 1
wins).

21.	P—B 4

Black is desperate and resorts to
an attacking gesture which only
weakens him further.

22. B—Q 1 !	

Very fine. The threat is B×P
followed by B—Kt 6 and Q—R 5.

22.	Q—B 1

23. B×P	Q—Q 1

Or 23. ...R—Q 1 ; 24. B—
Kt 6, R—B 3 ; 25. Q—R 5 and
wins.

24. Q—K 3	P—B 5

The compulsory loss of a second Pawn is conclusive. Black's menacing gestures cannot affect the outcome.

25. Q×R P   Q—R 5

The quiet continuation ...R—K 2 would be hopeless.

26. B×R   B×P
27. Q—B 2   B×P dbl ch
28. K×B   P—B 6 ch
29. Q×P

White gets more than enough material for the Queen.

29. ......   R×Q
30. K×R   Q—R 6 ch
31. K—K 2   Q—Kt 5 ch
32. K—Q 2   Q—Kt 7 ch
33. K—B 1   P—K Kt 4

Now that the checks are over, White's superior force quickly tells in his favour.

34. B—Kt 6   P—Kt 5
35. B—K 4   Q—Kt 6
36. R—K 2   P—Kt 4
37. R(K 2)—K B 2   Q—K 6 ch
38. K—B 2   P—Kt 6

Tarrasch announced mate in five : 39. R—B 8 ch, K—Kt 2 ; 40. R (B 1)—B 7 ch, K—R 3 ; 41. R—R 7 ch, K—Kt 4 ; 42. R—Kt 8 ch, K—B 3 (if 42. ...K—B 5 ; 43. R—R 4 mate) ; 43. R—Kt 6 mate.

48. MONTE CARLO, 1903
RUY LOPEZ

ONCE more Tarrasch puts the Bishops to good use. There is a good deal to be learned from such apparently unpretentious games.

	White	*Black*
	S. TAUBENHAUS	DR. S. TARRASCH

1. P—K 4   P—K 4
2. Kt—K B 3   Kt—Q B 3
3. B—Kt 5   Kt—B 3

The Berlin Defence. At this time it had already lost much of its vogue.

4. O—O   Kt×P
5. P—Q 4   Kt—Q 3
6. B×Kt   Q P×B
7. P×P   Kt—B 4
8. Q—K 2

For the more customary Q×Q ch see Game no. 20.

8. ......   Kt—Q 5 !
9. Kt×Kt   Q×Kt
10. Kt—B 3

R—Q 1 would be answered in the same way.

10. ......   B—K Kt 5 !

Forcing the exchange of Queens, with a favourable ending in view.

11. Q—K 3   Q×Q
12. B×Q   B—Kt 5
13. Kt—K 4   B—K B 4

It is already clear that Black has the initiative. White's game is not bad, but his position is destined to drift towards defeat unless he can exchange his Knight for one of the Bishops or else make good use of the King's side majority of Pawns.

14. P—Q B 3   B—K 2
15. Kt—Kt 3   B—Q 6

By means of his manœuvres with the Bishops Tarrasch has weakened

White's Q 3, which will serve as a valuable invasion point later on.

| 16. K R—Q 1 | O—O—O |
| 17. R—Q 2 | |

The Tournament Book recommends Kt—R 5—B 4, which is better than the text ; although Black would still retain his positional advantage.

| 17. ...... | P—Q B 4 |
| 18. P—K B 4 | P—K R 4 |

Preventing Kt—R 5 and also beginning the process of cutting down the Knight's mobility.

| 19. Q R—Q 1 | P—B 5 |

Now the Q B is strongly entrenched.

20. K—B 2	P—R 5
21. Kt—K 2	P—Q B 4
22. Kt—Kt 1	K—B 2
23. Kt—B 3	K—B 3

The King is headed for K 5 and eventually Q 6.

| 24. Kt—K 1 | B—K 5 |
| 25. K—K 2 | |

Here the Tournament Book rightly recommends R × R followed by P—K Kt 4. While the Bishops should have no trouble in holding back White's King's side Pawns, the passive policy pursued in the text is quite barren of any hope.

25.	R × R ch
26. R × R	R—Q 1
27. R × R	B × R

The removal of the Rooks has

only enhanced the power of Black's Bishops.

| 28. Kt—B 3 | |

P—K Kt 4 could still have been tried.

| 28. ...... | B—Kt 8 ! |

An important move, which ensures White's having to capture when Black eventually plays ... P—Q Kt 5.

29. P—Q R 3	B—Q 6 ch
30. K—K 1	B—K 5
31. K—K 2	B—Q 6 ch
32. K—K 1	B—K 5
33. K—K 2	B—Q 6 ch

The rule about claiming a draw after three-fold repetition did not apply in Continental tournaments.

34. K—K 1	K—Q 4
35. B—B 2	P—R 6 !
36. P—K Kt 3	

If 36. P × P, P—Q Kt 3 ; 37. B—K 3, K—K 5 ; 38. K—B 2, P—Kt 3 is very much in Black's favour.

36.	P—Q Kt 3
37. Kt—Kt 1	B—B 4
38. Kt—B 3	K—K 5
39. Kt—Q 2 ch	

Or 39. Kt—Kt 5 ch, B × Kt ; 40. P × B, K—Q 6 ! ; 41. K—Q 1, B—Kt 5 ch ; 42. K—B 1, K—K 7 and wins.

39.	K—Q 6
40. Kt—B 1	B—K 5
41. Kt—K 3	B—K 2

Black has now made all the necessary preparations, and wins easily by advancing his Queen's side majority of Pawns.

42. P—K Kt 4   P—Q Kt 4
43. P—Kt 5   P—R 4
44. K—Q 1

White is helpless against the Pawns.

44. ......   P—Kt 5
45. B P×P   B P×P
46. P×P   P×P
47. Kt—B 2

A last hope : if now 47. ...P—Kt 6 ? ? ; 48. Kt—K 1 mate !

47. ......   P—B 6
48. P×P

Or 48. K—B 1, P—Kt 6 ; 49. Kt—Q 4, B—R 6 ! and wins.

48. ......   P—Kt 6

White resigns. A well played ending by Tarrasch.

49. MONTE CARLO, 1903
RUY LOPEZ

WHITE is so overawed from the very start that he finds himself on the de-fensive very quickly. Tarrasch takes the initiative and utilises it to build up an amusing *Zugzwang* position in which White is starved out of moves.

| *White* | *Black* |
| H. WOLF | DR. S. TARRASCH |

1. P—K 4   P—K 4
2. Kt—K B 3   Kt—Q B 3
3. B—Kt 5   P—B 4
4. P—Q 3

This timid reply is of little value. Kt—B 3 would be more aggressive.

4. ......   P×P
5. P×P   Kt—B 3
6. O—O

There is nothing in 6. B×Kt, *e.g.* 6 ...Kt P×B ; 7. Kt×P, Q—K 2 and Black recovers the Pawn advantageously.

6. ......   P—Q 3
7. Q—Q 3   B—Kt 5
8. B—Kt 5

The pin is rather pointless. Tarrasch recommends P—Q R 3, so as to have a retreat for the K B after B—Q B 4 ; the posting of the K B on this diagonal would be rather inconvenient for Black.

8. ......   B—K 2
9. Q Kt—Q 2   Q—Q 2

Castling would lose a Pawn ; 10. B×Q Kt, P×B ; 11. Q—B 4 ch.

10. P—K R 3 ?

Another thoughtless move which at once gives Black a target for attack.

10. ......   B—R 4
11. P—R 3

Finally deciding on B—Q B 4—but he wishes to guard against ... Kt—R 4 in reply.

11. ......   P—K R 3 !
12. B—K 3   P—Kt 4 !

This advance demonstrates that White's 10th move was a mistake.

13. P—K Kt 4

He continues to meet his opponent half-way ! Kt—R 2 was relatively better.

13. ......   B—Kt 3
14. K R—Q 1   P—K R 4 !
15. Kt × Kt P

15. B × Kt P, P × P ; 16. Kt—R 4, P × P ! ; 17. Kt × B, K R—Kt 1 (Tarrasch) is likewise favourable for Black.

15. ......   P × P

On 15. ...Kt × Kt P White has a good reply in 16. Q Kt—B 3.

16. B—Q B 4   Kt—Q 1

Naturally he does not permit B—K 6.

17. Q—Kt 3   P × P

Black has won a Pawn and his attack continues. Although the K R P never makes another move, it plays an important rôle.

18. P—K B 3   Kt—Kt 5 !

This Knight cannot be captured, and meanwhile Black threatens to

win a piece by 19. ...Kt × B ; 20. Q × Kt, R—R 4.

19. Kt—K 6 ! ?   Kt × B
20. Kt—Kt 7 ch   K—B 1
21. Kt—K 6 ch   Kt × Kt
22. B × Kt   B—B 2 !

Winning the exchange — a stronger course than 22. ....P—R 7 ch ; 23. K—R 1, Kt × R ; 24. B × Q, Kt—B 7 ch ; 25. K—Kt 2, P—R 8(Q) ch ; 26. R × Q, Kt × R ; 27. Q × P and the unfortunate position of Black's Knight, coupled with the awkward grouping of his other pieces, makes the win difficult.

23. B × B   Kt × R
24. R × Kt   B—R 5

White has parted with the exchange, but he has consolidated his position and can barricade himself by bringing his Bishop to Kt 4. Black must rely on the K R P and his powerful grip on the weak black squares.

25. B—K 6   Q—Kt 2 ch
26. B—Kt 4   P—Kt 3
27. Q—Q 5   R—K 1
28. Kt—B 1   Q—Kt 4
29. Q—Kt 7   R—K 2
30. Q × R P

The win of this Pawn is an irrelevance ; the game will be decided on the other wing.

30. ......   Q—B 5
31. K—R 1

Otherwise ...R—Kt 1 wins at once.

31. ......   R—Kt1
32. Q—R 6   K—Kt 2

Black gets the King out of the way before undertaking the final attack. If 32. ...R×B ?; 33. Q—B 8 ch.

33. Q—Q 3   B—B 7 !

The Bishop is transferred to a stronger diagonal.

34. Q—K 2   K—R 1 !
35. R—Q 2

Capture of the Bishop would give Black an easy win: 35. Q×B ?, R×B; 36. Kt—K 3 (otherwise ...R—Kt 7), R—Kt 6; 37. R—K B 1, R—B 2 etc. (38. Kt—B 5, R—Kt 7).

35. ......   R—B 2 !
36. P—R 4

If 36. P—B 3, P—Kt 4 ! creates a retreat for the Bishop.

36. ......   B—Q 5

Threatening ...R×B.

37. R—Q 1   R(B 2)—Kt 2 !

...B×P would relax the pressure, permitting Kt—K 3—B 5.

38. P—B 3   B—B 7
39. Kt—R 2

If 39. R—Q 2, R×B !; 40. P× R, R×P ; 41. Q×B, Q×P ch ; 42. K—R 2, R—Kt 7 ch (Tarrasch). This is one of the many variations which illustrate the usefulness of the R P.

39. ......   Q—Kt 6 !

Apparently burning his bridges, as the Bishop's position becomes more precarious than ever. However, the continued penetration on the black squares and the new mating threat keep White sufficiently occupied.

40. Q—B 1   B—K 6 !
41. Q—K 2

Not 41. Q×P ch ?, Q×Q ; 42. B×Q, R—Kt 8 ch and mate next move.

41. ......   R—B 2 !

White cannot move his Knight or Bishop, while if 42. Q—B 1, R×B ! ; 43. Kt×R, R×P wins. Or if 42. Q—Q B 2, R×B ! ; 43. Kt×R, Q×P ch wins.

42. R—K B 1   R—B 5 !
43. P—Kt 3

White has nothing left but Pawn moves : if 43. Q—Q B 2, R(Kt 1) ×B ! ; 44. Kt×R, Q×Kt and wins. If 43. R—Q 1, R(Kt 1)× B ! ; 44. Kt×R, R×B P and wins.

43. ......   P—B 3
44. P—B 4   B—B 4
45. R—Q Kt 1   B—B 7

45. ...R(Kt 1)×B !, as in the previous note, was also possible.

46. Q—B 1   R(Kt 1)×B !

White resigns. If 47. P×R, B—K 6 followed by ...R—B 7. If 47. Kt×R, Q×P ch ; 48. K—R 2, B—Kt 6 ch ; 49. K—Kt 1, P—R 7 ch (at last !) ; 50. Kt×P, B×Kt ch ; 51. K×B, R—R 5 ch etc. A highly interesting encounter.

50. MONTE CARLO, 1903

RUY LOPEZ

THERE are days during a chess tournament when a master, possibly because of fatigue, is disinclined to give of his best. There are other days when he is able to put forth his finest efforts, when he is able to play in an inspired mood and produce such a game as the following one.

White	Black
H. N. PILLSBURY	DR. S. TARRASCH

1. P—K 4   P—K 4
2. Kt—K B 3   Kt—Q B 3
3. B—Kt 5   P—B 4

One of the many lively lines of play with which Marshall freshened the somewhat stuffy atmosphere that prevailed in master chess during the first decade of the present century. Tarrasch adopts this unsound continuation not because of any profound faith in it, but rather by way of announcing his aggressive intentions.

4. Kt—B 3   Kt—B 3

Apparently best. After 4. ... P×P ; 5. Q Kt×P, Kt—B 3 ; 6. Kt×Kt ch, P×Kt (risky, but after 6. Q×Kt ; 7. O—O White has too many threats : 8. P—Q 4, or 8. B×Kt followed by 9. Kt×P) ; 7. P—Q 4, P—Q 3 ; 8. O—O, B—Q 2 ; 9. R—K 1, Q—K 2 ; 10. P×P, Q P×P ; 11. B×Kt, B×B ; 12. Kt×P ! (Sergeant—Spielmann, Margate, 1938). White should win.

5. P×P   P—K 5
6. Q—K 2 ?

Weak. A few years later Leonhardt introduced the following advantageous continuation : 6. Kt—Kt 5 !, P—Q 4 ; 7. P—Q 3, B×P (if 7. ...P—K R 3 ; 8. Kt—K 6 is in White's favour) ; 8. P×P, P×P ; 9. Q—K 2, B—Q Kt 5 ; 10. B—Q 2, Q—K 2 ; 11. B×Kt ch, P×B ; 12. Q—B 4 etc.

6. ......   Q—K 2
7. B×Kt

This gives Black two formidable Bishops and a strong Pawn centre, but if 7. Kt—Kt 5, P—Q 4 ; 8. P—Q 3, P—K R 3 ! with a good game for Black :

I. 9. Kt—K 6, B×Kt ; 10. P×B, Q×P ; 11. P×P, P×P ; 12. P—B 3, O—O—O ; 13. P×P, Kt—Q 5 etc. or 13. B×Kt, Q×B ; 14. P×P, B—Kt 5 etc.

II. 9. P×P !?, P×Kt ; 10. P—K 5, B×P ! (not 10. ...Kt—Kt 1 ; 11. Kt×P, Q—Q 1 ; 12. Q—B 4 with a powerful attack, 12. ...B—Q 2 being refuted by P—K 6) ; 11. P×Kt, Q×Q ch ; 12. K×Q, P×P ; 13. Kt×P, O—O—O with a magnificent game for the material sacrificed.

7. ......   Kt P×B
8. Kt—K R 4   P—Q 4
9. P—Q 4   P—Q R 4 !

Preventing White from castling because of the threat of ...B—R 3.

10. B—Kt 5   .

With the seemingly formidable threat of B×Kt followed by Q—R 5 ch.

10. ......   B—R 3 !
11. B×Kt   Q×B
12. Q—R 5 ch   K—Q 2 ! !

Much stronger than the pedestrian ...Q—B 2. The text involves the speculative sacrifice of a whole Rook.

13. Kt—Kt 6   Q×Q P !

Tarrasch points out that 13. ... P×Kt would be weaker, and he gives the following continuations after 14. Q×R :

I. 14. ...Q×Q P ;   15. Q—R 3 with a satisfactory defence.

II. 14. ...P×P ; 15. O—O—O, Q—Kt 4 ch ; 16. K—Kt 1, Q×P ; 17. K R—Kt 1, Q×B P ; 18. Kt—R 4, R—K 1 ; 19. R×P ch, B×R ; 20. Q×B ch, K—Q 1 ; 21. Kt—B 5, B—B 1 and White has at least a draw by perpetual check.

III. 14. ...Q—Kt 4, 15. P×P, Q×P(Kt 7) ; 16. O—O—O and again White is much better off than in the text continuation.

14. Kt×R   B—B 4

The position continues to grow more complicated ! 14. ...B—Kt 5 would yield a strong attack, but the adventurous text is even more powerful.

15. Q—R 4

After this White is only the exchange ahead. However, 15. Q—B 7 ch, K—B 1 ; 16. Kt—Q 1, K—Kt 2 leads to the same result ; while if 15. Kt—B 7, Q×P ch ; 16. K—Q 1, B—K 6 ; 17. Kt—K 5 ch, K—Q 3 ; 18. Kt—B 7 ch, K—K 2 ; 19. Kt—K 2 (or Kt—Kt 1), B—Q 6 ! ; 20. P×B, P×P ; 21. Kt—Kt 5, Q—B 7 ch ; 22. K—K 1, P—Q 7 ch wins.

15. ......   R×Kt
16. R—Q 1   Q—Kt 5
17. Q—Kt 4

Pillsbury's inability to castle makes his defence difficult, but he is putting up a gallant fight.

17. ......   K—Q 1
18. Q×Kt P   R—K 1
19. Q—B 6 ch   K—Q 2
20. P—Q R 3 ! ?

The propitiatory sacrifice 20. R×P ch, P×R ; 21. Q×B would be inadequate, says Tarrasch, as Black would have a choice of three good continuations : 21. ...Q×P, 21. ...P—K 6 or 21. ...P—Q 5.

20. ......   Q—Kt 3 !

Not 20. ...Q×Kt P ? ; 21. Kt
Q P ! and wins.

21. R—Q 2

Q—R 4 would be no better because of ...Q×P.

| 21. ...... | P—K 6 ! |
| 22. P×P | B×K P |

White's position is hopeless. If
now 23. K—Q 1 (or 23. R—K 2),
Q×P wins ; or if 23. Q—B 7 ch,
R—K 2 ; 24. R×P ch, P×R ; 25.
Q×R ch, K×Q ; 26. Kt×P ch,
K—Q 3 and wins (Tarrasch).

23. Kt×P

His best chance.

23.	B×R ch
24. K×B	Q—B 7 ch
25. K—Q 1 .	

Not 25. K—B 3 ? ?, R—K 6 ch !

25.	Q—K 7 ch
26. K—B 1	P×Kt
27. R—Q 1	

Pillsbury's counterattack is over,
but he hangs on grimly for many
moves !

27.	P—B 3
28. Q—R 4	Q×P
29. Q×P ch	R—K 2
30. Q—R 4	

White's Queen will head eventually for Q R 7, but the expedition
will prove none too profitable.

30.	Q—K 5
31. Q—R 8	Q×P
32. Q—R 8	B—B 1
33. Q—R 7 ch	K—K 1

34. Q×P	Q—B 5 ch
35. K—Kt 1	Q×P
36. Q—B 5	B—Kt 2 !

Tarrasch does not care for 36.
...K—Q 2 ; 37. P—B 4, while 36.
...B—Q 2 ; 37. P—R 4 appears
risky because of the passed R P.
Hence he resigns himself to this
highly unsatisfactory position for
the Bishop.

37. P—Kt 4

Pillsbury naturally strives for
further simplification by exchange
of *Pawns*—his only drawing chance.

| 37. ...... | Q—K 7 |
| 38. R—R 1 | R—K B 2 ! |

From now on, Black concentrates
on the task of forcing a further exchange of *pieces*.

| 39. R—R 8 ch | K—Q 2 |
| 40. R—R 6 | |

Threatening to win with 41. Q—
Q 6 ch. 40. Q—Kt 6 ? would be
a blunder because of 40. ...R—
B 8 ch and wins.

| 40. ...... | R—B 8 ch |
| 41. K—Kt 2 | Q—K 2 |

Preventing Q—Q 6 ch and threatening ...Q—Kt 2 ch.

| 42. Q—Q 4 | R—K 8 |

Threatening ...Q—K 4. Black
is gradually consolidating his position by threats of exchange.

43. R—R 5	K—B 2
44. Q—B 4 ch	K—Kt 3
45. Q—Q 4 ch	P—B 4 !

Permitting a further exchange of Pawns, but only because the position of White's King becomes insecure and Black's Bishop comes to life—at last !

46. P×P ch

If 46. Q—B 2, Q—K 6 is very strong.

46.	Q×P
47. R—R 6 ch	B—B 3
48. Q—B 6	Q—Kt 4 ch
49. K—B 3	Q—B 5 ch
50. K—Kt 2	Q—Kt 4 ch
51. K—B 3	Q—B 5 ch

Black is gaining considerable time on the clock with these repetitions.

52. K—Kt 2	Q—Kt 4 ch
53. K—B 3	R—K 6 ch
54. K—Q 2	R—K 7 ch
55. K—Q 1	R—K 1

Threatening mate in three beginning with ...Q—Kt 8 ch.

| 56. K—Q 2 | Q—K 7 ch |
| 57. K—B 1 | |

If 57. K—B 3, Q—K 4 ch forces the exchange of Queens at once.

| 57. ...... | Q—K 8 ch |
| 58. K—Kt 2 | Q—K 4 ch |

At last Black has attained his heart's desire.

| 59. Q×Q | R×Q |
| 60. R—R 4 | |

Although White has only one Pawn for the piece, most players would encounter considerable difficulty in demonstrating a win for Black. Although Tarrasch's procedure here is characterised in high degree by what Hercule Poirot calls "the order and the method", the ending is anything but dry. What we notice about this ending (at least at the first view) is its inordinate difficulty ; but Tarrasch's play is so clear and so logical that the ending seems rather easy after all ! Black begins with the basic idea that his opponent can never allow an exchange of Rooks ; for once that happens, White's King will be helpless against Black's King and Bishop and will sooner or later have to lose both Pawns by *Zugzwang*.

The fact that White cannot exchange Rooks gives Black's forces great power ; for it means that Black can consistently improve the position of his pieces by constantly offering an exchange of Rooks. White will always have to withdraw, and in this way Black can carry out a steady policy of encroachment. (One caution to be observed is, of course, that Black must not allow the exchange of his Pawn.)

Now what is to be the object of Black's attack ? Clearly, the B P. The best way to attack it will be to place Black's Rook on the seventh rank and his Bishop at K 5 or K B 4. This will reduce White's Rook to complete passivity on the Q B file. Black can then advance his King with decisive effect.

60.	R—K 5
61. R—R 8	K—B 4
62. R—Q B 8	

Hampering Black by pinning his Bishop ; Black at once removes this annoyance.

62.	......	R—K 1
63.	R—B 7	K—Q 3
64.	R—K R 7	B—Kt 4
65.	K—B 3	

He must try to prevent ...K—Q 5 after Black's King gets to Q B 4.

| 65. | ...... | B—R 5 |

The plan of attack begins to unfold : ...R—B 1 ch is threatened.

66.	R—R 2	R—K 5
67.	R—Kt 2	K—B 4
68.	R—R 2	R—K 6 ch
69.	K—Kt 2	B—Kt 4 !

In order to take the seventh rank. Black's constriction policy is making progress.

70.	R—R 8	R—K 7
71.	R—B 8 ch	K—Q 5
72.	K—Kt 3	B—B 5 ch
73.	K—Kt 2	B—Q 6 !

Now the Pawn is attacked twice ; but more important is the fact that at K B 4, this Bishop will be performing still another function.

| 74. | K—Kt 3 | B—B 4 |
| 75. | R—B 7 | R—K 1 !! |

This retreat is the winning move ! Its significance, as will be seen, is that it forces an advantageous entry for Black's King.

76. P—B 3 ch

Just the move that White has been trying to avoid, but now "he must bite into the sour apple".

Black was threatening to force the exchange of Rooks with R—Q B 1 (hence 74. ...B—B 4 ; and 75.

...R—K 1 !!). If 76. R—Q Kt 7, R—Q B 1 wins the B P ; on other moves of White's Rook along the rank, Black wins the B P with ... R—Kt 1 ch (Tarrasch).

| 76. | ...... | K—Q 6 |
| 77. | R—B 5 | R—Kt 1 ch |

Still another point of 75. ... R—K 1 !! : White's King can no longer protect the B P.

78.	K—R 4	B—K 5
79.	R—B 7	K—B 7
80.	R—B 6	B—Q 6

...P—Q 5 also wins, but Tarrasch prefers the "theoretical" move.

81.	R—B 5	B—B 5
82.	K—R 5	K×P
83.	P—R 4	R—R 1 ch

White resigns. Even those readers who have a distaste for endgame play will be fascinated by Black's accurate and luminous play !

51. MONTE CARLO, 1903

RUY LOPEZ

TARRASCH's Knight manœuvres are a revelation of what can be accomplished with this piece in the hands of a master. The whole conception is novel and has many piquant fine points.

| *White* | *Black* |
| DR. S. TARRASCH | S. TAUBENHAUS |

1.	P—K 4	P—K 4
2.	Kt—K B 3	Kt—Q B 3
3.	B—Kt 5	Kt—B 3

The Berlin Defence, which had already lost much of its popularity by the time this game was played.

4. O—O	Kt × P
5. P—Q 4	B—K 2
6. Q—K 2	Kt—Q 3
7. B × Kt	Kt P × B
8. P × P	Kt—B 4 ?

Black confuses his defences. The text is playable after 7. ...Q P × B (see Game 20), but is out of place here. 8. ...Kt—Kt 2 should have been played.

| 9. Q—K 4 | P—Kt 3 |

...Kt—R 3 has been tried here, although after 10. B × Kt Black is burdened with an unenviable Pawn position.

10. Kt—Q 4

The simplest, although 10. P—K Kt 4, Kt—Kt 2 ; 11. B—R 6 is also attractive.

10.	Kt × Kt
11. Q × Kt	O—O
12. B—R 6	R—K 1
13. Kt—B 3	B—Kt 4

This leads to an ugly weakness on the black squares. However, Black had no good way of bringing out his Q B or of parrying White's automatic attack by Kt—K 4, P—K B 4 etc.

| 14. B × B | Q × B |
| 15. Kt—K 4 ! | |

Highly unexpected, since P—B 4 would lead to an easily winning attack without any loss of material. Black must accept the offer.

| 15. ...... | Q × P |
| 16. Kt—B 6 ch | K—B 1 |

Here and later, Black has little choice. If 16. ...K—Kt 2 ?, 17. Kt × R ch wins right off. If 16. ...K—R 1 ; 17. Q—K R 4 wins easily.

| 17. Q—K R 4 | R—K 3 |

If 17. ...R—K 2 ? ; 18. Q—R 6 mate (very neat !). If 17. ...R—Q 1 ; 18. either R—K 1 wins at once.

18. Kt × R P ch   K—K 1

Amusing would be 18. ...K—Kt 1 ; 19. Kt—Kt 5, R—K 2 (or 19. ...R—K 1 ; 20. Q—R 7 ch and mate next move) ; 20. Q R—K 1, Q × R ; 21. Q—R 7 ch, K—B 1 ; 22. Q—R 8 mate.

19. Kt—Kt 5   Q—B 3

...B—R 3 offers better defensive chances.

20. Q—R 6   R—K 2

One possibility after 20. ...R—K 4 is 21. P—K B 4, R—K 7 ; 22. K R—K 1, B—R 3 ; 23. R × R ch, B × R ; 24. R—K 1, Q—Q 5 ch ;

25. K—R 1, Q—Q 7; 26. Q—R 8 ch, K—K 2; 27. Q—K 5 ch and wins.

21. Kt—R 7   Q—R 1

The only move to prevent mate and save the Queen.

22. Q—R 4   Q—Kt 2

If 22. ...Q—K 4; 23. Kt—B 6 ch, K—Q 1; 24. P—K B 4! (stronger than Q—R 8 ch), Q—K 6 ch; 25. K—R 1 followed by either R—K 1 and wins. White's play with the Queen and Knight has been very clever, and now he is able to bring a new piece into the attack.

23. K R—K 1   R—K 3

Or 23. ...P—K B 4; 24. P—K B 4 with the winning threat R×R ch followed by R—K 1.

24. Kt—Kt 5   R—K 2

He could have prolonged his resistance by giving up the exchange with some such move as ...P—Q 4. However, there would have been no doubt about the ultimate result.

25. R×R ch   K×R
26. R—K 1 ch   Resigns

If 26. ...K—Q 1 ?; 27. Kt×P mate. If 26. ...K—B 1; 27. Kt—R 7 ch, K—Kt 1; 28. R—K 8 ch and wins. Against 26. ... K—Q 3 Chernev gives the following: 27. Kt—K 4 ch, K—K 3; 28. Kt—B 6 ch, K—B 4 (if 28. ... K—Q 3; 29. Q—Q 4 mate); 29. Q—K 4 ch, K×Kt; 30. Q—K 5 mate. If 27. ...K—Q 4; 28. R—Q 1 ch, K—B 5 (if 28. ...K—K 4; 29. Q—K 7 ch, K—B 4;

30. Q—Kt 5 ch, K×Kt; 31. P—B 3 mate, or 28. ...K—K 3; 29. Kt—B 5 ch etc.); 29. Kt—Q 6 ch, K—B 4; 30. Q—B 4 ch, K—Kt 3; 31. Q—Kt 4 ch, K—R 3; 32. R—Q 5, P×R; 33. Q—Kt 5 mate.

Apparently Taubenhaus had had enough of the Knight moves and preferred not to be shown these variations !

52. OSTEND, 1905

QUEEN'S GAMBIT DECLINED

THIS game takes an amusing course. Black makes threatening gestures and finally succeeds in posting his forces in aggressive positions. But at the decisive moment, Tarrasch expertly extracts the venom from the attack and leaves Black helpless.

White	*Black*
DR. S. TARRASCH	P. S. LEONHARDT

1. P—Q 4	P—Q 4
2. P—Q B 4	P—K 3
3. Kt—Q B 3	Kt—K B 3
4. B—Kt 5	B—K 2
5. Kt—B 3	O—O
6. P—K 3	Kt—K 5

The merits of this defence, closely associated with Dr. Lasker's name, have been disputed for forty years. Modern theory considers it adequate for equalising.

7. B×B	Q×B
8. P×P	

8. Kt×Kt, P×Kt; 9. Kt—Q 2, P—K B 4 followed eventually by ...P—K 4 gives Black an easy game. The same is true of 8. B—

Q 3, Kt×Kt; 9. P×Kt, P×P;
10. B×P, P—Q B 4.

8.	Kt×Kt
9. P×Kt	P×P
10. Q—Kt 3	R—Q 1

The moderns favour ...Q—Q 3
here. If then 11. P—B 4, P×P;
12. B×P, Kt—B 3; 13. Q—B 3;
B—Kt 5 with fighting chances.

| 11. P—B 4 | P×P |

Many years later, Wolf introduced the alternative line 11. ...
Kt—B 3; 12. P×P, Q—Kt 5 ch;
13. Kt—Q 2, Q×Q; 14. Kt×Q,
Kt—Kt 5; 15. R—B 1, Kt×Q P.
White's game is theoretically preferable because of his open files and
Pawn centre; but in actual practice Black's stubborn defence has
managed to preserve equality.

| 12. B×P | Kt—B 3 |

Threatening ...Kt×P as well as
...Kt—R 4.

| 13. Q—B 3 | B—Kt 5 |

Now threatening ...B×Kt followed by ...Kt×P. 13. ...Q—
Kt 5 would be answered by 14.
Q R—B 1 leaving White with a
good game.

| 14. O—O ! | |

Apparently very risky, for Black
can continue with 14. ...B×Kt;
15. P×B, R—Q 3. But in that
event 16. K—R 1, R—R 3; 17.
R—K Kt 1, Q—R 5; 18. R—Kt 2
gives White a fine game.

| 14. ...... | R—Q 3 |

Now threatening 15. ...B×Kt;
16. P×B, R—R 3 and White has
no good defence against ...Q—R 5.

| 15. Kt—Q 2 ! | |

The Knight will play an important defensive rôle.

| 15. ...... | R—K 1 |
| 16. K R—B 1 | |

Making room for the Knight.
15. ...R—R 3 would have been
answered in the same way.

| 16. ...... | R—R 3 |
| 17. Kt—B 1 | Kt—Q 1 |

Hoping to make the Q B P safe
by ...P—Q B 3 and at the same
time bring the Knight to the King's
side by ...Kt—K 3.

| 18. P—Q 5 ! | |

Now the Knight is stalemated,
and ...P—Q B 3 can be met by
19. P—K 4, giving White a passed
Q P sooner or later (if 19. ...Q×
P ?? 20. R—K 1 wins the Queen).

18.	Q—Kt 4
19. Q—Q 4	B—B 6
20. Kt—Kt 3	

Tarrasch naturally avoids the
weakening move 20. P—Kt 3 ?
which would be answered by ...
Q—R 4.

| 20. ...... | R—K 5 ? ! |
| 21. Q—Q 3 | R(K 5)—R 5 |

Black has played very ingeniously
to obtain a . . . lost game !

| 22. Q—B 5 ! | |

22. P×B, R×P ; 23. P—B 4, Q—R 5 ; 24. Q—K 4 was also good enough, but the text is even more forcing.

22.	Q—B 3
23. Q×Q	P×Q
24. P×B	R×P
25. B—B 1	P—B 3
26. B—Kt 2	Resigns

The Rooks and Knight are stalemated. If 26. ...R(R 3)—R 5 ; 27. Kt—B 1 ; if, instead, 26. ... R(R 7)—R 5 ; 27. Kt—B 5. A sorry *débâcle* !

53. OSTEND, 1905

QUEEN'S GAMBIT DECLINED

THIS game, admirably contested by both players, abounds in fascinating play. Tarrasch shows himself a master of all parts of the game : superior opening strategy, skilful augmentation of the opening advantage, resourceful defensive play and a finely handled ending.

| *White* | *Black* |
| DR. S. TARRASCH | S. ALAPIN |

| 1. P—Q 4 | P—Q 4 |
| 2. P—Q B 4 | P—K 3 |

3. Kt—Q B 3	Kt—K B 3
4. B—Kt 5	B—K 2
5. Kt—B 3	Kt—K 5
6. B×B	Q×B
7. P×P	Kt×Kt
8. P×Kt	P×P
9. Q—Kt 3	P—Q B 3

Regarding the opening, see the previous game.

| 10. P—K 3 | O—O |
| 11. R—Q Kt 1 ! | |

Hampering the development of Black's Bishop—a difficulty which Alapin solves in a novel manner.

11.	Kt—Q 2
12. B—Q 3	Kt—B 3
13. O—O	Kt—K 5
14. P—B 4	P×P
15. B×P	P—K Kt 3 ! ?

A puzzling move, but its motivation is quite logical. Black wants to play ...P—B 3 in order to prevent Kt—K 5 and also in order to bring his K R to K B 2, protecting the Q Kt P and thus making possible the development of the Bishop. It will be interesting to study Tarrasch's procedure against this plan.

16. R—Kt 2

Guarding against ...Kt—Q 7 in the event of his Knight moving, and also preparing for the possibility of doubling on a file.

16.	K—Kt 2
17. B—Q 3	P—B 3
18. R—B 1	R—B 2
19. Q—B 2 !	

Practically forcing the Knight's retreat, after which White can continue with his indicated advance in the centre.

| 19. ...... | Kt—Q 3 |
| 20. P—K 4 | R—B 1 |

An apparently pointless loss of time.

| 21. P—K R 3 | B—K 3 |
| 22. Q—Kt 1 ! | |

Threatening to win at least a Pawn with P—K 5.

| 22. ...... | R—B 2 |
| 23. R—K 1 | |

White's initiative in the centre becomes ever more threatening.

| 23. ...... | Q—Q 1 ? ! |

Losing a Pawn, but part of a far-sighted plan.

24. P—K 5	P×P
25. P×P	Kt—Kt 4
26. B×Kt	P×B
27. R×P	R×Kt !

This is the move that Black has been playing for. 27. ...B× K R P would be much weaker because of 28. R×P.

| 28. P×R | Q—Kt 4 ch |
| 29. K—R 1 ! | |

This looks risky, but Tarrasch has calculated well. If instead 29. K—B 1 ?, B—B 5 ch and wins.

| 29. ...... | B×K R P |

If now 30. R—Kt 1, Q—R 5 threatening ...B—B 8 mate as well as ...B—B 4 ch winning the Queen. But White has a way out.

| 30. R×P ch | K—R 1 |

If 30. ...K—R 3 ; 31. Q—B 1 breaks the attack.

| 31. R—Kt 8 ch | K—Kt 2 ! |

The only chance, for if 31. ... R×R ; 32. Q×R ch, K—Kt 2 ; 33. R—K Kt 1, Q—R 5 ; 34. R— Kt 3 and White wins easily.

| 32. Q—Kt 7 ch | K—R 3 |

33. P—B 4 !

The saving move. If now 33. ...Q—R 4 ; 34. Q×R, B—Kt 5 ch ; 35. K—Kt 1, B—B 6 ; 36. Q×B and wins.

33.	Q—Kt 7 ch
34. Q×Q	B×Q ch
35. K×B	R×R
36. K—B 3	

Just as important as White's material advantage is his positional superiority : his passed K P forces Black's Rook into passivity, and the effective centralising possibilities for his King will make it possible for him to secure two passed Pawns.

| 36. ...... | K—Kt 2 |
| 37. R—Q 1 ! | |

Tying down the hostile Rook to the defence of the second rank.

37. ......   R—Kt 2
38. P—B 5 !

Giving up a Pawn but only temporarily. White will soon have two
united passed Pawns.

38. ......   P×P
39. K—B 4   K—B 1
40. P—B 3

Not 40. K×P because of ...
R—B 2 ch.

40. ......   R—K B 2
41. P—K 6   R—B 2
42. K×P   K—K 2

White's King must be kept out
of K B 6.

43. R—Q 5

To stop ...R—B 4 ch. The
rest is easy.

43. ......   P—K R 4
44. P—B 4   P—R 5
45. K—K 5   P—R 6
46. P—B 5   P—R 7
47. P—B 6 ch   K—K 1
48. R—Kt 5 !   Resigns

For if 48. ...R—B 1 ; 49. P—
B 7 ch, K—K 2 ; 50. R—Kt 7 ch,
K—B 1 ; 51. K—B 6, P—R 8(Q) ;
52. P—K 7, mate ! ! ! Tarrasch's
superb competence in the endgame
was never shown to better advantage.

54. OSTEND, 1905

(3rd Brilliancy Prize)

SICILIAN DEFENCE

ALTHOUGH there is nothing very
brilliant about this game, it richly

deserved a special prize because of
Tarrasch's forceful exploitation of
his lead in development. Maróczy,
it is true, does not show to much advantage ; but such uncongenial
positions do not lend themselves to
able handling by the defence.

White	Black
G. MARÓCZY	DR. S. TARRASCH

1. P—K 4   P—Q B 4
2. Kt—K B 3   P—K 3
3. P—Q 4   P—Q 4

One of the many original variations popularised by Marshall at
this time. The inadequacy of this
line of play came to be recognised
in due course, with the result that
it gradually disappeared from master practice.

4. K P×P   K P×P
5. B—Kt 5 ch

This apparently strong move has
unpleasant consequences. Bearing
in mind Black's coming sacrifice of
a Pawn (the real point of the variation, as far as Marshall was concerned), the proper course would
have been : 5. Kt—B 3, Kt—
Q B 3 ; 6. B—K 2, Kt—B 3 ; 7.
O—O, B—K 2 ; 8. B—K 3, B—
K 3 ; 9. P×P, O—O ; 10. Kt—
Q 4, Kt×Kt ; 11. B×Kt, Q—
B 2 ; 12. B—K B 3, K R—Q 1 ;
13. P—Q Kt 4 with a winning
game for White (from a game Leonhardt—Tarrasch, played in the
same tournament two weeks later).

5. ......   Kt—B 3
6. O—O   Kt—B 3
7. R—K 1 ch   B—K 2

The Pawn sacrifice is here vir-

tually forced, for 7. ...B—K 3
would be answered by 8. Kt—Kt 5.

8. P×P   O—O
9. B—K 3   B—Kt 5
10. P—B 3

White has to rely on this move,
together with P—Kt 4, to retain
the extra Pawn. But in order to
maintain such a Pawn formation
against ...P—Q R 4, it is necessary
to play B×Kt. In doing this,
however, White will give his opponent two Bishops, strengthen the
Q P, and expose himself to an irritating pin. This simple sequence
of cause and effect throws light on
the difficulties of White's position.

10. ......   Kt—K 5
11. B×Kt   P×B
12. P—Q Kt 4   B—B 3

Black has a beautiful development, while the advantage of
White's extra Pawn is destined to be
of strictly minor importance.

13. B—Q 4

Intending 14. B×B, Q×B ; 15.
Q—Q 4.

13. ......   R—K 1 !

A subtle rejoinder. The idea is
that if 14. B×B, Q×B ; 15. Q—
Q 4, B×Kt ; 16. Q×Q, Kt×Q ;
17. R×R ch, R×R ; 18. P×B,
R—K 8 ch and White is lost.

14. P—Q R 4

Apparently with the idea of playing R—R 2—Kt 2 followed by P—
Kt 5. But White will be too much
occupied on the other wing.

14. ......   B×B
15. P×B

The alternative 15. Q×B, B×
Kt ; 16. P×B, Q—Kt 4 ch does
not look very attractive.

15. ......   B×Kt !
16. P×B

After this weakening of the White
King's position, the game is apparently lost. 16. Q×B, Kt×Q B P ;
17. R×R ch, Q×R ; 18. Kt—Q 2
offered good chances of equalising.

16. ......   Q—Kt 4 ch
17. K—B 1   Kt—B 3

Now Black threatens ...Kt—
R 4—B 5.

18. R—K 3

This returns the Pawn and proves
futile for defensive purposes ; the
alternative 18. R—R 3, Kt—R 4 ;
19. P—B 4, Kt×P ; 20. R—K
Kt 3 is, however, none too promising.

18. ......   R×R
19. P×R   Q×P
20. R—R 3   Q—B 5
21. Q—Q 2   Q—B 4
22. R—Kt 3

White seems to have consolidated
his game somewhat, but the attack
soon gathers new momentum.

22. ......   R—K 1

Threatening (among other things)
23. ...Q—R 6 ch ; 24. K—Kt 1
(if 24. Q—Kt 2 ? ?, R—K 8 ch),
Kt—Kt 5 ; 25. Kt—R 3, Kt×P
and wins.

23. K—Kt 2

Guarding against this threat, and also making possible the reply 24. R—K 3 ! to 23. ...Kt—R 4. But Tarrasch has a stronger reply.

23. ......   R—K 3 !

Rendering R—K 3 impossible and thus threatening ...Kt—R 4 in real earnest. In addition ...R—Kt 3 ch will be available. The concentration against White's helpless King has become overwhelming.

24. Kt—R 3   Kt—R 4
25. R—K 3   R—Kt 3 ch
26. K—B 2   P—K R 3

White must now succumb quickly.

27. R—K 5   Q—R 6
28. K—K 3   Kt—B 3
29. Q—K 2

...Kt—Kt 5 ch would now suffice ; but Tarrasch has an even stronger move.

29. ......   R—Kt 7 !

White resigns, for if 30. Q—K 1, Kt—Kt 5 ch ; 31. K—Q 3, Q×P ch wins. Tarrasch has carried out the attack very forcefully.

55. OSTEND, 1905

RUY LOPEZ

QUEEN and Pawn endings are notoriously difficult to play well. That is why Tarrasch's superlatively able handling of the concluding portion of this game merits high praise.

White	*Black*
DR. TARRASCH	G. MARCO

1. P—K 4	P—K 4
2. Kt—K B 3	Kt—Q B 3
3. B—Kt 5	P—Q R 3
4. B—R 4	Kt—B 3
5. O—O	P—Q 3
6. P—Q 4	P×P

Transposing into a kind of Steinitz Defence. 6. ...P—Q Kt 4 is also possible, but leads to rather a dull and unpromising game for Black after 7. P×P, P×P ; 8. Q×Q ch etc.

7. Kt×P	B—Q 2
8. Kt—Q B 3	B—K 2
9. K Kt—K 2	

Thus Tarrasch announces that he intends to keep Black's game in as cramped a state as possible by avoiding exchanges.

9.	O—O
10. Kt—Kt 3	R—K 1

More exact was 10. ...P—Q Kt 4 ; 11. B—Kt 3, Kt—Q R 4 ; this would at least give Black the consolation of the two Bishops.

11. P—Q R 3

Now White is able to preserve his K B—for some time to come.

11.	......	B—K 3
12.	Kt—Q 5	P—Q Kt 4
13.	B—Kt 3	Kt—Q R 4
14.	B—R 2	P—B 3
15.	Kt × B ch	Q × Kt
16.	B—Q 2	

Black has freed his game somewhat, but at the cost of weakening
his Queen's side Pawns.

| 16. | ...... | Kt—B 5 |

...Kt—Kt 2 would be answered
by P—Kt 4, virtually stalemating
the Knight.

| 17. | B—B 3 | P—Q R 4 |
| 18. | B × Kt | |

Realising that his K B is now useless and Black's Knight is too well
entrenched, White decides to exchange.

| 18. | ...... | B × B |
| 19. | R—K 1 | |

Having consumed a great deal of
time up to this point, Tarrasch did
not dare to venture on the stronger
but more complicated 19. Kt—B 5.

19.	......	B—K 3
20.	Q—Q 2	P—R 5
21.	Q R—Q 1	Q R—Q 1
22.	Kt—B 5	

A formidable stroke, to which,
however, Black has an adequate
defence.

| 22. | ...... | B × Kt |
| 23. | P × B | Q—B 1 ? |

This apparently secure retreat
proves fatal. Correct was 23. ...
Q—Q 2 ! (Marco's suggestion) and
Black should be able to hold the
position.

| 24. | B × Kt | P × B |
| 25. | Q—B 3 ! | |

Forcing the gain of a Pawn.
However, the presence of only the
heavy pieces gives Black excellent
drawing prospects.

25.	......	R × R ch
26.	R × R	R—K 1
27.	R—Q 1	Q—K 2
28.	P—R 3	P—B 4
29.	Q—Kt 3 ch	K—B 1
30.	R × P	Q—K 8 ch
31.	K—R 2	Q—Q B 8

It is difficult to find a convincing
continuation for White. If 32.
R × P, R—K 8 ; 33. Q—Q Kt 8 ch,
K—Kt 2 ; 34. R—B 6, R—R 8 ch;
35. K—Kt 3, Q—Kt 4 ch ; 36.
K—B 3, Q × B P ch ; 37. Q—B 4,
Q × Q ch ; 38. K × Q, R—Q Kt 8
with good drawing chances.

| 32. | R—Q 5 ! | |

The only winning move, says
Tarrasch. The chief point is that
after 32. ...R—K 8 ? ; 33. R—
Q 8 ch wins at once.

32.	......	Q × Kt P
33.	Q—Q 6 ch	K—Kt 2
34.	Q × P	R—K 4
35.	R × R	P × R

Interesting would be the King and Pawn ending after 35. ...Q× R ch ; 36. Q×Q, P×Q ; 37. P— Q B 3 (otherwise ...P—Kt 5 wins right off), K—B 3 ; 38. P—Kt 4, K—K 2 ; 39. K—Kt 3, K—Q 3 ; 40. P—R 4, K—Q 4 ; 41. P—Kt 5, K—B 5 ; 42. P—R 5, K×P ; 43. P—Kt 6 and wins.

36. P—Q B 3

...P—Kt 5 must be prevented. Superficially viewed, the win seems extremely difficult for White ; yet Tarrasch forces his opponent's capitulation after only nine more moves !

36. ......   K—B 3

Tarrasch points out that if 36. ...P—B 3 (or 36. ...Q—K 7 ; 37. Q—K 3 and wins) ; 37. Q— K 7 ch, K—Kt 1 ; 38. Q×B P, Q×R P ; 39. Q—K 6 ch followed by P—B 6 Black is lost.

37. P—Kt 4   Q—B 8
38. Q—Q 6 ch   K—Kt 4
39. Q—Q 8 ch !

Much more effective than 39. Q×P ?, Q—B 5 ch ! ; 40. Q× Q ch, K×Q leaving White with a very difficult game on his hands.

39. ......   K—B 5
40. Q—Q 3   P—K 5

If 40. ...Q—K 8 ; 41. Q— Kt 3 ch wins the Queen.

41. Q—Kt 3 ch   K—Kt 4
42. P—R 4 ch

Q—K 3 ch is also good enough, but Tarrasch prefers to weave a mating net.

42. ......   K—B 3
43. Q—Q 6 ch   K—Kt 2
44. P—B 6 ch   K—Kt 3
45. Q—K 5   Resigns

Mate is unavoidable. A clever ending by Tarrasch.

56. OSTEND, 1905

QUEEN'S GAMBIT DECLINED

MARSHALL weakens his position in his impetuous search for a quick attack. Careless play soon leads to loss of material, and Tarrasch winds up with a fine ending.

White	Black
F. J. MARSHALL	DR. S. TARRASCH
1. P—Q 4	P—Q 4
2. P—Q B 4	P—K 3
3. Kt—Q B 3	Kt—K B 3
4. B—Kt 5	B—K 2
5. P—K 3	O—O
6. Kt—B 3	Q Kt—Q 2

Here we have one of Tarrasch's infrequent adoptions of the Orthodox Defence, in which he had no faith.

7. Q—B 2   P—B 3

Despite its timid appearance, this is more of a fighting move than 7. ...P—B 4, which leads to a lifeless game for Black after 8. B P×P.

8. P—Q R 3   R—K 1
9. P—K R 4

This move, typical of Marshall's devil-may-care attacking style, appears frequently in his games of this period. It has the possible drawback of committing White to an attacking policy before he is fully prepared for it.

9. ......   Kt—B 1

Too passive. ...P×P at once, followed by ...Kt—Q 4, was indicated.

10. Kt—K 5   P×P
11. B×P   Kt—Q 4

The only chance for Black to free himself from his sadly cramped position.

12. B×B   Q×B
13. P—K 4

Much stronger was 13. Kt—K 4 ! The text is powerful in appearance, but it leaves the Q P in somewhat a shaky state—a circumstance which Tarrasch later turns to advantage.

13. ......   Kt—Q Kt 3
14. B—R 2   B—Q 2
15. Kt—Q 3

In order to restrain the characteristic freeing move ...P—Q B 4.

15. ......   K R—Q 1

Beginning to "observe" the Q P. Although Black's game is still cramped, his pieces are gradually coming into play.

16. O—O—O   B—K 1
17. Kt—K 2   Kt—B 1

In order to play ...Kt—Q 3—Kt 4. Black is stealthily acquiring the initiative !

18. Q—B 5

Admitting defeat for his middle game plans, Marshall tries his luck with the ending. ...Q×Q ? would be a poor reply because after 19. P×Q White would be rid of the weak Q P and would in turn have a commanding grip on Q 6.

18. ......   P—Q Kt 3
19. Q×Q   Kt×Q
20. Kt—K 5

Apparently with a view to provoking Black's reply.

20. ......   P—B 3

Tarrasch does not fear any weakening effects from this move, and the accuracy of his judgment is soon borne out.

21. Kt—Q 3   B—B 2
22. K—Kt 1

Marshall seems to have lost the thread of the game. "Overprotection" of the Q P by doubling the Rooks on the Q file was in order.

22. ......   R—Q 3
23. R—Q B 1 ?

An oversight which costs a Pawn.

23. ......   P—K 4
24. B×B ch   K×B
25. P—Q Kt 4

In order to prevent ...P—Q B 4 after ...P×P, thus artificially isolating Black's Q P. But Tarrasch has a more effective continuation.

25. ......   Kt—K 3 !
26. P—Q 5   P×P
27. K R—Q 1   Q R—Q 1

Not 27. ...P×P ?; 28. Kt×P ch.

28. P×P	R×P
29. Kt—Kt 2	R×R
30. R×R	R×R ch
31. Kt×R	Kt—K B 4
32. P—Kt 3	Kt(K 3)—Q 5
33. Kt×Kt	Kt×Kt

The ending is easily won for Black, but Tarrasch's impeccable handling of the remaining play lends it interest.

34. K—Kt 2	K—K 3
35. K—B 3	Kt—Kt 4 ch
36. K—Kt 3	K—Q 4
37. P—R 4	Kt—Q 5 ch
38. K—B 3	K—K 5
39. P—Kt 5	

If 39. K—Q 2, K—B 6; 40. K—Q 3, P—K R 4! followed by ...P—K Kt 4! with an easy win.

39.	K—B 6
40. K—Q 3	Kt—K 3

Beginning a combination eleven moves deep which forces the win neatly.

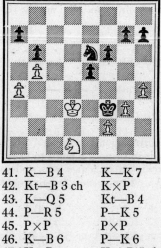

41. K—B 4	K—K 7
42. Kt—B 3 ch	K×P
43. K—Q 5	Kt—B 4
44. P—R 5	P—K 5
45. P×P	P×P
46. K—B 6	P—K 6
47. K×P	Kt—R 5 ch !

The point of the combination.

48. Kt×Kt	P—K 7
49. Kt—B 5	

49. Kt—Kt 2 (so that if 49. ... P—K 8(Q)?; 50. Kt—Q 3 ch) would be answered in the same way.

49.	K—K 6
50. K—R 7	

Marshall continues to fight on bitterly, although resignation would be more to the point.

50.	P—K 8(Q)
51. P—Kt 6	Q×P
52. P—Kt 7	P—B 4

For if 53. P—Kt 8(Q), Q×Q ch; 54. K×Q, P—B 5; 55. Kt—R 4, P—B 6; 56. Kt—Kt 2, K—K 7 and the Pawn must queen.

53. Kt—K 6	Q×P !
54. P—Kt 8(Q)	Q—R 5 ch
55. K—Kt 6	Q—Kt 6 ch
56. K—B 7	Q×Q ch
57. K×Q	P—B 5
58. Kt×Kt P	P—B 6
59. Kt—R 5	P—B 7
60. Kt—Kt 3	P—R 4
61. K—B 7	P—R 5
62. Kt—B 5 ch	K—B 5

White resigns—at last! An interesting ending.

57. OSTEND, 1905

RUY LOPEZ

THIS is one of the most celebrated games of Tarrasch's mature period. Rarely has an advantage in space been exploited so convincingly and with such refined methods.

White	Black
DR. S. TARRASCH	R. TEICHMANN

1.	P—K 4	P—K 4
2.	Kt—K B 3	Kt—Q B 3
3.	B—Kt 5	P—Q R 3
4.	B—R 4	Kt—B 3
5.	O—O	B—K 2
6.	R—K 1	P—Q 3
7.	P—B 3	O—O
8.	P—K R 3	B—Q 2
9.	P—Q 4	P—R 3

The general outlines of the coming play are fairly clear. White's position is somewhat freer, and Black must try to rearrange his pieces so that they will function more harmoniously. He therefore plans to bring his K B to K Kt 2.

10.	B—B 2	R—K 1
11.	Q Kt—Q 2	B—K B 1
12.	Kt—B 1	P—K Kt 3
13.	Kt—Kt 3	B—Kt 2
14.	B—K 3	K—R 2
15.	Q—Q 2	Q—K 2
16.	P—Q 5 !	

The game really begins here, the previous play being more or less public property. The text has the function of cramping Black's game, and it is also the prelude to a contemplated advance of White's Queen's side Pawns with the object of *opening a file and taking command of it*.

16.	......	Kt—Q 1
17.	P—B 4	P—Q R 4
18.	P—Kt 3 !	

White wants to play P—Kt 4, but the immediate 18. P—R 3 would be faulty because of the reply ...P—R 5 !, crippling White's Queen's side activity. This motif is common knowledge nowadays, but it

was not so well known forty years ago.

18.	......	P—Kt 3
19.	P—R 3	Kt—Kt 2

Teichmann is setting up his barricades against the anticipated P—Kt 4 and P—B 5.

20.	P—Kt 4	R—R 2 !

In order to double Rooks on the Q R file, so that White will have to be on his guard against ...P×P.

21.	Q—B 3 !	

Immediately parrying the potential threat.

21.	......	Kt—Kt 1
22.	Kt—Q 2	K R—R 1
23.	P—B 3	Kt—B 3

Black's position is difficult, his choices exiguous and his prospects dreary. He could play ...P×P here and exchange all the Rooks; but then White would play a dangerous invasion rôle on the Q R file.

24.	B—Kt 3	B—K 1
25.	Q R—B 1	Kt—Q 2

Preventing P—B 5.

26.	Q—B 2 !	

Changing his methods. He intends to bring a Knight to Q Kt 5, forcing an exchange which should have advantageous repercussions.

26.	......	B—B 1
27.	Kt—K 2	B—Kt 2
28.	Kt—B 3	Kt—B 3
29.	Kt—Kt 5 !	B×Kt

Avoiding this exchange would leave Black with too cramped a game. But now White has two potentially strong Bishops, pressure on the white squares and an annoying grip on the Q B file. It is this last factor which soon induces Black to exchange all the Rooks.

| 30. | P×B | Kt—K 1 |
| 31. | Q—Q 3 | P×P |

This exchange can always be forced by Kt—B 4 and B—Q 2. Black cannot afford to push on with ...P—R 5, for then the R P could be attacked too many times (say by White's placing the Knight on Q Kt 2, the K B at B 2 and the Queen at Q 1). *Note throughout how White's greater freedom multiplies his choice of action, while Black's cramped position restricts his possibilities.*

32.	P×P	Kt—Q 1
33.	Q—B 1 !	Q—Q 2
34.	R—R 1	Q—B 1

Had Teichmann accepted the temporary Pawn sacrifice the following continuation would have been likely : 34. ...R×R ; 35. R×R, R×R ; 36. Q×R, Q× Kt P ; 37. B—R 4 !, Q—K 7 ; 38. Kt—B 1, Kt—K B 3 (if 38. ...P— Q Kt 4 ; 39. Q—Q 1 !, Q—B 5 ; 40. Q—Kt 3 !, Q—K 7 ; 41. Q— B 2 !, Q×Q ; 42. B×Q, regaining the Pawn with a favourable ending) ; 39. Q—B 3, Q—R 7 ; 40. Q×B P, Q×B ; 41. Q×Kt, Q× P ; 42. B×P, Kt—K 1 ; 43. K— R 2, P—B 3 ; 44. Kt—K 3 and White still has the advantage.

| 35. | R×R | R×R |
| 36. | R—R 1 | R×R |

Not 36. ...Q—R 1 ; 37. R— R 6 !

| 37. | Q×R | Q—Kt 1 |
| 38. | Q—R 6 | Kt—K B 3 |

It is clear that the best that Black can hope for is a draw ; yet within the limitations of his position, he seems to be so firmly entrenched that White can make no headway. All the more worthy of praise, therefore, are the subtle manœuvres by which Tarrasch reduces his opponent to helplessness.

39. B—Q B 4 ! !

This pointless-looking move is the key to White's plan.

39.	......	K—Kt 1
40.	P—Kt 3 !	K—B 1
41.	P—R 4	Kt—Q 2
42.	B—B 1	K—K 1
43.	B—R 3	

Thus the last five moves have resulted in the posting of this Bishop on a splendid diagonal.

| 43. | ...... | B—B 1 |
| 44. | Kt—B 4 ! | |

Now threatening Q—R 1— Q B 1. Black must therefore move

the R P, which will allow the opening of new lines.

44.	......	P—R 4
45.	P—Kt 4 !	B—K 2
46.	B—B 2	B—B 3

...P×P would have maintained control of Black's K B 4, but it would have other drawbacks.

47.	P×P	P×P
48.	K—R 1	Q—Kt 2
49.	Kt—K 3 !	Kt—B 1
50.	Kt—B 5	

Now the Knight also has obtained a magnificent post. But that is not the end of Black's tribulations, for the weakness of his R P will soon plague him.

50.	......:	Q—Kt 1
51.	Q—R 1 !	Kt—Kt 3
52.	B—Kt 3	B—R 1
53.	K—R 2	Q—Kt 2
54.	B—Kt 2	Q—B 1
55.	Q—Q B 1 !	

Just at the right moment. He gains time for the following invasion with the Queen because of the threatened Kt×P ch.

| 55. | ...... | Q—Q 2 |
| 56. | B—R 3 ! | K—B 1 |

Forced. Black's game is going steadily downhill.

57.	Q—R 6 ch	K—Kt 1
58.	Q×P	Q—K 1
59.	Q—Kt 5	K—B 1
60.	P—R 5	Kt—B 5
61.	B—R 4 !	P—B 3
62.	Q—R 6 ch	K—Kt 1
63.	B×P !	

Seemingly dangerous.

63.	......	Kt—B 2
64.	Kt—K 7 ch !	Q×Kt
65.	Q×B ch	Kt×Q
66.	B×Q	Kt—B 2
67.	B—K 6	Kt×R P
68.	B—Q 8	Resigns

The play beginning with Tarrasch's 39th move is a model for the utilisation of superior mobility.

58. OSTEND, 1907

RUY LOPEZ

THE *Year Book of Chess* describes this as "an interesting and well-played game by both masters, Tarrasch keeping wonderfully cool under trying circumstances, and winning the game with his customary skill and resource."

| *White* | *Black* |
| DR. S. TARRASCH | A. BURN |

1.	P—K 4	P—K 4
2.	Kt—K B 3	Kt—Q B 3
3.	B—Kt 5	P—Q R 3
4.	B—R 4	Kt—B 3
5.	O—O	P—Q Kt 4
6.	B—Kt 3	B—K 2
7.	P—Q 4	P—Q 3
8.	P—Q R 4	

An unusual move. P—B 3 would turn the game into more orthodox channels.

8.	......	B—Kt 5
9.	P—B 3	O—O
10.	Q—Q 3	

P—Q 5 would be clearer and safer. But Tarrasch wants to maintain the tension.

| 10. | ...... | Q—Q 2 ! |

Interesting play. If now 11.
R P×P, R P×P; 12. R×R, R×
R; 13. Q×P, B×Kt; 14. P×B,
Kt×Q P ! with advantage.

11. B—Kt 5 ! ?

A speculative Pawn sacrifice
which is, perhaps, not quite sound.
P—Q 5 was still in order.

11.	B×Kt
12. Q×B	

White has little choice, for if 12.
P×B ?, Q—R 6 threatening ...
Kt—K Kt 5 ; and if 13. B×Kt,
B×B followed by ...B—Kt 4—
B 5.

12.	K P×P
13. R P×P	Kt—K 4

Permitting White to regain the
Pawn eventually. Correct was 13.
...R P×P ; 14. R×R, R×R, for,
as Marco points out, Black need not
fear 15. B×Kt, B×B ; 16. P—
K 5, Q P×P ; 17. B—Q 5, R—
R 3. Tarrasch would have had to
play 15. Q—Q 3, with questionable compensation for the Pawn.

14. Q—Q 1	Q P×P
15. Kt×P	P×P
16. R×R	R×R
17. P—B 4 !	

Now commences a stern battle for
the initiative. The text is not easy
to answer, for 17. ...Kt(K 4)—
Kt 5 ? loses a piece after 18. P—
K 5, while 17. ...Kt—Kt 3 allows
White to regain the Pawn advan-
tageously with 18. B×P ch ! (18.
...K×B ; 19. B×Kt, B×B ; 20.
Q—Q 5 ch etc.)

17.	Kt—B 5
18. P—K 5	Kt—K 1

Not 18. ...P×P ? ; 19. Q×Q
winning a piece ; nor 18. ...Kt—
K 6 ? ; 19. Q—B 3 etc.

19. B×B	Q×B
20. Kt×P	P×P !

For 21. B×Kt is answered by
...Q—B 4 ch

21. Q—Q 5 !	Kt—Kt 3
22. Q×P	Q—Kt 5 !

Best. ...Q×Q ? would lose the
K B P.

23. R—K 1   P—Kt 3

The threat of Q×Kt ch was best
answered by ...Kt—Q 2, to which
Tarrasch would have replied with
Q—K 4, with about equal chances.

24. Kt—Q 4

With the murderous threat of
Kt—B 6 and Kt—K 7 ch. But
Black has a formidable reply.

24. ......   Kt—Kt 2

Apparently decisive : Black
threatens ...R—K 1 as well as ...
P—B 4.

25. R—Q 1 !

Defending himself against the first threat; the second is only a sham.

25. ......   P—B 4

If 25. ...R—K 1; 26. Q×P, R—K 8 ch; 27. K—B 2 and wins.

26. B×P ch !

This move saves the game. A dramatic situation !

26. ......   K×B
27. Kt—B 6   Q—Kt 6 ?

Doubtless in time pressure, Burn overlooks the fatal effect of this move. Correct was 27. ...Q—Kt 4 !; 28. Q—K 7 ch, K—Kt 1; 29. R—Q 8 ch, R×R; 30. Q× R ch, K—B 2; 31. Kt—K 5 ch, K—K 3; 32. Q—Kt 8 ch, K—B 4; 33. Q×Kt, Q×P and Black draws.

28. Q—K 7 ch   K—Kt 1
29. R—Q 8 ch   R×R
30. Q×R ch   Kt—K 1

If 30. ...K—B 2; 31. Kt—K 5 ch, K—K 3; 32. Q—Kt 8 ch winning the Queen (compare the previous note).

31. Q×Kt ch   K—Kt 2
32. Q—K 5 ch   K—R 3

Or 32. ...K—Kt 1; 33. P—B 5 !, P×P; 34. Kt—K 7 ch and wins.

33. Kt—K 7 !

Threatening mate in three beginning with Kt—B 5 ch.

33. ......   Q—Q 8 ch

Black has no choice : he must steer into a lost ending.

34. K—B 2   Q—Q 5 ch
35. Q×Q   P×Q
36. Kt—B 6   P—Q 6
37. Kt—K 5   P—Q 7
38. K—K 2   Kt—Q 4
39. P—K Kt 3   Resigns

For if 39. ...Kt—K 6; 40. K×P, Kt—B 8 ch; 41. K—K 2, Kt×R P; 42. P—Q Kt 4 wins. A highly interesting game.

59. OSTEND, 1907

FOUR KNIGHTS' GAME

TARRASCH takes advantage of the opponent's exposed position to execute a crushing attack with very simple means.

White DR. S. TARRASCH	Black D. JANOWSKI
1. P—K 4	P—K 4
2. Kt—K B 3	Kt—Q B 3
3. Kt—B 3	Kt—B 3
4. B—Kt 5	B—Kt 5

The favoured continuation now-adays is Rubinstein's 4. ...Kt—Q 5, against which there is no known way of obtaining an advantage.

5. O—O	O—O
6. P—Q 3	P—Q 3
7. B—Kt 5	Kt—K 2

And here the moderns prefer 7. ...B×Kt; 8. P×B, Q—K 2. The text continuation, while more difficult, is also playable.

8. Kt—K R 4

8. B×Kt, P×B ; 9. Kt—K R 4,
Kt—Kt 3 ; 10. Kt×Kt, R P×Kt ;
11. P—B 4, B—B 4 ch ; 12.K—
R 1, K—Kt 2 gives Black good
chances.

| 8. ...... | P—B 3 |
| 9. B—Q B 4 | B—Kt 5 |

Not so good as 9. ...P—Q 4 ;
10. B—Kt 3, Q—Q 3 and Black
stands well.

| 10. P—B 3 | B—K 3 |
| 11. B×Kt | P×B |

If 11. ...B×B ? ? ; 12. B×Kt
wins a piece. Black's position is
already seriously compromised.

12. B×B	P×B
13. P—B 4	Kt—Kt 3
14. Kt×Kt	P×Kt
15. Q—Kt 4	

The direct assault begins.

15.	Q—K 1
16. P—B 5	P×P
17. P×P	B×Kt

Janowski was always reluctant to
surrender a Bishop for a Knight,
but he realises that White's Knight
has more useful possibilities than
the Bishop in this position.

18. P×B	K—Kt 2
19. R—B 3	R—R 1
20. P×P	Q—K 2

...Q×P would be refuted by
Q—Q 7 ch
Against the plausible 20. ...R—
R 3, Tarrasch had prepared the fol-
lowing pretty continuation : 21.
R×P !, K×R ; 22. R—B 1 ch,
K—Kt 2 ; 23. R—B 7 ch, Q×R
(if 23. ...K—Kt 1 ; 24. Q—Kt 5

followed by Q—B 6 wins) ; 24.
P×Q ch, K×P ; 25. Q—Q 7 ch
and wins.

21. P—K R 4	P—Q 4
22. Q R—K B 1	Q R—K B 1
23. P—R 5	R—R 3

It is not easy to see how White is
to make further headway, as his
advanced Pawns are apparently so
well blockaded.

24. R(B 1)—B 2	R(R 3)—R 1
25. Q—B 5 !	Q—Q 3
26. P—Kt 4 !	

The further advance of this Pawn
will very quickly prove decisive.
An attempt to prevent P—Kt 5
would end catastrophically : 26.
...K—R 3 ? ; 27. P—Kt 7 !, K×
P ; 28. Q—Kt 6 mate !

26. ......   Q—K 2

27. P—Kt 5 !

As will be seen, the consequences
of this move have been calculated
right down to the last detail.

27.	P×P
28. Q×R ch	R×Q
29. R×R	Q×R

There is nothing to be done against the threat of R—B 7 ch. If for example 29. ...Q—Q 3 ?; 30. R(B 2)—B 7 ch, K—R 3; 31. R—R 7 mate. Or 29. ...Q—B 4; 30. P—Q 4 and Black is helpless.

Black's last hope is that Tarrasch will play 30. R×Q ?, K×R leading to a drawn King and Pawn ending. Instead there follows:

30. P—R 6 ch !   Resigns

For if 30. ...K—Kt 1; 31. P—R 7 ch, K—Kt 2; 32. R×Q etc. A delightful game.

60. OSTEND, 1907

RUY LOPEZ

IN this game the gradual cramping of Black's position takes on a tragi-comic aspect and ends logically enough with the stalemating of Black's Queen !

White	Black
DR. S. TARRASCH	A. BURN

1. P—K 4	P—K 4
2. Kt—K B 3	Kt—Q B 3
3. B—Kt 5	P—Q R 3
4. B—R 4	Kt—B 3
5. O—O	B—K 2
6. R—K 1	P—Q Kt 4
7. B—Kt 3	P—Q 3
8. P—Q R 4	

Unusual at this point. It is probably best answered by ...R—Q Kt 1.

8. ...   B—Kt 5

Threatening ...Kt—Q 5, but committing Black to the maintenance of the pin.

9. P—B 3	O—O
10. P—R 3 !	

Forcing a decision.

10. ......   B—Q 2 ?

Burn does not rise to the occasion. ...B—R 4 had to be played. If then 11. P—Q 4 White's centre would be rather shaky, while if 11. P—Q 3, R—Kt 1 could be tried with a view to creating complications with ...P—Q 4.

11. P—Q 4	Q—B 1
12. B—Kt 5	

Threatening 13. R P×P, R P×P; 14. R×R, Q×R; 15. P×P, P×P; 16. B×Kt winning a piece.

12.	R—Kt 1
13. R P×P	R P×P
14. Q Kt—Q 2	R—K 1
15. K—R 2	

White has an appreciably freer position, and now plans to increase his advantage in space by means of Kt—K Kt 1 and P—K B 4.

15. ......   B—Q 1 ?

A fantastic move. More reasonable was 15. ...P—R 3 and if 16. B—K 3, B—B 1 followed by ...P—Kt 3 and ...B—Kt 2. If 16. B—K R 4, Kt—K R 2 could have been played.

16. Q—B 2

16. P—Q 5, Kt—K 2; 17. B×Kt, P×B; 18. P—K Kt 4 is not so good as it looks because of ...P—B 3 with good counterplay for Black.

16.	P—R 3
17. B—K 3	B—K 2
18. Kt—K Kt 1	P—Kt 4 ?

Suicide. Since P—K B 4 cannot be prevented, it is pointless (to say the least) for Black to weaken his position in this way.

19. P—Kt 3	B—B 1
20. P—K B 4	Kt P×P
21. Kt P×P	P×B P
22. B×P	Kt—Q 1
23. R—K B 1	

In addition to his other advantages, White now has the use of the K B file, and this soon proves decisive. Black's pieces wander around aimlessly and have no scope.

| 23. ...... | Kt—K 3 |
| 24. B—K 3 | |

Tarrasch does not even bother to win a Pawn with B×R P.

24.	B—Kt 2
25. R—B 2	Kt—R 2
26. Q R—K B 1	R—K 2
27. Q—Q 1	Q—B 1

Hoping to defend the King—but the results are catastrophic.

| 28. K Kt—B 3 | B—K 1 |

Burn seems sardonically bent on constructing a suimate position. However, his game was already beyond good and evil.

| 29. Kt—R 4 | Kt(K 3)—Kt 4 |
| 30. Kt—Kt 6 | Resigns |

Black's Queen is prettily stalemated—a conclusion for which

Black deserves as much credit as does his opponent !

61. OSTEND, 1907

QUEEN'S GAMBIT DECLINED
(IN EFFECT)

THIS bitterly fought game was played in the semi-final round, when Tarrasch needed a win to make almost certain of the first prize. While his play was not perfect, he displayed commendable courage and resourcefulness and thoroughly deserved to win.

| *White* | *Black* |
| DR. S. TARRASCH | M. TCHIGORIN |

| 1. P—Q 4 | P—Q 4 |
| 2. Kt—K B 3 | P—Q B 3 |

Unusual but quite playable.

3. P—K 3

A tame continuation which leaves Black with a satisfactory game. 3. P—B 4 is more enterprising.

| 3. ...... | B—Kt 5 |

K

Freeing his Q B, which so often suffers from early and lasting imprisonment in this opening. ... B—B 4 was also good.

4. P—B 4	P—K 3
5. Kt—B 3	Kt—Q 2
6. B—Q 3	K Kt—B 3
7. O—O	B—Q 3

Black has achieved an excellent development, and it is not easy to see how his opponent can obtain any initiative.

8. P×P

Or 8. P—K 4, P×K P ; 9. Kt× P, Kt×Kt ; 10. B×Kt, P—K 4 (Tarrasch) and Black stands well.

8.	K P×P
9. P—K 4	P×P
10. Kt×P	Kt×Kt
11. B×Kt	O—O
12. Q—B 2 !	

As he is badly hampered by the pin and his Q P shows signs of becoming a serious weakness, Tarrasch decides on a speculative Pawn sacrifice which will give him the initiative and rid him of the pin—and the Pawn.

12. ......   P—K B 4

If at once 12. ...B×Kt ; 13. B×B, Q—R 5 ; 14. P—K R 3, Q×Q P ? ; 15. R—Q 1, Q—K 4 ; 16. Q—Q 3, Q—R 7 ch ; 17. K— B 1 and Black cannot save the piece (Tarrasch).

13. Q—Kt 3 ch	K—R 1
14. B—B 2	B×Kt
15. Q×B	Q—R 5
16. P—K Kt 3	Q×P
17. R—Q 1	

Now White's object is clear. He has two strong Bishops and gains time for developing his pieces favourably.

17. ......   Q—B 4

...Kt—K 4 is too risky.

18. Q—K 2

Q—Q 3 leads to nothing because of ...Kt—K 4 !

18.	Kt—B 3
19. B—K 3	Q—K 4
20. Q—Q 3	

20. B×B P would regain the Pawn but relax the pressure : after 20. ...B—B 4 followed by ... Q R—K 1 Black would have a fine game.

20.	Kt—Q 4
21. B—Q 4	Q—K 2
22. R—K 1	Q—Kt 4

At last Black seems ready to pursue his own plans.

23. P—Q R 3

Preventing ...Kt—Kt 5.

23. ......   Q R—Q 1

With formidable possibilities on the Q file which, surprisingly enough, lead to nothing in the further course of the game.

24. K—R 1   Q—R 3

Preparing for ...P—B 5. White cannot play 25. P—B 4 because of 25. ...Kt×P ; 26. P×Kt, B× B P, threatening mate and also ... P—B 4.

25. Q—K B 3   Q—Q 7

...P—B 5 would be answered
by P—K Kt 4.

26. Q—Q 1 ! ?   Q—Kt 4

A difficult decision for Black.
26. ...Q×Q ; 27. Q R×Q would
lead to an interesting and difficult
ending in which Black's extra Pawn
would be largely outweighed by
White's strong Bishops and generally superior mobility.

27. P—B 4 !   Kt×P

This sacrifice looks promising,
but it is ultimately refuted by Tarrasch's fine play. But the passive
alternative ...Q—R 3 would not
have been congenial to a player of
Tchigorin's aggressive temperament.

28. B—K 3 !

Tchigorin apparently expected
only 28. P×Kt ? which would turn
out disastrously for White after 28.
...Q×P :
I. 29. B—K Kt 1, B—Kt 5 ; 30.
P×B, R×Q ; 31. B×R (forced !),
Q×P and Black has Queen and four
Pawns against Rook and two
Bishops.

II. 29. R—K 2, B—B 2 ; 30.
R—Q 2, R×B ! and wins.

28. ......   Q—B 3
29. P×Kt   B×B P

If 29. ...B—Kt 5 ; 30. P×B,
R×Q ; 31. Q R×R, Q×P ; 32.
B—B 5, R—K Kt 1 ; 33. B×B P
and Black's Pawns are inadequate
compensation for the magnificent
positions of White's pieces, which
must soon lead to further gains of
material.

30. Q—B 3

30. B×B, R×Q ; 31. Q R×R,
Q×P would be relatively favourable for Black, as he would have
Queen and three Pawns against
three pieces.

30. ......   B×B
31. Q×B   Q×P

The following play is highly instructive. Black's four Pawns
ought to outweigh the Bishop, but
White's greater mobility enables
Tarrasch to demonstrate the value
of the Bishop and the worthlessness
of the Pawns !

32. Q R—B 1   P—Q R 3
33. Q—K 7 !

The key to the following play.
White threatens B×P or Q R—Q 1.

33. ......   Q—B 6

So that if 34. Q×P ?, Q—
B 6 ch ; 35. K—Kt 1, R—Q 7 and
wins. However, the more conservative ...R—Q Kt 1 offers better
chances.

34. R—K 3	Q—B 5
35. R—K Kt 1	Q—Q 4 ch
36. R—Kt 2 !	

Not 36. B—K 4, Q—B 2, forcing the exchange of Queens under relatively favourable circumstances. White has built up a promising attacking game, for example if 36. ...R—B 2 ; 37. Q—R 4 (threatening B—Kt 3), Q—R 4 ; 38. B—Kt 3, K R—Q 2 ; 39. Q×P ch !, K× Q ; 40. R—R 3 mate (Tarrasch).

36.	Q—B 2
37. B—Kt 3 !	

Decisive. White wins a Pawn.

37.	Q×Q
38. R×Q	P—K Kt 3
39. R×Q Kt P	R—Q Kt 1

Practically forced.

40. R×R	R×R
41. R—Kt 3 !	

Not 41. B—B 4, R—Kt 8 ch ; 42. R—Kt 1, R×R ch with splendid drawing chances.

41.	P—B 4

Although Black has three Pawns (two of them passed) for the piece, he should lose in the long run. The factors involved in the winning process may be conveniently summed up as follows :

(1) White must make the weight of his extra piece tell ; he must place his pieces to the best advantage, threaten the hostile Pawns, provoke their advance, force them into an optimum position in which any change is for the worse.

(2) White's King must be played to a *centralised* position (say K 5 or

Q 5 or Q B 4) where it can add to the pressure on Black's game.

(3) White's Pawns seem insignificant at present, yet White must avoid exchanging them ; for without them he cannot possibly win.

(4) Another reason why White must avoid Pawn exchanges is that his whole play is oriented about winning Black's Pawns ; *exchanges* would therefore be a negation of his policy.

42. R—Q 3

Taking an open file.

42.	P—Q R 4
43. K—Kt 2	

Advancing the King to the centre.

43.	K—Kt 2
44. K—B 3	K—B 3

Black follows suit ; he tries to hold as much terrain as possible.

45. P—K R 4

In order to penetrate further with K—B 4 followed (after providing for his Bishop) by R—Q 6 ch and K—K 5.

45.	R—Kt 3

...P—Kt 4 would weaken the K B P ; the why and wherefore of this will be set forth later. The text guards the third rank.

46. B—B 2

White dallies with the idea of a frontal attack on the Q B P (R—B 3) but this proves impracticable.

46.	K—K 4

Threatening ...P—Q B 5. If 47. R—B 3, K—Q 5.

47. B—Kt 3   K—B 3
48. B—B 4

Now the Bishop is self-supporting and the Rook becomes active.

48. ......   P—R 3
49. K—K 3

Not 49. K—B 4 ?, P—Kt 4 ch. Exchange of Pawns is to be avoided.

49. ......   P—Kt 4

Inevitable; if for example 49. ...R—B 3; 50. R—Q 7 with such unpleasant threats as R—Q R 7.

50. P—R 5 !

The key to the ending; Black's K R P is now the decisive weakness. The Q B P, K B P and K R P can now be attacked both in turn and simultaneously.

50. ......   R—B 3
51. R—Q 7   R—Kt 3
52. R—K R 7   K—K 4
53. R—K 7 ch   K—Q 3

Or 53. ...K—B 3; 54. R—B 7 and wins.

54. R—K 6 ch   K—B 2
55. R—K 5 !

55. R—Kt 6 also wins; but the text is more "theoretical" as a path is created for White's King.

55. ......   P—B 5 ch
56. K—K 4   R—Q B 3

Or 56. ...K—B 3; 57. R—

K 6 ch, K—B 2; 58. R—Kt 6 ! followed by K—Q 5 and wins.

57. R—K 7 ch   K—Q 1

If 57. ...K—Kt 3; 58. R—Kt 7 followed by R—Kt 6 and K—Q 5. The text loses even more quickly.

58. R—K Kt 7   R—Q 3
59. K—K 5   R—Q 5
60. B—Q 5   P—B 6
61. K—Q 6   K—B 1
62. R—Kt 8 mate

62. OSTEND, 1907

RUY LOPEZ

This game is perhaps the most bitterly contested of Tarrasch's whole career. The ending abounds in tricky and instructive play, and the struggle is so bitter that the outcome is uncertain until the 79th move !

White	*Black*
Dr. S. Tarrasch	D. Janowski

1. P—K 4	P—K 4
2. Kt—K B 3	Kt—Q B 3
3. Kt—B 3	Kt—B 3
4. B—Kt 5	B—K 2
5. O—O	P—Q 3
6. P—Q 4	Kt—Q 2

Tchigorin's favourite defence.

7. Kt—K 2   O—O
8. Kt—Kt 3

A careless move, as the sequel proves. P—B 3 was indicated, as in Game 103.

8. ......   Kt×P !

Completely unexpected, since maintenance of the centre is the basic idea of the whole variation. However, Janowski alertly realises that Tarrasch's last move has forfeited the initiative.

9. Kt×Kt	P×Kt
10. Q×P	B—B 3
11. Q—Q 1	R—K 1

Black has gained time, he has freed his game, he has posted his K B on a magnificent diagonal and his "observation" of the K P creates further difficulties. Fully aware of the danger, Tarrasch bends all his energies toward achieving equality.

12. P—Q B 3

Making possible the eventual development of the Q B.

12.	P—Q R 3
13. B—R 4	

Better than 13. B—Q 3, Kt—B 4 followed by ...B—R 5.

13.	P—Q Kt 4
14. B—Kt 3 !	

If 14. B—B 2, Kt—B 4 followed by ...B—Kt 2 with a strong initiative for Black.

14.	B—Kt 2
15. B—Q 5 !	P—B 3

Perhaps ...B×B followed by ...Kt—Kt 3 was more promising. But Janowski apparently believes he can accomplish more by avoiding the exchange.

16. B—Kt 3	Kt—B 4
17. B—B 2	P—Q 4

Black naturally wants to rid himself of the weak Q P and in addition he anticipates a favourable ending because of his lead in development.

18. P×P	Q×P
19. Q×Q	P×Q
20. B—K 3	

...P—Q 5 must not be permitted.

20.	Kt—K 3
21. Kt—B 5	Q R—Q 1
22. Q R—Q 1	P—Kt 3
23. Kt—Q 4	Kt×Kt
24. P×Kt	R—Q B 1

Now Black hopes to derive some advantage from the Q B file. But Tarrasch's judiciously timed play ruins this hope.

25. B—Q 3	R—K 3
26. R—B 1	R(K 3)—B 3
27. R×R	R×R
28. R—R 1 !	

This move has a double purpose. It prepares for the entry of White's King, and for counterplay in the form of P—Q R 4. The position is now level, but from this point on, Black's difficulties mount steadily.

28.	B—B 1
29. K—B 1 !	B—B 4
30. K—K 2	

Just in time. 30. B×B ? would permit Black to occupy the seventh rank after ...P×B.

30.	B×B ch
31. K×B	R—B 5 !

A good move. If White wants to try for a win, he must weaken his position by advancing the Q Kt P.

32. P—Q Kt 3   R—B 3
33. P—Q R 4 !   P—Kt 5

Practically forced : if 33. ...
R—Kt 3 ; 34. P×P, P×P (not 34.
...R×P ; 35. R×P, R×P ch ;
36. K—B 2 and wins) ; 35. R—
R 7 (threatening R—Q 7), P—Kt 5;
36. B—R 6, R—Kt 1 ; 37. R—
Q 7, R—Kt 4 ; 38. R—B 7, R—
Kt 1 ; 39. R—B 5, R—Q 1 ; 40.
R—Kt 5, B—K 2 ; 41. B—Q 2
and wins.

34. B—Q 2   P—Q R 4

Again unavoidable : if 34. ...
B—K 2 ; 35. R—K 1, B—Q 3 (if
35. ...K—B 1 ; 36. R—K 5, R—
Q 3 ; 37. R×B etc.) ; 36. R—
K 8 ch, K—Kt 2 ; 37. P—R 5,;
K—B 3 ; 38. R—Q R 8 followed
by R—R 7—Kt 7.

But now both of Black's Queen's
side Pawns are on black squares and
therefore subject to potential attack
by White's Bishop.

35. R—K 1

R—Q B 1 would lead to a quick
draw, but now it is Tarrasch who
feels justified in playing for a win.

35. ......   R—B 1 ?

According to Tarrasch, 35. ...
K—B 1 would lose because of 36.
B—R 6 ch, B—Kt 2 ; 37. B×B ch,
K×B ; 38. R—K 5. However,
after 38. ...R—B 6 ch ; 39. K—
K 2, R×P ; 40. R×P, R—Kt 7
ch ; 41. K—B 3, R—Kt 6 ch ; 42.
K—B 4, R—Kt 7 ; 43. K—Kt 3,
R—Q 7 how is White to win ? !
Black is not yet lost, but the draw
has become much more difficult.

36. P—Kt 4 !

Since his Bishop cannot move
from Q 2, Tarrasch strives to increase the mobility of his Rook.
The text threatens 37. P—Kt 5,
B—Kt 2 ; 38. R—K 7.

36. ......   P—R 3 !

If 36. ...P—Kt 4 ; 37. P—B 4,
P×P ; 38. P—Kt 5 ! with advantage.

37. P—R 4 !   B×R P
38. R—K 5   R—Q 1

This is of course better than 38.
...B×P ; 39. R×P, R—R 1 ; 40.
B×R P and White should win.

39. B×R P   K—R 2

If 39. ...B×P ; 40. B—Kt 5,
R—Q 2 (or 40. ...R—Q B 1 ; 41.
B—B 6 !) ; 41. R—K 8 ch, K—
R 2 ; 42. R—R 8 etc.
Or 39. ...B—B 3 ; 40. B—
Kt 5 ! ; B×B ; 41. R×B, K—
B 1 ; 42. R—K 5, R—Q 3 ; 43.
P—Kt 5, R—Q 2 ; 44. P—B 4, R—
Q 3 ; 45. K—K 3, R—Q 2 ; 46.
P—B 5, P×P ; 47. R×B P, R—
Q 3 ; 48. K—B 4, K—K 2 ; 49.
K—K 5, R—Q 1 ; 50. R—B 6 and
wins (Tarrasch).

40. B—Q 2

Not 40. B—Kt 5 ? ?, B×B ; 41.
R×B, P—B 3.

40. ......   B—B 3

If 40. ...B×P ; 41. R—K 7,
K—Kt 2 ; 42. R—R 7.

41. R—K 1   R—Q 2 !

Not 41. ...R—Q B 1 (to prevent R—Q B 1—B 5); 42. P—Kt 5, B—Kt 2; 43. R—K 7 etc.

42.	R—Q B 1	K—Kt 2
43.	B—B 4	B—Q 1
44.	R—B 6	

Tarrasch has succeeded in tying up his opponent's pieces, but Janowski has covered all his weaknesses and further progress hardly seems possible.

44.	......	P—B 3
45.	B—Q 6	K—B 2
46.	B—B 5	P—Kt 4
47.	K—Q 2	

So that after B—Kt 6 and the exchange of Bishops, Black's Rook will not reach Q B 6 with a check. It is clear that B—Kt 6 is White's last winning chance, and Tarrasch is understandably dilatory in resorting to this final possibility.

47.	......	B—B 2
48.	K—B 2	B—Q 1
49.	K—Q 2	B—B 2
50.	K—K 2	B—B 5
51.	R—R 6	

Not 51. B—Kt 6, R—K 2 ch; 52. K—Q 3, R—K 8; 53. B×P, R—Q 8 ch winning the Q P.

51.	......	B—B 2
52.	K—Q 3	B—Q 1
53.	R—B 6	B—B 2
54.	K—B 2	B—Q 1
55.	K—Q 2	B—B 2
56.	B—Kt 6	

At last! The game now enters into its most critical stage.

56.	......	B×B
57.	R×B	R—B 2
58.	R—Q 6	

White now wins a Pawn, but it is not clear that this will suffice for victory.

58.	......	R—B 6
59.	R×P	R×P
60.	R×R P	K—K 3
61.	R—K B 5	R—Q R 6

At first sight the ending appears to be an easy win, but Black's resources soon make themselves felt.

62.	P—R 5	K—K 2
63.	K—B 2	K—K 3
64.	R—Kt 5	K—Q 3
65.	K—Kt 2	K—K 3
66.	R—Kt 6 ch	

Tarrasch points out that after 66. R×Q Kt P, R×P; 67. R—Kt 6 ch, K—Q 4; 68. R×P, K×P the draw is unavoidable.

| 66. | ...... | K—Q 4 ! |

After 66. ...K—B 2; 67. R×P, R×P; 68. K—Q 3 White should win.

| 67. | R×B P | K—B 5 ! |

The key to Black's play in the ending. The text enables the Q Kt P to become a threat which should ensure Black the draw.

68. R—B 5

Exhaustive analysis by Tarrasch failed to disclose a win. He gives the following alternatives : 68. P—R 6, R—Kt 6 ch ; 69. K—B 2, R—B 6 ch ; 70. K—Q 2, R—Q 6 ch ; 71. K—K 2, R—Q R 6.

I. 72. R—K Kt 6, P—Kt 6 ; 73. R×P, P—Kt 7 ; 74. R—B 5 ch, K×P ; 75. R—Q Kt 5, K—B 6 ; 76. P—B 4, R×P ; 77. P—B 5, R—R 5 (threatening ...R—Kt 5) ; 78. R×P, K×R ; 79. K—B 3, K—B 6 ; 80. P—B 6, K—Q 5 ; 81. K—B 4 (if 81. P—B 7, R—R 8 ; 82. K—B 2, R—R 1), K—Q 4 ch ; 82. K—B 5, R—R 8 ; 83. P—Kt 5, R—B 8 ch ; 84. K—Kt 6, K—K 3 and Black wins—85. K—Kt 7, R—B 7 ; 86. K—Kt 6, R—B 4 ; 87. K—R 6, K—B 2 ; 88. P—Kt 6 ch, K×P ; 89. P—Kt 7, R—K Kt 4 or 86. K—R 7, K—B 2 ; 87. P—Kt 6 ch, K×P ; 88. P—Kt 7, R—R 7 ch ; 89. K—Kt 8, R—K Kt 7 ; 90. K—R 8, K—B 2 and wins.

(Note that in the above variation White is a tempo behind the text play which begins with his 79th move, where his King is on K 3 instead of on K 2. This makes the difference between defeat and victory !)

II. 72. P—B 4, P—Kt 6 ; 73. P×P, P—Kt 7 ; 74. R—Q Kt 6, K—B 6 followed by ...R×P and draws ; or 73. P—B 5, P—Kt 7 ; 74. R—Q Kt 6, K—B 6 ; 75. K—K 3, R—Kt 6 ; 76. R×R ch ; K×R ; 77. P—R 7, P—Kt 8(Q) ; 78. P—R 8(Q), Q—K 8 ch and the ending is drawn.

68.	R—Kt 6 ch
69. K—B 2	R—B 6 ch
70. K—Q 2	R—Q 6 ch
71. K—K 2	R×P

If 71. ...P—Kt 6? ; 72. R—B 5 ch, K×P ; 73. R—Q 5 ch wins.

72. P—R 6

Not 72. R×P, P—Kt 6 ; 73. R—Kt 8, P—Kt 7 ; 74. R—Kt 8, K—B 6 ; 75. P—R 6, R×P ; 76. P—R 7, R—Q R 5 and White (!) must play for a draw with 77. R—B 8 ch, K—Q 5 ! ; 78. R—Q Kt 8, K—B 6 ; 79. R—B 8 ch etc. (Tarrasch).

72.	R—Q 1
73. R×P	P—Kt 6
74. R—Kt 7	P—Kt 7
75. R—Kt 7	K—B 6
76. P—B 4	R—Q R 1 !

This holds the draw, whereas 76. ...K—B 7 ; 77. P—B 5, P—Kt 8 (Q) ; 78. R×Q, K×R ; 79. P—B 6, R—Q R 1 ; 80. P—B 7 etc. would lose for Black.

| 77. P—B 5 | R×P |
| 78. K—K 3 | R—Q R 5 ? |

With this plausible move (which threatens ...R—Kt 5 or ...R×P) Janowski robs himself of the fruits of his hitherto tenacious defence.

The correct drawing method, says Tarrasch, was 78. ...R—R 8 ! ; 79. R×P, K×R ; 80. P—B 6, R—K B 8 ; 81. P—Kt 5, K—B 6 (not 81. ...R—B 4 ? ; 82. K—K 4 !, R×Kt P ; 83. P—B 7, R—Kt 5 ch ; 84. K—K 3, R—Kt 6 ch ; 85. K—B 2) ; 82. K—K 4, K—B 5 ; 83. K—K 5, K—B 4 ; 84. K—K 6, R—K 8 ch ; 85. K—Q 7, R—K B 8 ; 86. K—K 6, R—K 8 ch ; 87. K—B 7, K—Q 3 ; 88. P—Kt 6, R—K Kt 8 ; 89. P—Kt 7, K—K 4 etc.

79. R×P !

Now White wins by one tempo !

79. ......   K×R
80. P—B 6 !

For if 80. ...R×P ; 81. P—B 7
etc. The struggle of the Rook
against the two Pawns will have
exciting and instructive features.

80. ......   R—R 8

Too late ! The Rook has taken
an extra move to get to this square,
and as a result defeat cannot be
staved off.

81. P—Kt 5   R—K B 8
82. K—Q 4   K—Kt 6

Or 82. ...R—B 4 ; 83. K—
K 4 ! etc.

83. K—K 5

K—Q 5 !, fending off Black's
King, would have been more exact.
The text makes the win harder.

83. ......   K—B 5
84. P—Kt 6   R—K 8 ch
85. K—Q 6   R—Q 8 ch

85. ...R—K Kt 8 would have
led to a prettier finish : 86. P—
Kt 7 ! (not 86. P—B 7 ?, R×P ch ;
87. K—K 5, R—Kt 4 ch ; 88. K—
K 4, R—Kt 8 ! and Black draws),
K—Q 5 ; 87. K—B 6 ! (not 87.
K—K 7 ?, K—K 4 and draws ; nor
87. P—B 7 ?, R—Kt 3 ch ! and
draws), K—B 5 (if 87. ...R—Kt 3 ;
88. K—Kt 5 !) ; 88. K—Q 7, K—
Q 4 ; 89. K—K 8, K—K 3 ; 90.
P—B 7, R—Q R 8 ; 91. P—B 8
(Kt) ch ! and wins ! (Tarrasch).

86. K—K 6   R—K 8 ch
87. K—B 7   Resigns

A superb battle, worthy of the

occasion which produced it. Despite Tarrasch's slip in the opening,
victory rightly went to the man
with the greater ability and better
nerves.

63. HAMBURG, 1910

THREE KNIGHTS' GAME

TARRASCH nurses his advantage in
mobility until his opponent is sad-
dled with a fatal positional weakness. From then on, it is only a
question of time until Black's game
collapses.

White	*Black*
DR. S. TARRASCH	R. TEICHMANN

1. P—K 4   P—K 4
2. Kt—K B 3   Kt—Q B 3
3. Kt—B 3   B—Kt 5

One can understand Black's
eagerness to avoid the Four
Knights', which in those days was
still a potent weapon.

4. B—Kt 5   K Kt—K 2
5. O—O   O—O
6. P—Q 4   P×P

It is usually inferior policy to give
up the centre in such situations because of the gain in mobility which
the opponent obtains. In the previous round Tarrasch, playing the
black pieces against Schlechter, had
continued 6. ...P—Q 3 ! ; 7. P—
K R 3 (otherwise ...B—Kt 5 is
annoying), P—Q R 3 ; 8. B—K 2,
P×P ; 9. Kt×P, Kt×Kt ; 10.
Q×Kt, B—Q B 4 and Black had an
easy game.

7. Kt×P   P—Q 3

As Tarrasch points out, the continuation 7. ...P—Q 4 ; 8. P×P, B×Kt would not be good because of 9. P×B, Q×P ; 10. Kt×Kt, P×Kt ; 11. Q×Q, P×Q ; 12. B—R 3 winning the exchange.

8. B—K 3   Kt×Kt

More promising than this colourless move seems ...B×Kt, in the hope of making White's Pawn weakness tell in the endgame.

9. B×Kt   B—R 4
10. Q—B 3

A good move. The aggressive posting of the Queen soon pays dividends.

10. ......   B—Kt 3
11. B×B   R P×B
12. Q R—Q 1

By means of perfectly simple moves, Tarrasch has secured and maintained a considerable lead in development.

12. ......   Kt—Kt 3

Black must do something about the threat of P—K 5.

13. Q—Kt 3   B—Q 2 ?

After this, Teichmann soon finds himself in a hopeless predicament. There was probably nothing better than 13. ...P—K B 4, although after 14. B—B 4 ch, K—R 1 ; 15. P—B 4 the outlook for Black's game is very poor.

Tarrasch points out that if 13. ...Q—R 5 ; 14. Q×Q, Kt×Q ; 15. P—Q R 3 (in order to play Kt—Q 5) Black has no satisfactory move; if 15. ...B—K 3 ; 16. P—B 4,

P—K B 4 ; 17. P—K Kt 3, Kt—Kt 3 ; 18. P—K Kt 4 !

14. B×B   Q×B
15. P—K 5 !   K R—Q 1

Black is now left with an isolated Q P which must eventually lead to his downfall.

16. P×P   P×P
17. R—Q 2   Q—K 3

...Kt—K 4 ? at once would be a blunder, for then 18. Kt—Q 5 would force the gain of some material.

18. K R—Q 1   Kt—K 4
19. R—K 2   Q—B 5
20. P—Kt 3

White wants to establish the following cast-iron position on the Queen's side : Pawns at Q R 4, Q Kt 3 and Q B 4. Such a formation would free the Pawns from the need for protection by pieces, and would at the same time exert the maximum pressure on Black's game.

20. ......   Q—B 3
21. P—Q R 4   R—K 1
22. Kt—Q 5   Kt—Kt 3

Not 22. ...R—K 3 ? for then 23. P—K B 4 wins.

23. R(K 2)—Q 2   R—K 3
24. P—Q B 4

White has the desired position. Black can merely move to and fro and wait for the inevitable result.

24. ......   Q R—K 1
25. P—R 3   Q—B 4

26. K—R 2   P—R 3
27. Kt—K 3

The Knight is brought into position to menace the Q P.

27. ......   Kt—K 4
28. R—Q 5   Q—R 6

This has all the marks of a time-pressure move. The Queen is soon in serious difficulties, and while it is being extricated, the Q P is lost. But it could not have been held for very long in any event.

29. Kt—B 5   R—Kt 3
30. Q—Q B 3   Q—R 7

White threatened to win the Queen with R—Q R 1.

31. R(Q 5)—Q 2   Q—R 6
32. R × P   R × R
33. R × R !

Stronger than Kt × R.

33. ......   P—Kt 3

34. P—B 4 !

Decisive. The rest is mopping up.

34. ......   P × Kt
35. P × Kt   R—K 3

The attempt to guard the weakened King's side proves hopeless.

36. Q—Kt 3 ch   K—R 2
37. Q—B 4   K—Kt 2

Or 37. ...R × R ; 38. P × R, K—Kt 3 ; 39. P—Q 7, Q—K 2 ; 40. Q—B 7. If 37. ...K—Kt 3 ; 38. R—Q 3 wins.

38. R—Q 7   R—K 2
39. R—Q 3   R—K 3
40. Q × P   Q—B 4
41. R—Q 7   Q × P ch
42. Q × Q ch   R × Q
43. R—Q 6

43. R × P, R—K 3 ; 44. P—Q Kt 4 was also good enough. White could then continue with P—Kt 5 followed by R—B 7 and P—B 5.

After the text, Black resigned, since 43. ...R—K 3 ; 44. R × R, P × R leaves him with a lost King and Pawn ending.

64. HAMBURG, 1910

QUEEN'S GAMBIT DECLINED

THE first meeting between two great masters results in products of variable quality. In the present instance, Tarrasch's superiority is only too well marked ; his youthful opponent comes off a painfully second best.

White   *Black*
DR. S. TARRASCH   DR. A. ALEKHINE

1. P—Q 4   P—Q 4
2. Kt—K B 3   P—K 3
3. P—K 3

Preparing to adopt the symmetrical variation of the Queen's Gambit Declined.

3.	P—Q B 4
4. P—B 4	Kt—K B 3
5. Kt—B 3	P—Q R 3

An inexactitude which creates difficulties for Black. ...Kt—B 3 would have been simpler and better.

6. Kt—K 5	Kt—B 3
7. Kt×Kt	P×Kt
8. B—Q 3	B—K 2
9. O—O	O—O
10. Kt—R 4 !	

Black is beginning to be faced with difficulties as a result of his inexact opening play.

| 10. ...... | B P×P |
| 11. K P×P | Q—B 2 |

Relying on his next move—but Tarrasch is not impressed.

| 12. P—B 5 ! | P—K 4 |
| 13. Kt—Kt 6 | R—R 2 |

Forced, for if 13. ...R—Kt 1 ; 14. P×P, Q×P ; 15. Kt×B followed by B×P wins a Pawn. Or if 14. ...Kt—Kt 5 ; 15. Kt×B, Q×Kt ; 16. Q—B 2, P—Kt 3 ; 16. B—K B 4 and wins.

14. P×P	Q×P
15. R—K 1	Q—Kt 1
16. Q—B 2	P—R 3

In order to free the Knight from the defence of the K R P.

17. Kt×B	R×Kt
18. B—Q 2	R—K 1
19. R—K 2 !	

Threatening to obtain an unpleasant bind by doubling the Rooks on the K file.

19.	Kt—Kt 5
20. P—K Kt 3	Kt—K 4
21. B—K B 4	B—Kt 4 !

An ingenious resource : B×B is to be answered by ...Kt—B 6 ch. However, Tarrasch manages to retain his advantage.

22. B×Kt !	R×B
23. Q R—K 1	R×R
24. R×R	P—Q R 4

Black is rightly concerned about the weakness of his Queen-side Pawns, but the text is inferior to the Tournament Book's suggestion of 24. ...R—K 2 ; 25. R×R, B×R ; 26. B×P, Q—Kt 5. After 27. P—Q R 3, Q×B P ; 28. Q×Q, B×Q ; 29. B—Kt 7 Black would come out a Pawn down, but he would have the drawing chances which are inherent in an ending with Bishops on opposite colours.

| 25. Q—R 4 | Q—R 1 |
| 26. P—Q Kt 4 ! | B—K 2 |

Not 26. ...P×P ?? ; 27. Q×R !

27. P—Kt 5 !	P×P
28. B×P	K—R 2
29. P—B 6	

Tarrasch has secured a formidable passed Pawn which ties up Black's pieces.

29.	B—B 3
30. Q—B 2 ch	P—Kt 3
31. Q—Q B 5 !	

Black's position has become extremely uncomfortable. The text

is stronger than 31. P—B 7, Q—
Q B 1 ; 32. Q—B 6, B—Kt 2 ! 33.
R—B 2, B—K 4 ! 34. Q×P, R×
P ! ; 35. Q×P ch, R×Q ; 36. R×
Q and White has no more than a
draw.

31. ......   Q—Q Kt 1
32. R—K 8 !

This is stronger than 32. Q×P,
Q—B 2 etc.

32. ......   Q×R

Black has little choice, for if 32.
...Q—B 2 ; 33. Q—B 8 wins.

33. Q×R   B—K 4

If 33. ...B—Q 1 ? ? ; 34. P—
B 7 wins. Or 33. ...Q—K 8 ch ;
34. B—B 1, winning.

34. Q×P   Q—K 2
35. Q—K 1   Q—B 3
36. P—Q R 4

Despite White's two passed
Pawns, the win is anything but
easy.

36. ......   B—B 2
37. P—R 5   K—Kt 2
38. P—R 6   Q—Q 5
39. K—Kt 2   Q—B 4

If 39. ...B—Kt 3 ; 40. Q—
K 3 !, Q×Q ; 41. P×Q and the
advance of either passed Pawn wins.
This motif appears again and again
throughout the following play.

40. Q—R 1 ch   P—B 3 !

If 40. ...K—Kt 1 ? ; 41. P—
R 7 wins. If 40. ...K—R 2 ; 41.
P—R 7, B—Kt 3 ! ; 42. Q—B 6 !,

B×P ; 43. Q×B P ch, K—R 1 ;
44. P—B 7 wins.

41. Q—Kt 2 !

Against 41. P—R 7 Black has the
clever resource 41. ...B—Kt 3 ! ;
42. P—R 8(Q), Q×P ch ; 43. K—
R 3 (not 43. K—R 1 ? ?, Q—B 6
mate !), Q—B 4 ch and White cannot avoid the draw.

41. ......   B—Kt 3
42. Q—K 2   K—B 2
43. B—R 4

43. ......   K—B 1 ?

This loses quickly. 43. ...Q—
R 4 ? would likewise lose in quick
time after 44. Q—Kt 5 !
But 43. ...K—Kt 2 would have
required very fine play to force the
win. There are a number of win-
ning methods, but the following is
the clearest : 44. Q—B 2 !, Q—
R 4 ; 45. P—B 7 !, B×P ; 46. Q—
B 6, Q—Kt 3 ; 47. Q—Q 7 ch,
K—R 1 ; 48. B—B 6 !, Q×P ; 49.
B×P and Black is helpless ! Or
46. ...P—R 4 ; 47. Q—Q 7 ch,
K—R 3 ; 48. Q—K 8, Q—Kt 5 ;
49. Q—R 8 ch, K—Kt 4 ; 50. P—
R 4 ch, K—B 4 ; 51. Q—B 8 ch,
K—K 5 ; 52. B—B 2 ch and wins.

44. Q—K 3 !   Q—Kt 5

There was no saving move.

45. Q×P ch   K—K 2

Or 45. ...K—B 2 ; 46. Q—R 7 ch, K—B 1 ; 47. B—B 2, Q—B 4 ; 48. Q—R 6 ch, winning easily.

46. Q—Kt 7 ch   K—K 3
47. Q—Q 7 ch   K—K 4
48. Q—K 8 ch   K—Q 5

If 48. ...K—Q 3 ? ; 49. Q—B 8 ch wins the Queen. If 48. ... K—B 4 ; 49. B—B 2 ch with the same result.

49. Q—K 3 ch   K—B 5
50. Q—Kt 3 ch !

Nicely played.

50. ......   Q×Q
51. B×Q ch   Resigns

For the advance of the passed Pawns decides. A fine game by Tarrasch.

65. SAN SEBASTIAN, 1911

SICILIAN DEFENCE

BURN loses the initiative early in the game, after which his position goes steadily downhill. Black makes good use of his advantage to build up a winning game.

White	*Black*
A. BURN	DR. S. TARRASCH

1. P—K 4   P—Q B 4
2. Kt—Q B 3   P—K 3
3. Kt—B 3   Kt—Q B 3
4. P—Q 4   P×P
5. Kt×P   Kt—B 3

6. K Kt—Kt 5   B—Kt 5
7. P—Q R 3

A variation which does not give Black much difficulty. 7. Kt—Q 6 ch, K—K 2 ; 8. Kt×B ch, R×Kt ; 9. B—Q 3 seems worth trying, for it would be interesting to see whether White's Bishops would compensate for the weakness of his Pawn structure after 9. ...B×Kt ch.

7. ......   B×Kt ch
8. Kt×B   P—Q 4
9. P×P

The modern preference is for B—Q 3. The isolation of Black's Q P does not weigh very heavily against the opportunity to develop the Bishop.

9. ......   P×P
10. B—Q 3

B—K Kt 5 is strong only in appearance ; see Game 126.

10. ......   O—O
11. O—O   B—Kt 5 !

Taking advantage of the opportunity created by White's 9th move. B—K 2 is probably best in reply, but painfully passive.

12. P—B 3   B—K 3
13. R—K 1   R—K 1
14. Q—Q 2 ?

B—K B 4 or B—K Kt 5 would cost a Pawn after ...Q—Kt 3 ch. But K—R 1 was surely preferable to the time-wasting text.

14. ......   P—Q 5
15. Kt—K 4   B—B 4
16. Q—B 4

White's position is uncomfortable. If 16. Kt×Kt ch, Q×Kt; 17. B×B, Q×B and Black must gain the K file.

| 16. ...... | B×Kt |
| 17. P×B | |

Giving Black a strong post for his pieces at K 4. However, if 17. B×B, Kt×B; 18. R×Kt, R×R; 19. Q×R, Q—Q 2 followed by ... R—K 1 with clear advantage to Black.

17.	Kt—K 4 !
18. Q—R 4	Q—Kt 3
19. B—K Kt 5	K Kt—Q 2
20. P—Q Kt 4	Q R—B 1

White's Bishops are ineffectual and his Queen's side is weak. Black's positional advantage has become decisive.

21. B—Q 2

...R—B 6 had to be prevented, but the text loses a Pawn.

21.	Kt×B
22. P×Kt	Kt—K 4
23. Q—Kt 3	Q—R 3
24. P—Kt 5	

He prefers to lose the Q Kt P instead of the Q P; for in the latter event, the K P would be weak and Black's Q P would be passed.

24.	Q×Kt P
25. B—R 6	Kt—Kt 3
26. B—Q 2	R—B 7

In addition to his material advantage, Black is working up a powerful attack. White's days are numbered.

27. B—Kt 4	Kt—K 4
28. K R—Q 1	R—K 3
29. Q R—B 1	Q—B 3
30. R—Kt 1	Q—B 2

Protecting the Knight and thus threatening ...R—K Kt 3.

| 31. B—Q 2 | R—K Kt 3 |
| 32. Q—R 3 | P—K R 3 ! |

Making a loophole for the King so as to assure his Queen freedom of action.

| 33. K—R 1 | Kt—Kt 5 |
| 34. K—Kt 1 | P—Kt 3 ! |

Tarrasch bides his time, since his opponent is helpless. The text line is more forcing than 34. ...Kt—K 6; 35. B×Kt, R(Kt 3)×P ch; 36. Q×R, R×Q ch; 37. K×R, P×B; 38. R—Kt 2 and White will win the K P.

35. K R—Q B 1

If 35. Q R—B 1, R×B! wins. Or if 35. P—Kt 3, Kt—K 4 is decisive.

| 35. ...... | Kt×P ! |

For if 36. Q×Kt, Q×Q ch; 37.

K×Q, R×B etc. (note the importance of Black's ...P—K R 3).

36. P—K 5	Kt—Kt 5
37. B—B 4	Kt×P
38. K—R 1	P—B 3
39. Q—K 6 ch	K—R 2
40. Q—B 5	Q—B 3
41. Q—K 4	

White resigned without awaiting his opponent's reply, for after 41. ...Q×Q ; 42. P×Q, R(Kt 3)×P further play would be quite hopeless.

66. SAN SEBASTIAN, 1912
RUY LOPEZ

IN this game, Tarrasch produced one of the abiding classics of his favourite variation. The play against White's trapped Bishop is original, and the task of smashing Spielmann's well-barricaded position is handled impeccably by Tarrasch.

White	Black
R. SPIELMANN	DR. S. TARRASCH
1. P—K 4	P—K 4
2. Kt—K B 3	Kt—Q B 3
3. B—Kt 5	P—Q R 3
4. B—R 4	Kt—B 3
5. O—O	Kt×P
6. P—Q 4	P—Q Kt 4
7. B—Kt 3	P—Q 4
8. P—Q R 4	

An old-fashioned move which has disappeared from master play. The normal 8. P×P, B—K 3 ; 9. P—B 3 is preferable.

8.	Kt×Q P !
9. Kt×Kt	P×Kt
10. Kt—B 3 ! ?	

Berger's interesting suggestion. 10. Q×P, B—K 3 followed by ... P—Q B 4 gives Black a perfectly satisfactory game.

10.	Kt×Kt !

Better than 10. ...P×Kt ; 11. B×P etc.

11. P×Kt	P—Q B 4 !

White must now strive for equality, as the position of his K B is insecure.

12. R P×P	B—K 2

...P—B 5 could be answered by B—R 4.

13. Q—B 3 ?	

True to his temperament, Spielmann plays an attacking move. Only the utmost caution could save him here, says Tarrasch, who recommends 13. B P×P, P—B 5 ; 14. B—R 4, O—O ; 15. P×P, R×P ; 16. P—Q B 3 followed by the development of the Q B and the retreat of the K B to B 2.

13.	B—K 3
14. R×P	O—O !
15. P×P	P—B 5
16. B—R 2	

If 16. B—R 4, B—Q 2 ! wins a piece. But now the Bishop is buried alive.

16.	R×R
17. P×R	Q—R 4
18. B—Kt 1	P—B 6 !

A pitiable position for the Bishop. However, White's game is solid and capable of prolonged passive resist-

L

ance, so that Tarrasch's problem in the following phase is far from simple.

19. Q—Kt 3	R—B 1
20. P—B 4	B—K B 4
21. R—K 1	B—B 3
22. K—R 1	

Hoping for 22. ...Q×P ? ; 23. Q×P !

22.	P—R 3 !

22. ...B×Q P might easily be a boomerang, for example 23. B—K 3, B×B ; 24. Q×B, P—R 3 ; 25. P—R 7, R—R 1 ? ; 26. Q—K 8 ch etc.

23. P—R 3	R—Kt 1
24. B—K 3	Q×P

If 24. ...Q—R 8 ; 25. P—R 7 leads to much the same position.

25. R—Q 1	Q—R 8
26. Q—K 1	B—K 5
27. K—R 2	B—K 2
28. Q—B 1	P—B 4

Preventing P—B 5. Black is virtually a piece to the good, but just how this advantage is to be made to tell is not yet clear. Before Tarrasch can undertake decisive action, he must create more weaknesses in the hostile camp.

29. R—K 1	B—R 5 !
30. P—Kt 3	

Weakening his position ; but after 30. R—Q 1, R—Kt 3 (threatening ...R—Kt 3), P—Kt 3 would have to be played in any event.

30.	B—K 2
31. B—B 2	B—Q 3
32. R—B 1	K—R 2 !

Tarrasch was strongly tempted to play 32. ...P—Kt 4, but renounced it because of the following variation : 33. B—K 3, P×P ; 34. B×P, B×B ; 35. Q×B, R×B ; 36. Q×R P !, R×R ; 37. Q—Kt 6 ch, K—B 1 ; 38. Q—B 6 ch, K—K 1 ; 39. Q—K 6 ch, K—Q 1 ; 40. Q—Q 6 ch, K—B 1 ; 41. Q—B 6 ch, K—Kt 1 ; 42. Q—Kt 6 ch, K—R 1 ; 43. Q—B 6 ch, K—R 2 ; 44. Q—B 7 ch, K—R 3 ; 45. Q—B 6 ch, K—R 4 ; 46. Q—B 5 ch, K—R 5 ; 47. Q—R 7 ch, K—Kt 5 ; 48. Q—B 5 ch and strangely enough Black cannot evade the perpetual check !

33. R—K 1	R—Kt 3
34. R—B 1	B—R 6
35. R—K 1	Q—Kt 7

The pressure now mounts steadily.

36. Q—K 2	R—Kt 5

Threatening to reduce White to helplessness by playing ...R—R 5, ...B—Q 3 and ...R—R 8.

Tarrasch considered the sacrifice of the Queen here, but discarded it because after 36. ...Q×B ? ! ; 38. R×Q, R×R ; 38. P—Kt 4, R—Q B 8 ; 39. Q—R 6, B—Q Kt 7 ; 40. P×P (threatening perpetual check), B×K B P ; 41. Q—Q 6, B—K 5 ; 42. P—B 5 !, B×K B P ; 43. Q×P the position is still quite unclear.

37. R—Kt 1

Possibly with some hope of getting an attack with P—Kt 4.

37.	R—Kt 3
38. R—K 1	Q—Kt 4 !

Confronting White with a difficult choice. If 39. B—R 2, Q× Q ; 40. R×Q, R—Kt 7 ; 41. B— Kt 3, R×B ; 42. P×R, P—B 7 and wins. If 39. Q—Q 1, Q—B 5 followed by ...B—Q 3—B 2, ... R—Kt 5 and ...B—Kt 3, winning the Q P.

39. Q—R 5

Trying for counterattack, for instance 39. ...B—Q 3 ; 40. B— R 2 !, B×Q B P ; 41. Q—B 7, B— K 5 ; 42. R×B, B P×R ; 43. B×P and White has at least a draw (Tarrasch).

39. ......   Q×B !

But now the sacrifice is sound, and it forces the win in pretty style.

40. R×Q   R×R
41. P—Kt 4 .

If 41. B—Kt 1, R—Q B 8 winning easily.

41. ......   B—B 8 ! !

White resigns. The following elegant possibilities are indicated by Tarrasch :
I.   42. K—Kt 1,   B—K 6 ch ; 43. K—R 2, B×P ch ;   44. B— Kt 3, R—R 8 mate.

II.   42. B—K 1, B×P ch ; 43. K—Kt 1, B—Kt 6 forcing mate or winning the Queen.
III. 42. K—Kt 3, P—Kt 3 ; 43. Q—R 4, B×P ch ; 44. K×B, P— Kt 4 ch etc.

67. SAN SEBASTIAN, 1912

SICILIAN DEFENCE

This game is chiefly notable for the remarkably stubborn attitude of both players—Tarrasch concentrates on the enemy's weaknesses for many moves, and Marshall defends a lost cause with his customary fighting spirit. This has frequently broken the will of lesser masters, but it fails against Tarrasch.

| *White* | *Black* |
| F. J. Marshall | Dr. S. Tarrasch |

1. P—K 4   P—Q B 4
2. P—Q Kt 4

Marshall always thought well of openings which involved a Pawn sacrifice, and the Wing Gambit was no exception.

2. ......   P×P
3. P—Q R 3   P—K 3

This leads to a cramped game ; ...P—Q 4 is the move preferred.

4. P×P   B×P
5. P—Q B 3   B—K 2
6. P—Q 4   P—Q 3

...P—Q 4 looks more natural; but after 7. P—K 5 Black would have difficulties in developing his King's side.

7. Kt—B 3   Kt—Q B 3
8. B—K 3   P—Q Kt 3

White threatened to win the
Q R P by P—Q 5.

9. B—Q Kt 5   B—Q 2
10. P—Q 5   P×P
11. P×P   Kt—R 4

Ordinarily a Knight is very
poorly posted here, but the pressure
on White's Q B 4 offers some compensation. White's Q B P is already a target for future attack.

12. Kt—R 3   Kt—B 3
13. O—O   O—O
14. R—K 1   R—K 1
15. B—Q 3   Kt—Kt 5

Tarrasch feels uncomfortable in
his cramped position and therefore
decides to give up the extra Pawn,
achieving freedom in the process.

16. B—K B 4   B—K B 3 !
17. Q—B 2   Q—B 2 !
18. B×P ch   K—R 1
19. B—B 5   Kt—K 4 !
20. B×Kt

Kt×Kt would lose a Pawn without compensation.

20. ......   P×B
21. Q R—Q 1   Q R—B 1

The situation has cleared, and we
can now appraise the results of
Black's Pawn sacrifice. He has
freed his game and has strong pressure on the Q B file.

22. B×B   Q×B
23. P—B 4   Kt—Kt 2 !
24. R—K 3   Kt—Q 3

An ideal situation for the Knight ;

it blockades White's passed Pawn
and simultaneously attacks White's
Q B P.

25. Q R—K 1   P—K 5
26. Kt—Q 2

Apparently the K P is lost, but
Tarrasch has calculated well.

26. ......   B—Q 5 !
27. R—R 3 ch

27. R(K 3)—K 2, P—B 4 is even
more favourable for Black.

27. ......   K—Kt 1
28. Kt—Kt 3

If 28. Kt×P ?, Q—B 4 ! wins a
piece.

28. ......   B—K 4
29. P—B 3

If 29. Kt—Q 2, P—B 4 and
Black continues to apply the pressure on the Queen's side.

29. ......   Q—R 5
30. P—B 4

Desperation.   Tarrasch could
now simply capture the Pawn, but
he prefers to steer directly for an
advantageous ending.

30. ......   B—B 3
31. Kt—Q 2   Q×Q
32. Kt×Q   P—Q Kt 4 !

This move, which has been in the
air for some time, gives Black a winning passed Pawn.

33. R(R 3)—K 3   P×P
34. Kt×K P   Kt×Kt
35. R×Kt   R×R
36. R×R   P—B 6

This far-advanced Pawn will eventually cost White his Knight.

37. P—Kt 4 P—Kt 3

Black naturally does not allow his Bishop to be driven off the diagonal.

38. P—Kt 5 B—Kt 2
39. R—R 4

The only hope—and a faint one at that. If, instead, R—K 1—Q 1, Black plays his King to Q 3 and wins.

39. ...... R—B 4
40. R×P R×P
41. R—R 8 ch B—B 1
42. Kt—K 3

Giving up the Knight, for after 42. R—R 1, R—Q 7 ; 43. R—Q B 1, B—B 4 ch ! ; 44. K—R 1, B—Q 3 ; 45. Kt—K 1, B×P ; 46. R×P, R—Q 8 ; 47. R—B 8 ch, K—Kt 2 ; 48. R—K 8, B—Q 7 the end would be in sight.

42. ...... P—B 7
43. Kt×P

Not 43. R—R 1 ? ?, B—B 4 etc.

43. ...... R—Q 8 ch
44. K—B 2 R—Q 7 ch
45. K—Kt 3 R×Kt
46. P—R 4 K—Kt 2

Despite White's material disadvantage, the ending is not easy for Black to win. White's attempt to exchange with P—R 5 must be stopped, and a method for confiscating the K B P must be found. Tarrasch's manœuvres in the following play are highly instructive.

47. R—Q 8 R—B 5

In order to prevent P—R 5 after the eventual K—Kt 4.

48. R—Q 7 B—R 6
49. R—Q 3 B—Kt 5
50. K—B 3 B—K 8

...R—B 6 ? would allow White to draw after the exchange of Rooks.

51. K—Kt 4 B—R 4
52. R—Q 1 B—B 2
53. R—K B 1 K—B 1

Now that White's Rook is pinned to the defence of the B P, Black's King is free to advance.

54. R—B 3 R—K 5
55. R—B 1 K—K 2
56. R—B 3 K—K 3
57. R—B 1 B—Kt 1
58. R—B 3 B—Q 3
59. R—B 1 B—B 2
60. R—B 2 R—K 8

Decisive : He threatens ...R—Kt 8 ch followed by ...K—B 4. White cannot play 61. R—K Kt 2 because of 61. ...R—K B 8 while if 61. P—B 5 ch ?, P×P ch ; 62. R×P ?, R—Kt 8 ch wins.

61. R—B 2	B—Q 3
62. R—K Kt 2	R—K B 8
63. R—K 2 ch	K—Q 4
64. R—Q 2 ch	K—B 4
65. R—B 2 ch	K—Kt 4
66. K—R 3	R—B 6 ch

Now White's resignation is in order.

67. K—Kt 2	R×P
68. K—R 3	R—B 6 ch
69. K—Kt 2	R—Kt 6 ch
70. K—B 2	R—K R 6
71. R—Kt 2 ch	K—B 3
72. R—B 2 ch	B—B 4 ch
73. K—Kt 2	R×P

And wins. Marshall played on for another 17 moves, but the reader cannot be expected to emulate his interest in this position.

68. BRESLAU, 1912

RUY LOPEZ

A BITTERLY fought game in which Tarrasch scores a well-earned victory. The struggle is arduous and interesting in all its phases.

White	Black
R. TEICHMANN	DR. S. TARRASCH
1. P—K 4	P—K 4
2. Kt—K B 3	Kt—Q B 3
3. B—Kt 5	P—Q R 3
4. B—R 4	Kt—B 3
5. O—O	Kt×P
6. P—Q 4	P—Q Kt 4
7. B—Kt 3	P—Q 4
8. P×P	B—K 3
9. P—B 3	B—K 2
10. R—K 1	Kt—B 4

At the time this game was played, the Breslau Variation (10. ...O—

O ; 11. Kt—Q 4, Kt×K P !? ; 12. P—B 3, B—Q 3) had not yet been invented, or at any rate had not yet become public property. Tarrasch was therefore reluctant to play the normal move 10. ...O—O because of the expected reply 11. Kt—Q 4.

11. B—B 2	B—Kt 5

Anticipating White's next move, he creates a retreat at K 3 for the K Kt.

12. P—Kt 4	

Rather questionable because of the resulting weakness of the Queen's side. Better is 12. Q Kt—Q 2 and, if 12. ...P—Q 5 ; 13. Kt—Kt 3 with a good game.

12.	Kt—K 3
13. P—Q R 4	R—Q Kt 1
14. P×P	P×P
15. R—R 6	

By means of the foregoing moves, Teichmann has opened up the Q R file and laid the basis for pressure on Black's Q Kt P and Q P. The game has already reached a critical stage and Tarrasch must play with great care to hold the position together.

The immediate 15. B—Kt 3 would have been answered by ... P—Q 5.

15.	Q—Q 2
16. P—R 3	B—R 4
17. B—Kt 3	R—Q 1 !

But not 17. ...P—Q 5 ? because of the continuation pointed out in the Tournament Book : 18. B× Kt, Q×B ; 19. R×Kt !, Q×R ; 20. Kt×P !, Q—K Kt 3 (if 20. ...

B×Q ; 21. Kt×Q coming out with two pieces for the Rook) ; 21. P—Kt 4, Q×Kt ; 22. P×B with a winning attack.

18. Kt—R 3

If 18. B×P, Kt×Kt P !

18. ......   O—O

White threatened 19. Kt×P, Kt×Kt P ? ; 20. P×Kt, Q×Kt ; 21. B—R 4.

19. Kt—B 2

Threatening P—Kt 4 followed by B—K 3 with a very powerful game.

19. ......   Kt—Kt 1 !
20. R—R 7   Q—B 3 !

In this highly critical situation Tarrasch hits on the logical counterchance.

21. Q—Q 3

The Tournament Book castigates this move and recommends 21. Q Kt—Q 4 for, if 21. ...Q×P ; 22. P—Kt 4, B—Kt 3 ; 23. R—K 3, Q×P ; 24. B—R 3, Q×B ; 25. R×Q, B×R ; 26. Kt×P with a winning game.

However, Tarrasch would have answered 21. Q Kt—Q 4 with ... Q—Kt 3 ; 22. R—R 5, Kt×Kt ; 23. Q×Kt, P—Q B 4 ! with considerable advantage.

21. ......   B—Kt 3
22. Q—K 3

Q—Q 2 would have been somewhat better, although not wholly satisfactory.

22. ......   B×Kt
23. B×B   P—Q 5 !

With this long-awaited move, Tarrasch seizes the initiative.

24. Q—Q 3   P—Kt 3
25. B—Kt 2

If 25. P×P, B×P ; 26. R—Q 1, B—B 4 ; 27. R—R 5, B×P and Black has a won game.

25. ......   P×P
26. Q×P   Q×Q
27. B×Q   Kt—-B 3

Black now wins a Pawn.

28. R—Kt 7   B×P !
29. B×B   Kt×B
30. B—Kt 3   R—Kt 1 !
31. R×R   R×R

Although Black has two united passed Pawns, Tarrasch must continue to play well, as Teichmann puts up a courageous struggle all the way.

32. B×Kt   P×B
33. R—Q B 1

Or 33. Kt—Q 4, P—B 4 ! ; 34. R—Kt 1 (if 34. Kt×K P, Kt—Q 6 and the passed Pawns win easily),

Kt—Q 6 ; 35. R×P, R×R ; 36.
Kt×R, Kt×K P and wins.

| 33. ...... | Kt—Q 4 |
| 34. Kt—Q 4 | |

White strives to prevent the advance of the deadly Pawns.

34.	P—Kt 5
35. Kt—Kt 3	Kt—B 6
36. R—R 1	

If 36. K—B 1, R—R 1 ; 37. K—
K 1, R—R 6 ; 38. Kt—B 5, P—
Kt 6 ; 39. R×Kt, P—Kt 7 ; 40.
R—Q Kt 3, R—R 8 ch and wins.

| 36. ...... | P—B 4 ! |

Wins a piece.

37. Kt×P	P—Kt 6
38. Kt×Kt P	R×Kt
39. R—R 6	Kt—K 7 ch
40. K—R 2	Kt—B 5

Despite the win of the piece, the ending is still difficult. But Tarrasch continues to play it admirably.

41. P—Kt 3	Kt—Q 6
42. P—B 4	R—Kt 7 ch
43. K—Kt 1	Kt—B 4
44. R—B 6	Kt—K 5
45. R—B 8 ch	K—B 2

45. ...K—Kt 2 ;   46. R—B 7
ch, K—R 3 ? is not good because of
47. P—Kt 4, threatening P—Kt 5
ch etc.

| 46. R—B 7 ch | K—B 1 ! |
| 47. P—Kt 4 | |

If 47. R×P, Kt×P followed by
...Kt—R 4 wins.

47.	Kt—Kt 6
48. R—B 8 ch	K—K 2
49. R—B 7 ch	K—K 1
50. R×P	Kt—K 7 ch
51. K—B 2	Kt×P ch
52. K—B 3	

If 52. K—Kt 3, Kt—Q 6 wins.

| 52. ...... | Kt×P ! |

A neat concluding touch.   If 53.
R×Kt, R—Kt 6 ch ; 54. K—Kt 2,
R×R ; 55. K×R, P—Kt 4 ; 56.
K—Kt 3, K—Q 2 ; 57. K—B 3,
K—B 3 ;   58. K—K 4, K—B 4,
winning the K P in due course.

| 53. R—R 6 | R—Kt 6 ch |
| 54. K—K 4 | R—Kt 5 ch |

White resigns, for if 55. K—K 3,
Kt—B 5 with an easy win. A
hard-fought battle.

69. BRESLAU, 1912

FRENCH DEFENCE

ALTHOUGH Duras achieved an enviable degree of success in international play, he never bothered to make a careful study of the openings. The result was that he often indulged in adventurous experiments which turned out poorly. In the present encounter, Tarrasch incisively exploits his opponent's unsatisfactory handling of the opening and the early middle game.

| *White* | *Black* |
| DR. S. TARRASCH | O. DURAS |

1. P—K 4	P—K 3
2. P—Q 4	P—Q 4
3. Kt—Q B 3	B—Kt 5

A defence which was later popularised by Nimzovich in the '20s. White's best chance of retaining the initiative is 4. P—K 5.

4. P×P	P×P
5. B—Q 3	Kt—K B 3

...Kt—K 2 is better. It enables Black to answer B—Kt 5 with ... P—K B 3, and also makes ...B— K B 4 possible. The text on the other hand exposes Black to an uncomfortable pin.

6. B—Kt 5	P—K R 3
7. B—R 4	P—B 4

A violent attempt to gain the initiative which leaves Black with a positionally inferior game.

8. P×P !	O—O

Surprisingly tame for Duras. The continuation indicated was 8. ...P—Q 5 ; 9. P—Q R 3, B— R 4 ; 10. P—Q Kt 4, P×Kt ; 11. P×B, Q×P ; 12. B×Kt, P×B ; 13. Q—B 3, Kt—Q 2 ; 14. P—B 6 with interesting complications.

9. Kt—K 2	B×P

...P—Q 5 ? would be answered by Kt×P.

10. O—O	B—K 3
11. Q—Q 2	Kt—B 3
12. Q R—Q 1	K—R 1

If instead 12. ...P—Q 5 ; 13. B×Kt, Q×B ; 14. Kt—K 4, Q— K 2 ; 15. Kt×B followed by pressure on the Q P. With the text Duras intends a risky freeing manœuvre.

13. K—R 1 !	P—K Kt 4 ?!

As White's last move prepared for P—B 4—5, Duras feels that the text, despite its weakening character, is unavoidable.

14. B—Kt 3

The Tournament Book shows that sacrificing the Bishop would lead to no more than a draw : 14. B×P, P×B ; 15. Q×P, Kt— K Kt 5 ; 16. Q—R 5 ch, K—Kt 2 ; 17. Q—R 7 ch, K—B 3 ; 18. Q— R 4 ch, K—K 4 ; 19. Q—Kt 3 ch, K—B 3 ; 20. Q—R 4 ch etc.

14.	Kt—K R 4

Apparently very strong, the idea being to answer 15. P—B 4 advantageously with ...B—K Kt 5 followed by ...R—K 1 and B—K 6.

15. B—Kt 5 !	P—R 3

This loses a Pawn, but there was no wholly satisfactory continuation. If 15. ...Kt—K 2 ; 16. B—K 5 ch, P—B 3 ; 17. B—Q 4 and Black's game is full of ugly weaknesses. If 15. ...Kt—B 3 ; 16. P—B 4 with a strong game, or if 15. ...Kt×B ch ; 16. B P×Kt !

16. B×Kt	P×B

17. Kt×P !

A clever move which Black has overlooked.

17.	P×Kt

...Q×Kt ? would be even worse.

18. Q—B 3 ch	K—Kt 1
19. Q×B	R—B 1
20. Q—R 3	R×P
21. Kt—Q 4	R—B 1
22. Q×P	Q—B 3

...R—R 1 would be answered by Kt×B. The position is now cleared ; White is a Pawn ahead and has two united passed Pawns. The win, which is only a question of time, is engineered by Tarrasch in patient and instructive fashion.

23. Q—K 2	Q—Kt 3
24. K R—K 1	K R—K 1
25. Q—B 3	Kt—B 3

Duras avoids :..Kt×B ch, because he has some hopes of obtaining an ending with Bishops on opposite colours.

26. Q—Q 3	Q×Q

Black was doubtless reluctant to exchange Queens, but 26. ...Q—Kt 2 ; 27. B—K 5 or 26. ...Q—R 4 ; 27. P—B 3 (leaving his Queen badly out of play) would have been even more unpleasant.

27. R×Q	B—Q 2
28. R×R ch	R×R
29. P—B 3	P—R 4
30. K—Kt 1	R—Q B 1
31. R—Q 1	

Note that Tarrasch is in no great hurry to begin the advance of the Queen's side Pawns. In such endings, it is more important to place one's pieces in the most favourable positions.

31.	P—R 5
32. B—B 2	R—R 1
33. R—R 1	Kt—R 4
34. B—K 3	P—B 3
35. P—Q Kt 3	

Now the Pawns are ready to advance.

35.	Kt—Kt 2
36. P—R 4	Kt—B 4
37. K—B 2 !	

Permitting Duras to exchange Knights, as he is satisfied that the ending can be won easily despite the Bishops on opposite colours.

37.	Kt×Kt
38. B×Kt	K—B 2
39. P—R 5	B—Kt 4
40. P—Q Kt 4	B—B 5
41. B—B 5	P—B 4

Now White's King gets a beautifully centralised post at Q 4 ; however, if 41. ...R—K 1 ; 42. P—R 6, B—Kt 4 ; 43. P—R 7, B—B 3 ; 44. R—R 6, B—R 1 ; 45. R—Kt 6 followed by R—Kt 8.

42. K—K 3	K—K 3
43. K—Q 4	K—Q 2
44. R—K 1	R—K Kt 1

If 44. ...R—K 1 ; 45. R×R, R×R ; 46. K—K 5 and wins.

45. R—K 7 ch	K—B 3
46. R—K 6 ch	K—B 2

Or 46. ...K—Kt 2 ; 47. P—R 6 ch etc.

47. P—R 6	P—Kt 5
48. R—K 7 ch	K—Kt 1

If 48. ...K—B 3 ; 49. R—Q
Kt 7 threatening P—Kt 5 ch. The
Pawns are irresistible.

49. P—Kt 5 !   P—R 6

White announced mate in three :
50. B—Q 6 ch, K—R 1 ; 51. P—
Kt 6, or 50. ....K—B 1 ; 51. P—
R 7 etc.

70. BRESLAU, 1912

FRENCH DEFENCE

Tarrasch's superior positional insight carries the day here. The
original peregrinations of his pieces
foreshadow the arrival of the hyper-
modern style.

White	*Black*
Dr. S. Tarrasch	M. Lowtzky

1.	P—K 4	P—K 3
2.	P—Q 4	P—Q 4
3.	Kt—Q B 3	Kt—K B 3
4.	B—Kt 5	B—K 2
5.	P—K 5	K Kt—Q 2
6.	B × B	

In recent years 6. P—K R 4 has
become more and more popular.

6.	......	Q × B
7.	Q—Q 2	O—O
8.	P—B 4	P—Q R 3

Too slow. The modern con-
tinuation is 8. ...P—Q B 4 ! ; 9.
Kt—B 3, Kt—Q B 3 ; 10. P—K
Kt 3, P—B 3 ; 11. P × K B P, Kt ×
B P ! ; 12. B—Kt 2, P × P ; 13.
K Kt × P, P—K 4 ! (Black does not
care to submit to the weak Pawn
configuration K 3 and Q 4, and
therefore frees himself at the cost of
a Pawn) ; 14. Kt × P, K Kt × Kt ;

15. B × Kt ch, K—R 1 ; 16. Kt—
K 2, B—Kt 5 ; 17. O—O—O,
Q R—Q 1 ; 18. P—B 4, Kt—Kt 5 ;
19. P—Q R 3, Kt × B (A. Steiner—
Stahlberg, Ujpest, 1934) with ad-
vantage to Black.

9.	Kt—B 3	P—Q B 4
10.	P—K Kt 3	Kt—Q B 3
11.	B—Kt 2	P—Q Kt 4

If instead 11. ...P—B 3 ; 12.
K P × P, Kt × B P ; 13. O—O and
since Black is a tempo short, he cannot adopt the freeing variation
shown in the previous note.

He would therefore be left with
a weak Pawn formation in the
centre ; hence he prefers to strive
for counterplay on the Queen's side.

12.	O—O	P × P

...P—B 5 would be bad on two
counts : (*a*) *Black has no "targets"
on the Queen's side*, so that a general
advance there could not force the
opening of a file ; (*b*) *it would
stabilise the centre*, permitting White
to proceed with P—K Kt 4 and
P—B 5.

13.	Kt—K 2 !	

This gives White a better game
than he would obtain after 13.
K Kt × P, Q—B 4 ; 14. Kt—K 2
etc.

13.	......	Kt—Kt 3

Practically forcing the following
move, which leaves White with a
backward Pawn on the open Q B
file. However, this is a difficulty
which can be endured without too
much trouble.

14.	P—Kt 3	B—Q 2
15.	Q Kt × P	

White has two positional advantages : his pieces cannot be driven off Q 4, and Black's Bishop has virtually no scope.

15. ......   Q—B 4
16. R—B 2 !

A many-sided move. Most players would have adopted the mechanical rejoinder K—R 1, but not so Tarrasch : the text relieves the pin, guards the Q B P (see the note to White's 13th move) and makes room for the Bishop at K B 1.

16. ......   Q R—B 1

As will later be apparent, ... K R—B 1 is preferable.

17. Kt×Kt   R×Kt
18. Q—Q 4 !

White feels equally comfortable in a middle game or in an ending, for in either, his positional advantages will prove valuable.

18. ......   K R—B 1

...R—R 1 would have been better, here or next move.

19. B—B 1 !   Kt—R 1
20. P—Q R 4 !   P×P ?

This soon leads to a lost game. ...Kt—B 2 was relatively better. Note that because of his previous omissions, Black cannot play 20. ...P—Kt 5 (21. Q×Q, R×Q ; 22. B×P).

21. R×P

Black may have expected 21. Q×Q, R×Q ; 22. B×P, R(B 1)—B 2 ; 23. P×P, R—R 2 recovering the Pawn.

21. ......   P—Q R 4
22. Q—R 1 !

The winning move. The Q R P must fall, but Black apparently has strong counterplay.

22. ......   Q—Kt 3

If 22. ...Q—K 6 White continues 23. B—Q 3 !, R×P ; 24. B×R, R×B ; 25. Q—Q 4, Q×R ch ; 26. Q×Q, R×Q ; 27. R×P and wins (Tarrasch points out that if in this variation 23. Kt—Q 4 Black can save himself with 27. ... R×B ch !).

23. Kt—Q 4   R×P

The sacrifice of the exchange is virtually compulsory ; if 24. ... R—B 4 ; 25. P—Q Kt 4, B×R ; 26. P×R, Q—Kt 5 ; 27. P—B 3 winning the Bishop !

24. Kt×R   R×Kt

Not 24. ...B×R ? ; 25. Q×B and Black cannot capture the Knight.

25. R—Q 4	R×R
26. K×R	Kt—B 2
27. Q—B 3	

White wants to unpin his Rook, after which his material advantage will tell effectively.

| 27. ...... | P—Kt 3 |

A loophole is needed, but ...P—R 3 was a bit better.

| 28. Q—K 3 | B—Kt 4 |

Exchanges only help the stronger side, but there was no doubt about the outcome in any event.

29. R—Q 1	Q—Kt 2
30. Q—B 5	B×B
31. R×B	Kt—Kt 4
32. R—Q R 1	Q—R 3

Or 32. ...P—Q 5 ; 33. R×P, Kt—B 6 ; 34. Q—R 3 and wins.

33. R—R 4

Stronger than 33. P—Q Kt 4 ?, P—R 5 etc.

| 33. ...... | P—Q 5 |
| 34. R—B 4 ! | |

34. P—Q Kt 4 ? would have been a mistake because of 34. ...Kt—B 6.

| 34. ...... | K—Kt 2 |

Otherwise Q—Q B 8 ch wins easily.

| 35. Q—B 6 ! | Q—R 2 |

As ...Q×Q would be tantamount to resignation, Black prefers to play on with a Rook down ! Naturally a pointless proceeding.

36. Q×Kt	P—Q 6 ch
37. Q—B 5	Q—Kt 2
38. R—Q 4	Q×P
39. R—Q 8	Q—Kt 7 ch

"Hoping" for 40. K—B 3 ? ?, Q—K 7 mate.

| 40. K—Kt 1 | P—Kt 4 |

If 40. ...K—R 3 ; 41. P—Kt 4 wins.

41. Q—B 8 ch	K—Kt 3
42. Q—Kt 8 ch	K—B 4
43. Q×B P ch	K—Kt 5
44. Q×P ch	K—B 6
45. Q—Q 5 ch	K—Kt 5
46. Q—Q 7 ch	K—B 6
47. Q×P ch	K—Kt 5
48. Q—Q 1 ch	K—B 4
49. Q—Q 7 ch	K—K 5
50. Q—Q 3 mate	

71. ST. PETERSBURG, 1914

RUY LOPEZ

THE inclusion of two celebrated masters of the Victorian period—Blackburne and Gunsberg—gave this great tournament a certain historical flavour. Unfortunately the older players, being long past their prime, could not live up to their reputations. Nevertheless the encounter between distinguished players who had met for the first time more than a quarter of a century earlier, has a sentimental value which lends the following game attractive qualities.

White	Black
Dr. S.	J. H
Tarrasch	Blackburne

1. P—K 4	P—K 4
2. Kt—K B 3	Kt—Q B 3
3. B—Kt 5	Kt—Q 5

Blackburne shared his country-man Bird's predilection for un-orthodox lines of play.

4. Kt×Kt	P×Kt
5. P—Q 3	P—K Kt 3
6. P—Q B 3	

Tarrasch is anxious to remove the Q P at once because of its hamper-ing effect on White's development.

6.	B—Kt 2
7. O—O	Kt—K 2
8. P×P	B×P

It is clear that Black will have to lose a tempo later on retreating this Bishop ; but if he had played ... P×P, the exchange would have strengthened White's centre.

| 9. Kt—B 3 | P—Q B 3 |
| 10. B—Q B 4 | P—Q 3 |

Against 10. ...P—Q 4 Tarrasch contemplated 11. P×P, P×P ; 12. Q—R 4 ch !, B—Q 2 ; 13. B—Q Kt 5, B—Kt 2 ; 14. B—Kt 5 with a fine game.

| 11. B—K 3 ! | B—Kt 2 |

...B×B would give White an open K B file and seriously weaken Black's black squares.

| 12. Q—B 3 | O—O |
| 13. B—Kt 3 | |

White wants to play Q—Kt 3, which cannot be done at once be-cause of the reply ...P—Q 4 win-ning a piece.

| 13. ...... | K—R 1 |
| 14. Q—Kt 3 | B—K 3 |

Black had intended 14. ...P—K B 4, but the reply 15. B—Kt 5 would have been troublesome.

| 15. B×B | P×B |
| 16. Q—R 3 | P—K 4 |

On 16. ...Q—Q 2 or ...P—Q 4 White has advantageous replies in 17. B—Kt 5 and 17. B—R 6.

| 17. B—Kt 5 | B—B 3 |

Not caring for the threatened Q—K 6.

| 18. B—R 6 | B—Kt 2 |
| 19. B×B ch | K×B |

Tarrasch's manœuvres have re-sulted in a weakening of the black squares, which he will turn to his advantage later on.

| 20. Q R—Q 1 | P—B 4 |

Black cannot permit the opening of the centre by P—Q 4. But now he has a marked weakness on the white squares as well.

| 21. Kt—K 2 | Kt—B 3 |
| 22. P—B 4 | Q—K 2 |

After this the advance of the B P proves formidable. However, 22. ...P×P ; 23. R×P !, R×R (else White doubles Rooks on the file) ; 24. Kt×R, Kt—Q 5 ; 25. Kt—K 6 ch, Kt×Kt ; 26. Q×Kt, threatening 27. R—K B 1, gives White a decisive advantage. If 26.

...Q—B 2 ; 27. P—Q 4 ! with much the better game.

23. P—B 5 !   Kt—Q 5
24. Kt—B 3   Q—Kt 4

Or 24. ...P×P ; 25. P×P, Q—Kt 4 ; 26. Kt—K 4, Q—Q 1 ; 27. P—B 6 ch with a winning attack.

25. P×P   P×P

After 25. ...Q×P ; 26. Q—Q 7 ch would still win a Pawn.

26. Q—Q 7 ch   K—R 3
27. Q×Q P   Q R—Q 1

Blackburne must have relied on 27. ...Q—K 6 ch ; 28. K—R 1, R×R ch ; 29. R×R, Q×Q P ; but in that event 30. R—B 3 ! (Tarrasch) forces Black's resignation.

28. Q×R ch

Quite right. White's Rooks will be so strong that Black will be glad to remove them at the earliest opportunity.

28. ......   R×Q
29. R×R   K—Kt 2
30. R—B 2

Not 30. Q R—K B 1, Kt—B 4.

30. ......   Q—R 4
31. Q R—K B 1   P—K Kt 4
32. P—K R 3

32. Kt—Q 5 ? would be premature because of ...Kt—K 7 ch ; 33. K—R 1, Kt—Kt 6 ch.

32. ......   Kt—K 3

Black wants to block the K B file with ...Kt—B 5.

33. R—B 7 ch

Forcing a won ending, for if 33. ...K—Kt 1 ; 34. Kt—Q 5 wins, while if 33. ...K—R 1 ; 34. R (B 1)—B 6 is decisive.

33. ......   Q×R
34. R×Q ch   K×R
35. Kt—Q 5

The endgame which follows is handled by Tarrasch in his usual instructive manner. Eventually he will make the win clear by playing P—K Kt 3 and P—K R 4, but first he must bring his King to the centre and utilise the Knight to exploit the weaknesses in Black's camp.

35. ......   P—Kt 4
36. K—B 2   Kt—Q 5
37. Kt—K 3   K—K 3
38. K—K 1

White wishes to dislodge Black's Knight from its strong post.

38. ......   P—R 4

Blackburne advances the Queen's side Pawns in the hope of exchanging the Pawns on that wing.

39. K—Q 2	P—R 5
40. Kt—B 2	Kt—B 3
41. Kt—K 1 !	

Tarrasch wants to post his Knight at K B 3, where it will function at maximum power : attacking the K Kt P and K P and keeping Black's Knight out of Q 4.

41.	Kt—Q 5
42. K—K 3 !	

After 42. Kt—B 3 ?, Kt×Kt ; 43. P×Kt the King and Pawn ending would be a draw.

42.	K—B 3
43. Kt—B 3	Kt—K 3
44. P—K Kt 3	

Preventing ...Kt—B 5.

44.	Kt—B 1
45. Kt—Kt 1 !	

Heading for Q B 3. The advanced position of Black's Queen's side Pawn hastens his downfall.

45.	Kt—Q 2
46. Kt—K 2	P—Q Kt 5

Otherwise Kt—B 3 wins a Pawn. But now the Knight is headed for a fine post at Q B 4.

47. Kt—Kt 1 !	Kt—Kt 3
48. Kt—B 3	P—B 5

Blackburne realises that after 48. ...Kt—Q 2 ; 49. Kt—Q 2, K—Kt 3 ; 50. Kt—B 4, K—R 3 ; 51. K—B 3, K—R 4 ; 52. P—Kt 4 ch, K—R 3 (not 52. ...K—R 5 ? ? ; 53. K—Kt 2 followed by Kt—Q 2

—B 3 mate !) ; 53. K—Kt 3, Kt—Kt 3 ; 54. P—R 4, K—B 3 ; 55. P×P ch, K×P ; 56. Kt—Q 2 followed by Kt—B 3 ch, White's gradual but steady penetration would prove irresistible.

49. P—Q 4 !	P—B 6

If 49. ...P×P ch ; 50. K×P wins easily.

50. P×P ch	K—Kt 3
51. P×P	P—Kt 6
52. P×P	P×P

Or 52. ...P—R 6 ; 53. Kt—Q 4, P—R 7 ; 54. Kt—B 2 etc.

53. Kt—Q 2	P—Kt 7
54. K—Q 3	

Black threatened ...Kt—B 5 ch. The rest is easy.

54.	K—B 2
55. K—B 2	K—K 3
56. K×P	K×P
57. K—B 2	Kt—Q 2
58. K—Q 3	Kt—B 4 ch
59. K—K 3	Kt—K 3
60. Kt—B 3 ch	K—B 3
61. P—K 5 ch	K—B 4

Else K—K 4 wins easily.

62. Kt—Q 4 ch	K×P
63. Kt×Kt	Resigns

A well-played game by Tarrasch. Curiously enough, the K R P was not advanced throughout the whole ending ! The clever handling of White's Knight proved to be the decisive factor.

72. ST. PETERSBURG, 1914

(Second Brilliancy Prize)

QUEEN'S GAMBIT DECLINED

HERE is another of the famous Tarrasch games. He plays throughout with magnificent verve, while his deadly rival Nimzovich ruins his own position with over-subtle moves.

| *White* | *Black* |
| A. NIMZOVICH | DR. S. TARRASCH |

1.	P—Q 4	P—Q 4
2.	Kt—K B 3	P—Q B 4
3.	P—B 4	P—K 3
4.	P—K 3	

Obligatory, according to Tarrasch! The modern masters have rightly discarded this timid move in favour of 4. B P×P, K P×P; 5. Kt—B 3, Kt—Q B 3; 6. P—K Kt 3, Kt—B 3; 7. B—Kt 2 etc.

4.	......	Kt—K B 3
5.	B—Q 3	Kt—B 3
6.	O—O	B—Q 3
7.	P—Q Kt 3	O—O
8.	B—Kt 2	P—Q Kt 3
9.	Q Kt—Q 2	

In order to leave a clear diagonal for the fianchettoed Bishop. But the Q Kt accomplishes nothing throughout the game.

9.	......	B—Kt 2
10.	R—B 1	

More to the point would have been 10. Kt—K 5 and, if 10. ... Q—K 2; 11. P—Q R 3.

10.	......	Q—K 2

Threatening ...B P×P followed by ...B—R 6.

11. B P×P ?

Freeing Black's game at one stroke. B—R 1 was better.

11.	......	K P×P
12.	Kt—R 4	

In order to force the following weakening move.

12.	......	P—Kt 3

As will be seen, the weakening of the long diagonal has little significance.

13. K Kt—B 3   Q R—Q 1

Tarrasch wants to play ...Kt—K 5; however, after 13. ...Kt—K 5; 14. P×P he would be unable to retake with the Pawn because of 15. B×Kt, P×B; 16. Kt×P. Hence the preparatory Rook move.

14. P×P

Continuing with fatal consistency. Nimzovich hopes to develop pressure against the "hanging Pawns".

14.	......	P×P
15.	B—Kt 5	

Threatening 16. B×Kt, B×B; 17. P—Q Kt 4, B—Kt 4; 18. P×P, B×P; 19. R—K 1 followed by Kt—Q 4 with a strong game.

15.	......	Kt—K 5 !

Tarrasch strengthens his position and parries the threat at the same time. If now 16. B×Kt, B×B;

M

17. P—Q Kt 4, B—Kt 4 ; 18. P×
P, Kt×Q B P ; 19. R—K 1, Kt—
Q 6, winning the exchange.

16. B×Kt ?

Continuing his plan with little
suspicion of what is to come.

16. ......   B×B
17. Q—B 2

Nimzovich is still convinced that
he can demonstrate Black's Pawns
to be weak.

17. ......   Kt×Kt !
18. Kt×Kt

Or 18. Q×Kt, P—Q 5 ! ; 19.
P×P, B×Kt ; 20. P×B, Q—R 5
and wins.

18. ......   P—Q 5 !
19. P×P ?

The only chance was 19. P—K 4,
Q—R 5 ; 20. P—Kt 3, Q—R 6
with good attacking chances for
Black but with some defensive possibilities for White. After the
feeble text, Tarrasch triumphs with
a slashing attack reminiscent of a
famous Lasker combination.

19. ......   B×P ch ! !
20. K×B   Q—R 5 ch
21. K—Kt 1   B×P ! !

Nimzovich is being brutally punished for the absence of his pieces
from the King's side !

22. P—B 3

This feeble move is all that he has
left. If instead 22. K×B, Q—
Kt 5 ch ; 23. K—R 1, R—Q 4 ;
24. Q×P, R—R 4 ch ! ; 25. Q×
R, Q×Q ch ; 26. K moves, Q—
Kt 4 ch winning the Knight.

22. ......   K R—K 1 !

Threatening ...R—K 7 with
fatal effect.

23. Kt—K 4

There is nothing else : if 23. Q—
Q 3, Q—Kt 6 wins. If 23. K R—
K 1, R×R ch ; 24. R×R, Q×
R ch ; 25. K×B, Q—K 7 ch ; 26.
K moves, R—Q 4 and wins.

23. ......   Q—R 8 ch
24. K—B 2   B×R
25. P—Q 5

Despair ; if 25. R×B, Q—R 7
ch wins the Queen.

25. ......   P—B 4 !

Stronger than 25. ...Q—Kt 7
ch ; 26. K—K 3, Q×Q ; 27. R×
Q, P—B 4.

26. Q—B 3

Nimzovich has finally carried out
his idea of attack on the long
diagonal ; the only flaw is that the
game is lost !

If instead 26. Kt—B 6 ch, K—B 2 ; 27. Kt×R, R×Kt and mate follows.

| 26. | ...... | Q—Kt 7 ch |
| 27. | K—K 3 | R×Kt ch ! |

One murderous blow after another.

28. P×R   P—B 5 ch

In the heat of the battle, Tarrasch misses 28. ...Q—Kt 6 ch ; 29. K—Q 2, Q—B 7 ch ; 30. K—Q 1, Q—K 7 mate.

29.	K×P	R—B 1 ch
30.	K—K 5	Q—R 7 ch
31.	K—K 6	R—K 1 ch
32.	K—Q 7	

Or 32. K—B 6, Q—R 5 mate.

32. ......   B—Kt 4 mate

A pretty finish to a victory which must have been particularly gratifying to Tarrasch.

73. ST. PETERSBURG, 1914

RUY LOPEZ

THE outstanding feature of this game is the triumph of an idea. Tarrasch forces an ending which is easily won, but he fails to find the quickest winning line and is therefore faced with considerable technical difficulties. He thereupon devises a brilliant winning method which is as logical as it is simple. However, the actual process requires accuracy of the highest order. All these factors combine to produce an exceptionally instructive game.

	White	*Black*
	DR. O. S.	DR. S.
	BERNSTEIN	TARRASCH
1.	P—K 4	P—K 4
2.	Kt—K B 3	Kt—Q B 3
3.	B—Kt 5	P—Q R 3
4.	B—R 4	Kt—B 3
5.	O—O	Kt×P
6.	P—Q 4	P—Q Kt 4
7.	B—Kt 3	P—Q 4
8.	P×P	B—K 3
9.	Q Kt—Q 2	

A departure from the almost obligatory P—B 3.

| 9. | ...... | Kt—B 4 |
| 10. | P—B 3 | B—K 2 |

Tarrasch does not care for ... Kt×B, for after 11. Kt×Kt and 12. B—K 3 White would proceed with the occupation of Q B 5.

11. Q—K 2

11. B—B 2 or R—K 1 would be answered in the same way. White's most promising course is apparently the speculative Pawn sacrifice 11. Kt—Q 4, Kt×P ; 12. P—K B 4 etc.

| 11. | ...... | P—Q 5 ! |
| 12. | B×B | P×B |

...Kt×B ? would not be good because of 13. Q—K 4.

13.	P×P	Kt×Q P
14.	Kt×Kt	Q×Kt
15.	Kt—Kt 3	

White's position is already inferior—if 15. Kt—B 3, Q—Q 6 ! and Black has a number of well-defined advantages : Queen's side majority, the better Bishop, and open files. The text yields pressure against Black's Q R P at the cost of a doubled and isolated Q Kt P.

| 15. ...... | Kt × Kt |
| 16. P × Kt | O—O |

An unfortunate position for White, who cannot develop his Bishop. If 16. Q—K 3, B—B 4 or 16. K—R 1, Q R—Q 1 ; 17. P—B 4, Q—Q 6 maintains Black's advantage.

| 17. R—Q 1 ? | R × P ! |
| 18. B—K 3 | |

He has little choice, for if 18. Q × R ?, Q × R ch ; 19. Q—B 1, B—B 4 ch wins—or 18. R × Q, R × Q and the K P falls, ...B—B 4 being threatened.

18.	R × Q
19. B × Q	P—B 4
20. B—B 3	P—Kt 5
21. K—B 1	

If 21. R—Q 2 ? ?, R—K 5 winning a piece.

| 21. ...... | R—K 5 |

If 21. ...R—B 7 ; 22. R—Q 2 !

| 22. B—K 1 | R × P |

...R—K 6 looks even stronger.

| 23. B—Kt 3 | R—Q 4 |

Tarrasch underestimates the difficulty of the coming ending. ... R—K 6 was preferable.

| 24. R × R | P × R |
| 25. R—Q 1 | P—B 5 ! |

Rising to the occasion. If 25. ...R—Q 1 ; 26. R—R 1, P—Q 5 ; 27. R × P, P—Q 6 ; 28. R—R 1, P—Q 7 ; 29. K—K 2 would involve Black in considerable difficulties.

Likewise, after 25. ...P—Q 5 ; 26. K—K 2, B—B 3 ; 27. K—Q 3, Black is confronted with serious difficulties because his passed Pawn is blockaded.

26. R × P	P × P
27. R—Q 3	P—Q R 4
28. R × P	P—R 5
29. R—K 3	B—B 3

If now 30. B—K 5, R—K 1 wins easily.

| 30. R—K 2 | P—R 6 ? |

Probably because of time pressure, Black misses a quick win by 30. ...R—Q B 1 ! ; 31. B—B 4 (if 31. B—Q 6, P—R 6 ! ; 32. P × P, P—Kt 6 ; 33. R—K 1, P—Kt 7 ; 34. B—B 4, B—B 6 ! ; 35. R—Kt 1, R—B 1, winning the Bishop), R—B 1 ! and wins because of the threat of ...B × P : if 32. B—Q 6 ?, B—K 2 ch ; if 32. K—K 1, B × P ; 33. B—Q 6, B—B 6 ch ; if 32. P—K Kt 3, P—Kt 4 wins ; if 32. R—K B 2, B × P etc.

| 31. P × P | P × P |
| 32. R—R 2 | B—Kt 7 |

Now Black threatens ...R—Q B 1—B 8 ch—Q R 8.

33. B—Q 6

The win now seems difficult, but there are two clear winning methods, one suggested by Nimzovich, and the one actually worked out by Tarrasch.

Nimzovich's method is simpler, and might have unfolded in the following manner : 33. ...K—B 2; 34. K—K 2, K—K 3; 35. B—Kt 4, K—Q 4; 36. K—Q 3, R—R 5; 37. B—B 8, K—B 3; 38. K—B 2, K—Kt 4; 39. K—Kt 3, R—R 1; 40. B—K 7 (if 40. B×P, R×B ch; 41. R×R, B×R; 42. K×B, K—B 5 wins), R—K 1; 41. B—Kt 5 (if 41. B×P, B×B followed by the exchange of Rooks and ...K—B 5), P—R 3; 42. B—Q 2, R—K 7 and wins.

The method selected by Tarrasch is much more laborious, but it has a certain logic behind it : his idea is to eliminate White's Kt P. The result will be that when the Kings are placed in opposition, with White's King on the third rank, Black will be able to play ...R—K B 6 ch, driving White's King back and making possible the decisive entry of his own King.

33.	K—B 2
34. K—K 2	R—R 3
35. B—B 5	R—R 4
36. B—Kt 4	R—R 5
37. B—B 5	K—K 3
38. K—Q 3	K—B 4

...K—Q 4 would have transposed into the alternative (and quicker) winning line.

39. B—B 8	K—Kt 5
40. K—K 3	

If 40. K—B 2, R—B 5; 41. B×R P, B×B; 42. R×B, R—B 7 ch followed by ...R×P and wins.

40.	R—R 3 !

Not 40. ...R—Q B 5; 41. B×R P, R—B 6 ch; 42. K—Q 2 and draws.

41. B—B 5	P—R 4 !
42. K—K 4	P—R 5 !
43. K—K 3	

If 43. K—Q 5, R—R 4 !; 44. K—B 4, R×B ch !; 45. K×R, K—B 5 followed by ...K—K 6—B 7 and wins.

43.	R—R 5
44. B—Q 6	P—R 6
45. P×P ch	

Now Black has obtained the square K B 6 for a Rook check. 45. P—Kt 3 would lead to the same result, and would in fact be even worse, as Black could switch plans and go after the vulnerable R P.

45.	K×P
46. K—B 3	K—R 5
47. B—K 7 ch	K—R 4
48. K—K 3	P—Kt 4
49. B—B 5	K—Kt 3
50. B—Q 6	K—B 4

Black is making steady headway.

51. B—B 5	K—K 3
52. K—B 3	K—B 4 !

Tarrasch recoils in time from a faulty plan with a subtle flaw : 52. ...K—Q 4; 53. B—K 7, K—B 5; 54. B×R P ! !, R×B ch; 55. R×

R, B×R ; 56. P—R 4 ! and Black cannot win ! Or 54. ...B×B ; 55. R—K Kt 2 !, R—R 4 (if 55. ... B—K 2 ; 56. R—Kt 4 ch draws) ; 56. P—R 4 !, P×P ; 57. R—Kt 4 ch and draws (Tarrasch).

53. K—K 3

If 53. K—Kt 2, K—K 5 ; 54. B—K 7, K—Q 6 ; 55. K—B 3, K—B 6 ! (if 55. ...K—B 7 ? ; 56. B×R P !, R×B ; 57. R×R ch, B×R ; 58. P—R 4 ! or 55. ... K—B 5 ? ; 56. B×R P !, B×B ; 57. R—K Kt 2 !, drawing in either case) followed by ...K—Kt 6 and wins.

If 53. K—K 2, K—K 5 ; 54. B—K 7, P—Kt 5 ; 55. K—Q 2, K—Q 4 (not 55. ...K—Q 5 ? ? ; 56. B—B 6 ch) ; 56. K—Q 3, R—K B 5 followed by ...R—B 6 ch with the ideal winning position (Tarrasch).

| 53. ...... | R—K 5 ch |
| 54. K—B 2 | |

If 54. K—B 3, R—B 5 followed by ...R—B 6 ch and the penetration of Black's King to Q Kt 6 is assured. If 54. K—Q 3, R—K R 5 ; 55. B—Q 6, R—R 6 ch ; 56. B—Kt 3, K—Kt 5 followed by ... R×B ch (Tarrasch).

54.	R—Q R 5
55. K—K 3	R—R 5
56. B—Q 6	R—R 6 ch
57. B—Kt 3	B—K 4 !

For if 58. R×P, B×B wins.

| 58. K—B 3 | P—Kt 5 ch ! |

At last achieving his objective, as

White's King must leave the third rank.

59. K—Kt 2

Not 59. K—B 2 ? ?, B×B ch ; 60. P×B, R—R 7 ch.

59.	B—Kt 7
60. K—B 2	K—K 5
61. K—K 2	

Provoking 61. ...R×B ? which would only draw ; 62. P×R, K—Q 5 ; 63. K—Q 2, K—B 5 ; 64. K—K 3, K—Kt 6 ; 65. R×P ch and 66. K—B 4 (Tarrasch).

61.	R—R 3
62. K—Q 2	R—R 1
63. B—B 7	

Or 63. K—B 2, R—K B 1 ; 64. K—Kt 3, R—B 6 ch followed by ...R×B and wins.

| 63. ...... | R—K B 1 |
| 64. B—Kt 3 | R—B 6 |

The winning situation aimed for by Tarrasch in the diagrammed position !

65. B—Kt 8	K—Q 4
66. K—B 2	K—B 5
67. B—Kt 3	R—B 6 ch
68. K—Q 2	K—Kt 6
69. R×B ch	

A last trap : if 69. ...K×R ? ? ; 70. B—K 5 wins.

| 69. ...... | P×R |

White resigns. An absorbing endgame.

74. MANNHEIM, 1914

RUY LOPEZ

AFTER a quiet beginning, there follows a neatly played ending which Tarrasch handles precisely and effectively.

White	*Black*
DR. S. TARRASCH	O. DURAS

1.	P—K 4		P—K 4
2.	Kt—K B 3		Kt—Q B 3
3.	B—Kt 5		K Kt—K 2

The Cozio Defence, one of the old discredited lines of play in this opening.

4.	Kt—B 3		P—K Kt 3

Black would do better to transpose into the Steinitz Defence with 4. ...P—Q 3 ; 5. P—Q 4, B—Q 2.

5.	P—Q 4		P×P
6.	Kt×P		

Too tame. Much stronger is 6 Kt—Q 5 (threatens Kt—B 6 mate !), Kt×Kt (if 6. ...B—Kt 2 ; 7. B—Kt 5 and Black's game is compromised) ; 7. P×Kt regaining the Pawn with considerable advantage.

6.	......		B—Kt 2
7.	B—K 3		O—O
8.	Q—Q 2		P—B 4

Now Black is well on the way to freeing himself.

9.	P×P		Kt×Kt
10.	B×Kt		B×B
11.	Q×B		P—B 3
12.	B—Q 3		

12. P×P !, P×B ; 13. P×P ch, K×P ; 14. Kt×P looks like a more promising course : White has three united passed Pawns, while Black's King is exposed and his Q P is weak.

12.	......		Kt×P
13.	B×Kt		R×B
14.	O—O		P—Q 4
15.	Q R—K 1		B—Q 2

The position is fairly level : Black has the Queen's side majority of Pawns, but his Bishop has little scope.

16.	R—K 2		Q—B 3
17.	Q—Q 2		R—K B 1
18.	P—B 3		R—B 2
19.	Kt—Q 1		R—R 4

Duras overestimates his position. The text is pure loss of time.

20.	Q—K 1		Q—B 5
21.	Q—Kt 3 !		

Forcing a favourable ending, as ...Q—Q R 5 could be answered by Q—Kt 8 ch.

21.	......		Q×Q
22.	P×Q		R(R 4)—B 4
23.	Kt—B 2		R(B 4)—B 3
24.	K R—K 1		P—B 4

Hoping to play ...B—B 3 followed by ...P—Q 5 with good prospects ; Tarrasch's simple but vigorous play scotches this plan.

25.	P—K Kt 4 !		P—K R 3

If 25. ...B—B 3 ; 26. P—Kt 5 followed by Kt—Kt 4 with a strong position. But ...K—Kt 2 was doubtless preferable to the text.

26. R—K 5

One would expect 26. ...B—B 3 in reply, but then comes 27. P—Kt 5 !, R—Q 3 (if 27. ...P×P ; 28. Kt—Kt 4 wins the exchange) ; 28. Kt—Kt 4, winning a Pawn.

26.	R—R 3
27. R×P	R×R P
28. Kt—Q 3	P—B 5

If 28. ...P—Kt 3 ; 29. Kt—K 5, B—K 3 ; 30. R—Q 6 wins.

29. Kt—K 5   B—B 3

Again if 29. ...B—K 3 ; 30. R—Q 6 wins.

30. R—Q 8 ch !

Stronger than 30. Kt×R, K×Kt ! followed by ...R×P and Black's passed Q R P will be ample compensation for the exchange.

30.	R—B 1
31. Kt×B	P×Kt
32. R—Q 6 !	

Tarrasch continues to play very simply and clearly. 32. R×R ch, K×R ; 33. R—K 6 would only draw ; White needs the combined action of both Rooks.

32.	K—B 2
33. R×B P	R×P
34. R—R 1 !	

This is the move that makes the win clear.

34. ......   R—Q R 1

The position is hopeless. If 34. ...R×P ; 35. R×P ch, K—Kt 1 ; 36. R×P ch, K—R 1 ; 37. R×P ch, K—Kt 1 ; 38. R—Q B 6 winning easily. Or 35. ...K—K 1 ; 36. R—B 8 mate. As the game goes, Duras puts up a surprisingly good fight.

35. R(R 1)—R 6 !   R×P

Black resigns himself to the loss of his threatened Pawns.

36. R—B 7 ch	K—B 1
37. R—B 6 ch	K—Kt 1
38. R×P ch	K—R 1
39. R×P ch	K—Kt 1
40. R—Kt 6 ch	

The powerful cooperation of White's Rooks bears out Tarrasch's judgment in evading an exchange at move 32.

40.	K—B 1
41. R—B 6 ch	K—Kt 1
42. R—Q R 6 !	

Tarrasch is unconcerned about the Q B P. He has just one tempo to hold it back, but that tempo is sufficient.

42.	P—B 6
43. R(R 6)×P	R×R
44. R×R	R—K 7
45. R—Q B 7	P—B 7

Threatening ...R—K 8 ch followed by ...P—B 8 (Q).

46. K—R 2   K—B 1
47. P—Kt 5   K—K 1
48. P—Kt 6   K—B 1

If 48. ...K—Q 1 ; 49. R×P !, R×R ; 50. P—Kt 7 and wins. What a tableau of helplessness !

49. P—B 4   K—Kt 1

Praying for 50. P—B 5 ? ? whereupon ...R—B 7 draws.

50. K—Kt 3 !   Resigns

An unpretentious ending which blends clarity with logic in an attractive manner.

75. GOTHENBURG, 1920

CENTRE COUNTER GAME

In this game we have one of the many fine examples of Tarrasch's ability to turn a lead in development into a won game. So clear and convincing is Tarrasch's handling of this game that the loser has praised Tarrasch's play unstintedly.

White	Black
Dr. S. Tarrasch	J. Mieses

1. P—K 4   P—Q 4
2. P×P   Q×P

Although this defence is rarely adopted because most players view the early development of the Queen with disfavour, Mieses has achieved some fine victories with it.

3. Kt—Q B 3   Q—Q R 4
4. P—Q 4   P—K 4

A bold attempt, in typical Mieses fashion, to seize the initiative. Tarrasch is content to develop with gain of time.

5. Kt—B 3 !   B—Q Kt 5

...B—K Kt 5 was doubtless better, in order to continue with ... Kt—Q B 3 and ...O—O—O.

6. B—Q 2   B—Kt 5
7. B—K 2

Still developing, although 7. P—Q R 3 ! would have been even more embarrassing to meet.

7. ......   P×P

7. ...Kt—Q B 3 looks promising, but then Black has no good reply to 8. P—Q R 3 ; for example, 8. ...K B×Kt ; 9. B×B, winning the K P ; or 8. ...B—Q 3 ; 9. P—Q Kt 4, Q—Kt 3 ; 10. Kt—Q 5, winning the Queen ; or 8. ... Q B×Kt ; 9. B×B (if 9. R P×B, B×B), Kt×P ; 10. P×B, Q×R ; 11. Q×Q, Kt×P ch ; 12. K—K 2 and wins.
If (instead of 7. ...Kt—Q B 3 or the text) 7. ...Q B×Kt ; 8. B× B, P—Q B 3 ; 9. P—Q R 3 with advantage.

8. Kt×P   Q—K 4

No matter how Black plays, his development is bound to be badly in arrears.

9. Q Kt—Kt 5 !

Mieses must now exchange his developed pieces.

9. ......   B×B

He has no choice, as White threatens B×B or Kt×P ch. If 9. ...B—Q 3 ; 10. Kt×B ch, P×Kt; 11. Kt—Kt 5 with considerable advantage.

10.	Q×B	B×B ch
11.	K×B	Q×Q ch
12.	K×Q	Kt—Q R 3

A poor square for the Knight, but if 12. ...K—Q 1 ; 13. Q R—Q 1, Kt—Q 2 ; 14. K R—K 1, K Kt—B 3 ; 15. K—B 3, P—Q R 3 ; 16. Kt—B 3 and Black's position is destined to remain permanently uncomfortable.

| 13. K R—K 1 | O—O—O |

Desperation ; if 13. ...K—Q 1 ; 14. Q R—Q 1, K—B 1 ; 15. K—B 3 with a winning position. Or 13. ...K—B 1 ; 14. Q R—Q 1 and Black's position is very difficult.

| 14. Kt×P ch ! | K—Kt 1 |

Expecting 15. Kt(R 7)—Kt 5, P—Q B 3.

15.	Kt(R 7)—B 6 ch !	P×Kt
16.	Kt×P ch	K—B 1
17.	Kt×R	K×Kt

Tarrasch's little combination has given him a winning endgame. An agile Rook and two Pawns are more than a match for two awkwardly placed Knights which are incapable of cooperation. White's goal will now be two united passed Pawns on the Queen's side, but first he will improve the position of his King and reduce the Knights to virtual helplessness.

| 18. Q R—Q 1 ch | K—K 1 |

If 18. ...K—B 1 ; 19. K—B 3 and the K R penetrates into Black's game.

| 19. K—Q 3 ch | Kt—K 2 |
| 20. K—B 4 |

The King is strongly posted here, as will be seen.

| 20. ...... | P—R 4 |

Seeing no prospect of developing the Rook in normal fashion, Mieses intends ....R—R 3. But he soon changes his mind.

21. R—Q 3	Kt—Kt 1
22. R(Q 3)—K 3	Kt—B 3
23. P—Q Kt 4	P—B 3
24. P—B 4

Preventing ...Kt—K 4 ch in answer to P—Kt 5.

| 24. ...... | K—B 2 ! |

A neat trap. If 25. P—Kt 5, Kt—R 4 ch ; 26. K—Kt 4, Kt—Q 4 ch ; 27. K×Kt, R—R 1 mate !

| 25. P—Q R 4 | R—Q Kt 1 |
| 26. P—B 3 | R—Q 1 |
| 27. R—Q 3 ! |

Black must either yield the open file or else permit an exchange which will make clear the helplessness of his Knights.

| 27. ...... | R×R |
| 28. K×R | K—K 1 |
| 29. P—R 5 |

The advance of the Pawn practically stalemates one of the Knights.

29.	......	K—Q 2
30.	P—R 6	Kt—Q 4
31.	R—Q R 1 !	Kt—R 2

Not 31. ...Kt×B P ch ? ; 32. K—K 4 followed by P—R 7, winning a piece. Now that one of the Knights cannot move, the other Knight must be dislodged by means of P—B 4. Observe how Black's game goes downhill.

| 32. | P—Kt 3 | P—B 3 |
| 33. | R—R 4 | Kt—Kt 3 |

Otherwise P—B 4 follows.

| 34. | R—R 5 | P—Kt 3 |

Or 34. ...Kt—Q 4 ; 35. K—B 4 followed by K—Kt 3 and P—B 4.

| 35. | P—B 4 | Kt(Kt 3)—B 1 |
| 36. | R—R 1 | |

The Rook has completed its work on the Q R file ; the occupation of the seventh rank is now in order.

36.	......	Kt—Q 3
37.	K—Q 4	Kt(Q 3)—B 1
38.	K—B 5	

The King is now posted for the kill.

| 38. | ...... | K—B 2 |

Not 38. ...Kt—Q 3 ? ; 39. R—Q 1, Kt—B 1 ; 40. R×Kt ch !, Kt×R ; 41. P—R 7.

| 39. | R—K 1 | Kt—Kt 3 |

Or 39. ...K—Q 2 ; 40. P—Kt 5 and wins.

| 40. | R—K 7 ch | Kt—Q 2 |

| 41. | R×Kt ch ! | Resigns |

If 41. ...K×R ; 42. P—Kt 5 ! wins easily. But 42. K—Kt 6 ? would only draw because of 42. ... Kt—B 1 ch ; 43. K—Kt 7, Kt—Q 3 ch ; 44. K—Kt 8, Kt×P ; 45. P—R 7, Kt—Kt 3 ; 46. K—Kt 7, Kt—R 1 ! ; 47. K—Kt 8 ! (47. K×Kt ?, K—B 2 loses for White) etc. A finely played game by Tarrasch.

76. GOTHENBURG, 1920

QUEEN'S GAMBIT DECLINED

(IN EFFECT)

THIS methodical masterpiece is one of the great Tarrasch games. The contrast between Tarrasch's systematic execution of a correct strategical plan and Breyer's extemporised continuation of one that is faulty is striking.

| *White* | *Black* |
| J. BREYER | DR. S. TARRASCH |

| 1. | P—Q 4 | P—Q 4 |
| 2. | P—K 3 | |

This move has disappeared from master play, as the obvious reply

...B—B 4 gives Black a perfectly satisfactory game.

2. ......   Kt—K B 3
3. Kt—K B 3   P—K 3
4. Q Kt—Q 2   B—Q 3
5. P—B 4   P—Q Kt 3

...P—B 4 is also playable and even simpler.

6. Q—B 2   B—Kt 2

Deliberately provoking P—B 5, says Tarrasch, otherwise he could have played ...P—B 4 or ...Q Kt —Q 2 or ...Q—K 2 here.

7. P—B 5 ?

A strategical error, as the further course of the game demonstrates. P—Q R 3 or B—Q 3 was in order.

7. ......   P×P

In order to get control of the centre, Tarrasch allows his opponent to establish a threatening phalanx of Queen's side Pawns.

8. P×P   B—K 2
9. P—Q Kt 4   O—O

Not the most exact : 9. ...P— Q R 4 ! would force 10. P—Kt 5, weakening the Q B P ; whereas after the text, White has time for P—Q R 3, so as to answer ...P— Q R 4 with B—Kt 2.

10. B—Kt 2   P—Q R 4
11. P—Kt 5 ?

As shown above, P—Q R 3 was indicated here. After the text, Tarrasch concentrates on the Q B P ; but the execution of this plan is laborious.

11. ......   P—B 3

Naturally, he cannot allow P— B 6.

12. P—Q R 4   Q Kt—Q 2
13. B—Q 4   R—K 1 !

...R—B 1 would not be good because of P—Kt 6 followed by Kt—Kt 3 and Black's Q R P cannot last very long. The text is played to prepare for ...P—K4, which will drive back White's Q B and thus strengthen the pressure against his Q B P.

14. R—B 1   B—K B 1
15. Q—Kt 2   Kt—Kt 5 !

The contemplated advance of the K P will not only drive back White's Q B—it will also make room for a Black Knight at K 3. How this comes about is interesting to observe.

16. P—R 3   Kt—R 3
17. Kt—Kt 3   P—B 3
18. Q—R 3   P—K 4
19. B—B 3   Q—B 2

Black has made a great step forward in finally achieving the advance of the K P. Now he prepares to increase the pressure on the Q B P, the immediate threat being ...P×P followed by ...B×P.

20. B—Kt 2

Not 20. P—Kt 6 ?, Q×P.

20. ......   K R—B 1

Relentlessly maintaining the pressure. 20. ...P×P ; 21. B× KtP, B—B 3 would not be so good, for example 22. Q—R 2 !,

B×B; 23. P×B, P—R 5; 24.
Q Kt—Q 2, Kt×P; 25. Q×P ch
followed by B—R 3 with advantage (Tarrasch).

21. Q—R 2 !

Not 21. P—Kt 6 ?, Kt×Kt P ;
22. P×Kt, B×Q and wins.

21. ......   Q—Q 1 !

21. ...P×P ? would be refuted
by 22. P—B 6 !, winning a piece.

22. P—Kt 6

Now the attack on the Q B P is
apparently at an end. But Tarrasch has seen more deeply into the
position.

22. ......   B—K 2 !

Preparing a new onslaught on the
Q B P. If 23. B—R 3, Q—B 1 !,
threatening ...Kt×Kt P !

23. Q—Kt 1   Q—B 1 !
24. Q—B 2   Kt—B 2!

Tarrasch intends to bring the
Knight to K 3, attacking the Q B P
for the fourth time. White appears
to have no defence, for if 25. B—
R 3, Kt×Kt P. But Breyer finds
a new resource. Unfortunately his
position is so bad that his ingenuity
turns out to be wasted.

25. P—R 4 !   Kt—Q 1
26. P—Kt 3   Kt—K 3
27. B—K R 3

If Black captures the Q B P, he
loses the exchange. But Tarrasch
is fully prepared.

27. ......   Kt(K 3)×P !
28. Kt×Kt   Kt×Kt
29. B—R 3

The commentators have recommended 29. B×R, R×B; 30.
O—O. But in that case Black
would still have a won game, for
example 30. ...B—R 3; 31. K R
—Q 1, B—Q 6 !; 32. Q—B 3 (if
32. R×B, Kt×R; 33. Q×Kt,
P—K 5), B—K 7, or 32. Q—Q 2,
P—K 5 etc.

29. ......   Kt—Q 6 ch !

After this Black remains the exchange down, but he has two terrible Bishops and devastating pressure.

30. Q×Kt   B×B
31. B×R   R×B
32. R—R 1   B—Kt 5 ch
33. Kt—Q 2   P—K 5
34. Q—Kt 3

34. Q—K 2, R—R 1 ; 35. O—
O, B—R 3 is equally hopeless for
White.

34. ......   P—Q B 4
35. K—Q 1   P—B 5
36. Q—R 2   Q—Q 3
37. K—K 2   B—R 3

Black's command of the board is crushing.

38. P—Kt 7	R—Kt 1
39. K—Q 1	R×P
40. P—B 3	

Pointless. White should resign.

40.	K—R 1
41. P×P	P×P
42. K—B 1	Q×P
43. Kt—B 1	Q—K 8 ch
44. K—B 2	Q—B 6 ch
45. K—Q 1	Q—Q 6 ch
46. K—B 1	R—Q 2

At last White resigns. Tarrasch: "One of my best—and hardest—games".

77. BERLIN, 1920

ALBIN COUNTER GAMBIT

AN interesting feature of this beautiful game is the number of fine variations which take place in the notes rather than over the board. There are not many players who could so easily outwit a master of Tartakover's splendid tactical abilities.

White	Black
DR. S.	DR. S.
TARRASCH	TARTAKOVER

| 1. P—Q 4 | P—Q 4 |
| 2. P—Q B 4 | P—K 4 |

Tartakover's adoption of this counter gambit is consistent with his fondness for playing variations whose reputation and soundness are dubious.

| 3. Q P×P | P—Q 5 |
| 4. Kt—K B 3 | P—Q B 4 |

The customary continuation is 4. ...Kt—Q B 3, when White continues with 5. Q Kt—Q 2 and the fianchetto of his K B. But Tartakover, true to his style, prefers the unconventional text, which results in a passed Q P.

5. P—K 3	Kt—Q B 3
6. P×P	P×P
7. B—Q 3	K Kt—K 2

In a later game against Grünfeld at Carlsbad, 1923, Tartakover continued 7. ...B—Kt 5 ; 8. O—O, Q—B 2 ; 9. P—K R 3, B×Kt ; 10. Q×B, Kt×P ; 11. R—K 1, B—Q 3 ; 12. B—B 4, Kt—K 2 ; 13. B×Kt, B×B ; 14. Kt—R 3 !, P—Q R 3 ; 15. P—B 5 ! with advantage to White.

If 7. ...Kt×P ? ; 8. Q—K 2 !, P—B 3 ; 9. Kt×Kt, Q—R 4 ch ; 10. K—Q 1 ! and White wins a Pawn.

| 8. Q Kt—Q 2 | B—Kt 5 |
| 9. Q—Kt 3 | |

Tarrasch loses no time getting rid of the pin.

| 9. ...... | Q—B 2 |
| 10. O—O | O—O—O |

Black's King is somewhat exposed here, but Tartakover is not the man to shun risks.

| 11. R—K 1 | Kt—Kt 3 |
| 12. P—K R 3 ! | |

B×Kt would retain the Pawn but it would give Black two Bishops weaken the white squares, expose White to a possible attack on the K R file, and leave his development in arrears. Tarrasch wisely prefers a continuation which will bring his pieces into play and give him good attacking chances.

12. ......   B—K 3

Since Black can still regain the K P (for after 13. B×Kt, R P×B he would threaten ...Kt—R 4 as well as ...R—R 4), he naturally prefers to retain both Bishops.

13. B—K 4 !   K Kt×P

Black decides to win back the Pawn, for after 13. ...B—K 2 the following plausible continuation suggested by Tartakover would be unfavourable for him : 14. B—Q 5 !, B×B ; 15. P×B, Q Kt×P ; 16. Kt×Kt, Kt×Kt ; 17. Kt—B 3, Kt×Kt ch ; 18. Q×Kt and Black cannot stop to defend the B P because of the threat of 19. B—B 4 and 20. Q R—B 1 (if 19. ...B—Q 3 ; 20. B—Kt 5 !).

14. Kt×Kt   Q×Kt !

14. ...Kt×Kt would be inferior because of 15. Q×P ch !, Q×Q ; 16. B×Q ch, K×B ; 17. R×Kt, B—Q 3 ; 18. R—K 1 and now :
I. 18. ...Q R—K 1 ; 19. Kt—K 4 !, B—K B 1 ; 20. P—Q Kt 3, B×R P ; 21. P×B, P—B 4 ; 22. P—B 3.
II. 18. ...B—Q Kt 5 ; 19. P—R 3 !, B×Kt ; 20. B×B, B×B P ; 21. R—K 7 ch, K—R 3 ; 22. R—Q B 1, R—Q B 1 ; 23. R—Q 7.
In both these variations, pointed out by Tartakover, White has the advantage.

15. Kt—B 3 !

Here, however, the pseudo-sacrifice of the Queen would not be good : 15. Q×P ch, K×Q ; 16.

B×Kt ch, K×B ; 17. R×Q, B—Q Kt 5 ; 18. P—Q Kt 3, B—B 6 ; 19. R—Kt 1, K R—K 1 and Black's two Bishops, his passed Pawn and the generally superior position of his pieces outweigh the Pawn minus (Tartakover).

15. ......   Q—Q B 4

How is White to defend the Q B P ? 16. B—Q 3 or Kt—Q 2 can be effectively answered by ... Kt—R 4.

16. B—B 4 !

16. ......   B—Q 3

Seeing through Tarrasch's profound combination. If 16. ...B× B P ; 17. Q×B ! !, Q×Q ; 18. B—B 5 ch, R—Q 2 (or 18. ...Q—K 3 ; 19. R×Q, P×R ; 20. B×P ch, R—Q 2 ; 21. Kt—K 5, Kt×Kt ; 22. B×Kt and the Q P falls with an easy win for White) ; 19. R—K 8 ch, Kt—Q 1 ; 20. Kt—K 5 and wins (Tarrasch).

17. B×Kt !

Just at the right moment, when Black must retake with the Pawn and thus expose his King still more.

17. ......   P×B
18. B×B   R×B
19. Kt—K 5

Not best. Correct was 19. Kt—
Q 2 and if ...Q—Kt 3 ; 20. Q—
R 3, P—Q B 4 ; 21. R—K 5, R—
B 3 ; 22. Kt—K 4, B×B P ; 23.
R—Q B 1, Q—R 3 ; 24. R×P !
and wins, or 23. ...B—R 3 ; 24.
R(K 5)×P with a winning attack.

19. ......   K R—Q 1 ?

19. ...P—B 3 ; 20. Kt—Q 3,
Q×P ? is refuted by 21. Q—R 3,
R—Q 2 ; 22. Q R—B 1, Q—Q 4
(or 22. ...Q×P ; 23. R×P ch) ;
23. Kt—B 4 losing a piece for
Black.
But 19. ...Q—Kt 3 ! would
have given Black a satisfactory
game : 20. Q—R 3, P—Q B 4 ;
21. Kt—Q 3, R—B 3 ; 22. Q R—
B 1 (not 22. R—K 5 ?, B×B P ;
23. Kt×P, P—B 3 ; 24. Kt—R 4,
Q—R 3 ; 25 K R—K 1, B—Kt 4
with a good game), K—Kt 2 and the
outcome is unclear.

20. Q—R 4 !

The winning move, the imme-
diate threat being 21. P—Q Kt 4,
Q—Kt 3 ; 22. P—B 5 winning a
Rook.

20. ......   P—Q 6

His only hope, but not one to be
despised. If 20. ...Q—Kt 3 ; 21.
P—B 5 !, Q×B P ; 22. Q R—B 1
wins. If 20. ...P—Q R 4 ; 21.
P—R 3 followed by 22. P—Q Kt 4
wins.

21. P—Q Kt 4   Q—Q 5
22. Kt×Q B P !

The strongest move. 22. P—
B 5 would be less forcing because of
22. ...P—Q 7 !

22. ......   R×Kt
23. Q×R ch   K—Kt 1
24. P—B 5

White must push the attack with
all speed because of the menacing
advance of the Q P.

24. ......   P—Q 7
25. K R—Q 1   B—B 4

25. ...B—B 5 is no better : 26.
P—Kt 5 !, R—Q 2 (or 26. ...Q—
Q 4 ; 27. R×P ! !, Q×R ; 28.
P—Kt 6, R—Q 2 ; 29. P×P ch,
K×P ; 30. Q—Kt 6 ch, K—R 1 ;
31. R—Kt 1, while if 28. ...Q—
Q 2 ; 29. P×P ch, K×P ; 30.
Q—Kt 6 ch, K—R 1 ; 31. Q—
R 5 ch followed by R—Kt 1 ch and
wins) ; 27. P—Kt 6 !, P—Q R 3 ;
28. Q—B 3 and wins.

26. Q—Kt 5 ch !   K—B 2

If 26. ...K—B 1 ; 27. P—B 6
wins the Bishop ; if 26. ...K—
R 1 ; 27. P—B 6, B—B 1 ; 28.
P—B 7 and wins.

27. Q—R 5 ch   K—Kt 1

Now come six smashing Pawn
moves which decide the issue.

28. P—Kt 5 !   B—B 7

If instead 28. ...R—Q 4 ; 29.
P—B 6, Q—Kt 3 (or 29. ...B—
B 7 ; 30. P—B 7 ch, K—B 1 ; 31.
Q—R 6 ch, K×P ; 32. Q—B 6 ch
and wins) ; 30. Q×Q ch, P×Q ;
31. P—B 3, B—B 7 ; 32. P—Q
R 4, R—Q 5 ; 33. K—B 2 with a
won ending (Tartakover).

29. P—Kt 6 !   R—Q 2

If 29. ...P×P ; 30. Q×P ch
with a mating attack.

30. P×P ch   K—R 1

Or 30. ...R×P ; 31. Q×P
winning easily.

31. P—B 6   R—Q 4
32. P—B 7   B—B 4

An inglorious retreat, but if 32.
...R×Q ; 33. P—B 8(Q) ch, winning the Bishop.

33. P—B 8 (Q) ch ! B×Q
34. Q—B 7   R—Q Kt 4

Black should resign.

35. Q×B ch   K×P
36. P—Q R 4   R—Q B 4
37. Q—Kt 4   Q×R
38. R×Q   R—B 8 ch
39. Q—Q 1   Resigns

Tartakover : "A magnificent victory". The march of the Pawns
has been remarkable.

78. BERLIN, 1920

FRENCH DEFENCE

DESPITE its length, this well-con-
tested game, with its striking conclusion, is absorbing from beginning
to end. Both players commit in-
exactitudes, but their ingenuity in
difficult situations makes the game
memorable.

| *White* | *Black* |
| P. S. LEONHARDT | DR. S. TARRASCH |

1. P—K 4   P—K 3

2. P—Q 4   P—Q 4
3. Kt—Q B 3   Kt—K B 3
4. B—Kt 5   B—Kt 5
5. P×P

An old-fashioned reply which
allows Black to obtain a promising
position.

5. ......   Q×P
6. B×Kt   P×B

Also good is 6. ...B×Kt ch ; 7.
P×B, P×B ; 8. Kt—B 3, P—
Q Kt 3 ! ; 9. P—K Kt 3, B—R 3 !;
10. B—Kt 2, Kt—Q 2 ; 11. Kt—
R 4, Q—Q R 4 ! etc.

7. Q—Q 2   Q—Q R 4
8. K Kt—K 2   B—Q 2
9. O—O—O   Kt—R 3

A surprising move from Tarrasch, who always preached the inadequacy of this development.
Simple and good was 9. ...B—B 3;
10. K—Kt 1, Kt—Q 2 followed by
...O—O—O.

10. Q—B 4   B—K 2
11. P—K Kt 3   O—O—O

If 11. ...B—B 3 ; 12. P—Q 5 !,
B×P ; 13. Kt×B, P×Kt ; 14.
Kt—B 3, P—B 3 ; 15. R—K 1 is
very promising.

12. B—Kt 2

The fianchettoed Bishop is very
strongly posted here. The following play will demonstrate whether
Black's two Bishops compensate for
his cramped position and potentially
weak King's side Pawns.

12. ......   P—B 3

To close the White Bishop's

diagonal and prepare for ...Kt—Kt 5—Q 4.

13. K—Kt 1 !   Q—B 2

If 13. ...Kt—Kt 5 ; 14. R—Q B 1, Kt—Q 4 ? ; 15. Kt×Kt, B P×Kt ; 16. P—B 4 with a winning attack. But 13. ...Kt—B 2 ; 14. R—Q B 1, Kt—Kt 4 ! would have been much better. Black's unfortunate Knight is now out of play for many moves to come (Tarrasch).

14. Q—R 6   Q R—Kt 1

Not caring for 15. Q—Kt 7.

15. K R—K 1   B—Q 1 ?

Tarrasch criticises this ultra-cautious move and recommends ...Kt—Kt 5.

16. P—Q R 3 !   P—K B 4
17. Q—K 3   K—Kt 1
18. B—R 1

In order to play Kt—B 1 without allowing ...P—B 5.

18. ......   B—Kt 4
19. Q—B 3

Not 19. P—B 4 for after the Bishop's retreat Black would have strong counterplay in ...P—R 4—5.

19. ......   B—B 1
20. Kt—B 1   R—Q 1
21. Kt—Kt 3   B—R 3
22. R—Q 3   B—Kt 2
23. K R—Q 1   Q—K 2

In order to play ...Kt—B 2, but White's reply threatens Q×Q B P !

24. Kt—R 5   Q—B 2
25. P—Q Kt 4 K—R 1

Making way for the unhappy Knight. Black's position is cramped but very solid.

26. Kt—B 4   R—Q 2
27. Kt—R 4   K R—Q 1

Of course not 27. ...P—Kt 4 ? ; 28. Q×P ch.

28. P—B 3   Kt—Kt 1

Now ...P—Kt 4 is threatened.

29. Kt—B 5   R—K 2
30. K—B 2 ?

The thirtieth move ! Kt—K 3 should have been played.

30. ......   P—Kt 3 !

Now Black's Bishops come to life, and a desperate struggle for the initiative ensues.

31. Kt—Kt 3   B—Q R 3 !
32. Kt(Kt 3)—Q 2 B—R 3
33. K—Kt 3   R—Q B 1

Threatening ...Q—Q 1—Q 4.

34. P—Q R 4   Q—Q 1
35. Kt—K 5 !

35. P—Kt 5, B—Q Kt 2 would give Black good chances. Leonhardt prefers a more active course, even if it means losing the exchange.

35. ......   B×R
36. Q×B   B×Kt
37. R×B   P—B 3
38. Kt×P   Kt×Kt
39. P—Kt 5   K—Kt 1
40. P×Kt

A formidable Pawn which will need constant watching. The chances for both sides are approximately even.

40. ......   Q—Q 3
41. Q—Kt 5

Preventing the return of the exchange with ...R×P.

41. ......   K—B 2
42. P—Q B 4

Leonhardt intends P—Q 5, which will give him two united passed Pawns. Fortunately, Tarrasch will be able to blockade the dangerous Pawns.

42. ......   R—Q Kt 1
43. B—Kt 2

Intending to play B—R 3 after Black answers P—Q 5 with ...P—K 4.

43. ......   R—K Kt 2
44. P—B 4

To prevent ...P—B 5. But now Tarrasch gets counterplay.

44. ......   P—K R 4
45. R—Q 3   P—R 5
46. Q—R 6   K—Q 1
47. P—Q 5   R P×P
48. R P×P   R—R 2
49. R—K 3   P—K 4

Tarrasch seems to have made considerable headway and is apparently well on the way to victory. Now comes an inspired finish.

50. R—K 1 !

Intending to save himself with R—K R 1, which would force the

exchange of Rooks and keep Black fully occupied guarding the R P.

50. ......   R—K Kt 2

50. ...P—K 5 looks more promising but would not be any stronger: 51. R—K R 1 !, R×R ; 52. B×R, Q—B 2 ; 53. B—Kt 2, K—K 2 ; 54. B—R 3, R—Kt 1 ; 55. B×P, R× P ch ; 56. K—B 2, R—Kt 7 ch ; 57. K—B 3 !, P—K 6 (if 57. ... Q×P ; 58. Q×P ch gives White at least a draw) ; 58. Q—Kt 7, K— Q 3 ; 59. Q—R 8 (threatening 60. Q—B 8 ch, Q—K 2 ; 61. Q×Q ch, K×Q ; 62. P—B 7 and wins), P— K 7 (if 59. ...Q—K 2 ? ; 60. Q— Kt 8 ch, K—B 4 ; 61. P—B 7 and wins) ; 60. Q—B 8 ch, Q—K 2 ; 61. Q×Q ch, K×Q ; 62. K— Q 2, K—Q 3 ; 63. P—R 5 ! with a likely draw. Black dare not play 63. ...P×P ? because of 64. P— B 5 ch, K—B 2 ; 65. P—Q 6 ch, K×P ; 66. B—K 4 ch (Tarrasch).

51. R—K R 1 ! !   R×P ch

Tarrasch accepts the "gift" of the Bishop. However, he shows that there was nothing better :

I. 51. ...Q—B 2 ? ;   52. P—

Q 6 !, Q×Q P ; 53. R—R 8 ch,
K—K 2 ; 54. Q×P ch, K—K 3 ;
55. B—Q 5 ch and wins.

II. 51. ...R—Kt 1 ; 52. R—
R 7 and wins.

52. B—B 3 ! !

This problem move saves the
game.

52. ......   R×B ch
53. K—B 2

How is Black to continue ?
If 53. ...Q—B 1 ; 54. Q×P
wins. If 53. ...Q—R 6 ; 54. R—
R 8 ch, K—K 2 ; 55. Q×P ch,
K—Q 3 ; 56. Q×R ch, K—B 4,
Q—B 8 ch and wins.

53. ......   R—B 7 ch

Tarrasch points out that 53. ...
R—B 6 ch ! ! would also have
drawn !

54. K—Q 1   R—B 8 ch ! !

Echoing the theme of White's
52nd move !

55. R×R   Q—R 6
56. R—B 2

The perpetual check cannot be
avoided. If 56. Q×P, Q—Q 6 ch
etc. If 56. P—B 5, Q×P ; 57.
Q×P, Q×P ch ; 58. K—K 2, Q—
K 5 ch etc.

56. ......   Q—Q 6 ch
57. K—B 1   Q—B 6 ch

Drawn. A superb finish.

79. BERLIN, 1920

FOUR KNIGHTS' GAME

In this game Spielmann shows none
of his famous attacking brilliance ;
it is Tarrasch who makes the sparkling moves and displays ingenuity
and resourcefulness.

White	*Black*
Dr. S. Tarrasch	R. Spielmann

1. P—K 4	P—K 4
2. Kt—K B 3	Kt—Q B 3
3. Kt—B 3	Kt—B 3
4. B—Kt 5	B—Kt 5
5. O—O	O—O
6. P—Q 3	P—Q 3
7. B—Kt 5	B×Kt

A decade earlier, in the tournament at Hamburg, Spielmann had
demonstrated, against the same opponent, the excellence of the defence 7. ...Kt—K 2 ; 8. B×Kt,
P×B ; 9. Kt—K R 4, P—B 3 ; 10.
B—Q B 4, Kt—Kt 3 ; 11. Kt×Kt,
R P×Kt ; 12. P—B 4, B—B 4 ch ;
13. K—R 1, K—Kt 2.   Apparently he was now fearful of some
theoretical innovation.

8. P×B   P—K R 3

Simpler is 8. ...Q—K 2 ; 9.
R—K 1, Kt—Q 1 ; 10. P—Q 4,
P—B 3 with good chances.

9. B—K R 4   Q—K 2
10. Q—Q 2

Preventing ...P—Kt 4 for some
time to come.

10. ......   Kt—Q 1
11. P—Q 4   Kt—K 3 ? !

Not 11. ...Kt×P ? ; 12. B×Q
and White wins a piece.

The text involves an apparently promising Pawn sacrifice, but it undergoes a sharp refutation at Tarrasch's hands. The best line was 11. ...K—R 1, intending ...R—K Kt 1 and ...P—Kt 4.

12. P×P	P×P
13. Kt×P	Kt—B 4
14. Q—B 4 !	P—Kt 4

Spielmann accepts the challenge, since other moves will leave him a Pawn down without compensation. If 14. ...Kt(B 4)×P ? ; 15. Q× Q Kt wins.

15. B×P	P×B
16. Q×P ch	K—R 2
17. Q—R 4 ch	K—Kt 2
18. Q—Kt 5 ch	K—R 2
19. Q—R 4 ch	K—Kt 2
20. Q—Kt 5 ch	K—R 2
21. Q—R 4 ch	K—Kt 2
22. Q—Kt 3 ch	K—R 2
23. Q—R 4 ch	K—Kt 2
24. Q—Kt 3 ch	K—R 2
25. Q—R 4 ch	K—Kt 2
26. Q—Kt 5 ch	K—R 2

Having indulged in his old sport of demonstrating that he has a draw whenever he wants it, Tarrasch now gets down to business.

27. B—B 4 !

Threatens B×P !

27. ......   B—K 3

Overlooking White's clever reply. 27. ...Kt—K 3 offered better defensive chances.

| 28. Kt—Kt 4 ! | B×Kt |
| 29. P—K 5 | Kt—Kt 1 |

If 29. ...R—K Kt 1 ; 30. Q— R 4 ch, K—Kt 3 ; 31. P×Kt, Q— Q 2 ; 32. P—B 4 with an easy win.

30. Q×B   Kt—K R 3

If 30. ...Q×P ; 31. K R—K 1, Q—Q 3 ; 32. Q—R 5 ch, Kt—R 3 ; 33. Q R—Q 1, Q—Q B 3 ; 34. R—K 5 and wins.

| 31. Q—R 5 | R—K Kt 1 |
| 32. P—B 4 | Q—Q 2 |

Black has beaten off the attack, but his game has no future. Tarrasch now calmly prepares the advance of his powerful King's side Pawns, and there is little that Black can do about it.

| 33. R—B 2 ! | Q R—K B 1 |
| 34. P—K R 3 | Q—B 4 |

Keeping the Queens on the board might have been preferable, although in any event the paucity of moves at Black's disposal would have exasperated a less volatile player than Spielmann.

| 35. Q×Q ch | Kt×Q |
| 36. P—Kt 4 | Kt—K 6 |

In the ending which follows, the Knights play a miserable rôle.

37. B—Q 3 ch   K—Kt 2

Spielmann avoids ...Kt×B, as he does not want to straighten out White's Pawns.

38. R—B 3	Kt—Q 4
39. B—B 5	Kt—K 2
40. B—Q 3	R—Q 1

...Kt—Q 4 was again indicated.

41. K—Kt 2	R—Q 4
42. R—K 1	

Tarrasch intends to eliminate the hostile K B P by advancing his K P in due course ; he will then have three overwhelming united passed Pawns.

42.	R(Kt 1)—Q 1
43. R(K 1)—K 3	Kt—B 3
44. K—Kt 3	P—R 3
45. P—K R 4	P—Kt 4

Too late.

46. P—Kt 5 !	P—Kt 5
47. B—K 4	Kt×B
48. R×Kt	R—B 4
49. P×P	R×B P
50. P—B 5	Kt—Q 5

Black's pieces have at last become active, but they cannot accomplish anything against the terrible Pawns.

51. R—B 1	Kt—K 7 ch
52. K—Kt 4	R—Q 6
53. R—B 3	R—Q 8

...R×R is no better.

54. P—K 6 !	R—Kt 8 ch
55. K—R 5	K—B 1

Of course, if 55. ...Kt—Kt 6 ch ; 56. R×Kt, R×R ; 57. P—K 7.

56. P×P	K×P
57. P—Kt 6 ch	K—B 1
58. K—R 6	Kt—Kt 6
59. P—Kt 7 ch	K—B 2
60. R—Kt 4	Resigns

A well-played game by Tarrasch.

80. PISTYAN, 1922

DUTCH DEFENCE

WHITE mangles the opening so badly that Tarrasch is able to take the initiative at an early stage and demolish the enemy's seriously compromised position.

White	*Black*
Z. VON BALLA	DR. S. TARRASCH

1. P—Q B 4	P—K 3
2. P—Q 4	P—K B 4
3. Kt—Q B 3	Kt—K B 3
4. P—Q R 3	

This timidity is out of place. P—K Kt 3 followed by B—Kt 2 was in order.

4.	P—Q Kt 3
5. P—B 3	

A naive attempt to minimise the power of Black's fianchettoed Bishop. The result, thanks to White's slow development, is a seriously endangered King's side.

5.	B—Kt 2
6. B—Kt 5	B—K 2
7. P—K 3	Kt—R 4 !
8. B×B	Q×B
9. Q—B 2	

So as to answer ...Q—R 5 ch with Q—B 2.

9. ......   O—O
10. B—Q 3   P—B 4 !

A powerful thrust at White's
shaky centre. 11. P—Q 5 would
simply be answered by ...P×P.

11. K Kt—K 2

After this he will be unable to
castle, but if instead 11. Kt—R 3
(to prevent Black's next move), the
reply 11. ...P×P ; 12. P×P,
Kt—Q B 3 is embarrassing.

11. ......   Q—Kt 4 !
12. K—B 2   Kt—Q B 3
13. P—K R 4

Driving Black's Queen away
from its commanding position ; on
the other hand, the K R is now tied
to the defence of the K R P.

13. ......   Q—B 3

Forcing the following exchange,
which gives Black the Q Kt file.

14. P×P   P×P
15. Q R—K B 1   Kt—K 4 !
16. K—K 1   Q R—Kt 1
17. R—R 3   B—R 3 !

Threatening ...R×P.

18. Kt—Q 1   P—Q 4 !

The final, convincing stroke
which completes the disintegration
of White's miserable position.

19. P—Q Kt 3   K R—Q 1

Black now threatens to win with
20. ...P×P ; 21. B×Q B P, B×
B ; 22. P×B, Kt—Q 6 ch.

20. Kt—B 1   P×P
21. B×Q B P   Kt×B
22. P×Kt   Q—R 8 !

Threatening ...R—Kt 8 with
fatal effect.

23. Kt—Q 3   Q×P
24. Kt(Q 1)—Kt 2 Q R×Kt !

Putting a merciful end to White's
resistance.

25. Kt×R   Q×P ch

White resigns, as he must lose the
Queen.

81. PISTYAN, 1922

SICILIAN DEFENCE

THIS is one of those curious games
in which a colourless opening leads
to a barren position devoid of any
prospects for Black. Even as
early as the fifth move, the unpromising character of his position is
clear.

White   *Black*
DR. S. TARRASCH   A. SELESNIEFF

1. P—K 4   P—Q B 4
2. Kt—Q B 3   P—K 3

The simplest continuation against White's second move is 2. ...Kt—Q B 3 ; 3. P—K Kt 3, P—K Kt 3 ; 4. B—Kt 2, B—Kt 2 ; 5. K Kt—K 2, P—K 3 ; 6. P—Q 3, K Kt—K 2 with a good game for Black.

3. P—K Kt 3   P—Q 3

Too stodgy. Black fears the isolated Q P which would result from 3. ...P—Q 4 ; 4. P×P, P×P ; 5. P—Q 4. Black would have a fine, free game to compensate for the Pawn weakness.

4. B—Kt 2   Kt—K B 3
5. K Kt—K 2   B—K 2

Black's game is cramped and lifeless.

6. O—O   Kt—B 3
7. P—Q 3

At this stage, Tarrasch avoids P—Q 4, which, after ...P×P, would give Black counterchances on the Q B file.

7. ......   B—Q 2
8. P—K R 3   Q—Kt 3

This is pointless : the more conservative ...Q—B 2 was in order.

9. R—Kt 1 !

Preparing for B—K 3, after which P—Q Kt 4 ! will be a real threat.

9. ......   Kt—Q 5
10. K—R 2   B—B 3
11. P—B 4   P—K R 4 ?

An error of judgment. As Black has no chances of King's side attack, he should castle at this juncture.

12. B—K 3   Kt×Kt

Else P—Q Kt 4 is very strong.

13. Q×Kt   Q—B 2
14. P—Q 4

White is now ready to open up the game in order to utilise his superior development.

14. ......   P×P
15. B×P   P—K 4

Weakening the Q P and the square Q 4. But after Black's unfortunate 11th move, there can be no satisfactory continuation.

16. B—K 3   P—Q Kt 3
17. Q R—Q 1   R—Q B 1
18. R—B 2

The striking power of White's forces increases steadily.

18. ......   Q—Kt 2
19. Kt—Q 5 !

Since Black can hardly avoid exchanging now (if 19. ...B—Q 1 ; 20. Kt×Kt ch wins a Pawn), Tarrasch succeeds in opening an attack on Black's helpless King.

19. ......   B×Kt
20. P×B   Kt—Q 2
21. P—B 4   B—B 3
22. P—Kt 3   Q—R 3
23. B—K 4 !   P—R 5 ?

Relatively best was 23. ...P—Kt 3 ; 24. Q R—K B 1, O—O. After the text, White's K B plays too powerful a rôle.

24. P—K Kt 4   P×P

The object of Black's previous

move was to follow up with this exchange and thus gain the strong square K 4 for his pieces. But normal strategical considerations are of little value in a position which has been compromised so grievously.

25. B×BP   B—K 4

If 25. ...Kt—K 4 ; 26. P—Kt 5, B—K 2 ; 27. B—B 5 and wins.

26. B—B 5 !

Decisive.

26. ......   P—B 3
27. B×B   Q P×B

If 27. ...B P×B ; 28. B×Kt ch, K×B ; 29. R—B 7 ch winning in quick time.

28. P—Kt 5 !   P—Kt 4

A despairing attempt to have the Queen participate in the "defence".

29. Kt P×P   K Kt P×P
30. P—Q 6 !   Resigns

White has too many threats ; the deadliest is Q—Kt 4.

82. PISTYAN, 1922
DUTCH DEFENCE

TARRASCH plays this game with a youthful freshness which is remarkable. His much younger opponent finds himself baffled at every turn !

White	*Black*
P. JOHNER	DR. S. TARRASCH
1. P—Q 4	P—K 3
2. P—Q B 4	P—K B 4
3. P—K Kt 3	Kt—K B 3
4. B—Kt 2	P—B 3
5. Kt—K B 3	P—Q 4

The Stonewall Variation, a line of play to which Tarrasch was partial in his later years.

6. Q—B 2   B—K 2

...B—Q 3 is more customary, but Tarrasch shows that the text development can also be put to good use.

7. O—O	O—O
8. P—Kt 3	Kt—K 5
9. B—Kt 2	Kt—Q 2
10. Kt—K 1	

White wants to play P—B 3 in order to eject the hostile Knight and to prepare for P—K 4. Tarrasch meets this plan very cleverly.

10. ......   B—Kt 4 !

So as to answer 11. P—B 3 ? with ...B—K 6 ch.

11. Q—Q 3   Q—Kt 3 !

With P—B 3 in the offing, the Queen is well posted here.

12. P×P ?

Always a poor move in this variation, as it frees Black's game appreciably. Kt—B 2 or K—R 1 should have been played.

12. ......   K P × P
13. Kt—B 2   R—B 2

Preparing for the eventual doubling of the Rooks, and also avoiding a pin by B—Q R 3 after his next move.

14. P—B 3   Kt—Q 3
15. Kt—B 3   P—B 5 !

Forestalling the contemplated P—K 4.

16. P × P   B × P
17. P—K 3

17. P—K 4 is less good than it appears, for example 17. ...P×P ; 18. P×P, Kt—K 4 ; 19. Q—K 2, B—Kt 5 or 18. Kt×P, Kt×Kt ; 19. Q×Kt, Q—B 2 followed by ...Kt—B 3—with considerable advantage for Black in either event.

17. ......   B—R 3
18. B—Q R 3   Kt—Kt 4 !
19. Kt × Kt   P × Kt
20. P—B 4

The attempt to concentrate on the Q P proves futile, and in addition the text hands over K 4 to the enemy. But P—K 4 would still be inadequate.

20. ......   Kt—B 3
21. B—B 5   Q—B 3
22. P—B 5 ?

In his zeal to bottle up the Q B, White places his K B P on a square where it is bound to be lost very shortly.

22. ......   P—R 4

Preventing Kt—Kt 4 and threatening to trap the Q B with ...P—Kt 5.

23. B—Q R 3   Kt—K 5
24. B × Kt

A sad choice : the elimination of the Bishop weakens White's King's side, but the continued presence of Black's Knight would prove unbearable. Tarrasch now concludes with a series of powerful strokes.

24. ......   P × B
25. Q—Q 2   P—Kt 5
26. P—Q 5   Q—B 3
27. B—B 1   B × P
28. K—R 1

If 28. Kt—Q 4, Q R—K B 1 ; 29. Kt × B (R × B is answered in the same way), Q—Kt 3 ch with a winning game.

28. ......   Q R—K B 1 !

Realising that his position is hopeless, Johner resigns. While it is true that his pieces are ineffectually bunched together and his King is exposed, this decision comes as a surprise. However, in the Tour-

nament Book, Teichmann gives the
following likely variations : 29.
Kt—Q 4, B—R 6 ! !

I. 30. R×Q, R×R ; 31. Kt—
K 2, R—B 8 ch ; 32. Kt—Kt 1,
R×Kt ch ; 33. K×R, R—B 8
mate.

II. 30. R—K Kt 1, Q—R 5 ;
31. B—Kt 2, R—B 7 ; 32. Q—
K 1, B—B 8 and mate follows.

83. TEPLITZ-SCHOENAU, 1922

SICILIAN DEFENCE

TARRASCH had very poor luck in this
tournament, and threw away a number of well-earned wins. This
game was his only victory in the
tourney, and it must have consoled
him for his reverses in other games.
It is a complex, arduous struggle in
which the veteran clearly outplays
his youthful opponent all the way.

| *White* | *Black* |
| DR. S. TARRASCH | F. SÄMISCH |

1. P—K 4	P—Q B 4
2. Kt—Q B 3	Kt—Q B 3
3. P—K Kt 3	P—Q 3
4. B—Kt 2	B—Q 2

The beginning of a series of
peculiar and time-wasting manœuvres. Simple and logical is 4.
...P—K Kt 3 and 5. ...B—Kt 2.

| 5. K Kt—K 2 | Q—B 1 |

Intending ...B—R 6, which
Tarrasch at once prevents.

| 6. Kt—B 4 | B—Kt 5 |

Spending a tempo to provoke

White's reply, which blocks the
diagonal of the fianchettoed Bishop.

7. P—B 3	B—Q 2
8. P—Q 3	P—K Kt 3
9. Q Kt—Q 5	B—Kt 2
10. P—B 3	R—Kt 1
11. O—O	P—K R 4 ?

Thoughtlessly weakening the
King's side in the hope of playing
...P—R 5. Much better was ...
P—K 3 followed by ...K Kt—K 2
and ...O—O with a normal
development.

| 12. P—K R 4 | Kt—R 3 |

Further waste of time, as the
Knight has no prospects here.

| 13. K—R 2 | P—Q Kt 4 |

Counterplay on the Queen's side
is Black's best chance in this variation.

14. B—Q 2	P—R 4
15. B—R 3	P—K 3
16. Kt—K 3	Kt—K 2

Another "clever" move, the
object being to play ...P—Q 4 !
But Tarrasch's next move foils this
plan, hence ...Kt—Kt 1—K 2 was
better.

17. R—K 1 !	Q—R 3
18. B—K B 1	Q—R 2
19. R—Kt 1	Kt—B 3
20. Q—K 2	

Tarrasch, like his adversary, has
indulged in a great deal of groping
manœuvring ; the fact remains that
White's pieces have been developed
much more purposefully and have
much more promising perspectives.
This will soon become clear.

20.	......	Kt—Kt 1
21.	Kt—R 3	K Kt—K 2
22.	B—Kt 2	P—R 5
23.	P—K B 4 !	

At last Tarrasch shows his cards. The K B's diagonal is once more significant, and such possibilities as P—B 5 or P—K 5 are in the air.

| 23. | ...... | P—R 6 |

...P—B 4 would leave a bad weakness at Black's K 3. Black cannot very well castle, for then P—Kt 4 would initiate a smashing attack ; hence nothing remains but action on the Queen's side.

| 24. | P—Kt 3 | P—Kt 5 |
| 25. | P×P ! | |

Stronger than P—B 4, which would deprive White's Knights of access to Q B 4.

| 25. | ...... | Kt×P |

The Q B P soon becomes seriously weak, but 25. ...P×P ; 26. Kt—B 4, Q—B 2 ; 27. Q R—B 1 would leave White with a fine initiative.

| 26. | Kt—B 4 ! | Kt×R P |

Black has little choice : if 26. ... Kt—B 1 ; 27. B×Kt followed by P—B 5. If 26. ...Q—R 3 ; 27. P—K 5, P—Q 4 (or 27. ...P×P ; 28. P×P, Kt×P ; 29. Kt—Q 6 ch, K—B 1 ; 30. Q—B 2, Kt—B 4 ; 31. Kt×Kt, followed by Q× P ch and Q R—R 1) ; 28. Kt—Q 6 ch, K—B 1 ; 29. Kt—K Kt 5, B—K 1 ; 30. B×Kt followed by Q R—B 1 (the Tournament Book). In all cases, White has a clear advantage.

| 27. | Kt×P ch | K—B 1 |
| 28. | P—K 5 | Kt—Q 4 |

The Tournament Book points out that Black's game is really hopeless in the long run because of the poor position of his pieces on the King's side. It offers the following alternatives :

I.   28. ...B—R 3 ;   29. Q—B 2, Kt—Kt 5 (B—K 3 was threatened) ;   30. B×Kt, R×B ;   31. K R—Q B 1, R—Q 5 ;   32. P—Q Kt 4 ! with advantage.

II.   28. ...Kt—B 4 ; 29. Kt× Kt, K P×Kt (if 29. ...Kt P×Kt ; 30. B—K B 3 is good enough) ; 30. Q—B 2 followed by B—K 3. Black dare not play 30. ...R—B 1 because of 31. R—Q R 1, winning a piece.

III.   28. ...Kt—B 3 ; 29. B× Kt, B×B ; 30. Kt—K Kt 5, B—K 1 ; 31. Q—B 2, Kt—Kt 5 ; 32. B×Kt, R×B ; 33. Kt(Kt 5)—K 4, R—Q 5 ;   34. K R—Q B 1, R× P ? ; 35. Kt×Q B P, winning a Rook.

IV.   28. ...Kt—Kt 5 ; 29. B× Kt, P×B ; 30. Kt—K Kt 5, B—K 1 ; 31. K R—Q B 1 with much the better game.

| 29. | B×Kt | P×B |

If now 30. Kt×P ?, B—Kt 5 !

| 30. | Q—B 3 ! | B—Kt 5 |

The natural move 30. ...B—K 3, says the Tournament Book, would not do because of 31. P—B 5, P×P ; 32. Kt×P(B 5), Q—Q 2 ; 33. Kt×B and now :

I.   33. ...K×Kt ; 34. B—Kt 5 !, B×Kt ; 35. B—B 6 ch, K—Kt 1 ;   36. P—K 6, B×P ; 37. Q—B 4 !, K—R 2 ; 38. Q—Kt 5 and wins.

II. 33. ...B×Kt; 34. P—K
6, B—Kt 5; 35. Q—B 4 !, Q—Kt
2; 36. P—K 7 ch, K×Kt; 37.
Q—Kt 5 ch, K—R 2; 38. Q—R 6
ch, K—Kt 1; 39. P—K 8(Q) ch,
R×Q; 40. R×R mate.

31. Q×P   B—K 3

White threatened 32. Kt×P,
Q×Kt; 33. Q—Q 6 ch.

32. Q—B 3   Kt—Kt 5

If 32. ... B×Kt P; 33. Kt—
K Kt 5 followed by P—B 5 etc.

33. B×Kt   P×B
34. Kt—K Kt 5   K—Kt 1
35. Kt×B   P×Kt
36. R—K 2

P—Kt 4 is in the air, but it would
be premature here: 36. P—Kt 4,
P×P; 37. Q×P, Q—K 2; 38.
K—Kt 3, R—R 4 followed by ...
K—R 2 with a much better game
for Black than he gets in the text.

36. ......   K—R 2
37. R—Q B 1   K R—Q 1
38. P—Kt 4 ! ?

This leads to risky and exciting
play. 38. R(B 1)—B 2 would have
avoided the following complications, leading to an easier win.

38. ......   R×Kt

If instead 38. ...P×P; 39.
Q×P, R×Kt; 40. P×R, P—R 7;
41. R×K P, P—R 8(Q); 42. Q×
P ch, K—R 1; 43. R—K 8 ch !,
R×R; 44. Q×R ch, K—R 2; 45.
R×Q, Q×R (if 45. ...B×R;
46. Q—K 7 ch !); 46. Q—K 4 ch
followed by Q×P and wins (the
Tournament Book).

39. P×R   P—R 7
40. R×K P   P—R 8(Q)
41. R×Q   Q×R
42. Q—K 4

The Tournament Book points out
that Black has no satisfactory move:
I. 42. ...P×P; 43. Q×P ch,
K—Kt 1 (if 43. ...K—R 1; 44.
P—Q 7, R—K B 1; 45. Q—R 5 ch,
K—Kt 1; 46. Q—Q 5 ! and wins);
44. P—Q 7, R—K B 1; 45. R—
K 8, Q—B 3 (mate was threatened);
46. R×R ch, Q×R; 47. Q—K 6
ch, K—R 2 (if 47. ...K—R 1; 48.
Q—K 8 wins); 48. Q—K 4 ch,
K—R 3 (forced); 49. K—Kt 3 !,
B—B 3; 50. P—R 5 !, K×P (or
50. ...Q—Kt 2; 51. Q—K 8 and
wins); 51. Q—R 7 ch, Q—R 3;
52. Q—B 5 ch and wins.
II. 42. ...Q—Kt 7 ch; 43.
K—Kt 3, Q×P; 44. Q×P ch,
K—Kt 1; 45. R—K 8 ch, R×R;
46. Q×R ch, K—R 2; 47. Q×
P ch, K—Kt 1; 48. Q—K 8 ch,
K—R 2; 49. Q—K 4 ch followed
by P—Q 7 and wins.

42. ......   Q—K B 8
43. Q×P ch   K—Kt 1
44. R—K 8 ch   R×R
45. Q×R ch   B—B 1
46. Q—K 6 ch   K—R 2

Or 46. ...K—Kt 2; 47. Q—

K 5 ch, K—Kt 1 ; 48. Q—Q 5 ch,
K—Kt 2 ; 49. Q—Kt 5 ch, K—
B 2 ; 50. Q×P ch with an easy
win. Black's hope of a perpetual
check is futile.

47. Q—B 7 ch	B—Kt 2
48. Q×P ch	B—R 3
49. Q—B 5 ch	K—Kt 1

If 49. ...K—Kt 2 ; 50. K—
Kt 3 !, Q—Kt 8 ch ; 51. K—B 3,
Q—R 8 ch ; 52. K—K 3, Q—K 8
ch ; 53. K—Q 4, Q—B 6 ch ; 54.
K—K 4 wins easily.

| 50. Q—Q 5 ch | K—B 1 |
| 51. P—Kt 5 ! | |

The B P does not signify.

| 51. ...... | Q×P ch |
| 52. K—R 3 | B×P |

Or 52. ...Q—B 8 ch ; 53. K—
Kt 4, Q—K 7 ch ; 54. K—B 5 etc.

53. P×B	Q—K 6 ch
54. K—Kt 4	Q—Kt 8 ch
55. K—B 5	Q—B 7 ch
56. K—Kt 6	Resigns

A highly enjoyable game.

84. VIENNA, 1922

(Special Prize)

CARO-KANN DEFENCE

It has often been observed that life
imitates art, and this charming
game is a case in point. The ending harks back to a famous Troitzky
composition (*White* : King on Q 5,
Bishop on K R 6, Pawn on K Kt 7 ;
Black : King on K B 2, Pawns on
K 2 and K R 2. *Solution* : 1.

P—Kt 8(Q) ch, K×Q ; 2. K—
K 6, K—R 1 ; 3. K—B 7 and wins).

| *White* | *Black* |
| Dr. S. Tarrasch | R. Réti |

| 1. P—K 4 | P—Q B 3 |

In the palmy days of Hyper-
modernism, this move was considered one of the "refutations" of
1. P—K 4.

2. Kt—Q B 3	P—Q 4
3. Kt—B 3	Kt—B 3
4. P×P	

4. P—K 5 is more in the spirit of
the variation, but after 4. ...Kt—
K 5 Black's game is satisfactory.
With his next move, Tarrasch returns to more orthodox ground.

4.	P×P
5. P—Q 4	B—Kt 5
6. P—K R 3	B×Kt

Apparently Réti shrinks from the
obscure complexities of 6. ...B—
R 4 ; 7. B—Kt 5 ch, Kt—B 3 ; 8.
P—K Kt 4, B—Kt 3 ; 9. Kt—K 5,
R—B 1 ; 10. P—K R 4 etc.

| 7. Q×B | P—K 3 |

...Kt—B 3 would have been
more energetic.

| 8. B—Q 3 | Kt—B 3 |
| 9. B—K 3 | B—K 2 |

...Q—Kt 3 looks more promis-
ing than it actually is, for after 10.
O—O !, Q×Kt P ? ? ; 11. Kt—
Kt 5 threatens K R—Kt 1 as well
as Kt—B 7 ch, while if 10. ...
Kt×P ? ? ; 11. Q—B 4, B—B 4 ;
12. Kt—R 4 and White annexes a
piece.

10. O—O   O—O

At last threatening ...Kt—Q Kt 5, which would have been ineffectual previously because of B—Kt 5 ch.

11. P—R 3

Preventing ...Kt—Q Kt 5 but creating a target on which Black at once trains his guns. White must counter with some action on the King's side, thus presaging an exciting struggle.

11. ......   P—Q R 3

The apparently freeing move 11. ...P—K 4 would only lead to a weak Q P after 12. P×P, Kt×P ; 13. Q—B 5, Kt×B (not 13. ...Kt—B 5 ? ; 14. Kt×P !) ; 14. Q×Q Kt.

12. Kt—K 2   P—Q Kt 4
13. B—K B 4   Q—Kt 3
14. P—B 3   Kt—Q R 4
15. Q R—Q 1 !   Kt—B 5
16. B—B 1

Black's Q Kt has a beautiful post at Q B 5. By way of partial compensation, White is able to guard the Q Kt P in the most economical manner.

16. ......   Q—B 3

With a futile hope of being able to play ...Kt—K 5. But time is lost and the Queen's position here turns out to have some unfortunate aspects. ...P—Q R 4 was preferable.

17. Kt—Kt 3   P—Q R 4
18. K R—K 1 !   P—Kt 5 ?

Underestimating the strength of White's 20th move. ...R—R 2 or ...K R—K 1 should have been played.

19. R P×P   P×P
20. Kt—B 5 !   P×Kt

This ultimately turns out to be unsatisfactory because of the resulting weakness of the black squares. However, the alternatives are not pleasant :

I. 20. ...B—Q 3 ? ; 21. Kt×P !, K×Kt ; 22. B—R 6 ch ! and wins.

II. 20. ...K R—K 1 ; 21. Kt×B ch, R×Kt ; 22. B—Kt 5 !, Kt×P ; 23. B×Kt, P×B ; 24. B×P ch ! and wins. For example 24. ...K—Kt 2 ; 25. Q—Kt 4 ch !, K—R 1 ; 26. R—K 3 ! !, Kt×R ; 27. R—Kt 3 and mate follows.

III. 20. ...B—Q 1 ; 21. B×Kt, Q×B ; 22. Kt—K 3, Q—B 1 ; 23. P—B 4 !, P×P ; 24. Kt×P with a vastly superior position.

21. R×B   P×P
22. P×P   P—Kt 3

Now both players have weaknesses, but, as will be seen, Black's are far more serious.

23. B—R 6 !   Kt—Kt 7

Ingeniously striving for complications. If instead 23. ...K R—K 1 ; 24. R×R ch, Kt×R (or 24. ...R×R ; 25. P—Kt 4 !) ; 25. B×Kt, Q×B ; 26. Q—K 3 ! with a powerful grip on the black squares.

24. R—Kt 1 !   Kt×B
25. Q×Kt !

Better than 25. B×R, which

would part with the valuable Q B
and give Black the pleasant choice
between 25. ...K×B ; 26. R—
K 3, Q×P ; 27. R×Kt, Q—B 7
followed by ...Kt—K 5 or (still
better) 25. ...Q×P ! ; 26. R—
K 3, R—R 8 ! ; 27. R×R, Q×R
ch ; 28. K—R 2, Kt—K 8 ! ; 29.
Q—K 2, K×B ; 30. Q×Kt, Q×P
etc.

25. ......   K R—Kt 1

After 25. ...K R—K 1 White
could maintain the pressure with
26. R(K 7)—Kt 7. Réti can hardly
be blamed for failing to foresee the
problem-like winning continuation
which Tarrasch is preparing. The
winning process is classic in its convincing economy of means and
simplicity of procedure.

26. R×R ch   R×R
27. Q—Kt 3   R—Q 1

Or 27. ...R—K 1 ; 28. Q—K 5
(threatens Q×Kt !) and White has
a winning game.

28. Q—K 5

Interestingly enough, White has
a mating attack which can be parried only by recourse to a lost ending.

28. ......   R—R 1

The alternatives are interesting :

I. 28. ...R—Q B 1 ; 29. P—
Q B 4 ! !, P×P ; 30. P—Q 5 !, Q—
R 3 ; 31. P—Q 6 and wins.
II. 28. ...R—Q 3 ; 29. R—
Kt 7 ! ! and Black is lost :
  (A) 29. ...Q×R ; 30. Q×R,
Kt—Q 2 ; 31. Q—K 7, Q—B 1 ;
32. P—K B 4, Kt—B 1 ; 33. Q—
K 5, Kt—K 3 ; 34. Q×Q P and
wins.
  (B) 29. ...R—Q 1 ; 30. Q—
K 7 and wins.
  (C) 29. ...Kt—K 1 ; 30. R—
Kt 8, R—K 3 ; 31. Q—Kt 7 mate.
  (D) 29. ...R—K 3 ; 30. R—
Kt 8 ch (or Q×Kt !), R—K 1 ; 31.
Q×Kt !

29. R—B 7 !   Q—K 3

Black has no choice in view of the
threatened Q—K 7.

30. Q×Q   P×Q
31. R—Kt 7 ch   K—R 1
32. R—K 7   K—Kt 1

...Kt—Kt 1 ? ? allows mate on
the move !

33. P—B 3 !

33. R×K P, K—B 2 would allow
Black to free himself. The text is
played to prevent ...Kt—K 5—
part of the programme of constriction which will starve Black of
moves.

33. ...   Kt—K 1

No better is 33. ...R—K 1 ; 34.
R—Kt 7 ch, K—R 1 ; 35. R—
K B 7, Kt—R 4 ; 36. P—Kt 4,
K—Kt 1 (if 36. ...Kt—Kt 6 ; 37.

K—B 2, Kt—R 8 ch ; 38. K—Kt 2 winning the Knight) ; 37. R—R 7, Kt—B 3 ; 38. R—Kt 7 ch, K—R 1 ; 39. R—K B 7—or 33. ... Kt—R 4 ; 34. P—Kt 4, Kt—Kt 6 (if 34. ...Kt—B 3 ; 35. R—Kt 7 ch, K—R 1 ; 36. R—K B 7) ; 35. K—B 2, Kt—R 8 ch ; 36. K—Kt 2, R—R 8 ; 37. R—Kt 7 ch. K—R 1 ; 38. R—K B 7 (Tartakover) and White wins nicely in either event.

34. K—R 2 !

Beginning a delightful journey by the King which provides the finishing touch to Black's cramped position.

34.	Kt—Q 3
35. R—Kt 7 ch	K—R 1
36. R—Q 7 !	Kt—Kt 4

...Kt—K 1 would be no better.

37. K—Kt 3	Kt×B P
38. K—B 4	Kt—Kt 4
39. K—K 5	R—K 1
40. K—B 6	Resigns

For if 40. ...K—Kt 1 ; 41. R—Kt 7 ch, K—R 1 ; 42. R—Kt 7, Kt—Q 3 ; 43. R—Q 7, Kt—Kt 4 ; 44. K—B 7, R—K Kt 1 ; 45. R—Q 8 ! A striking triumph for the Tarrasch constriction strategy !

85. VIENNA, 1922

RUY LOPEZ

SOME opening moves are so obviously disadvantageous and lead so clearly to disaster that their adoption by a first-class master constitutes a psychological puzzle. Here, for example, Bogolyubov's 9th move spells utter ruin.

| *White* | *Black* |
| E. BOGOLYUBOV | DR. S. TARRASCH |

1. P—K 4	P—K 4
2. Kt—K B 3	Kt—Q B 3
3. B—Kt 5	P—Q R 3
4. B—R 4	Kt—B 3
5. O—O	Kt×P

Once more Tarrasch adopts his beloved defence.

6. P—Q 4	P—Q Kt 4
7. B—Kt 3	P—Q 4
8. P×P	B—K 3
9. Kt—B 3 ? ?	

As the deadly consequence of this move (the permanent exclusion of the K B) is easily foreseen, it is hard to understand Bogolyubov's avoidance of 9. P—B 3.

| 9. ...... | Kt×Kt |
| 10. P×Kt | Kt—K 2 |

In order to play ...P—Q B 4—5.

11. P—Q R 4 ?

The resulting opening of the Q R file makes a bad position still worse. 11. B—R 3, Kt—B 4 ; 12. B×B, K×B ; 13. P—Kt 4, Kt—R 3 ; 14. P—R 3, P—Q B 4 is, however, singularly unattractive.

| 11. ...... | P—Q B 4 |
| 12. B—R 3 | P—B 5 |

From now on, White is in effect a piece behind.

| 13. B—R 2 | Kt—B 4 |

As Black can permit himself a

o

number of luxuries in a position of this type, the loss of castling does no harm.

14. B×B   K×B
15. P×P   P×P

A new danger for White has cropped up : should Black succeed in doubling on the Q R file, the Bishop will be lost. The position reminds one of Game 66.

16. P—Kt 4

True to his style, Bogolyubov makes a dashing attempt to fix his opponent's attention on the King's side.

16. ......   Kt—R 5
17. Kt—Q 4   P—R 4
18. P—B 3   K—Kt 1
19. Q—K 2   R—K R 3

It is obvious that the loss of castling has done Black no harm. If now 20. Kt×P ?, R—R 4 wins some material !

20. P—R 3   P×P
21. B P×P

21. ......   R—R 6 !

This seals the fate of the Bishop. If now 22. Kt×P, Q—Kt 3 ch;

23. Kt—Q 4, Q—R 3 and the Bishop is lost. If 22. Q—K 1, Q—R 4 ; 23. Q—Kt 1, Q×P (or ... B—Q 2 followed by ...R—R 3) and wins.

22. Q—K 3   Q—R 1
23. R—B 6

An attempted swindle which is easily refuted.

23. ......   R×B
24. Q R×R   Q×R
25. R×R   P×R
26. Q×P

If 26. Kt×B, Q—Kt 8 ch ; 27. K—B 2, P×Kt ; 28. Q×P, Q×P ch followed by ...Kt—Kt 3.

26. ......   Kt—Kt 3
27. K—B 2   Q—R 2
28. K—K 2   Q—K 2
29. Kt—B 3   B—Q 2
30. Q—K 3   K—Kt 2
31. Q—Q 4   P—B 3
32. Q×Q P ? ?

A merciful conclusion to White's sufferings.

32. ......   Kt—B 5 ch
Resigns.

86. CARLSBAD, 1923
RUY LOPEZ

TARRASCH'S opponent attempts to create complications, but the older master soon turns them to his advantage. This is a good example of the Tarrasch Defence.

White   *Black*
O. CHAJES   DR. S. TARRASCH

1. P—K 4   P—K 4
2. Kt—K B 3   Kt—Q B 3

3. B—Kt 5	P—Q R 3
4. B—R 4	Kt—B 3
5. O—O	Kt×P
6. P—Q 4	P—Q Kt 4
7. B—Kt 3	P—Q 4
8. P×P	B—K 3
9. P—B 3	B—K 2
10. Q Kt—Q 2	

Regarding 10. R—K 1 and its sequel, the Breslau Variation, see the following game.

10.	O—O

In Game 68 Tarrasch played ... Kt—B 4 at this point. If White answers the text with 11. Kt×Kt, Black can play either 11. ...P× Kt ; 12. B×B, P×B or 12. ... P×Kt ; 13. B—Q 5, Kt×P !

11. B—B 2	P—K B 4

After 11. ...Kt—B 4 White has the interesting continuation 12. Kt—Q 4 !, Kt×P ; 13. P—K B 4!, B—Kt 5 ; 14. Q—K 1, B—R 5 ; 15. Q×Kt, R—K 1 ; 16. Kt— B 6!, Q—Q 2 ; 17. P—B 5 ! with a winning position (Bogolyubov— Réti, Stockholm, 1919).

12. Kt—Kt 3	

12. P×P e.p., Kt×P(B 3) ; 13. Kt—Kt 5, B—K Kt 5 gives Black a satisfactory game.

12.	Q—Q 2
13. Q Kt—Q 4	Kt×Kt
14. Kt×Kt	

After 14. P×Kt, P—B 4 ; 15. P×P, B×P Black's free position, as so often happens in this variation, outweighs the somewhat ragged state of his Pawns.

14.	P—B 4
15. Kt×B	Q×Kt
16. P—B 3	Kt—Kt 4
17. B×Kt	

This leads to Bishops on opposite colours, but White wants to play P—K B 4 without allowing ... Kt—K 5. Chajes was also probably anxious to rid himself of the Q B, which would be sadly limited in scope after 17. P—K B 4.

17.	B×B
18. P—K B 4	B—Q 1 !

The Bishop will take up a fine post at Q Kt 3.

19. Q—B 3	B—Kt 3

The advance ...P—Q 5 is now in the air.

20. Q R—Q 1	Q R—Q 1
21. K—R 1	

Maróczy comments in the Tournament Book that, without having committed a positive error, White is left with the inferior game.

21.	R—Q 2

A superfluous preparatory move. He could have played ...P—B 5 followed by ...P—Q 5, saving a tempo.

22. P—K R 3	P—B 5
23. P—K Kt 4	

Chajes believes in energetic measures, all the more so since 23. R—Q 2, P—Q 5 ; 24. P×P, B×P ; 25. K R—Q 1, K R—Q 1 would leave Black a fine game without any compensating counterplay for White.

23. ......   P—Kt 3
24. P×P   P×P
25. R—Q 2   P—Q 5

This must be played at once; else White might continue with K R—Q 1.

26. P×P   R×P
27. R—Kt 2 ch K—R 1
28. Q—R 3   Q—R 3 !

Parrying White's threat and threatening ...R—Q 6 !

29. R—B 3   R—K 1
30. Q×P

Since 30. B×P would be answered more than satisfactorily with ...R×B P, Chajes strives to give the game a new turn. The play now becomes very critical.

30. ......   Q—Q B 3 !

31. Q—R 3

The only defence against the double threat of ...R—R 1 and ... Q×R. Maróczy refutes 31. R(B 3)—K Kt 3 ?! with 31. ... R—Q 7 ! (not 31. ...R—R 1 ; 32. Q—R 3 !) ; 32. B×P (if 32. Q—R 3, R×B ; 33. Q—K 7 ?, R—

B 8 ch ; 34. K—R 2, Q×R ch etc.), R×R ; 33. R×R, R—K Kt 1 ; 34. B—Kt 4, P—R 4 ; 35. Q—R 3, P×B ; 36. P×P, B—B 4 ; 37. Q—Q B 3, P—Kt 5 etc.

31. ......   B—B 4

...P—Kt 5 would be answered by Q—R 4.

32. P—Kt 4

Forced !

32. ......   B×P
33. Q—R 7   R—Q 2
34. Q—B 2   R—K B 1
35. Q—Kt 3 ?

Fatal ; he should have played 35. Q—B 1, with some defensive chances.

35. ......   B—K 8 !
36. Q—Kt 5

Equivalent to resignation, but after 36. R(B 3)—B 2, B×R ; 37. Q×B, R—K Kt 1 or 36. R(Kt 2)—B 2, R—K Kt 1 ; 37. Q—R 2, B× R ; 38. Q×B, R—Q 7 White's game would be hopeless.

36. ......   Q×R
37. B×P   B—R 5
38. Q—Kt 4   R—Q 8 ch
39. K—R 2   Q×Q
40. B×Q   R—K B 8
41. P—B 5   R—B 7
42. P—B 6   R×R ch
43. K×R   P—B 6
44. B—Q 1   R—Q 1

White resigns. He could have spared himself the last eight moves.

87. CARLSBAD, 1923

RUY LOPEZ

This game is played with a verve which is astounding in an old man. So resounding a victory with one of his favourite variations must have given Tarrasch special pleasure.

White	Black
H. Wolf	Dr. S. Tarrasch

1. P—K 4	P—K 4
2. Kt—K B 3	Kt—Q B 3
3. B—Kt 5	P—Q R 3
4. B—R 4	Kt—B 3
5. O—O	Kt × P
6. P—Q 4	P—Q Kt 4
7. B—Kt 3	P—Q 4
8. P × P	B—K 3
9. P—B 3	B—K 2
10. R—K 1	O—O
11. Kt—Q 4	Kt × K P !

The famous Breslau Variation. For 11. ...Q—Q 2 ?? see Game 16.

12. P—B 3	B—Q 3
13. P × Kt	B—K Kt 5

Black has only a Pawn for the piece and he must therefore mass his pieces rapidly for a powerful attack. White's material advantage is deceptive, for his development has been retarded and Black has many hidden resources.

14. Q—Q 2

The alternative is 14. Q—B 2, P—Q B 4 ; 15. B × P (or 15. Kt × P, P × Kt ; 16. B × P, Q—R 5 ; 17. R—B 1, R—R 3 ! ; 18. B—K B 4, P—B 5 ; 19. Kt—R 3, B—B 4 ch ; 20. K—R 1, Kt—Q 6 ; 21. Kt × Kt P, P—Kt 4 ; 22. B—B 7, Kt—

B 7 ch ; 23. R × Kt, B × R ; 24. B × P, R—Q B 3 ; 25. B—K 2, B × B ; 26. Q × B, R × B with advantage to Black), P × Kt ; 16. B × R, Q—R 5 ; 17. R—B 1, P—Q 6 ; 18. Q—B 2, Q × Q ch (Teichmann-John, Breslau, 1913) with equal chances.

14.	Q—R 5
15. P—K R 3	

P—Kt 3 would create painful weaknesses.

15.	P—Q B 4 !

In a game played the previous year between the same opponents at Teplitz-Schönau, the continuation had been 15. ...B—Q 2 ; 16. B × P, P—B 3 ; 17. B—Kt 3, P—Q B 4 ; 18. Kt—B 5, B × Kt ; 19. P × B, Kt—Q 6 ; 20. R—K 3, P—B 5 ; 21. B—B 2, B—B 4 ; 22. B × Kt, P × B ; 23. Q—K B 2, Q—B 3 ; 24. K—B 1, Q R—K 1 ; 25. Q—B 3, B × R ; 26. B × B, Q—K 2 ; 27. K—B 2, Q—R 5 ch ; 28. K—B 1, Q—K 2 ; 29. K—B 2 and the game was abandoned as a draw on the following move. This is a fine example of the variation.

16. P × B

The *Laröbok* points out that 16.
Q—K B 2, Q×Q ch; 17. K×Q,
B—Q 2!; 18. Kt—B 5, B×Kt;
19. P×B, Kt—Q 6 ch; 20. K—
B 1, Kt×R; 21. K×Kt, B—Kt 6
ch; 22. K—B 1, K R—K 1; 23.
B—Q 2, R—K 4 is in Black's
favour. The text, on the other
hand, leads to a kind of game in
which White is beset with intang-
ible difficulties. Such positions are
both tiring and discouraging, which
explains why Wolf eventually drifts
into a lost game.

16. ......   P×Kt
17. Q—K B 2   Q×P

Decidedly more promising than
...Q×Q ch followed by ...Kt—
Q 6 ch.

18. B—Q 1

In order to play Q×P without
having to fear ...Kt—B 6 ch.
The text has been criticised as too
passive, but the position is perplex-
ing. Thus if 18. Q—B 5, Q—R 5;
19. Q—B 2 (not 19. R—B 1, Kt—
Kt 5), Kt—B 6 ch!; 20. P×Kt,
B—Kt 6; 21. Q—K 2, B×R; 22.
B×P, Q R—Q 1; 23. P×P, K R
—K 1; 24. B—K 3, R—Q 3 and
wins.

18. ......   Q—Kt 3
19. Q×P

White seems to be safe now, but
Tarrasch's clever reply revives the
attack.

19. ......   B—B 2!

Threatens ...B—Kt 3.

20. B—K 3

If 20. Q×P, Q R—Q 1; 21.
Q—Kt 3, Kt—Q 6 with a winning
game.

20. ......   P×P

Now Black has two Pawns for the
piece, and his King's side Pawns
can become very dangerous.

21. Kt—Q 2   P—B 4

Threatening to win a piece with
...P—B 5.

22. Q—B 5

Gaining time for B—Q 4 in due
course.

22. ......   Q R—B 1
23. R—K B 1   Kt—Q 6

He could have won the Queen
here with 23. ...Kt—B 6 ch and
24. ...B—R 7 ch, but the cost
would have been fantastic.

24. Q—Q 5 ch   K—R 1
25. R—B 2

White is only too ready to part
with surplus material in view of the
fearful threat of ...Q—Kt 6.

25. ......   Kt×R

25. ...Q—Kt 6? would have
been pointless because of 26. Kt—
B 1.

26. B×Kt

Wolf must have been relieved to
see the last of the terrible Knight!

26. ......   K R—Q 1
27. Q—Kt 7   Q—Q 3
28. Kt—B 1   R—R 1

Threatening to win the Queen with ...K R—Q Kt 1.

29. B—Q Kt 3   K R—Q Kt 1

Tarrasch's play lacks incisiveness hereabouts ; it is not easy to make further headway and the clock ticks away inexorably in such situations.

30. Q—Q 5   R—K B 1
31. B—B 5 ?

Weak. White's best chance was to exchange Queens and rely on his two Bishops in the struggle to hold back Black's powerful King's side Pawns.

31. ......   Q—R 3 !

Wolf must have overlooked the consequences of this strong (and necessary !) move, reckoning only on the feeble 31. ...Q × Q ? which would lose the exchange in amusing fashion.

32. B × R ?

This loses without any chance of a fight for the draw ; but White's position had already become desperate in any case. A likely possibility was 32. B—Q 4, P—B 5 ! ; 33. Q × K P, P—B 6 ! ; 34. P × P, Q R—K 1 ; 35. Q—Q 3, Q—Kt 4 ch ; 36. K—R 1, Q—R 4 ch ; 37. K—Kt 2, R—B 4 and wins.

32. ......   R × B

Now White must give back the exchange, in view of the terrible threat ...B—Kt 3 ch. If 33. P—K Kt 3, B—Kt 3 ch ; 34. K—Kt 2, P—B 5 wins in quick time.

33. R—Q 1   B—Kt 3 ch
34. R—Q 4   Q—K B 3
35. Kt—K 3   P—Kt 3

Note how comfortably Black can proceed in the absence of White's Q B. Tarrasch's plan is simple and irresistible : Black's King's side Pawns will advance triumphantly, escorted if need be by the King.

36. Kt—B 2   K—Kt 2
37. K—B 1   B × R
38. Kt × B

Q × B would not alter the result, as White's pieces would be helpless against the Pawns.

38. ......   K—R 3
39. Kt—K 6   R—K 1
40. Q—Q 6   P—Kt 4
41. P—Kt 4 ? !

Breaking up the Pawns, but to no avail.

41. ......   P × P ch
42. K—K 1   R—K 2
43. B—Q 5   K—Kt 3 !

A sardonic invitation to 44. B × P ch, K—B 2 ; 45. B—Q 5, R × Kt etc.

44. K—Q 1   P—K 6
45. Kt—B 8 ch   K—Kt 2
46. Kt—K 6 ch   K—Kt 3
47. Kt—B 8 ch   K—B 4
48. Q—Q 8   Q—K 4
49. Q—B 8 ch   K—B 5

"My King likes to go for a walk".

50. Q—B 5   K—Kt 6
51. K—B 1

A last trap : if 51. ...P—K 7 ? ; 52. Q—Kt 1 ch draws.

51. ......   K—R 5 !

White resigns. A highly interesting game.

88. TRIESTE, 1923

INDIAN DEFENCE

THIS is one of the games in the great Tarrasch tradition. He systematically exploits his advantage on the Queen's side until Black is reduced to a state of virtual *Zugzwang*. All this is accomplished by far from obvious moves.

White	*Black*
DR. S. TARRASCH	F. D. YATES

1. Kt—K B 3	Kt—K B 3
2. P—Q 4	P—K Kt 3
3. P—B 4	B—Kt 2
4. Kt—B 3	P—Q 3
5. P—K 4	Kt—B 3

Burn's famous move, during the early post-war years highly thought of, but nowadays rarely encountered ; its objectives (opening the K B's diagonal and working the Q Kt around to Q B 4 after provoking P—Q 5) are plausible in theory, but have very little practical value.

6. P—K R 3 !

The old Tarrasch theme : ... B—Kt 5 is prevented ; the Q B accomplishes nothing during the game, and Black's position is encumbered with a useless piece.

6.	O—O
7. B—K 3	P—K 4

This violates one of the underlying ideas of 5. ...Kt—B 3, since

the diagonal of Black's K B is now permanently blocked.

8. P—Q 5	Kt—Kt 1
9. Q—Q 2	Q Kt—Q 2

...Kt—K 1 would have been better, as Tarrasch's excellent 12th move demonstrates.

10. B—Q 3	P—Q R 4
11. B—B 2	Q—K 2
12. B—Kt 5 !	

Preventing Black's natural counterplay, which consists in retreating his K Kt and advancing ...P—K B 4. Black eventually succeeds in driving the irritating Q B away from K Kt 5, but in the process he displaces his pieces to such an extent that any possible counter-attack has little value.

12.	Kt—B 4
13. P—Q Kt 3 !	

Beginning the process of ejecting Black's Q Kt from Q B 4.

13.	R—K 1
14. O—O	Q—B 1
15. P—R 3	P—R 3

At last Black has succeeded in removing the Q B ; but he has paid a heavy price in the awkward position of his pieces.

16. B—K 3	B—Q 2

The alternative was 16. ...P—Kt 3 ; 17. P—Q Kt 4, Kt—Kt 2, with much the same kind of Pawn structure and strategical features as in Game 57 !

17. P—Q Kt 4   P × P

After 17. ...Kt—R 3 White could proceed advantageously with Kt—Q R 4 or Kt—Q Kt 5.

18. P×P	R×R
19. R×R	Kt—R 3
20. R—Kt 1	Kt—R 4

Hoping for some counteraction on the King's side. The following advance could have been prevented by 20. ...P—Kt 3, but after 21. B—Q 3 (threatening P—B 5), R—R 1 ; 22. Q—Kt 2 followed by R—R 1 Black would have a strategically lost game.

Now comes a fine stroke by Tarrasch.

21. P—Kt 5 !

Wholly unexpected, and obviously the result of a profound understanding of the position. The natural procedure is to play for P—B 5, but Tarrasch sees an opportunity to proceed even more effectively.

| 21. ...... | Kt—B 4 |
| 22. P—Kt 6 ! | |

The point. If Black captures, he is left with a miserably weak Q Kt P

and Q P ; he therefore chooses what is apparently the lesser evil.

| 22. ...... | P—Q B 3 |
| 23. B×Kt ! | |

Since White's remaining Bishop will apparently have little scope, it required real courage and considerable foresight to make this move.

| 23. ...... | P×B |
| 24. P×P | B×B P |

Allowing White to invade Q 5, but ...P×P would free White's Q Kt P, as well as saddle Black with two very weak Q B Ps.

| 25. Kt—Q 5 ! | R—Q 1 |
| 26. R—Q 1 | K—R 2 |

Kt—K 7 ch was threatened.

| 27. Q—K 3 | B×Kt |

If 27. ...R—R 1 ; 28. Q—B 3 followed by R—R 1 with a winning advantage.

28. B P×B	Q—Q 3
29. R—Kt 1	B—B 3
30. R—Kt 5	B—K 2
31. Q—B 3	

Every move tells. White steadily increases the pressure until further resistance becomes impossible.

| 31. ...... | P—B 3 |
| 32. Kt—Q 2 ! | |

The Knight is to go to Q R 5.

| 32. ...... | Kt—B 5 |
| 33. K—B 1 | Kt—K 3 |

Heading for Q 5—generally a

powerful post, but it has no importance here on account of the following formidable concentration of
White's forces.

34. Kt—B 4	Q—Q 2
35. R—R 5	Kt—Q 5
36. B—R 4	Q—B 1
37. R—R 7	P—B 4

Despair—the Q Kt P cannot be
protected adequately.

38. Kt—R 5	K—R 1
39. Kt×P	P×P

If the Rook moves, P—Q 6—7
wins easily.

40. Kt×R	B×Kt
41. P—Kt 7	Resigns

A strategical masterpiece.

89. MÄHRISCH-OSTRAU, 1923

NIMZOVICH OPENING

BOGOLYUBOV'S exaggerated optim-
ism has become proverbial. In
the following game he comes a
cropper when he underestimates
Tarrasch's familiarity with hyper-
modern strategy !

White	*Black*
E. BOGOLYUBOV	DR. S. TARRASCH

1. Kt—K B 3	Kt—K B 3
2. P—Q Kt 3	P—K Kt 3

Doubtless an unexpected reply
from Steinitz's contemporary !

3. B—Kt 2	B—Kt 2
4. P—K 4	

This is against the spirit of the
opening. P—K Kt 3 or P—K 3
would be more logical.

4.	P—Q 3
5. P—Q 3	O—O
6. Q Kt—Q 2	P—K 4
7. P—Kt 3	

7. P—Q 4, P×P ; 8. Kt×P,
R—K 1 would at once cede the
initiative to Black.

7.	B—Q 2
8. B—Kt 2	Q—B 1
9. P—K R 3	

White's reluctance to part with
his none too effective K B is difficult to understand. 9. O—O, B—
R 6 ; 10. Kt—K 1 (intending P—
K B 4) was far more promising.

9.	R—K 1
10. Q—K 2	

Bogolyubov's unfortunate 9th
move prevents him from castling
and thus securing a normal development.

10.	P—Q R 4

Intending to open the Q R file,
and thus leaving White little choice.

11. P—Q R 4	Kt—B 3
12. P—K Kt 4 ?	

As the sequel demonstrates, this
seriously compromises White's
game. O—O—O was in order,
with a complicated middle game to
follow.

12.	P—R 4 !
13. P—Kt 5	Kt—K R 2
14. Kt—B 4	Kt—B 1

The Knight is headed for the magnificent square K B 5.

15. Kt—K 3	Kt—K 3
16. Kt—Q 5	Kt—Kt 5
17. Kt × Kt	P × Kt
18. B—Q B 1	

A pathetic admission that his treatment of the opening has been faulty ; but he has no choice.

| 18. ...... | P—Kt 4 ! |
| 19. P—R 5 | |

As a result of Tarrasch's clever advance of the Q Kt P, White's Q R P has been weakened irretrievably, and must soon be lost.

| 19. ...... | P—Q B 4 |
| 20. O—O | |

Losing some material by force, but it hardly matters in view of the unavoidable loss of the Q R P (... Q—B 2 etc.).

20.	Kt—B 5 !
21. B × Kt	P × B
22. K—R 2	

Since moving his Q R would lose the K R P, Bogolyubov desperately decides to give up the exchange, hoping for some compensation on the black squares.

| 22. ...... | B × R |
| 23. R × B | Q—B 2 |

Carrying out the death sentence.

24. Q—Q 2	R × R P
25. R—K Kt 1	R—R 7
26. R—Q B 1	

| 26. ...... | P—Q 4 ! |

This breakthrough must have come as a surprise to White. If now 27. P × P, Q—Q 3 and the Knight dare not move because of ...P—B 6 ch.

| 27. P—K 5 | P—Q 5 |
| 28. Q × B P | B—B 3 |

With a view to ...B × Kt followed by ...Q × P.

29. R—K 1	R × B P
30. Kt—Q 2	B × B
31. K × B	R × Kt !

Rudely smashing White's hope of getting some play with Kt—K 4— B 6 ch.

32. Q × R	R × P
33. R × R	Q × R
34. P—B 4	

Or 34. K—Kt 1, Q—Q 4 winning a Pawn.

34.	Q—Q 4 ch
35. K—Kt 3	Q × P
36. P—B 5	P—B 5
37. K—R 4	Q × P
38. Q × P	Q × P
39. Q—Q 6	Q—B 7 ch

White resigns. A good game by Tarrasch against feeble opposition.

90. MÄHRISCH-OSTRAU, 1923

(Third Brilliancy Prize)

FALKBEER COUNTER-GAMBIT

It is curious that, despite all the extensive research which has been lavished on the openings, inferior lines of play persist for decades. So prevalent is this condition that when some great master refutes one of these faulty variations, he is rightly praised for his originality and profundity.

| *White* | *Black* |
| R. Spielmann | Dr. S. Tarrasch |

| 1. P—K 4 | P—K 4 |
| 2. P—K B 4 | P—Q 4 |

Throughout his career, Tarrasch was convinced that this move constitutes the refutation of the King's Gambit.

3. K P × P	P—K 5
4. P—Q 3	Kt—K B 3
5. P × P	

In recent years Keres has scored some sensational successes with 5. Kt—Q 2, but after 5. ...B—K B 4 ! Black has a satisfactory game.

5.	Kt × K P
6. Kt—K B 3	B—Q B 4
7. Q—K 2	

The crucial position. The old continuation 7. ...B—B 7 ch ; 8.

K—Q 1, Q × P ch ; 9. K Kt—Q 2, P—K B 4 ; 10. Kt—B 3, Q—Q 5 ; 11. Kt × Kt, P × Kt ; 12. P—B 3, Q—K 6 was drastically refuted by Réti in a game with Breyer in the Budapest Tournament, 1917 ; 13. Q—R 5 ch !, K—B 1 ; 14. B—B 4 !, Q × K B P ; 15. Q—Q 5, B—Kt 5 ch ; 16. K—B 2, K—K 1 ; 17. Kt × P, Q—B 4 ; 18. R—B 1, P—B 3 ; 19. Q—Q 3, resigns.

As for 7. ...B—B 4, the *Handbuch* curtly dismisses it because of 8. P—K Kt 4.

| 7. ...... | B—B 4 ! |
| 8. P—K Kt 4 ? | |

Spielmann snaps at the bait. Correct is 8. Kt—B 3, Q—K 2 ; 9. B—K 3 with about even chances.

| 8. ...... | O—O |

The point ! The terribly exposed position of White's King ensures the soundness of the sacrifice.

| 9. P × B | R—K 1 |
| 10. B—Kt 2 | |

A master of the attack such as Spielmann realises that after 10. Q—Kt 2, Q × P ! ; 11. B—K 2, Kt—Q B 3 ; 12. Kt—B 3, Q × B P

White's game must soon collapse; for example 13. Kt—K R 4, Q—B 3; 14. Kt×Kt, Q×Kt ch; 15. Q—Kt 3, Q—K 2; 16. Kt—B 3, Kt—Q 5 and wins.

10.	Kt—B 7
11. Kt—K 5	Kt×R
12. B×Kt	Kt—Q 2 !

Because of the presence of both his King and Queen on the K file, White cannot avoid the loss of his K Kt. But it would be an error for Black to play 12. ...P—K B 3 because of 13. P—Q 6 !, P×P; 14. B—Q 5 ch, K—B 1; 15. Q—R 5 etc.

13. Kt—Q B 3	P—K B 3
14. Kt—K 4	P×Kt
15. Kt×B	Kt×Kt
16. P×P	Q—R 5 ch

White's centre looks imposing, but he is actually on the brink of disaster; if now 17. K—Q 1, Q—Q 5 ch etc.

| 17. K—B 1 | R—K B 1 ! |

The K B P must fall (if 18. P—B 6, Q R—K 1 !).

| 18. K—Kt 1 | Q—Q 5 ch |
| 19. B—K 3 | |

Or 19. Q—K 3, Q—Q 8 ch.

19.	Q×K P
20. R—K 1	Kt—Q 2
21. Q—B 4	K—R 1
22. B—K 4	Q R—K 1
23. B—Q 4	Q—B 5
24. R—K 2	Kt—B 3

Naturally disregarding the transparent booby trap 24. ...R×B ?;

25. R×R, Q×R; 26. B×P ch etc.

| 25. B×Kt | P×B ! |

The opening of the K Kt file leads to a speedy decision.

26. P—K R 3

Refusing to give his opponent the pleasure of answering 26. R—K 1 with ...R—Kt 1 ch; 27. K—R 1, Q—B 6 ch ! and mate in two.

| 26. ...... | R—Kt 1 ch |

White resigns. A most instructive game.

91. MERAN, 1924

(First Brilliancy Prize)

QUEEN'S GAMBIT DECLINED

IT must be frankly admitted that this game hardly deserved a brilliancy prize. Nevertheless, Tarrasch's forthright and consistent utilisation of his advantage cannot fail to evoke admiration.

| White | Black |
| DR. S. TARRASCH | E. COLLE |

1. P—Q 4	P—Q 4
2. P—Q B 4	P—K 3
3. Kt—Q B 3	P—Q B 3
4. Kt—B 3	Kt—B 3

After 4. ...P×P; 5. P—K 3, P—Q Kt 4; 6. P—Q R 4, B—Kt 5; 7. B—Q 2, B×Kt; 8. B×B, P—Q R 4; 9. P×P, P×P White has the advantageous reply 10. P—Q 5 ! (much stronger than

10. P—Q Kt 3, B—Kt 2; 11. P×
P, P—Kt 5).

5. B—Kt 5	B—K 2
6. P—K 3	Q Kt—Q 2
7. B—Q 3	P×P
8. B×B P	P—Kt 4
9. B—Q 3	P—Q R 3
10. O—O	

Black is anxious to round out his
Pawn position with ...P—B 4;
hence the continuation 10. P—
Q R 4, P—Kt 5; 11. B×Kt, Kt×
B; 12. Kt—K 4 naturally suggests
itself.

10.	P—B 4
11. Q—K 2	P—B 5?

The idea of acquiring the Queen's
side majority is seductive but very
risky, as it gives White a free hand
in the centre. ...B—Kt 2 was
better.

12. B—B 2	B—Kt 2
13. P—K 4	

The natural reaction; see the
previous note.

13.	O—O
14. P—K 5	Kt—Q 4
15. Q—K 4	

While Black's Queen's side Pawns
are idle throughout the game, White
has already obtained a strong attack. 15. ...P—B 4 cannot be
played, for then 16. P×P e.p. wins
a Pawn.

15.	P—Kt 3
16. Q—R 4	P—B 3

Leaving the K P in a fatally
weak state, but the alternative 16.
...R—K 1; 17. Kt—K 4 (threaten-

ing Kt—Q 6) is anything but attractive.

17. P×P	B×P
18. Kt—K 4	B×B
19. Q Kt×B	Q—K 2
20. Q R—K 1	

White's pressure against the K P
(a lasting target) gives him an easy
game. If now 20. ...Kt—B 5;
21. Kt×K P !, or 20. ...R—B 5;
21. R×P !

20.	R—B 3
21. P—K Kt 3 !	

Apparently very risky because of
the diagonal of Black's Bishop.
However, Kt—Q 2 could not be
played at once because of ...R—
B 5 in reply.

21.	R—K 1
22. Kt—Q 2	Kt—Kt 5
23. B—K 4	B×B

Or 23. ...Kt—Kt 3; 24. B×
B, Q×B; 25. Kt×R P.

24. Kt(Q 2)×B	K R—B 1

25. Kt—Q 6 !

This clever move induces Black
to give up the exchange, for after

25. ...R—Kt 1 ; 26. R×P Black's game would be in ruins.

25. ......   P—K 4

Desperately hoping to obtain some counterplay.

26. Kt×R   R×Kt
27. P×P   Kt—Q 6

Of course if 27. ...Kt×K P ? ; 28. R×Kt ! Or if 27. ...Kt× R P ; 28. P—B 4 followed by P— B 5 with fatal effect.

28. R—K 2   P—K R 4

But not 28. ...Kt(Q 2)×P ; 29. P—B 4, Q—B 4 ch ; 30. K—Kt 2 and wins.

29. P—B 4   Q—B 4 ch
30. K—Kt 2   Kt—B 3
31. P—K R 3   P—Kt 5

Hopeless.

32. Kt—B 3 !   Q—B 3
33. K—R 2

Threatening to win with 33. Kt—Q 4.

33. ......   Kt—K 5
34. P—B 5 !

Now the position is too much for Black to cope with, although he makes a valiant attempt.

34. ......   Kt×K P

Hoping for 35. R×Kt ?, Kt× Kt ch etc., or 35. Q×Kt ?, Kt— Kt 5 ch.

35. Kt—Q 4 !

Winning the piece. Black is determined, however, to have one last fling before he resigns.

35. ......   Q—Q 4
36. R×Kt   Kt—Kt 5 ch
37. R×Kt   P×R
38. Q×P   R—K 5
39. Q×P ch   Resigns

Black's 11. ...P—B 5 ? was the primary cause of his downfall.

92. BRESLAU, 1925
QUEEN'S GAMBIT DECLINED

It is difficult to put one's finger on Black's decisive mistake in this game. Perhaps the chief responsibility should be assigned to his policy of indecisive drifting.

White	*Black*
Dr. S. Tarrasch	B. Moritz

1. P—Q 4   Kt—K B 3
2. P—Q B 4   P—K 3
3. Kt—Q B 3   P—Q 4
4. B—Kt 5   B—K 2
5. P—K 3   Q Kt—Q 2
6. Kt—B 3   O—O
7. R—B 1   P—B 3
8. Q—B 2   P—Q R 3

...Kt—K 5, with the object of easing Black's defence through exchange, has been popular at this point in recent tournament play.

9. P×P   K P×P
10. B—Q 3   R—K 1
11. O—O   Kt—B 1
12. P—K R 3   Kt—K 5

The customary freeing manœuvre in this variation—but it does not quite succeed in its purpose.

13. B—K B 4   Kt×Kt
14. P×Kt

In more recent times, the alternative 14. Q×Kt has been given preference, with a view to initiating the famous Queen-side minority attack (P—Q Kt 4 etc.). The simpler text also has its points.

14. ......   B—Q 3
15. B×B   Q×B
16. P—B 4   P—Q Kt 4

In an earlier game Grünfeld—J. Bernstein, Carlsbad 1923, the continuation was 16. ...P×P; 17. B×P, B—K 3; 18. Kt—Q 2; White had the advantage because of his pressure on the Q Kt file and the possibility Kt—Kt 3—B 5.

The text move rids Black of the weakness on Q Kt 2 but leaves him vulnerable on the Q B file.

17. P×Q P   P×P
18. Q—B 5   R—Q 1

A highly disagreeable situation for Black; if he exchanges Queens, the pressure on the Q B file and the fact that his Bishop has little mobility result in a hopeless ending for him.

19. Kt—K 5   Kt—K 3

If 19. ...B—Kt 2; 20. Q×Q, R×Q; 21. R—B 7, P—B 3; 22. R×B, P×Kt; 23. P×P and wins.

20. Q—B 2   P—Kt 3

This permits a quickly decisive attack. There was apparently nothing better than the uninspired but safer ...Kt—B 1.

21. P—B 4   B—Kt 2

If 21. ...P—B 4; 22. P—K Kt 4 with a devastating attack; or if 21. ...P—B 3; 22. B×K Kt P and wins. ...Kt—Kt 2 offered more defensive chances.

22. P—B 5   Q R—B 1

Black has been reduced to desperation, for 22. ...Kt—B 1 is at once refuted by 23. P×P, B P×P; 24. Kt—B 7.

23. P×Kt !

Not too difficult to see, but nevertheless elegant and forceful.

23. ......   R×Q
24. P×P ch   K—B 1

24. ...K—Kt 2 would be little better, for after 25. R×R, R—K B 1; 26. Q R—B 2 followed by P—K R 4 ! and P—R 5 Black could not hold out very long.

25. R×R   R—B 1
26. Q R—B 2   R—Q 1

He is helpless against White's next move.

27. B×K Kt P !   P×B
28. R—B 6   Q—R 6
29. Kt×P ch   K—Kt 2

30. P—B 8(Q) ch	R×Q
31. Kt×R	Q×P ch
32. K—R 2	B—B 1
33. R—Kt 6 ch	Resigns

For if 33. ...K—R 1 ; 34. R—B 7. Tarrasch's play has been admirably simple and to the point.

93. SEMMERING, 1926

QUEEN'S PAWN GAME

THIS game is an example of clean-cut exploitation of weak and vacillating treatment of a cramped position.

White	*Black*
DR. S. TARRASCH	DR. W. MICHEL
1. P—Q 4	Kt—K B 3
2. P—Q B 4	P—K 3
3. Kt—K B 3	B—Kt 5 ch
4. B—Q 2	B×B ch

...Q—K 2 is slightly better.

5. Q Kt×B

Not the best, as 5. Q×B reserves the stronger square Q B 3 for the Q Kt.

5. ......   P—Q 4

But this is likewise not best, as it now stamps White's move as a good one ! The text has the drawback of creating a Pawn configuration which hampers the development of Black's remaining Bishop. Preferable, therefore, was ...P—Q 3, intending an eventual ...P—K 4.

| 6. P—K 3 | Q Kt—Q 2 |
| 7. R—B 1 ! | |

Tarrasch's strategy is now directed towards preventing the freeing moves ...P—B 4 or ...P—K 4.

7.	O—O
8. Q—B 2	P—B 3
9. B—Q 3	R—K 1

Kmoch claims that Black's best course is to resign himself to the impossibility of freeing his game at this point, and continuing with ...Q—K 2, ...R—Q 1, ...Kt—B 1, ...B—Q 2—K 1 and ...Q R—B 1. But such a continuation is hardly pleasing in over the board play !

| 10. O—O | Kt—B 1 |

A sorry move, but if 10. ...P—K 4 ; 11. B P×P, leaving Black with an isolated Q P, as the price to pay for freeing his game.

11. P—K 4 !	P×K P
12. Kt×P	Kt×Kt
13. B×Kt	R—K 2

The advance of the K P has enhanced the superior mobility of White's forces.

| 14. Q R—Q 1 | Q—B 2 |
| 15. K R—K 1 | B—Q 2 |

The freedom secured by 15. ...P—Q B 4 ; 16. P×P, Q×P would be deceptive : White would have the Queen's side majority of Pawns, control of the Q file, and an extended diagonal for his Bishop.

16. Kt—Kt 5 !

A subtle move. By forcing the advance of one of the King's side Pawns, Tarrasch prevents the man-

œuvre ...P—B 3 followed by ...
B—K 1—Kt 3.

16.	......	P—K R 3
17.	Kt—B 3	B—K 1
18.	P—B 5 !	

A new phase begins. White submits to a backward Q P and the surrender of his control of Q 5, in order
to cramp Black's game still more,
and to prepare a powerful post at
Q 6 for his Knight.

18.	......	Kt—Q 2
19.	Kt—K 5	Kt—B 3

After 19. ...Kt×Kt ; 20. P×
Kt White would continue with R—
Q 6 and have a strategically won
game.

20. Kt—B 4 !	Kt—Q 4 ?

Feeble. Kmoch points out that
...B—Q 2 would be better, so as to
play ...Kt—K 1 after the arrival at
Q 6 of White's Knight.

21. Kt—Q 6	P—Q Kt 3 ?

There was still time for ...Kt—
B 3—K 1.

22. B×Kt !	B P×B ?

The final mistake. After 22. ...
K P×B White would continue with
P—Q Kt 4, maintaining a marked
positional advantage, but the text is
even worse for Black, as it creates a
passed Q B P for White.

23. P—Q Kt 4	R—Q 1
24. R—Q B 1	P×P

If 24. ...R×Kt ; 25. P×R,
Q×P ; 26. P—Q R 3 and White's
control of the Q B file will decide
the issue.

25. Kt P×P	Q—R 4
26. Q—B 3	

Black should decline this offer to
exchange Queens ; as we shall see
in the remaining play, White's
occupation of the Q Kt file leaves
his opponent without adequate
defence.

26.	......	Q×Q
27.	R×Q	R—B 2

Or 27. ...R—Kt 1 ; 28. R—
Q Kt 3, R×R ; 29. P×R followed
by R—R 1 and P—Q Kt 4—5 with
an easy win.

28. R—Q Kt 3	B—B 3
29. P—B 4	K—B 1
30. K R—Kt 1	K—K 2
31. K—B 2	P—K R 4
32. R—Kt 8	R(B 2)—Q 2

Otherwise White continues victoriously with R×R and R—Kt 8
ch ! But Black cannot hold out
much longer against Tarrasch's
systematic pressure.

33. K—Kt 3	P—B 3
34. R—B 8 !	R×R

The exchange was compulsory ;
but now White makes rapid headway.

35. Kt×R ch	K—B 2
36. R—Kt 3	R—B 2
37. Kt—Q 6 ch	K—Kt 3

If 37. ...K—Kt 1 ; 38. R—
Kt 8 ch, K—R 2 ; 39. R—Q B 8 !
winning with ease.   The text allows
a clever finish.

38. R—K 3	B—Q 2
39. P—B 5 ch !	P×P
40. R—K 7	P—B 5 ch
41. K×P	Resigns

Black has no way of preventing
the loss of a piece (42. P—B 6).
An instructive game.

94. SEMMERING, 1926
INDIAN DEFENCE

In his notes, Réti expresses almost
idolatrous admiration for the exactitude and freshness of the veteran's
play in this highly interesting game.

| *White* | *Black* |
| K. Gilg | Dr. S. Tarrasch |

1. P—Q 4	Kt—K B 3
2. P—Q B 4	P—K 3
3. Kt—Q B 3	B—Kt 5
4. Kt—B 3	

If White is indifferent to the possible doubling of his Q B P, he has
better moves at his disposal than the
text.   Such moves as 4. P—Q R 3
or 4. P—K 3 make it possible to
bring the K Kt to K 2, with the
idea of playing for P—B 3 or P—
K 4.   In comparison, the immediate Kt—B 3 is rather lifeless.

| 4. ...... | Kt—K 5 |
| 5. Q—Q 3 | |

Since this move does not force a
decision as regards the pin, and
since the text has certain tactical
inconveniences, Q—B 2 would be
preferable.

5.	P—K B 4
6. P—K Kt 3	P—Q Kt 3
7. B—Kt 2	B—Kt 2
8. O—O	Kt×Kt
9. P×Kt	B—K 5 !

In effect, Tarrasch has reached a
favourable variation of the Dutch
Defence.   The well-timed text
causes White to lose time by blocking the development of his Q B.

| 10. Q—Q 2 | B—K 2 |
| 11. Kt—K 1 | |

Inevitable, as the hostile Q B was
too well placed.   But White remains without compensation for the
weakness of his Queen's side Pawns.

11.	B×B
12. Kt×B	O—O
13. Q—Q 3	Kt—B 3
14. R—K 1	

A superfluous preparatory move.
P—K 4 could have been played at
once, although Black's game would
have been quite satisfactory.

| 14. ...... | Kt—R 4 ! |

So that if 15. P—K 4 ?, P×P ;
16. R×P, Kt×P !

| 15. B—K 3 | Q—B 1 |
| 16. P—B 5 ? ! | |

Otherwise ...Q—R 3 is ex-
tremely unpleasant.   In playing the
text, White hopes for 16. ...P×P ;
17. P×P, when his newly opened
lines would compensate for his
ragged Pawns.   But Tarrasch plays
a much stronger line.

| 16. ...... | P—Q 4 ! |

Forcing the establishment of his
Knight on the important square
Q B 5.

17. P×P e.p.	P×P
18. B—Q 2	P—Q 4
19. P—B 3	Q—B 5 !
20. Q—K 3	

Putting an end once more to his plans for P—K 4. However, the exchange of Queens would lead to a lost ending, while if 20. Q—B 2, Q R—B 1 (threatens ...Q×P ch) ; 21. P—K 3 (not 21. Q R—B 1, B—R 6), P—Q Kt 4 and Black has a strategically won game.

20.	Q—B 3
21. Q—Q 3	

White has nothing better, but he has allowed Black to win a whole tempo.

21.	Kt—B 5
22. B—B 4	

Apparently provoking the following thrust, which turns out to be quite useful for Black.

22.	P—K Kt 4 !
23. B—B 1	R—B 2 !

He is fully prepared for P—K 4, as will be seen.

24. P—K 4	B P×P
25. P×P	Q R—K B 1

Black's control of the K B file is quite formidable.

26. P—K 5	R—B 6
27. B—K 3	P—Kt 5

Threatening ...B—Kt 4 with decisive effect. As Gilg feels the noose tightening about his neck, he decides to part with a Pawn for temporary relief.

28. Q—K 2	Kt×B
29. Kt×Kt	Q×P

30. Q R—Q 1	P—K R 4
31. R—Q 3	Q—B 2
32. R(Q 3)—Q 1	B—Kt 4
33. Kt—Kt 2	Q—B 6 !

Now White finds himself in *Zugzwang*. He cannot move either Rook or the Knight, so only Queen moves remain ; but that possibility is only an illusion.

34. Q—Kt 5	R—B 7

White resigns, for the threat of 35. ...R×Kt ch ; 36. K×R, Q—B 6 ch ; 37. K—Kt 1, B—K 6 ch is decisive. If he tries 35. R—Q 3, there follows 35. ...Q×R ch ! ; 36. Kt×Q, R—B 8 ch and mate next move.

The most interesting feature of this game has been Tarrasch's clever exploitation of his opponent's weakness on the white squares (Q B 5 and K B 6). White's indifferent opening play has been duly punished.

95. SEMMERING, 1926

INDIAN DEFENCE

TARRASCH'S tactical finesses in this game must have filled his younger opponent with chagrin !

White   *Black*

             MARQUIS
             S. ROSSELLI
DR. S. TARRASCH   DEL TURCO

1. P—Q 4   Kt—K B 3
2. P—Q B 4   P—K 3
3. Kt—K B 3   P—Q Kt 3
4. B—Kt 5

A colourless continuation, which should not offer Black any difficulties.

4. ......   B—Kt 2
5. Kt—B 3   B—Kt 5
6. Q—Kt 3   P—B 4

Very tame. More promising is 6. ...B×Kt ch ; 7. Q×B, P—K R 3 ; 8. B—R 4 (or 8. B×Kt, Q×B with equality), P—K Kt 4 ; 9. B—Kt 3, Kt—K 5 ; 10. Q—B 2, P—K R 4 ! with lively complications.

7. P—Q R 3   B×Kt ch
8. Q×B   Kt—R 3

After this, quite a bit of time elapses before the Q Kt really gets into play ; but Black is reluctant to block the diagonal with the more natural ...Kt—B 3.

9. P—K 3   P—R 3
10. B—R 4   O—O
11. B—Q 3   R—B 1
12. P—Q Kt 4 !

Intending 13. Q P×P, P×P ; 14. P—Kt 5 with a strong game. Black now proceeds to counterplay, but in so doing he opens up the position and thereby increases the usefulness of White's Bishops.

12. ......   P—Q 4
13. Q P×P   Q P×P
14. B×P   P×P
15. P—Kt 5 !

Establishing a useful Queen's side majority.

15. ......   Kt—B 2
16. O—O   Q Kt—Q 4

...B×Kt would be of no value ; White would have two Bishops and attacking chances on the K Kt file, while the "weakness" of his K B Ps would be insignificant.

17. Q—B 2   Kt—Kt 3
18. K R—Q 1   B—K 5
19. Q—K 2   Q Kt—Q 4

20. K B×Kt !

Highly unexpected. 20. ...B×B ? would be refuted by 21. P—K 4 with a winning game.

20. ......   P×B
21. Kt—K 5 !   P—Kt 4

Some kind of weakening of the Pawn position was inevitable. Kt—Kt 4 was threatened, and if 21. ...Q—Q 3 ; 22. B×Kt and Black must retake with the Pawn ; or, if 21. ...B—B 4 ; 22. Kt—B 6, Q—Q 2 ; 23. B×Kt, P×B ; 24. R×P !

22. B—Kt 3   P—Q 5
23. P×P   P×P
24. Kt—Kt 4 !   Kt×Kt
25. Q×B   P—B 4
26. Q—K 6 ch

26. Q×Q P, Q×Q ; 27. R×Q, P—B 5 is not good enough for White. If then 28. P—B 3 ?, Kt —K 6 wins the exchange.

26. ......   K—R 2
27. P—R 3   R—K B 3

Black has no choice : he must part with a Pawn.

28. Q—K 2   P—B 5
29. Q×Kt   P×B
30. P×P

Stronger than 30. Q×P(Kt 3) ; Tarrasch means to utilise the K B file, if the opportunity arises.

30. ......   R—Q 3

Not 30. ...P—Q 6 ? ; 31. Q— K 4 ch etc.

31. R—Q 3   R—B 6
32. R—K B 1 !   R×R ? ?

The second rank had to be protected. After the text, Black's resistance collapses. White has a mating attack.

33. R—B 7 ch   Resigns !

If 33. ...K—Kt 1 ; 34. Q—B 5 forces mate. If 33. ...K—R 1 ; 34. Q—B 5, Q—K Kt 1 ; 35. Q— K 5 ch leads to mate. If 33. ... K—Kt 3 ; 34. Q—B 5 ch, K—R 4 ; 35. P—Kt 4 ch, K—R 5 ; 36. Q— B 2 ch, R—Kt 6 ; 37. K—R 2 and mate next move !

96. SEMMERING, 1926
INDIAN DEFENCE

THOUGH Tarrasch was 64 when this game was played, he conducted the attack with all the verve of a youthful prodigy. His play throughout was bright and original.

	White	Black
	DR. S. TARRASCH	J. DAVIDSON

1. P—Q 4   Kt—K B 3
2. Kt—K B 3   P—K Kt 3
3. Kt—B 3 .

A welcome deviation from the almost obligatory 3. P—B 4. The present game goes far to indicate that White need not suffer from obstructing the advance of the Q B P.

3. ......   B—Kt 2

...P—Q 4 would stop White's next move at least temporarily, but would have the serious drawback of perceptibly weakening Black's grip on the black squares.

4. P—K 4   O—O
5. B—K Kt 5   P—K R 3 ?

A thoughtless weakening move, in view of the fact that White has not castled yet. ...P—Q 3 followed by ...Q Kt—Q 2 was in order.

6. B—K B 4   P—Q 3
7. Q—Q 2   K—R 2
8. O—O—O !

Quite right. White has excellent attacking prospects on the King's side, while Black's chances of countering on the other wing are slight indeed.

8. ......   P—Q R 4

An empty gesture.

9. B—Q 3   Kt—R 3
10. P—K 5 !   Kt—K Kt 1
11. P—K R 4   Kt—Kt 5

White's attack is now proceeding

in full force, so that even this simplifying manœuvre holds out no hope.

12. P—R 5 !	Kt×B ch
13. Q×Kt	B—B 4
14. P×P ch	P×P
15. Q—K 3	P—R 4

The threat was Kt—Kt 5 ch followed by P—B 3 and P—K Kt 4 ; but the text truly meets White halfway !

16. Kt—Kt 5 ch	K—R 1
17. P—B 3	Kt—R 3
18. P—K Kt 4	

The crucial point. After 18. ...P×P ; 19. K Kt—K 4 wins easily.

| 18. ...... | B×Kt P |

This attempt to propitiate the enemy proves futile.

| 19. P×B | Kt×P |

20. R×P ch !

Elegant demolition of Black's flimsy barricades. If 20. ...P× R ; 21. Q—K 4 wins quickly.

| 20. ...... | K—Kt 1 |
| 21. Q—R 3 ! | P×R |

22. Q×P	Kt—R 3
23. Q—Kt 6	R×B
24. Q—R 7 ch	

Now Black's Queen is lost, and the complete collapse of his game cannot be postponed much longer.

24.	K—B 1
25. Kt—K 6 ch	K—B 2
26. Kt×Q ch	R×Kt
27. P—K 6 ch	K—B 1
28. Kt—Q 5	R—B 7
29. R—Kt 1	Resigns

A delightful game.

97. LONDON TEAM TOURNAMENT, 1927

QUEEN'S GAMBIT DECLINED

THIS game has ironic overtones : despite Tarrasch's lifelong advocacy of the strength of the isolated Q P, he demonstrates its weakness here in classic style.

White	*Black*
	MARQUIS
	S. ROSSELLI
DR. S. TARRASCH	DEL TURCO
(Germany)	(Italy)
1. P—Q 4	P—Q 4
2. Kt—K B 3	P—K 3
3. P—B 4	Kt—Q 2
4. Kt—B 3	K Kt—B 3
5. P—K 3	

A favourite with Tarrasch, this move became quite popular with such masters as Flohr, Rehevsky and Fine during the pre-war years. Although it is less aggressive than 5. B—Kt 5, it embodies certain finesses which are often lost on second-rate players.

| 5. ...... | B—K 2 |

...P—B 4 is better. Black cannot yet be certain whether K 2 or
Q 3 is the Bishop's best square.

6. B—Q 3   O—O
7. O—O   P—B 4

And here 7. ...P×P ; 8. B×P,
P—Q R 3 should have been played.
The text is apparently quite in
order, but its disadvantageous
points soon become manifest.

8. P—Q Kt 3   P—Q Kt 3
9. B—Kt 2   B—Kt 2
10. Q—K 2

Despite the symmetrical character of the Pawn position, White
has the better game. This is due
to the fact that Black has no wholly
satisfactory position for his Queen
(had he played ...B—Q 3, he could
ape White's moves and play ...Q—
K 2).

10. ......   Kt—K 5
11. Q R—Q 1   P—B 4

White threatened to undermine
the position of the advanced Knight
by a double exchange of Pawns in
the centre. The text gives the
Knight additional support, but
creates new weaknesses.

12. B P×P !   K P×P
13. B—R 6 !

Increasing the striking power of
his Rook on the Q file, and also
striving to remove an important
support of Black's Q P.

13. ......   Kt×Kt

After 13. ...B—Q B 3 there
could follow 14. P×P, Q Kt×P ;
15. B—B 4 with an extremely uncomfortable game for Black.

14. B×Kt   Q—B 1
15. B×B   Q×B
16. P×P   Kt×P

To recapture with the Pawn is
generally better in such positions ;
but after 16. ...P×P ; 17. Q—
Q 3,   Kt—Kt 3 ;   18. B—R 5
Black's position would be difficult.

17. Q—Kt 2 !   B—Q 3

...B—B 3 would lead to much
the same kind of position.

18. B—K 5 !

Tarrasch is naturally interested
in removing Black's Bishop and
thus depriving the latter's black
squares of adequate protection.
The following forced exchange
yields White's Queen a magnificently centralised post.

18. ......   Q R—Q 1
19. B×B   R×B
20. Q—K 5 !   Kt—K 5
21. R—B 1   Q—Q 2

Black can now play in various
ways, but he must invariably lose by
sheer weight of positional inferiority.

22. R—B 2 !

A simple but invincible plan : he
intends to double Rooks on the Q B
file, followed by R—B 7.

22. ......   R—B 1 ?

Fatal, but if 22. ...R—K 1 ; 23.
Q—B 4, R—Q B 1 ; 24. R×R ch,
Q×R ; 25. Kt—Q 4, R—K B 3 ;
26. Q—K 5 with a winning advantage.

23. R×R ch !   Q×R
24. Kt—Q 4

Not only threatening the B P, but also menacing the win of a piece with P—B 3. There is no defence to the two-fold threat.

24. ......   R—Q 1
25. Kt×P   Resigns

Black's quick surrender is justified. If 25. ...Q—Q 2 ; 26. R—Q 1, Kt—B 3 ; 27. Kt—K 7 ch, K—B 2 ; 28. Kt×P, Kt×Kt ; 29. P—K 4, Q—Kt 5 ; 30. P—B 3 ! (not 30. R×Kt ? ?, Q—Q 8 ch !), Kt—K 6 ; 31. Q—B 7 ch !

98. MUNICH, 1932

BIRD'S OPENING
(IN EFFECT)

THIS and the following game are interesting as examples of Tarrasch's tournament play at the age of 70. They are the last tournament games of which we have record.

White	*Black*
SCHWARZ	DR. S. TARRASCH
1. P—K 3	P—Q 4
2. P—K B 4	P—K Kt 3
3. Kt—K B 3	B—Kt 2
4. P—Q 4	Kt—K B 3

The opening has turned into a Dutch Defence (Stonewall Variation) with colours reversed.

White's extra tempo gives him the opportunity to seize the initiative in the centre.

5. P—B 4   P—B 3

Black must maintain a Pawn in the centre, but ...P—K 3 would hardly do because it would block the Q B's development.

6. Kt—B 3   O—O
7. B—Q 3   B—B 4 !

Well played. If White exchanges Bishops, he is left with the inferior Q B (blocked by White Pawns on black squares) and he strengthens Black's hold on the centre.

8. O—O

He defers a decision. After 8. B—K 2, P—K R 4 or 8. B×B, P×B ; 9. P×P, P×P ; 10. Q—Kt 3, P—Kt 3 (followed by ...Kt—B 3 —Q R 4) Black would have an excellent game.

8. ......   P—K 3

Now that the Q B has been developed, this move is permissible.

9. P—Q R 3

Apparently intending a Queen's-side advance.

9. ......   Q Kt—Q 2
10. Kt—K 5

10. P—B 5, P—Q Kt 3 ; 11. P—Q Kt 4, P—Q R 4 ; 12. R—Kt 1 looks more promising.

10. ......   Kt×Kt
11. B P×Kt   Kt—Q 2

Black is now on the point of freeing himself with ...P—B 3.

Tarrasch points out that 12. P—K 4, P×K P ; 13. Kt×P, P—B 3 ; 14. P×P, Kt×P would now leave White's Q P weak and recommends

as the latter's best course 12. Q—
K 2, P—B 3 ; 13. K P×P, Kt×
P ; 14. B—Q 2. Instead, White
embarks on an interesting but
faulty plan.

12. B×B	Kt P×B
13. P×P	B P×P
14. Q—B 3	P—B 3 !

Falling in with his opponent's
intentions.

15. Kt×P ? !

Expecting 15. ...P×Kt ; 16.
Q×P ch, K—R 1 ; 17. P—K 6,
Kt—K 3 ; 18. Q×B P with three
Pawns (two of them passed) and a
promising game for the sacrificed
piece.
But Tarrasch smashes this hope
very neatly.

15.	P×P !
16. Kt—Kt 4	

16. Kt—B 3 would simply lose a
Pawn, while 16. P×P ? would not
yield adequate compensation for the
piece after 16. ...P×Kt. Hence
the Knight's inglorious retreat.

16.	P—Q R 4
17. Kt—R 2	

If 17. Kt—B 2, Q—B 2 ; 18.
Q—K 2, Q R—B 1 ; 19. R—B 2,

Kt—B 3 (threat : ...Kt—K 5)
with decisive advantage (Tarrasch).

17.	P×P
18. P×P	

Tamely resigning himself to the
loss of a Pawn. Tarrasch points
out, however, that after the plausible continuation 18. Q×Kt P, Kt
—B 4 ; 19. Q—Kt 5, Q—K 2 ; 20.
P×P, B×P ch ; 21. K—R 1, Kt—
K 5 ; 22. Q—K 2, Q—R 5 White
would have no good continuation
against the double threat of ...
Kt—Kt 6 ch and ...Kt—B 7 ch.

18.	B×P ch
19. K—R 1	Q—R 5
20. B—B 4	

Not 20. Q×Kt P ?, B—K 4 ;
21. P—R 3, Q—Kt 6 with a winning position.

20.	Kt—B 4
21. Q R—B 1	Kt—K 5
22. P—K Kt 3	Q—B 3

With both a material and positional advantage in his favour,
Black's victory is only a question of
time.

23. R—Q B 2   Q R—B 1

If 23. ...B×Q Kt P ; 24. R—
Q Kt 1 recovers the Pawn.

24. Kt—B 3

Leading into a lost ending, but
the more patient 24. K R—B 1,
R×R ; 25. R×R, P—K 4 would
not be much better.

24.	B×Kt
25. P×B	R×P

Not 25. ...Kt×P ? ; 26. K R—
B 1 etc.

26. R×R	Q×R
27. Q×Q	Kt×Q

28. B—Q 2 . Kt—Q 4
29. R—K 1

Losing a tempo ; B×P at once would be slightly better.

29. ...... K—B 2
30. B×P R—Q R 1
31. B—Kt 4

White has no choice—but the ensuing Rook and Pawn ending is hopeless.

31. ...... Kt×B
32. P×Kt R—R 5
33. R—Q Kt 1 P—K 4
34. R—Kt 2 K—K 3

Black has an easy time of it, all his forces being well placed.

35. K—Kt 2 P—K 5
36. K—B 2 K—K 4
37. P—R 4

Weakening the K Kt P and thus hastening the end.

37. ...... P—R 4 !
38. P—Kt 5 P—B 5

Decisive, for White must either allow his opponent two passed Pawns or resign himself to the loss of the R P after 39. P×P ch, K×P followed by ... K—Kt 5.

39. R—B 2 P—B 6
40. K—K 3

40. R—B 5 ch, K—Q 5 ; 41. R×P, R—R 7 ch would only transpose into the text continuation.

40. ...... R—R 6 ch
41. K—B 2 R—Kt 6
42. R—B 5 ch K—Q 5

White resigns, for if 43. R×P, R—Kt 7 ch ; 44. K—Kt 1, P—K 6 etc. Tarrasch's play has been effectively simple.

99. MUNICH, 1932

QUEEN'S GAMBIT DECLINED

CURIOUSLY enough, this is the only game in the present collection in which we see the Schlechter-Rubinstein Variation against Tarrasch's famous defence. Despite the great master's passionate advocacy of that defence, its yield of useful tournament points was not very great.

White	Black
BENZINGER	DR. S. TARRASCH

1. P—Q 4 P—Q 4
2. P—Q B 4 P—K 3
3. Kt—K B 3 P—Q B 4
4. B P×P K P×P
5. P—K Kt 3 Kt—Q B 3
6. B—Kt 2 Kt—B 3
7. O—O B—K 2
8. P×P B×P

With very few exceptions, the pundits have held that White's pressure on the isolated Pawn outweighs the freedom of Black's position and the mobility of his pieces. Tarrasch steadfastly held the contrary view.

9. B—Kt 5

If White intends Q Kt—Q 2, he should play that move at once : 9. Q Kt—Q 2, O—O ; 10. Kt—Kt 3, B—Kt 3 ; 11. Q Kt—Q 4 etc.

9. ...... B—K 3
10. Q Kt—Q 2 ?

Now this move is a serious inexactitude. Kt—B 3 was in order, transposing into one of the normal lines.

10. ...... P—K R 3 !

Forcing the exchange of the Q B

as a result of White's last move.   If
11. B—B 4, Kt—K R 4.

11.	B×Kt	Q×B
12.	Kt—Kt 3	B—Kt 3
13.	Q—Q 2	O—O

Black has definitely had the better
of the opening : he has two Bishops
and a quicker development, while
his Q P is in no danger.

| 14. | K R—Q 1 | Q R—B 1 |
| 15. | P—Q R 3 | |

If 15. Q Kt—Q 4, Kt×Kt ; 16.
Kt×Kt, R—B 5 gaining time for
doubling on the Q B file. 15.
Q R—B 1 could be answered by ...
P—Kt 4, whereupon 16. Q Kt—
Q 4 ? would lose a piece : 16. ...
Kt×Kt ; 17. Kt×Kt (or 17. R×
R, Kt×Kt ch), R×R etc.

| 15. | ...... | K R—Q 1 |
| 16. | Q Kt—Q 4 | |

Otherwise Black gains too much
ground with ...P—Q 5.

| 16. | ...... | Kt×Kt |
| 17. | Kt×Kt | R—B 5 ! |

Positionally decisive : neither
Kt×B nor Kt—Kt 3 is possible,
and if 18. P—K 3, B×Kt ; 19.
P×B, K R—Q B 1 ; 20. Q R—B 1
(otherwise ...R—B 7), R×R ; 21.
R×R, R×R ch ; 22. Q×R, Q×P
and wins.

| 18. | Kt—B 3 | P—Kt 4 ! |

Also good enough was 18. ...
K R—Q B 1 ; 19. Q R—B 1, B—
R 4 ! ; 20. P—Q Kt 4, B—Kt 3.
But the text is more energetic.

19. P—R 3

If 19. P—K 3, B—Kt 5 ; 20.
Q—K 2, K R—Q B 1 and White's
position is most unpleasant.

| 19. | ...... | P—Kt 5 ! |
| 20. | P×P | R×P |

Threatening ...R×P.

21. K—B 1

Or 21. P—K 3, P—Q 5 opening
up new avenues of attack.

| 21. | ...... | P—Q 5 |

The Q P threatens to continue
its advance.

| 22. | B—R 3 | R—K 5 |
| 23. | B—Kt 2 | |

23. B×B, P×B was somewhat
better for White—though of course
not wholly satisfactory.

| 23. | ...... | P—Q 6 ! |
| 24. | P×P | |

P—K 3 was no better, for then
...B—Kt 5 would be decisive.

| 24. | ...... | R×P |
| 25. | Q—B 2 | |

If 25. Q×R, B—B 5. But now
Tarrasch decides the game with a
few telling strokes.

25.	......	R×Kt !
26.	Q×R	R×P ch
27.	K—K 1	Q×P !

Even stronger than the more
"brilliant" ...R—B 8 ch. White
resigns, as he has no defence to the
murderous threats of ...Q—B 6 ch
or ...B—R 4 ch.

A brightly played little game by
the veteran.

PART 2

MATCH GAMES

100. MATCH, 1893

(Fourth Game)

FRENCH DEFENCE

SINCE both grandmasters were at their peak when this match was contested, it is no wonder that their meeting produced so much superb chess. Of the many fine games they produced, this monumental struggle is perhaps the most celebrated example.

White	*Black*
M. TCHIGORIN	DR. S. TARRASCH

| 1. P—K 4 | P—K 3 |

Tarrasch resorted to his tried and true French Defence repeatedly during the match, apparently because he did not care to sample Tchigorin's famed wizardry with the Evans and King's gambits.

| 2. Q—K 2 |

Tchigorin's favourite continuation in this opening; the move has been experimented with by other masters, notably Tartakover, but no one brought to it the same uncanny mastery of middle-game complications.

| 2. ...... | P—Q B 4 |
| 3. P—K Kt 3 |

Curiously enough, Tchigorin, the great gambit specialist, was one of the pioneers in the adoption of the fianchetto !

3.	Kt—Q B 3
4. Kt—K B 3	B—K 2
5. B—Kt 2	P—Q 4
6. P—Q 3	Kt—B 3
7. O—O	O—O
8. Kt—B 3

Even today, the originality of Tchigorin's play is still striking. He hopes for ...P—Q 5, which will stabilise the centre and thus increase the strength of his later advance of the K B P.

| 8. ...... | P—Q R 3 |
| 9. B—Kt 5 ! | P—R 3 ? |

Tarrasch succumbs to the provocation inherent in Tchigorin's last move. Better was 9. ...P—Q 5; 10. Kt—Q 1, Kt—Q 2 and Black is in much better shape than after the text to withstand White's coming attack, as there are no Pawn targets on the King's side.

| 10. B—B 4 | P—Q Kt 4 |
| 11. K R—K 1 | P—Q 5 |

Black's last two moves have been played with a view to later counter-action on the Queen's side. Tchigorin is now in a position, however, to play for the advance P—K B 4—5 followed by P—K Kt 4—5 with decisive effect.

12. Kt—Q 1	Kt—Q 2
13. K—R 1	R—K 1
14. R—K Kt 1	P—K 4
15. B—Q 2	Kt—B 1
16. Kt—K 1

Tchigorin's ponderous preparations for the menacing King's side advance have now been completed.

16. ......   Kt—K 3 ?

Curiously enough, Tarrasch fails to criticise this time-robbing manœuvre, which squanders precious tempi in a critical situation. ... Kt—K R 2 would have been much more to the point.

17. P—K B 4   B—Kt 2
18. P—B 5   Kt—Kt 4
19. Kt—B 2   R—Q B 1
20. Q—R 5 ?

Dallying with the idea of an eventual sacrifice at K R 6. Tarrasch recommends 20. P—K R 4 followed by Kt—B 3, Q—B 2 and P—K Kt 4, or by Kt—B 3, B—K B 1, Q—R 2 and P—K Kt 4—in either case with an attack which he admits could hardly be parried.

20. ......   Kt—K R 2 !

White threatened 21. Kt—Kt 4, B—B 1 (otherwise 22. P—K R 4, Kt—K R 2 ; 23. B×P !) ; 22. P—B 6, P—Kt 3 ; 23. Kt×P ch, K—R 2 ; 24. Kt×P ch, P×Q ; 25. Kt×Q etc.

21. Kt—B 3   P—B 5

Black's only counterchance. Watch it grow !

22. B—K B 1

Against 22. Kt—Kt 4 (threatening B×P), Tarrasch considers that ...B—B 1 or ...B—Kt 4 would yield an adequate defence.

22. ......   P×P
23. P×P   Kt—Kt 4

24. B×Kt   B×B
25. Kt—Kt 4

White has achieved an ideal attacking position, the threat being 26. P—K R 4, B—B 3 ; 27. Kt× B ch, Q×Kt ; 28. P—K Kt 4 followed by P—Kt 5.

25. ......   K—B 1 ! !

A very fine defensive move, which has the two-fold object of removing the King from the danger zone if need be, and also of posting the Knight at the strong defensive bulwark K Kt 1. Tarrasch gives the following variations :
I. 26. P—K R 4, B—B 3 ; 27. Kt×B, Q×Kt ; 28. P—K Kt 4, K—K 2 ; 29. P—Kt 5, P×P ; 30. P×P, Q—Q 3 followed by occupation of the K R file.
II. 26. P—K R 4, B—B 3 ; 27. Kt(B 3)—R 2, B—K 2 ; 28. Kt× R P, P×Kt ; 29. Q×R P ch, K—Kt 1 ; 30. Kt—Kt 4, P—B 3 ! ; 31. Q—Kt 6 ch, K—R 1 ; 32. Kt—R 6, R—B 1 ; 33. Kt—B 7 ch, R× Kt ; 34. Q×R. Both sides have chances and the outcome is difficult to foresee.

26. B—K 2   B—B 3
27. P—K R 4   Q—Q 3
28. Kt(B 3)—R 2 Kt—K 2 !

If now 29. Kt×B, Q×Kt threatening to capture the B P ; or 29. Kt×R P, P×Kt ; 30. Q×R P ch, K—Kt 1 ; 31. Kt—Kt 4, R—B 3 (Tarrasch) with a satisfactory defence.

29. Q R—K B 1   Kt—Kt 1

With the Knight on this square, Black's K R 3 and K B 3 are fairly well guarded and he can await

White's eventual P—K Kt 5 with composure.

30. B—Q 1	R—B 2
31. B—Kt 3	K R—B 1
32. Kt—B 2	B—Q 1

Still preventing P—Kt 4 ? ? which would be answered by ... Kt—B 3 winning the Queen !

33. Q—K 2	P—Q R 4 !
34. Kt—B 3	P—R 5
35. B—Q 1	B—Q B 3 !

Beginning a fine manœuvre aimed at getting this Bishop to Q Kt 6 and thus making possible an invasion on the seventh rank. But Tchigorin is now ready for the long-heralded advance on the King's side, which comes dangerously near to victory, despite his previous losses of time and Black's substantial counterplay on the other wing. This indicates that if Tchigorin had followed the proper plan on move 20, Black's chances of escaping with a whole skin would have been slight indeed.

36. P—K Kt 4 ! P—B 3

Postponing P—Kt 5 for some time (because of the eventual ... Q—R 3 ch) and also making room for the Q B at K B 2.

37. Kt—R 3	B—K 1
38. Q—R 2	B—B 2
39. P—R 3	B—Kt 6
40. Kt—B 2	B×B
41. Kt×B	R—B 7

The logical conclusion of the plan initiated with Black's 33rd move.

42. Q—Kt 3	P—Kt 5
43. P×P	Q—R 3 !

This unexpected interpolation gives Black a mighty passed Q R P, since White cannot permit the fall of the Q P.

44. Kt—B 2

Or 44. Kt—K 1, R—Q 7 ; 45. Q—B 3, R—B 8 and the Knight must leave Q 1 after all.

44.	R×P
45. P—Kt 5	

At last. Both players have reached their respective goals, and the final phase is one of extraordinary tension and difficulty.

45.	R P×P
46. P×P	R(B 1)—B 7
47. Kt—Kt 4	

Not 47. P×P, B×P ; 48. Kt× K P ?, B×Kt ; 49. Q×B, Q— R 3 ch.

47. ...... Q—Q 3 !

The K P is safe, as may be seen from the following variations :
I. 48. P×P, B×P ; 49. Kt×B, Q×Kt and the K P is immune because of the reply ...Q—R 3 ch.
II. 48. P×P, B×P ; 49. Kt×

P ? ?, B×Kt ; 50. Kt×B, Q—R 3 ch.

Note how the Rooks on the seventh cooperate indirectly in the defence of the Black King !

48. P×P ?

While this does not definitely lose, it makes White's task very difficult. The correct move 48. Q—R 3 ! was later pointed out by Tchigorin and analysed by Tarrasch in the following masterly fashion :

I.   48. ...Q—B 2 ! ; 49. P×P (if 49. Q—R 8, Q—B 2 ! ; 50. Kt—R 6 ?, Q—R 4 ch and wins. Without Black's Queen manœuvre, Kt—R 6 would be fatal for him), B×P ! (Tchigorin refutes 49. ...P×P ? with 50. Kt—R 6, Kt×Kt ; 51. Q×Kt ch, K—K 1 ; 52. R—Kt 8 ch, K—Q 2 ; 53. R—Kt 7 ch, B—K 2 ; 54. Q×P, Q—Q 3 ; 55. Q—R 4) ; 50. Kt×B, P×Kt ; 51. R×Kt ch (if 51. Q—R 8, Q—B 2 ; 52. R—Kt 6, R—B 2 ; 53. Kt—R 2, R(B 2)—B 7 ; 54. Kt—Kt 4, P—R 6 ; 55. R×P ?, R—R 7 ch ! ; 56. Kt×R, Q×R or 55. Kt—R 6 ?, R—R 7 ch ; 56. K—Kt 1, Q×R ch ! ; 57. P×Q, R(Kt 7)—Kt 7 mate), K×R ; 52. R—Kt 1 ch, Q—Kt 2 ! ; 53. R×Q ch, K×R ; 54. Q—Kt 4 ch, K—B 1 ; 55. Q—Kt 6, R—Kt 8 ch ; 56. Kt—Kt 1 and now :

I.   56. ...R(Kt 8)—Kt 7 ; 57. Q×P ch, K—Kt 1 and White must take a draw because of the mating threat on his K R 2 ; for if 58. Kt—B 3, R—Kt 8 ch ; 59. Kt—Kt 1, R(Kt 8)—Kt 7 ; or 58. Q×P (Q—R 4 allows the same continuation), R—R 7 ch ! and the R P queens ; or 58. Q—Kt 6 ch, K—R 1 ; 59. Q—R 6 ch, K—Kt 1 ; 60. P—Kt 5, P—R 6 ; 61. P—Kt 6, P—R 7 ; 62. P—Kt 7, R×P or ... P—R 8(Q).

II.   56. ...R(B 7)—B 8 ; 57. Q×P ch, K—Kt 1 ; 58. Q—Q 8 ch (if 58. Q×P, R×Kt ch ; 59. K—R 2, R—R 8 ch ; 60. K—Kt 3, R(R 8)—Kt 8 ch ; 61. K—B 3, R(Q Kt 8)—B 8 ch with a draw by perpetual check ; or 61. K—R 4 ?, R—R 8 ch ; 62. K—Kt 5, R(Kt 8)—Kt 8 ch ; 63. K—B 6, R—R 3 ch ; 64. K—K 7, R—Kt 2 ch ; 65. K—K 8, R—R 1 losing for White), K—R 2 ; 59. Q—Q 7 ch, K—R 3 (or 59. ...K—R 1 ; 60. Q×R P, R×Kt ch ; 61. K—R 2, R(Q Kt 8)—K B 8 and White must submit to perpetual check, as any attempt by his King to escape the draw would lead to mating possibilities) ; 60. Q×R P, R×Kt ch ; 61. K—R 2, K—Kt 4. Again White cannot avoid a draw, for if 62. Q—B 2 ?, R—R 8 ch ; 63. K—Kt 2, R(Kt 8)—Kt 8 ch ; 64. K—B 3, R—R 6 ch ; 65. K—B 2, R—R 7 ch, winning the Queen. Or if 62. P—B 6 ?, K—B 5 ; 63. P—B 7, R—R 8 ch ; 64. K—Kt 2, K—K 6, forcing mate.

48. ......   B×P
49. Q—R 3

Now the threat is 50. Kt×B, P×Kt ; 51. R×Kt ch or 50. ...Q×Kt ; 51. R—Kt 6, Q—K 2 ; 52. P—B 6, P×P (if 52. ...Kt×P ; 53. Q—R 8 ch) ; 53. Q R—K Kt 1, Q—B 2 ; 54. Q—R 8 and wins.

49. ......   P—R 6 !

Contemplating the Queen sacrifice which follows, else Black could transpose into one of the earlier drawing variations : 49. ...Q—B 2 ; 50. Kt×B, P×Kt ; 51. R×Kt ch, K×R ; 52. R—Kt 1 ch, Q—K 2 !

50. Kt×B   Q×Kt

51. R—Kt 6   P—R 7 !
52. R×Q ch ?

After this the game cannot be saved. Tarrasch recommends 52. Kt—Kt 5 ! (threatening Kt—R 7 ch), with the following likely continuation : 52. ...K—K 2 ; 53. R×Q, P×R ; 54. Q—R 7 ch, K—Q 3 ; 55. Kt—B 7 ch, K—B 3 ; 56. Kt—Q 8 ch, K—Kt 4 ! ; 57. Q—Q 7 ch, K×P ; 58. Q—Q 6 ch, K—B 6 ; 59. Q—R 3 ch and it is difficult to see how Black can avoid a perpetual check.

52. ......   P×R
53. R—Q 1

More complicated, but no better, would be 53. Q—Kt 3, R—Kt 8 ; 54. Kt—K 1 (if 54. R—Kt 1, R×R ch ; 55. Q×R, R—Q Kt 7 ; 56. Kt—Q 2, R×Kt, transposing into the text), R—B 2 ! (stronger than ...P—R 8(Q)) ; 55. R—Kt 1, R—R 2 ch ; 56. K—Kt 2, P—R 8(Q). Or 53. R—K Kt 1, R—Kt 8 ; 54. Kt—K 1, P—R 8(Q) (if 54. ...R—B 2 ; 55. Q—R 8) ; 55. Q—Kt 3, R×Kt ! (the only winning move : 55. ...Q—R 7 would not be good enough because of 56. Q—Kt 7 ch, K—K 1 ; 57. Kt×R) ; 56. Q×Kt ch, K—K 2 ; 57. Q—K 6 ch, K—Q 1 ; 58. Q×P ch, K—B 1 ; 59. Q—K 6 ch, K—Kt 2 ; 60. Q—Q 5 ch (or 60. Q—Q 7 ch, R—B 2 ; 61. Q—Kt 5 ch, K—R 2), R—B 3 ; 61. Q—Kt 5 ch, K—R 2 (Tarrasch) and White's checks are exhausted.

53. ......   R—Kt 8
54. Q—B 1   R(B 7)—Q Kt 7
55. Kt—Q 2   R×R
56. Q×R   R×Kt
57. Q—Q B 1

If 57. Q—R 1, R—Q B 7 ! ; 58. P—Kt 5, Kt—K 2 ; 59. P—Kt 6, Kt—B 3 and Black wins easily by advancing his King to Q Kt 6. White is practically in *Zugzwang*, as Queen moves are answered by ...R—Q Kt 7—Kt 8, while the King cannot cross beyond K B 1, for then ...R—R 7 wins the Queen. The text is not much better.

57. ......   R×P
58. K—Kt 2

Queen checks would be futile.

58. ......   R—Q B 6
59. Q—Q R 1

Or 59. Q—Kt 2, R—B 7 ch !

59. ......   R—B 7 ch
60. K—B 3   P—Q 6

If now 61. K—K 3, P—Q 7 ; 62. K—K 2, R—B 8 and wins.

61. Q—Q 1   R—Q Kt 7
62. Q—R 4   P—Q 7

White resigns, as he is helpless against ...R—Kt 8. A masterpiece of truly heroic dimensions ! Note how useful a rôle was played by Black's Knight at K Kt 1, although it was stationary for 33 moves !

101. MATCH, 1893

(Fifth Game)

RUY LOPEZ

Tchigorin cuts a pitiable figure in this game. Tarrasch outplays him all the way, and concludes with a smashing attack. Rarely has a great master been defeated in such incisive style.

White	Black
Dr. S. Tarrasch	M. Tchigorin

1.	P—K 4	P—K 4
2.	Kt—K B 3	Kt—Q B 3
3.	B—Kt 5	P—Q R 3
4.	B—R 4	Kt—B 3
5.	Kt—B 3	B—Kt 5
6.	Kt—Q 5	B—R 4 ?

The first false step. The Bishop has no future here and remains out of play for the rest of the game. 6. ...B—K 2, as played in Game 30, is the proper move.

7.	O—O	P—Q Kt 4

7. ...P—Q 3, followed by ... B—K Kt 5 and ...Kt—Q 2 as in the seventh game of the match, is somewhat better.

8.	B—Kt 3	P—Q 3
9.	P—Q 3	B—K Kt 5
10.	P—B 3	Kt—K 2 ?

A plausible mistake which is refuted brilliantly. Tarrasch gives 10. ...Kt—Q 2 as relatively best, but White's position would still have remained preferable.

11.	Kt×P !	P×Kt

If 11....B×Q ; 12. Kt×Kt ch, K—B 1 (not 12. ...P×Kt ? ; 13. B×P ch, K—B 1 ; 14. B—R 6 mate) ; 13. either Kt—Q 7 ch and wins.

12.	Kt×Kt ch	P×Kt
13.	Q×B	Kt—Kt 3

A hopeless situation for Black ; he cannot play ...Q×P ? because of R—Q 1.

14.	B—Q 5	R—Q Kt 1
15.	P—K B 4	

Tarrasch naturally opens new lines to exploit Black's weaknesses.

15.	......	P—B 3

Since normal play offers no hope, Tchigorin embarks on wild adventures.

16.	B×Q B P ch	K—K 2
17.	B—Q 5	

Black threatened ...Q—Kt 3 ch winning the Bishop.

17.	......	P—Kt 5
18.	P×K P	Q—Kt 3 ch
19.	K—R 1	Kt×P
20.	Q—R 5	

Planning a fine finish.

20.	......	Kt—Kt 3

The threat was 21. R×P !, Q×R (or 21. ...K×R ; 22. Q—Kt 5 mate) ; 22. B—Kt 5 etc.

21.	R×P !	K×R
22.	B—Kt 5 ch	K—Kt 2

Or 22. ...K—K 4 ; 23. B—K 7 ch and mate follows.

23. Q—R 6 ch   K—Kt 1
24. R—K B 1   R—K B 1
25. B—K B 6   Q×B
26. R×Q   Resigns

Black cannot stave off the piquant "epaulette" mate by 27. R×Kt ch, P×R; 28. Q×P mate! Note that Black's K B had no share in the play after the unfortunate retreat to Q R 4.

102. MATCH, 1893

(Sixth Game)

FRENCH DEFENCE

THIS game is one of the finest examples of Tarrasch's powers as a master of position play. There is a deceptive simplicity about the way in which pressure is applied on White's game with cumulatively crushing force.

White   *Black*
M. TCHIGORIN   DR. S. TARRASCH

1. P—K 4   P—K 3
2. Q—K 2   P—Q B 4
3. P—K Kt 3   Kt—Q B 3
4. B—Kt 2   Kt—Q 5
5. Q—Q 3

Q—Q 1 is more natural, but then Black could play ...P—Q 4 with an excellent game.

5. ......   B—K 2

The continuation 5. ...P—Q 4; 6. P—Q B 3 (if 6. P×P, P×P; 7. P—Q B 3, B—B 4; 8. Q—K 3 ch, Kt—K 3 with a good position), P×P; 7. B×P, Kt—Q B 3 is rather unclear.

6. Kt—Q B 3

P—Q B 3 was in order.

6. ......   B—B 3

Threatening ...P—B 5. 7. Q Kt—K 2 should now be played, but instead Tchigorin loses additional time.

7. Kt—Kt 5   Kt×Kt
8. Q×Kt   Q—Kt 3!

The exchange of Queens would give Black a fine game, for example 9. Q×Q, P×Q; 10. P—Q 3, P—Q Kt 4; 11. P—Q B 3, Kt—K 2; 12. B—K 3, P—Q 3; followed by ...Kt—B 3 and ...P—Kt 5 and Black clearly has the initiative (Tarrasch).

9. Q—K 2   P—Q 3
10. Kt—B 3   B—Q 2
11. P—B 3

11. P—Q 3? would be a mistake because of 11. ...B×P; 12. R—Q Kt 1, B—B 6 ch. The text, however, is not the best. Tarrasch points out that the proper course was either 11. O—O or else 11. P—K 5, P×P; 12. Kt×P, B×Kt; 13. Q×B, Kt—B 3.

11. ......   B—Q Kt 4
12. P—Q 3   Q—R 3!

Forcing a backward Q P in White's camp. Tchigorin's position becomes ever more uncomfortable.

13. P—B 4   B—B 3
14. O—O   P—R 3!

The routine ...Kt—K 2 would be answered by B—Kt 5, whereby White would relieve the pressure somewhat.

15. B—K 3   Q—Kt 3

White was on the point of playing either P—Q 4 ! or P—K 5 !

16. Q R—Kt 1 !   P—Q R 4

White threatened P—Q Kt 4.

17. P—Q R 3 ?

A grave strategical blunder, as Black's reply demonstrates. K R —Q 1 was better.

17. ......   P—R 5 !

Stifling any hope of a possible P—Q Kt 4.

18. K R—Q 1   P—K 4

Tarrasch must have been reluctant to play this move, for it makes a hole of his Q 4, so that his contemplated occupation of White's Q 4 can be copied by White. However, it was essential to prevent P— Q 4.

19. Kt—Q 2   Kt—K 2

Both Knights are heading for Q 5.

20. Kt—B 1   B—Q 2
21. B—Q 2   Kt—B 3
22. B—Q B 3   Kt—Q 5
23. B×Kt ?

Tchigorin exchanged Bishops for Knights almost invariably, but the text seriously compromises his game. The proper course was to retreat the Queen, play Kt—K 3 and *then* B×Kt. White's Knight would then reach Q 5, forcing a similar exchange, with a symmetrical Pawn position in the centre and Bishops on opposite colours and a draw as the likely result.

23. ......   B P×B

Now White's Knight cannot reach Q 5 !

24. B—B 3   Q—B 2

Tarrasch has in mind a whole series of far-reaching manœuvres which will exploit his positional advantages. The magnificent Bishops will play an important rôle in these plans.

25. B—Kt 4   B—B 3

Black naturally avoids exchanges.

26. K R—B 1   B—K Kt 4
27. R—B 2   Q—K 2

To prevent P—B 5.

28. Q—K 1   P—R 4 !

This and Black's 31st move explain why he has avoided ...O—O.

29. B—Q 1   Q—K 3
30. P—B 3   B—Q 1
31. Q—B 2   P—R 5
32. Q—Kt 2

Tarrasch suggests P—B 4 as somewhat better, although equalisation would be too much for White to hope for.

32. ......   R—K R 3 !
33. P—K Kt 4

Tchigorin's patience is exhausted. This move is inevitable, but it should have been postponed. White's Bishop is now hopelessly ineffective, and his Pawn position is fixed, so that Black can now quietly plan the three Pawn moves which, in conjunction with the powerful action of Black's Bishops, are to smash the hostile position. The three moves are ...P—Q Kt 4, ... P—K B 4 and eventually ...P—Q 4.

33.	......	B—K Kt 4
34.	P—R 3	K—B 1
35.	Q—K 2	K—Kt 1
36.	Q—K 1	P—K Kt 3 !
37.	R—Kt 2	R—K R 2 !
38.	B—B 2	R—Kt 2

Black's last two moves were necessary preparations for ...P—B 4. Note, by the way, how cruelly White's position suffers from the absence of his black-square Bishop.

39. Q—Q 1	Q—Q 2

Guarding the Q R P so that the Q R can be switched to the King's side.

40. Q—K 1

White is helpless: if 40. P—Kt 4, P×P e.p.; 41. R×P, B—R 5 winning the Q R P.

40.	......	P—B 4
41.	B—Q 1	R—K B 1
42.	B—K 2	P×K P
43.	B P×P	R(Kt 2)—B 2

A new advantage for Black: unassailable control of the K B file.

44. Q—Q 1	P—Kt 4 !

This Pawn must be captured, else Black captures, isolating White's K P and making his own Q P passed.

45.	P×P	B×Kt P
46.	Kt—R 2	B—K 6 ch
47.	K—R 1	P—Kt 4
48.	Kt—B 1	P—Q 4 !

Decisive.

49. Kt—Q 2

If 49. Kt×B, P×Kt; 50. Q—Q B 1, P×P; 51. P×P, B—Q 6!; 52. B×B, Q×B; 53. Q—B 2, R—B 8 ch; 54. R×R, R×R ch; 55. K—R 2, Q×Q; 56. R×Q, R—Q 8; 57. R—Kt 2, R—Q 7; 58. K—Kt 1, P—K 7; 59. K—B 2, P—K 8(Q) ch and wins (Tarrasch).

49.	......	B—B 3
50.	P×P	B×P

Black's operations on the long diagonal will soon have murderous effect.

51. Kt—K 4	Q—B 3
52. R—R 1	

White is helpless.

52.	......	R—B 5
53.	K—R 2	R×Kt !

The Q B is more valuable than the Rook !

54. P×R   B×P
55. B—B 1   B×R
56. B×B   R—B 7
57. Q—R 1   P—K 5

Threatening ...Q—Q 3 ch and
mate next move.

58. Q—Q Kt 1   Q—Q 3 ch
59. K—R 1   R×B !

White resigns, mate being unavoidable. A positional masterpiece of the highest order.

103. MATCH, 1893

(Seventeenth Game)

RUY LOPEZ

IN this game Tarrasch's alert and
well-timed handling of the attack
puts his opponent to shame. This
is one of the famous Tarrasch
games in which each move blends
so neatly with the next one that it is
difficult to appreciate the artistry
which produced these moves.

White	*Black*
DR. S. TARRASCH	M. TCHIGORIN

1. P—K 4   P—K 4
2. Kt—K B 3   Kt—Q B 3
3. B—Kt 5   P—Q R 3
4. B—R 4   Kt—B 3
5. Kt—B 3   P—Q 3

An improvement on Tchigorin's
play in earlier games.

6. P—Q 4   Kt—Q 2

A continuation of which the great
Russian was extremely fond, although Janowski was the only other
famous master to whom this move

appealed. The notion of blocking
the Q B's development and of risk-
ing a ragged Pawn position after
B×Kt followed by P×P, has been
repugnant to most players.

7. Kt—K 2   P—B 3

Another cramping move which
enhances the uncomfortable nature
of Black's position and leaves his
K B with no future. ...B—K 2
seems preferable.

8. P—B 3   Kt—Kt 3
9. B—Kt 3   Kt—R 4

White's K B must be driven
away from the vital diagonal, but
this manœuvre is not without risk.

10. B—B 2   B—K 3 ? !

At first sight it seems that White
can play P—Q 5 followed by P—
Q Kt 4, eventually winning the
"trapped" Knight; however, Tchigorin has planned its rescue very
cleverly. The only trouble with
this plan is that by merely avoiding
it White obtains a clear positional
advantage !

11. O—O !

Tarrasch points out that there is
nothing to be gained from the
tempting 11. P—Q 5, B—Q 2 (or
...B—B 2) ; 12. P—Q Kt 4, Kt
(R 4)—B 5 ; 13. B—Kt 3 (if 13.
P—Q R 4, P—Q R 4 ; 14. B—
Kt 3, P—B 3 or 14. P—Kt 5, P—
B 3), P—B 3 ; 14. P×P (or 14.
Q—Q 3, P×P ; 15. P×P, R—
B 1), P×P ; 15. Q—Q 3, B—K 3.
The Knight is firmly entrenched
and White has merely succeeded in
weakening his own Pawns.

11. ......   B—B 2

12. Kt—K 1 !

Intending to increase his superior
mobility still further with P—
K B 4.

12. ......   P—Kt 4

Crossing White's plan, but at the
cost of weakening his game still
more and making the prospects of
his K B worse than ever.

13. P—Q Kt 3 !

Preparing to cut off Black's Q Kt
with P—Q 5 followed by P—
Q B 4.

13. ......   Kt—B 3

Getting the Knight back in good
time and intending ...Kt—K 2—
Kt 3—B 5. However, White, who
has no weaknesses and whose development has been much more
effective, turns out to be the first to
carry out this plan.

14. Kt—Kt 3   P—K R 4
15. B—K 3   Kt—K 2
16. P×P !

Just at the right moment : Black
must recapture with the Q P, so as
to avoid the loss of the K Kt P.
This means that he will be left with
a weak K B P and will have to submit to pressure on the Q file.

16. ......   Q P×P
17. Q—B 3   Kt—Q 2

Tchigorin later recommended
...Q—Q 3 before this move, in
order to facilitate castling on the
Queen's side, but in that event also
he would have been exposed to
attack.

18. Kt—B 5   Kt×Kt

The Knight was too well placed
at K B 5 to be permitted to remain
on such a dominating square.

19. P×Kt !

Giving up the pressure on the
K B P in return for utilisation of the
valuable square K 4.

19. ......   P—B 3
20. Q—K 2   Q—R 4

Provoking the following "weakening" move.

21. P—Q Kt 4 !   Q—B 2
22. B—Kt 3 !

Played with masterly judgment.
No matter how Black continues, he
must part with his good Bishop, so
that his white squares are weak and
he is left with the ineffectual K B.

22. ......   B—K 2

Relatively best was 22. ...B×
B ; 23. P×B, P—R 5 ; 24. P—
K B 4, Kt P×P ; 25. B×P, O—
O—O. Both players would then
have attacking chances, remarks
Tarrasch, with the outcome prob-
able in favour of White, who would
have hostile weaknesses against
which to operate. The course indicated for him would be Kt—B 2,
P—B 4 and P—Kt 5 (after the retreat of his Bishop).

23. B×B ch   K×B
24. Q—B 4 ch   K—Kt 2
25. P—K R 4 !

The outlook is bad for Black's
King ! The text casts a strong

light on the sad effects of Black's omission of ...P—R 5.

25.	P×P
26. Kt—B 3	Kt—B 1

Here it would have been somewhat better to play ...Q R—K Kt 1 followed by ...R—R 2 and ...K—R 1. Tchigorin apparently does not appreciate the force of the coming attack.

27. Kt×R P	R—K 1
28. Q R—Q 1	

As will be seen, the Q file is the highway to the attack.

28.	B—Q 1

Or 28. ...B—Q 3 ; 29. Q—Q 3, R—Q 1 ; 30. B—B 5 !, B—K-2 ; 31. Q—Kt 3 ch, K—B 2 ; 32. Kt—Kt 6 and wins (Tarrasch). The text is sheer waste of time, and Tarrasch rightly recommends ... P—Kt 4 hereabouts in order to drive away White's Queen from its powerful post at Q B 4.

29. B—B 5 !	B—K 2

No better would be 29. ...Q—B 2 ; 30. Q×Q ch, K×Q ; 31. B×Kt, K R×B ; 32. Kt—Kt 6, R—K Kt 1 ; 33. R—Q 7 ch, B—K 2 ; 34. R×P followed by R—Q 1—Q 7 etc. (Tarrasch).

30. R—Q 3 !	

Now comes a devastating attack, executed by Tarrasch in really impeccable style.

30.	B×B
31. R—Kt 3 ch	K—R 2
32. P×B !	

White's Queen's side Pawns are not handsome, but the text maintains the pressure and allows the utilisation of the Queen on two important diagonals.

32.	R—K 2

The only defence against the threat of 33. Q—K 2, K—R 3 ; 34. Kt—Kt 6 and wins.

33. R—Q 1 !	

33. Q—K 2 would be premature : 33. ...R—Kt 2 ! ; 34. Q× P ch.?, K—R 1 and the Knight is lost.

33.	R—Kt 2
34. R×R ch	

34.	K×R

Tarrasch refutes 34. ...Q×R with 35. R—Q 3, R—Kt 1 (if 35. ...Q—Kt 5 ; 36. Q—B 7 ch, Q—Kt 2 ; 37. Q—K 8 followed by R—Kt 3 and wins) ; 36. R—Kt 3, Q—R 1 ; 37. R—R 3 !, R—Kt 5 (if 37. ...Q—Kt 2 ; 38. Kt—Kt 6, K—R 3 ; 39. R×P ch !, K× R ; 40. Q—R 4 mate. If 37. ... K—R 3 ; 38. Kt—B 3, threatening R×P ch !) ; 38. Q—B 7 ch, K—

R 3 (if 38. ...R—Kt 2 ? ; 39. Q×
P ch, K—Kt 1 ; 40. Q×Q ch, K×
Q ; 41. Kt—Kt 6 ch, K—Kt 1 ;
42. R—R 8 ch, K—B 2 ; 43. R×
Kt mate. If 38. ...Q—Kt 2 ;
39. Q—K 8, K—R 3 ? ; 40. Q×
P ch ! etc. or 39. ...R—Kt 4 ; 40.
R—Q 3 followed by R—Q 8 or 39.
...Q—Kt 4 ; 40. Q×Kt, R×Kt ;
41. Q—B 7 ch, K—R 1 ; 42. P—
B 4 ! !, P×P ; 43. R—Q 3, Q—
Kt 2 ; 44. R—Q 8 ch, K—R 2 ;
45. Q—K 8 and wins) ; 39. Q×P
ch !, K×Q ; 40. Kt—B 3 ch and
mate next move !

35. R—Q 3   Kt—R 2

No better is 35. ...K—R 3 ; 36.
R—Kt 3 (threatening 37. Kt—
Kt 6, Kt×Kt ; 38. R×Kt ch, K—
R 2 ; 39. Q—K 2 etc.), Q—Q 1 (if
36. ...R—R 2 ; 37. Q—Kt 8 etc.
or 36. ...Q—Q 2 ; 37. Q—K 2
followed by Kt—Kt 6 and wins) ;
37. Q—B 7, R—R 2 ; 38. Q—
Kt 6 ch ! and mate follows (Tarrasch).

36. Q—K 6   R—Q 1

The play that follows is forced.

37. R—Kt 3 ch   Kt—Kt 4
38. R×Kt ch !   P×R
39. P—B 6 ch   K—R 2

If 39. ...K—R 1 ; 40. Kt—
Kt 6 ch wins.

40. Q—B 5 ch   K—R 1

Or 40. ...K—Kt 1 ; 41. P—
B 7 ch, Q×P ; 42. Q×P ch.

41. P—B 7 !

Much stronger than 41. Kt—
Kt 6 ch, K—Kt 1 ; 42. Kt—K 7

ch, K—B 2 ; 43. Q—Kt 6 ch, K—
K 3 etc.

41. ......   P×Kt

Or 41. ...K—Kt 2 ; 42. Q—
Kt 6 ch, K—B 1 ; 43. Q—Kt 8
ch, K—K 2 ; 44. Kt—Kt 6 ch. If
41. ...R—K B 1 ; 42. Q—B 6 ch.
leads to mate.

42. Q—Kt 6

Leaving Black completely helpless !

42. ......   R—Q 8 ch
43. K—R 2   P—K 5 ch
44. P—Kt 3   P×P ch
45. K—Kt 2

The simplest, although Tarrasch
points out that 45. P×P, R—Q 7
ch ; 46. K—Kt 1, R—Q 8 ch ; 47.
K—Kt 2, R—Q 7 ch ; 48. K—B 1,
R—Q 8 ch ; 49. K—K 2, R—Q 7
ch ; 50. K×R, Q—Q 1 ch ; 51.
K—K 1, Q—K B 1 ; 52. K—K 2
wins easily for White.

45. ......   Q×P
46. Q×Q and wins

Tchigorin dragged out this hopeless ending for another ten moves.
One of Tarrasch's finest games.

104. MATCH, 1894

(First Game)

GIUOCO PIANO

THE way in which Black slowly
secures the initiative in this rather
lifeless opening is remarkable. But
we must remember that the ability

to make something out of nothing is peculiarly the hallmark of the modern master.

	White	*Black*
	C. A. WALBRODT	DR. S. TARRASCH
1.	P—K 4	P—K 4
2.	Kt—K B 3	Kt—Q B 3
3.	B—B 4	B—B 4
4.	O—O	Kt—B 3
5.	P—Q 3	P—Q 3
6.	P—B 3	B—Kt 3

The object of this rather mysterious move is to discourage White from playing B—K 3, since the natural reply ...B—Kt 3 has already been made. But Walbrodt, who was a connoisseur of drawish lines, is not sufficiently fastidious for such considerations.

7. P—Q Kt 4

An unwarranted weakening of the Pawn structure which was popular at the time this game was played.

| 7. | ...... | B—K 3 |
| 8. | B×B | |

Tarrasch always viewed this exchange as a mistake, relying on the open file to prove more than ample compensation for the weakening of his Pawn formation.

8.	......	P×B
9.	P—Q R 4	P—Q R 3
10.	B—K 3	B—R 2 ?!

Rather than create a symmetrical and hence drawish Pawn position with ...B×B, or weaken his own position by allowing White to exchange on Kt 6, Tarrasch loses several tempi with this rather clumsy retreat. Such repulsive-looking moves can be made only by pathetically incompetent tyros or by first-rate masters !

11.	B×B	R×B
12.	Q—Kt 3	Q—Q 2
13.	Kt—Kt 5	Kt—Q 1
14.	P—K B 4	P—R 3

Played in order to force the Knight back to R 3, where it will be out of play for some time to come. On the other hand, the weakening of Black's K Kt 3 may be troublesome later on. At all events, 15. P×P ? would lose a Pawn because of the simple reply ...P×P.

| 15. | Kt—R 3 | O—O ! |

...P×P would bring White's K Kt into the game once more. Tarrasch therefore reconciles himself to the hideous doubled K P which would result from 16. P×P, comforting himself with the consoling reflection that he would thereby continue to freeze White's K Kt out of the game, and also exert pressure on White's Q P.

| 16. | Kt—Q 2 | Kt—B 2 |

A modest post, but, says Tarrasch, on the more natural square Q B 3 the Knight would always be menaced by the possibility of P—Kt 5.

| 17. | Q R—K 1 | Q R—R 1 |
| 18. | Kt—B 3 | K—R 2 |

In order to guard K Kt 3 ; but the move turns out to have subtle tactical significance later on.

| 19. | P×P | P×P |
| 20. | P—Q 4 | P×P |

21. P—K 5   Kt—Q 4
22. Kt×P !

White's advance in the centre has given him the freer game and his prospects are quite promising now. The mode of recapture in the text makes possible a subsequent P—B 4 to drive Black's Knight away from its advantageous central position.

22. ......   Q R—K 1
23. R—K 4 ?

Superficial : R—K 2 was much better.

23. ......   Kt—Q 1
24. R—Q 1

Threatening 25. Kt×P. If 24. ...P—B 3 ; 25. P—B 4, Kt—Kt 3 ; 26. Kt—B 5, Q—Q B 2 ; 27. Kt—Q 6 with a winning position.

24. ......   Kt—Q B 3 !

Cleverly calculated. If 25. Kt×P, Q×Kt ; 26. Q×Kt, R—Q 1 ! winning the Queen. Or if 26. R×Kt, Kt—K 2 winning the exchange. However, with the Rook on K 2 (see the note to White's 23rd move), White could extricate himself in

this latter variation by Q—B 2 ch. An interesting finesse !

25. Kt—B 3

If instead 25. P—B 4, Kt(Q 4)×P ; 26. Kt×Kt, Q×Kt ; 27. Q×Kt, Q×R. A most unfortunate Rook !

25. ......   P—Q Kt 4

In order to take the sting out of P—B 4 ; now the Knight can no longer be driven away from Q 4.

26. P×P ?

Walbrodt has lost his grip on the position ; 26. P—B 4 would have yielded better prospects, because of Black's isolated Q R P.

26. ......   P×P
27. P—B 4   P×P
28. R×P   K—Kt 1

White was threatening to win a piece with Q—B 2 ch.

29. Kt—B 4   Kt(B 3)—K 2
30. Q—Q 3   P—B 3

A Roland for White's Oliver ! Black threatens to win a piece with ...Q—R 2 ch.

31. Q—Q 4 ?

Losing the exchange, although this is not clear until the 35th move. Kt×Kt was doubtless best, with about even chances.

31. ......   Kt—B 4
32. Q—B 5   Kt(B 4)—K 6
33. Kt×Kt

If 33. Q×Kt(K 3), Kt×Q ; 34. R×Q, Kt×R etc.

33. ......   Kt×R(Q 8)
34. Kt—B 4

Threatening R—Q 4.

34. ......   Kt—B 6 !

A move whose consequences Walbrodt had apparently not fully examined. 34. ...Kt—Kt 7 would be inadequate because of 35. R—Q 4 and 36. Q—B 2.

35. R—Q 4

Tarrasch had foreseen that 35. Kt—Kt 6 would not regain the exchange because of the continuation 35. ...Q—Q 8 ch ; 36. K—B 2, Q—B 7 ch ; 37. K—Kt 1 (if 37. K—B 1, Q—K 7 ch ; 38. K—Kt 1, Q—K 8 ch ! !), R×Kt ; 38. P×R, Q×Kt ch etc.

35. ......   Kt—Q 4
36. Kt—Q 3   R—R 1

In addition to his material advantage, Black now has a good attack.

37. P—R 3   R—R 8 ch
38. K—R 2   R—R 7
39. K—R 1

This allows a quickly decisive return of the exchange. Tarrasch suggests Kt(Q 3)—K 1 to prolong his resistance.

39. ......   R×Kt
40. P×R   Q—K B 2
41. Kt—K 1

White's pieces are all unfortunately situated for defensive purposes.

41. ......   R—R 8

Threatening ...Q×P ch as well as ...R×Kt ch.

42. R—Q 1   R×R
    Resigns

An eventful encounter after a dull start.

105. MATCH, 1894

(Second Game)

PETROFF DEFENCE

THE turning-point of this game occurs at Black's fourteenth move. Instead of adopting the indicated positional line of play, Walbrodt strikes out blindly with a crude attacking move which compromises his game irretrievably.

White	*Black*
DR. S. TARRASCH	C. A. WALBRODT
1. P—K 4	P—K 4
2. Kt—K B 3	Kt—K B 3
3. Kt×P	P—Q 3
4. Kt—K B 3	Kt×P
5. P—Q 4	P—Q 4
6. B—Q 3	B—K 2
7. O—O	O—O
8. R—K 1	

This simple move is not easy to meet. If the attacked Knight retreats, 9. Kt—K 5 gives White a clear initiative. If 9. ...P—K B 4 ; 10. P—B 4 (or Kt—K 5) is distinctly in White's favour.

8.	B—K B 4
9. P—B 4	P—Q B 3
10. Q—Kt 3	

Maintaining the pressure. 10. P×P, P×P ; 11. Q—Kt 3 looks

attractive, but after 11. ...Kt—
Q B 3 White could not very well
play 12. Q×Kt P ? because of 12.
...Kt—Kt 5 !

10. ......   P×P
11. B×P

Not 11. Q×Kt P ? ?, P×B ; 12.
Q×R, Q—Kt 3 and White's Queen
is lost.

11. ......   Kt—Q 3
12. B—B 1

The best retreat for the Bishop.
It does not make another move
throughout the game, but nevertheless plays a useful rôle.

12. ......   Kt—Q 2
13. B—K B 4   Kt—Kt 3
14. Kt—B 3   P—Kt 4 ?

Such a move on the part of a
master is almost worse than a palp-
able blunder. Instead of the text,
which ruins Black's King's side, the
proper continuation was 14. ...
B—K 3 ; 15. Q—B 2, Kt—Q 4 ;
16. Kt×Kt, B×Kt ; 17. Kt—
K 5 : Black's position would be
somewhat cramped but free from
organic weakness.

15. B—Kt 3   K—R 1
16. P—Q 5 !

Very strong. If now 16. ...
P×P ; 17. Kt×Q P, Kt×Kt ; 18.
Q×Kt followed by Q R—Q 1 and
Black should succumb rapidly. He
therefore avoids the opening up of
the central sector.

16. ......   P—B 4
17. P—Q R 4 !

A difficult move to answer, since

17. ...P—Q R 4 would be refuted
by 18. R×B.

17. ......   P—Kt 5
18. Kt—Q 2   R—B 1
19. P—R 5   Kt—R 1

If 19. ...Kt—Q 2 ; 20. B×Kt,
B×B ; 21. Kt—B 4 with a winning game.

20. Kt(B 3)—K 4 !

Not 20. B×Kt, B×B ; 21. Q×
P, B×P ch ! ; 22. K×B, Q—R 5
ch ; 23. K—Kt 1, P—Kt 6 ! ; 24.
P×P (if 24. Kt—B 3 ? ?, P×P
mate), Q—Q 5 ch, regaining the
sacrificed piece.

20. ......   P—Kt 3

A pathetically feeble reply, but
Tarrasch points out that 20. ...
Kt×Kt ; 21. Kt×Kt, B×Kt ;
22. R×B, P—B 4 would be an-
swered by 23. R×B !, Q×R ; 24.
Q—B 3 ch, K—Kt 1 ; 25. P—Q 6,
Q—Q 2 ; 26. B—B 4 ch, R—B 2 ;
27. Q—B 6, R—K 1 ; 28. B—K 5,
R×B ; 29. Q×R and wins.

21. P×P   P×P
22. R—R 7 !   R—B 2

R×B was threatened. If 22.

...Kt—B 2 ; 23. Kt×Kt, B×Kt ; 24. Kt—B 4, B×B; 25. Q×B (Tarrasch) with a winning position.

23.	R×Kt !	Q×R
24.	Kt×Kt	B—Kt 3
25.	Kt×P ch	B×Kt
26.	B×R	B×P
27.	R×B !	

As will be seen, White obtains more than enough material for the Queen.

| 27. | ...... | B×Q |
| 28. | B—K 5 ch | R—B 3 |

Forced ! (if 28. ...K—Kt 1 ; 29. R—Kt 7 ch leads to mate).

29.	B×R ch	K—Kt 1
30.	Kt×B	Q—Q 4
31.	Kt—B 1	Q—Q 3

Black could not have lasted very long in any event : if 31. ...P—B 5 ; 32. Kt—K 2, P—Kt 4 ; 33. Kt—B 4, Q—Q 7 ; 34. Kt—K 6 etc.

| 32. | R—Kt 7 ch | K—B 1 |
| 33. | B—K 7 ch | Resigns |

Tarrasch's play has been simple, logical and forceful.

106. MATCH, 1894

(Fourth Game)

PETROFF DEFENCE

THIS game is short but "meaty". Once more Walbrodt's unfortunate treatment of the opening leaves him in lasting difficulties.

| *White* | *Black* |
| DR. S. TARRASCH | C. A. WALBRODT |

| 1. | P—K 4 | P—K 4 |
| 2. | Kt—K B 3 | Kt—K B 3 |

Apparently the thought of a Ruy Lopez terrified Walbrodt !

3.	Kt×P	P—Q 3
4.	Kt—K B 3	Kt×P
5.	P—Q 4	P—Q 4
6.	B—Q 3	Kt—Q B 3
7.	O—O	B—K 2
8.	R—K 1	Kt—B 3

Thus far Walbrodt has improved on his play in the second game, but the text is a superficial move which leaves White with a clear initiative. 8. ...B—K Kt 5 should be played.

| 9. | B—K B 4 | O—O |

Here or on the next move. ... B—K Kt 5 should be tried.

| 10. | P—B 3 | |

White is ahead in development, his K B is posted more aggressively and in general White's position has a promising character which is quite lacking in Black's game. Walbrodt is naturally uneasy and tries to disentangle himself.

10.	......	B—Q 3
11.	Kt—K 5	R—K 1
12.	Kt—Q 2	Kt—K Kt 5

Still seeking exchanges.

| 13. | Q Kt—B 3 | Q Kt×Kt |

This turns out unsatisfactorily, but Tarrasch shows that the obvious 13. ...P—B 3 would be no better : 14. Kt×Q Kt, P×Kt ; 15. B×B,

R×R ch (or 15. ...P×B; 16.
Q—B 2, P—Kt 3; 17. B×P); 16.
Q×R, P×B (if 16. ...Q×B??;
17. Q—K 8 ch, Q—B 1; 18. B×
P ch); 17. Q—Kt 1, P—Kt 3; 18.
P—K R 3, Kt—R 3; 19. B×P
and wins.

14. P×Kt !

Preventing ...Kt—B 3, so that
Black is exposed to a dangerous attack and his Knight is endangered.

14. ......   B—Q B 4
15. B—Kt 3   Kt—R 3

Otherwise 16. Q—B 2, P—
K Kt 3; 17. Q—Q 2 leaves the
Knight in a cruel predicament.

16. Q—B 2 !   P—K Kt 3

Tarrasch has forced a *weakening
of the black squares* which is bound
to prove fatal.

17. B—K B 4   Kt—B 4
18. K—R 1 !

Tarrasch does not care for the
obvious P—K Kt 4 at this stage,
but intends to dislodge the Knight
by Kt—Q 4. The King move is
the beginning of a deep plan to
drive away the Knight.

18. ......   P—Q B 3
19. Q—Q 2 !   B—K 3
20. Kt—Q 4 !   Q—Q 2

20. ...Kt×Kt; 21. P×Kt,
B—K 2 (not 21. ...B×P; 22.
B×P with advantage to White.
With White's King still at Kt 1
Black would have still had a re-
source in ...B×P ch) would have
been better, as the Knight plays a
miserable rôle throughout the game.

21. B—K Kt 5 !   B—B 1

Tarrasch points out that Black's
best course was 21. ...Kt×Kt (not
21. ...B—K 2; 22. B×Kt, Q B×
B; 23. B—B 6 ! and 23. ...B×B?
will not do, for example, 24. P×B,
R×R ch; 25. R×R, R—K 1; 26.
R×R ch, Q×R; 27. Kt×B, P×
Kt; 28. Q—Kt 5 ch and mate next
move. Note also that if 22. ...
K B×B?; 23. B×B wins a piece);
22. P×Kt, B—K 2; 23. B—B 6 !,
B×B; 24. P×B, Q—Q 1; 25.
Q—Kt 5 or 23. ...B—K B 4; 24.
Q—R 6, B—B 1; 25. B×B, Q×
B; 26. Q—R 4 with a good attack
in either case.

22. Q—B 4 !   Kt—Kt 2

Since the unfortunate position of
the Knight soon proves fatal, Black
should have tried 22. ...Kt×Kt;
23. P×Kt, B—K B 4 although
White would retain his advantage.

23. Q—R 4

Black is helpless in the long run
against the coming attack, which, in
a number of variations, involves the
sacrifice of White's Queen.

23. ......   P—Q R 3

The immediate ...P—Q B 4 ?
would cost the exchange (24. B—
Kt 5).

24. R—K 3   P—Q B 4
25. Kt×B   Q×Kt

There is no satisfactory move : if
25. ...P×Kt; 26. P—K Kt 4 !,
K R—B 1; 27. R—R 3, Kt—K 1;
28. B×Kt P and wins. If 25.
...Kt×Kt; 26. B—B 6 followed
by P—K B 4—5.

26. P—K Kt 4   P—K R 4

Or 26. ...P—Q 5 ; 27. R—R 3, P—K R 4 ; 28. R—K Kt 1 (the simplest) with an easy win for White.

27. R—K Kt 1 !

Threatening 28. P×P, Kt×P ; 29. Q×Kt ! P×Q ; 30. B—B 6 ch and wins.

27. ......   P×P

Tarrasch refutes the alternative 27. ...P—Q 5 with 28. B P×P, B P×P ; 29. R—R 3, Q—Q 4 ch ; 30. P—B 3,   R×P ;   31. P×P, Kt×P ; 32. Q×Kt !, P×Q ; 33. B—B 6 ch, B—Kt 2 ; 34. R×B ch, K—B 1 ; 35. R(R 3)—Kt 3, R—K 8 ch : 36. K—Kt 2, K—K 1 ; 37. R—Kt 8 ch, K—Q 2 ; 38. R× R and wins.

28. R×P   Q R—B 1

Equivalent to resignation. However, Tarrasch demonstrates that there is no prospect of resistance :
I. 28. ...Kt—B 4 ;   29. B× Kt, Q×B ; 30. B—B 6, B—Kt 2 ; 31. R—R 3, B×B ; 32. P×B.
II. 28. ...Kt—R 4 ; 29. B— B 6, Kt×B (if 29. ...B—Kt 2 ;

30. Q×Kt !, P×Q ; 31. R×B ch, K—B 1 ; 32. B—R 7, Q—Kt 5 ; 33. R(K 3)—Kt 3 ! wins) ; 30. P×Kt followed by R—R 3 etc.
III. 28. ...B—K 2 ; 29. B— B 6 followed by R—R 3.
IV. 28. ...P—Q 5 ; 29. R— R 3, Kt—R 4 ; 30. B—B 6.

29. B—B 6   B—K 2
30. R—R 3   B×B

Or 30. ... Kt—R 4 ; 31. B× Kt P and Black can resign.

31. Q—R 8 mate

Tarrasch has been inexorable in exploiting the weakness on the black squares provoked by his 16th move.

107. MATCH, 1894

(Seventh Game)

RUY LOPEZ

THIS is one of those endlessly instructive Tarrasch games in which the apparently only slight slips of the opponent are utilised to build up an impressive victory.

White	*Black*
C. A. WALBRODT	DR. S. TARRASCH

1. P—K 4	P—K 4
2. Kt—K B 3	Kt—Q B 3
3. B—Kt 5	P—Q R 3
4. B—R 4	Kt—B 3
5. Kt—B 3	B—B 4

...B—K 2 is better, as the text could be answered favourably by 6. Kt×P etc.

6. P—Q 3   P—R 3

Not caring for the pin which would result from B—K Kt 5.

7. B—K 3   B×B

Tarrasch generally avoided this exchange (see, for example, the first game of the match), but in this case no prepossessing alternative suggests itself.

8. P×B   P—Q 3
9. Kt—Q 5

This leads to nothing. O—O would have been more to the point.

9. ......   O—O
10. P—B 4 ?

The consequences of this move are unpleasant. Kt×Kt ch should have been played, with equal chances.

10. ......   Kt×Kt !
11. B P×Kt   Kt—K 2

It is now clear that Walbrodt has committed a serious strategical blunder : White's Bishop is hemmed in by his own Pawns, and Black has good chances with the possibility of ...P—Q B 3 or ... P—K B 4.

12. O—O

Walbrodt must have anticipated playing 12. Q R—B 1 here to prevent ...P—Q B 3. However, Tarrasch would have continued 12. ... P—Q B 3 ! all the same, for after 13. P×P, P×P ; 14. B×P, R—Kt 1 White could not maintain the extra Pawn against the simultaneous threats of ...R×P and ...Q—Kt 3.

12. ......   P—Q B 3
13. B—Kt 3

P×P would have been better, although it would have signified an admission that White's plan of the game has been faulty.

13. ......   P×P
14. P×P

Better would have been 14. B× P. 14. ...Kt×B ; 15. P×Kt, P—B 4 would have left Black with a comfortable game, but White would at least have been rid of the hapless Bishop.

14. ......   Q—Kt 3
15. Q—K 2   P—Q R 4 !
16. K—R 1   P—R 5
17. B—B 4   Q—R 4
18. P—Q Kt 4 ! ?

An inspired move for a player with Walbrodt's wooden style. The idea is that after 18. ...Q× Kt P ; 19. Q R—Kt 1, Q—R 4 ; 20. R—Kt 5, Q—B 2 ; 21. K R— Kt 1 followed by Q—Kt 2, White has strong pressure on the Q Kt file and the development of Black's Bishop must be postponed indefinitely.

18. ......   P×P e.p.
19. P—K 4 !   Kt—Kt 3

19. ...P—B 4 would be premature because of 20. Kt×P !, P× Kt ; 21. P—Q 6 ch.

20. B×P   B—Kt 5 !

A good idea. White's Knight is to be exchanged, so that he will be left with his ineffectual Bishop.

21. Q—K 3   B×Kt
22. R×B

R

Q×B was a bit better, as the Rook is needed on the first rank.

22. ......   Q R—B 1
23. P—Q 4 ?

In a positional sense, this move is fatal, as it opens up a dominating post at K 4 for the Knight. However, White's game was inferior in any event.

23. ......   P×P
24. Q×Q P   Kt—K 4
25. R(B 3)—B 1   R—B 6
26. Q R—B 1   K R—B 1

Asserting his mastery over the Q B file and thus assuring the following systematic penetration of White's defences.

27. R×R   R×R
28. P—K R 3   R—Q 6
29. Q—B 2   Q—B 6

White is helpless in the face of the threatened ...R—Q 7. Tarrasch gives a highly interesting analysis of the possibilities resulting from 30. R—Q 1, R×R ch ; 31. B×R, Q—B 8 !

I. 32. Q—B 2 (not 32. Q—K 1 ?, Kt—Q 6 followed by ... Q×B !), Q×Q ; 33. B×Q, K—B 1 ; 34. K—Kt 1, K—K 2 ; 35.

K—B 2, K—B 3 ; 36. K—K 3, Kt—Kt 3 with an easily won ending :

(A) 37. P—Kt 3, K—K 4 ; 38. B—Q 3, Kt—K 2 ; 39. B—B 2, P—K Kt 3 (threatening to win the Q P with ...P—B 4) ; 40. P—Kt 4, P—B 4 ; 41. Kt P×P, P×P ; 42. P×P, Kt×Q P ch ; 43. K—B 3, P—Kt 3 ; 44. K—Kt 3, Kt—K 6. On other moves instead of 44. K—Kt 3, Black can play ... P—R 4 and ...Kt—K 2 winning the B P.

(B) 37. K—Q 4, Kt—B 5 ; 38. K—B 4, K—K 2 ! ; 39. K—Kt 5, K—Q 2 ; 40. K—Kt 6, K—B 1 and wins.

II. 32. Q—B 1, Kt—Q 2 ; 33. K—R 2 (not 33. B—K 2, Q×Q ch; 34. B×Q, Kt—B 4), Kt—B 3 ; 35. Q—B 3, Q—B 5, winning the K P.

III. 32. Q—Q 4,   Kt—Q 2 ; 33. K—R 2, Kt—B 4 ; 34. B—B 3 (if 34. P—Kt 3, Q—Kt 8 wins), Q—B 5 ch ; 35. K—R 1, P—B 4, winning the K P.

IV. 32. Q—K 2, Kt—B 5 ; 33. K—R 2, Kt—K 6 ; 34. B—Kt 3, Kt—B 8 ch ; 35. K—Kt 1, Kt—Kt 6 ch ; 36. Q—Q 1, Q×Q ch followed by ...Kt×P.

These variations are instructive because they cast a strong light on the weakness of White's K P and the helplessness of his Bishop.

30. K—R 2   Kt—B 6 ch

An experiment.

31. K—R 1   Kt—K 4
32. K—R 2   R—Q 7
33. Q—B 4

33. Q—Kt 3, Q—Q 5 ; 34. Q—B 4, Q—Kt 7 leads to the same position.

33. ......   Q—Kt 7
34. Q—Kt 3   R—K 7
35. B—Q 1

A bitter decision, but if 35. R—
B 4 (not 35. R—K 1 ?, R×R ; 36.
Q×R, Kt—B 6 ch), Q—B 8 ; 36.
R—B 2, R—K 8 ; 37. Q—B 4, R—
R 8 ch ; 38. K—Kt 3, Q—B 6 ch
(Tarrasch) and wins.

35. ......   R×P
36. R—B 2   Q—B 8
37. R—B 1   R—Q 5
38. Q—Kt 3   · P—K Kt 3 !

This fine move, calculated eight
moves ahead, leads to an impressive
finish.

39. B—K 2   Q—Kt 4
40. Q×P   R—Q 7

If now 41. R—K 1 (not 41. R—
B 2 ?, Q—K 6), Q—B 5 ch ; 42.
K—Kt 1, Q—K 6 ch ; 43. K—
B 1, Kt—Q 6 ; 44. Q—B 8 ch, K—
R 2 and wins. Without 38. ...
P—K Kt 3 ! White would have a
perpetual check here ! (Tarrasch).

41. Q—R 6   Q—K 6
42. B—Q 1

Or 42. B—Kt 5, Q—K 5 fol-
lowed by ...Kt—B 6 ch.

42. ......   Q—K 5
43. R—K Kt 1   Q—B 5 ch
44. K—R 1   Kt—Q 6

The threat of ...Kt—B 7 mate
is decisive. Again, without 38. ...
P—K Kt 3 !, White would have 45.
Q—B 8 ch, K—R 2 ; 46. B—B 2.

45. Q—B 8 ch   K—R 2
46. R—K 1   Kt×R
47. Q—B 8   Q—B 8 ch

Resigns. Tarrasch has utilised
his advantage in superior style.

108. MATCH, 1905

(Fifth Game)

QUEEN'S PAWN GAME

TARRASCH'S exploitation of his opponent's inferior second move is inexorable. This is one of the games
in which Tarrasch reduced such a
procedure to a fine art.

White	Black
F. J. MARSHALL	DR. S. TARRASCH

1. P—Q 4   P—Q 4
2. Kt—Q B 3

This move was experimented
with by Mieses and Breyer, but the
results were unimpressive. The
blockade of White's Q B P is a violation of the familiar positional rule
that this Pawn must always be free
to advance in Q P openings.

2. ......   Kt—K B 3
3. Kt—B 3

B—Kt 5 is more forceful.

3. ......   P—K 3
4. Kt—K 5

An unfortunate idea. B—Kt 5
was still preferable.

4. ......   P—B 4 !
5. P—K 3   Kt—B 3
6. B—Kt 5   B—Q 2
7. Kt×B

Loss of time and a tame sequel to
the two moves with the Knight.
7. Kt×Kt held out better equalis-

ing prospects (7. ...B×Kt; 8. B×B ch, P×B; 9. O—O followed by Kt—R 4).

7.	......	Q×Kt
8.	O—O	B—Q 3
9.	P—Q Kt 3	

A dangerous move which weakens White on the Q B file. But how else can his Queen's Bishop be developed?

| 9. | ...... | Q—B 2 ! |

Gaining time and at the same time forcing the advance of one of White's King's side Pawns, which will be useful later on.

| 10. | P—K R 3 | O—O |
| 11. | B—Kt 2 | P×P ! |

Opening the Q B file for subsequent exploitation, and at the same time closing the diagonal of White's Queen's Bishop.

| 12. | P×P | Q—Kt 3 ! |

Another good move, forcing the following exchange, which does away with White's Bishop-pair and removes the best protection of White's Q B P.

13.	B×Kt	Q×B
14.	Q—Q 3	Q R—B 1
15.	Q R—B 1	

...B—Kt 5 was threatened.

| 15. | ...... | B—B 5 |
| 16. | Q R—K 1 | P—Q R 3 |

Contemplating ...P—Q Kt 4—5. Black's game is rich in prospects, whilst the position of White's pieces is suitable only for defensive or waiting moves.

17.	P—Q R 4	R—B 2
18.	R—K 2	R—Kt 1
19.	P—Kt 3	B—Q 3
20.	P—B 4	

Marshall has played into his opponent's hands with his last two moves: the hope of King's side action proves vain, but the weaknesses created by the Pawn moves will plague White later on.

20.	......	P—Q Kt 4
21.	P×P	P×P
22.	R—R 1	

Best under the circumstances. 22. P—B 5 would be answered powerfully by ...P—Kt 5 and ... Kt—K 5.

22.	......	P—Kt 5
23.	Kt—Q 1	R—R 1
24.	R×R ch	Q×R
25.	P—B 4	P×P e.p.
26.	Kt×P	R—Kt 2

White is at last rid of the weak Q B P, but the Q Kt P is now equally feeble.

27.	Kt—R 4	Q—Kt 1
28.	R—K 3	Kt—K 5
29.	K—Kt 2	P—B 4

Strengthening the Knight in its dominating post. White is in a bad way, as his pieces are virtually helpless.

30.	R—B 3	P—R 3
31.	P—R 4	K—R 2
32.	R—K 3	Q—Q B 1
33.	R—K 2	Q—K 1 !

Tarrasch is now ready for the decisive manœuvre ...Q—Kt 3—

Kt 5 followed by ...P—Kt 4, which explains his renunciation of the otherwise attractive sacrifice 32. ...B×P!? Marshall finds the only, albeit none too promising method of prolonging the game.

34. Kt—B 5	B×Kt
35. P×B	Kt×B P
36. Q×P ch	P×Q
37. R×Q	R×P

White's simplification has been of no avail.

38. B—Q 4	Kt—K 5
39. K—R 2	R—Q 6
40. B—K 5	Kt×P
41. R—K B 8	

Or 41. R—K 7, Kt—R 4 ; 42. R—Q 7, K—Kt 1 ; followed by ...K—B 1—K 1, and Black wins without too much trouble.

41.	K—Kt 3
42 R—Q 8	Kt—K 5 !

With mating intentions. If now 43. R—Q 7, K—R 4 ; 44. R× Kt P, K×P etc.

43. P—R 5 ch	K×P
44. B×P	K—Kt 5
45. R—K Kt 8	R—R 6 ch
46. K—Kt 2	R—Kt 6 ch

The position has amusing possibilities : if 47. K—R 1, K—R 6 followed by ...Kt—B 7 mate ; or 47. K—R 2, K—B 6 ; 48. K—R 1, Kt—B 7 ch ; 48. K—R 2, R—Kt 7 mate.

47. K—B 1	K—B 6

An ingenious conclusion. Any move by White is fatal !

48. K—K 1	R—Kt 8 mate

Tarrasch has outplayed his opponent all the way.

109. MATCH, 1905

(Seventh Game)

VIENNA GAME

(IN EFFECT)

DESPITE its colourless opening, Tarrasch was extremely fond of this game. The Rook and Pawn ending is unquestionably one of the finest in master play.

White	*Black*
F. J. MARSHALL	DR. S. TARRASCH

1. P—K 4	P—K 4
2. B—B 4	Kt—K B 3
3. Kt—Q B 3	B—B 4

Tarrasch hopes for something more interesting than 3. ...Kt× P ; 4. Q—R 5, Kt—Q 3 ; 5. Q× K P ch, Q—K 2 etc.

4. P—Q 3	P—Q 3
5. Kt—R 4	

Strangely tame for Marshall.

One would expect from him the natural and aggressive 5. P—B 4.

5.	B—Kt 3
6. Kt×B	R P×Kt
8. P—B 4	B—K 3 ! ?

An interesting move, which reveals, as in Game 104, that Tarrasch does not fear a doubled and isolated K P.

8. B×B	P×B
9. P×P	P×P
10. Kt—B 3	Kt—B 3
11. O—O	O—O

The position has drawish implications despite Black's three open files ; the material left on the board offers little prospect of successful action.

12. P—Q R 3	Q—Q 3
13. B—K 3	Kt—K Kt 5
14. Q—K 2	Kt×B
15. Q×Kt	Kt—Q 5
16. Kt×Kt	Q×Kt
17. Q×Q	P×Q
18. R×R ch	K×R

After this blood-letting, an early draw seems to be in order. Yet Black has a slight advantage in the circumstance that his Rook can be utilised for aggressive action against the hostile Pawns. Fine gives the following variation to show how passive play might lead to White's downfall : 19. K—B 2, K—K 2 ; 20. K—Kt 3, P—K 4 ; 21. K—B 3, P—Q Kt 4 ; 22. K—K 2, P—Kt 5 ; 23. K—B 2, R—R 5 ; 24. K—K 2, P—Q Kt 4 ; 25. K—B 2, K—Q 3 ; 26. K—K 2, P×P ; 27. R×P (if 27. P×P, P—Kt 5), R× R ; 28. P×R, K—B 4 ; 29. K— Q 2, K—Kt 3 ; 30. K—B 1, K— R 4 ; 31. K—Kt 2, K—R 5 ; 32. K—R 2, P—B 4 ; 33. K—Kt 2, P—B 5 ; 34. K—R 2, P—Kt 4 ! ; 35. K—Kt 2, P—K Kt 5 ; 36. K— R 2, P—B 6 ; 37. P—R 3, P— Kt 6 ! ; 38. P—R 4, P—R 4 ; 39. K—Kt 1, K×P and wins.

| 19. R—B 1 ch | K—K 2 |
| 20. R—B 4 ? |

This superficial move starts White well on the way to loss, and he must now bend every effort to draw. The simple continuation 20. K—B 2, R—R 4 (the King and Pawn ending after ...R—B 1 ch would be drawn) ; 21. K—K 2, R—Q B 4 ; 22. K—Q 2 would have sufficed to maintain equality.

| 20. ...... | R—R 4 ! ! |

The key to the following play : Black's Rook is to be manœuvred along the fourth rank in order to weaken White's Pawns. Lasker imitated this procedure in a famous ending against Marshall two years later.

21. K—B 1

If Marshall intended 21. P—K 5, he now renounces it because of the sequel 21. ...R×K P ; 22. R×P, R—K 7 ; 23. R—Q B 4, P—B 4 and Black's formidable position on the seventh rank gives him fine winning prospects.

| 21. ...... | R—Q B 4 |
| 22. R—B 2 | R—Q Kt 4 ! |

The "softening-up" process begins !

| 23. P—Q Kt 3 | R—K R 4 ! |

Gaining time for the following important move.

24. P—R 3   P—Q Kt 4 !

Black now threatens ...R—Q B 4—B 3—R 3.

25. P—Q Kt 4 ?

Panic. White should have avoided this new weakness by bringing his King to Q Kt 2. Black would have retained the initiative, but a direct win would not be in sight. After the text, White will be unable to save the game.

25. ......   R—Kt 4
26. R—B 4   P—K 4

White threatened 27. P—K R 4, R—Kt 3 ; 28. P—K 5, with fatal consequences for Black.

27. R—B 2

Not 27. R—B 5, R×R ch ; 28. P×R, K—B 3 ; 29. P—Kt 4, K—Kt 4 ; 30. K—Kt 2, K—B 5 and Black wins the ending.

27. ......   R—Kt 3
28. R—B 5   R—K 3

...R—K B 3 would only draw.

29. K—K 2   P—K Kt 3

Driving away the Rook in order to resume the contemplated attack on the Queen's side.

30. R—B 1   R—R 3
31. R—Q R 1

Now White pays the penalty for his inaccurate play : he must guard the Q R P with his Rook, whereas if he had played properly, he could use the King for this menial purpose.

31. ......   P—Kt 3 !

Beginning the decisive advance against White's chief weakness.

32. K—Q 2   R—R 5
33. P—B 3

This opens the gates to the enemy, but if 33. K—B 1, R—R 1 ; 34. K—Q 2 (if 34. K—Kt 2, R—K B 1 ! wins), K—Q 3 with much the same kind of ending.

33. ......   P—B 4 !

Now the crisis is reached.

34. B P×P

Fine treats the alternative 34. Kt P×P as follows : 34. ...P×P ; 35. K—B 2, P—B 5 ! ; 36. B P× P, P×P ch ; 37. K×P, R×Q P ch ; 38. K—K 3, R—R 5 ; 39. R—Q Kt 1 (the loss of a Pawn is unavoidable), R×R P ch ; 40. K—B 2, R—R 4 ; 41. K—K 3, K—Q 3 ; 42. R—Q 1 ch, K—B 3 ; 43. R—Q 5, R—R 7 and wins.

Tarrasch also gives the following possibility : 34. R—Q Kt 1, R× R P ; 35. Kt P×P, P×P.

I. 36. R×P, R×P ; 37. R—
Kt 7 ch, K—Q 3 ; 38. R—Kt 6 ch,
K—Q 2 ; 39. R—Kt 7 ch, K—
B 3 ; 40. R—K 7, K—Q 3 ; 41.
R×R P, P—B 5 ; 42. P×P, R—
K Kt 6 with a won ending.

II. 36. P×P, R—R 7 ch ; 37.
K—K 1, B P×P ; 38. R×P, K—
B 3 ; 39. R—Kt 6 ch, K—Kt 4 ;
40. R—K 6, K—B 5 ; 41. R—
B 6 ch, K—Kt 6 ; 42. R—K 6,
K×P ; 43. R×P, K×P ; 44. R—
Q 5, P—R 4 ; 45. R×P, P—R 5
with an easy win.

Black's greater mobility and preferable Pawn structure tell every
time in his favour.

34. ......   P×Kt P ! !

An amazing reply ! Despite
White's three passed Pawns he will
have a lost game.

35. Q P×P   K—K 3
36. P—Q 4

Tarrasch demonstrates that the
alternative 36. K—B 2, P×P ; 37.
K—Kt 3, R—Q 5 ; 38. K—B 3,
K×P would also be unavailing :
I. 39. R—Q 1 (not 39. R×
P ? ?, P—Kt 5 ch), R—R 5 ; 40.
K—Kt 3, K—Q 5 ; 41. R—Q R 1,
K×P ; 42. P—K 5, R—K 5 ; 43.
R×P, R×P and wins.
II. 39. R—Q 1, R—R 5 ; 40.
R—Q R 1, P—Kt 5 ch ; 41. K—
Kt 3, P—Q Kt 4 ; 42. R—Q 1,
P—R 7 ; 43. R—Q R 1, K—Q 5 ;
44. R×P, R×R ; 45. K×R, K×
P ; 46. P—K 5, K—B 7 ; 47. P—
K 6, P—Kt 6 ch ; 48. K—R 3,
P—Kt 7 ; 49. P—K 7, P—Kt 8
(Q) ; 50. P—K 8(Q), Q—Kt 6
mate.
III. 39. K—B 2, P—Kt 5 ; 40.
R—Q 1, R—Q 1 ; 41. K—Kt 3,
R—Q R 1 ; 42. K×P, P—R 7 ;

43. R—Q R 1, K—Q 5 ; 44. K—
Kt 3, K×P ; 45. P—K 5, R—
K 1 ; 46. R×P, R×P and wins.

36. ......   P×P

A peculiar Pawn position ! Although White has managed to maintain material equality, he must soon
succumb, as his Pawns are immo-
bilised.

37. K—B 3   P—R 7 !

White is now without resource.
He must lose the triple mass of
Pawns in exchange for Black's simi-
lar set of Pawns ; but then Black's
King's nearness to the King's side
Pawns will be decisive.

38. P—Kt 4

King moves are no better, Fine
points out :
I. 38. K—Kt 3, R×P ; 39.
R×P, K×P ; 40. R—R 7, P—
R 4 ; 41. R—K 7 ch, K—B 5 ; 42.
R—K 6, P—Kt 4 ; 43. R×P, R×
P ; 44. R×P, R—K 4 ; 45. R—
Kt 8, K—Kt 6 ; 46. R—K R 8,
P—R 5 and wins.
II. 38. K—Q 3, R—R 6 ch ;
39. K—B 2, R—K Kt 6 ! ; 40. R×
P, R×P ch ; 41. K—Kt 3, R×R ;
42. K×R, P—Kt 4 ; 43. K—Kt 3,
P—R 4 ; 44. K—Kt 4, P—Kt 5 ;
45. P×P, P×P ; 46. K×P, P—
Kt 6 ; 47. P—Q 5 ch, K×P ; 48.
K—B 6, P—Kt 7 and wins.

38. ......   P—Kt 4
39. K—Q 3   P—Kt 5
40. K—B 4   P—Kt 6 ch
41. K×P

Or 41. K—B 3, R×P !

41. ......   R×P
42. R×P   R×P

43. R—R 6	R—K 6 ch
44. K—B 2	R×R P
45. R×P ch	K×P
46. R—Kt 4	R—K 6
47. K—Q 2	R—K 5

White resigns, for after 48. R—Kt 7, K—B 5 ! ; 49. R×P, K×P Black has a well-known book win. It is curious that the pressure on White's obviously weak Queen's side Pawns did not win by itself, but was only a means towards ultimately winning on the other wing.

110. MATCH, 1905

(Tenth Game)

FRENCH DEFENCE

IN this game Tarrasch puts his redoubtable opponent to shame. Marshall is on the defensive all the way, and it is Tarrasch who indulges in sparkling and ingenious play.

White	*Black*
DR. S. TARRASCH	F. J. MARSHALL

1. P—K 4	P—K 3
2. P—Q 4	P—Q 4
3. Kt—Q B 3	Kt—K B 3
4. P—K 5	

Tarrasch had so high an opinion of the McCutcheon Variation 4. B—Kt 5, B—Kt 5 (just becoming popular after the turn of the century) that he resorted for several years to Steinitz's outmoded continuation.

4.	K Kt—Q 2
5. P—B 4	P—Q B 4
6. P×P	Kt—Q B 3
7. P—Q R 3	

This creates what may become a serious weakness in the event of Queen's side castling, but Tarrasch wants to guard his K B from exchange (7. B—Q 3, Kt—Kt 5).

7.	B×P
8. Q—Kt 4	O—O
9. Kt—B 3	

If 9. B—Q 3, B×Kt ; 10. R×B, Q—Kt 3 ; 11. Kt—K 2, Kt—B 4 with about even chances.

9.	Kt—Q 5
10. B—Q 3	P—B 4
11. Q—R 3	P—Q R 3

In the Nuremberg Tournament of the following year, Spielmann played 11. ...Kt×Kt ch ; 12. Q×Kt, B—Kt 3 ! ; 13. Kt—K 2, Kt—B 4 ; 14. B—K 3, B—Q 2 against Tarrasch with an excellent position.

12. B—Q 2	P—Q Kt 4

True to his style, Marshall is playing for an attacking formation against White's intended castling on the Queen's side. If the attack does not materialise, Black will be in a bad way because of the ineffectual position of his Q B.

13. O—O—O	Kt×Kt
14. Q×Kt	B—Kt 2

A superficial "developing" move which does nothing for the Bishop and at best makes room for a Rook at Q B 1. 14. ...Kt—Kt 3 (guarding against Kt×Q P) was a far better move, as will soon be apparent.

15. Kt—K 2	Q—Kt 3
16. P—Q Kt 4 !	

Apparently suicidal, but in reality a very powerful stroke.

16. ......   B—K 2
17. Q—K 3 !

If Black exchanges Queens, his Knight and Q B are virtually helpless, while White gets a magnificent square at Q 4 for his Knight and the promising possibility of a breakthrough by P—Kt 4 etc.

17. ......   K R—B 1

Black resigns himself to the exchange if it will result in the posting of his Knight at Q B 5.

18. Kt—Q 4   Kt—B 4 ? !

An astounding move, but what to do ? If 18. ...Kt—B 1 ; 19. Kt ×B P with clear advantage. If 18. ...P—Q R 4 ; 19. B×Kt P etc. On other moves, White has a choice between P—Kt 4 or Kt—Kt 3 as highly promising continuations.

19. B×B P !

Also good enough was 19. P× Kt, B×P ; 20. B—B 3, B×P ch ; 21. B—Kt 2 (not 21. K—Q 2 ?, R×B ! ; 22. K×R, Q—R 4 ch ; 23. K—Kt 3, Q—Kt 5 ch ; 24.

K—R 2, Q—Kt 7 mate) etc. But the text is much sharper and clearer.

19. ......   P×B
20. Kt×B P

White regains the piece and remains two Pawns to the good.

20. ......   B—B 1
21. P×Kt   Q—Kt 3

There is little choice : if 21. ... Q×P (not 21. ...B×P ? ; 22. Kt—K 7 ch followed by 23. Kt× R !) ; 22. Q×Q, B×Q ; 23. B— Kt 4 with an easy win.

22. Kt—Q 6   B×Kt
23. K P×B   R—K 1

Exchanging the two Rooks for the Queen would be a hopeless speculation : 23. ...R×P ? ; 24. Q× R, R—Q B 1 ; 25. P—B 5 !, Q× B P ; 26. P—Q 7 ! and wins.

24. Q—K Kt 3   Q×Q

The Bishops on opposite colours are his last hope.

25. P×Q   B—B 3
26. Q R—K 1 !

Tarrasch does not fear the following exchanges, as he anticipates little difficulty from the resulting endgame.

26. ......   R×R ch
27. R×R   R—K 1
28. R×R ch   B×R
29. P—Kt 4   K—B 2
30. B—B 3   P—Kt 3
31. P—B 5 !

Now White has a third passed

Pawn. Black's King is tied to the King's side, while the Bishop must always be on guard against P—Q B 6.

| 31. ...... | B—B 3 |
| 32. B—Q 4 | P—Q R 4 |

Else White's King would eventually reach Q R 5.

33. K—Q 2	P—Kt 5
34. R P×P	R P×P
35. K—K 3	P—Kt 4

Momentarily preventing White King's penetration to K 5. But this cannot be staved off for long.

36. P—Kt 3	P—R 3
37. B—R 8	K—Kt 1
38. B—K 5	K—B 2
39. K—Q 4	B—Kt 2

Or 39. ...K—Kt 1 ; 40. B—B 6, K—B 2 ; 41. B—Q 8, K—Kt 2 ; 42. B—R 5 winning easily.

40. B—Kt 7 !	P—R 4
41. P×P	P—Kt 5
42. P—Q 7	Resigns

A simple but instructive ending : White's control of the black squares was just as important as his material advantage.

111. MATCH, 1905

(Fourteenth Game)

PETROFF DEFENCE

SIMPLE but vigorous positional chess by Tarrasch carries the day. At no time does Marshall have an opportunity for the tactical fireworks which made him a feared opponent.

| White | Black |
| DR. S. TARRASCH | F. J. MARSHALL |

1. P—K 4	P—K 4
2. Kt—K B 3	Kt—K B 3
3. Kt×P	P—Q 3
4. Kt—K B 3	Kt×P
5. P—Q 4	B—Kt 5

A novelty. Since the customary ...P—Q 4 gives White control of K 5 and sometimes allows P—B 4 as a powerful reaction, Marshall renounces the second advance of the Q P and tries a different system of development.

6. B—Q 3	Kt—K B 3
7. O—O	B—K 2
8. R—K 1	

Black's game is cramped and his K B in particular faces a barren existence. His only compensation is the pin on White's K Kt, which Tarrasch intends to remove by Q Kt—Q 2—B 1—Kt 3 followed by P—K R 3.

8.	O—O
9. Q Kt—Q 2	Kt—B 3
10. P—B 3	P—Q 4

Marshall realises that the pin cannot be maintained much longer, and that he must have recourse to the further advance of the Q P if he is to gain a measure of freedom. Thus the great connoisseur of this defence admits defeat !

11. Kt—B 1   Q—Q 2
12. Kt—Kt 3   B—Q 3
13. P—K R 3 !   Q B × Kt

Tarrasch points out there is no wholly satisfactory move, for if 13. ...B—R 4 ; 14. B—B 5, Q—Q 1 ; 15. Kt × B, Kt × Kt ; 16. B × P ch, K × B ; 17. Kt—Kt 5 ch, K—Kt 3 ; 18. Q—Q 3 ch, P—B 4 ; 19. R—K 6 ch, Kt—B 3 ; 20. P—K Kt 4 wins. If 13. ...B—K 3 ; 14. Kt—K 5 or 13. ...K B × Kt ; 14. P × Q B, B—Q 3 ; 15. B—B 5 followed by P—Kt 5—in either case with considerable advantage.

14. Q × B   B × Kt

Marshall cannot have had any illusions about the following unequal struggle between two Bishops and two Knights ; unfortunately, the prospect of Kt—B 5 was too unpleasant to face. The necessity for this hard choice is the consequence of Tarrasch's masterly opening play.

15. P × B

Q × B was also quite good.

15. ......   Q R—K 1

Black is still afflicted with a choice of unfavourable continuations. He now plays for a double exchange of Rooks, although this procedure will only enhance the power of the Bishops and in fact lead to the loss of a Pawn. But it is difficult to find any other way of continuing the game.

16. B—K Kt 5   R × R ch
17. R × R   R—K 1
18. R × R ch   Kt × R
19. B—B 5   Q—Q 3
20. Q—K 2 !

White's game plays itself. The loss of a Pawn by Black is now inevitable.

20. ......   K—B 1

20. ...Kt—B 3 is equally disagreeable : 21. B × Kt, P × B ; 22. Q—Kt 4 ch etc.

21. B—B 4   Q—K 2

...Q—B 3 would also lose a Pawn after 22. B—Q 7.

22. Q—Kt 5   P—Kt 4

What follows is desperation. Marshall vainly strives for complications.

23. B—Q 2   P—K R 3
24. Q × Kt P   Q—K 7
25. Q × Kt   Q × B
26. Q × P ch   K—K 2
27. Q—B 6 !

Tarrasch already has in mind the subsequent victorious advance of his K R P. The text is the necessary preliminary to useful simplification.

27. ......   Q × Kt P
28. Q—B 5 ch   K—Q 1

Or 28. ..K—B 3 ; 29. Q × Q P, K—Kt 2 ; 30. B—Q 7 and wins.

29. Q × Q P ch   Kt—Q 3
30. B—Kt 4   Q × B P

30. ...P—K B 3 is refuted by 31. Q—K 6 ; while if 30. ...Q—Q 7 ; 31. P—B 4, Q×R P ; 32. Q×P ch followed by P—B 5 winning easily.

31. Q×P ch	K—K 1
32. Q—K 5 ch	K—B 1
33. K—R 2	Q—B 5
34. P—R 3 !	

Tarrasch points out that the plausible continuation 34. P—K R 4, Q×R P ; 35. P—R 5, Q—Q 7 ; 36. Q—R 8 ch, K—K 2 ; 37. P—R 6, Kt—K 1 ! ; 38. P—R 7 is not good enough to win : 38. ... Q—R 3 ch ; 39. B—R 3, Kt—B3 etc.

| 34. ...... | Q—Kt 4 |

So that, if 35. Q×Q ?, Kt×Q and Black wins a Pawn. At the same time he threatens 35. ...Q×Q ; 36. P×Q, Kt—B 5 etc.

35. B—K 2	Q—Kt 7
36. P—Q R 4	Q—B 7
37. P—R 4 !	

But now this advance decides the game very quickly.

| 37. ...... | Q×P |
| 38. P—R 5 | Q—K 1 |

No better is 38. ...Q—B 7 ; 39, Q—R 8 ch, K—K 2 ; 40. B—B 3. Kt—K 1 ; 41. P—Kt 4 !, Kt—B 3 ; 42. P—Kt 5, Kt—R 2 ; 43. P—Kt 6, P×P ; 44. Q×Kt ch—or 41. ...Q—Q 7 ; 42. Q—K 5 ch, K—B 1 ; 43. P—Kt 5 and wins (Tarrasch).

| 39. Q—R 8 ch | K—K 2 |
| 40. Q—K 5 ch | K—Q 1 |

If 40. ...K—B 1 ; 41. Q—R 8 ch, K—K 2 ; 42. Q—Kt 7, Q—K B 1 ; 43. P—R 6, Kt—K 1 ; 44. Q—K 5 ch, K—Q 1 ; 45. P—R 7, Kt—Kt 2 ; 46. Q—B 6 ch, winning easily.

41. P—R 6	Q—B 1
42. Q—B 6 ch	K—K 1
43. P—R 7	Kt—K 5

It would have been more gracious to resign.

| 44. B—Kt 5 ch | Resigns |

For it is mate next move. An impressive game by Tarrasch.

112. MATCH, 1908

(Third Game)

RUY LOPEZ

THIS is one of the few games of the match in which Tarrasch did himself justice. So able a judge as Teichmann says : "He deserves great praise for his accurate and economical defence, as well as for the forceful way in which he presses his counterattack."

White	*Black*
DR. E. LASKER	DR. S. TARRASCH
1. P—K 4	P—K 4
2. Kt—K B 3	Kt—Q B 3
3. B—Kt 5	P—Q R 3
4. B—R 4	Kt—B 3
5. O—O	B—K 2

At the time this game was played, Tarrasch did not care very much for the defence (5. ...Kt× P) with which his name is associated.

6. R—K 1	P—Q Kt 4
7. B—Kt 3	P—Q 3
8. P—B 3	Kt—Q R 4
9. B—B 2	P—B 4
10. P—Q 4	Q—B 2
11. Q Kt—Q 2	Kt—B 3

Black wishes to bring about a clarification of the Pawn position in the centre.

12. P—K R 3

The modern masters prefer to interpolate P—Q R 4 hereabouts.

12. ......   O—O

To play for the win of a Pawn here would be futile : 12. ...B P× P ; 13. P×P, Kt×Q P ; 14. Kt× Kt, P×Kt ; 15. Kt—B 3 etc.

13. Kt—B 1

Lasker continues his development at the cost of a Pawn, apparently convinced that he will later regain it without any difficulty. The sacrifice is nowadays considered unsound.

13. ......   B P×P

Tarrasch accepts the challenge.

14. P×P   Kt×Q P

The alternative, perhaps even more favourable, is 14. ...P×P ; 15. B—Kt 5, P—R 3 ; 16. B— K R 4, R—K 1 ; 17. R—B 1, Q— Kt 3 ; 18. Q—Q 2, B—K 3 ; 19. B—Kt 1, Kt—K 4 (Leonhardt–Rubinstein, San Sebastian, 1911).

| 15. Kt×Kt | P×Kt |
| 16. Kt—Kt 3 | |

This turns out unsatisfactorily. In the fifth game, Lasker adopted the stronger move 16. B—Kt 5 with the continuation 16. ...P— R 3 ; 17. B—K R 4, Q—Kt 3 ; 18. Q—Q 3, P—Kt 4 ? ; 19. B— K Kt 3, B—K 3 ; 20. Q R—Q 1, K R—B 1 ? (...B×Q R P ! should have been played) ; 21. B—Kt 1 with a winning game for White.

The correct continuation after 16. B—Kt 5 would have been 16. ...Kt—Q 4 ; 17. B×B, Kt×B ; 18. Kt—Kt 3, B—K 3 ; 19. Kt— K 2, Kt—B 3 ; 20. R—Q B 1, Q— Kt 3 ; 21. Q—Q 2 (Q—Q 3 is answered by ...Kt—Kt 5), P— Q 4 ; 22. P×P, B×Q P ; 23. Q R—Q 1, Q R—Q 1 and the Q P cannot be captured.

16. ......   Kt—Q 2

Making room for the defence of the Q P by ...B—B 3 and at the same time opening promising perspectives to the Knight (...Kt— K 4 or ...Kt—B 4). The move requires some courage, however, as it permits such formidable replies as Kt—B 5 and (later on) B—Q 5.

17. B—Kt 3	Q—Kt 3
18. Kt—B 5	B—B 3
19. B—K B 4	

Tarrasch refutes Schlechter's recommendation 19. B—Q 5, R— R 2 ; 20. P—Q Kt 3, with Kt— K 4 ! ; 21. B—Kt 2 (if 21. Kt× P(Q 4), Q×Kt ; 22. Q×Q, Kt— B 6 ch ; 23. P×Kt, B×Q, winning a Pawn), B×Kt ; 22. P×B, P— Q 6 ! ; 23. B×Kt, B×B ; 24. Q R—B 1, Q—Q 5 with a winning game.

19. ......   Kt—K 4 !

Tarrasch carefully avoids the plausible pitfall 19. ...B—K 4 ; 20. B×B, P×B ; 21. Q—Kt 4, Q—K B 3 (White threatened not only mate, but the win of a piece as well with Kt—K 7 ch) ; 22. Q R—B 1 with a decisive attack, for example 22. ...P—Kt 3 ; 23. R—B 6, Q—Q 1 ; 24. R×P ch ; or 22. ...Kt—Kt 1 ; 23. R×B, R×R ; 24. Kt—R 6 ch ; or 22. ...B—Kt 2 ; 23. R—B 7 etc. ; or 22. ...P—K R 4 ; 23. Q—Kt 3, P—R 5 ; 24. Q—Kt 4 etc.

20. B—Q 5

If instead 20. Kt×P(Q 4), Kt—B 5 ! ; 21. B—K 3, Kt×B ; 22. P×Kt, B—Kt 2 with conclusive positional advantage : two Bishops plus pressure on White's ungainly isolated K P.

20. ....   R—R 2
21. Q—Kt 3

Or 21. Kt×P(Q 4), Kt—B 5 ; 22. B—K 3, Kt×B ; 23. P×Kt, B—Kt 2 and Black still has the advantage.

21. ....   R—B 2

Taking the open file and at the same time parrying the threat 22. Kt×P(Q 4) !, Q×Kt ; 23. B—K 3.

22. P—Kt 4

Something drastic must be tried, since tamer moves will no longer do ; if, for example, 22. Q R—B 1, B×Kt ; 23. P×B, K R—B 1 with an easy game.

22. ....   P—Kt 3

Boldly forcing the issue : Lasker must now play desperately for some compensating attack.

23. Kt—R 6 ch   K—Kt 2
24. P—Kt 5   B—Q 1

The Bishop retreats all the way to permit the Q R to guard the second rank if need be.

25. Q—Kt 3   P—B 3 !

This beats off the attack and makes it possible for Black to seize the initiative.

26. Kt—B 5 ch ! ?

Lasker still tries for a "swindle". If now 26. ...P×Kt ; 27. P×P dbl ch, K—R 1 ; 28. B—R 6 with a powerful attack.

He naturally avoids 26. P—K R 4 (the threat was 26. ...P×P ; 27. B×P, B×B ; 28. Q×B, Kt—B 6 ch), P×P ; 27. P×P, R×B ! ; 28. Q×R, B×P and wins.

26. ....   K—R 1
27. Kt—R 4 ?

After this his position crumbles rapidly under Tarrasch's brutal strokes. 27. P×P, B×P ; 28. Kt—R 6 was relatively best.

27. ......   P×P
28. B×P   B×B
29. Q×B   P—Q 6 !
30. K—R 1

If 30. Q—Kt 3 or R—K 3, R—
B 7 is decisive, while 30. Q—K 3
leads to a hopeless ending.

30. ......   R—B 7

Or 30. ...Q×P ; 31. R—K B 1,
Q×R ch ; 32. R×Q, R×R ch ;
33. K—Kt 2, R—B 1 ; 34. Q—
R 6, R—K Kt 2 followed by ...
P—Kt 4 with an easy win (Tar-
rasch).

31. R—K 3

If 31. P—B 4, Q—B 7 ; 32. Kt
—Kt 2, Kt—B 6 and wins. The
attack on the seventh rank is devastating.

31. ......   K R×P

With the terrible threat 32. ...
R—R 7 ch ; 33. K—Kt 1, K R—
Kt 7 ch ! ; 34. Kt×R, Kt—B 6 ch!
winning the queen.

32. Kt—Kt 2

If 32. Kt—B 3 ? !, R×Kt ; 33.
R×R, R—R 7 ch ! wins.

32. ......   P—Q 7
33. R—K Kt 1   R—Q B 8

The position is ripe for resignation.

34. Q—K 7   R×R ch

...R(B 7)—B 8 was even
stronger.

35. K×R   P—Q 8(Q) ch

Who could have prophesied such
a fate for the sickly Q P ? !

36. K×R   Q—B 6 ch
37. K—K 1   Q—R 4 ch

...Kt—Q 6 ch ! (Tarrasch) wins
even more neatly, for example 38.
K—Q 2, Q—R 4 ch ; 39. K×Kt,
Q—Q 8 mate. But White is beyond good and evil in any event.

38. R—B 3   B×P

In order to be able to check with
the Bishop at Kt 5 later on.

39. Q×P   Q(R 4)×R ch

Black is again threatened with
mate, but his attack hits home first.

40. P×Q   Q×B P ch
41. K—K 2

If 41. K—Q 1, B—Kt 5 mate !

41. ......   Q—B 7 ch
42. K—K 3   Q—Q 6 ch
43. K—B 4   P—Kt 4 ch !

So that if 44. K×Kt, Q—B 6
mate !

44. K×P   Kt—B 2 ch

White resigns. Rarely has
Lasker been beaten in such sensational style !

113. MATCH, 1908

(Tenth Game)

RUY LOPEZ

WHILE it must be admitted that
Lasker is not seen here at his best,

Tarrasch's keen and accurate play results in a well-earned win.

	White	Black
	Dr. S. Tarrasch	Dr. E. Lasker
1.	P—K 4	P—K 4
2.	Kt—K B 3	Kt—Q B 3
3.	B—Kt 5	Kt—B 3
4.	O—O	Kt × P

In the second and fourth games of the match, Lasker transposed into the Steinitz Defence with 4. ...P—Q 3. In both cases, despite ultimate defeat, Tarrasch established such an impressive opening advantage that one readily understands Lasker's switch to a more open, if more dangerous, opening system.

5.	P—Q 4	B—K 2
6.	Q—K 2	Kt—Q 3
7.	B × Kt	Kt P × B
8.	P × P	Kt—Kt 2
9.	Kt—B 3	O—O
10.	R—K 1	

Modern theory prefers 10. Kt— Q 4 ! with the likely sequel 10. ... B—B 4 ; 11. R—Q 1, B × Kt ; 12. R × B, P—Q 4 ; 13. P × P e.p., P × P ; 14. P—Q Kt 4 !, Q—B 3 ; 15. B—K 3, B—B 4 ; 16. Q R— Q 1, P—Q R 3 ; 17. P—Kt 4 ! (Schlechter—Réti, Vienna, 1914) and the position is much in White's favour.

10.	......	Kt—B 4
11.	Kt—Q 4	Kt—K 3
12.	B—K 3	Kt × Kt
13.	B × Kt	P—Q B 4 ! ?

The Rio de Janeiro Variation, at the time a fashionable novelty. It gives Black a fine free position at the cost of a ragged Pawn formation ; and in any event it is definitely preferable to the continuation in a famous game between Pillsbury and Tarrasch at Vienna, 1898 : 13. ... P—Q 4 ; 14. Kt—R 4 ! when White's bind on Q B 5 gives him a strategically won game.

14.	B—K 3	P—Q 4
15.	P × P e.p.	B × P
16.	Kt—K 4	

Q R—Q 1, as played by Tarrasch in a later game of the match, is even stronger.

16.	......	B—Kt 2

16. ...B × P ch ; 17. K × B, Q— R 5 ch ; 18. K—Kt 1, Q × Kt looks promising, but after 19. B × P, Q × Q ; 20. R × Q followed by R—K 7 White has the better ending.

17.	Kt × B	

17. Kt × P ? would be a serious blunder : 17. ...B × Kt ; 18. B × B, Q—Kt 4 and Black wins a piece.

17.	......	P × Kt
18.	Q R—Q 1	Q—B 3
19.	P—Q B 4	K R—K 1

Despite his weak Q P, Black has a playable game : his Bishop is threatening (the manœuvre ...R— K 3 followed by ...Q—K 2 and ...R—Kt 3 is in the offing), his development is easy, and he can rely on the Bishops on opposite colours for drawing possibilities. Nevertheless, the weakness of his Q P is irksome, and the variation is one which can recommend itself only to a supremely resourceful and self-confident master like Lasker.

20.	Q—Kt 4 !	

A strong move. Tarrasch points out that Black dare not play 20. ... Q×P ? because of 21. R—Kt 1, Q—B 6 ; 22. K R—Q B 1, Q—R 6 ; 23. B—R 6 ! (not 23. R×B ?, Q×R ch ; 24. B×Q, R—K 8 mate), P—Kt 3 ; 24. Q—B 4 and Black cannot save his Bishop because of the threat of Q—B 6. Or if 20. ...R—K 5 ; 21. Q—Q 7, Q×P ; 22. P—B 3 ! (not 22. R—Kt 1 ?, R×B !) followed by R—Kt 1 and wins.

20. ......   B—B 3 ?

This leads to a lost game. Correct was ...R—K 3 with a playable position.

21. R—K 2 !

A move which is as powerful as it is simple. It prepares for the doubling of the Rooks on the Q file, guards the Q Kt P and prevents 21. ...R—K 3, which would be refuted by 22. B—Kt 5, Q—Kt 3 (with White's K R on K 1, Black could save himself by ...R×R ch) ; 23. R×R, P×R ; 24. R×P etc.

21. ......   R—K 5

Lasker studied the position for an hour before making this move. It turns out to be inadequate, but against the plausible 21. ...Q R—Kt 1 Tarrasch planned 22. P—Q Kt 3 with strong pressure.

22. Q—Kt 3

Now that the Q P is menaced, one would have expected Black to seek compensation with 22. ...R×P. In that event Tarrasch would have continued 23. R×P, R—Q 1 ; 24. R×R ch, Q×R ; 25. P—K R 3 ! and White has much the better game because of the threat of B—R 6. If 25. ...K—R 1 ; 26. R—Q 2, Q—K 2 ; 27. Q—Kt 8 ch wins ; if 26. ...Q—Q B 1 ; 27. Q—Q 6 with a winning position.

22. ......   Q—K 3

Threatening ...R—Kt 5.

23. P—K R 3 !

Guarding against the threat, and also freeing his forces from the defence of the first rank. 23. R×P, Q×P ; 24. K R—Q 2, R—Kt 5 ? 25. R—Q 8 ch, B—K 1 ; 26. Q×R, Q×Q ; 27. R×R would also win for White, but Black can improve on this variation with 24. ...R—K 3 (if then 25. R—Q 8 ch, R—K 1 ; 26. B—R 6 ?, Q—Q B 8 ch), so that the text is clearer and more exact.

23. ......   R—Q 1

Or 23. ...Q×B P ; 24. B—R 6, P—Kt 3 ; 25. R×R, Q×R ; 26. R×P and Black's weaknesses will prove fatal (the immediate threat is 27. R×B, Q×R ; 28. Q—K 5, P—B 3 ; 29. Q—K 7 and mate follows).

24. K R—Q 2   R—K 4

If 24. ...Q×B P ; 25. B—R 6, P—Kt 3 ; 26. R×P, R×R (or 26. ...R—Q B 1 ; 27. R×B etc.) ; 27. Q×R and wins. Or 24. ...R×P ; 25. R×P, R×R ; 26. R×R, Q— K 1 ; 27. B—R 6, P—Kt 3 ; 28. Q—Kt 5. The usefulness of 23. P—K R 3 ! is now obvious.

25. B—R 6 !

This move has been in the air for some time and is now played with decisive effect. If 25. ...Q×B ; 26. Q×R etc.

25. ......   Q—Kt 3

...P—Kt 3 is answered in the same way.

26. B—B 4 !

Q×Q would give Black a loophole, while 26. Q×R ? ? would allow mate.

26. ......   R—K 3
27. B×P   Q—R 4

...P—K R 4 was somewhat better without offering any real hope.

28. Q—Kt 4

Avoiding the clever trap 28. B— K 5 ? Q×R ch ; 29. R×Q, R× R ch ; 30. K—R 2, R—Kt 3 and Black wins !

28. ......   Q×Q
29. P×Q   R—K 5
30. B×P   R×R

Or 30. ...R—K 8 ch ; 31. R× R, R×R ; 32. P—Kt 4 !, R×R P ; 33. P—Kt 5, B—Q 2 ; 34. R—

Q 1, B—K 1 ; 35. R—Q 8, R— K 7 ; 36. B×P (Tarrasch) and White wins easily.

31. R×R   P—K R 4
32. R—Q 6   Resigns

The win is only a question of time, in view of White's considerable material and positional superiority.

114. MATCH, 1908

(Twelfth Game)

FOUR KNIGHTS' GAME

WITH one exception, Tarrasch's play is irreproachable throughout this fine ending. It is true that Lasker blunders badly early in the game, but only the greatest masters ever succeeded in fully exploiting Lasker's mistakes—and such triumphs were few and far between.

| *White* | *Black* |
| DR. S. TARRASCH | DR. E. LASKER |

1. P—K 4	P—K 4
2. Kt—K B 3	Kt—Q B 3
3. B—Kt 5	Kt—B 3
4. Kt—B 3	

Perhaps suspecting some improvement in Lasker's handling of the Berlin Defence.

| 4. ...... | B—Kt 5 |
| 5. O—O | P—Q 3 ? |

A careless move which seriously compromises Black's game.

6. Kt—Q 5	B—B 4
7. P—Q 4	P×P
8. Kt×P	B×Kt

Doubtless a reluctant decision, but against 8. ...B—Q 2 Tarrasch gives 9. Kt—B 5 !, B×Kt (if 9. ... Kt×Kt ; 10. Kt×P ch with advantage) ; 10. P×B, Kt×Kt (if 10. ...O—O ; 11. B—Kt 5 smashing up Black King's side formation) ; 11. Q×Kt and Black, in order to save a pawn, must lose the privilege of castling.

9. Q×B   O—O
10. Kt×Kt ch   Q×Kt

After ...P×Kt, Black would speedily succumb in the middle game. But the resulting endgame is also much in White's favour : he has two Bishops, the freer game and possibilities of pressure on the doubled and isolated K B P.

11. Q×Q   P×Q
12. B—K R 6   R—K 1
13. K R—K 1   P—R 3
14. B—K B 1

The best retreat for the time being. Tarrasch points out that he does not fear 14. ...Kt—Kt 5 because of 15. R—K 3 ! K—R 1 (not 15. ...Kt×B P ? ? ; 16. R—Kt 3 ch) ; 16. R—K Kt 3, R—K Kt 1 ; 17. B—Q 2, Kt×B P ; 18. R—Q B 1 etc.

14. ......   K—R 1

This will turn out to be loss of time, as the K B P needs guarding. However, the move is unavoidable as part of a complex regrouping plan.

15. B—Q 2 !   Kt—K 2

White intends B—B 3. Since ...K—Kt 2 would then be answered by R—K 3—Kt 3 ch, and

...R—K 3 by B—Q B 4, Black must needs protect the threatened Pawn with the Knight. This explains Lasker's 14th move.

16. B—B 3   Kt—Kt 1
17. P—B 4

It is instructive to see how Tarrasch steadily increases his advantage in space, creating a position which is too much even for Lasker's proverbial defensive skill.

18. ......   K—Kt 2

The King must depart from the terrible diagonal.

18. R—K 3   K—B 1
19. B—Q 3   B—Q 2
20. Q R—K 1   B—Kt 4

Since his pieces are relatively ineffectual, Lasker's eagerness to exchange is understandable.

21. P—K 5 !   B×B
22. R×B   B P×P

The opening up of the position is unfavourable for Black, but the alternative 22. ...Q R—Q 1 ; 23. P×Q P, R×R ch ; 24. B×R, P× P ; 25. B—Kt 4 is uninviting.

23. P×P   P×P
24. R×P   P—Kt 3

Despite its simplicity, the position remains terribly difficult for Black. If 24. ...R×R ; 25. B× R, followed by R—Q 7 with a won game.

25. R—K R 5 ?

Good enough, but not the best. Tarrasch later pointed out that 25.

R—K Kt 5 ! would have been decisive, the threat being 26. B—Kt 7
ch, K—K 2 ; 27. R—K 5 mate !
Here are the possibilities he indicates :

I. 25. ...R—K 2 ? ;   26. R
(K 3)—Kt 3 winning the Knight.

II. 25. ...R—K 3 ;   26. R—
Q 7, R—B 1 (if 26. ...R—K 2 ? ;
27. R×Kt ch) ; 27. R—Kt 7 and
wins.

III. 25. ...K—K 2 ; 26. R—
Kt 7, P—R 3 ; 27. R—K 3 ch, K—
B 1 ; 28. R—B 3, R—K 2 ; 29.
R(B 3)—Kt 3 again winning the
Knight.

IV. 25. ...P—K B 3 ; 26. R—
Q 7, Kt—K 2 (if 26. ...P×R ? ;
27. B—Kt 7 mate !) ;   27. B×P
etc.

| 25. ...... | P—R 3 |
| 26. B—Q 2 | R—K 3 |

...Q R—Q 1 would have offered
better chances, the strongest reply
being 27. R(R 5)—Q 5 (Tarrasch).

| 27. R—Q 7 | R—B 1 |

No better is 27. ...Kt—B 3 ;
28. R×R P, Kt×R ; 29. R—R 8
ch, K—K 2 ; 30. R×R, R—K 7 ;
31. B—B 3, P—R 4 ; 32. P—
K R 4 !, R×P ; 33. P—R 5, R—
K 7 ; 34. P—R 6 etc. (Tarrasch).
If then 34. ...Kt—B 1 ; 35. R×
Kt !

28. R—K B 5	R—K 2
29. R×R	K×R
30. R—K 5 ch	K—B 3
31. B—B 3	K—Kt 3
32. R—K 3	R—Q 1

...P—K B 3 would have been
better for purposes of passive defence, but after the reply 33. R—
Q 3 followed by 34. R—Q 7,

White's advantage would still have
been considerable.

33. R—Kt 3 ch	K—B 4
34. R—Kt 7	K—K 3
35. R—R 7 !	

This soon leads to the win of the
K R P. The following play has to
be calculated precisely.

| 35. ...... | P—Q B 4 |

If instead 35. ...R—Q 8 ch ;
36. K—B 2, R—B 8 ; 37. R—R 8,
R×P ch ; 38. K—Kt 3 !, Kt—
K 2 ; 39. R×P ch, K—Q 2 ; 40.
R—K B 6, K—K 1 ; 41. R—B 2 !
and the passed K R P decides in
White's favour (Tarrasch).

| 36. K—B 2 | P—Kt 4 |
| 37. K—K 2 | P—Kt 5 |

Now that White is fully protected against invasion by the hostile Rook, he can go after the K R P
in earnest.

| 38. B—Q 2 | R—Q 5 |

A curious variation would be 38.
...K—B 3 ; 39. B×P ! K—Kt 3 ;
40. R—R 8 and White is safe !

| 39. P—K Kt 3 ! | R—Kt 5 |

Resigning himself to the inevitable, for if 39. ...K—B 3 ; 40.
B×P, K—Kt 3 ; 41. R—Kt 7 ch
etc.

40. B×R P	Kt—B 3
41. R—R 8	R—Q B 5
42. K—Q 1	Kt—Kt 5

At last the Knight has become
active ; White is thrown on the
defensive for some time.

43. B—B 4	K—B 4
44. P—Kt 3	R—B 6
45. B—Q 2	R—B 6

Now the position looks threatening, but Tarrasch has a powerful resource.

| 46. R—R 5 ch | K—K 5 |

If 46. ...K—K 3; 47. R×P, Kt×P; 48. B×P, R×K Kt P; 49. R—B 6 ch, K—Q 4; 50. R×P, P—B 4; 51. R—K B 6, K—K 5; 52. P—R 4, winning easily.

| 47. R—R 4 ! | |

Much more conclusive than 47. R×P, Kt×P; 48. B×P, R×K Kt P; 49. R—B 6, P—B 4 and White must play with great care.

| 47. ...... | K—B 4 |

Tarrasch analyses the alternative 47. ...R—B 8 ch as follows : 48. K—K 2, R—B 7 ch; 49. K—K 1, K—B 6; 50. R×Kt, R—K 7 ch; 51. K—Q 1, R×B ch; 52. K×R, K×R; 53. K—K 3 ! (not 53. P—K R 4 ?, P—B 4; 54. K—K 3, K×P !; 55. P—R 5, P—B 5 ch etc.), K—R 6; 54. K—B 4, K×P; 55. P—Kt 4, K—R 6; 56. K—B 5, K—R 5; 57. P—Kt 5, P—R 4; 59. K—B 6, K—R 4; 59.

K×P, K×P; 60. K—K 6, K—B 5; 61. K—Q 5, K—K 6; 62. K×P, K—Q 7; 63. K—Kt 5, K×P; 64. K×P, K—B 6; 65. K—R 4 and wins.

48. P—K R 3	Kt—B 3
49. R—B 4 ch	R×R
50. B×R	K—K 5

The ending is easily won because of White's extra Pawn, his passed K R P and the weakness of Black's Queen's side. But Lasker fights on grimly.

| 51. K—K 2 | P—B 5 |

Hoping for 52. P×P ? K—Q 5. Tarrasch has a much stronger reply.

| 52. B—Kt 5 ! | Kt—Q 4 |

Other Knight moves are answered by B—K 7, winning another Pawn.

| 53. P×P | Kt—B 6 ch |
| 54. K—Q 2 ! | |

Tarrasch points out that after 54. K—B 2, K—Q 5; 55. B—B 6 ch, K×P; 56. B×Kt, K×B; 57. P—K R 4, K×P; 58. P—R 5, K—Kt 7; 59. P—R 6, K×P; 60. P—R 7, P—Kt 6; 61. P—R 8(Q), P—Kt 7 the ending would be drawn.

| 54. ...... | K—B 4 |

If 54. ...Kt×P; 55. B—B 6 and Black is helpless.

55. B—B 4	Kt×P
56. P—B 5	K—K 3
57. P—B 6	Kt—B 6
58. K—Q 3	Kt—Q 4

Or 58. ...P—R 4; 59. K—B 4

winning easily. The rest is hopeless.

59.	K—B 4	Kt—K 2
60.	K—B 5	P—R 4
61.	P—B 7	K—Q 2
62.	K—Kt 5	Kt—B 4
63.	K×P	Kt—Q 5
64.	K×P	Kt×P ch
65.	K—B 4	Resigns

A bitter struggle.

115. MATCH, 1911

(Fourth Game)

RUY LOPEZ

A HIGHLY interesting game, ably
conducted for the most part by Tarrasch. The fine finish is both
logical and brilliant.

| *White* | *Black* |
| DR. S. TARRASCH | C. SCHLECHTER |

1.	P—K 4	P—K 4
2.	Kt—K B 3	Kt—Q B 3
3.	B—Kt 5	P—Q R 3
4.	B—R 4	Kt—B 3
5.	O—O	P—Q 3

A move somewhat off the beaten
track which was greatly favoured by
Janowski and Rubinstein.

| 6. | R—K 1 | P—Q Kt 4 |
| 7. | B—Kt 3 | B—K 2 |

But this routine move is not the
best.   Correct is 7. ...Kt—Q R 4;
8. P—Q 4, Kt×B (not 8. ...P×
P ? ; 9. P—K 5 !, P×P ; 10. Kt×
P, B—K 3 ; 11. Kt×P and wins) ;
9. R P×Kt, Kt—Q 2 with a good
game for Black. If 10. P×P,
Kt×P (not 10. ...P×P ; 11. Q—
Q 5) etc.

8. P—Q R 4 !

Much stronger than the obvious
8. P—B 3.

8. ...... R—Q Kt 1

This surrender of the Q R file
brings disagreeable consequences in
its train, but the alternative 8. ...
P—Kt 5 ; 9. P—R 5 ! would also
have its unpleasant features.

9.	P×P	P×P
10.	P—B 3	O—O
11.	P—Q 4	P×P

A master of Schlechter's stature
would be reluctant to yield the
centre in this manner, but something must be done about White's
threat to win a piece with P—Q 5.

12. P×P B—Kt 5

The alternative was 12. ...P—
Q 4 ; 13. P—K 5, Kt—K 5 ; 14.
Kt—B 3, Kt×Kt ; 15. P×Kt, B—
K Kt 5 etc.

13. Kt—B 3 Kt—Kt 5

...B×Kt ; 14. P×B would only
strengthen White's centre and give
him attacking chances.   The text is
played with a view to ...P—B 4,
which would enable Black to assert
himself in the centre. Tarrasch's
reply momentarily prevents ...
P—B 4.

| 14. | B—K B 4 | Kt—Q 2 |
| 15. | P—R 3 ! | B×Kt |

Compulsory, since ...B—K 3 ?
loses a piece and 15. ...B—R 4 ;
16. P—Kt 4, B—Kt 3 would leave
the Q B permanently out of play.

16. Q×B P—B 4

If now 16. P×P, Kt×P ; 17. B—Q 1, Kt(Kt 5)—Q 6 ; 18. R—K 2, B—B 3 (threatening ...Kt×Kt P) and Black has seized the initiative. Tarrasch therefore temporarily sacrifices a Pawn in order to maintain his grip on the position.

17. Kt—Q 5 !   Kt×Kt
18. B×Kt   P×P
19. R—R 7 !

Tarrasch utilises the Q R file to exert uncomfortable pressure on Black, who cannot free his Queen and Bishop.

19. ......   Kt—K 4
20. Q—Q Kt 3   B—B 3

Gladly returning the Pawn in order to diminish the pressure, which would become unbearable after some such continuation as 20. ...Q—K 1 ; 21. R—Q B 1 followed by K R—B 7.

21. B×Kt   B×B ?

The more solid 21. ...P×B offered decidedly better prospects of resistance. The text gives Tarrasch the idea of advancing his King-side Pawns to exploit the insecurity of Black's Bishop—a plan which he executes with commendable virtuosity.

22. P—Kt 3 !   Q—Kt 3
23. R×P   K—R 1
24. K—Kt 2

The King is to guard the Pawns as they advance.

24. ......   R×R
25. B×R   Q—B 4

Taking the open file.

26. P—B 4   B—B 3
27. R—K 2 !

Beginning a complicated manœuvre to drive Black's Queen from the Q B file. If now 27. ...R—Q B 1 ; 28. Q—Q 3 followed by B—Kt 3 threatening R—Q B 2.

27. ......   Q—B 8

Intending to answer 28. R—Q B 2 with ...Q—K 6 ; at the same time he prepares for ...R—R 1—R 8.

28. Q—Q 3 !

A fine move which combines attack and defence.

28. ......   Q—B 2

Retreating ingloriously because of the threatened P—K 5 (one sees now how disadvantageous Black's 21st move was). 28. ...R—R 1 ? would be refuted by 29. P—K 5, R—R 8 ? ; 30. R—Q B 2 !, Q—R 8 ch ; 31. K—B 2, Q—Kt 8 ch ; 32. K—B 3, R—B 8 ch ; 33. K—Kt 4 and wins. A finely calculated resource !

29. B—Kt 3   P—Kt 3

This weakening move can always be forced by B—B 2.

30. R—Q B 2   Q—Q 2
31. P—Kt 4 !

Tarrasch has achieved his goals : he commands the open Q B file and his King's side attack is proceeding beautifully.

31. ......   R—K B 1
32. P—Kt 5   B—Kt 2
33. K—Kt 3 ?

But this is a sad oversight. 33. R—B 2 should have been played, as Black can now draw with 38. ... R×P ! ! ; 34. K×R, B—K 4 ch ; 35. K—B 3, Q×P ch ; 36. K—K 2, Q—Kt 7 ch ; 37. K—Q 1, Q—Kt 8 ch and the perpetual check cannot be avoided.

33. ......   Q—R 2 ?

Schlechter misses his grand opportunity and soon succumbs.

34. R—B 1   P—R 3

This hastens the end, which could not be staved off for very long in any event.

35. P—R 4   P—R 4

Otherwise 36. P—K 5, K—R 2 ; 37. P—R 5 wins.

36. P—B 5   P×P

Desperately hoping for counter-attack via the K file. After 36. ... B—K 4 ch ; 37. K—R 3, Q—Q 2 ; 38. B—K 6 White wins without any difficulty.

37. P×P   R—K 1

38. P—B 6 ! !   B×P

If 38. ...R—K 6 ch ; 39. Q× R, P×Q ; 40. R—B 8 ch, B—B 1 ; 41. R×B ch, K—R 2 ; 42. B—B 2 mate ! If 38. ...B—B 1 ; 39. Q—Kt 6 wins.

39. P×B   Q—Q 2

Or 39. ...R—K 6 ch ; 40. Q× R, P×Q ; 41. R—B 8 ch, K—R 2 ; 42. B—B 2 ch, K—R 3 ; 43. R—R 8 ch and mate next move.

40. Q—Kt 6   Resigns

Despite the inexactitude on move 33, this was a game of which Tarrasch was justifiably proud.

116. MATCH, 1916

(First Game)

FRENCH DEFENCE

A HIGHLY interesting game, in which we see the clash of two contrasting personalities and two opposing ideas. Although the game should have ended in a draw, Tarrasch's superior handling of the middle game complications proves decisive.

White   *Black*
DR. S. TARRASCH   J. MIESES

1. P—Q 4   P—K 3

Mieses had won an excellent game from Tarrasch some months earlier, using a favourite form of the French. He therefore continued to use it throughout the match, but with little success.

2. P—K 4

Although Tarrasch could have

played 2. P—Q B 4 or Kt—K B 3, he gladly accepts the challenge to transpose into the French.

2. ......   P—Q 4
3. Kt—Q B 3   P×P

According to Tarrasch, this is a serious blunder which surrenders the centre. According to Mieses, it is a good move which creates room for Black's pieces. The struggle between these two points of view makes for interesting chess.

4. Kt×P   Kt—Q 2
5. Kt—K B 3   K Kt—B 3
6. B—Q 3   Kt×Kt
7. B×Kt   Kt—B 3
8. B—Kt 5   B—K 2
9. B×Kt

Tarrasch is reluctant to lose a tempo, but the retreat B—Q 3 was doubtless stronger. Analogous positions invariably proved to be in White's favour in later games of the match.

9. ......   P×B

At the cost of some weakness in his Pawn structure and insecurity of his King, Black takes the riskier but more promising course. The text has the virtue of keeping White's Knight out of K 5 and thereby greatly cutting down its mobility.

10. Q—K 2   P—B 3

A cramping move, but White was threatening B×Kt P !

11. O—O—O ? !

White likewise selects the more enterprising but dangerous course.

Tarrasch strongly condemns this move and recommends O—O, making possible a storming attack with Pawns if Black castles on the Queen's side ; while if he castles on the King's side, the position of his King will not be quite safe.

11. ......   Q—B 2
12. K R—K 1   B—Q 2
13. K—Kt 1   O—O—O

White's last two moves have been more or less in the nature of waiting moves. But now that he knows the definite location of Black's King, attacking measures are in order.

14. P—B 4   B—Kt 5 !

A subtle gain of time. Foreseeing that White will play P—B 5 followed eventually by R—K 3—Kt 3, Mieses first drives away the K R from the K file.

15. R—R 1   B—Q 3

Superfluous provocation.

16. P—B 5

Courageous play. White follows up his attacking plan, despite the resulting weakness of his Q P, the renunciation of his control of Q 5, and the avenues of counterattack opened up to Black. Such a move requires more courage from a modern master than the most daring sacrificial combinations !

16. ......   B—B 1
17. Q—B 4   B—Kt 2
18. Q—R 4   K—Kt 1
19. B—B 2

Not 19. R—Q 3 ?, P—B 4 winning a piece.

19. ......   B—Q B 1

The Bishop retreats in order to play an important defensive rôle and at the same time White's Q P is kept under observation.

20. R—Q 3   R—Q 2
21. R—R 3   P—Q R 3

Creating a target for White's attack, but it is not easy to exploit this weakness, for example, 22. R—K 1, P—K 4 ; 23. K R—K 3, P× P ; 24. R(K 3)—Kt 3, K—R 1 ; 25. B—Q 3, B—B 1 ; 26. R—Kt 6, B×P ; 27. B×R P, P×B ; 28. R×P ch, B×R ; 29. Q×B ch, B—R 2 and White is lost (Tarrasch).

22. R—Kt 3   K—R 2
23. R—Kt 6   K R—Q 1
24. Q—R 5

Making room for the advance of the Q R P, and also preparing to answer the eventual ...P—B 4 and the ensuing capture of the Q P with R×R P ch winning the Queen, for example 24. ...P—B 4 ; 25. P—Q Kt 4, B×P ? ; 26. Kt×B, R× Kt ; 27. R×R P ch etc.

24. ......   R—K 2
25. P—Q Kt 4 ! ?

Now it is a question of do or die. White has committed himself irrevocably to the outcome of his attack.

25. ......   P—B 4

Now White's attack must pause while he protects the Q P.

26. R—Q 1   P—K 4

The tension mounts steadily !

27. P—Q R 4   P—K 5

After 27. ...P×P ; 28. B—Q 3, B—R 3 (to prevent R—Q B 1) ; 29. K—R 2, intending R—Q Kt 1—2 —B 2 White's attack would continue with unabated force. After the text, on the other hand, Tarrasch sees himself compelled to sacrifice the Knight, for any move with this piece would lead to the collapse of his game.

28. P—Kt 5

28. ......   P×Kt ?

This loses. According to Tarrasch, there was a draw with 28. ...K—Kt 1 ! ; 29. P×B P, P× Kt ; 30. P×Kt P, B×KtP ; 31. P—B 6, R—Q 4 ! ; 32. Q—Kt 4, R×P ; 33. R×R, B×R ; 34. R× B ch, Q×R ; 35. P×Q, R×P ; 36. Q×R ch, K×Q ; 37. P×P etc.

29. R×R P ch !   P×R
30. P—Kt 6 ch   K—R 1

A move that smacks of time pressure. 30. ...K—Kt 1, so as to answer P×Q ch with ...R×P, was somewhat better.

31. P×Q   R(Q 1)—Q 2
32. B×P   R×B P
33. B×B   R×B
34. Q×P ch

The unfortunate position of Black's King renders his position hopeless.

34.	......	K—Kt 1
35.	P×P	R—Q 2
36.	K—B 2	Resigns

For if 36. ...B×P ; 37. R—Kt 1 ch, K—B 2 ; 38. Q—Kt 6 mate ; if 36. ...R×P ; 35. Q—Kt 6 ch, K—R 1 ; 36. Q—R 5 ch followed by R—Kt 1 ch and mate ; if 36. ...R—Kt 2 ; 37. R—Q Kt 1, R×R ; 38. K×R, B×P ? ; 39. Q—Kt 6 ch, K—R 1 ; 40. Q—R 5 ch followed by 41. Q—Kt 4 ch etc. An interesting and tremendously difficult game.

117. MATCH, 1916

(Third Game)

(Brilliancy Prize)

FRENCH DEFENCE

A DELIGHTFUL brevity. Tarrasch refutes his opponent's inferior opening very quickly, and winds up the game with a neat finesse.

| *White* | *Black* |
| DR. S. TARRASCH | J. MIESES |

| 1. P—Q 4 | P—K 3 |

Undiscouraged by the first game, Mieses again angles for the French Defence.

2. P—K 4	P—Q 4
3. Kt—Q B 3	P×P
4. Kt×P	Kt—Q 2
5. Kt—K B 3	K Kt—B 3
6. B—Q 3	B—K 2
7. O—O	Kt×Kt
8. B×Kt	Kt—B 3
9. B—Q 3	

As is customary in this variation, Black's position is somewhat cramped. ...P—B 4 is the best attempt for equality.

| 9. ...... | P—Q Kt 3 ? |

Most untimely, as Tarrasch immediately demonstrates.

| 10. Kt—K 5 ! | O—O |

After 10. ...B—Kt 2 ; 11. B—Kt 5 ch, K—B 1 ; 12. B—B 6 White has gained command of Q B 6, as in the text, but with the additional advantage that he has prevented Black from castling.

| 11. Kt—B 6 | Q—Q 3 |
| 12. Q—B 3 ! | |

A subtle move. Most players would have continued 12. Kt×B ch, Q×Kt ; 13. Q—B 3, but after 13. ...R—Kt 1 followed by ...B—Kt 2 Black would have a fair game. But after the text, as Tarrasch points out, the threat of Kt×B ch compels Black to play . .B—Q 2, thus forfeiting his Q B's best diagonal.

| 12. ...... | B—Q 2 |

If 12. ...Kt—Q 4 ; 13. Kt×B ch, Q×Kt ; 14. P—B 4 etc.

| 13. Kt×B ch | Q×Kt |
| 14. B—K Kt 5 | |

By means of quite simple moves White has obtained two Bishops, the better development, a good attacking game and a lasting initiative.

| 14. ...... | Q R—B 1 |

Intending ...P—B 4 and at the same time taking the sting out of Q—K 4 !

| 15. K R—K 1 | K R—K 1 ? |

Mieses evidently does not realise the gravity of the situation : White's pieces are all posted for a decisive attack and only the utmost care can hold the position temporarily. ...P—K R 3 was best, but as Tarrasch shows, the natural move 15. ...P—B 4 was no longer feasible because of 16. Q—R 3, P—K R 3 ; 17. B×P, P×B (or 17. ...P—B 5 ; 18. B×Kt P, K×B ; 19. Q—Kt 3 ch, K—R 1 ; 20. Q—R 4 ch, K—Kt 2 ; 21. Q—Kt 5 ch, K—R 1 ; 22. Q—R 6 ch, K—Kt 1 ; 23. R—K 5 and wins) ; 18. Q×R P, P×P ; 17. P—Q Kt 4 ! (preventing ...R—B 4) followed by R—K 5 with a winning attack.

16. Q—R 3 !

As already intimated, Black has no satisfactory defence. On 16. ...P—K R 3 White sacrifices with B×P and obtains a devastating attack. On 16. ...P—Kt 3 there follows 17. Q—R 4, K—Kt 2 ; 18. R—K 4 followed by R—B 4 and wins. On 16. ...P—K 4 ; 17. B×Kt ! wins a piece. Black therefore decides to part with the K R P, but Tarrasch is after higher game.

16.	......	Q—Q 3
17.	B×Kt	P×B
18.	Q—R 6 !!	

Nailing down the hapless Black King. Mate in four is threatened, beginning with B×P ch etc.

| 18. | ...... | P—K B 4 |
| 19. | R—K 3 | Q×P |

Desperately striving to prevent the mate at his K Kt 2. If instead 19. ...P—K B 3 ; 20. R—Kt 3 ch is murderous.

| 20. | P—Q B 3 ! | Resigns |

For no matter how he plays, he must lose the Queen or be mated. A fine example of straightforward exploitation of a superior position.

118. MATCH, 1916

(Fourth Game)

SCOTCH GAME

Tarrasch considers this the finest game of the match. It is an impressive example of what the two Bishops can accomplish in a fairly open position.

| | *White* | *Black* |
	J. Mieses	Dr. S. Tarrasch
1.	P—K 4	P—K 4
2.	P—Q 4	P×P
3.	Kt—K B 3	Kt—Q B 3
4.	Kt×P	Kt—B 3
5.	Kt×Kt	Kt P×Kt
6.	P—K 5	

An unusual move, adopted in the realisation that the more customary 6. Kt—B 3, B—Kt 5 leaves Black with an easy game. The text, on the other hand, has the possible drawback of resulting in a weakening of the K P because of its precipitate advance.

| 6. | ...... | Q—K 2 |
| 7. | Q—K 2 | Kt—Q 4 |

The Queen moves on both sides are quite unusual and forecast rather a slow development for both players, the development of Black's K B being hampered for some time and the same being true for some while of White's Queen's side.

6. Kt—Q 2

The earlier move here was 8. P—Q B 4, allowing Black a good reply with ...B—R 3. The text has the merit of avoiding this pin and also making the Knight available for future protection of the advanced K P.

8. ......   Kt—B 5

Not bad, but the line of play adopted by Tarrasch in Game 120 is still better. However, the Knight tour is attractive, as it leads to an attack on the K P without loss of time.

9. Q—K 3

If 9. Q—K 4, Kt—Kt 3 ; 10. P—K B 4 (not 10. Kt—B 4 ?, P—Q 4, winning a piece, while if 10. Kt—B 3, P—B 3 ; 11. B—K B 4, Q—Kt 5 ch !, winning a Pawn), P—Q 4 with an excellent position.

9. ......   Kt—Kt 3
10. P—K B 4   P—B 3
11. B—Q 3

Apparently very powerful, for after the following exchange, Black's Pawn formation is in a pitiable state. Black's two Bishops and open lines are more than ample compensation, however ; therefore White would have done better to play 11. Kt—B 3, P×P ; 12. P×P, P—Q 3 ; 13. P×P with only a slightly inferior ending.

11. ......   P×P
12. B×Kt ch   P×B
13. P×P   B—R 3 !

Far from being despondent over the wretched state of his Pawn position, Tarrasch sets about making good use of the two Bishops. The text is an excellent beginning, as White is prevented from castling.

14. P—Q Kt 3

It is becoming apparent that the development of White's Queen's side will be a very slow process. If 14. Kt—B 3, Q—Kt 5 ch ; 15. P—B 3, Q—Kt 4 ! ; 16. Kt—Q 4, Q—Q 4 (Tarrasch) and Black has a very promising game.

14. ......   Q—B 4 !
15. Q×Q

Since this brings out Black's other Bishop with gain of time, Mieses must have exchanged with the greatest reluctance. However, 15. Q—K 4 would not do because of 15. ...Q—B 6 ! (...O—O—O is good enough, but the text is sharper) ; 16. R—Q Kt 1 (not 16. Q×P ch ? ?, K—Q 1 ; 17. Q R—Kt 1, Q—K 6 ch and mate follows), R×P !

15. ......   B×Q
16. Kt—B 3   O—O

Tarrasch sees that the K B file will be far more useful to him than the K R file. In addition, the removal of his King makes it possible for him to utilise the K file at just the right moment.

17. B—Kt 2   P—Q 3 !

The combination of the two-Bishop pressure and the K P's

difficult position makes White's game unbearable. Thus if 18. P× P, Q R—K 1 ch and White's King is battered in the centre ; if 18. P— B 4, B—Kt 5 ch ; 19. K—Q 1, P— Q 4 ! ; 20. P×P, Q R—Q 1 ! and again White's King is under the crossfire of the enemy's pieces ; or 18. O—O—O, B—K 7 winning a Pawn (Tarrasch). This last possibility would, however, have assured White a longer resistance than the line of play actually adopted.

18. Kt—Q 4   P×P

Calmly ignoring White's desperate attempt at counterattack.

19. Kt—K 6

Not 19. Kt×P ?, B—Kt 2 and Black wins the exchange.

19. ......   B—B 7 ch
20. K—Q 2   R—B 2
21. P—B 4

The attempt to maintain material equality with 21. B×P ? would lead to a débâcle after 21. ...R— K 2 ; 22. Kt×B P, R—Q 1 ch ; 23. K—B 1, B—Kt 2 ; 24. B— B 4, B—K 6 ch ; 25. B×B, R×B and the Knight is lost (Tarrasch).

21. ......   R—K 1

22. Kt—Kt 5   R—Q 2 ch
23. K—K 2   B—Q 5

Despite the fact that Mieses has managed to close the Q B's diagonal, his situation is still a dismal one.

24. Q R—Q 1   P—B 4 !

A move with two functions. It reinforces the K B's position and opens an effective diagonal for the other Bishop.

25. Kt—K 4

With the shallow threat of Kt×P. Tarrasch disposes of the alternative 25. B×B with 25. ...B P×B ; 26. Kt—K 4, R(Q 2)—Q 1 ; 27. Kt—B 5, B—B 1 ; 28. P—K R 3, P—K 5 etc.

25. ......   R—B 2
26. B—R 3

Losing quickly, but if instead 26. B×B, K P×B ; 27. K—Q 3, R— B 4 winning easily, for if 28. R— K 1, R(B 4)—K 4 followed by ... B—Kt 2, or if 28. P—Q Kt 4, P× P ; 29. K×P, R—B 5 ; 30. Q R— K 1, B—Kt 2 (Tarrasch). In either case Black wins a piece.

26. ......   B—Kt 2 !
27. K—Q 3

Amusing would be 27. Kt×P, R—B 7 ch ; 28. K—Q 3, R×R P ; 29. B—Kt 4 (if 29. Kt×B, R×B and wins, and if 29. K R—K 1, B—B 1 ; 30. B—Kt 4, P—Q R 4, winning a piece), P—Q R 4 and Black loses a piece.

27. ......   R—Q 2 !
28. Kt—B 3

Black was threatening to win the Bishop with ...B—Kt 7 ch. The enormous power of Black's position is illustrated by the following piquant variation given by Tarrasch : 28. B—B 1, R(K 1)—Q 1 ! ; 29. Q R—B 1 (...B—Kt 8 ch was threatened), B—R 8 ch ! ; 30. K—K 3, R—Q 6 ch, winning the Knight.

| 28. ...... | B×P |
| 29. K R—K 1 | B—B 6 |

29. ...B—B 7 ch would be answered by 30. K—K 2, but after the text, 30. R—Q 2 would be followed by 30. ...B—B 7 ch ; 31. K—B 2, R×R ch ; 32. K×R, B×R ch.

30. Kt—K 2

Since he must lose at least the exchange, he tries a last trap : if 30. ...B—B 7 ch ; 31. K—B 2, R×R ; 32. R×R, B×Kt ; 33. R—Q 2, regaining the piece.

| 30. ...... | B—Kt 7 ch |
| 31. K—K 3 | R×R |

White resigns, for if 32. R×R, B×Kt ; 33. K×B, B×B with a piece ahead. A fine demonstration of the Bishops' powers.

119. MATCH, 1916

(Fifth Game)

FRENCH DEFENCE

THIS time Tarrasch's attack is momentarily—but only momentarily—interrupted by the exchange of Queens. The game casts a strong light on the difficulties encountered by Black in this variation.

White	*Black*
DR. S. TARRASCH	J. MIESES
1. P—K 4	P—K3
2. P—Q 4	P—Q 4
3. Kt—Q B 3	P×P
4. Kt×P	Kt—Q 2
5. Kt—K B 3	K Kt—B 3
6. B—Q 3	Kt×Kt
7. B×Kt	Kt—B 3
8. B—Kt 5	

B—Q 3 would be more exact, since Black could now force an exchange with ...P—K R 3.

| 8. ...... | B—K 2 |
| 9. B—Q 3 | |

Switching from 9. B×Kt, as played in the first game. The text has more lasting effect.

| 9. ...... | P—B 4 |

This is best answered by P×P.

10. O—O	P×P
11. Kt×P	O—O
12. R—K 1	

Kt—B 3 was better—see the next note.

| 12. ...... | Kt—Q 4 ? |

In a later game against Grünfeld (Kaschau, 1918) Mieses played the superior line 12. ...Q×Kt ! ; 13. B×P ch, Kt×B ; 14. Q×Q, B×B ; 15. Q R—Q 1, B—B 3 ; 16. Q—Q Kt 4, P—K 4 ; 17. P—Q B 3, Kt—Kt 4 and it is up to White to maintain equality.

| 13. Q—R 5 ! | P—K Kt 3 |

Some kind of weakening move was unavoidable : if 13. ...P—K R 3 ? ; 14. B×P ; if 13. ...P—B 4 ? ; 14. B×B, Q×B ; 15. Kt×B P, R×Kt ; 16. B×R, P—K Kt 3 ; 17. B×P, P×B (if 17. ...Kt—B 3 ; 18. B×P ch wins) ; 18. Q×Kt and wins.

14. B×B   Kt×B

14. ...P×Q would lead to a lost ending, and 14. ...Q×B ? ? would be a serious blunder because of 15. Q×Kt.

15. Q—R 4   Kt—B 4

This move soon turns out to be quite inadequate, but Tarrasch dismisses 15. ...Kt—B 3 with 16. Q×Q, Kt×Q ; 17. Q R—Q 1, B—Q 2 ; 18. B—K 4, R—B 1 ; 19. P—Q B 3, Kt—B 3 ; 20. Kt× Kt, B×Kt ; 21. B×B, R×B ; 22. R—Q 7 with clear advantage. 15. ...B—Q 2 was best, but Black's disadvantage, the result of his inferior development and weakness on the black squares, would have remained.

16. Kt×Kt   Kt P×Kt

After 16. ...K P×Kt White would have the comfortable choice between 17. Q×Q, R×Q ; 18. R—K 7 and 17. R—K 7, R—K 1 (not 17. ...B—K 3 ; 18. Q R—K 1 threatening Q R×B !) ; 18. Q R—K 1, R×R ; 19. Q×R, Q× Q ; 20. R×Q, in either event with a won ending.

17. Q—R 6 !   K—R 1

Black is in a bad way because of the threatened R—K 3—Kt 3 ch.

If he tries 17. ...P—B 3 ; 18. R—K 3, R—B 2 ; 19. Q R—K 1 (threatening B×P), Q—Q 4 (or 19. ...B—Q 2 ; 20. B—B 4, winning the K P) ; 20. P—Q B 4, Q—B 4 ; 21. P—Q Kt 4, Q×Kt P ; 22. B× P, P×B (if 22. ...B—Q 2 ; 23. B×P ch, R×B ; 24. R—Kt 3 ch, K—R 1 ; 25. Q—B 6 ch and mate next move) ; 23. R—Kt 3 ch, K—R 1 ; 24. R—K 8 ch and mate follows.

18. Q R—Q 1 !

Decisive, as ...B—Q 2 would be refuted by B—Kt 5. Black can ward off the attack only at the cost of ruinous loss of material.

18. ......   Q—K 2

If 18. ...Q—K 1 ? ; 19. Q—B 6 ch, K—Kt 1 ; 20. R—K 3, P—B 5 ; 21. B×P ch etc.

19. B×P   P—B 3
20. B×R P   Q—Kt 2
21. Q×Q ch   K×Q
22. B—Q 3   P—K 4
23. P—Q Kt 3 !

Much stronger, of course, than 23. B—K 4, B—K 3 ; 24. B×P, Q R—Kt 1 etc.

23. ......   R—K 1
24. B—Kt 5   R—K 2

Leads to a mating attack ; but 24. ...R—B 1 ; 25. B—Q 7 would be quite hopeless.

25. R—Q 8   P—R 3
26. B—B 4   R—Q B 2
27. R—K 3   P—Kt 4
28. R—Kt 3 ch   K—R 3
29. B—Q 5 !

Even quicker than 29. B—Q 3, P—B 4 ; 30. B×P, B×B ; 31. R×R.

29. ......   Q R—R 2

After 29. ...R—Kt 1 Tarrasch intended to wind up as follows : 30. R—R 8 ch, R—R 2 ; 31. R(R 8)—Kt 8, R—Q B 2 ; 32. R(Kt 8)—Kt 6 ch etc.

31. R—R 8 ch	R—R 2
32. R×B	Resigns

The course of this game convincingly demonstrates that the defence adopted by Mieses requires the very best play on Black's part if catastrophe is to be avoided.

120. MATCH, 1916

(Tenth Game)

SCOTCH GAME

An exciting and difficult game. The powerful thrusts of both players produce a steady stream of violent shocks and counteractions, with the outcome of the game in doubt right to the very end. A delightful game to study and to analyse.

White	*Black*
J. Mieses	Dr. S. Tarrasch
1. P—K 4	P—K 4
2. P—Q 4	P×P
3. Kt—K B 3	Kt—Q B 3
4. Kt×P	Kt—B 3
5. Kt×Kt	Kt P×Kt
6. P—K 5	Q—K 2
7. Q—K 2	Kt—Q 4
8. Kt—Q 2	B—Kt 2

Varying from Game 118. Black's idea is to castle as soon as possible and begin the attack on the K P.

9. Kt—Kt 3   O—O—O ! ?

The move is by no means without risk, but Tarrasch considers the difficulties well worth while, considering the powerful offensive he will soon start in the centre.

10. P—Q B 4

True to his style, Mieses plays for attack—not that he has much choice ; If 10. B—Q 2, R—K 1 ; 11. P—K B 4, P—B 3 and Black has achieved his objective in the centre ; or 10. Kt—R 5 ?, Q—Kt 5 ch and Black wins a couple of Pawns.

10. ......   Kt—Kt 3

...B—R 3 looks attractive, but it allows White to obtain a strong attack with 11. Q—K 4, Kt—Kt 3 (if 11. ...Kt—B 3 ; 12. Q—K 3, Kt—Kt 5 ; 13. Q×P, Q×P ch ; 14. K—Q 1, B—Kt 2 ; 15. Kt—R 5 and wins) ; 12. P—Q B 5, B× B ; 13. P×Kt, B—R 3 ; 14. P× R P (Tarrasch).

11. B—Q 2	R—K 1
12. P—B 4	P—B 3 .

White's position is apparently desperate, for if 13. B—B 3, Kt—R 5 !, or if 13. P×P, Q—B 2 ; 14. B—K 3, B—R 3 with considerable advantage to Black. But Mieses finds a clever resource.

13. P—Q R 4 !

The chief threat is 14. P—R 5, Kt—R 1 ; 15. P—R 6, winning a piece !

13. ......   B—R 3

Parrying the threat and beginning an attack of his own.

14. Q—K 4

Also possible was 14. P—R 5 ! ?, after which the plausible 14. ...B×P ? would be wrong, for after 15. Q—K 3, B×B (not 15. ...B×Kt ? ; 16. Q×B and the Knight cannot move because of mate with B—R 6 ch etc. Or if 15. ...Kt—Q 4 ? ; 16. Q×P and wins) ; 16. R×B, Kt—Q 4 ; 17. Q×P (Tarrasch) and White has a splendid position.

However, Tarrasch intended to answer 14. P—R 5 ? ! with 14. ... Kt×P ! This mode of capture is quite feasible despite the apparent danger involved, for example 15. R—B 1, P—Q 4 (White dare not capture *en passant*, as this would lose the Queen after ...Q—B 2 or ...Q—Q 2) ; or 15. Q—B 2, K—Kt 1 followed by ...P—Q 4 and the Knight is quite safe !

After the text, however, White threatens P—R 5 or P—Q B 5 so strongly that it is difficult to see a good continuation for Black.

14. ......   Q—B 2 !

A many-sided move which defends satisfactorily against White's threats and also renews Black's.

15. P—Q B 5

There is no longer time for simple defence, for if 15. R—B 1, P×P ; 16. P×P (better P—K B 5), B—Q 3 ; 17. B—B 4, K R—B 1 ; 18. B—Kt 3, B×P ; 19. B×B, Q—B 4 and White's position is in ruins (Tarrasch).

15. ......   B×B
16. P×Kt   Q×Kt

Plausible, but not the best. The right way, Tarrasch points out, was 16. ...R P×P and if 17. P—R 5 (the only hope of attack), P—Q Kt 4 ! (not 17. ...B P×P ? ; 18. R P×P, K P×P ? ; 19. R—R 8 ch) ; 18. P—R 6 (if 18. Kt—Q 4 ?, B—B 5 followed by ...B—Q 4), Q×Kt (18. ...B—B 5 ? ; 19. Kt—R 5 !, B—Q 4 ; 20. P—R 7 ! wins for White) ; 19. Q—Q 4, B× P ; 20. Q—R 7, P—Q B 4 and the attack is beaten off.

17. P×R P

Now begins a new, and for Black, very dangerous phase. His King is exposed and his development is still in arrears, with the result that the natural move ...P×P is deferred for a long time to come.

17. ......   K—Kt 2
18. R×B   P—Q 4 !

Much stronger, says Tarrasch, than 18. ...Q—Q 4 ; 19. Q×Q, P×Q ; 20. O—O—O !, P×P ; 21. P×P, R×P ; 22. R—B 7, R—K 2 ; 23. Q R—B 1, R×R ; 24. R×R and White's aggressive position will soon lead to the advantageous recovery of the Pawn (Tarrasch).

19. R—B 3 !   Q—Kt 3
20. Q—B 2   Q—Kt 8 ch

Gaining time against the threat of R—Q Kt 3.

21. R—B 1

21. K—K 2 looks attractive, for after 21. ...Q×R ? ; 22. R—Kt 3 ch White has a mating attack ; but Black continues with 21. ...Q×P ch ! ; 22. R—B 2, Q—Kt 5 ch (even stronger than ...Q—K 5 ch); 23. K—B 1, Q—R 6 ch ; 24. K—Kt 1, P×P (Tarrasch) and Black's attack is the more effective.

21. ......   Q×Kt P !

Apparently very risky, but its chief virtue is that it provides against 22. R—B 1 (22. ...P—Q 5 !).

22. Q—Kt 3 ch   K—R 1

This is much safer than 22. K× P ; 23. B—K 3 ch. As frequently happens in such situations, the formidable Pawn helps to protect the enemy King !

23. O—O—O ! ?

With one stroke White brings his King into "safety" and throws into relief the desperate character of his opponent's position :   ...B—B 4 cannot be played because of Q—B 2 ;   ...B—K 2 is advantageously answered by R—Kt 1 and R×P ; in addition, P—K 6 may become a dangerous menace.

23. ......   P×P !

This calm reply is best.   In the event of 24. P×P, Black intends... Q—Kt 3 with a satisfactory defence.

24. R—Kt 1   Q—K 7

The Queen hastens back to aid the defence of the somewhat isolated King.

25. Q R—K 1   Q—R 3
26. P×P   Q×P(R 2)

Black now threatens ...R×P.

27. Q—B 2   P—B 4 !
28. R—Kt 3   P—Kt 3
29. R—Kt 3   P—B 3

White was threatening R—Kt 5. Tarrasch is finally consolidating his position.

30. P—R 5   B—K 2

At last Black's Rooks can head for the Queen's side.

31. R—Kt 6   R—Q Kt 1 !

Tarrasch gladly dispenses with the extra Pawn in order to obtain a strong attacking position.

32. R×P   R—Kt 4 !
33. Q—Q 3

Beginning a highly interesting and complex manœuvre, the object of which is to bring the Queen to K 6 with the apparently murderous threat of R—R 6.   As the further course of the game demonstrates, Black has just enough time to refute this plan ; hence the more prosaic 33. R—B 1, Q—Q 2 ; 34. R—Kt 6, R×R ; 35. P×R, K—Kt 2 should have been tried.   White would have come out a Pawn down, but he could have put up a considerably longer fight.

33. ......   P—B 5
34. Q—K R 3   K R—Q Kt 1 !
35. Q—K 6

The crisis.   The finish is thrilling.

35. ......   R×Kt P !

Very pretty.   If now 36. R—R 6, R—Kt 8 ch ; 37. K—B 2, R(Kt 1)—Kt 7 ch ; 38. K—B 3, B—Kt 5 mate !   Or if 36. Q×Q P, R—Kt 8 ch ; 37. K—B 2, R(Kt 1)—Kt 7 ch ; 38. K—B 3, B—Kt 5 ch ; 39. K×P, R—B 7 ch ; 40. K—Kt 5 (if 40. K—Q 3, R×B ch wins the Queen), Q×P mate.

36. K—Q 1   R×B ch !
37. K×R   Q—Q 5 ch

White resigns, for if 38. K—K 2, R—Kt 7 ch ; 39. K—B 3, R—B 7 ch ; 40. K—Kt 3, Q—R 5 mate.   A very exciting, complicated, fascinating struggle—like most of the games of this match.

PART 3
OTHER GAMES

121. BRESLAU, 1880 ?

CARO-KANN DEFENCE
(IN EFFECT)

THIS is one of the earliest of Tarrasch's recorded games. He plays here with all the assurance of a self-confident youngster.

White	Black
DR. S. TARRASCH	T. VON SCHEVE

1.	P—K 4	P—Q 4
2.	P×P	P—Q B 3
3.	P—Q 4	

A move which illustrates a lifelong tendency of Tarrasch's play. He placed so much emphasis on quick and effective development that he accepted Pawn sacrifices in the opening only when there was overwhelming justification for such acceptance.

3.	......	P×P
4.	B—Q 3	Kt—Q B 3
5.	B—K 3	Kt—B 3
6.	Kt—K B 3	

In modern games with this variation, it is customary to play P—K R 3 in such positions to prevent ...B—Kt 5—a motif derived from the games of the mature Tarrasch (see, for example, Game 84).

6.	......	B—Kt 5
7.	P—K R 3	B×Kt

...B—R 4 followed in due course by ...B—Kt 3 would have been better.

8.	Q×B	Q—Kt 3

The contemplated win of a Pawn turns out badly. ...P—K 3 was preferable.

9.	O—O	Q×Kt P

Not 9. ...Kt×P ? 10. Q—B 4, Kt—K 3 ; 11. Q—R 4 ch and wins.

10.	Kt—Q 2	Kt×P ?

This is altogether too risky. ...Q—Kt 3 should have been played, although White's lead in development would have given him dangerous attacking prospects.

11.	Q—B 4	Kt—K 3

If 11. ...Kt—B 3 ; 12. Q—B 7 ! and the threat of Q R—Kt 1 is difficult to meet.

12.	Q—R 4 ch	Kt—Q 2
13.	Q R—Kt 1	Q—B 6
14.	R×P	Kt—B 2

15.	B—Q 4	

Decisive.

277

15.	......	Q×Kt
16.	R×Kt	R—Q 1
17.	Q×Kt ch !	R×Q
18.	R—B 8 ch	R—Q 1
19.	B—Kt 5 mate	

The neat finish is reminiscent of a famous Morphy game.

122. BERLIN, 1880 ?

KING'S GAMBIT DECLINED

IT is enjoyable to observe how young Tarrasch batters down the defences of his more experienced opponent.

| *White* | *Black* |
| T. VON SCHEVE | DR. S. TARRASCH |

1.	P—K 4	P—K 4
2.	P—K B 4	B—B 4
3.	Kt—K B 3	P—Q 3
4.	P—B 3	B—K Kt 5
5.	P—Q 4 ?	

Foolhardy, as the sequel shows. Marshall's line 5. P×P, P×P ; 6. Q—R 4 ch ! is far better.

5.	......	P×Q P
6.	P×P	B×Kt
7.	Kt P×B	Q—R 5 ch

White's King is destined to find no refuge for the rest of the game—the consequence of his fifth move.

8.	K—K 2	B—Kt 3
9.	Kt—B 3	Kt—Q B 3
10.	B—K 3	Kt—B 3
11.	Kt—R 4	

This costs a Pawn. Relatively better was 11. B—Kt 2, so that if 11. ...Kt—K R 4 ; 12. Kt—Q 5.

11.	......	Kt—K R 4 !
12.	Kt×B	R P×Kt
13.	P—Q 5	Kt—K 2

Now White has no recourse against the double threat of ... Kt—Kt 6 ch or ...Kt×P ch.

| 14. | K—Q 2 | Kt×B P |
| 15. | Q—B 2 | O—O ! |

Played in true gambit style. Black is not worried about a Pawn or two.

16. Q×P

| 16. | ...... | Kt(B 5)×P ! |

A far-seeing sacrifice. Tarrasch depends on the open Q B and K files to drive home his attack. White's helpless King and his lack of development are of course contributory factors.

| 17. | P×Kt | Kt×P |
| 18. | Q—B 4 | |

If 18. Q—B 2, Q—Kt 5 ch ; 19. K—K 2, K R—K 1 wins. Or if 19. K—Q 3, K R—K 1 ; 20. B—B 2, Q—K B 5 etc.

| 18. | ...... | Q—B 3 ! |
| 19. | B—Q 3 | |

Tarrasch points out that against
19. B—Q 4 Black continues 19.
...Q—B 5 ch ; 20. K—K 2, Q R
—B 1 ; 21. Q×Kt (if 21. Q—Q 3,
Kt—Kt 5), R—B 7 ch ; 22. K—
Q 3, Q—Q 7 ch ; 23. K—K 4, R—
K 1 ch ; 24. K—B 5, R—K 4 ch
etc. Or if 19. R—Q Kt 1, Q×P
wins.

The best chance, however, was
19. Q—Q 4, Kt×B ; 20. Q×Q
(not 20. K×Kt ?, K R—K 1 ch ;
21. K—Q 3, Q×P ch and wins),
Kt×B ch ; 21. K R×Kt, P×Q ;
22. K R—K 1 and Black's broken
Pawn position gives White some
drawing prospects.

| 19. ...... | Q×P ch |
| 20. Q—B 2 | |

If 20. B—B 2, Kt×B ; 21. K×
Kt, Q R—B 1.

| 20. ...... | Q—Kt 5 ch |
| 21. K—K 2 | K R—K 1 |

Regaining the piece with an easy
win.

22. B×P ch	K—R 1
23. B—K 4	Kt×B
24. K×Kt	P—Q 4
25. K R—Q Kt 1	Q—K 2
26. R×P	P×B

If now 27. P×P, Q R—B 1 and
White must allow either ...Q—
B 4 ch or ...Q×P ch.

27. P—B 4	Q R—B 1
28. Q—Q Kt 2	Q—B 4 ch
29. Q—Q 4	Q—K R 4
30. R—K B 1	R—B 7 !

White resigns ; the mating
threats are too much for him.

123. BERLIN, 1880 ?

EVANS GAMBIT DECLINED

From Winawer's sorry display here,
one would hardly guess that he was
at the height of his fame at the time
this game was played. He divided
first prize with Zukertort at Paris in
1878, and with Steinitz at Vienna
in 1882, shared the third prize with
Tchigorin at Berlin in 1881 and
captured the first prize at Nuremberg in 1883. Despite this impressive record, he receives short
shrift from his youthful opponent.

White	*Black*
Dr. S. Tarrasch	S. Winawer
1. P—K 4	P—K 4
2. Kt—K B 3	Kt—Q B 3
3. B—B 4	B—B 4
4. P—Q Kt 4	B—Kt 3

A lifeless continuation ; one
would expect the more enterprising
...B×P from a player with Winawer's imaginative style.

| 5. O—O | P—Q 3 |
| 6. P—Q R 4 | P—Q R 4 |

...P—Q R 3 is almost always
better in analogous situations.
Black is drifting into a very cramped
position.

7. P—Kt 5	Q Kt—K 2
8. P—Q 4	P×P
9. Kt×P	Kt—K B 3
10. Kt—Q B 3	O—O ?

A careless move which leads to a
serious King's side weakness. Better would have been ...Kt—Kt 3,
in order to answer B—Kt 5 with
...P—R 3.

11. B—Kt 5	Kt—Kt 3
12. Kt—Q 5	Kt—K 4
13. B×Kt	P×B
14. Kt×B	P×Kt
15. B—Q 5	

The exchanges have given White an easily won game : Black's Pawns are shattered and his King exposed, while White's Bishop is unassailably centralised.

| 15. ...... | K—R 1 |
| 16. R—R 3 ! | |

This unusual but efficacious method of developing the Q R is often seen in Tarrasch's early games.

16.	R—K Kt 1
17. P—K B 4	Kt—Kt 3
18. Kt—B 5 !	

White does not bother with the win of the K B P, as he wishes to concentrate on higher game.

| 18. ...... | Q—B 2 |
| 19. R—R 3 | R—Kt 2 |

Or 19. ...B×Kt ; 20. P×B, Kt—B 1 ; 21. R—K 1 and Black is unbearably cramped.

20. Kt×R	B×R
21. Kt—R 5	B—K 3
22. Kt×P	Q—B 6
23. P—B 5 !	

This forces the issue. If now 23. ...Q×Kt ; 24. P×B winning easily. Tarrasch winds up the game neatly and forcefully.

23.	B×B
24. P×Kt	Q—K 6 ch
25. K—R 1	B×P

26. Q—R 1 !

A very fine and decisive move. The obvious 26. R—K 1 would be answered by 26. ...B×P ch ; 27. K×B, Q—Kt 4 ch ; 28. Kt—Kt 4, P—B 4 etc.

26. ......   B×P ch

The loss of the Bishop was inevitable, in view of the threatened Kt—Kt 4 ch.

| 27. K×B | Q—Kt 4 ch |
| 28. K—R 1 | B P×P |

28. ...R P×P ; 29. Kt—K 4 ch, Q—K 4 ; 30. Q×Q ch, P×Q ; 31. R×P, K—Kt 1 (otherwise 32. Kt—B 6) ; 32. R×P would be quite hopeless ; while if 28. ... Q×K Kt P ; 29. Kt—R 5 ch is decisive.

| 29. Kt—K 8 ch ! | Q—K 4 |
| 30. R—B 8 mate | |

An artistic finish.

124. BERLIN, 1880 ?

PIERCE GAMBIT

THIS typically dashing Gambit is a cogent reminder that Tarrasch was a fellow townsman of the great Anderssen. Tarrasch's opponent here was a brother of the later World's Champion, and himself a strong player.

	White	*Black*
	DR. B. LASKER	DR. S. TARRASCH
1.	P—K 4	P—K 4
2.	Kt—Q B 3	Kt—Q B 3
3.	P—B 4	P×P
4.	Kt—B 3	P—K Kt 4
5.	P—Q 4	B—Kt 2
6.	B—B 4	

Neither player has selected the most aggressive line (5. ...P—Kt 5 ; or 6. P—Q 5 followed by 7. P—Q 6).

| 6. | ...... | P—Q 3 |
| 7. | O—O | P—K R 3 |

Compare the previous note. White is relying on his strong centre, while Black means to avoid breaking up his King's side chain of Pawns. As will be seen, Black's judgment of the position turns out to be correct.

| 8. | Kt—K 2 | Q—K 2 |
| 9. | P—B 3 | B—Q 2 |

Black wants to get his King into safety with ...O—O—O. 9. ... Q×P is answered by 10. Kt×B P.

| 10. | P—Q Kt 4 | O—O—O |
| 11. | B—Q 3 | R—B 1 |

Playing for ...P—B 4, so as to have more room for his pieces.

| 12. | Q—B 2 | P—B 4 ! |

This advance is useful even at the cost of a Pawn.

13.	P×P	Q—B 3
14.	P—Kt 4	P×P e.p.
15.	Q Kt×P	P—Kt 5 !

Regaining the Pawn, for if now 16. Kt—K 1, Kt×Q P ! or, if 16. Kt—R 5, Q—B 2 with good attacking chances. Thus White's 10th had no attacking value and has actually helped Black.

| 16. | P—Kt 5 | P×Kt |
| 17. | P×Kt | B×Q B P |

Black's attacking possibilities have multiplied enormously : he has opened the K Kt file, his Q B is effectively posted, and his K B P is an important asset for attacking purposes.

18.	B—Q B 4	Kt—K 2
19.	B—K 6 ch	K—Kt 1
20.	R—Kt 1	P—K R 4
21.	Kt—K 4	

| 21. | .... | K R—Kt 1 ! ! |

Very pretty play ! White has no good defence :

I. 22. B×R, Q×P ; 23. P—Q 5, R×B ; 24. P×B, B—Q 5 ch ; 25. K—R 1, Q—R 6 ! ; 26. B—B 4, Q—Kt 7 ch ; 27. Q×Q, P×Q mate.

II. 22. Kt×Q, B×Kt ch ; 23.

K—R 1 !, P—B 7 ch ; 24. P—Q 5,
Kt×Q P ; 25. Q—K 4 !, Kt—K 2;
26. Q×B, R—Kt 8 ch ! ; 27. R×
R, P×R(Q) ch ; 28. K×Q, Kt×Q
(Tarrasch) and Black wins the ending, as White's K B P cannot last
very long.

22. R×P	Q×B ! !
23. P×Q	B×P ch
24. K—B 1	R×R ch
25. K—K 2	R—Kt 7 ch
26. K×R	R×Q
27. P×B	R—B 6 ch

Black has regained the Queen and
his attack continues unabated. If
now 28. B—K 3, Kt—Q 4 ! and
Black wins a piece—although the
K P will require careful attention.

28. K—B 4	Kt—Kt 3 ch

White resigns, for if 29. K—B 5,
R—B 6 ch ; 30. K×Kt, B—K 5 ch.
A highly interesting game.

125. BERLIN, 1880 ?

SICILIAN DEFENCE

THIS is the earliest example of what
Tarrasch calls his "Pattsetzung-
stil" (the policy of restricting the
opponent's moves until he is helpless).

White	*Black*
DR. S. TARRASCH	MÜNCHOFF

1. P—K 4	P—Q B 4
2. Kt—K B 3	Kt—K R 3 ?

After this it is painfully apparent
that Black knows virtually nothing
about opening play.

3. P—Q 4	P—K 3
4. P—Q 5	

Beginning the process of cramping Black's position. Very few
players could resist the temptation
to play B×Kt ; but Tarrasch realises that Black's K Kt will have to
lose time in getting to a better
square.

4.	P—Q 3
5. P—B 4	P—K 4
6. B—Q 3	Kt—Kt 5

...P—K Kt 3 is more logical.

7. Kt—B 3	Kt—Q R 3
8. P—Q R 3	B—K 2
9. O—O	P—R 3
10. P—R 3	Kt—B 3
11. Kt—K R 2	P—K Kt 4

Preventing P—B 4. Black's objective is now to block the position
as much as possible, in the hope of
thus minimising the effect of his
lack of mobility.

12. P—Q Kt 4 !	B—Q 2

Naturally, if 12. ...P×P ; 13.
P×P, Kt×Kt P ? ; 14. Q—R 4 ch
wins a piece.

13. P—Kt 5	

Tarrasch shows a great deal of
confidence in making this move.
Most players would prefer 14. R—
Kt 1, keeping alive the possibility
of opening a file on the Queen's
side.

13.	Kt—B 2
14. B—Q 2	B—K B 1
15. P—Q R 4	B—Kt 2
16. P—R 5	O—O
17. Kt—K 2	

White's next step is to prepare
the occupation of the important
square K B 5.

17. ......   Kt—R 2
18. Kt—Kt 3 !   P—B 3

Avoiding 18. ...P—B 4 ; 19. P×P, P—K 5 ; 20. B×K P, B× R ; 21. Q×B—which would lead to a quick win for White because of the fatally weakened long diagonal.

19. R—K 1 !   Q—K 2
20. Kt(R 2)—B 1

Heading for K B 5.

20. ......   K—R 1
21. Kt—K 3   Kt—K 1
22. P—Kt 6 !

Alertly played. The Q Kt can no longer return to Q B 2, and thus *both* Black Knights are now stalemated !

22. ,.....   P—R 3

Exchanging would only help White.

23. Kt(K·3)—B 5   Q—B 2
24. B—K 2 !

Note how the pressure is inexorably augmented.

24. ......   R—K Kt 1
25. B—R 5   Q—B 1

Tarrasch remarks proudly that such positions are rare indeed ! Black is trussed up, and yet the position is so blocked that it is not easy to hit on the decisive stroke. Tarrasch solves the problem by the next five moves, which prepare for the sacrifice Kt×Q P !

26. Q—B 1 !   R—Q 1
27. Q—R 3   B—B 1
28. B—K 3   R—Q 2
29. Q R—B 1   R—Q 1
30. K R—Q 1   B—Q 2

Now White is ready.

31. Kt×Q P !   Kt×Kt

Or 31. ...Q×Kt ; 32. B×B P, Q—Kt 1 ; 33. B—K 7 followed by P—B 5—6 etc.

32. B×B P   B—B 1
33. B—K Kt 4 !   B×B
34. P×B   R—Q 2
35. Kt—B 5   Q—Q 1

Or 35. ...Kt×Kt ; 36. B×Q, B×B. In any case White's Pawns cannot be held back for long.

36. B×Kt   Kt—B 1
37. P—B 5   Kt—Kt 3
38. P—B 6   P×P
39. P×P   R×B
40. Q×R   Q×Q
41. R×Q   Resigns

126. HALLE, 1883 ?

SICILIAN DEFENCE

A FINE example of the unequal struggle between speedy development versus time-wasting Pawn grabbing. The evaluation of the opening play revolves about one of the vexing questions which were the subject of so much dispute throughout Tarrasch's lifetime : the strength or weakness of the isolated Q P.

White	Black
B. RICHTER	DR. S. TARRASCH

1. P—K 4	P—Q B 4
2. Kt—K B 3	P—K 3
3. Kt—B 3	Kt—Q B 3
4. P—Q 4	P×P
5. Kt×P	Kt—B 3
6. K Kt—Kt 5	B—Kt 5
7. P—Q R 3	

The attractive-looking 7. Kt—Q 6 ch can be answered by 7. ... K—K 2 !; 8. B—K B 4, P—K 4 ; 9. Kt—B 5 ch, K—B 1 ; 10. B—K Kt 5, P—Q 4 ! and Black has the better game.

7.	B×Kt ch
8. Kt×B	P—Q 4
9. P×P	

9. B—Q 3 is considered White's best course, and if 9. ...P×P ; 10. Kt×P, Kt×Kt ; 11. B×Kt, Q×Q ch ; 12. K×Q with the better ending for White. The text leaves Black with an isolated Q P, but by way of compensation he gets a fine development and a free game.

9.	P×P
10. B—K Kt 5	

In view of what follows, B—Q 3 would be more prudent.

10.	O—O !
11. B×Kt	

The contemplated win of the Q P has catastrophic consequences, but White's position is difficult in any event. A famous game between Pillsbury and Mieses (Paris, 1900) continued as follows : 11. B—K 2, P—Q 5 !; 12. Kt—K 4, Q—R 4 ch !; 13. P—Q Kt 4, Q—K 4 !; 14. Kt×Kt ch, P×Kt ; 15. B—R 6, P—Q 6 !!; 16. P×P, Kt—Q 5 ; 17. B×R, K×B ; 18. R—R 2, B—K 3 ; 19. R—Q 2, R—K 1 ; 20. O—O, B—Kt 6 ; 21. Q—Kt 1 !, B—Q 4 !; 22. B—Q 1, B×P !; 23. K×B, Q—Kt 4 ch ; 24. K—R 1, Q×R ; 25. B—Kt 4, Q—B 5 ; 26. R—Kt 1, P—B 4 ; 27. B—R 5, Kt—B 6 ; 28. B×Kt, Q×B ch ; 29. R—Kt 2, R—K 7 ? (...R—Q 1 wins) ; 30. Q—Q B 1, Q×Q P ; 31. Q—B 5 ch, R—K 2 ; 32. Q—B 8 ch : drawn by perpetual check.

11.	Q×B
12. Q×P ?	R—K 1 ch
13. B—K 2	B—Kt 5
14. P—B 3	Q R—Q 1

Black develops with terrifying rapidity. He has all his pieces in play, and a quick finish is indicated.

15. Q—Q B 5   Kt—Q 5 !

If now 16. P×B, Kt×P mate ! Or 16. Q R—B 1, B×P and wins.

16. O—O—O	B—B 4
17. R—Q 2	

17. B—Q 3, B×B ; 18. R×B, Kt—Kt 6 ch is slightly more inviting.

17. ......   Q—K R 3

To this there is no reply.

18. K—Q 1   Kt—Kt 6 !

White resigns. 19. R×R being answered by ...Q—B 8 mate. A bright little game.

127. NUREMBERG, 1883

DANISH GAMBIT

A CONDESCENDING attitude toward one's opponent is a very bad influence on one's play. Schwarz was a highly conservative player, so that his choice of opening was bound to recoil on him.

White	*Black*
J. SCHWARZ	DR. S. TARRASCH

1. P—K 4	P—K 4
2. P—Q 4	P×P
3. P—Q B 3	Q—K 2

This unusual move is by no means bad, as White is puzzled to find a good method of guarding the K P.

4. P—B 3

An ugly move which is sadly out of place in a gambit ! White should have continued in true gambit style with 4. P×P, Q×P ch ; 5. B—K 2, Q×Kt P ; 6. B—B 3. Less good would be 4. Kt—B 3, Q×P ch ; 5. B—K 2, P—Q 6 ! ; 6. Q×P, Q×Q and Black is a Pawn ahead with an easy game.

4.	P—Q 4 !
5. Q×P	Kt—Q B 3 !

Black's play, by contrast, is anything but timid.

6. B—Q Kt 5

Or 6. Q×Q P, B—K 3 with a fine game for the Pawn sacrificed.

6.	P×P
7. P×P	Kt—B 3
8. P—K 5	B—Q 2

White's position is already in a bad way.

9. B×Kt	B×B
10. Kt—B 3	R—Q 1
11. Q—K 3	

Or 11. Q—K B 4, B×Kt ; 12. P×B, R—Q 4 and the K P falls. By the text White manages to save his K P, but loses his King in the process !

11.	Kt—Kt 5
12. Q—Kt 5	Q—Q 2
13. O—O	

This can hardly be called a blunder, since White's game has already been seriously compromised.

13.	......	B—B 4 ch
14.	K—R 1	Kt—B 7 ch
15.	R×Kt	Q—Q 8 ch
16.	Kt—Kt 1	Q×Kt ch !
17.	K×Q	R—Q 8 mate

A fascinating lesson on the subject of gambit play.

128. LEIPZIG, 1883

KING'S GAMBIT

TARRASCH'S play in this game is a dramatic contrast to that of Schwarz in the previous one. Tarrasch shows here a real mastery of the spirit of gambit play, and he spares no expense to accomplish his aims.

| *White* | *Black* |
| F. RIEMANN | DR. S. TARRASCH |

1.	P—K 4	P—K 4
2.	P—K B 4	P×P
3.	Kt—K B 3	B—K 2

The old-fashioned Cunningham Gambit, which has completely disappeared from master play.

| 4. | B—B 4 | B—R 5 ch |
| 5. | K—B 1 | |

The older and more venturesome continuation was 5. P—Kt 3, P× P ; 6. O—O, P×P ch ; 7. K—R 1.

| 5. | ...... | P—Q 4 |

Black at once announces his policy of playing for open lines and ignoring material considerations.

| 6. | B×P | Kt—K B 3 |
| 7. | Kt—B 3 | |

7. B×P ch, K×B ; 8. Kt×B,

Kt×P or 7. Kt×B, Kt×B would be in Black's favour.

7.	......	Kt×B
8.	Kt×Kt	B—Kt 5
9.	Kt×P	Kt—B 3

Now Black is actually a Pawn down, but he is so pleased with his position that he considers the cost worth while.

| 10. | P—K R 3 | B×Kt |
| 11. | Q×B ? | |

Superficial ; he should have played P×B.

| 11. | ...... | Kt—Q 5 |

If now 12. Q—Q 1 ?, Q—B 3 wins a piece.

| 12. | Q—Kt 4 | Kt×P |

This cannot be answered by 13. Q×P ? because of ...B—B 3.

| 13. | R—Q Kt 1 | O—O |
| 14. | P—Q 4 | P—K B 4 ! |

Instead of accepting the Pawn offer, Black chooses to sacrifice a piece !

| 15. | P×P | Q×P ! |
| 16. | Q×B | Q R—K 1 ! ? |

Certainly more adventurous than
...Q—Q 8 ch followed by ...
Q×R.

Close examination of the position
reveals how difficult White's game
has become. If now 17. P—
K Kt 4, R—K 8 ch ; 18. Q×R,
Kt×Q ; 19. K×Kt, Q—K 5 ch,
winding up with Queen for Rook.

17. B—Q 2	Q×B
18. Q—B 2	Kt—K 6 ch
19. K—Kt 1	

White is lost : the disagreeable
position of his King has crippled
his game throughout.

| 19. ...... | Q—Q 5 |
| 20. Kt—K 2 | |

Or 20. P—K Kt 4, R—K 5 ; 21.
Kt—K 2, Q—Q 6 ; 22. Kt—B 3,
Kt×Kt P ; 23. P×Kt, R×P ch ;
24. K—R 2, R×P and wins (Tarrasch).

20.	Q—Q 6
21. Kt—B 3	R×P
22. Q—Kt 3	Q R—K B 1
23. R—K 1	R—B 8 ch

If now 24. K—R 2, R×R ; 25.
Q×R, Kt—B 8 ch and White must
give up the exchange, for if 26.
K—Kt 1, Q—Q 5 ch and mate follows (Tarrasch).

| 24. R×R | R×R ch |
| 25. K—R 2 | |

Now comes a pretty finish.

| 25. ...... | Kt—Kt 5 ch ! |
| 26. Q×Kt | |

Or 26. P×Kt, R×R ch winning
the Queen.

26.	Q—Q 3 ch
27. P—Kt 3	Q—Q 7 ch
28. Kt—K 2	R—B 7 ch
29. K—Kt 1	Q—K 8 mate

129. NUREMBERG CHESS CLUB CHAMPIONSHIP, 1887–88

ODDS OF PAWN AND MOVE*

THIS game is played in true odds
style : an unsound sacrifice
triumphs over a weak defence.
The pseudo-dangerous peregrinations of Black's King add a touch of
piquancy.

| *White* | *Black* |
| K. ECKART | DR. S. TARRASCH |

| 1. P—K 4 | Kt—Q B 3 |

Together with 1. ...P—Q 3,
this constitutes the best defence at
these odds.

2. P—K B 4	P—K 4
3. Kt—K B 3	P×P
4. B—B 4	B—B 4

Apparently played with the following "swindle" in mind.

5. P—Q 4	Kt×P ? !
6. Kt×Kt	Q—R 5 ch
7. K—B 1	P—Q 4

Black must develop quickly if he
is to secure any compensation for
the lost material.

| 8. P×P | B—K Kt 5 |
| 9. B—Kt 5 ch | |

A feeble reply ; 9. Q—Q 3
should have been played, with a
satisfactory defence.

* Remove Black's K B P.

9. ......   P—B 3 !

Apparently White has not real-ised that this move is possible.

10. P×P   O—O—O !
11. P×P ch   K×P
12. B—B 6 ch   K—Kt 3
13. Q—Q 3   R×Kt

Black has regained the sacrificed piece and, contrary to appearances, his King is quite safe.

14. Q—Kt 5 ch   K—B 2
15. Q—Kt 7 ch   K—Q 3
16. Kt—B 3

Allowing a pretty finish, but 16. B—B 3, B×B ; 17. Q×B, R—Q 8 ch ! would be conclusive.

16. ......   Q—B 7 ch !
17. K×Q   R—Q 8 ch
18. B—K 3   B×B mate

130. NUREMBERG CHESS CLUB CHAMPIONSHIP, 1888

RUY LOPEZ

THE manner in which Tarrasch provokes hostile weaknesses and then trains his guns on them is highly instructive.

White   *Black*
M. KÜRSCHNER   DR. S. TARRASCH

1. P—K 4   P—K 4
2. Kt—K B 3   Kt—Q B 3
3. B—Kt 5   Kt—B 3
4. O—O   Kt×P
5. R—K 1

P—Q 4 is far more promising ; the text does not offer Black any serious difficulties.

5. ......   Kt—Q 3
6. Kt×P   Kt×Kt
7. R×Kt ch   B—K 2
8. B—B 1

One of Steinitz's eccentricities. In a similar position in Game 44 Tarrasch played B—Q 3.

8. ......   O—O
9. Kt—B 3   Kt—K 1

Beginning a long and somewhat awkward regrouping manœuvre, but the improved position of his pieces is well worth the effort.

10. Q—K 1 ?

Obviously the Queen is useless here. P—Q 4 was preferable.

10. ......   B—Q 3
11. R—K 2   P—Q B 3
12. P—Q Kt 3

A further error of judgment. As White will have to advance his Q P eventually in order to make room for his Queen and secure coopera-tion for his Rooks, it would be more logical to play P—Q 4.

12. ......   B—B 2
13. B—Kt 2   P—Q 4

Black has rearranged his pieces

very nicely and he will actually take the initiative with his next move.

14. P—Q 4

See the note to White's 12th move. The future prospects of his Q B are dark indeed.

14. ......   Q—Q 3
15. P—Kt 3

Creating—unavoidably, to be sure—a weakness which Tarrasch will soon begin to exploit.

15. ......   B—Kt 5
16. R—K 3   Kt—B 3
17. Q—Q 2   P—Q Kt 4

In order to answer a possible P—Q R 4 (intending B—Q R 3) with ...P—Kt 5.

18. B—Kt 2   P—K R 4 !

Tarrasch now turns his attention to the weakened King's side. The manner in which his Knight is now brought into the attack is novel— and clever.

19. P—K R 4   B—B 4
20. Q R—K 1   Kt—Kt 5
21. R(K 3)—K 2   Kt—R 3 !
22. B—B 3   B—K Kt 3
23. Q—Kt 5

This sortie is repulsed with ease.

23. ......   Kt—B 4

This completes the rather complicated manœuvre begun with Black's 18th move.

24. Kt—Q 1   B—Q 1
25. Q—Q 2   Kt×Kt P !

The bomb explodes. Black gets a good attack and three Pawns for the piece.

26. P×Kt   Q×P ch
27. B—Kt 2   B×R P
28. Kt—B 2

B—R 3 (Tarrasch) was White's last hope. After the text Black simply continues to pile up the pressure.

28. ......   P—R 4 !
29. B—B 1   B—B 3
30. P—B 3   P—K R 5
31. Q—K 3   B—R 4 !
32. Kt—R 1   Q—Kt 3
33. R—K B 2

33. ......   Q R—K 1 !

By far the finest move in the game. Tarrasch does not fear his resulting material disadvantage, as his Queen will be more than a match for his opponent's scattered forces.

34. Q×R   R×Q
35. R×R ch   K—R 2
36. K—R 2   B—Kt 5

Otherwise B—K R 3 wins.

37. B—B 4

But not 37. B—K R 3, B×B ; 38. K×B, Q—K Kt 8 and wins !

37. ......   P—Kt 5 !

This move, postponed so long, has a highly disintegrating effect on White's game.

38. B—Q 2	P—R 6 !
39. B×R P	B×B
40. K×B	P×P
41. B—K 3	

Not 41. B×P, Q—Q 6 ch etc. The passed Q B P now decides the issue very quickly.

| 41. ...... | P—B 7 |

Threatening ...B×P !

42. R—B 4	B—Kt 4
43. Kt—Kt 3	Q—R 3 ch
44. K—Kt 4	B×R
45. B×B	Q×B ch

White resigns. The neat conclusion is in keeping with Black's excellent play throughout.

131. NUREMBERG, 1888

RUY LOPEZ

HERE is one of Tarrasch's finest games, and one of the most instructive examples in chess literature of the power of the two Bishops. An off-hand game of this character was virtually unknown among the older players !

| *White* | *Black* |
| B. RICHTER | DR. S. TARRASCH |

1. P—K 4	P—K 4
2. Kt—K B 3	Kt—Q B 3
3. B—Kt 5	Kt—B 3
4. O—O	Kt×P
5. Q—K 2	

It cannot be stressed too often that P—Q 4 is White's strongest move here. See, for example, Game 118.

| 5. ...... | Kt—Q 3 |

A favourite move with Tarrasch, who often played it in analogous situations.

6. B×Kt	Q P×B
7. Q×P ch	Q—K 2
8. R—K 1	

Since Black's Queen and K B are awkwardly situated and since the ending is very promising for Black because of his two Bishops, 8. Q—B 3 would be preferable.

8.	Q×Q
9. R×Q ch	B—K 2
10. P—Q 3	P—B 3
11. R—K 1	K—B 2

Black has an easy game and he will soon begin to make his Bishops tell in his favour.

| 12. B—B 4 | P—K Kt 4 ! |

A significant move. The proper way to make use of the two Bishops is to follow a policy of restriction which will leave the enemy's Knights with less and less scope. The text has the future virtue of compelling White to commit himself on the further disposition of the Q B. After 13. B—Kt 3, the Bishop would lose contact with the Queen's side.

| 13. B—Q 2 | B—Kt 5 |
| 14. Kt—Q 4 | P—Q B 4 ! |

Another characteristic move. Now White's Knights no longer have access to Q 4.

15. Kt—K 2   Kt—Kt 4

Threatening ...B×Kt followed
by ...Kt—Q 5. 16. Q Kt—B 3
was probably White's best reply.

16. B—B 3   Q R—Q 1
17. Kt—Q 2   Kt—Q 5 !

Forcing White's reply, which
gives Black two Bishops against two
Knights.

18. B×Kt   P×B
19. P—Q R 3

To prevent ...B—Kt 5. But
the move creates a slight weakness
which later on is finely exploited by
Tarrasch.

19. ......   P—Q B 4
20. Kt—K Kt 3   P—K R 4 !
21. P—K B 3   B—Q 2
22. R—K 2   P—Kt 4

From now on, White must reckon
with the possibility of ...P—B 5.

23. Q R—K 1   B—K B 1 !

Well played. As Tarrasch wisely
comments, ...K R—K 1 would
sooner or later lead to exchanges,
which would somewhat relieve
White's cramped position.

24. Kt(Kt 3)—K 4   R—K Kt 1

Preparing to drive White's
Knight away from K 4. The constriction increases apace.

25. Kt—Q Kt 3   R—B 1
26. Kt(K 4)—Q 2   B—Q 3
27. Kt—K 4   B—B 1
28. Kt(K 4)—Q 2   P—B 4
29. R—K 5   B—Q 3
30. R(K 5)—K 2

Beating a hasty retreat, for after
30. R—Q 5, R—Kt 3 the advanced
Rook's predicament would be embarrassing.

30. ......   R—Q R 1

Black's next objective is to en-
force ...P—R 4—5. The position
of the Knights becomes more
painful with every move.

31. Kt—R 5   Q R—Kt 1
32. Kt(R 5)—Kt 3   P—R 5
33. K—R 1

White is reduced to miserable
waiting moves.

33. ......   R—K Kt 3 !
34. K—Kt 1   B—K 3 !

Tarrasch needs to accomplish
only two more objectives to reduce
White to impotence : the Pawn
advances ...P—R 4—5 and ...P—
Q B 5.

35. R—B 2   R—Q R 1
36. R(B 2)—K 2   P—R 4
37. Kt—Kt 1   P—R 5
38. Kt(Kt 3)—Q 2

At last Black is ready for the
decisive thrust.

38. ......   P—Q B 5 !

White is defenceless : if 39. P×
P, P×P and his Q Kt P soon falls.

| 39. | Kt—B 1 | R—Q B 1 |
| 40. | K—R 1 | P—B 6 ! |

Taking advantage of White's 19th
move.

| 41. | P×P | P×P |

Threatening 42. ....P—Q Kt 5 ;
43. P×P, B×Kt P followed by ...
P—Q R 6 and White must give up
a piece !

| 42. | Kt—K 3 | P—Q Kt 5 |
| 43. | Kt—B 4 | |

Or 43. P×P, B×Kt P followed
by ...P—Q R 6 etc.

43.	......	B×Kt
44.	P×B	R×P
45.	R—K 3	P×P
46.	Kt×B P	B—Kt 5

White resigns. "Many people
will find this game very boring,
since 'nothing seems to happen' for
the first 37 moves. Yet I look upon
the game as one of my finest
achievements ; the connoisseur will
endorse my judgment" (Tarrasch).

*

132. NUREMBERG, 1888

ODDS OF PAWN AND MOVE *

NOWHERE is the immense gap between the first-rate master and the
fairly good amateur so clearly
demonstrated as in odds games.
Despite his material inferiority, the
master usually has the game well in
hand by the fifteenth move !

* Remove Black's K B P.

White	Black
L.	DR. S.
REGENSBURGER	TARRASCH

1.	P—K 4	P—Q 3
2.	P—Q 4	Kt—K B 3
3.	Kt—Q B 3	Kt—B 3
4.	B—K Kt 5	

Almost always a pointless move
when the opponent has an open K B
file. B—Q B 4 was better.

4.	......	P—K 3
5.	Q—Q 2	B—K 2
6.	Kt—B 3	O—O
7.	O—O—O	P—Q 4
8.	P—K 5 ?	

Either 8. B—Q 3 or 8. P×P,
P×P ; 9. Kt—K 5 was much more
promising. The text creates a
barricade behind which Black can
develop comfortably.

8.	......	Kt—K Kt 5
9.	B×B	Q×B
10.	P—K R 3	Kt—R 3
11.	B—Q 3	

Waste of time. Better was B—
K 2 followed by P—K Kt 4.

| 11. | ...... | Kt—Q Kt 5 |
| 12. | B—K 2 | P—B 4 |

A difficult move to answer : 13.
P×P, Q×P would leave Black with
an excellent position.

| 13. | Kt—Q Kt 5 | P—B 5 ! |

Contemplating a storming attack
with the Queen's side Pawns later
on. The fact that White can post
his Knight on Q 6 is by no means
adequate compensation, as this post
is untenable. Note that the re-

covery of the Pawn by ...Kt×P ch does not interest Tarrasch.

14. P—Q B 3	Kt—B 3
15. Kt—Q 6	Kt—B 4
16. Kt×B ?	

An error of judgment; the removal of the relatively harmless Bishop is much weaker than Kt×Kt.

16.	Q R×Kt
17. P—K Kt 4	Kt—R 3
18. Q R—B 1	P—Q Kt 4

With both players striving for attack, the position becomes extremely interesting.

19. Kt—Kt 5	P—Kt 5
20. P—K R 4	Kt—B 2 !

White was threatening Q—B 2, forcing the weakening Pawn advance ...P—Kt 3.

21. Kt×Kt	R×Kt
22. P—Kt 5 ?	

A feeble move which ruins White's attacking chances. P—B 4, angling for P—B 5, was the proper continuation.

22.	P—Q R 4
23. P—R 5	K R—B 1

Preventing White from opening a file on the King's side. P—Kt 6 can now be answered by ...P—R 3.

24. B—Kt 4 ?

Another weak move. Tarrasch prefers B—Q 1, in order to hold back Black's Q R P.

24.	P—R 5
25. P—B 4	P—R 6 !

Full speed ahead ! The game now enters a very exciting phase.

26. P—B 5	P×P ch
27. K—Kt 1	

Despite this precautionary measure, White's King is soon smoked out.

27.	Kt P×P
28. Q×B P	Q×P !
29. K R—Kt 1 !	P×P !

Intending a surprisingly powerful Queen sacrifice.

30. B×P

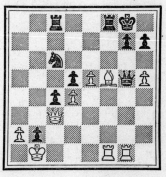

30.	R×B !
31. R×Q	R×R ch

The manner in which Black's forces now cooperate to bring about the win is highly interesting.

32. K×P	R—Kt 1 ch
33. K—B 2	

If 33. K—R 3, K R—Q Kt 8 ! and White can resign.

33.	Kt—Kt 5 ch
34. K—Q 2	R—B 7 ch
35. K—K 1	

If 35. K—K 3, Q R—K B 1 ;

36. R—Kt 3, Kt—B 7 ch wins ; or if 35. K—Q 1, Kt—Q 6 etc. (Tarrasch).

35. ......   R×P
36. R—Kt 3   Kt—B 7 ch
37. K—B 1

Tarrasch points out that if the King goes to the second rank, 37. ...Kt—R 6 ch wins the Queen ; while if 37. K—Q 1, R—Kt 8 ch with the same result.

37. ......   R—Kt 8 ch
38. K—Kt 2   Kt—K 6 ch
39. K—B 3

Or 39. K—R 3, R—R 8 mate.

39. ......   R—Kt 6
40. Q×Kt

If 40. Q—B 1, Kt—B 8 ch leads to mate.

40. ......   R×Q ch
41. K×R   R—R 6 ch

White resigns, for if 42. K—B 2, R×R ; 43. K×R, P—B 6 and the Pawn marches on. White's Queen has been curiously helpless all through the attack.

133. BRESLAU, 1889

FOUR KNIGHTS' GAME

THIS game is interesting because of the way Tarrasch evolves a powerful attack from a seemingly barren position. He works out his problems here with an impressive economy of means.

	White	Black
	L. PAULSEN	DR. S. TARRASCH

1. P—K 4   P—K 4
2. Kt—K B 3   Kt—Q B 3
3. Kt—B 3   Kt—B 3
4. B—Kt 5   B—Kt 5
5. O—O   O—O
6. P—Q 3   P—Q 3
7. B×Kt

This and the next three moves constitute one big blunder which exemplifies a certain ponderous timidity characteristic of Paulsen's play.

7. ......   P×B
8. B—Q 2   R—K 1
9. P—Q R 3   B—R 4
10. P—R 3   R—Kt 1
11. R—Kt 1   P—B 4

Intending to proceed energetically with ...P—B 3, ...P—Q 4 and ...B—B 2. Paulsen decides to forestall this advance, but comes to grief very quickly.

12. Kt—K R 2   P—B 3
13. P—B 4   P×P
14. R×P ?

Despite its plausible aspect, this move is a serious mistake which meets with a harsh rejoinder. B×P should have been played.

14. ......   P—Q 4

Intending ...B—B 2, which would win a Pawn.

15. Kt—Kt 4

P×P was his best chance. After the text, Black gets a clear advantage by force.

15. ......   Q B×Kt
16. P×B   P×P !

Obvious, but really unanswerable. On 17. P×P there follows

17. ...R×Kt P !; 18. R×R, B×
Kt and wins, or if 17. Kt×P, Kt×
Kt ; 18. B×B, Q—Q 5 ch ; 19.
K—R 2, Q—Q 3 ; 20. P—Kt 3,
Kt×P ! (Tarrasch) and wins.

17. P—Kt 5   B×Kt !

For if 18. B×B, Kt—Q 4 with a
Pawn ahead.

18. P×B   R×R
19. Q×R   P—K 6 !

The extra Pawn becomes formidable ! White cannot play B×P because of ...Kt—Q 4.

20. B—K 1   Kt—Q 4
21. R—K Kt 4   Q—Q 2
22. R—K 4

If 22. R—Kt 3, Kt—B 5 is a
strong reply.

22. ......   R×R
23. P×R   Kt—Kt 3

As White has no good defence
against the threatened ...Q—Kt 5,
he evolves the following counterchance, which is, however, effortlessly repulsed by Tarrasch.

24. P—R 4 ? !   Q—Q 1 !

Guarding against the mating
threat and threatening the doomed
Kt P.

25. P—R 5   Kt—B 5
26. P—R 6   P—Kt 3 !

Freeing the Queen from guarding
against the mating threat ; if now
27. Q—Kt 7, Q—Q 8 ; 28. K—
B 1, Kt—Q 7 ch and wins.

27. K—B 1   K—Kt 2 !

But not 27. ...Kt—Q 7 ch ? 28.
B×Kt, Q×B ; 29. Q—Kt 8 ch,
K—Kt 2 ; 30. Q—K 5 ch with
perpetual check.

28. K—K 2   Q×P
29. P—Kt 3   Q—Kt 5 ch

Now comes a playful finish in
which Tarrasch makes every move
tell.

30. K—Q 3

Or 30. K—B 1, Kt—Q 7 ch ;
31. B×Kt, P×B and wins.

30. ......   Kt—K 4 ch
31. K×P   Q—B 6 ch
32. K—Q 2   Kt—B 5 ch
33. K—B 1   Q—K 7 !

White resigns, mate being unavoidable.

134. NUREMBERG, 1889–90 ?

RUY LOPEZ

THIS is one of the rare games in
which Tarrasch, who loved the
initiative, is on the defensive almost
all through. The way in which he

wards off a vexing attack is well
worthy of study.

| White | Black |
| M. Kürschner | Dr. S. Tarrasch |

1. P—K 4	P—K 4
2. Kt—K B 3	Kt—Q B 3
3. B—Kt 5	P—Q 3

Tarrasch had a lifelong aversion
to this defence ; but at the time, his
admiration for Steinitz doubtless
influenced the choice of the text.

4. P—Q 4	B—Q 2
5. P—B 3	Kt—B 3
6. Q—K 2	B—K 2
7. O—O	O—O
8. B—Kt 5	R—K 1
9. Q Kt—Q 2	P—K R 3

Black's game is very cramped—
just the kind of position which Tarrasch always strove to avoid.

| 10. B—K R 4 | P—R 3 |
| 11. B—Q 3 | |

11. B—R 4 ? would be answered
by ...Kt×Q P ! ; while if 11.
K B×Kt, B×B ; 12. P×P, P×P ;
13. Kt×P, B—Kt 4 ! ; 14. P—
Q B 4, Kt×P ! and Black stands
well.

| 11. ...... | P×P |
| 12. P×P | |

Seemingly stronger than Kt×P ;
but in reality, Black is now able to
free himself.

| 12. ...... | Kt—Q Kt 5 ! |
| 13. B—Kt 1 ? | |

Curiously enough, this plausible
move must lead to a loss of material.

| 13. ...... | B—Kt 4 |
| 14. Kt—B 4 | |

Although this costs a piece, it
permits White to put up a better
fight than some such move as
Q—Q 1.

| 14. ...... | P—Q 4 ! |
| 15. P×P | K Kt×P |

White must lose a piece ! If 16.
B×B, R×B ; 17. K Kt—K 5, P—
K B 3

16. Q—K 4	B×B
17. Q—R 7 ch	K—B 1
18. Q—R 8 ch	K—K 2
19. R—K 1 ch	K—B 3
20. Q Kt—K 5 !	

Very pretty. If 20. ...R×Q ;
21. Kt—Kt 4 mate. White's attack requires careful treatment by
his adversary.

20.	B—Q 2
21. Q—R 7	B—K Kt 4
22. P—K R 4	B—B 5
23. P—K Kt 3	B×Kt
24. P×B ch	K—K 2

White's attack is petering out, but
he now picks up several Pawns
while continuing to maintain pressure.

25. Q×Kt P	B—K 3
26. P—R 3	Kt—Q B 3
27. Q×P	R—R 1
28. Q—Kt 5 ch	K—Q 2
29. Q—Q 2	K—B 1
30. R—Q 1	Q Kt—K 2
31. B—K 4	P—Q B 3

Tarrasch has consolidated his
game, and the King is safe on the
Queen's side.

32. Kt—Q 4	K—Kt 1
33. Q—B 2	K—R 2
34. R—Q 3	Q—Kt 3
35. Q R—Q 1	Q R—Q 1

White's best chance is doubtless P—Q Kt 4, aiming for an eventual P—Q R 4 etc. The move he actually makes has been amply provided for by his wary opponent.

36. R—Kt 3 ?

36. ......   Kt—K 6 !

This pretty move has great simplifying value for Black. The main point is that if 37. P×Kt, B×R ; 38. Kt×B, R×R ch ; 39. Q×R, Q×P ch followed by ... Q×B (Tarrasch).

37. R×Kt	R×Kt
38. R×R	Q×R
39. Q—K 2	B—B 5
40. B—Q 3	B×B
41. R×B	Q—Q B 5
42. Q—K 3 ch	K—Kt 1
43. R—Q 7	

White wants to force P—K 6, which would give him three united passed Pawns. However, Tarrasch foils him with a cleverly worked out attack.

43.	Q—K 3
44. R—Q 6	Q—B 4
45. P—K 6	Kt—Q 4
46. Q—Q 4	R—K 1
47. P×P	Q×P

Ironically enough, White's advance of the K P now proves his undoing : he is helpless against the coming attack on the K B file. Thus if 48. Q—Q 2, Q—B 6 to be followed by ...R—K 7.

48. K—Kt 2	R—K 7
49. Q—R 8 ch	K—R 2
50. Q—Q 4 ch	P—Kt 3
51. R×P	Kt—K 6 ch
52. K—R 3	Q—B 4 ch

White resigns, a quick mate being inevitable. An interesting game.

135. NUREMBERG, 1889–90 ?

ODDS OF PAWN AND MOVE *

TARRASCH'S opponent puts up an honourable if unduly timid resistance until one faulty move leaves him without a satisfactory defence.

White K. ECKART	*Black* DR. S. TARRASCH
1. P—K 4	P—Q 3
2. Kt—K B 3	Kt—Q B 3
3. P—Q 4	Kt—B 3
4. B—Q 3	

This development of the Bishop is not timely. 4. Kt—B 3 would be better, reserving the development of the Bishop to B 4 or Kt 5.

4.	P—K 4
5. P—B 3	B—K 2
6. P—Q 5	

This is also questionable. It blocks the Bishop, leaving Black safe from attack and free to obtain a good development.

* Remove Black's K B P.

6.	......	Kt—Q Kt 1
7.	P—K R 3	O—O
8.	Q Kt—Q 2	Q Kt—Q 2
9.	Q—K 2	Kt—R 4

A good move. White must now provide against ...Kt—B 5.

10.	P—K Kt 3	Q—K 1
11.	Kt—B 1	Q—B 2
12.	Kt—Kt 5	B×Kt
13.	B×B	

White has two Bishops, but they cannot be of much use to him unless the position is opened up.

| 13. | ...... | Kt—B 4 |
| 14. | B—B 2 | P—Q Kt 3 |

Intending 15. ...B—R 3 ; 16. P—Q B 4 ?, B×P !

| 15. | O—O—O | P—R 4 |
| 16. | Kt—Q 2 | P—Kt 4 |

Tarrasch is playing for a Pawn advance against the White King. 17. Q×P ? would be answered by 17. ...B—R 3 ; 18. Q—B 6, Q R—Kt 1 and wins.

17.	B—K 3	P—Kt 5
18.	B×Kt	P×B
19.	Kt—B 4	

P—Q B 4 would have been safer, as it would have made it impossible for Black to open a file on the Queen's side. However, the text should yield satisfactory results if followed up correctly.

| 19. | ...... | P×P |
| 20. | P×P | |

Black's Queen's side Pawns are in a sorry case so his attack is now a case of "do or die".

| 20. | ...... | P—Kt 3 |

In order to relieve the Queen of the task of guarding the Knight.

| 21. | R—Q 2 | R—Kt 1 |
| 22. | B—Kt 3 | |

22. Kt×K P was also possible. If then 22. ...Q—Kt 2 ; 23. Kt—B 6, B—R 3 ; 24. Q×B, Q×P ; 25. Kt×R, R×Kt ; 26. Q—Q 3, Q—Kt 7 ch ; 27. K—Q 1, Q—R 8 ch (Tarrasch) ; 28. K—K 2 and White has weathered the storm.

22.	......	B—R 3
23.	Q—K 3	P—R 5
24.	Kt×P !	

This is quite playable, despite its risky appearance.

24.	......	Q—Kt 2
25.	B—B 4	Q×Kt
26.	B×B	R—Kt 3
27.	P—K B 4	Q—Kt 2
28.	B—B 4	K R—Kt 1
29.	K—B 2 ?	K—R 1

There is nothing to be gained by checking, which would only drive the King to the excellent square Q 3.

30. P—K 5 ?

Threatening to win a piece with P—Kt 4, but completely missing the force of Black's excellent reply. Correct was 30. P—Kt 4, Kt—B 3 ; 31. P—K 5 and White should win.

30. ......   Q—B 1 !

With the powerful threat of ... R—Kt 7 ch ; 32. K—Q 3, Q—B 4 ch.

31. K—Q 3

Since this loses quickly, 31. R—Q B 1 should have been tried, despite Black's advantageous continuation 31. ...Q—B 4 ch and 32. ... Q×R P.

31. ......   Q—B 4 ch
32. K—K 2   Kt×Kt P ch

Doubtless a painful surprise for White.

33. Q×Kt   Q—K 5 ch
34. Q—K 3   Q×R
35. P—K 6

Apparently White's position is full of fight, but the end comes quite suddenly.

35. ......   R—Kt 7 !
36. P—K 7   R×R ch
37. K×R

If 37. Q×R, Q—K 5 ch wins.

37. ......   R—Kt 7 ch
38. K—Q 3   Q—Kt 8 mate

A pretty conclusion to an enterprising but unsound attack.

136. NUREMBERG 1889–90 ?

VIENNA GAME
(IN EFFECT)

HERE is a game in which rapid development tells the whole story. White loses too much time in the opening with "pretty" but ineffectual Queen moves.

White   *Black*
M. KÜRSCHNER   DR. S. TARRASCH

1. P—K 4   P—K 4
2. B—B 4   Kt—K B 3
3. Kt—Q B 3

P—Q 3 is more effective, as the text allows the following advantageous exchange.

3. ......   Kt×P
4. B×P ch ?

Although Black is deprived of the possibility of castling, this does not prove too great a hardship. His powerful centre and accelerated development are more than adequate compensation.

4. ......   K×B
5. Kt×Kt   P—Q 4
6. Q—R 5 ch

In another game between the same players, contested during this period, the continuation was 6. Q—B 3 ch, K—Kt 1 ; 7. Kt—K 2, B—K 3 (the bait is too obvious !) ; 8. Kt(K 4)—Kt 3, Kt—B 3 ; 9. P—Q R 3, Q—Q 2 ; 10. P—R 3, B—Q B 4 ; 11. O—O, P—K R 4 ; 12. Kt—R 1, R—K B 1 ; 13. Q—Kt 3, P—R 5 ; 14. Q—R 2, P—K 5 ; 15. P—Q 3, B—Q 3 ; 16. B—B 4, R×B ; 17. Kt×R, P—K Kt 4 and White resigned.

| 6. ...... | K—Kt 1 |
| 7. Q—K 2 | P—K R 3 |

Now the Knight must move.

| 8. Kt—Kt 3 | Kt—B 3 |
| 9. P—Q 3 | Kt—Q 5 |

Possibly premature, but Black can afford such luxuries.

10. Q—Q 1	B—Q B 4
11. B—K 3	K—R 2
12. P—Q B 3	R—K 1
13. P—K R 3	

13. P×Kt ?, P×P would of course be unfavourable, but 13. K Kt—K 2 would have been better.

13.	Q—R 5
14. K Kt—K 2	Kt×Kt
15. Q×Kt	P—Q 5 ! ?

Enterprising play. He cedes K 4 to White's pieces, in order to cramp the latter's position.

| 16. B—Q 2 | B—Q 2 |
| 17. Kt—K 4 | B—K B 1 ! |

A fine move. The more obvious ...B—Kt 3 would leave the Bishop staring along a dead diagonal.

18. O—O—O

O—O also has its drawbacks, for example, 18. ...R—K 3 ; 19. Q—Kt 4, Q—K 2 threatening ...R—K Kt 3, with a strong attack.

| 18. ...... | R—K 3 |

The Rook at once opens a heavy attack against White's King.

| 19. K→Kt 1 | R—R 3 |
| 20. B—B 1 | B—K 3 |

Both Bishops are now trained menacingly on the vulnerable castled position. If now 21. P—Q B 4, P—Q Kt 4 is a powerful reply.

21. P—R 3	P—Q Kt 4
22. P—B 3	R—Kt 1
23. P—K Kt 4	Q—Q 1

Black judiciously removes the Queen to the other wing, thus forestalling P—Kt 5.

| 24. P—Kt 5 | Q—Q 4 |
| 25. K—B 2 | |

Trying to escape the mounting fury of the attack. But flight is futile.

25.	Q P×P
26. Kt×P	Q—Kt 6 ch
27. K—Q 2	P—Kt 5

Every move makes the position of White's King still more precarious.

| 28. P×P | B×Kt P |

Threatening ...B×Kt ch followed by ...R—R 7 ch. White has no good reply.

| 29. Q×P | R—R 7 |
| 30. P×P | |

Hoping that the mating threat will keep Black occupied. But Tarrasch has a neat forced win.

30.	......	R×P ch !
31.	B×R	Q×B ch
32.	K—K 3	B×Kt
33.	Q—K 4 ch	

Or 33. Q×Q B, B—Q 5 ch ; 34. K—B 4, R—B 1 ch ; 35. K—Kt 5, Q—Kt 7 ch ; 36. Q—Kt 4, B—K 6 ch ; 37. K—R 5, P—Kt 3 ch and the game is over.

33.	......	P—Kt 3
34.	Q×B	B—Q 5 ch
35.	K—B 4	

If 35. K—K 4, Q—K 7 ch ; 36. K—Q 5, R—Q 1 ch and wins.

35.	......	R—B 1 ch
36.	K—Kt 5	Q—Kt 7 ch
37.	Q—Kt 4	R—B 4 ch
		and wins.

137. NUREMBERG, 1889–90 ?

ODDS OF QUEEN *

IT goes without saying that only execrable play can result in the odds-receiver being mated in twelve moves ; nevertheless, the manner in which this mate is engineered has a captivating quality.

| *White* | *Black* |
| DR. S. TARRASCH | C. SCHROEDER |

| 1. | P—K 4 | P—K 4 |
| 2. | P—K B 4 | P—Q 3 |

Needlessly conservative. 2. ... P×P, ...P—Q 4 and ...B—B 4 are all good replies.

* Remove White's Queen.

| 3. | P—Q 3 | P—K B 4 |
| 4. | Kt—Q B 3 | B P×P |

Opening up lines for the opponent's pieces. ...Kt—K B 3 should be played.

| 5. | Q P×P | P—Q R.3 |

Pointless. A developing move was in order.

6.	P×P	P×P
7.	Kt—B 3	B—Q Kt 5
8.	B—Kt 5	

Of course not 8. Kt×P ? ?, Q—Q 5 etc.

| 8. | ...... | Q—Q 3 |

Black systematically neglects his development. ...Kt—K B 3 should have been played.

| 9. | R—Q 1 | Q—K Kt 3 ? ? |

Up to this point, Black's errors have all been theoretical in character. His last blunder, however, is at once fatal. He should have played 9. ...Q—K 3 or, even more prosaically, 9. ...B×Kt ch ; 10. P×B, Q×R ch etc., breaking the back of any attacking possibilities available to his opponent. Now Tarrasch announces mate in three.

10. R—Q 8 ch   K—B 2
11. B—B 4 ch   Q or B—K 3
12. Kt×P mate !

A finish as pretty as it is drastic.

138. NUREMBERG, 1889–90 ?

FRENCH DEFENCE

It is always worth while to observe expert practitioners of this defence avoiding the drawing perils of the Exchange Variation. In this game Tarrasch proves once more that it takes two to make a draw, and that if either player is imbued with fighting spirit, even the stodgiest variation is bound to take on new life.

| *White* | *Black* |
| M. Kürschner | Dr. S. Tarrasch |

1. P—K 4   P—K 3
2. P—Q 4   P—Q 4
3. P×P   P×P
4. B—Q 3   B—Q 3
5. Kt—K B 3   Kt—K B 3
6. O—O   O—O
7. P—B 3   B—K Kt 5 !

Putting an end to the symmetry, an important consideration if Black wishes to play for a win. In later years Nimzovich was to improve on this system by castling on the Queen's side.

8. B—K 3   Q—Q 2
9. Q Kt—Q 2   Kt—B 3
10. Q—B 2   Q R—K 1
11. Kt—R 4   Kt—K 2
12. B—K Kt 5   Kt—Kt 3 ? !

He submits to the weakening of his Pawn position for the sake of opening the K Kt file and seeking complications.

13. Q B×Kt   P×B
14. Kt—B 5 ?

Feeble. Correct was 14. B—B 5, forcing the elimination of Black's Q B, after which White's control of K B 5 would create serious problems for his opponent.

14. ......   B—B 5 !

Good. White prevents Kt—R 6 ch and also threatens to win a piece with ...K B×Kt.

15. Kt—Q Kt 3

This Knight will be useless for the remainder of the game. Kt—K Kt 3 was relatively better.

15. ......   Kt—K 2

The hostile Knight must be removed from its advantageous post.

16. Kt—B 5   Q—B 1
17. Kt×Kt ch   R×Kt
18. B×P ch ?

A serious error of judgment, since the open K R file is bound to give Black powerful attacking chances. However, White's game had already become inferior, with his Knight out of play and the possibility of controlling K B 5 having vanished. Note that if 18. P—K R 3, B×P ! ; 19. P×B, Q×P ; 20. P—B 3, B—K 6 ch ; 21. R—B 2, K—R 1 wins for Black.

18. ......   K—Kt 2
19. B—Q 3   R—R 1
20. P—K Kt 3

Apparently White is quite safe now.

20. ......   R×P!!

A very fine sacrifice which is followed up impeccably by Tarrasch. White cannot reply 21. P×B be-because of ...Q—K R 1 ! and wins.

21. K×R   Q—R 1 ch
22. B—R 7

The only chance. If 22. K—Kt 1, Q—R 6 ! (not 22. ...B—B 6 ; 23. B—R 7) ; 23. P—B 3 (...B—B 6 was threatened), B—K 6 ch ; 24. R—B 2, B×P and mate follows.

22. ......   R—K 7
23. Kt—K 6 ch ? !

An interesting albeit inadequate resource. On 23. Q—Q 3 Tarrasch intended 23. ...R—Q 7 ; 24. Q—Kt 1, P—B 4 ; 25. K—Kt 2, Q×B ; 26. R—R 1, Q—Kt 3 with a winning attack, the chief threat being 27. ...B—B 6 ch ! ; 28. K×B, Q—Kt 5 ch ; 29. K—Kt 2, Q×P ch and mate next move. If 27. Q—Kt 1, B—K 6 ; 28. R—K B 1, P—B 5 with an irresistible attack.

23. ......   R×Kt

23. ...P×Kt would of course

be answered by 24. Q—Kt 6 ch and 25. Q×B.

24. P×B

Or 24. K—Kt 2, R—K 7 ; 25. Q—Q 3, R—Q 7 ; 26. Q—Kt 1, P—K B 4 ; 27. R—R 1, B—K 6 (Tarrasch) and wins.

24. ......   P—K B 4
25. R—R 1   Q×B ch
26. K—Kt 2   Q—Kt 3

Gaining important time, as ... Q 8 ch is threatened.

27. K—B 1   B—B 6 !

The beautiful point of the attack, and much stronger than ...B—Q 8 ch.

28. R—R 2

Unfortunately he cannot play 28. R—K Kt 1 because of ...Q×R ch ; 29. K×Q, R—K R 3 and mate follows.

28. ......   Q—Kt 5 !

Another fine move, the threat being 28. ...B—K 7 ch ; 29. K—K 1, B—Q 6 ch and mate follows.

29. Q—Q 2

White is helpless. If 29. R—K 1, Q—Kt 8 ch !! forces mate, and if 29. Q—B 1, B—K 7 ch ; 30. K—K 1, B—Q 6 ch etc.

29. ......   R—K Kt 3

White resigns, as mate cannot be prevented. A brilliantly executed attack.

139. NUREMBERG, 1889–90 ?

TWO KNIGHTS' DEFENCE

WHITE's neglect of his development gives Tarrasch time to build up a murderous attack with his two Bishops.

White	Black
K. ECKART	DR. S. TARRASCH
1. P—K 4	P—K 4
2. Kt—K B 3	Kt—Q B 3
3. B—B 4	Kt—B 3
4. Kt—B 3	

Better is 4. O—O or 4. Kt—Kt 5.

| 4. ...... | Kt×P |
| 5. O—O | |

5. B×P ch, K×B ; 6. Kt×Kt, P—Q 4 is much in Black's favour, but there is no good reason for the Pawn sacrifice. 5. Kt×Kt, P—Q 4 ; 6. B—Q 3 should have been played.

| 5. ...... | B—K 2 |

This in turn is unduly conservative. 5. ...Kt×Kt is quite playable and leaves White no compensation for the Pawn.

6. Kt×Kt	P—Q 4
7. B—Kt 5	P×Kt
8. Kt×P	Q—Q 4
9. Kt×Kt	P×Kt
10. B—R 4	

A primitive attempt to keep the doubled and isolated Q B P under observation ; but the K B is put out of play thereby. Much better was 10. B—K 2, O—O ; 11. P—Q 3 with an interesting struggle in prospect between Black's mobility and an attempt to exploit his Pawn weaknesses.

| 10. ...... | O—O |
| 11. R—K 1 ? | |

Plausible as this move may seem, it constitutes a serious loss of time from which White never recovers. The proper course was 11. P—Q 3, P×P ; 12. Q×P, Q×Q ; 13. P×Q with reciprocal Pawn weaknesses in a position in which White should be able to hold his own.

| 11. ...... | B—Q B 4 |

Already threatening ...B×P ch or ...Q—Q 5.

| 12. B—Kt 3 | Q—B 4 |
| 13. Q—K 2 | B—R 3 ! |

Played in the style of the "good old days". Obviously the Q B is immune. These continued gains of time are ominous for the future of White's game.

| 14. P—B 4 | |

An ugly move, but he has no choice.

| 14. ...... | Q R—K 1 |
| 15. R—B 1 | |

If instead 15. P—Q 3, B—Kt 5 ! ; 16. B—Q 2, B×B ; 17. Q×B, P×P with a Pawn to the good ; but not 15. ...P×P ? ; 16. Q×R, Q×P ch ; 17. K—R 1, R×Q ; 18. R×R ch, B—B 1 ; 19. B—Kt 5 !, P—Q 7 (if 19. ...P—B 3 ? ; 20. P—B 5 ch etc.) ; 20. R—K Kt 1 ! (not 20. B—K 7 ? ?, Q—K 8 ch and not 20. R—Q 1 ?, P—Q B 4 ; 21.

B×P, B—Kt 2 !) and Black, being unable to prevent B—K 7, has a lost game ! (Tarrasch).

15. ......   Q—Kt 3 !

Beginning the regrouping of his pieces for the final attack. White's pitiable inability to develop makes the outcome absolutely certain.

16. B—B 2   B—B 1 !
17. K—R 1   B—K Kt 5
18. Q—K 1   Q—R 4
19. B×P   B—K 7 !

...P—K B 4 would be less conclusive because of P—B 3.

20. B×P   R—K 3
21. B—Q 7   R—K R 3

Black's attack has reached the decisive stage. If now 22. B—R 3, Q×B !; 23. P×Q, B—B 6 ch ; 24. K—Kt 1, R—Kt 3 mate.

22. P—K R 3   P—B 4 !

Black threatens 23. ...Q× P ch !; 24. P×Q, B—B 6 ch ; 25. K—R 2, B—Q 3 ch ; 26. K—Kt 1, R—Kt 3 mate.

23. P—Q 4   B—B 6 !

Forcing White's reply.

24. K—R 2   B—Q 3 ch
25. K—Kt 1   Q×P !
26. Q—K 6 ch

A last try.

26. ......   K—R 1 !
27. P×Q   R×P
Resigns

140. NUREMBERG CHESS CLUB CHAMPIONSHIP, 1889–90

ODDS OF KNIGHT *

HERE is a game which towers over the usual odds—encounter. The final combination is unusually fine, and the preceding play underlines the contrast between the master, who makes the most of his development, and the inexperienced player, who lets his advantage slip through his hands.

White   *Black*
DR. S. TARRASCH   K. MEISER

1. P—K 4   P—Q 4

The best defence at these odds ; but Black follows it up very lamely.

2. P—K 5   P—Q 5

There is no need for this, which incidentally opens a useful diagonal for White. Simply ...P—Q B 4 followed by ...Kt—Q B 3 and ... B—B 4 should have been played.

3. P—K B 4   P—Q B 4
4. B—B 4   Kt—Q B 3
5. Kt—B 3   B—Kt 5 ?

A typical tyro's mistake ; ... Kt—R 3 was in order.

* Remove White's Q Kt.

x

6. B×P ch	K×B
7. Kt—Kt 5 ch	K—K 1
8. Q×B	Kt—R 3
9. Q—R 3	Q—Q 2

It would have been simpler and stronger to post the Queen on the best available square by ...Q—Q 4.

| 10. Q—Q Kt 3 | Kt—R 4 |
| 11. P—K 6 | Q—B 3 |

Since Black has reason to fear tactical complications, it would have been prudent to return the piece with ...Kt×Q. But it is characteristic of odds-receivers that they part with material only unintentionally.

| 12. Q—K R 3 | R—Q 1 |

Black loses valuable time, as will soon be apparent. Correct was 12. ...P—K Kt 3 ; 13. O—O, B—Kt 2 ; 14. P—B 5, O—O.

| 13. O—O | P—K Kt 3 |
| 14. P—B 5 ! | |

Beginning a strong attack. If now 14. ...Kt×P ; 15. R×Kt, P×R ; 16. Q—R 5 mate.

| 14. ...... | B—Kt 2 |
| 15. P×P | R—Q 4 |

Black does not have much choice. If 15. ...P×P ; 16. Q—Q 3, Kt—B 4 ; 17. R×Kt. One can now appreciate how critical was Black's loss of time on move 12.

| 16. Kt—B 7 ! | Kt×Kt |
| 17. Kt P×Kt ch | K—B 1 |

White has two Pawns for the piece, and the far-advanced Pawn

at K B 7 gives him magnificent attacking prospects.

| 18. P—Q 3 | P—K R 3 |

B—R 6 was a strong threat.

| 19. B—Q 2 | P—Kt 3 |
| 20. Q—Kt 3 ! | |

Primarily threatening Q—Kt 8 ch and thus gaining time for the coming combination. Tarrasch is marshalling his forces for the attack in clever style.

20.	Kt—Kt 2
21. Q R—K 1	Kt—Q 1
22. R—K 4 !	R—Q 3

The K P is adequately protected (22. ...Kt×K P ? ; 23. R×Kt, Q×R ; 24. Q—Kt 8 ch and mate follows).

| 23. R—Kt 4 ! | Kt×K P |

This loses prettily, but there was no good move ; 23. ...R—R 2 would be refuted by 24. R×B or B×P.

| 24. R×B ! | |

The beginning of a charming combination.

24.	Kt×R
25. B×P !	K R×B
26. Q×Kt ch	

Tarrasch has made way for the passed Pawn in a manner which could not be excelled even by Nimzovich !

26.	K×Q
27. P—B 8(Q) ch	K—Kt 3
28. Q—B 7 ch	K—Kt 4
29. Q—B 5 ch	K—R 5
30. P—Kt 3 mate	

Truly a triumph of mind over matter !

141. NUREMBERG CHESS CLUB CHAMPIONSHIP, 1889–90

GIUOCO PIANO

Tarrasch considered this game a good example of the then "modern" strategy of playing for an accumulation of small advantages. In those early days, when the Steinitzian theories were met with ridicule more often than not, such games as this one had a freshness and originality which are far from obvious today.

White	*Black*
Dr. S. Tarrasch	K. Eckart

1. P—K 4	P—K 4
2. Kt—K B 3	Kt—Q B 3
3. B—B 4	B—B 4
4. P—B 3	Kt—B 3
5. P—Q 3	

The Giuoco Pianissimo, with which Tarrasch occasionally experimented. His victory here is due to his skill in manœuvre rather than to the opening.

5. ...•...	P—Q 3
6. B—K 3	B—Kt 3
7. Q Kt—Q 2	O—O
8. Q—K 2	B—K 3
9. B—Q Kt 5	

He wants to preserve the Bishop, which will play an unobtrusive but important rôle later on.

9.	B×B

An exchange which always came in for severe criticism from Tarrasch, who felt that the open K B file was far more important than any possible weakening of the Pawn structure. He therefore recommends the immediate ...Kt—K 2 as preferable.

10. P×B	Kt—K 2
11. P—Q 4	P—B 3
12. B—Q 3	Kt—Kt 3
13. O—O	Q—K 2
14. Kt—Kt 5	Kt—Q 2

Tarrasch suggests the withdrawal of the Bishop as better, since the ensuing exchange enables White to post his Bishop on a more effective diagonal.

15. Q—R 5	P—K R 3
16. Kt×B	Q×Kt
17. P—K R 3	Q—K 2
18. B—B 4	Kt—R 1

A very timid reply to the threat of Q×Kt. ...K—R 2 followed by ...Kt—B 3 and counterplay in the centre against White's K P was the proper course.

19. R—B 2	Kt—B 3
20. Q—B 3	Q R—Q 1
21. B—Kt 3	Q R—K 1 ?

...P—Q 4 (blocking out the

Bishop) should have been played, leaving Black with a fair game. The idea of exerting pressure on the K P turns out to be inadequate because of the miserable positions to which Black's Knights are soon consigned.

22. R—K 1   Kt—Kt 3
23. P—K Kt 4   Kt—R 5
24. Q—Kt 3   Kt—Kt 3

And not 24. ...P—K Kt 4 ? ; 25. Q R—K B 1 and wins.

25. Q R—K B 1   Kt—R 1

Increasing the protection of his K B P in order to be able to capture the K P.

26. B—B 2   Q—K 3
27. R—B 5 !

Intending P—Kt 5. Against 27. ...Q×R P Tarrasch would have played 28. P—Kt 5, Kt—R 4 ; 29. Q—B 3 (also good is 29. Q—R 4, P—K Kt 3 ; 30. Kt P×P), P—K Kt 3 ; 30. B—Kt 3, Q×P ; 31. B×P ch with the rapid collapse of Black's game in prospect.

27. ......   Kt—R 2
28. B—Kt 3   Q—Q 2
29. P—K R 4   P—K Kt 3

Black expects the Rook to retreat, whereupon he can await eventualities, answering P—Kt 5 with ...P—K R 4 and P—R 5 with ...P—K Kt 4. But Tarrasch has a surprising reply.

30. P×P !   R×P

If 30. ...P×R ; 31. P×P ch, Kt—Kt 4 ; 32. P × Kt wins easily.

31. R×R   P×R
32. Kt—B 4   K—Kt 2

The influence of the Bishop on the diagonal makes ...P—B 3 ? impossible.

33. Kt×P   Q—B 2
34. Q—B 4

Threatening Kt×Kt P ! Black misses the point, but his game was hopeless. It is true that White's "extra" Pawn is of no great value ; the decisive factor is the wretched position of Black's Knights.

34. ......   P—B 3 ?
35. Kt×Kt P   Q×Q
36. Kt×Q   R—Q Kt 1
37. P—K 5 !   P×P

There was no defence to the threatened Knight check.

38. Kt—R 5 ch   Resigns

If 38. ...K—Kt 3 ; 39. B—B 2 ch forces mate. A drastic finish !

142. NUREMBERG, 1889–90 ?

EVANS GAMBIT

THE Evans Gambit has unquestionably had more analysis lavished on it than any other opening, and the investment has been repaid by the production of more beautiful games than have resulted from any other opening. Here is a case in point.

White	Black
DR. S. TARRASCH	C. KELZ

1.	P—K 4	P—K 4
2.	Kt—K B 3	Kt—Q B 3
3.	B—B 4	B—B 4
4.	P—Q Kt 4	B×P
5.	P—B 3	B—R 4
6.	P—Q 4	P×P
7.	O—O	P×P

The famous Compromised Defence — the most extensively analysed line of play in this famous Gambit. The analyses generally produced a good game for Black, but in actual play the defence was almost always seriously handicapped by the difficulty of developing the Queen-side forces.

8.	Q—Kt 3	Q—B 3
9.	P—K 5	Q—Kt 3

Not 9. ...Kt×P because of 10. R—K 1, P—Q 3 ; 11. Q—R 4 ch.

10.	Kt×P	K Kt—K 2
11.	B—R 3	R—Q Kt 1

Contemplating the following thrust of the Q Kt P in order to drive away White's Bishops from their menacing diagonals. As the game goes, Black's harried King never has a chance to castle ; but 11. ...O—O also has its drawbacks because of the considerable delay involved in coordinating Black's pieces.

12.	Kt—Q 5 !	Kt×Kt
13.	B×Kt	P—Q Kt 4
14.	P—K 6 !	

This clever sacrifice of a third Pawn (an ingenious manœuvre which Tarrasch credits to Dufresne) makes White's attack irresistible.

14.	......	B P×P
15.	B×Kt	P×B
16.	Kt—K 5	Q—K 5

Forced—like most of Black's moves hereabouts.

17. Q—Kt 3 !

Decisive. If 17. ...R—Kt 1 ; 18. Q—Kt 5, P—Kt 5 (or 18. ...B—Kt 5 ; 19. B×B, Q×B ; 20. Kt×P) ; 19. Q R—Q 1, B—R 3 ; 20. R—Q 7.

17.	......	P—Kt 3
18.	Q—Kt 5	P—Kt 5
19.	Q R—Q 1 !	O—O

Black has apparently castled into safety, but nothing could be further from the truth !

20.	B—Kt 2	R—Kt 4

Apparently a valid defence, but now White's control of the long diagonal leads to a pretty finish.

21. Kt—B 7 ! !

Not 21. Kt—Kt 4 ?, says Tarrasch, because of ...Q×P ch !

21. ......   P—K 4

It is clear that Black cannot go in for 21. ...R×Q ; 22. Kt—R 6 mate, nor 21. ...R×Kt ; 22. R—Q 8 ch, R—B 1 ; 23. Q—B 6.

22. Kt—R 6 ch   K—R 1

If 22. ...K—Kt 2 ; 23. Q—K 7 ch wins. After. the text, Tarrasch heads straight for the mate.

23. R—Q 8   K—Kt 2
24. R×R   K×R
25. Q—B 6 ch   K—K 1
26. Kt—Kt 8   Resigns

A pleasing finish. White's Knight has worked wonders.

143. NUREMBERG, 1890

FRENCH DEFENCE

CAREFUL examination of Tarrasch's less famous games often leads us to revise our estimate of him. In the following game, for example, he shows a thorough understanding of the favourite Nimzovich strategy of surrendering the centre in order to occupy it with pieces. This game was played about fifteen years before Nimzovich made his appearance in international competition !

White	*Black*
DR. S. TARRASCH	M. KÜRSCHNER

1. P—K 4   P—K 3
2. P—Q 4   P—Q 4
3. Kt—Q 2

A move with which Tarrasch experimented frequently at this time. For the reply 3. ...P—Q B 4, see Game 18.

3. ......   Kt—K B 3
4. P—K 5   K Kt—Q 2
5. B—Q 3   P—Q B 4
6. P—Q B 3   Kt—Q B 3

Plausible but not very promising. Black's best chance here is apparently the modern Russian move ...P—Q Kt 3 ! intending ...B—R 3. The exchange of Bishops is practically unavoidable in that event, so that Black removes his most ineffectual piece and White's most useful attacking one ; in addition, White's white squares are somewhat weakened.

7. Kt—K 2   Q—Kt 3
8. Kt—B 3   P—B 3

If instead 8. ...P×P ; 9. P×P, B—Kt 5 ch ; 10. K—B 1 ! and Black's game remains cramped.

9. K P×P   Kt×B P

Steinitz recommends 9. ...Kt P ×P, which would, however, leave Black in a sorry state after 10. Kt—B 4.

10. O—O   B—Q 3
11. P×P   Q×B P

The K B is kept at Q 3 to support the contemplated ...P—K 4.

12. Q Kt—Q 4 !

Beginning the struggle between two strategical concepts : White occupies the centre with his pieces, while Black occupies the centre with his Pawns. The following play therefore revolves about the possibility of Black's successfully playing ...P—K 4.

12. ...... O—O

After 12. ...P—K 4 there might follow 13. Kt×Kt, P×Kt ; 14. Kt×P !, B×Kt ; 15. R—K 1, Kt—K 5 ; 16. Q—R 5 ch, K—Q 1 ; 17. B×Kt, P×B ; 18. R×P, B—Q 3 ; 19. B—Kt 5 ch, K—B 2 ; 20. Q—B 7 ch with a winning attack.

13. Q—K 2 R—K 1

Now 13. ...P—K 4 would be answered by 14. Kt×Kt, P×Kt ; 15. Kt×P, R—K 1 ; 16. B—K B 4, Kt—Kt 5 ; 17. B×P ch, K×B ; 18. Q—B 2 ch, K—Kt 1 ; 19. Kt—Q 3 with a winning game (Tarrasch).

Steinitz considers, however, that 13. ...B—Q 2 followed by ...Q R—K 1 would have been a stronger preparation for ...P—K 4.

14. B—K 3 Q—R 4

White threatened to win the Queen with Kt—Kt 3.

15. Kt—K Kt 5 !

An unexpected diversion which initiates a profoundly conceived attack. If now 15. ...P—K 4 ; 16. Kt×Kt, P×Kt ; 17. B×P ch, Kt×B ; 18. Kt×Kt, K×Kt ; 19. Q—R 5 ch, winning the Rook.

15. ...... B—Q 2

Against 15. ...P—K R 3 White has the fine reply 16. P—K B 4 !, with consequences which will become clear later on in the game.

16. Q—B 2 P—K R 3
17. B—R 7 ch K—B 1

He does not care for 17. ...K—R 1 ? ? ; 18. Kt—B 7 mate.

18. P—K B 4 !

Since ...P×Kt would allow White to regain the piece advantageously, he is able to take the sting out of ...P—K 4 with this excellent move.

18. ...... R—K 2
19. P—Q Kt 4 Q—Q 1

Black has no choice (if 19. ...Q—B 2 ? ; 20. Kt—Kt 5, Q—Kt 1 ; 21. Kt×B, Q×Kt ; 22. B—Q B 5).

20. Q R—K 1 P—Q Kt 3 ?

Steinitz suggests ...Q—B 1 followed by ...Kt—Q 1. The text offers no resistance.

21. Kt×Kt B×Kt
22. B—Q 4

A move that would have gladdened Nimzovich's heart.

22. ...... Kt×B

There was no good move : if 22. ...Q—Q 2 ; 23. B×Kt, P×B ; 24. Q—Kt 6 wins ; or if 22. ...Q—K 1 ; 23. Kt—B 3 followed by Kt—K 5, winning very quickly.

23. Q×Kt P×Kt

Tarrasch now announced mate in eight moves, as follows :

[See diagram next page]

24. Q—R 8 ch   K—B 2
25. P×P ch   K—Kt 3

If 25. ...B—B 5 ; 26. R×B ch,
K—Kt 3 ; 27. R×P ch, R×R ;
28. Q×P ch, K—R 4 ; 29. Q—
R 7 ch, K×P ; 30. R—B 5 ch, K—
Kt 5 ; 31. Q—R 3 mate.

26. R—B 6 ch   P×R

Or 26. ...K×P ; 27. P—R 4
ch, K—Kt 5 ; 28. R—Kt 6 ch,
K—B 5 ; 29. P—Kt 3 ch and mate
next move.

27. Q×P ch   K—R 4

Or 27. ...K—R 2 ; 28. P—
Kt 6 ch, K—R 3 ; 29. B—K 3 ch,
B—B 5 ; 30. B×B ch, K—R 4 ;
31. Q—Kt 5 mate.

28. Q—R 6 ch   K—Kt 5
29. P—R 3 ch   K—Kt 6
30. B—B 2 ch   K—B 5
31. Q—B 6 mate

144. NUREMBERG CHESS CLUB CHAMPIONSHIP, 1890–91

QUEEN'S GAMBIT DECLINED

BLACK's mishandling of the early
middle game soon leads to a lost
position. As so often happens in
Tarrasch's games with amateurs,
White's exploitation of his opponent's mistakes is most instructive.

| *White* | *Black* |
| DR. S. TARRASCH | M. KÜRSCHNER |

1. Kt—K B 3	P—Q 4
2. P—Q 4	P—K 3
3. P—K 3	P—Q B 4
4. P—B 4	Kt—K B 3
5. Kt—B 3	Kt—B 3
6. B—K 2	

Very tame ; ...Kt—K 5 would
be a good reply, or else ...B—Q 3
followed by ...P—Q Kt 3.

6.	P—Q R 3

Planning ...Q P×P, which will
only result in an improvement of
the position of White's K B.

7. O—O	Q P×P
8. B×P	P—Q Kt 4
9. B—Kt 3	B—Kt 2
10. Q—K 2	P—B 5

This allows White more freedom
in the centre.

11. B—B 2	B—Kt 5 ?

A very weak move, after which
Black soon finds himself in serious
difficulties. His tenth move having released all pressure on the
centre, a powerful reaction in the
form of P—K 4—5 may be expected. He should therefore adopt
the logical course of 11. ...Q—
B 2 ! If then 12. P—K 4, P—
K 4 ; 13. P—Q 5, Kt—Q R 4 with
fair chances ; or 11. ...Q—B 2 ;
12. P—Q R 4, P—Kt 5 ; 13. Kt—
K 4, Kt—Q R 4 again with good
counterplay.

12. P—Q R 4 !   B×Kt

12. ...Q—Kt 3 ;   13. R—Q 1,
O—O ; 14. P—K 4 would also be
unsatisfactory for Black.

13. P×B   O—O
14. P—K 4

The game has taken a very bad
turn for Black : his opponent has
two Bishops, a strong centre and
prospects of a powerful attack.
Moreover he cannot be prevented
from forcing a serious weakness in
Black's King's side.

14. ......   P—R 3

Black could not have been very
happy in making this move ; but
in any event, allowing White to play
P—K 5 and Q—K 4 and answering
the resulting threat with ...P—
Kt 3 would have been catastrophic.
In the absence of Black's K B, the
weakening of the black squares
would have been unbearable.

15. P—K 5   Kt—Q 4
16. Q—K 4   P—B 4
17. P×P e.p.   Q×P
18. B—R 3

Gaining a useful tempo for the
attack.

18. ......   K R—K 1
19. Q—R 7 ch   K—B 2
20. Kt—K 5 ch ! Kt×Kt
21. P×Kt   Q—Kt 4

21. ...Q×P ; 22. B—Kt 6 ch,
K—B 3 ; 23. B×R, R×B ; 24.
Q R—K 1 would leave Black with
the exchange down and still subject
to a powerful attack. The text
loses in a different but no less
interesting manner.

22. P—B 4 !

So that if 22. ...Kt×K B P ;
23. R×Kt ch, Q×R ; 24. B—
Kt 6 mate ! But Black has an
interesting reply.

22. ......   Q×P ch ? !

It is a pity that this clever move
is not quite good enough.

23. K×Q   Kt—B 3 ch
24. K—B 2   Kt×Q
25. B×Kt   P—Kt 3

One would now take for granted
that Black must regain the piece
with little difficulty. But Tarrasch
scotches this plan effectively.

26. P—B 5 !

The banal R—K Kt 1 would
have been answered by ...B—K 5.

26. ......   K P×P

Or 26. ...Kt P×P ; 27. R—
Kt 1 followed by B—Kt 6 ch.

27. R—K Kt 1   R—K 3
28. Q R—Q 1 !   B—B 1

If Black guards against R—Q 7
ch by playing 28. ...B—B 3, there

follows 29. B×P ch, R×B; 30.
R×R, K×R; 31. R—Q 6 ch.

29. R—Q 8!

White can now afford to part
with the K B.

29. ......   K—Kt 2
30. R×P ch   R×R
31. B×R   P—Kt 5

An intermezzo which in no way
affects the winning process.

32. B×P   P—Q R 4
33. B—Q 6   K×B
34. P—K 6   R—R 3
35. P—K 7   Resigns

A very easy game to understand,
but none the less a highly interesting one.

145. NUREMBERG CHESS CLUB CHAMPIONSHIP, 1890–91

QUEEN'S GAMBIT DECLINED

WHITE's play is an illuminating
study in progressive deterioration.
He starts out with a good position,
but his timidity prevents him from
playing the best moves. The
initiative soon slips from his hands,
and he soon finds himself exposed
to a devastating attack.

White W. HAHN	*Black* DR. S. TARRASCH
1. P—Q 4	P—Q 4
2. P—Q B 4	P—Q B 3
3. Kt—Q B 3	Kt—B 3
4. P—K 3	B—B 4
5. Q—Kt 3	B—B 1

The retreat of the Bishop is a
bitter pill for Black to swallow; 5.
...Q—Kt 3 is very likely his best
move at this point.

6. B—Q 3   P—K 3
7. K Kt—K 2

An unnaturally passive move.
Kt—B 3 is simpler and stronger.

7. ......   B—Q 3
8. B—Q 2   O—O
9. O—O—O

Castling on this wing is unob-
jectionable, but in view of the proverbial instability of positions in
which heterogeneous castling is a
feature, White would have been
better advised to castle on the other
side. Since he is not prepared to
continue in aggressive style, he
ought not to commit himself unduly.

9. ......   Q Kt—Q 2
10. Q—B 2

P—K 4 was in order. Black is
now able to seize the initiative.

10. ......   P×P
11. B×P   P—K 4
12. B—Q 3

Tarrasch prefers P—K 4 here or
on the next move. As White plays,
his Q B soon becomes worthless.

12. ......   R—K 1
13. Kt—K 4   Kt×Kt
14. B×Kt   Kt—B 3
15. B—B 5   P—K 5!
16. B×B   R×B

Now White's Bishop is useless,
and he is threatened with the opening of the Q B file.

17. Kt—B 3   Q—K 2
18. P—B 3

White hopes for some relief from
the resulting Pawn exchange, but
his hopes are soon dashed.

18. ......   P×P
19. P×P   Kt—Q 4
20. Kt—K 4

White's position is steadily getting worse. If 20. Kt×Kt ?, P×
Kt ; 21. B—B 3, P—Q Kt 4 wins
a piece. If 20. P—K 4, Kt—Kt 5 ;
21. Q—Kt 1 (on other moves,
Black continues with ...Kt—Q 6
ch and ...Kt—B 7), P—Q B 4 ;
22. P—Q 5, P—B 5 with a good
attack.

20. ......   P—Q B 4 !
21. Q—Q 3   P—B 5 !

Stronger than 21. ...P×P ch ;
22. K—Kt 1 and White regains the
Pawn with a fair game.

22. Q—K 2   P—B 4
23. Kt×B   Q×Kt
24. P—K 4

...Kt×P was threatened. But
Black is now ready for the final
assault.

24. ......   P—B 6 !
25. Kt P×P   Q—R 6 ch
26. K—Kt 1   R—K 3
27. K—R 1   Kt—Kt 5 !

Irresistible. If 28. P×Kt, R—
B 7 wins. If 28. B—B 1, Q×B P
ch ; 29. B—Kt 2 (or 29. Q—Kt 2,
Kt—B 7 ch ; 30. K—Kt 1, R—
Q Kt 3), Kt—B 7 ch ; 30. K—
Kt 1, R—Q Kt 3. White's game
now collapses very quickly.

28. B—K 1   R×B P !
29. B×R   Q×B ch
30. Q—Kt 2   Kt—B 7 ch
31. K—Kt 1   R—Q Kt 3
32. Q×R   Kt—R 6 mate

146. NUREMBERG CHESS CLUB CHAMPIONSHIP, 1890-91

ODDS OF ROOK AND KNIGHT *

A game played at such enormous
odds has little to offer, apart from
its pretty finish. However, it is
instructive to observe the effects of
Black's negligence in forcing exchange. For the odds-receiver, this
is a matter of life and death !

White	*Black*
Dr. S. Tarrasch	O. Liebhardt

1. P—K 4   P—K 4
2. Kt—K B 3   Kt—Q B 3
3. B—B 4   B—B 4
4. P—B 3   Kt—B 3

As Black will not have, the cus-

* Remove White's Q R and Q Kt and
place his Q R P at Q R 3.

tomary resource of ...B—Kt 5 ch two moves later, it would be more sensible to hold up the advance of White's centre Pawns by playing ...P—Q 3 instead of the text.

5.	P—Q 4	P×P
6.	P×P	B—Kt 3
7.	P—Q 5	Kt—Q R 4 ?

Very thoughtless : the Knight will either be lost, or else cut off for the rest of the game. ...Kt—K 2 was better, although the reply P—Q 6 would block Black's development for a long time to come.

| 8. | B—Q 3 | P—Q 3 |
| 9. | P—R 3 ! | |

Highly interesting ! As an experienced odds-giver, Tarrasch knows that his primary task is to avoid exchanges. 9. P—Q Kt 4 would win a piece, but would allow the simplifying ...B—Kt 5, crushing White's potential attacking chances and still leaving Black a Rook to the good.

| 9. | .... | P—B 4 |
| 10. | O—O ! | |

Here and on the next few moves, White could regain a piece by 10. P—Q Kt 4, P—B 5 ; 11. P×Kt, P×B ; 12. P×B. But this would involve the loss of an important attacking piece, so Tarrasch again refrains from decreasing the disparity in material.

10.	....	P—K R 3
11.	P—Q Kt 4	P—B 5
12.	B—Kt 1 !	

See the previous note. Of course, this policy of deliberately avoiding the win of the piece cannot be

recommended for serious chess ! But odds-play has its own special rules and psychological features.

12.	....	Kt—Kt 6
13.	B—Kt 2	B—Q 2
14.	Q—K 2	B—Kt 4

It is characteristic of inexperienced players that they rarely realise the value of developing new pieces. Here ...Q R—B 1 would be more useful—unless Black intends to castle on the Queen's side.

15.	P—K 5	P×P
16.	Q×P ch	Q—K 2
17.	Q—Kt 3	O—O

A case of "castling into it". Black's position is safe enough objectively, but since White's pieces are trained on the King's side, the attack will tax Black's slight defensive skill. ...O—O—O was therefore more to the point, as White would be left without any attacking goals.

18.	R—K 1	Q—Q 1
19.	Kt—R 4	B—B 2
20.	P—B 4	Kt—R 4

...R—K 1 would break the attack. If then 21. R×R ch, Kt×R ; 22. Kt—B 5, P—B 3 ; 23. Kt×P ch, K—B 1 and the attack is over.

| 21. | Q—Kt 4 | Q×P ? |

Throwing away an easy win. After 21. ...B×P ; 22. Q×Kt, Q—Kt 4 the attack would be over.

| 22. | Kt—B 5 | Q—Q 7 |

Apparently the resource that Black relied on, but it proves to be a broken reed. However, Black had no choice, in view of the threats of Q×Kt and Kt—K 7 ch.

| 23. | Kt×P ch | K—R 1 |
| 24. | Kt×P ch ! | K—Kt 1 |

If 24. ...R×Kt ; 25. Q×Kt ch and mate in two.

25.	B—R 7 ch	K×B
26.	Q×Kt ch	K—Kt 1
27.	Q—R 8 ch	K×Kt
28.	Q×P mate	

Black has been effectively punished for his failure to court exchanges.

147. NUREMBERG, 1890–92 ?

VIENNA GAME

HERE we have another instance of the resounding success of a sacrifice whose soundness is rather dubious. There is some compensation in the fact that the attack is piquant and original.

| *White* | *Black* |
| M. KÜRSCHNER | DR. S. TARRASCH |

| 1. | P—K 4 | P—K 4 |
| 2. | Kt—Q B 3 | Kt—Q B 3 |

In more modern times, 2. ... Kt—K B 3 has been played almost exclusively, so that 3. P—K Kt 3 can then be answered by 3. ... P—Q 4.

3.	P—K Kt 3	Kt—B 3
4.	B—Kt 2	B—B 4
5.	P—Q 3	P—Q R 3
6.	P—B 4	

Somewhat risky ; Kt—Q 5 or B—K 3 would be preferable.

| 6. | ...... | P—Q 3 |
| 7. | P—B 5 | |

This very quickly leads to critical play, as Tarrasch makes a strenuous attempt to break up White's advanced Pawns.

7.	......	P—K Kt 3
8.	P—K Kt 4	P—K R 4 !?
9.	B—Kt 5	

Not 9. P—Kt 5, Kt—K Kt 5 winning at least a Pawn. 9. P—K R 3 could have been answered by 9. ...R P×P ; 10. R P×P, R×R ; 11. B×R, P—Q 4 !

| 9. | ...... | Kt—Q 5 !? |

Preparing for the following daring Queen sacrifice, which Tarrasch must already have had in mind when playing his previous move.

| 10. | Kt—Q 5 | Kt×Kt |
| 11. | B×Q | Kt—K 6 |

Although at the moment Black has only a minor piece for the Queen, his opponent must play with great care.

12. Q—Q 2 Kt(Q5)×P ch
13. K—K 2

Forced.

13. ...... Kt—Q 5 ch
14. K—B 2 ?

Not 14. K—K 1 ?, B—Kt 5 !, regaining the Queen. But the clearest and simplest way to break the attack was 14. K×Kt !, Kt—Kt 6 ch ; 15. K—K 2, Kt×Q ; 16. B—B 6.

14. ...... Kt×P ch
15. K—Kt 3 ?

Here again White misses his way. 15. K—B 1 had to be played, leaving Black with two minor pieces and three Pawns against the Queen. The further course of the game would have been extremely difficult and interesting, whereas the text, surprisingly enough, loses very quickly.

15. ...... P×P

16. Q—Kt 5

Strangely enough, White has no good move. If 16. P×P, Kt×P ch ; 17. K—B 3, K×B leads to a winning attack. Or if 16. B—

Kt 5, P—R 5 ch ! ; 17. B×P (if 17. K—R 3, Kt—B 7 ch ! ; 18. Q×Kt, P—B 5 mate !), P—B 5 ch ; 18. Q×P (if 18. K—R 3, Kt—B 7 mate), P×Q ch ; 19. K×P (if 19. K—R 3, Kt—B 7 mate), R×B and White can resign.

16. ...... P—R 5 ch !

The same motif : if 17. K—R 3, Kt—B 7 mate.

17. Q×P P—B 5 ch
18. K—R 3 Kt mates

The Knight can administer mate by going to K B 7, K 6, or K B 3. A diverting finish !

148. NUREMBERG, 1892
RUY LOPEZ

THIS game is extremely interesting from the psychological point of view. White comes out of the opening with a clear advantage, but he gradually allows the initiative to slip through his fingers. The manner in which Tarrasch seizes his opportunity and gradually augments his advantage makes the latter half of the game quite absorbing.

White	Black
M. HARMONIST	DR. S. TARRASCH

1. P—K 4	P—K 4
2. Kt—K B 3	Kt—Q B 3
3. B—Kt 5	Kt—B 3
4. O—O	B—K 2
5. Kt—B 3	P—Q 3

As is well known, Tarrasch adopted this defence on only a very few occasions because of his dislike for cramped positions.

6. P—Q 4	P×P
7. Kt×P	B—Q 2
8. Kt×Kt	

B×Kt is more frequently played.

8.	P×Kt
9. B—Q 3	O—O
10. P—K R 3	

This careful move is superfluous. 10. P—B 4, P—Q 4 ; 11. P—K 5, B—B 4 ch ; 12. K—R 1, Kt— Kt 5 ; 13. Q—K 1 would be quite satisfactory for White.

10.	Kt—K 1

Black hopes to free himself with ...P—K B 4, but this objective is not easy to achieve.

11. Q—R 5	P—Kt 3
12. Q—K 2	Kt—Kt 2

12. ...P—K B 4 ? ; 13. P×P, B×P would lose a Pawn : 14. B×B, R×B ; 15. Q—B 4 ch.

13. R—K 1	

Still preventing ...P—K B 4, for if 13. ...P—K B 4 ? ; 14. P×P and the K B is attacked.

13.	B—B 3
14. B—K 3	

B—Q 2 was better, as the sequel demonstrates.

14.	R—Kt 1 !

If now 15. Q R—Kt 1, R×P !

15. Kt—Q 1	P—B 4

Preferring to strengthen the pressure rather than win a Pawn with

15. ...B×Kt P ; 16. Kt×B, R× Kt ; 17. B—Q 4, R—Kt 5 ; 18. P—Q B 3, R—R 5 and Black's Q R is in an awkward situation.

16. P—Q B 3	

White's Knight has no moves. Tarrasch now steadily improves his game.

16.	R—K 1 !
17. P—B 3	B—R 5

So that if 18. B—B 2, Kt—R 4 intending ...Kt—B 5.

18. Kt—B 2	P—B 4

At last Tarrasch has succeeded in playing this move, and has a distinctly more promising position.

19. P—Q Kt 4	

White chafes under his enforced passivity and strikes out with more energy than judgment in a futile attempt to free himself.

19.	P×Kt P
20. B×P	R—Kt 2
21. B—B 4 ch	K—R 1
22. B—Q 4	P—B 4 !

In order to avoid the loss of a Pawn, White must now part with his Q B, after which the power of Black's Bishops becomes still greater. The backwardness of Black's Q P does not matter.

23. B×Kt ch	K×B
24. B—Q 5	R—Kt 3
25. B P×P	R×Kt P
26. Q R—Kt 1	Q—Kt 3
27. Q—B 2	R—Q Kt 1
28. R—Kt 3	B—R 5
29. Q—Kt 2 ch	B—B 3

Black's Bishops are functioning magnificently.

30. R×R   P×R !

A fine move. Most players would have retaken with the Queen, in order to hold the Q Kt file and keep the passed Q B P. But Tarrasch readily renounces these advantages, for the control of the diagonal leading to White's King is more than ample compensation.

31. Q—B 1

If 31. Q—K 2, R—K 1 in conjunction with ...B—Q 5 and ... Q—B 4 would be decisive.

31. ......   B—Q 5
32. R—K 2   P×P
33. B×P

After 33. P×P, R—K B 1 the pressure would soon prove too much for White.

33. ......   R—K 1
34. Q—Q 2

...P—Q 4 was threatened. If 34. Q—K 1, B—Kt 4 wins the exchange, as Rook moves are answered by ...P—Q 4.

34. ......   B—Kt 4

White resigns, for if 35. B—Q 3, R×R wins a piece, or if 35. R— K 1, P—Q 4 ; 36. B moves, B× Kt ch ; 37. Q×B, R×R ch etc. A classic instance of the power of the Bishops.

149. NUREMBERG, 1892 ?

RUY LOPEZ

ANOTHER example of Tarrasch's famous constriction technique. His opponent goes astray in the opening and is never able to overcome this handicap. Black's difficulties point to the need for playing the opening with an eye to the later play. In this game one feels that Harmonist's treatment of the opening was completely lacking in foresight.

White   *Black*
DR. S. TARRASCH   M. HARMONIST

1. P—K 4   P—K 4
2. Kt—K B 3   Kt—Q B 3
3. B—Kt 5   Kt—B 3
4. O—O   Kt×P
5. P—Q 4   B—K 2
6. P—Q 5 ! ?

A novelty ; he varies from the almost obligatory 6. Q—K 2

6. ......   Kt—Q 3
7. Kt—B 3

Stronger than 7. B×Kt ?, Q P× B ; 8. P×P, P—B 3 ; 9. P×P, B×P ; 10. B—K 3, O—O (Tchigorin-Zukertort, London, 1883) and Black has an excellent game.

7. ......   P—K 5

Tarrasch recommends 7. ... Kt×B ; 8. Kt×Kt, Kt—Kt 1 as preferable.

8. Kt—Q 2   Kt × B

Alternatives here are 8. ...P—K 6 !? or 8. ...Kt—Q 5 ; 9. B—R 4, O—O ; 10. K Kt × P, Kt × Kt ; 11. Kt × Kt, Kt—B 4 ; 12. B—B 4 (Tarrasch-Taubenhaus, Frankfort, 1887) with a somewhat freer game for White.

9. Kt × Kt   Kt—K 4
10. Kt × K P

Less energetic than 10. P—Q 6 ! P × P ; 11. Kt × K P, O—O ; 12. Kt(Kt 5) × Q P (Tarrasch-Metger, Nuremberg, 1888) with a wretched position for Black. But even the quieter text move leaves White with a clearly preferable game.

10. ......   P—Q 3
11. P—K B 4   Kt—Kt 5
12. P—K R 3   Kt—R 3

12. ...Kt—B 3 appears more natural, but after 13. Kt × Kt ch, B × Kt ; 14. R—K 1 ch, B—K 2 ; 15. Q—K 2 Black will not be able to castle.

13. Kt—Q 4 !

So that if 13. ...O—O ; 14. P—B 5 with a magnificent attacking position.

13. ......   Kt—B 4
14. Kt × Kt   B × Kt
15. Kt—Kt 3   B—Q 2

Black has rid himself of the misplaced Knight, but the cardinal defect of his position—its cramped character—still remains.

16. P—B 5

Now Black's two Bishops will play a sorry rôle throughout the game !

16. ......   O—O
17. Q—Kt 4   B—K B 3

White was threatening 18. B—R 6, B—K B 3 ; 19. Kt—R 5, winning the exchange.

18. Kt—R 5   K—R 1
19. B—Q 2   R—B 1

After 19. ...B × P ; 20. Q R—Kt 1 White would regain the Pawn advantageously and eventually utilise the Q R for the attack by means of R—Kt 3—Kt 3.

20. Q R—K 1   P—B 3

A feeble attempt at counterplay which is defeated easily enough.

21. Kt × B   Q × Kt
22. B—B 3

A splendid post for the Bishop. White's superiority must prove decisive very quickly.

22. ......   Q—R 3
23. R—K 7   R—B 2

Or 23. ...Q R—Q 1 ; 24. R—B 3, followed by R—Kt 3 and wins.

24. K R—K 1   P × P

24. ...P—B 3 would be of no
avail : 25. B—R 5, P—Q Kt 3 ;
26. B—Q 2 ! P—K Kt 4 ; 27. P×
P winning a piece.

25. R×B !   R×R
26. P—B 6   Resigns

26. ...K R—Q 1 is refuted by
27. Q×R ! An instructive game.

150. NUREMBERG, 1892

RUY LOPEZ

IN this game Tarrasch effortlessly
refutes an old-fashioned line of play
in this opening. In recent years
we have seen many revivals of old
moves that were discarded decades
ago, but it is safe to say that 8. ...
Kt—K 2 will never be disinterred.

White	*Black*
DR. S. TARRASCH	S. TAUBENHAUS

1. P—K 4   P—K 4
2. Kt—K B 3   Kt—Q B 3
3. B—Kt 5   Kt—B 3
4. O—O   Kt×P
5. P—Q 4   P—Q R 3
6. B—R 4   P—Q Kt 4

Black has transposed from the
Berlin Defence into Tarrasch's
favourite variation.

7. B—Kt 3   P—Q 4
8. P×P   Kt—K 2 ?

Surely an extraordinary notion !
Black holds up his development by
wasting two moves to bring this
Knight to an inferior position !
...B—K 3 is of course simpler and
better.

9. P—Q R 4   B—K 3
10. Q—K 2   P—Q B 3
11. P—B 3

Preserving the K B in the event
of ...Kt—Q B 4.

11. ......   Kt—Kt 3
12. Kt—Q 4 !

Gaining time for the advance of
the K B P. In the event of 12.
...Q—Q 2 there might follow 13.
P×P, B P×P ; 14. Kt×P !

12. ......   B—Q 2
13. P×P   R P×P
14. R×R   Q×R

The foregoing exchanges have
removed Black's Queen from the
scene of action. What now follows
leads to a surprisingly abrupt conclusion.

15. B—B 2   Kt—B 4
16. P—K B 4   B—K 2

Loses a piece. 16. ...Kt—K 3 ;
17. Kt×Kt !, P×Kt ; 18. Q—R 5,
K—B 2 ; 19. P—B 5 (not 19. B×
Kt ch ?, P×B ! ; 20. Q×R, B—
B 4 ch) likewise offered little hope.

17. P—B 5   Resigns

If 17. ... Kt—B 1 ; 18. P—B 6
wins a piece ; or if 17. ...Kt—
K R 5 ; 18. P—K Kt 3 with the
same result.

151. NUREMBERG, 1892

EVANS GAMBIT

THIS is a romantic game of the cut-
and-thrust type. Tarrasch displays courage and ingenuity in
warding off a dangerous attack until
he is finally able to seize the initiative.

| White | Black |
S. TAUBENHAUS	DR. S. TARRASCH
1. P—K 4	P—K 4
2. Kt—K B 3	Kt—Q B 3
3. B—B 4	B—B 4
4. P—Q Kt 4	B×P
5. P—B 3	B—R 4
6. P—Q 4	P×P
7. O—O	P×P

Having accepted the gambit, Tarrasch decides to make a thorough
job of it and go in for the celebrated
"Compromised Defence". Black
wins two Pawns, but in return he
must submit to a troublesome backwardness in development.

8. Q—Kt 3	Q—B 3
9. P—K 5	Q—Kt 3

Not 9. ...Kt×P because of 10.
R—K 1, P—Q 3 ; 11. Q—R 4 ch.

10. Kt×P	K Kt—K 2
11. Kt—K 2	

B—R 3 is more forceful.

11.	P—Q Kt 4

An attempt to gain some freedom
by offering one of the extra Pawns.
White prefers to concentrate on his
attack.

12. B—Q 3	Q—K 3
13. Q—Kt 2	Kt—Kt 3
14. Kt—B 4	Kt×Kt
15. B×Kt	P—K R 3
16. K R—Q 1	P—R 3
17. Q R—B 1	

Without having any definite
threats, White continues to post his
pieces on favourable posts, thus
accentuating the uncomfortable
character of Black's position.

17.	B—Kt 2
18. B—K 4	

"Now that both players have
demonstrated what fine memories
they have," Tarrasch comments
drily, "the real play at last begins."

18.	B—Kt 3
19. Kt—R 4	O—O—O

White was threatening B—B 5.
But Black's troubles are only beginning.

20. P—R 4 ?	P×P ?

It is not clear how White would
reply to 20. ...P—Kt 4. If 21.
P×P, P×P ; 22. B—B 5, Q—K 2 ;
23. Q×P, P×B ; 24. R×Kt, B×
R ; 25. Q×B, K—Kt 1 ; 26. Q—
R 4, Q×Kt ; 27. R—R 1, Q×P
ch ; 28. K—R 1, P—B 3. Black
is safe.

21. B—Q 5	Q—Kt 5
22. B—K Kt 3	P—Kt 4
23. Kt—B 3	K R—B 1
24. R—B 4	Q—B 4
25. K R—Q B 1	

White's concentration of force on the Q B file is very menacing, but Tarrasch shows considerable confidence in his precarious position by resorting to the following daring counterstroke :

25.	P—B 3 ! ?
26. B—K 4	Q—K 3
27. P×P !	Q×P !

Not 27. ...P—Q 4, says Tarrasch, because of 28. B—B 5 !, Q×B ; 29. R×Kt !, B×R ; 30. R×B and it is difficult to meet the threat of 31. Q×B (if 30. ...K—Kt 2 ; 31. R×P ch wins, or if 30. ...Q—Q 6 ; 31. Q—B 1).

28. Kt—K 5 !

The Knight cannot be captured : 28. ...Kt×Kt ; 29. R×P ch, B×R ; 30. Q×B mate ; or 29. ...K—Kt 1 ; 30. R×B ch, K—R 1 ; 31. R×B ch etc.

28. ......   P—R 6 !

This lowly Pawn is destined to win the game ! If now 29. Q×P ?, B×P ch ; 30. K—R 1 (not 30. B×B ?, Q×B ch ; 31. K—R 1, Q—B 8 ch and mate follows), B×B and wins.

29. Q—B 2 !	P—Q 4 !
30. R×Kt	B×R
31. Kt×B ?	

The losing move. Tarrasch points out a forced draw by 31. B—B 5 ch !, Q×B ; 32. Q×B, K—Kt 1 ! ; 33. Kt—Q 7 ch !, K—R 2 ! ; 34. Kt×B, P×Kt ; 35. Q—B 7 ch, K—R 1 ; 36. Q—B 6 ch etc.

31. ......   P×B

| 32. Kt×R | Q×Kt |
| 33. Q—B 6 | |

Q×P at once would have saved time. Black now succeeds in beating off the attack.

33.	Q—Q 7
34. Q—K 6 ch	K—Kt 2
35. Q×P ch	K—R 2
36. Q—Q B 4	R—Q 1 !

Stronger than the greedy ...B×P ch which would leave the B P in a feeble state.

37. P—R 3   Q—Q 6 !

Forcing the exchange of Queens, for if 38. Q—K Kt 4, R—Q 5 ; 39. Q—B 8, Q×B ! ; 40. P×Q, R—Q 1 ch and wins (Tarrasch).

| 38. Q×Q | R×Q |
| 39. K—B 1 | |

White is helpless against the hitherto puny Q R P ! Thus if 39. B×P, B×B ; 40. R×P ch, K—Kt 3 ; 41. R—B 2 (or 41. R—B 1, P—R 7 ; 42. K—R 2, R—Q 7 ; 43. K—Kt 3, R—Kt 7 ; 44. R—Q R 1, K—Kt 4 and wins), R—Q 8 ch ; 42. K—R 2, K—Kt 4. White's Rook must remain on the second rank (else ...P—R 7) so

that ...K—Kt 5—Kt 6 is conclusive.

| 39. ...... | B—Q 5 |
| 40. R × P ch | |

If 40. K—K 2, R × B wins
easily.

40.	K—Kt 3
41. R—B 2	B—Kt 7
42. K—K 2	R—Kt 6

White resigns. A thrilling
struggle.

152. NUREMBERG, 1892 ?

GIUOCO PIANO

TARRASCH embarks on an attack
which is so daring and so surprising
that his opponent crumples up in
short order.

| *White* | *Black* |
| DR. S. TARRASCH | S. TAUBENHAUS |

1. P—K 4	P—K 4
2. Kt—K B 3	Kt—Q B 3
3. B—B 4	Kt—B 3
4. P—Q 3	B—B 4
5. P—B 3	P—Q 3
6. B—K 3	

The quiet opening play gives no
hint of the wild turn the game will
take later on.

6.	B—Kt 3
7. Q Kt—Q 2	B—K 3
8. B—Q Kt 5	

As in Game 141, Tarrasch
strives to preserve the valuable
Bishop.

| 8. ...... | O—O |

9. Q—K 2	Kt—K 2
10. P—Q 4	Kt—Kt 3
11. O—O	Kt—R 4
12. P—K Kt 3	

"He had to keep one of the ad-
verse Knights away from his weak
point at K B 4, and the necessity for
this advance is not pleasant for his
King's side ; but this is also the
initiation of a profoundly conceived
scheme" (Steinitz).

12. Kt × P ? would be a blunder
because of ...Q Kt—B 5 etc.

| 12. ...... | B—Kt 5 |
| 13. P—K R 3 ! ? | |

"The depth of this can only be
estimated after careful study of the
subsequent play and the intricate
entanglements arising from the
possibilities that were open to each
side" (Steinitz).

| 13. ...... | B × R P |
| 14. Kt—Kt 5 ! | B × R |

Likewise after 14. ...Q Kt—
B 5 ; 15. P × Kt, B × R ; 16. Q—
R 5 Tarrasch would have had a
powerful and probably winning
attack.

| 15. Q × Kt | P—K R 3 |
| 16. Kt × B ! | |

"The position judgment of which
this mode of recapture is the pro-
duct bears the stamp of mastery.
It was evidently selected in preference to the apparently strong 16.
R × B, but is more powerful than
the latter : 16. R × B, P × Kt ; 17.
B × P, Kt—K 2 ; 18. K—Kt 2,
P—K B 3 ; 19. B—B 4 ch, P—Q 4
etc." (Steinitz).

16.	P×Kt
17. B×P	

Despite his material advantage, Black has a lost game. His pieces do not cooperate properly, whereas all of White's pieces can be brought to bear powerfully on the hostile King.

17.	Kt—K 2

Against 17. ...Q—B 1 Tarrasch gives 18. B—Q B 4, P—Q B 3 (so as to answer Q×Kt with ...P—Q 4) ; 19. Kt—K 3, P×P ; 20. Kt—Kt 4 (threatening Kt—B 6 ch followed by Q×Kt ch etc.), P—Q 4 (if 20. ...B—Q 1 ; 21. Kt—R 6 ch) ; 21. K—Kt 2, P×B ; 22. R—K R 1, P—B 3 (if 22. ...R—K 1 ; 23. Q—R 7 ch and 24. Q—R 8 ch ! leads to mate) ; 23. Kt—R 6 ch, K—R 2 ; 24. Kt—B 5 ch, K—Kt 1 ; 25. Kt—Q 6 and wins.

18. Kt—K 3	P×P

Tarrasch points out that if 18. ...P—Q B 3 ; 19. B—Q B 4, Q—Q 2 ; 20. Kt—Kt 4 (threatens Kt—B 6 ch), P—Q 4 ; 21. Kt—B 6 ch, P×Kt ; 22. B×B P, Kt—Kt 3 ; 23. Q—R 6 wins.

19. Kt—Q 5	P—K B 3
20. B—Q B 4 !	Resigns

For if 20. ...R—B 2 ; 21. Kt×P ch and mate follows. If 20. ...Kt×Kt ; 21. B×Kt ch, R—B 2 ; 22. Q×R ch, K—R 1 ; 23. Q—R 5 mate. The rapidity with which Black's game collapsed from the diagrammed position speaks well for Tarrasch's judgment of the position.

153. NUREMBERG, 1892

ODDS OF PAWN AND MOVE *

TARRASCH manages his attack very cleverly so that it increases to a crescendo of crushing force. This is one of the most instructive games ever played at these odds.

White	*Black*
W. HAHN	DR. S. TARRASCH

1. P—K 4	P—Q 3
2. P—Q 4	Kt—K B 3
3. B—Q 3	

Premature. Kt—Q B 3 should have been played first, as the Bishop might have been more useful at Q B 4.

3.	P—K 4
4. P—Q B 3	Kt—B 3
5. B—K 3	B—K 2
6. Kt—B 3	Kt—K Kt 5 !

This useful move indicates that White's 5th move was a repetition of the error of his 3rd. Black gains time, as ...Kt×B can hardly be permitted because of its bad effect on White's Pawn structure.

The banal 6. ...O—O would

* Remove Black's K B P.

have been inferior because of P×P followed by B—B 4 ch forcing the exchange of Queens.

7. B—Q 2	O—O
8. P—K R 3	Kt—B 3
9. B—K 3	Q—K 1

A move often seen in positions where the K B P is not at K B 2. The Queen's next move wins immediately!

| 10. Q Kt—Q 2 | K—R 1 |
| 11. Q—B 2 | P—Q R 3 |

Tarrasch is waiting to see how White will castle.

| 12. O—O—O | P—Q Kt 4 |
| 13. Kt—Kt 3 | Kt—Q 2 |

In order to avoid the occupation of his Q B 4 after P×P. The proper reply to the text was P—Q 5 followed by Kt—R 5, leaving Black with little chance for obtaining the initiative.

| 14. K Kt—Q 2 ? | P×P ! |

Alertly played.   15. P×P allows ...Kt—Kt 5, while   15. B×P would lose a Pawn.

15. Kt×P	Kt×Kt
16. P×Kt	P—B 4
17. Kt—B 3	

Another timid move. P—Q 5 was best, so that Black's eventual ...P—B 5 would give White's pieces access to Q 4.

| 17. ...... | P—B 5 |
| 18. B—K 2 | Kt—Kt 3 |

Threatening 19. ...P—Q 4 ; 20. P—K 5, B—B 4 ; 21. Q—Q 2, P—

B 6 ! ;   22. P×P ?,   B—R 6 ch (Tarrasch).

19. P—K Kt 4 ?

P—Q 5 was still available.

19.	P—Q 4
20. P—K 5	P—Kt 5
21. Kt—K 1	

White strives for P—B 4 ; but the move has little value in any event, as Black's attack is developing with alarming rapidity.

| 21. ...... | B—Q 2 |

Already threatening to win the exchange with ...B—R 5, since P—Kt 3 would not be a feasible reply.

| 22. K—Kt 1 | P—Kt 6 ! |

In contrast to his opponent, Tarrasch plays with commendable energy.

23. Q—B 1

If instead 23. P×P, P×P ; 24. Q×P, R—Q Kt 1 and Black's attack should be decisive.

| 23. ...... | R—B 1 |
| 24. P—B 4 | P—B 6 ! |

To this there is no good reply : if 25. R P×P, P×P ; 26. Q×P, Kt—R 5 !

| 25. Kt P×P | P—Kt 7 ! |
| 26. Q—Q 2 | |

If 26. Q—B 2, B—R 5 wins ; if 26. Q×P, Kt—R 5 etc.

| 26. ...... | Kt—R 5 |

27. P—B 4   P×P
28. Kt—B 2

A despairing effort to hold back
the murderous B P.

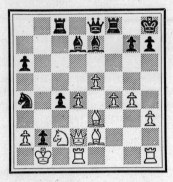

28. ......   B—Q B 3 !

Much stronger, says Tarrasch,
than the more obvious 28. ...P—
B 6 ? for after 29. Q—K 1, B—
Q B 3 White has a good counter in
30. P—Q 5.

29. R—R 2

If 29. P—Q 5, B×P ! Or 29.
K R—B 1, P—B 6 ; 30. Q—K 1,
B—Q 4 ; 31. B—B 3, B×P ch ! ;
32. K×B, P—Kt 8(Q) ch ; 33.
R×Kt, Kt—Kt 7 ; 34. R×Kt,
Q—R 5 ch and wins (Tarrasch).

29. ......   B—Q 4
30. P—B 5   P—B 6
31. Q—K 1   Kt—Kt 3

Making way for the fatal invasion
with the Queen.

32. P—B 6   Q—R 5
33. P—R 3   Q—Kt 6
34. B—Q B 4

Or "resigns".

34. ......   B×B
35. P×P ch   K×P
36. Kt—R 1   P—B 7 ch
37. Kt×P   Q—R 7 mate

154. NUREMBERG, 1892

KING'S INDIAN DEFENCE
(IN EFFECT)

The opening of this game is surprisingly modern, but the remainder
is characteristic Tarrasch. He plays
the opening perfectly and thus acquires a considerable positional advantage. Despite valiant attempts
at "swindling", Black finds that the
two Bishops are too much to con-
tend against.

White   *Black*
DR. S. TARRASCH   S. ALAPIN

1. Kt—K B 3   P—Q 4
2. P—Q 4   P—Q B 3
3. P—B 4   Kt—B 3
4. P—K 3   P—K Kt 3
5. Kt—B 3   B—Kt 2
6. Q—Kt 3 !

Thirty years later, the Queen
move came to be accepted as best
in the fashionable Grünfeld Variation. At the time the present game
was played, Grünfeld had not been
born !

6. ....   O—O
7. B—Q 2

Another "modern" move. Black
must not reply 7. ...Kt—K 5 ? because of 8. P×P, Kt×Kt ; 9. P×
P !, winning a Pawn.

7. ....   Q—Q 3

This does not turn out satisfac-

torily. ...P—Kt 3 is doubtless
better.

8. R—B 1	Q Kt—Q 2
9. P×P !	Kt×P
10. Kt×Kt	Q×Kt

Black's position is obviously difficult. If 10. ...P×Kt ; 11. B—
Kt 4, Q—K 3 ; 12. B—Kt 5 ! with
marked advantage for White.

11. B—B 4

11. Q×Q, P×Q ; 12. R—B 7
would yield White a won ending,
but the text development with gain
of time is tempting and equally
good.

11.	Q—K R 4
12. B—Kt 4	B—B 3
13. P—K 4	

White has such a commanding
position now that it requires all
Alapin's ingenuity to hold his
position together.

13. ......   P—R 4

A trap ; the plausible 14. B—
R 3 ? would be refuted by ...P—
Q Kt 4—5.

14. B—Q 2   Q—Kt 5

White was threatening P—K R 3
and P—Kt 4.

| 15. P—K 5 | B—Kt 2 |
| 16. P—K 6 | |

Tarrasch turned down the alter-
native 16. B×P ch, R×B ; 17.
P—K 6 because of the continuation
16. ...R×Kt ;   17. P×Kt ch ?,
R×Q ;   18. P—Q 8(Q) ch, K—
B 2 ; 19. P×R, Q×Kt P ; 20. R—

B 1, B—R 6 and wins ! As he subsequently pointed out, however, 17.
P×R ! (instead of 17. P×Kt ch ?)
is crushing.

16.	Kt—B 3
17. P×P ch	K—R 1
18. O—O	P—Q Kt 4

A necessary preliminary to the
recovery of the Pawn, but the state
of his Pawn position is deplorable.

19. B—Q 3

B—K 2 at once would have
saved time.

19.	B—K 3
20. Q—Q 1	B—Q 4
21. B—K 2	Kt—K 5

If 21. ...R×P ; 22. P—K R 3
and no matter where the Queen
retreats, White must win some
material (e.g. if 22. ...Q—K 3 ;
23. Kt—Kt 5 or if 22. ...Q—B 1 ;
23. B×P).

22. Kt—K 5   Q—R 5

A trappy position : Tarrasch
points out that 23. P—K Kt 3
would be refuted by 23. ...Kt×
Kt P !, while if 23. P—B 3, Kt—
Kt 6 ! or if 23. Kt×P, B×Kt ;
24. R×B, B×P, regaining the
Pawn.

23. P—B 4	B×Kt
24. B P×B	R×P
25. R×R	B×R

Black has regained the Pawn, for
if 26. R×P ?, Q—B 7 ch ; 27. K—
R 1, B—Q 4 and wins. But Tarrasch makes the superior position
tell very effectively.

26. Q—K 1 !   Q×Q ch

He has no choice.

| 27. B×Q | B—Q 4 |
| 28. B—K B 3 | K—Kt 1 |

The alternative 28. ...Kt—Kt 4;
29. B×B, P×B ; 30. R—B 5, P—
K 3 ; 31. R×Kt P, P—R 5 would
have held out longer without offering any real hope. After the text,
Tarrasch cuts off the Knight's
retreat.

| 29. P—K R 4 ! | K—B 2 |

Black must try to bolster the
Knight's position, which is menaced
by the threat R—B 2 !—K 2.

30. R—B 2 !	K—K 3
31. R—K 2	K—B 4
32. P—Kt 4 ch	K—B 5

Now everything is "protected",
but White announces mate in three :
33. K—Kt 2, and Black is helpless
against 34. R×Kt ch and 35. B—
Q 2 mate ! A sudden and amusing
finish.

155. NUREMBERG, 1892 ?
ODDS OF ROOK *

TARRASCH carries out the attack very
prettily here. The most effective

* Remove White's Q R.

feature of this game is, however, the
manner in which Tarrasch deploys
his forces to make up for the
absence of a vital piece ! Judged
by this standard, Black fails miserably.

White	*Black*
DR. S. TARRASCH	H. ROMBERG
1. P—K 4	P—K 3
2. P—Q 4	P—Q 4
3. P—K 5	P—Q B 4
4. P—Q B 3	P—B 5 ?

Poorly played. Black should
keep up the attack on the centre
with ...Kt—Q B 3, ...Q—Kt 3
etc.

5. B—K 2	P—Q Kt 4 ?
6. Kt—K R 3	P—Q R 4 ?
7. O—O	B—K 2

At last Black brings out a piece !

| 8. P—B 4 | P—B 4 |
| 9. P—K Kt 4 | |

Tarrasch is naturally eager to
open up avenues of attack.

| 9. ...... | B—R 5 ? |

More waste of time. Simply
...Kt—K R 3 followed by ...O—
O was correct.

10. P×P	P×P
11. B—B 3	B—K 3
12. P—Kt 3	R—R 2

Again ...Kt—K R 3 should have
been played.

| 13. Kt—R 3 | |

The development of the Knights
is peculiar ! The text should have
been answered by ...P—Kt 5,

13.	......	R—Kt 2 ?
14.	P×P	Kt P×P
15.	Kt×P	B—K 2

Inglorious conclusion of the Bishop's expedition.

16. Kt—Kt 5   B×Kt ?

This allows a winning attack, but it is true that after 16. ...Q—Q 2 ; 17. Kt×Q R P, R—B 2 ; 18. P—B 4 ! Black would have his hands full.

17. Kt—Q 6 ch   K—B 1

Or 17. ...K—Q 2 ? ; 18. Kt× R followed by Kt—B 5 ch and P×B.

18. P×B !

Tarrasch prefers to retain the powerfully posted Knight.

| 18. | ...... | R—Q B 2 |
| 19. | B×P ! | B×B |

Now White is a Rook and Bishop down, but the attack is well worth it.

20. R×P ch   Kt—B 3

Black cannot retain all his material : if 20. ...K—K 2 ; 21. B—R 3, K—Q 2 ; 22. Q—Kt 4, K—B 3 ; 23. P—B 4 ! with a devastating attack ; if 20. ...R—B 2 ; 21. Kt×R, B×Kt ; 22. P—K 6 ; or, if 20. ...B—B 2 ; 21. B—R 3 is crushing.

21. Kt P×Kt !

Stronger than 21. K P×Kt, for now White's Bishop enters the fray.

| 21. | ...... | P—Kt 3 |
| 22. | B—R 6 ch | K—Kt 1 |

Black is doing penance for his previous sins.

23. P—B 7 ch   B×P

If 23. ...R×P ; 24. Q—B 3 ! !, B×Q (if 24. ...R×R ; 25. Q× B ch forces mate ; if 24. ...P×R ; 25. Q—Kt 3 ch forces mate ; if 24. ...Q×Kt ; 25. R×R transposes into the main variation) ; 25. R× R, Q×Kt ; 26. R—Kt 7 ch, K—B 1 ; 27. P×Q, K—K 1 ; 28. R—K 7 ch, K—Q 1 ; 29. B—Kt 5, K—B 1 (Black is lost in any event) ; 30. R—B 7 mate (Tarrasch).

24. R×B !   R×R
25. Q—Kt 3

Forcing the win, which has been prepared by the previous sacrifices.

25. ......   Q—B 2

Kt×R would now win easily, but Tarrasch has a more elegant method.

26. P—K 6   R—K 2
27. Kt—K 8 ! !   R×Kt
28. P—K 7 ch and mate next move

Moral : note the utter worthlessness of Black's extra material !

156. NUREMBERG, 1892 ?

RUY LOPEZ

THIS game lacks brilliant features, but it is a fine example of the utilisation of a positional advantage.

White	Black
DR. S.	DR. K.
TARRASCH	HOLLÄNDER

1.	P—K 4	P—K 4
2.	Kt—K B 3	Kt—Q B 3
3.	B—Kt 5	P—Q 3
4.	P—Q 4	B—Q 2
5.	Kt—B 3	K Kt—K 2

A solid but cramped defence.

6.	O—O	Kt—Kt 3
7.	B—K 3	B—K 2
8.	Q—Q 2	O—O
9.	Q R—Q 1	B—Kt 5
10.	B—K 2	Q—K 1

Black has little prospect of putting his pieces to good use; the future development of the game will be dictated by White.

11.	P—K R 3	B × Kt

After 11. ...B—Q 2 ; 12. P—Q 5, Kt—Q 1 ; 13. P—K Kt 4 Black's game would be unbearably cramped.

12.	B × B	P × P

Continuing the exchanging policy so as to free his position.

13.	B × P	Kt × B
14.	Q × Kt	B—B 3
15.	Q—Kt 4	B × Kt

Or 15. ...R—Kt 1 ; 16. Kt—Q 5, B—Q 1 ; 17. K R—K 1 and White's game is appreciably freer.

16.	Q × B	Q—B 3

This creates a certain weakness in Black's Queen's side Pawns ; but the alternatives are not inviting.

17.	Q × Q	P × Q
18.	P—K Kt 3	P—B 3
19.	B—Kt 2	Kt—K 4

Loss of time ; he should have tried ...Q R—Kt 1 followed by ...P—Q B 4.

20.	P—Kt 3	Q R—K 1
21.	P—K B 4	Kt—Q 2

Black should have played ...Kt—Kt 3. The text permits a clever breakthrough which results in a won ending.

22.	P—K 5 !	B P × P

The weakness of his doubled Q B P and the unfortunate position of his Knight create irremediable difficulties for Black. He has little choice here if he wishes to save a Pawn, since if 22. ...P—Q 4 ; 23. P—B 4 ! and a Pawn is lost.

23.	B × P	R—K 2
24.	B × Kt	R × B
25.	P × P	R × R ch
26.	K × R	R—B 2 ch
27.	K—Kt 2	P × P

Black has managed to retain material equality, but the ending is lost for him.

28. R—Q 8 ch !   R—B 1
29. R × R ch   K × R

Now we have reached a King and Pawn ending in which White has the decisive advantage of a distant majority of Pawns. This advantage very quickly proves decisive.

30. K—B 3   K—K 2
31. K—K 4   K—Q 3
32. P—Q Kt 4 !   P—Q R 3

If Black keeps all his Pawns on their original squares, White's Queen's side Pawns advance to the fifth rank, after which P—Kt 6 will be decisive.

33. P—Q R 4   P—Kt 3
34. P—B 4   P—Q R 4

Desperation ; if 34. ...P—B 3 ; 35. P—Kt 5, R P × P ; 36. B P × P wins. Or 34. ...K—K 3 ; 35. P—Kt 5, P—Q R 4 ; 36. P—B 5 and wins.

35. P × P

Not 35. P—Kt 5 ?, K—B 4 and *Black* wins !

35. ......   K—B 4
36. K × P   Resigns

157. NUREMBERG, 1892 ?

ODDS OF ROOK *

BLACK plays well up to a point, but eventually allows his formidable opponent to work up a crushing attack.

* Remove White's Q R and place his Q R P at Q R 3.

White	*Black*
DR. S. TARRASCH	C. SCHROEDER

1. P—K 4	P—Q 4
2. P—K 5	P—Q B 4
3. P—K B 4	P—K 3
4. Kt—K B 3	P—Q 5
5. P—B 4	

Tarrasch's handling of the opening is not particularly scintillating, but this does not matter much in an odds game.

5.	P × P e.p.
6. Kt P × P	Kt—K 2
7. P—Q 4	P × P
8. P × P	Kt—Q 4
9. B—Q 3	Kt—Q B 3
10. O—O	Q—Kt 3

Unlike most players in his category, Black is developing his pieces systematically and effectively.

11. K—R 1	B—Q 2

Now threatening the Q P.

12. B—K 4	B—K 2
13. P—B 5 !	

In view of Black's excellent development and freedom from weaknesses, Tarrasch tries to create complications.

13.	P × P ?

This transaction does not turn out well for Black. ...O—O—O should have been played.

14. B × Kt	Q × Kt
15. B—Kt 3 !	Q—R 8 ?

In order to hinder P—Q 5. However, the move has sad consequences and therefore 15. ...Q—

K 5 ; 16. R—K 1, Q—Kt 5 should have been tried, although 17. P—Q 5 would have been unpleasant.

16. R—K 1 !   B×P

This is refuted by Tarrasch in fine style, but it is difficult to suggest something better. If, for example, 16. ...O—O—O ; 17. P—Q 5, Kt—R 4 ; 18. Q—B 2 ch followed by B—Kt 2 with advantage. If 16. ...O—O ; 17. P—Q 5, Kt—R 4 ; 18. P—K 6, P×P ; 19. Kt—K 5 with good attacking chances. The latter variation was, however, Black's best chance.

17. B×P ch !   K—B 1

If 17. ...K—Q 1 ? ? or ...K—K 2 ? ? ; 18. B—Kt 5 ch wins the Queen. If 17. ...K×B ; 18. Q—Kt 3 ch, K—K 1 (not 18. ...B—K 3 ? ; 19. Kt—Kt 5 ch) ; 19. B×B with a winning game.

18. Q—R 4   Q×B

Black has little choice. It is true that he has more than enough material for the Queen, but this state of affairs does not last very long.

19. R×Q   B×R
20. B—R 2   P—Q Kt 4

White threatened to win a piece with Q—B 4. If 20. ...R—B 1 ; 21. P—Q 5, Kt—Kt 1 ; 22. Q—Kt 4 ch winning easily.

21. Q×Kt P   Kt×K P

Equivalent to resignation.

22. Q—B 5 ch   K—K 1
23. Kt×Kt   R—K B 1
24. Q—Q 6   R—Q 1
25. Kt—B 6   Resigns

For if 25. ...B×Kt ; 26. Q—K 6 mate. The "Epaulette" Mate.

158. NUREMBERG, 1893 ?

FRENCH DEFENCE

BLACK plays the opening weakly and is bowled over mercilessly.

White   *Black*
DR. S. TARRASCH   M. KÜRSCHNER

1. P—K 4   P—K 3
2. P—Q 4   P—Q 4
3. B—Q 3   Kt—K B 3

...P—Q B 4 is more promising.

4. P—K 5   K Kt—Q 2
5. Kt—K B 3   P—Q B 4
6. P—B 3   Kt—Q B 3

And here ...P—Q Kt 3 (with a view to ...B—R 3) is worth considering.

7. O—O   P—B 3
8. R—K 1   P—B 4

Giving up his chances of initiative in the centre. ...B—K 2 followed by ...O—O was indicated.

9. B—K 3   P—Q B 5 ?

A fundamental positional blunder which completely removes the tension in the centre. ...B—K 2 was still in order.

Black is mistakenly under the impression that he is blocking the position and protecting himself from attack. Actually he is exposing himself to devastating counter-action.

| 10. B—B 2 | B—K 2 |
| 11. P—Q Kt 3 ! | P—Q Kt 4 ? |

There was nothing better than 11. ...P×P, although after 12. P×P followed by P—B 4, Black's centre would be under heavy attack.

12. P—Q R 4

Decisive.

12.	Kt P×P
13. P×B P	P×P
14. P—Q 5 !	

Black's position crumbles now with alarming rapidity.

14.	Q Kt×P
15. P×P	Kt×Kt ch
16. Q×Kt	Kt—Kt 3
17. Q×P	B—B 3
18. B—B 5 !	B—Kt 2

Allowing a pretty finish ; but if 18. ...Q—B 2 ; 19. Q—R 5 ch, P—Kt 3 ; 20. B×P ch winning easily.

| 19. Q—Kt 6 ch ! | P×Q |
| 20. B×P mate | |

159. NUREMBERG, 1893 ?
ODDS OF ROOK *

BLACK'S indifferent handling of the opening allows a concentration of murderous force against his King. So strong is this attack that even the disappearance of White's Queen does not diminish its ferocity !

| *White* | *Black* |
| DR. S. TARRASCH | H. ROMBERG |

1. P—K 4	P—K 4
2. Kt—K B 3	Kt—Q B 3
3. P—Q 4	P×P
4. B—B 4	B—B 4
5. Kt—Kt 5	

An old-fashioned continuation, discarded many decades ago. It promises success only against weak opposition.

| 5. ...... | Kt—R 3 |
| 6. Q—R 5 | O—O |

...Q—B 3, intending ...Q—Kt 3, would have been safer.

7. P—B 4   Q—K 1 ?

A curiously timid move which removes the Queen from active participation in the game. Tarrasch recommends ...P—Q 4 followed by ...B—K Kt 5.

8. O—O   P—Q 6 ch ?

* Remove White's Q R.

This meaningless check gives White's Q Kt access, via Q B 3, to the powerful square Q 5. Hence it would have been far wiser to omit the check and play ...P—Q 3 directly. Another good defensive idea was ...K—R 1 followed by ...P—B 3.

9. K—R 1   P×P
10. Kt—Q B 3   P—Q 3

There was still time for ...K—R 1 followed by ...P—B 3.

11. P—B 5   Kt—K 4
12. Kt—Q 5 !   K—R 1

Despite Black's material superiority and the fact that the game has barely begun, Black is already lost ! Tarrasch indicates the amusing alternative 12. ...Kt×B ; 13. Kt —B 6 ch, P×Kt ; 14. Q×Kt, P× Kt ; 15. P—B 6 and mate follows.

13. P—B 6   B—K Kt 5

At last a developing move. But it comes too late.

14. P×P ch   K×P
15. Q×Kt ch ! !

An admirably calculated sacrifice which forces the mate in all variations.

15. ......   K×Q
16. Kt—K 6 ch !

16. Kt×P dbl ch only draws : 16. ...K—Kt 3 ; 17. R—B 6 ch, K—Kt 2 ; 18. B—R 6 ch, K— Kt 1 ; 19. R—Kt 6 ch !, K×Kt (if 19. ...P×R ; 20. Kt—B 6 mate) ; 20. R—Kt 7 ch, K—K 3 ; 21. Kt —B 4 dbl ch etc.

16. ......   K—R 4

If 16. ...K—Kt 3 ; 17. R— B 6 ch and 18. R—R 6 mate.

17. Kt(Q 5)—B 4 ch   K—R 3

Or 17. ...K—R 5 ; 18. P— Kt 3 mate.

18. Kt—K 2 ch !

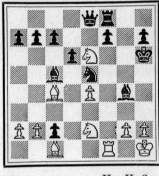

18. ......   K—Kt 3

Tarrasch points out that the somewhat stronger 18. ...K—R 4 would have held out longer and led to some fascinating possibilities : 19. R—B 6, Q×Kt ! (if 19. ... Kt—Kt 3 ; 20. Kt—Kt 3 ch, K— R 5 ; 21. B—Kt 5 mate. If 19. ...B×QKt ; 20. R—R 6 ch, K— Kt 5 ; 21. B×B mate. If 19. ... ...B×KKt ; 20. R—R 6 ch etc.) ; 20. B×Q, Kt—Kt 3 (if 20. ...B× Kt ; 21. R—R 6 mate) ; 21. B× B ch, K×B (if 21. ...K—R 5 ; 22. P—K R 3 leads to mate) ; 22. P—R 3 ch, K—R 5 (if 22. ...K— R 4 ; 23. R—B 5 ch, K—R 5 ; 24. B—Kt 5 ch, K—R 4 ; 25. P—Kt 4 mate) ; 23. K—R 2, B—B 7 (if 23. ...Kt—B 5 ; 24. R—R 6 ch, K— Kt 4 ; 25. B×Kt mate) ; 24. P— Kt 3 ch, B×P ch ; 25. Kt×B, Q R—K 1 ; 26. R—B 5 (threatening B—Kt 5 mate or R—R 5 mate), Kt—B 5 ; 27. R—R 5 ch, Kt×R ; 28. Kt—B 5 mate ! !

19. R—B 6 ch !   K×R
20. B—Kt 5 ch   K—Kt 3
21. Kt(K 2)—B 4 mate

Forceful demolition of weak opposition.

160. NUREMBERG, 1893 ?

ODDS OF KNIGHT *

BLACK plays weakly and the result is an attack which triumphs with surprising rapidity.

| *White* | *Black* |
| DR. S. TARRASCH | F. KOLB |

1. P—K B 4   P—K B 4
2. P—K 4

An eccentricity which is just as good or bad as the more customary openings at these considerable odds.

2. ......   P×P
3. P—Q 3   Kt—K B 3

Allowing White to gain time for development. ...P—K 6 was preferable.

4. P×P   Kt×P
5. B—Q 3   Kt—K B 3

5. ...P—Q 4 should be played (and, if 6. B×Kt, P×B ; 7. Q—R 5 ch, P—Kt 3 ; 8. Q—K 5, R—Kt 1 ; 9. Q×K P, Kt—B 3 followed by ...B—B 4). This game is a perfect example of how odds-receivers fritter away their advantage.

6. Kt—K B 3   P—K 3

Tarrasch suggests ...P—Q 3
    * Remove White's Q Kt.

followed by ...B—Kt 5, but the text is good enough.

7. Kt—Kt 5   B—B 4
8. B×P ?

Unsound, but luckily Black misses the proper reply.

8. ......   R—B 1 ?

Feeble. Correct was 8. ...Kt× B and if 9. Q—R 5 ch, K—K 2 and White is at a loss for a good reply.

9. B—Kt 6 ch   K—K 2
10. Q—K 2   P—Q 3

This leads to new troubles. ... Kt—B 3 should have been played first.

11. B—B 5   P—K 4
12. B×B   Q×B
13. P×P   Kt—Kt 5
14. P—K 6 !

The continuation 14. P×P dbl ch, K×P ; 15. Kt—K 4 ch, K—B 3 does not satisfy Tarrasch.

14. ......   Kt—K B 3
15. B—Q 2   Kt—B 3
16. O—O—O   Q—K 1

As is customary in such encounters, Black's material superiority is minimised by the unpleasant position of his King and the backwardness of his development.

17. B—B 3   K—Q 1
18. P—K R 4   Q—Kt 3 ?

After this plausible move, his position falls apart very rapidly. The patient course ...K—B 1— Kt 1 followed by ...P—R 3 and ...K—R 2 would have enabled Black to consolidate his position.

z

19. P—K 7 ch !   Kt × P
20. K R—K 1 !

Even stronger than the immediate Kt—K 6 ch.

20. ......   Kt—B 3

Tarrasch lists the following alternatives :

I. 20. ...R—K 1 ;   21. Kt—K 6 ch, K—B 1 ; 22. Kt × B, P × Kt ; 23. Q—K 6 ch, K—Kt 1 ; 24. Q × Q Kt etc.

II. 20. ...K Kt—Q 4 ;   21. Kt—K 6 ch, K—K 1 (or 21. ... K—Q 2 ; 22. Kt × B ch, P × Kt ; 23. Q × Kt ch) ; 22. Kt × P ch followed by Kt × Kt.

III. 20. ...Q Kt—Q 4 ;   21. Kt—K 6 ch, K—Q 2 ; 22. Q—Kt 5 ch etc.

21. Kt—K 6 ch   K—Q 2

Other King moves would lose too much material. Black is lost in any event, but the finish is a neat echo of a famous theme.

22. Kt × B ch   K—B 1
23. Q—K 6 ch   K—Kt 1

23. ...K—Q 1 ;   24. Kt × P mate would be amusing.

24. Kt—Q 7 ch   K—B 1
25. Kt × Kt dbl ch   K—Kt 1
26. Kt—Q 7 ch   K—B 1
27. Kt—Kt 6 dbl ch   K—Kt 1
28. Q—B 8 ch !   R × Q
29. Kt—Q 7 mate

A characteristic feature of such games : Black's Q R is still on its original square.

161. NUREMBERG, 1894
ODDS OF KNIGHT *

BLACK starts well, but he runs into difficulties and succumbs to a pretty finish.

White	*Black*
DR. S. TARRASCH	C. SCHROEDER

1. P—K 4	P—Q 4
2. P—K 5	P—Q B 4
3. P—K B 4	P—K 3

...B—B 4 is better.

4. Kt—K B 3	Kt—Q B 3
5. P—B 3	Q—Kt 3
6. B—Q 3	

A curious move. Tarrasch intends to play the more natural P—Q 4 later on, but he avoids it at this point because the pressure on his centre would be too embarrassing.

6.	B—Q 2
7. B—B 2	P—B 5

Creating new trouble for White, who will be unable to castle for some time to come.

8. P—Q Kt 3	P × P
9. P × P	P—Q 5

* Remove White's Q Kt.

Again preventing the natural move P—Q 4.

10. Q—K 2   P×P

Simply ...Kt—R 3 followed by further development would also be good.

11. P×P   Kt—R 3
12. Kt—Q 2   B—K 2
13. Kt—K 4   O—O

Up to this point Black has played well, but this is out of place. ...O—O—O would have brought Black's King into safety and maintained the advantage.

14. Q—Q 3

Threatening Kt—B 6 ch and mate next move.

14. ......   P—Kt 3

A serious weakness, but ...Kt—B 4 would not do because of P—K Kt 4.

15. Q—R 3

Of course not 15. Q×B ?, either R—Q 1 and White's Queen is lost.

15. ......   Kt—B 4

Or 15. ...K—Kt 2 ; 16. Kt—B 6 followed by P—B 5 ! with a winning attack.

16. P—K Kt 4   Kt—Kt 2

If 16. ...Kt—R 5 ; 17. Kt—B 6 ch wins.

17. Kt—B 6 ch   B×Kt
18. P×B   Kt—K 1
19. P—Kt 5

19. B—R 3 would be answered by 19. ...Q—R 4.

19. ......   K—R 1 ?

Running headlong into a mating attack. ...P—K R 4 ! should have been played.

20. Q—R 6 !   R—K Kt 1

There is no good defence against the following attack.

21. P—R 4   Kt—Q 3

Or 21. ...Q—B 4 ; 22. P—R 5 !, Q×P ch ; 23. K—Q 1, Q—Q 5 ch ; 24. K—K 2, Kt×P ; 25. P×P, Q—B 7 ch ; 26. K×Q, Kt—Kt 5 ch ; 27. K—K 1, Kt×Q ; 28. R×Kt, R—Kt 2 ; 29. B—Kt 2, P—K 4 ; 30. P×B P !

22. P—R 5   Kt—B 4

Too late !

23. Q×P ch !   K×Q
24. P×P dbl ch   K×P
25. R—R 6 mate

A pretty mate.

162. NUREMBERG, 1894

KIESERITZKY GAMBIT

THIS game is wound up very prettily by Tarrasch, but its most noteworthy incident is his curious chess blindness in missing an elegant mate. Despite this lapse, the game is so interesting that it well deserves publication.

White	*Black*
DR. S. TARRASCH	H. HIRSCHLER

1.	P—K 4	P—K 4
2.	P—K B 4	P×P
3.	Kt—K B 3	P—K Kt 4
4.	P—K R 4	P—Kt 5
5.	Kt—K 5	P—Q 3
6.	Kt×B P ! ?	

A venturesome sacrifice highly appropriate for "skittle" play. White speculates on the exposed position of the hostile King making the sacrifice worth while.

6.	......	K×Kt
7.	B—B 4 ch	K—Kt 3 ?

The more conservative 7. ... K—K 1 would make it much harder for White to work up an effective attack.

8.	P—Q 4	B—K 2
9.	B×P	Kt—K B 3
10.	P—R 5 ch !	K—Kt 2

If 10. ...Kt×P; 11. R×Kt !, K×R; 12. B—B 7 ch, K—R 5; 13. P—Kt 3 ch followed by mate !

11.	Kt—B 3	Kt—B 3
12.	P—K 5 !	

Foreseeing that even after the exchange of Queens he will remain with a powerful attack. The alternative was Q—Q 2 followed by O—O—O.

12.	......	P×P
13.	P—R 6 ch	K—B 1
14.	P×P	Q×Q ch
15.	R×Q	Kt—Q 2
16.	O—O	K—K 1

Black's King has had to make an arduous journey to get back to this square ! All of White's pieces are actively in play, and the existence of Black's King continues to be a miserable one.

17.	Kt—Q 5	B—B 4 ch

But not 17. ...either Kt×P ? ?; 18. B×Kt, Kt×B; 19. Kt×P mate ! This variation is more amusing than likely !

18.	K—R 1	B—Kt 3
19.	P—K 6 !	

This advance should have been quickly decisive.

19.	......	Kt(Q 2)—K 4
20.	Kt—B 6 ch	K—K 2
21.	B—K Kt 5 ! !	

A remarkable position with the Queens off : White sacrifices a second piece !

21.	......	Kt×B

Or 21. ...B×P; 22. Kt—R 5 ch !, K—K 1 ; 23. Kt—Kt 7 mate !

[*See diagram on next page.*]

22. Kt×Kt P ch ?

It is here that Tarrasch is stricken with an attack of chess blindness. He later pointed out the following lovely mate : 22. Kt—R 5 ch ! !,

K×P (if 22. ...K—K 1 ; 23. Kt
—Kt 7 mate) ; 23. R—B 6 ch, K—
K 2 (or 23. ...K—K 4 ; 24. B—
B 4 ch, K—K 5 ; 25. Kt—Kt 3
mate !) ; 24. R—B 5 ch !, K—K 3 ;
25. Kt—Kt 7 mate !

22. ......   K—K 1

If 22. ...K×P ; 23. R—B 6
ch, K—K 2 ; 24. R×Kt ch and
wins.

23. Kt—B 6 ch   K—K 2
24. Kt—Q 5 ch ? K—K 1

If 24. ...K×P ; 25. R—B 6
ch, K—Q 2 (not 25. ...K—K 4 ;
26. B—B 4 ch, K—K 5 ; 27. Kt—
B 3 mate) ; 26. Kt×B ch and
wins.

25. Kt—B 6 ch   K—K 2
26. Kt—Q 7 ch ? K—K 1

If 26. ...K×P ; 27. R—B 6
ch, K—K 2 ; 28. R×Kt ch wins.
Thus far the discovered checks
with the Knight have been inferior
in the sense that White has missed
the most elegant and most conclusive win.

27. Kt—B 6 ch   K—K 2
28. Kt—Kt 8 ch ? ?

Tarrasch's renunciation of his

cat-and-mouse policy is commendable, but the text is a genuine blunder, for after 28. ...K×P ! ; 29.
R—B 6 ch, K—K 4 White would
be embarrassed for an adequate
continuation. Best seems 30. R—
B 8, with the result of the game still
in doubt, despite Black's huge
material advantage.

28. ......   K—K 1 ? ?

Succumbing to the power of suggestion : Black thinks that the K P
is still sacrosanct.

29. R—Q 8 ch !   Kt×R
30. R—B 8 ch !

A finish with thunder and lightning !

30. ......   K×R
31. P—K 7 ch   Resigns

On 31. ...K—B 2 Tarrasch
gives 32. P×Kt(Q), K—Kt 3 ; 33.
Q—B 6 ch, K—R 4 ; 34. Kt—K 7,
B—Q 2 ; 35. B—B 4, K R—Kt 1 ;
36. Kt×R, R×Kt ; 37. Q—B 7
ch, R—Kt 3 ; 38. Q×B and wins.
A tragi-comic game !

163. NUREMBERG, 1904

RUY LOPEZ

TARRASCH's excellent play in this
game throws a strong light on his
skill in the handling of Bishops.
Note that the presence of the
Bishops of opposite colour does not
affect the outcome.

White ALLIES	*Black* DR. S. TARRASCH
1. P—K 4	P—K 4
2. Kt—K B 3	Kt—Q B 3

3. B—Kt 5	Kt—B 3
4. O—O	Kt × P
5. P—Q 4	B—K 2
6. P × P	

This unusual and weak move frees Black from any further worry about the course of the opening. 6. Q—K 2 should be played.

6.	P—Q 4
7. P—B 3 ?	

Another feeble move which foreshadows the delayed and ineffectual development of the Queen's side. Relatively better was 7. P × P e.p., Kt × Q P ; 8. B × Kt ch, P × B ; 9. Kt—Q 4 and the allies would have some compensation for the two Bishops in the weakness of Black's Pawns.

7.	O—O
8. B × Kt	

This and the next few moves are played with a view to forestall ... B—K Kt 5 and to remove the K Kt from its dominating position.

8.	P × B
9. Kt—Q 4	B—Q 2
10. P—B 3	Kt—B 4
11. Q—K 2	Kt—K 3
12. Kt × Kt	P × Kt !

Since this move seems to condemn the Q B to eternal passivity, most players would have retaken mechanically with the Bishop. But after 13. P—K B 4, P—K B 4 ; 14. B—K 3 followed by Q—K B 2 and Kt—Q 2—Kt 3, White would have a won game strategically.

13. P—K B 4 ?

This apparently natural move must be considered a decisive positional blunder. White should still have concentrated on the idea sketched out in the previous note.

Black is confronted with two interrelated problems : (1) how is he to dispose his Pawns to avoid pressure on his Q B 4 ? (2) how is the Q B to come into the game ? Tarrasch's solution of these problems is indicated by his prophecy to the spectators that, if the allies played P—K.B 4, they would eventually be mated at K Kt 2 !

13.	P—B 4 !
14. B—K 3	R—Kt 1
15. Q—Q 2	

In answer to the threat of ...B—Q Kt 4, one would expect 15. Q—K B 2. But then follows 15. ... P—Kt 4 ! ; 16. P—K Kt 3, P × P ; 17. P × P, B—K R 5 ; 18. Q—Kt 2 ch, K—R 1 ; 19. K—R 1, R—Kt 1 ; 20. Q—Q 2 (or Q—R 3), P—Q 5 ! and wins. Note how Black's Bishops suddenly come to life !

15.	B—Q Kt 4
16. R—Q 1	B—Q B 3

The possibility of ...P—Q 5 is already latent, the Q B is magnificently posted and Black's Pawns are safe from attack. Thus Tarrasch has solved the problems presented on move 13.

17. Kt—R 3

This miserable development of the Knight is the consequence of the allies' previous inaccuracies.

17. ......   Q—K 1 !

The Queen heads for K Kt 3 and

makes room for a Rook at Q 1.
The skilful manner in which Tarrasch carries out his plans makes the
game highly enjoyable.

18. Q R—Kt 1   R—Q 1
19. Q R—B 1

Directed against the coming
thrust of the Q P. If instead 19.
Kt—B 2, P—Q 5 ! ; 20. P×P, P×
P ; 21. B×P (or 21. Kt×P, B—
K 5 and Black wins at least the ex-
change), B—K 5 ; 22. Q—B 2,
Q—Kt 3 and wins.

19. ......   P—Q 5 !

Opening up the position advantageously.

20. P×P   P×P

If now 21. B×P, B—Q R 5 wins
some material.

21. B—B 2   B—Q R 5
22. R—K 1   P—B 4 !

...B×Kt is only superficially
tempting.

23. Kt—B 4   B—Q B 3
24. Kt—Q 6   R×Kt !

Quite right. The sacrifice of the
exchange allows Black to maintain
his B P and Q P and at the same
time gives him formidable attacking
chances.

25. P×R   B×Q P
26. B—Kt 3

If 26. P—K Kt 3 ?, B—Kt 2 !
(not 26. ...Q—R 4 ? ; 27. Q—
K 2 !) followed by ...Q—B 3 and
wins. The mating motif on K Kt 7
makes its appearance !

26. ......   P—K R 4 !
27. P—Kt 4 ! ?

A judicious attempt at counter-
play. If instead 27. P—K R 4,
Q—Kt 3 ; 28. Q—K B 2 (if 28.
K—R 2, B×B P ! wins : again the
mating motif !), B×B P ! etc. If
27. Q R—Q 1, Q—Kt 3 ; 28. R—
K B 1, Q—Kt 5 ; 29. Q—K B 2,
P—R 5 ! wins, or 27. Q—K 2,
B—Q 4, maintaining the pressure.

27. ......   P—R 5

Now Tarrasch regains the exchange and continues the attack
with undiminished vigour.

28. P×P   B—B 2 !
29. B×P   B×B P
30. Q×P   Q—R 4 !

An important gain of time which
makes possible his powerful 32nd
move.

31. B—Kt 3   B×R
32. R×B   Q—K 7

At last the mating motif has taken
tangible and brutal form. It will
be present constantly for the remainder of the game.

33. B—B 2   Q×P

In addition to the mating threat, Black has obtained a distant passed Pawn which will cooperate unobtrusively but effectively in the final attack.

34. Q—K 3

34. R—R 1 would be futile because of ...Q—B 7, when the Q R P would be immune from capture. If then 35. P—R 3, P—R 4 !; 36. R×P ?, Q—B 8 ch ; 37. K—R 2, Q—B 8 and wins.

| 34. ...... | P—R 4 |
| 35. R—K 1 | R—B 3 |

Not 35. ...B—Q 4 ; 36. P—B 6 !

36. R—K 2	Q—Q 4
37. B—Kt 3	P—R 5
38. R—Q 2	Q—B 5
39. P—R 3	

39. R—Q 8 ch ? would be a mistake because of 39. ...K—B 2 ; 40. R—Q 1 (if 40. P—R 3 ? ?, Q—K B 8 ch ; 41. K—R 2, Q×P mate), P—R 6 ! (also good is 40. ...Q—B 7 ; 41. Q—Q 2, Q×P ch) and White dare not play 41. Q×P because of 40. ...Q—K 7 (Tarrasch).

| 39. ...... | Q—Q B 8 ch |
| 40. K—R 2 | B—Q 4 |

Preventing R—Q 8 ch and threatening to advance the R P. The advance of White's B P need not be feared.

| 41. B—K 5 | R—Kt 3 |

Threatening ...R×P ch.

| 42. Q—Q 3 | R—Kt 4 |
| 43. R—Q B 2 | Q—Kt 8 |

Again threatening ...R×P ch, as well as ...R×B.

| 44. B—Kt 3 | R—B 4 ! |

44. ...P—R 6 would be premature because of 45. P—B 6, B×B P ; 46. Q—Q 8 ch etc.

45. R—B 3

If 45. P—B 6, B×B P etc.

| 45. ...... | Q—R 8 ! |

Threatening 46. ...P—R 6 ; 47. R×P, Q—Kt 7 and wins. The allies now play their last trump.

| 46. P—B 6 | R—B 8 |

Beginning the decisive phase. If now 47. B—Q 6, Q—K 8 and wins.

| 47. B—R 4 | R—R 8 ch |
| 48. K—Kt 3 | R—Q 8 |

Not 48. ...Q—K Kt 8 ? ; 49. P—B 7, Q×P ch ; 50. K—B 4 and White's King escapes ; or 49. ...R×P ch ; 50. K—Kt 4 ! and wins.

| 49. Q—K 3 | R—K 8 |
| 50. Q—Q 3 | Q—Kt 7 |

If now 51. P—B 7, Q×P ch ; 52. K—B 4, R—K 5 ch wins.

51. R—B 2

Not 51. Q—B 2 ?, R—K 6 ch and wins.

| 51. ...... | Q—K 4 ch |
| 52. K—B 2 | R—Q Kt 8 |

Threatening ...Q—K 8 mate. 53. Q—K 3 is answered by ...Q—

B 4 ch, while 53. Q—K 2 or 54.
R—K 2 is refuted by ...Q—
B 5 ch.

53. Q—Q 2   Q—K 5

Threatening mate in three.

54. K—Kt 3   R—Kt 6 ch
55. K—R 2

If 55. R—B 3, Q—K 4 ch wins.

55. ......   Q × B
56. P—B 7   Q—Kt 6 ch
57. K—Kt 1   R—Kt 8 ch
58. R—B 1   R × R ch
59. Q × R   Q × P mate

Q.E.D.! Tarrasch's insight into
the rôle of the Bishop at move 13
shows how a great master is guided
by intuitive perception of the essential feature of a given position.

164. COLOGNE, 1907
RUY LOPEZ

TARRASCH'S opponents do not give
him much trouble, but the pretty
finish is really striking.

White	*Black*
DR. S. TARRASCH	ALLIES

1. P—K 4	P—K 4
2. Kt—K B 3	Kt—Q B 3
3. B—Kt 5	P—Q R 3
4. B—R 4	Kt—B 3
5. O—O	P—Q 3
6. P—Q 4	P—Q Kt 4
7. B—Kt 3	

White can avoid the loss of a
Pawn here with 7. P × P etc. The
text is more enterprising.

7. ......   B—K 2

If 7. ...P × P; 8. Kt—Kt 5,
P—Q 4; 9. P × P, Kt × P; 10.
Kt × B P, K × Kt; 11. Q—B 3 ch,
K—K 3; 12. R—K 1 ch and wins.
   If 7. ...Kt × Q P; 8. Kt × Kt,
P × Kt; 9. P—Q B 3 (Q × P?
would, of course, lose a piece) with
good attacking chances for the
Pawn.

8. P—Q R 4	B—Kt 5
9. P—B 3	O—O
10. Q—Q 3	Kt—Q R 4

Burn's move 10. ...Q—Q 2 (as
in Game 58) is stronger.

11. B—B 2   .   B × Kt

Practically forced, since both the
K P and Q Kt P are under attack.
11. ...K P × P; 12. R P × P would
be in White's favour.

12. Q × B	P—B 4
13. Q—Q 3!	

Tarrasch wants to open up the
position with P—K B 4. If now
13. ...B P × P; 14. R P × P! (not
14. B P × P, Kt—B 3 threatening
...Kt × Q P as well as ...Kt—
Q Kt 5) with advantage.

13. ......   P—B 5

The alternative 13. ...P—Kt 5;
14. P—K B 4, P—B 5; 15. Q—
K 3, P—Kt 6 would also be unsatisfactory, for White's K B would
eventually reach a good post and
Black's Queen's side Pawns would
become weak.

14. Q—K 2   K P × P

This surrender of the centre does
not turn out well, but it is based on
a plausible idea. 14. ...Kt—Q 2

would have been better, but White's two Bishops and greater freedom would assure him a considerable advantage.

15. B P×P   Kt—B 3

Expecting 16. B—K 3, Kt—Q Kt 5 forcing the removal of the valuable K B.

16. R—Q 1 !

So that if 16. ...Kt—Q Kt 5 ; 17. P—K 5 !, Kt×B ? ; 18. P× Kt and wins.

16. ......   Q—B 2
17. P×P

Gaining time for the development of the Knight.

17. ......   P×P
18. R×R   R×R
19. Kt—B 3   R—Kt 1

Not 19. ...P—Kt 5 ; 20. Kt— Kt 5 followed by Q×P.

20. B—Kt 5

In order to gain command of Q 5. 20. B—B 4 was a good alternative.

20. ......   P—R 3

Waste of time, but the allies have no useful plan at their disposal.

21. B×Kt   B×B
22. Kt—Q 5   Q—Q 1
23. Q—K 3

White is now ready for the advance P—B 4 followed by P—K 5. His renunciation of the two Bishops in favour of the occupation of Q 5 has proved a wise decision.

23. ......   P—Kt 4 ?

A suicidal move which only enhances the strength of the ultimate advance of the B P.

24. P—K Kt 3   B—Kt 2
25. P—B 4   Kt—K 2
26. Kt—B 3

As usual, Tarrasch avoids an exchange which would relieve his opponent's cramped position.

26. ......   P×P

26. ...Kt—Kt 3 ; 27. P—B 5, Kt—K 2 ; 28. P—K 5 is equally uninviting.

27. P×P   P—Kt 5

This merely drives the Knight to participate in the coming decisive action on the K Kt file.

28. Kt—K 2   Kt—Kt 3
29. K—R 1   Q—R 5
30. R—K Kt 1   R—K 1

...K—R 1 here or next move may have been better.

31. Q—K B 3

Threatening to win a piece by advancing P—B 5—6.

31. ......   K—B 1

Fleeing to the Queen's side is apparently the safest course, but the allies are in for a stunning surprise.

32. Q—Kt 2   B—R 1
33. P—K 5   Kt×B P

Enabling White to win prettily, but if 33. ...P×P ; 34. B×Kt, P×B ; 35. Q P×P wins quickly.

34. Q—Kt 8 ch   K—K 2
35. P×P ch   K—Q 1

36. B—R 4 ! !

Very pretty. The allies resigned here. There is no move.

165. NUREMBERG, 1907

RUY LOPEZ

ALTHOUGH Tarrasch should have lost this game, it has been included as an interesting example of resourceful defence under trying conditions. White's play is an object lesson in the need for keeping consistently to the winning line once that the advantage has been clearly defined. Köhnlein's indecision at the critical juncture robs him first of a win and then of a draw.

White	*Black*
F. KÖHNLEIN	DR. S. TARRASCH

1. P—K 4   P—K 4
2. Kt—K B 3   Kt—Q B 3
3. B—Kt 5   P—Q R 3
4. B×Kt   Q P×B
5. Kt—B 3

Indicating that he prefers middle-game complications to further simplification by 5. P—Q 4, P×P ; 6. Q×P, Q×Q etc.

5. ......   B—Q B 4

Indirectly guarding the K P. 5. ...P—B 3 is generally accepted as best here. The disadvantage of the text is shown at move 7.

6. P—Q 3   Q—Q 3
7. B—K 3   B×B

Opening the K B file for White and giving him chances in the centre (later P—Q 4) as well. However, if 7. ...Kt—K 2 ; 8. P—Q 4, P×P ; 9. B×P ! and Black cannot avoid further exchanges which should leave White with a superior ending.

8. P×B   Kt—K 2
9. Q—K 2   P—B 3
10. Kt—K R 4

White renounces castling in favour of an immediate offensive ; in such a position it is difficult to decide which form of castling is preferable.

10. ......   B—K 3
11. P—K Kt 4

An interesting move. He intends Kt—B 5, and in the event of an exchange, the K Kt file will be opened for his Rooks. If ...P—K Kt 3, then Black's K B P will require constant attention.

11. ......   Q—Kt 5

Hoping to induce 12. O—O—O, after which Black can play for attack with ...Q—R 4 and ...P—Q Kt 4—5 (Tarrasch).

12. Kt—B 5 !

A speculative Pawn sacrifice

which leads to highly interesting play.

12.	Q×Kt P
13. K—Q 2	B×Kt

Not 13. ...Kt×Kt ? ; 14. Kt P ×Kt, B—B 1 (else the Q Kt P is lost) ; 15. Q R—K Kt 1, K—B 1 ; 16. R—Kt 3 with a splendid initiative.

14. Kt P×B	O—O—O

If instead 14. ...P—Q Kt 3 ? ? ; 15. P—Q R 3 ! and Black's Queen will be lost ! (Tarrasch).

15. P—Q R 4 !

Well played. Black's Queen is to be prevented from reaching Q R 4 (for example after 15. K R— Q Kt 1, Q—R 6 ; 16. R—Kt 3), which would be an effective post for hampering the movements of White's pieces.

15.	Q—Kt 5
16. P—R 5 !	

The point of White's previous move. As will be seen, the advanced Q R P is destined to play an important attacking rôle.

16.	K—Kt 1

In order to play Kt—B 1—Q 3 to protect the Q Kt P against White's intended doubling of his Rooks on the Q Kt file.

17. K R—Q Kt 1	Q—B 4
18. Kt—R 4 !	Q—R 2

A poor square for the Queen, but ...Q—Q 3 would prevent the intended Knight manœuvre, while 18.

...Q×R P ch the opening of the Q R file for White's Q R gives White formidable attacking chances. A possibility indicated by Tarrasch is (after 18. ...Q×R P ch) 19. K—B 1, Kt—B 1 ; 20. P—Q 4, P×P ; 21. Kt—B 5 !, Q×Kt ; 22. R×P ch !, K×R ; 23. Q×P ch, K—Kt 1 ; 24. Q—R 8 mate.

19. P—B 4 !

White continues to play very strongly. 19. ...Kt—B 1 is to be answered by 20. P—B 5 ; or if 19. ...K—R 1 ; 20. P—B 5, R—Q Kt 1 ; 21. Kt—Kt 6 ch ! and Black's Queen is trapped !

19.	P—B 4
20. Kt—B 3	

Good enough, but K—B 3 followed by Q—R 2—R 3 looks even more forceful.

20.	Kt—B 1
21. Kt—Q 5	Kt—Q 3

Threatening to win a Pawn with ...P—B 3.

22. K—B 3	P—B 3

The dominating Knight must be driven off, while at the same time Black begins a painfully involved manœuvre to get his Queen back into play. The weakening of Black's Q Kt 3 and the eventual loss of the Q B P constitute a small price to pay in return for this relief.

23. Kt—Kt 6	K—B 2
24. R—Kt 1 !	

A well-timed diversion. A simultaneous attack on both wings is advantageous for White because of his far greater mobility. Black's defence continues to be very onerous.

24. ......   Q R—K Kt 1

After ...Kt—K 1 the Knight would be tied to the defence of the K Kt P and the communication between his Rooks would be permanently disrupted.

25. Q—Q Kt 2

The logical course would have been to strengthen the King's side pressure still more, say by doubling the Rooks on the K Kt file. It is difficult to see how Black could ever have managed to free himself in that event.

25. ......   Q—Kt 1
26. Kt—R 4

After 26. Q—R 3, Q—K B 1 White would be unable to capture the Q B P because of ...Kt×P ch in reply. Compare the note to White's 20th move.

26. ......   P—K Kt 3
27. Kt×P   Q—R 2
28. Q—R 3   P×P
29. Q R—Kt 1

Planning a combination which is only good enough for a draw. 29. P×P was stronger, for if 29. ... Kt×K B P; 30. K R—K B 1 and White wins the K B P, leaving Black's game in a very critical state.

29. ......   P×P
30. Kt×Kt P ! ?   Kt×Kt
31. Q—K 7 ch   K—Kt 1
32. Q×B P   K—R 1
33. R×R ch   R×R
34. Q×B P

Threatening R—Kt 6. Black's position is still no bed of roses, but Tarrasch continues to defend with stubborn resourcefulness.

34. ......   P×P !
35. R—Kt 6   P—Q 7 !

The alternative, indicated by Tarrasch, was 35. ...R—Q 1 !; 36. R×P, P—Q 7; 37. R×Q ch, K×R; 38. Q—Kt 6 ch, K—R 1 ; 39. P—R 6, R—Q 6 ch ! ; 40. K× R (not 40. K—Kt 4 ?, Kt—Q 1 etc.), P—Q 8(Q) ch and Black draws by perpetual check.

36. K×P   R—Q 1 ch
37. K—B 3   R—Q 3
38. Q—B 7   R×R
39. P×R   Q—Kt 1
40. Q×R P ?

This loses. Tarrasch points out that 40. P—B 5 ! would still have left White with a draw ! The continuation might then have been 40. ...Q—Q 1 (not 40. ...Q×Q ? ? ; 41. P×Q and White wins) ; 41. K—B 2 (if 41. P—B 6, Q×Q ; 42. P×Q, Kt—Q 3 and White's Pawns are devaluated and he must lose ; or if 41. Q×K P, Q—Q 8 etc.), Q—Q Kt 1 ; 42. K—B 3, Q—Q 1 etc.

The fact that White still had a draw after several faulty moves demonstrates the vitality of the attack initiated with his twelfth move.

40. ......   Kt—B 4

After so much ineffectual wandering, the Knight at last takes a really important part in the concluding play. If now 41. Q— Kt 6, Q×P !

41. P—R 4   Q×P
42. Q—Kt 8 ch   K—Kt 2
43. Q—Q 5 ch   K—R 2
44. P—R 5

Q×P would have held out longer. The text loses by force.

44. ......   Kt—R 5 ch !

If now 45. K—Q 3, P—K 5 ch ! ! ; 46. K—Q 2, Q—Kt 5 ch ! and Black mates or wins the Queen. Likewise if 45. K—B 2, Q—Kt 7 ch ; 46. K—Q 3, P—K 5 ch ! ! wins the Queen.

45. K—Q 2   Q—Kt 5 ch
46. K—B 2

Or 46. K—Q 3, P—K 5 ch ! ! ; 47. K—Q 4, Q—Kt 7 ch again winning the Queen.

46. ......   Q—Kt 7 ch
47. K—Q 3   P—K 5 ch ! !

White resigns, as he must lose the Queen. If 48. Q×P, then 48. ... Kt—B 4 mate. The elegant finish must have been particularly sweet to Tarrasch after the laborious defensive task which preceded it.

166. COLOGNE, 1908

QUEEN'S GAMBIT DECLINED

TARRASCH was a past master in the art of demolishing an opponent's weak position. After White's all too timid treatment of the opening, he is steadily forced back into an indefensible situation.

White   *Black*
DR. OPPENHEIM DR. S. TARRASCH

1. P—Q 4   P—Q 4
2. P—Q B 4   P—K 3
3. Kt—Q B 3   P—Q B 4
4. P—K 3   Kt—K B 3
5. Kt—B 3   Kt—B 3
6. B—Q 3   P—Q R 3
7. B P×P

This move has its points, despite the fact that it frees Black's game.

7. ......   K P×P
8. O—O   B—Kt 5

At once indicating that he will strive for the initiative, regardless of whatever risks may be involved.

9. R—K 1 !

Despite its conservative appearance, this move is quite good. Thus if 9. ...B—K 2 ; 10. P×P, B×P ; 11. P—K 4 with an excellent game.

9. ......   P—B 5 ? !

Another aggressive move which might easily recoil on Black.

10. B—K 2   B—Q 3

If 10. ...B—K 2 ; 11. Kt—K 5 ! and White has distinctly the better game.

11. P—Q Kt 3 ?

Feeble. Tarrasch rightly recom-

mends 11. P—K 4 !, P×P ; 12.
B×P, B×Kt ; 13. Q×B, Kt×P ;
14. R×P ch etc.

11.	P—Q Kt 4
12. P×P	Kt P×P
13. Q—R 4	

Pure loss of time, but after 13.
P—K 4, B—Kt 5 White would be
at a loss for a good continuation.

13.	B—Q 2
14. Q—Q 1	O—O
15. Kt—Q 2	

Too slow, but White has nothing
more promising.

| 15. ...... | Q—R 4 |

Simple and strong. If now 16.
B—Kt 2, Q R—Kt 1 ; 17. Q—
B 1, R—Kt 2 followed by ...K R
—Kt 1 with a powerful initiative.

16. K Kt—Kt 1

Alas !

16. ......   B—K B 4

Now Black's Q Kt cannot be
prevented from reaching Q 6 or
Q B 7.

| 17. B—Q 2 | Q—B 2 |
| 18. P—Kt 3 | |

While White is lost in any case,
this weakening of the white squares
considerably diminishes his chances
of serious resistance.

18.	Kt—Q Kt 5
19. Kt—R 3	Kt—Q 6
20. B×Kt	B×B
21. Kt—B 2	Q—Q 2
22. R—Q B 1	

Or 22. K—Kt 2, Q—B 4 ; 23.
R—Q B 1, Q R—Kt 1 followed by
...R—Kt 7 with an easy win.

22. ......   Q—R 6

Now the weakness on the white
squares makes itself felt. The immediate threat is ...Kt—Kt 5.

23. Q—B 3

23. ......   Q R—Kt 1

Defending the Q P is too trivial a
consideration here. The text
threatens to win a piece with ...
R—Kt 7.

24. Kt×P

Amusing would be 24. K R—
Q 1, R—Kt 7 ; 25. Kt—K 1, Q—
B 8 mate !

24.	Kt×Kt
25. Q×Kt	R—Kt 7
26. Q×B	B—K 5 !

Decisive.

| 27. P—B 3 | B×P |
| 28. R—K 2 | B×R |

Threatening ...R×Kt.

| 29. B—Kt 4 | R—B 1 |
| 30. Q—B 4 | B—Q 6 |

White resigns, for if 31. Q—B 2, R—B 3 and White is helpless against ...R—B 3.

167. NUREMBERG, 1909

QUEEN'S GAMBIT
(IN EFFECT)

THIS game is highly instructive because of the way that Tarrasch repulses an inadequately prepared attack. An ingenious attack is always readily admired, but ingenious defence does not always meet with the appreciation which it deserves.

| *White* | *Black* |
| DR. S. TARRASCH | S. VOGEL |

1. P—Q 4	P—Q 4
2. Kt—K B 3	P—Q B 4
3. P—B 4	P—K 3
4. P—K 3	Kt—K B 3
5. Kt—B 3	Kt—B 3
6. B—Q 3	P—Q R 3
7. O—O	Q P × P

Once more Tarrasch has resorted to the colourless Symmetrical Variation. The text transposes into a variation of the Queen's Gambit, which generally turns out in White's favour.

| 8. B × B P | P—Q Kt 4 |
| 9. B—Kt 3 | |

The proper square for the Bishop is something of a problem. At Q 3 it is well posted for attack, but it blocks the later action of a White Rook at Q 1. The text, on the other hand, is less immediately ag-

gressive, but offers White's Rooks more scope.

9.	B—Kt 2
10. Q—K 2	P × P
11. R—Q 1	P—Q 6

This only helps White. Better was 11. ...B—K 2 and if 12. P × P, Kt—Q Kt 5 to be followed by ...Q Kt—Q 4.

| 12. R × P | Q—B 2 |
| 13. P—K 4 | |

This move, preparing for the development of the Q B, looks obvious ; yet its consequences have to be calculated very accurately.

| 13. ...... | B—B 4 |

13. ...P—Kt 5 ; 14. Kt—Q 1, Kt—K 4 ; 15. Kt × Kt, Q × Kt would not be good because of 16. B—R 4 ch, K—K 2 ; 17. P—B 3 followed by Kt—B 2 and P—B 4.

14. B—Kt 5 !

P—K R 3 would be safe but too slow. The text deliberately invites complications.

| 14. ...... | Kt—K Kt 5 |

Now White is apparently lost, for in addition to ...Kt×B P Black threatens ...Kt—Q 5 !

15. B—K R 4 !

Defending himself against the real threat and disregarding the sham.

15. ...... Kt—Q 5 ?

Castling was relatively better. Unfortunately Black is not so far-seeing as his famous adversary.

16. R×Kt   B×R
17. B—Kt 3 !   B—K 4

Forced, for if 17. ...Q—Q 1 ; 18. Kt×B wins.

18. Kt×B   Kt×Kt
19. Q—R 5 !

The point of Tarrasch's combination. The pinned Knight cannot be saved.

19. ......   O—O
20. B×Kt   Q—K 2
21. Q—Kt 4 !

The game can be won in many ways, but Tarrasch selects the quickest.

21. ......   P—Kt 3
22. Q—B 4   P—B 4

If 22. ...K R—K 1 ; 23. B—B 6, Q—B 1 ; 24. R—Q 1 followed by R—Q 3—R 3 and White wins easily.

23. Q—R 6 !

This is even stronger than the banal B—Q 6.

Black resigns, as he has no satisfactory defence to the threat of B× P ch. Tarrasch indicates the following possibility : 23. ...B—B 1 (if 23. ...R—B 2 ; 24. P×P etc.) ; 24. Kt—Q 5 !, Q—Q Kt 2 (or 24. ...P×Kt ; 25. B×P ch, R—B 2 ; 26. Q—Kt 7 mate ; while if 24. ...Q—K B 2 ;   25. Kt—B 6 ch, K—R 1 ;   26. Kt—Q 7 ch, K—Kt 1 ; 27. B×P followed by mate) ; 25. Kt—B 7, R—B 2 ;   26. R—Q 1, B—Q 2 ; 27. R×B, Q×P (if 27. ...R×R ; 28. B×P ch leads to mate) ; 28. Q—Kt 7 ch !, R×Q; 29. B×P ch, R—B 2 ;   30. B×R ch, K—B 1 ; 31. Kt—K 6 mate.

168. NUREMBERG, 1909

QUEEN'S PAWN GAME

TARRASCH wins this game with such ease that its chief attraction lies in the piquant winning method. A characteristic feature is his decisive utilisation of superior development.

White	*Black*
DR. S. TARRASCH	DR. E. DYCKHOFF
1. P—Q 4	P—Q 4
2. Kt—K B 3	P—Q B 4
3. P—B 4	B P×P

Black sets himself a thankless task : he loses times, cedes the opponent an early initiative and leaves himself exposed to lasting pressure. He should have followed in the master's footsteps by transposing into the Tarrasch Defence with 3. ...P—K 3.

4. P×P   Q×P

This involves a serious loss of time. 4. ...Kt—K B 3 was better.

5. Kt—B 3   Q—Q 1

The alternative 5. ...Q—Q R 4 ;
6. Kt×P is equally uninspiring.

6. Q×P   Q×Q

Black continues inexorably on the
road to perdition. 6. ...B—Q 2
followed by ...Kt—Q B 3 gives
better chances of obtaining a playable game.

7. Kt×Q   P—K 4 ?

7. ...B—Q 2 and if 8. K Kt—
Kt 5, Kt—Q R 3 ; 9. B—K 3, P—
Q Kt 3 should have been tried.
The consequences of the text are
disastrous.

8. K Kt—Kt 5   Kt—Q R 3
9. Kt—Q 5 !   Kt—Kt 5 ? !

A desperate attempt at counterplay. If instead 9. ...K—Q 1 ;
10. B—K 3, P—Q Kt 3 ; 11. O—
O—O, B—Q 2 ; 12. Kt×R P !
with a winning position.

10. Kt(Q 5)—B 7 ch K—Q 1
11. Kt×R   Kt—B 7 ch
12. K—Q 1   Kt×R

The superficial symmetry of the
position is amusing but misleading.
White's advantage in development
will enable him to rescue his
stranded Knight, whereas Black's
backward development seals the
doom of his Knight.

13. Kt×P

Threatening Kt×B followed by
Kt—Kt 6 ch etc.

13. ......   B—Q B 4

Or 13. ...B—K B 4 ; 14. P—
K 3, Kt—B 7 ; 15. P—Q R 3 and
the Knight is still trapped ! If 14.
...B—Kt 8 ; 15. B—B 4 followed
by P—Q Kt 4 and B—Kt 2.

14. Kt—Kt 5 !

After 14. Kt×B ?, K×Kt
White's Knight cannot escape.

14. ......   B—K 3
15. P—Q Kt 4 !   B×B P
16. B—Kt 2   Kt—Kt 6

Although the Knight is lost,
Black still hopes desperately to win
White's advanced Knight. If in-
stead 16. ...Kt—B 3 ; 17. Kt
(R 8)—B 7 !, B×P ; 18. B×Kt
(Tarrasch).

17. B×P !

Tarrasch prefers to increase his
advantage before capturing the
helpless Knight.

17. ......   P—B 3
18. B—B 7 ch   K—Q 2
19. P—K 3 !

Temporarily allowing the unfortunate Knight to escape its fate.

19. ......   Kt—R 8

Truly a comical situation, says
Tarrasch ! For lack of a better
move, the Knight voluntarily puts
its head in the lion's mouth once
more.

20. B—Q 3   B×K P
21. K—K 2   B—Kt 4
22. Kt—Kt 6 ch   K—B 3

Hoping to take advantage of the
apparently awkward position of

White's pieces, Black runs into a mating net.

23. P—Q R 4 !

Threatening 24. B—K 4 ch and mate next move.

| 23. ...... | P—B 4 |
| 24. P—R 5 ! | |

Guarding the Knight at Kt 6, in order to move away the Q B and thus threaten Kt—Q 4 mate or Kt—R 7 mate.

24.	Kt—Kt 6
25. B—K 5	Kt×P
26. P×Kt	Kt—B 3
27. R—Q Kt 1	Resigns

He is helpless against the threat of 28. Kt—Q 4 ch, K—B 4 ; 29. R—Kt 5 mate. If 27. ...B—Q 2 ; 28. Kt—Q 4 ch, K—B 4 ; 29. Kt ×B ch, Kt×Kt ; 30. R—Kt 5 mate ; or 27. ...K—B 4 ; 28. Kt—Q 4 and again mate cannot be prevented (Tarrasch). A delightful game !

169. NUREMBERG, 1910
RUY LOPEZ

TARRASCH was a past master of the art of exploiting microscopic advan-

tages. The skill he displayed in utilising a slight initiative was truly phenomenal, for most players would not even perceive the existence of such seemingly "trivial" factors.

White	*Black*
DR. S. TARRASCH	S. VOGEL
1. P—K 4	P—K 4
2. Kt—K B 3	Kt—Q B 3
3. B—Kt 5	P—Q 3
4. P—Q 4	B—Q 2
5. Kt—B 3	Kt—B 3
6. O—O	B—K 2
7. R—K 1	

Tarrasch never tired of preaching the inadequacy of the Steinitz Defence. Cramped positions, he insisted, carry within them the germ of defeat.

7.	P×P
8. Kt×P	Kt×Kt
9. Q×Kt	B×B
10. Kt×B	O—O
11. B—Kt 5	Kt—Kt 5

Black has decided on a policy of wholesale exchanges to minimise White's greater command of the board.

| 12. B×B | Q×B |
| 13. P—Q B 4 | |

In order to give added support to the Knight when it is eventually posted at Q 5. Note how at this point and in all the subsequent play, Tarrasch avoids driving away the Knight with P—K R 3—a move which so many amateurs would play instinctively. The move would not be good, for Black's main disadvantage is the decentralisation of this Knight. If White is to make any headway in this considerably simplified position, it will be through utilising this Knight's rôle of bystander.

13. ......   P—Q R 3

In order to exchange Queens, Black commits the strategical mistake which White avoids : *driving the hostile Knight into a centralised position.*

14. Kt—B 3   Q—K 4
15. Q×Q   P×Q

Here the opportunity presented itself to get the Knight back to the centre with 15. ...Kt×Q ; but then White would play 16. P—Q Kt 3 and drive the Knight away with P—B 4. White's Knight would then proceed to Q 5 (unless Black weakened his Q P by ...P—Q B 3), where it would be extremely annoying for Black. His Knight, on the other hand, would be unable to find an effective post.

16. Kt—Q 5 !

Despite the almost symmetrical character of the position, this move gives White a slight advantage, or at any rate the initiative. The Knight's invasion is not easy to answer satisfactorily, for if 16. ...Q R—B 1 ? ; 17. Kt—K 7 ch. Tarrasch recommends as best 16. ...Kt—B 3 ; 17. Q R—Q 1 (if 17. Kt×P, Q R—B 1), leaving White with a slight advantage.

16. ......   P—Q B 3 ?

This plausible move ejects the unpleasant intruder for a short time ; but the weakness thus created at Black's Q 3 soon makes itself noticeable.

17. Kt—K 7 ch   K—R 1

Now White must beware of having his Knight trapped by ...P—K Kt 3.

18. Kt—B 5   Q R—Q 1

Beginning the struggle for command of the Q file, which must end in Black's discomfiture, as he must also divert his forces to the protection of his weak Pawns.

19. Q R—Q 1   P—K Kt 3
20. Kt—Q 6   R—Q 2

Forced : White was threatening Kt×P ch as well as Kt×P, and ...Q R—Kt 1 would relinquish the Q file. The use of small, move-to-move tactical threats is an important device for attainment of large-scale strategical goals.

21. P—B 5 !

An important, many-sided move : it paralyses Black's Queen's side, strengthens White's grip on Q 6 and makes Q B 4 available for the Knight. Unfortunately White's next move cannot be prevented, for if 21. ...K R—Q 1 ? ; 22. Kt×P ch wins.

21. ......   K—Kt 1

...K—Kt 2 was somewhat better.

22. Kt—B 4 !   K R—Q 1

Confronted with an unpleasant choice of relinquishing the Q file or the K P, Black selects the latter alternative. 22. ...R—K 2 ; 23. R—Q 6 followed by K R—Q 1 would be decidedly in White's favour, but would at all events permit of a more stubborn resistance.

23. R×R   R×R
24. P—B 3

Finally the time has come for this move, which must now win some material.

24. ......   Kt—R 3
25. Kt×P   R—Q 7

Seeking counterplay, but he thereby leaves his Queen's side Pawns in the lurch.

26. Kt—B 4   R—Q B 7
27. P—Q Kt 3   R×P

Black has regained the Pawn— but the game is lost !

28. R—Q 1 !   P—R 4

Hoping for ...P—R 5, but there is no time for this.

29. R—Q 8 ch   K—Kt 2
30. R—Q R 8   P—R 5
31. R×P   R×R
32. P×R   Kt—Kt 1

The sad result, Tarrasch observes, of 11. ...Kt—Kt 5.

33. Kt—Q 6   K—B 3
34. Kt×Kt P   K—K 4
35. P—R 5   Kt—K 2
36. Kt—Q 6 !

And now the Q R P can no longer be held back.

36. ......   K—Q 5
37. P—R 6   Resigns

The exquisite precision of Tarrasch's play in this game should be studied with the greatest care.

170. NUREMBERG, 1910

QUEEN'S GAMBIT

In addition to its intrinsic interest, this game has a certain historic value because of Tarrasch's smashing refutation of an opening variation which was fashionable at the time.

White	Black
Dr. S. Tarrasch	R. Spielmann
1. P—Q 4	P—Q 4
2. Kt—K B 3	P—Q B 4
3. P—B 4	P—K 3
4. P—K 3	Kt—K B 3
5. Kt—B 3	Kt—B 3
6. B—Q 3	Q P×P
7. B×B P	P—Q R 3
8. O—O	P—Q Kt 4
9. B—Q 3	B—Kt 2
10. P—Q R 4 !	

This strong move brings Black's apparently strong Queen's side Pawns into disarray. The chief flaw in Black's development is the posting of his Q Kt at Q B 3 instead of at Q 2. Were this Knight at Q 2, Black could proceed with 10. ...P—Kt 5, driving back the Q Kt to Q Kt 1.

10. ......   P—B 5 ?

A risky decision characteristic of Spielmann's stormy style. If in-

stead 10. ...P—Kt 5 ; 11. Kt—
K 4 and Black's position is difficult.

11. B—B 2

In a game between Teichmann
and Spielmann at St. Petersburg
the previous year, the continuation
was 11. B—K 2, P—Kt 5 ; 12.
Kt—Kt 1, Kt—Q R 4 ; 13. Q Kt
—Q 2, R—B 1 ; 14. Kt—K 5, B—
Q 4 ; 15. P—Q Kt 3 (15. P—B 3
is answered by ...Kt—Q 2 !),
P—B 6 with a winning position for
Black.

The move selected by Tarrasch
is much stronger because (a)
White's Q Kt, on being attacked by
...P—Kt 5, can go to K 4 ; (b)
later on, White can react powerfully with P—K 4.

In the St. Petersburg Tournament Book, Lasker suggests the
even simpler course 11. P×P,
P×P ; 12. R×R, so as to avoid the
imprisonment of White's Q R
which results from the text.

11. ......   P—Kt 5
12. Kt—K 4   Kt—Q R 4
13. Kt×Kt ch   Q×Kt

Judging from the sequel, ...P×
Kt would have been preferable.

14. P—K 4   P—Kt 6

Seemingly very strong, since
White's Queen's side now presents
a fearfully constricted appearance.

15. B—Kt 1   B—Kt 5 ?

After this Black very soon has a
lost game. 15. ...Q—Q 1 was
somewhat better, although after 16.
B—Q 2 Black's position would be
definitely unsatisfactory because of
the exposed state of his Knight and
Q B P.

16. B—Kt 5 !   Q—Kt 3
17. B—Q 2 !   B×B

As a result of the finesse at
White's 16th move Black cannot
support the Bishop by Q—K 2.

Now that his Queen has been cut
off from the vital sector he finds
that he has a lost game. If 17. ...
Kt—B 3 ; 18. P—Q 5 wins a
piece !

18. Q×B   Kt—B 3
19. P—Q 5!

This energetic continuation
even stronger than the more obvious Q—B 3.

19. ......   Kt—Q 1

19. ...P×P ? would cost a
piece, and 19. ...R—Q 1 is
answered effectively by 20. Q—
B 3.

20. Kt—K 5   Q—R 4
21. Kt×Q B P   O—O

21. ...P×P would not do because of Kt—Q 6 ch.

22. Kt—Kt 6   R—R 2

A pitiable move, but he has
nothing better (if 22. ...R—Kt 1 ;
23. Kt—Q 7).

23. R—R 3

Once more we see this characteristic Rook development which appears so often in Tarrasch's games.
The Rook comes into action at
once, annexing the remaining weak
Pawn at the same time.

23. ......   P—B 4

A desperate move in a situation
beyond remedy.

24. P×B P   P×Q P
25. R×P   Q—B 2
26. R—Q 3

Winning still another Pawn.

26. ......   B—B 3

Not 26. ...Q×P ; 27. R—
K B 3 or 27. R—K R 3.

27. Kt×P   B×P

The game was lost in any event.

28. Kt—B 3 .   Resigns

There is no defence to the triple
threat of 29. Kt×B or 29. R×Kt
or 29. B—R 2.

171. NUREMBERG, 1910
RUY LOPEZ

TARRASCH outplays his opponent in
the opening and obtains a clear
advantage as a result. In the
second half of the game there follows a short, sharp skirmish in
which Tarrasch's tactical superiority carries the day.

White	*Black*
R. SPIELMANN	DR. S. TARRASCH

1. P—K 4   P—K 4
2. Kt—K B 3   Kt—Q B 3

3. B—Kt 5   P—Q R 3
4. B—R 4   Kt—B 3
5. Q—K 2

Probably played to avoid Tarrasch's favourite defence (5. ...
Kt×P in reply to 5. O—O) to
which Spielmann was himself rather
partial.

5. ......   P—Q Kt 4
6. B—Kt 3   B—B 4
7. P—Q R 4   R—Q Kt 1

Tarrasch must have been reluctant to yield the Q R file ; however,
if 7. ...P—Kt 5 ? ; 8. B×P ch !
follows.

8. P×P   P×P
9. Kt—B 3   O—O !

Ignoring the attack on the
Q Kt P, for after 10. Kt×Kt P,
P—Q 4 ; 11. P×P, P—K 5 ! or
11. Kt—B 3, B—K Kt 5 ; 12.
Q Kt×P, Kt—Q 5 ; 13. Q—B 4,
Kt×Kt ch ; 14. P×Kt, B×P with
a winning attack.

10. O—O   P—Q 3
11. P—R 3

Such a continuation as 11. Kt×
Kt P, B—K Kt 5 ; 12. P—B 3,
B×Kt ; 13. P×B, Kt—K R 4 ;
14. P—Q 4, P×P could hardly
appeal to an aggressive player like
Spielmann.

11. ......   Kt—K R 4

With the nasty double threat of
...Kt—Kt 6 or   ...Kt—B 5.
White has hardly anything better
than the following reply.

12. Kt×K P !?   Kt—B 5 !
13. Kt×Kt   Kt×Q ch
14. Kt×Kt   Q—K 1
15. Kt×R   B—Kt 2

...Q×P would be inferior because of 16. Kt—B 3, Q—Kt 2 ; 17. Kt—R 6.

16. P—Q 4

White has a Rook and two Knights for the Queen, but he cannot avoid parting with one of the Knights. Thus if 16. Kt—R 6, Q×P and the mating threat wins the Knight at K 7. Tarrasch considers that 16. P—Q 3 would have offered the best drawing chances.

16. ......   Q×P
17. Kt—B 4   R×Kt !

Best. If 17. ...P—Kt 4 ; 18. Kt—Q 7 ! (threatening Kt—B 6 ch) and White ends up with two Rooks for the Queen. Likewise if 17. ...B×P ; 18. Kt—Q 7, P—Kt 4 (or 18. ...R—Q 1 ; 19. B—Q 2, P—R 3 ; 20. P—Q B 3, R×Kt ; 21. P×B, P—Kt 4 ? ; 22. K R— K 1, Q×P ; 23. R—K 8 ch and wins) ; 19. Kt—Q 5, B×Kt ; 20. B×B, Q×B ; 21. Kt×R and again White has two Rooks for the Queen.

18. P×B   P—Kt 4
19. P×P   P×Kt
20. P—K B 3   Q—Q 5 ch
21. R—B 2

The only way to ensure the development of his Q B. If now 21. ...P×P ; 22. P—B 3, Q— B 3 ; 23. B—Q 2 and despite his material inferiority. White can put up considerable resistance, chiefly because of the weaknesses in Black's Pawn position. Tarrasch therefore selects a more enterprising if more risky course.

21. ......   P—B 4 !

This is played in order to keep his Queen's side Pawns intact, and to keep White's K B out of play.

22. P—B 4 ?

This loses very quickly. P—B 3 was his best chance.

22. ......   R—K 1 !
23. B—Q 2

23. K—B 1 is refuted by 23. ... Q—Q 6 ch, while if 23. P—Q 7, R—K 8 ch ; 24. K—R 2, Q×Q P and White is helpless.

23. ......   Q×Kt P !

Simple and decisive. Tarrasch shows that the plausible 23. ... R—K 7 ; 24. B—K 1, R×R ; 25. B×R, Q×Kt P is inferior because of 26. R—R 7 ! with the following possibilities :

I. 26. ...Q×B ; 27. R×B, Q—Q 8 ch ; 8. K—R 2, Q×Q P ; 29. R×Kt P followed by R×P and the winning chances are all on White's side.

II. 26. ...B—B 3 ; 27. P× P, B×Kt P ; 28. B×P ch etc.

III. 26. ...B—B 3 ; 27. P× P, Q×B ; 28. P×B, Q—Q 8 ch ; 29. K—R 2, Q×Q P ; 30. P— B 7, Q—Q B 3 ; 31. B×P and wins.

IV. 26. ...B—B 1 ; 27. R—
R 8, Q×B ; 28. R×B ch, K—
Kt 2 ; 29. B—Q 4 ch !, P×B ; 30.
P—Q 7, Q—Q 8 ch ; 31. K—R 2,
Q—K 8 (hoping for perpetual
check) ; 32. R—K 8 and wins.

24. R—K 1

Or 24. R—R 7, B—B 1 ; 25.
P—Q 7, B×P ; 26. R×B, Q×
K B ; 27. P×P, Q×Kt P and
wins.

24.	R×R ch
25. B×R	Q×B
26. P—Q 7	Q—Q 8
Resigns	

172. NUREMBERG, 1910

RUY LOPEZ

BLACK'S failure to castle makes his
early defeat inevitable, but the
manner in which Tarrasch drives
home the moral lends the game lasting interest.

White	*Black*
DR. S. TARRASCH	MOSBACHER
1. P—K 4	P—K 4
2. Kt—K B 3	Kt—Q B 3
3. B—Kt 5	P—Q R 3
4. B×Kt	

This early exchange was favoured by Lasker, who demonstrated that this variation has many
finesses despite its appearance of
simplicity.

| 4. ..... | Q P×B |
| 5. O—O | B—K Kt 5 |

...P—B 3 is Black's best course,
although the text is playable.

| 6. P—K R 3 | B×Kt ? |

Black should not give up his
Bishop-pair without some compensating consideration. Tarrasch suggests the interesting alternative 6. ...P—K R 4 ! ? ; 7. P—
Q 3 (after 7. P×B ?, P×P Black
would regain the piece with a
strong attack), Q—B 3 ! with the
intention of doubling White's
K B P and then keeping it permanently in that state by means of ...
B—Q 3.

| 7. Q×B | Kt—K 2 ? |

Black's development is too much
in arrears for such clumsy and time-
wasting moves. Correct was 7.
...Kt—B 3 and if 8. P—Q 3, B—
K 2 ; 9. Kt—B 3, O—O with an
inferior but playable position for
Black.

| 8. Q—Q Kt 3 ! | R—Q Kt 1 |
| 9. P—K B 4 ! | |

Tarrasch plays energetically to
open up the position, pointing out
that after the quieter 9. P—Q 3,
Kt—Kt 3 ; 10. P—K B 4, P×P ;
11. B×P, Kt×B ; 12. R×Kt,
B—B 4 ch ; 13. K—R 1, O—O ;
14. Kt—B 3, Q—K 2 Black would
not be too badly off.

| 9. ..... | Q—Q 5 ch |

Beginning a series of Queen
moves which loses a great deal of
time ; but it is not easy to suggest
a better line of play.

| 10. K—R 1 | Q×K P |
| 11. Kt—B 3 | |

Gaining time and improving on
11. P×P, Q—Q 4 etc.

11.	Q—Q 5
12. P×P	Kt—Q 4
13. P—Q 3	B—K 2

...Q×P ? would be bad because of 14. B—B 4 !

After the text, Black is ready to castle, so that Tarrasch must proceed energetically to maintain his grip.

14. Kt×Kt   Q×Kt

Or 14. ...P×Kt ; 15. B—B 4, O—O ; 16. P—K 6, B—Q 1 ; 17. P—K 7, B×P ; 18. B×P and Black's Pawns are in a bad way.

15. P—B 4   Q—Q 2

After 15. ...Q—K 3 ; 16. P—Q 4, O—O Black's tribulations would have been at an end ; but the text is also playable.

16. P—Q 4 ! ?   Q×Q P ?

But this is very bad. Correct was 16. ...O—O ; 17. Q—Kt 3, K—R 1 ; 18. B—K 3, P—B 3 and White's centre may yet turn out to be weak !

17. B—K 3   Q—Q 2

It is now too late for caution. However, if 17. ...Q×K P ; 18. B—R 7 (or 18. Q R—K 1 or 18. B—B 4) would give White a ·winning advantage because of the attack on the K file.

18. P—K 6 !

The finest move in the whole game.

18. ......   P×P

Or 18. ...Q×P ; 19. B—R 7, O—O (otherwise White will play Q R—K 1 to be followed by B—B 5) ; 20. B×R, R×B ; 21. Q R —K 1 and White soon wins.

19. Q R—Q 1   Q—B 1

He has nothing better, since 19. ...B—Q 3 ? is refuted by 20. P—B 5. Black's position is now a picture of helplessness.

20. B—R 7   R—R 1
21. B—Q 4   R—B 1

If 21. ...R—K Kt 1 ; 22. Q—K B 3 wins easily.

22. B×P   R—B 2
23. B—K 5   B—Q 3
24. R×R   K×R
25. Q—B 3 ch   Resigns

For if 25. ...K—K 1 ; 26. Q—R 5 ch wins. The Pawn sacrifices have achieved their object !

173. NUREMBERG, 1911
FRENCH DEFENCE

TARRASCH exploits his opponent's shortcomings with his accustomed virtuosity. As is usual in his games, Tarrasch's utilisation of his advantage is just as masterly as the way in which that advantage is gained and augmented.

White	*Black*
Dr. S. Tarrasch	F. Köhnlein
1. P—K 4	P—K 3
2. P—Q 4	P—Q 4
3. Kt—Q B 3	Kt—K B 3
4. B—Kt 5	B—K 2
5. P×P	

A simplifying move which gives White prospects only if his opponent handles the subsequent play inaccurately.

5.	P×P
6. B—Q 3	O—O
7. Q—Q 2	

Preparing for subsequent castling on the Queen's side and an attack against Black's King.

| 7. ...... | P—B 4 |

This is played primarily to open up the Q B file by way of discouraging White's intended castling. The move is open to the objection that it leaves an isolated Q P which will require careful attention on Black's part. The alternative was 7. ... Kt—B 3, in order to answer 8. Kt—B 3 or K Kt—K 2 with 8. ...Kt—Q Kt 5.

| 8. P×P | B×P |
| 9. K Kt—K 2 | |

Realising that 9. O—O—O would now have its drawbacks; there might follow 9. ...Q—R 4; 10. K—Kt 1, B—K 3 threatening ...P—Q 5. Tarrasch therefore prefers to rely on purely positional considerations.

9.	Kt—B 3
10. O—O	B—K 2
11. K R—K 1	

Played to prevent 11. ...B—K 3, on which Tarrasch gives the following plausible continuation, disastrous for Black : 12. Kt—B 4, Q—Q 2 ; 13. B×Kt, B×B ; 14. K Kt×P, Q B×Kt ; 15. Kt×B, B×P ? ; 16. Kt—B 6 ch, B×Kt ; 17. B×P ch winning the Queen !

| 11. ...... | Kt—Q Kt 5 ? |

From this point on, Black's game goes steadily downhill. The text is weak because it loses time, makes the development of the Q B a serious problem and facilitates White's pressure on the Q P.

The proper course, indicated by Tarrasch, was 11. ...P—Q 5 !; 12. Kt—Kt 5 (if 12. B×Kt, B× B ; 13. Kt—K 4, B—K 2 and Black stands well), B—Q Kt 5 ; 13. P—Q B 3, P×P ; 14. Q Kt× B P and Black has rid himself of the isolated Q P.

| 12. Kt—Q 4 | |

The Knight is always well posted here in such situations.

| 12. ...... | Kt×B |
| 13. Q×Kt | B—K Kt 5 |

White has a splendid development, while Black has difficulty getting his Q B into effective play.

| 14. P—K R 3 | B—R 4 |
| 15. Kt—B 5 ! | |

Tarrasch selects the clear and simple course instead of the more complicated and less conclusive 15. P—K Kt 4, B—Kt 3 ; 16. Q—B 3.

| 15. ...... | B—Q Kt 5 |

Hoping to guard the Q P indirectly ; a vain hope.

| 16. B×Kt | P×B |

This crucial weakening of the
King-side is enough to lose the
game, but the more natural 16. ...
Q×B ? would lose the K B after
17. Kt×Q P.

17. R—K 3   B×Kt

Even this move cannot save the
Q P. Black is in terrible straits.

18. Q×B   B—Kt 3

Black has no move. If 18. ...
R—B 1 ; 19. Q×R etc.

19. Kt—K 7 ch   K—Kt 2
20. Q—Q 4   R—K 1

Or 20. ...B×P ; 21. Kt×P
and Black is helpless against the
threat of R—K 7.

21. Q R—K 1   Q—Kt 3

Otherwise Kt—B 5 ch wins.

22. Q×P   Q R—Q 1

If 22. ...B×P ; 23. Kt—B 5
ch, K—B 1 ; 24. R×R ch, R×R ;
25. R×R ch, K×R ; 26. Kt—Q 6
ch and White mates or wins the
Queen. Or 22. ...Q×P ; 23.
Kt—B 5 ch, K—B 1 ? ; 24. Q—
Q 6 ch and mate follows.

23. Kt—B 5 ch

23. ......   K—B 1

If instead 23. ...B×Kt ; 24.
Q×B, R×R ; 25. R×R, Q×P
and now Tarrasch gives 26. P—
Q B 3 ! (stronger than 26. R—
Kt 3 ch, K—R 1 ; 27. P—Q B 3,
Q—B 8 ch ; 28. K—R 2, Q—R 3
etc.), Q—Kt 3 ; 27. R—Kt 3 ch,
K—B 1 (not 27. ...K—R 1 ? ; 28.
Q—Kt 4) ; 28. Q×R P, R—Q 8
ch ; 29. K—R 2, Q×P ; 30. R—
Kt 8 ch, K—K 2 ; 31. Q—K 4 ch,
K—Q 2 (if 31. ...K—Q 3 ; 32.
R—Q 8 ch) ; 32. Q×P ch, K—
K 3 ; 33. R—K 8 ch, K—B 4 ; 34.
Q—K 4 ch, K—Kt 4 ; 35. Q—
Kt 4 ch, K—R 3 ; 36. R—R 8
mate !

24. R×R ch

Tarrasch points out that this is
not only simpler but also stronger
than the flashy 24. Q—Q 6 ch, Q×
Q ;   25. R×R ch, R×R ;   26.
R×R ch, K×R ; 27. Kt—Q 6 ch,
K—Q 2 ; 28. Kt×Kt P, B×P and
White has a difficult ending on his
hands.

24. ......   R×R
25. R×R ch   K×R
26. Q—K 4 ch   Q—K 3

Tantamount to resignation ; but
if 26. ...K—B 1 ? ? 27. Q—K 7
ch forces mate, while if 26. ...K—
Q 2 ; 27. Q—K 7 ch wins easily.

27. Kt—Kt 7 ch   K—K 2
28. Q×P ch   Q—Q 2
29. Q×Q ch   K×Q
30. P—Q B 3   Resigns

White rescues the stranded
Knight with P—K Kt 4, remaining
two Pawns to the good with an
easy win.

174. NUREMBERG, 1912

FOUR KNIGHTS' GAME

A TYPICAL Tarrasch game which is instructive in all its phases. For amateurs who are often discouraged by the possibility of endless enemy checks in Queen and Pawn endings, Tarrasch's treatment of the endgame offers welcome consolation.

White	Black
DR. S.	C. VON BARDELEBEN
TARRASCH	A. LINDSTRÖM

1.	P—K 4	P—K 4
2.	Kt—K B 3	Kt—Q B 3
3.	Kt—B 3	Kt—B 3
4.	B—B 4	B—Kt 5

Tarrasch rightly criticises this move, which eventually involves Black in serious difficulties. 4. ...Kt×P equalises quickly and easily.

5. O—O	O—O

Since ...B×Kt will soon be necessary, the exchange is best made at once. After 5. ...B×Kt White must retake with the Q P, obtaining a somewhat less favourable Pawn position than after the text.

6. P—Q 3	B×Kt

As White is threatening B—K Kt 5 followed by Kt—Q 5, Black must choose between the text and 6. ...P—K R 3 ; 7. Kt—Q 5, B—B 4 ; 8. P—B 3, P—Q 3. The latter course is possibly preferable.

7. P×B	P—Q 3

Since the pin soon proves embarrassing, Black should have played either ...P—K R 3 or ...P—Q 4.

8.	B—K Kt 5	B—K 3
9.	B—Kt 3	Q—K 2
10.	R—K 1	Kt—Q 1

Copying a well-known Rubinstein manœuvre to free himself from the pin. The alternative was 10. ...P—K R 3 ; 11. B—K R 4, B×B ; 12. R P×B, K—R 1 ; 13. P—Q 4, R—K Kt 1 ; 14. P—Q 5, Kt—Q 1 followed by ...P—K Kt 4. The resulting position would be difficult to appraise : Black would be rid of the pin, but the effective posting of the Q Kt would be a serious problem.

11.	P—Q 4	B×B
12.	R P×B	Kt—K 3
13.	B×Kt !	P×B

A serious weakening move, but apparently Black had not foreseen that 13. ...Q×B would lose a Pawn after 14. P×P, P×P ; 15. Q—Q 5.

14.	Kt—R 4	Kt—Kt 2
15.	Q—Kt 4	K R—K 1

White was threatening to win at once with Kt—B 5 or Q×Kt ch.

Black's position is indefensible in the long run because of the lasting organic weakness of the King's side and the resulting exposure of the King. Tarrasch handles the position with his customary mastery of such situations.

16.	Kt—B 5	Q—B 1
17.	R—K 3	K—R 1
18.	Q—R 4 !	

Much stronger than the obvious R—Kt 3 or R—K R 3, which could be answered by ...Kt—K 3—Kt 4.

18.	......	Kt×Kt
19.	P×Kt	P—K R 3

The Pawn cannot be held, for if 19. ...Q—Kt 2 ; 20. R—Kt 3, while if 19. ...Q—K 2 ? ? ; 20. R—K R 3 wins at once.

20. P—Q 5

Once more Tarrasch introduces a favourite motif : he intends R—R 4—K Kt 4 with a devastating attack.

20. ......   P—K 5

In desperation the allies offer a Pawn in order to take the sting out of the attack. But Tarrasch prefers to keep up the pressure.

21. R—Kt 3   K—R 2
22. Q×B P   R—K 2
23. R—K 1   Q R—K 1
24. Q R—K 3   Q—R 1

Black must take some measures against the threatened doubling of White's Rooks on the K Kt file.

25. Q—R 4   R—K 4
26. P—B 6 !

The advance of the B P strengthens the attack appreciably.

26. ......   R—K Kt 1

Not 26. ...R×P : 27. P—R 3 and the allies are lost, for if 26. ... R—K Kt 1 ; 27. Q×K P ch wins.

27. P—Q B 4

Tarrasch points out that he could have won more rapidly with 27. R×R, K×R ; 28. R—Kt 3 ch, K—B 1 ; 29. R—Kt 7, P—K R 4 ; 30. Q—R 3, Q—R 3 ; 31. Q—B 8 ch, R—K 1 ; 32. R—Kt 8 ch, K×R ; 33. Q×R ch etc.

27. ......   R—Kt 3
28. R×R   P×R

The position of Black's King has improved, the advanced K B P looks precarious and the Queen and Pawn ending after 29. R×P, R×R ; 30. Q×R, Q×P would be long-winded and laborious. Tarrasch solves the difficulty with a very fine and unexpected move.

29. P—K Kt 4 !   K—Kt 1

Otherwise there follows 30. P—Kt 5 !, R×P ch (or 30. ...P—K R 4 ; 31. R×P winning easily) ; 31. Q×R, P×Q ; 32. R—R 3 ch, K—Kt 1 ; 33. P—B 7 ch ! etc.

If 29. ...P—K Kt 4 ; 30. Q×P ch !, K×Q ; 31. R—R 3 ch, K—Kt 3 ; 32. R×Q, K×P ; 33. R—R 7 and wins.

30. P—B 4 !   P×P e.p.

Slightly more hopeful would have been 30. ...P—K Kt 4 ; 31. P×P, R×Kt P ; 32. P—B 7 ch, K×P ; 33. R×P etc.

31. R×R   P×R

Now White has a clear majority of Pawns on the Queen's side, which will be important in some variations.

32. P—Kt 5   Q—R 2

They dare not play 32. ...
P×P ? ? because of 33. P—B 7 ch.
If 32. ...P—K R 4 ; 33. Q—R 3
wins outright.

33. Q—R 3

Another way was 33. Q×P, P—
Kt 3 ; 34. K—B 2 !, P—K 5 ; 35.
Q×Q ch, K×Q ; 36. P—Kt 4,
P—R 4 (or 36. ...K—Kt 1 ; 37.
P—B 5, P×P ; 38. P×P, K—B 2 ;
39. P—Q 6, P×P ; 40. P—B 6
etc.) ; 37. P×P, P×P ; 38. P—
B 5, P—R 5 ; 39. P—Q 6, P×P ;
40. P×P, P—R 6 ; 41. P—Q 7,
P—R 7 ; 42. P—Q 8(Q), P—R 8
(Q) ; 43. Q—K 7 ch and mate
next move. Note that the interpolation of 34. K—B 2 ! avoids the
queening of Black's Pawn with a
check.

33.	Q—B 2

If 33. ...P×P ? ; 34. Q—B 8
ch, K—B 2 ; 35. Q—Q 7 ch and
Black must resign.

34. Q×R P	P—Kt 3
35. Q—R 4	

Tarrasch points out that 35. Q—
R 3 would have won more rapidly,
for after 35. ...P—K 5 ; 36. Q—
K 6 the allies would be helpless :
36. ...Q×Q ; 37. P×Q followed
by P—R 4—5 etc.

35.	Q—B 1
36. K—B 2	Q—Kt 5

Black's best chance. Tarrasch's
play for the last few moves has been
none too exact, but the ending that
follows has interesting points.

37. P—B 7 ch	K×P
38. Q—R 7 ch	K—B 1
39. Q—R 8 ch	K—B 2

40. Q—B 6 ch	K—K 1
41. Q×K P ch	K—Q 1
42. Q—B 6 ch	K—B 1
43. K×P	Q—Q 7
44. Q×K Kt P	Q—Q 8 ch

The allies have a long series of
checks at their disposal, but the pur-
suit of White's King only leads to
their own downfall.

45. K—K 3

As will be seen, K—B 4 (move
52 !) initiates the winning plan.

45.	Q—Kt 8 ch
46. K—Q 3	Q—Q 8 ch
47. K—B 3	Q—R 8 ch
48. K—Q 2	Q—Q 5 ch
49. K—K 2	Q—Kt 5 ch
50. K—K 3	Q—Kt 8 ch
51. K—B 3	Q—Q 8 ch
52. K—B 4 !	

The King is headed for Q 7 !

52.	Q—Q 7 ch
53. K—K 5	Q×R P ch
54. K—B 6	Q—Q 3 ch
55. K—B 5	Q—R 7
56. Q—K 8 ch	K—Kt 2
57. Q—K 4	Q—B 7 ch

Black's efforts to stave off the
advance of the K Kt P lead to a different setting for their defeat.

58. K—K 6	K—Kt 1
59. Q—B 5	Q—B 4
60. Q—B 4	Q—Kt 8

Otherwise the passed Pawn advances.

61. K—Q 7	Q—B 4
62. P—Kt 4	

Here the allies resigned.

175. NAPLES, 1914

BIRD'S OPENING

THIS game concludes with what is perhaps the most artistic of all of Tarrasch's combinations. As in all the best Tarrasch games, shortcomings are punished by him not only inexorably but in the appropriate way.

White	Black
DR. S. TARRASCH	ALLIES

1.	P—K B 4	P—Q 4
2.	Kt—K B 3	P—Q B 4

The first of a number of opening transgressions. In this opening Black does better to avoid ...P—Q B 4 until he has castled.

3.	P—K 3	Kt—Q B 3

Even 3. ...P—Q R 3 would be preferable, in order to deprive White's K B of the following favourable development.

4.	B—Kt 5	B—Q 2
5.	O—O	P—K 3
6.	P—Q Kt 3	Q—B 2

This serves no useful purpose, unless they are already toying with the dubious notion of castling on the Queen's side. Normal development by means of ...Kt—B 3 and ...B—K 2 was in order.

7.	B—Kt 2	P—B 3

With the laudable object of preventing White from occupying or controlling K 5. However, the move loses time, weakens their Pawn position and delays the development of the King's side.

8.	P—B 4	Q Kt—K 2 ?

A further loss of time after which Black's game becomes definitely inferior. ...B—Q 3 and ...K Kt—K 2 should have been played.

9.	Kt—B 3	Kt—R 3

This miserable Knight plays a negligible rôle throughout the game —another consequence of Black's thoughtless development.

10.	R—B 1	B×B
11.	Kt×B	Q—Q 2
12.	Q—K 2	Kt—B 3
13.	P×P	P×P
14.	P—K 4 !	

Tarrasch strives to exploit his lead in development by opening up the position.

14.	......	O—O—O

Risky but apparently inevitable. After 14. ...P—Q 5 ; 15. P—K 5 would be unpleasant ; while if 14. ...P×P ; 15. Q×P ch and Black's King must move.

15.	P—K 5	

15. P×P, Q×P ; 15. P—Q 4 looks strong, but there follows 16. ...P—R 3 ! ; 17. Kt—R 3 (or 17. Kt—B 3, Kt×P etc.), P×P ; 18. Kt×P, B—B 4 with strong counterplay.

15.	......	P—R 3

15. ...P—Q 5 could be answered by 16. P×P, P×P ; 17. K Kt×P, P×Kt ; 18. B×P, B—K 2 ; 19. Kt×P ch, K—Kt 1 ; 20. Kt×Kt ch, P×Kt ; 21. B—Kt 6 with a strong attack.

16.	Kt—B 3	P—Q Kt 4

If 16. ...P—Q 5 ? ; 17. Kt—Q R 4 wins the Q B P.

17.	P—Q R 4	P—Kt 5

They have little choice : if 17.

...Kt—R 2 ; 18. P×P, P×P ;
19. R—R 1 and White should win.

18. Kt—Q 1 !

18. Q×P ch would allow the
exchange of Queens after ...Q—
Kt 2. Since he must win a Pawn
in any event, Tarrasch prefers to
keep the Queens on the board.

18. ...... K—Kt 2

After 18. ...P×P White would
have the pleasant choice between
19. Q×P ch and 19. Kt×P, Kt×
Kt ; 20. B×Kt, K—Kt 2 ; 21.
P—Q 4, R—B 1 ; 22. Kt—K 3
with a magnificent position.

19. P×P   P×P
20. B×P   R—K 1
21. Kt—K 3   R—K Kt 1

In return for the Pawn, the allies
have obtained open files and a pass-
able game. But this view of the
matter is deceptive.

22. Q—Q 3

Tarrasch wants to force ...P—
Q 5.

22. ......   Kt—Kt 5
23. Kt×Kt   Q×Kt
24. R—K B 2

Not 24. Q×K R P ch ? ?, R—
K 2 ! and wins.

24. ......   Q—Q 2
25. Kt—K 5   Kt×Kt
26. B×Kt   R—B 1

They realise that the B P is the
cardinal weakness of their game and
try to support it accordingly. But
Tarrasch overcomes their resistance
very cleverly.

27. Q—K B 3 !   K—Kt 3

In order to be able to answer P—
Q 4 with ...P—B 5.

28. P—Q 3

Preparing to double Rooks on the
Q B file.

28. ......   B—R 3 ?

They are under the erroneous
impression that the B P is adequately guarded. ...B—K 2 was
better.

29. K R—B 2   P—Q 5

White threatened 30. P—Q 4,
P×P ; 31. R—B 7, R×R ; 32.
R×R and wins (32. ...Q—Kt 5 ;
33. P—R 5 ch !).

30. P—R 5 ch !

The prelude to an exquisite combination. If 30. ...K×P ; 31.
R×P ch, R×R ; 32. R×R ch,
K—Kt 3 ; 33. R—B 4 winning
easily.

30. ......   K—Kt 4

31. B—B 7 ! !   Resigns.

White's last move is one of the
most beautiful ever played on the
chess-board. It illustrates the
famous Plachutta cutting-point
theme so dear to the hearts of
problemists : if 31. ...R×B ; 32.

Q—Kt 7 ch ! !, R×Q ; 33. R×P mate, or if 31. ...Q×B ; 32. R× P ch ! !, Q×R ; 33. Q—Kt 7 ch, K×P ; 34. R—R 1 mate ! Thus, if Black's Rook captures, the Queen's defence of Q Kt 2 is cut off ; if the Queen captures the Rook's defence of Q B 4 is cut off.

176. MUNICH, 1915

RUY LOPEZ

THE Breslau Variation, with its numerous scintillating possibilities, is a line of play which is particularly suitable for adoption against an amateur. Tarrasch was of course a past master of the brilliant resources of the variation, which apparently gives White an all too difficult game for over-the-board play.

White	Black
AMATEUR	DR. S. TARRASCH
1. P—K 4	P—K 4
2. Kt—K B 3	Kt—Q B 3
3. B—Kt 5	P—Q R 3
4. B—R 4	Kt—B 3
5. O—O	Kt×P
6. P—Q 4	P—Q Kt 4
7. B—Kt 3	P—Q 4
8. P×P	B—K 3
9. P—B 3	B—K 2
10. R—K 1	

Among the more frequently seen alternatives nowadays are 10. Q Kt —Q 2, 10. B—K 3 and 10. Q— K 2.

| 10. ...... | O—O |
| 11. Kt—Q 4 | Kt×K P |

Black prefers to sacrifice a piece rather than submit to the positional difficulties which result from 11 ...Kt×Kt ; 12. P×Kt etc.

| 12. P—B 3 | B—Q 3 |
| 13. P×Kt | B—K Kt 5 |

The Field points out that in later years, Tarrasch preferred the alternative 13. ...Q—R 5, a suggested continuation being 14. Q—Q 2, P—Q B 4 ; 15. Kt—B 5, B×Kt ; 16. P×B, Q R—K 1 ; 17. R— K 2, Kt—B 5 ; 18. B×Kt, B×P ch ; 19. K—B 1, B—Kt 6 ; 20. R—K 3, Q P×B ; 21. R×B, Q× R ; 22. Kt—R 3, R—K 4 and wins.

14. Q—B 2

For 14. Q—Q 2, see Game 87.

| 14. ...... | Q—R 5 |

And here the moderns prefer 14. ...P—Q B 4, with the consequences indicated in the game just quoted.

15. R—B 1

If 15. P—Kt 3, Q—R 4 ; 16. P×P, B—Q B 4 and Black's attack is very strong. Or 15. Q—B 2, Q×Q ch ; 16. K×Q, Kt—Q 6 ch ; 17. K—B 1, Kt×R ; 18. K× Kt, P×P and Black should win.

| 15. ...... | P—Q B 4 |

Leaving White little choice because of the threatened ...P—B 5.

16. B×P	P×Kt
17. B×R	R×B
18. P×P	

Black is the exchange and a Pawn down, but all his pieces are in active play and his concentration of force proves too much for the enemy to cope with.

| 18. ...... | R—Q B 1 |

This obvious but powerful move leaves White little choice, for if 19. Q—Kt 3, Kt—B 6 ch wins ; if 19. Q—Q 2, Kt—B 5 is decisive ; or if

19. Q—B 2, Q×Q ch ; 20. K×
Q, Kt—Q 6 ch etc.

19. Kt—B 3   Kt—B 3

20. P—K 5

Apparently very strong, this
move is brilliantly refuted. However, Tarrasch points out that if 20.
P—K Kt 3, Kt×P ; 21. P×Q,
Kt×Q ; 22. R—Kt 1, P—Kt 5 ;
23. Kt—Q 5, B—K 7 ; 24. R—
B 5, B—Q 6 Black has a splendid
game.

20. ......   Kt×Q P !
21. Q—K 4

White seems to have extricated
himself very nicely, since if 21.
...B—Q B 4 ; 22. B—K 3 etc.
But Tarrasch has a far stronger
resource.

21. ......   R×Kt !
22. R—B 4

Striving for counter-play. If
instead 22. P×R (22. Q×Kt ?,
B—Q B 4), Kt—K 7 ch ; 23. K—
R 1, Kt—Kt 6 ch etc.

22. ......   Kt—K 7 ch
23. Q×Kt

Leads to a spectacular finish, but
if 23. K—B 1, Kt×R ; 24. B×
Kt, R—B 5 with decisive material
advantage.

23. ......   B—B 4 ch
24. K—R 1   R—K R 6 ! !

This charming move forces the
game.

25. P×R

White could have prolonged the
game without affecting the outcome
by means of 25. P—K Kt 3, R×P ;
26. R×B, R×R ; 27. B—Q 2,
R—K 5 etc.

25. ......   B×Q
26. R×Q   B—B 6 mate

A delightful conclusion.

177. MUNICH, 1915
BIRD'S OPENING

THE dispute regarding the combinative powers of the older and
modern masters continues to rage
furiously, and will doubtless be a
perennial subject of controversy.
A game such as the following one,
with its magnificent combinative
finish, should furnish useful am-
munition !

| *White* | *Black* |
| DR. S. TARRASCH | SATZINGER |

1. P—K B 4	P—K 3
2. Kt—K B 3	P—Q 4
3. P—K 3	P—Q B 4

This is generally best omitted
until Black has castled, so as to
avoid White's B—Kt 5 ch, which
enables him to get rid of a piece
which is not likely to be useful.
However, after Black's inferior play
later on, White has even more
favourable perspectives than the
exchange of the K B.

| 4. P—Q Kt 3 | B—K 2 |
| 5. B—Kt 2 | B—B 3 |

A good move in positions where the exchange of Bishops can be forced. Since that is not the case here, the normal ...Kt—K B 3 would have been preferable.

6. Kt—K 5   B × Kt

Doubtless not expecting White's reply. ...Kt—Q 2 or ...Kt—K 2 would be much better.

7. P × B !

Giving himself an open K B file which subsequently proves useful.

7. ......   Kt—K 2

The Field points out that the crucial line 7. ...Q—R 5 ch ; 8. P—Kt 3, Q—K 5 ; 9. R—Kt 1, P—Q 5 ; 10. Kt—R 3, Q × P ; 11. Kt—B 4, Q—B 3 ; 12. P × P, P × P ; 13. Q—Kt 4, Kt—B 3 ; 14. B—Kt 2, P—K 4 ; 15. B × Kt ch, P × B ; 16. Q—K 2 winds up with White's regaining the lost Pawn with a superior position.

8. B—Q 3   Q Kt—B 3
9. O—O   O—O
10. Q—R 5

Tarrasch loses no time in proceeding to the attack. Black has slight prospect of successful resistance.

10. ......   Kt—Kt 3
11. R—B 3   Q Kt—K 2

Black is striving desperately to reinforce his threatened King's side. A curious variation is 11. ...Q—R 5 ; 12. B × Kt, Q—K 8 ch ; 13. R—B 1, B P × B (not 13. ...R P × B ? ; 14. Q—Kt 4 and wins) ; 14. Q × P ch etc. Also possible is 12. Q × Q, Kt × Q ; 13. B × P ch, K × B ; 14. R—R 3 etc.

12. Kt—B 3   P—Q R 3

As Black can do no more for his King, he tries a Queen's side advance with pathetically meagre results.

13. Q R—K B 1   P—Kt 4
14. Kt—Q 1 !

The transfer of this piece of the King's side is the decisive factor in the attack.

14. ......   B—Kt 2

The Field gives the following interesting variation after 14. ...P—B 5 : 15. Kt—B 2 !, P × B ; 16. Kt—Kt 4 (threatening 17. Kt—B 6 ch, P × Kt ; 18. K P × P and wins ; if 18. ...Kt—B 4 ; 19. R × Kt, P × R ; 20. Q—R 6. If 18. ...K—R 1 ; 19. P × Kt ch), Kt—B 4 ; 17. R—R 3, Kt(B 4)—R 5 (if 17. ...P—R 3 ; 18. R × Kt !, P × R ; 19. Kt × P ch ! P × Kt ; 20. Q × R P, R—K 1 ; 21. P—K 6 wins) ; 18. Kt—B 6 ch, P × Kt ; 19. K P × P, R—K 1 ; 20. Q—R 6 and wins.

15. Kt—B 2   P—B 5
16. Kt—Kt 4 !   P—B 4

If 16. ...P × B ; 17. Kt—B 6

ch wins. But the text allows an even more striking finish.

17. P×P e.p.	Kt—B 4
18. B P×P	Kt×Kt P
19. Q×P ch ! !	

Beginning a lovely six-move mate.

| 19. ...... | K×Q |
| 20. R—R 3 ch | K—Kt 1 |

If 20. ...Kt—R 4 ; 21. R× Kt ch, K—Kt 1 ; 22. R—R 8 ch !, Kt×R ; 23. Kt—R 6 mate !

21. Kt—R 6 ch	K—R 1
22. Kt—B 7 dbl ch	K—Kt 1
23. R—R 8 ch !	Kt×R
24. Kt—R 6 mate	

A highly unconventional conclusion !

178. MUNICH, 1915

RUY LOPEZ

TARRASCH scores an easy but instructive victory against inferior handling of his favourite defence.

White	*Black*
DR. S. TARRASCH	ALLIES
1. P—K 4	P—K 4
2. Kt—K B 3	Kt—Q B 3
3. B—Kt 5	P—Q R 3
4. B—R 4	Kt—B 3
5. O—O	Kt×P
6. P—Q 4	P—Q Kt 4
7. B—Kt 3	P—Q 4
8. P×P	B—K 3
9. P—B 3	B—K 2
10. B—K 3	O—O

The immediate ...Kt—R 4 is a promising alternative here.

| 11. Q Kt—Q 2 | Kt—R 4 |
| 12. B—B 2 | |

Kt×Kt would be answered by ...Kt×B.

12.	Kt×Kt
13. Q×Kt	Kt—B 5
14. Q—Q 3	P—Kt 3
15. B—B 1	

Too easygoing. White's best chance of maintaining the initiative is 15. B—R 6, Kt×Kt P ; 16. Q—K 2, R—K 1 ; 17. Kt—Q 4, Kt—B 5 ; 18. P—B 4 with strong attacking chances for the Pawn.

15.	B—K B 4
16. Q—K 2	B×B
17. Q×B	R—K 1 ?

An inexactitude which has painful consequences. ...P—K B 3 is the proper move here.

| 18. P—Q Kt 3 ! | Kt—Kt 3 |

The Knight now remains out of play for the rest of the game.

| 19. B—R 6 | B—B 1 |

Black's position is unsatisfactory at best, but the exchange of Bishops with its resulting weakening of Black's black squares, makes matters still worse.

| 20. Q—Q 2 | B—Kt 2 |
| 21. Q—B 4 | P—Q B 4 |

This bold advance is suitable only when Black's pieces are well posted. In the present situation, ...P—Q B 3 would have been advisable.

22. Q R—Q 1	Q—K 2
23. B×B	K×B
24. K R—K 1	

Tarrasch's play has been simple but forceful. He has all the play, and Black can find no good moves.

| 24. ...... | P—Q R 4 |
| 25. P—K R 4 ! | |

Apparently with a view to P—R 5, but his real intention is Kt—R 2—Kt 4—B 6.

25.	R—K Kt 1
26. Kt—R 2 !	P—R 4
27. Kt—B 3 !	

Now the Knight heads for Kt 5, since ...P—K R 3 is no longer at Black's disposal.

27.	Q—K 3
28. Kt—Kt 5	Q—B 4
29. Q—K 3 !	

This is even more rapidly decisive than the favourable ending that would result from 29. Q×Q, P×Q ; 30. Kt—R 3 followed by Kt—B 4.

| 29. ...... | Q R—Q B 1 |
| 30. P—K 6 ! | P×P |

If 30. ...P—B 3 ; 31. Kt—B 7 threatening Q—R 6 mate as well as Kt—Q 6.

| 31. Q×K P ! | Q×Q |

The exchange is unavoidable, as Q—K 7 ch is threatened as well as Q×Kt.

| 32. R×Q | Kt—R 1 |

...R—Kt 1 would be no better.

| 33. R—K 7 ch | K—B 1 |

Black is helpless ! If 33. ...K—B 3 ; 34. R—B 7 ch, K—K 4 ; 35. R—K 1 ch, K—Q 3 ; 36. R—K 6 mate.

34. R—B 7 ch	K—K 1
35. R—K 1 ch	K—Q 1
36. Kt—K 6 ch	K—K 1
37. R—Q Kt 7	Resigns

Black's King is in a mating net. If 37. ...R—R 1 ; 38. Kt—Kt 5 ch, K—B 1 ; 39. R(K 1)—K 7, and mate or ruinous loss of material follows. A smartly played finish.

179. MUNICH, 1916

GIUOCO PIANO

An instructive and pretty example of the dire effects of premature castling in this opening. Tarrasch's refutation is both precise and forceful.

White	*Black*
Professor	Dr. S.
Thoma	Tarrasch

1. P—K 4	P—K 4
2. Kt—K B 3	Kt—Q B 3
3. B—B 4	Kt—B 3
4. Kt—B 3	B—B 4

...Kt×P is an excellent alternative.

5. O—O

In this opening it is a well-known principle that castling should generally be deferred until Black has made his intentions clear. The underlying reason will soon become apparent.

5. ......   P—Q 3

So that if 6. P—Q 3, B—K Kt 5;
7. B—K 3, Kt—Q 5 and then, in
order to avoid the break-up of his
King's side Pawns, White will have
to cede the Bishop-pair to his opponent by playing 8. B×Kt. It
is true that after 8. ...B×B;
9. P—K R 3, B—R 4; 10. P—
K Kt 4, B—K Kt 3, White could
get a good game with 11. Kt×B,
P×Kt; 12. Kt—Q Kt 5, P—B 4;
13. P—B 4. Hence Black would
have to play 8. ...P×B; 9. Kt—
Q R 4, Q—Q 2; 10. Kt×B, P×
Kt with about even chances.

However, White fears the pin
unduly, and plays the timorous ...

6. P—K R 3?

After this "careful" move, Black
really gets an attack!

6. ......   P—K R 3!

Whereas White's last move weakened his castled position, Black's
advance of the K R P signifies the
beginning of a powerful attack.

7. P—Q 3   P—K Kt 4

This advance exposes the weakness of White's opening play. He
cannot avoid the opening of a file
against his castled King.

8. Kt—R 2   P—Kt 5

Achieving his object, for, if 9.
P—K R 4?, P—Kt 6.

9. P×P   R—K Kt 1
10. B—K 3

B×P would merely give Black an
additional open file and thereby
intensify his attack.

10. ......   Kt×Kt P
11. B×B   P×B
12. Q—B 3   Q—K 2

Provoking White's reply, which
has a surprising sequel.

13. Kt—Q 5   Kt×Kt!

For if 14. Kt×Q?, Kt×Q ch
wins a piece.

14. K×Kt   Q—R 5 ch
15. K—Kt 1   Kt—Q 5!

The most energetic reply.
White dare not play 15. Kt×P ch,
for after 15. ...K—Q 1 he would
have a lost game.

16. Q—R 5

A pretty move which has an even
prettier sequel.

16. ......   B—R 6!!

This charming move must have
left White thunderstruck!

17. Kt×P ch

If 17. Q×Q, Kt—B 6 ch; 18.
K—R 1, B×P mate!

17. ......   K—Q 2

Forced, but it wins a piece!

18. Q×P ch   K—B 3
19. Q—Q 5 ch   K×Kt
20. Q×K P ch

He cannot capture the B P, for he must be in a position to guard the K Kt P after its advance on move 23.

20. ......   K—Kt 3
21. Q—Q 6 ch   Kt—B 3
22. B×R   R×B
23. P—K Kt 3   Q—R 4

Before capturing the Rook, Black prefers to gain valuable time. The threat is of course ...Q—B 6.

24. P—K B 3   R—Kt 3

This interpolation serves to free the Knight for powerful action. White's three Pawns are inadequate compensation for the piece, since the active co-operation of Black's pieces cannot be withstood satisfactorily.

25. Q—B 4   B×R
26. R×B   Q—R 6
27. P—K Kt 4   Kt—Q 5
28. R—B 2

Allows a pretty finish, but if instead 28. K—B 2, Kt×Q B P wins easily.

28. ......   Kt×P ch
29. R×Kt   R×P ch
30. K—B 2   R×Q

White resigns. An attractive little game, played by Tarrasch with commendable verve.

180. MUNICH, 1922

FRENCH DEFENCE

TARRASCH'S enterprising Pawn sacrifices in the opening give the game its later character. Black's King's side is left exposed as a result of his opening play, and the weakness assumes a catastrophic aspect as soon as White has completed his development.

White	Black
DR. S. TARRASCH	DAUER

1. P—K 4   P—K 3
2. P—Q 4   P—Q 4
3. Kt—Q B 3   Kt—K B 3
4. B—Kt 5   B—Kt 5
5. P—K 5   P—K R 3
6. B—R 4

An old-fashioned move, the continuation 6. B—Q 2, B×Kt ; 7. P×B, Kt—K 5 ; 8. Q—Kt 4 being almost obligatory in modern play. However, Tarrasch has an interesting variation in mind.

6. ......   P—K Kt 4
7. B—Kt 3   Kt—K 5
8. B—Q 3 !?

The usual move is 8. Q—Q 3. The text move leads to highly interesting play, but it is hardly to be ventured against a first-clas opponent.

8. ......   Kt×Kt
9. Q—Q 2   Kt×P
10. P—Q B 3   Kt×P

This is perhaps too much of a good thing. 10. ...B—K 2 would save time and leave Black some reasonable prospect of being able to castle on the Queen's side.

11. P×Kt   B—K 2
12. Kt—K 2   Kt—Q 2
13. O—O   Kt—B 1
14. P—K B 4

White's plan of attack is clearly

laid out for him : pressure along
the K B file.

14.	Kt—Kt 3
15. R—B 2	P—Q B 4

Black's position is very difficult.
Burn, in *The Field*, here suggests
castling, which would at least have
the virtue of avoiding the losses of
time in which Black now indulges.

16. Q P×P	B×P
17. Kt—Q 4	B—K 2
18. Q R—K B 1	O—O

A perfect case of "castling into
it". However, 18. ...R—B 1 ;
19. Q—K 2 followed by Q—R 5
would likewise be unsatisfactory for
Black.

19. Q—K 2	P×P

There was no good defence
against White's threat of 20. Q—
R 5, K—Kt 2 ; 21. P×P, B×P ;
22. R×P ch.

20. B×P	K—Kt 2
21. Q—R 5	B—Kt 4

22. P—R 4 !

A pretty move which forces the
issue. If 22. ...Kt×R P ; 23.

B×B, Q×B ; 24. R×P ch and
mate follows.

22.	B×B

22. ...Kt×B ; 23. R×Kt, B×
R ; 24. R×B would only transpose
into the text.

23. R×B	Kt×R

Else follows R×P ch with murderous effect. If 23. ...Q—K 2 ;
24. R—B 6 wins quickly.

24. R×Kt	P—B 4

Can it be that Black has found a
cast-iron defence ? !

25. R—Kt 4 ch !	Resigns .

The demolition of Black's castled
position has been engineered in
impressive style.

181. MUNICH, 1925
QUEEN'S GAMBIT DECLINED

THIS game illustrates Tarrasch's
knack of finishing off inferior
opponents in elegant style. The
conclusion is curious for the number of elegant variations which
White manages to avoid !

White	*Black*
DR.	DR. S.
OTTENSOOSER	TARRASCH
1. P—Q 4	P—Q 4
2. Kt—K B 3	Kt—K B 3
3. P—B 4	P—B 3
4. P—K 3	P—K 3
5. Kt—B 3	Kt—K 5

As in the case of the Dutch Defence, this line of play was a favourite with Tarrasch in his later years.

6. Kt×Kt

A good line if followed up properly.

6. ......   P×Kt
7. Kt—Q 2   P—K B 4
8. B—K 2

Lifeless play. The proper course is 8. P—B 3 and if 8. ... B—Q 3 ; 9. P—K Kt 3 !, forcing ...P×P with an excellent game for White.

8. ......   B—Q 3
9. P—B 4   Kt—Q 2

As so often happens in the Stonewall Variation, the problem for both players is how to develop the Q B. Curiously enough, it is Black who solves the problem successfully, while White fails miserably.

10. P—B 5

A superficial notion. White plays for occupation of K 5, but in the process he permits Black occupation of the splendid square Q 4. However, it must be admitted that after White's previous colourless treatment of the opening, his position does not lend itself to any strikingly energetic procedure.

10. ......   B—B 2
11. Kt—B 4   Kt—B 3
12. Kt—K 5   O—O
13. O—O   Kt—Q 4
14. P—K Kt 4   Q—K 2
15. P×P ?

White's previous move was excellent, but this cannot possibly be right. He should have played 15. B—Q 2, intending a general Queen's side advance beginning

with P—Kt 4 ; or else 15. K—R 1 followed by R—K Kt 1.

15. ......   P×P

Tarrasch's position has been freed perceptibly, and his Q B has a good square now at K 3. We may therefore modify the note to Black's ninth move to say that it was not Black who solved the problem of his Q B, but that White solved it for him !

16. B—B 4   B—K 3
17. B×Kt

Another weak move. ...Kt× B P was not yet threatened, and White could have provided for all eventualities with 17. Q—K 2.

17. ......   B×B

The present position of this Bishop would have been unthinkable only four moves ago.

18. B—Q 2   B×Kt !

A masterly conception of which very few players would be capable. Despite the fact that Tarrasch parts with the Bishop-pair and permits Bishops on opposite colours, the text-move is very good. He obtains a strong attack, with the possibility of bringing his remaining Bishop into powerful action.

19. BP×B   Q—Kt 4 ch
20. K—R 1

Permitting a powerful attack with the motif of unmasking the terrible Bishop. If, however, 20. K—B 2, Black gets a fine attack with 20. ...Q—R 5 ch ; 21. K—Kt 1, P— K Kt 4 etc.

20. ......   P—B 5 !

Beginning the final phase of the attack. Capture of this Pawn would be fatal for White.

21. Q—K 1   R—B 4
22. R—B 2   Q R—K B 1
23. Q—K Kt 1   P×P

Now that Black has concentrated his forces overwhelmingly on the King's side, this capture is in order.

24. R×R

Burn, in *The Field*, refutes 24. Q×Q, with 24. ...P×R; 25. Q—K 3, R—B 6; 26. Q—K 2, P—K 6 and wins.

24. ......   Q×R
25. Q×P .

White's helplessness is touching. If 25. B×P, Q—B 6 ch wins.

25. ......   Q—Kt 5 !

In order to remove the blockader with ...R—B 6.

26. R—K Kt 1   Q—B 6 ch
27. R—Kt 2

Or 27. Q×Q, P×Q and White can resign.

27. ......   Q—Q 8 ch
Forcing White's reply.

28. R—Kt 1   R—B 8

White resigns, for if 29. K—Kt 2, R×R ch; 30. Q×R, Q—B 6 mate; if 29. B—K 1, Q×B 30. Q×Q, P—K6 mate. Meanwhile White has no defence against the threatened ...R×R ch followed by ...P—K 6 ch. A pleasing finish.

182. MUNICH, 1926
GIUOCO PIANO

WHITE combines a lackadaisical opening with time-wasting capture of the Q Kt P. Tarrasch's refutation is both elegant and incisive.

White	Black
PROFESSOR	DR. S.
GEBHARDT	TARRASCH

1. P—K 4	P—K 4
2. Kt—K B 3	Kt—Q B 3
3. B—B 4	Kt—B 3
4. P—Q 3	B—B 4
5. P—B 3	

This leads to a particularly slow development for White, as his Q Kt has to undertake a laborious trek to K Kt 3.

5.	P—Q 3
6. Q Kt—Q 2	O—O
7. Kt—B 1	B—K 3
8. B×B	

Opening an important file for Black and strengthening his position in the centre. B—Kt 3 is preferable.

8.	P×B
9. Q—Kt 3	

Loss of time. Kt—Kt 3 followed by O—O was in order.

9. ......   Q—Q 2 !

Tarrasch disdains the protection of the Q Kt P and therefore discards the more conservative ...Q—B 1.

10. Q×P ?

White's development is too backward to allow of such luxuries. There was still time for Kt—Kt 3.

10. ......   P—Q 4 !
11. Kt—Kt 3

Or 11. P×P, P×P ; 12. Q—Kt 3, Q R—Kt 1 ; 13. Q—B 2, P—K 5 ; 14. Kt—Kt 5, Kt—K 4 with a winning advantage.

11. ......   K R—Kt 1
12. Q—R 6

12. ......   Kt—Q Kt 5 ! !

A stunning surprise for White, who has no good reply.

13. P×Kt

The interpolation of 13. Kt×P, Q—K 1 would not materially alter the course of the game.

13. ......   B×Kt P ch
14. B—Q 2   R—Kt 3

The point. White's Queen is lost.

15. Kt×P   Q—K 1
16. Q×R   B×B ch
17. K×B   R P×Q
18. K R—Q B 1   Q—Kt 4

This leaves White without any good reply. The rest is simple.

19. R—B 2   P×P
20. P—B 4   P×P
21. R(B 2)—B 1

Or 21. Kt×P, R—Q 1 ; 22. R—B 3, Q×P ch etc.

21. ......   Q×P ch
22. K×P   R—R 6 ch

White resigns, as there is a quick mate in the offing.

183. MUNICH, 1932

RUY LOPEZ

A BRILLIANT little game, hardly to be expected from a 70-year-old veteran. A striking series of sacrifices, including the gift of both Rooks and the Queen, concludes this collection of Tarrasch's finest games in appropriate style.

White	*Black*
AMATEUR	DR. S. TARRASCH

1. P—K 4   P—K 4
2. Kt—K B 3   Kt—Q B 3
3. B—Kt 5   P—Q R 3
4. B—R 4   Kt—B 3
5. O—O   B—B 4

An adventurous but not quite sound defence. It always leads to interesting play.

6. Kt×P   Kt×P ? !

An experiment. If 6. ...Kt×
Kt ; 7. P—Q 4, Kt×P ; 8. Q—
K 2, B—K 2 ; 9. Q×Kt, Kt—
Kt 3 ; 10. P—Q B 4, O—O ; 11.
Kt—B 3 (Takács) and White has
the better game.

7. Kt×Kt   Q P×Kt
8. Q—B 3

Tarrasch gives 8. Q—K 2, Q—
K 2 ; 9. R—K 1, B—B 4 (if 9.
...B×P ch ; 10. Q×B !) ; 10.
P—Q 3, Kt—B 3 here as satisfac-
tory for Black ; however, after 11.
Q—Q 1, B—K 3 ; 12. B—Kt 3 he
is left with a serious weakness at
K 3.

8. ......   Q—R 5 !

The Knight cannot retreat because of 9. B×P ch etc. If, instead, 8. ...Q—Q 5 ; 9. Kt—B 3,
Kt×Kt ; 10. B×P ch ! and White
wins a Pawn.

9. Kt—B 3

If instead 9. P—Q 3, Kt×P ;
10. B×P ch, K—B 1 ! with advan-
tage. White's best is 9. B—Kt 3,
O—O with equality. If 9. P—
K Kt 3, Q—Kt 5 with a good game
(Tarrasch).

9. ......   Kt×Kt
10. B×P ch   P×B !

Stronger than 10. ...K—B 1 ;
11. Q P×Kt, P×B ; 12. Q×P,
and White regains the sacrificed

material, for if 12. ...B—Q 3 ; 13.
P—K Kt 3 (Tarrasch).

11. Q×Q B P ch   B—Q 2 !

12. Q×R ch

Modern Chess Openings recommends Blake's move 12. R—K 1
ch, but after Tarrasch's continuation 12. ...K—Q 1 ; 13. Q×R ch,
B—B 1 White is in difficulties because of the threat of ...Q×B P ch.

12. ......   K—K 2
13. Q×R ?

This loses quickly. 13. Q—B 3,
Kt—Kt 4 ; 14. P—B 3 followed
by 15. P—Q 4, was better.

13. ......   Kt—K 7 ch
14. K—R 1   B×P

Although White is the double
exchange ahead, he is helpless
against the threat of mate.

15. P—K R 3   Q×P ch !
16. P×Q   B—B 3 ch
17. K—R 2   B—Kt 6 mate !

A charming finish.

INDEX OF PLAYERS

INDEX OF OPENINGS

(The numbers refer to games)

C C

Printed in Great Britain by
Butler & Tanner Ltd.,
Frome and London

19- 1878